8 Men and a Lady

8 Men and a Lady

Profiles Of The Justices Of The Supreme Court

A ZENITH EDITION

NATIONAL PRESS
Bethesda, Maryland

LIBRARY OF CONGRESS CATALOGING-IN-PUBLICATION DATA

Eight men & a lady: profiles of the justices of the U.S.
Supreme Court by the staff of the National Press.
288 p. 15 x 23 cm (a Zenith Edition)
Includes index.
ISBN 0-915765-69-1: $19.95
1. Judges--United States--Biography.
2. United States Supreme Court--History.
I. National Press (Firm: U.S.)
II. Title: Eight men and a lady.
KF8744.E38 1990
347.73'2634--dc20
"B"
"347.3073534" 89-12689
CIP

PRINTED IN THE UNITED STATES OF AMERICA

Chapter One

Introduction

As this book goes to press, Justice William Brennan has announced his resignation from the Supreme Court. During his 34 years on the bench, the Court has shifted, first to the left under Earl Warren, then to the right under Chief Justices Burger and Rehnquist. Brennan became the leading liberal jurist, often in dissent; his voice will be greatly missed. Hopefully, his replacement will not merely be an echo of the three Reagan appointees, but will be an independent voice. When William J. Brennan was appointed by President Eisenhower, his liberal views were unknown. President Bush's nominee may possess similarly hidden qualities which will preserve the Court's balance and independence.

David Souter, the president's nominee to fill Justice Brennan's shoes, should be compared to the man he intends to replace. Only by undertanding Justice Brennan's role on the Court can the importance of his replacement be evaluated. Brennan's key role on the

Supreme Court, his friendships and pursuasiveness, will be nearly impossible to replicate.

The Court's rulings are often the last word on the most compelling issues of the day, from abortion rights to euthanasia, and from freedom of religion to flag burning. Until the 1987 Senate hearings concerning the nomination of Robert Bork to the Supreme Court, the confirmation process was not rigorous; nominees were not interrogated on the constitutional doctrines and methods of interpretation which guided them. Judge Souter should not be allowed to sit on the nation's highest tribunal until the Senate Judiciary Committee knows where he stands on matters of great constitutional significance. In the words of columnist George Will, we [the American people] should not buy "a pig in the poke."

The Supreme Court is the most secretive branch of our government and also its members are not well known to the public. The Court's decision-making process—its internal debates, conferences, meetings, draft opinions—is conducted behind closed doors, and are almost never publicly revealed. Only final written opinions are available to the public, and these opinions become bound into the formal decisions of the Supreme Court of the United States.

According to a recent *Washington Post* survey, more than two-thirds of all Americans cannot name a single Supreme Court justice, yet a majority of the American public knows that Joseph Wapner is the judge on "The People's Court" television show. We hope that this book will change this. By examining how the individual justices make decisions, how they come out on various issues, and by providing background of the justices, concerned citizens, students and lawyers can learn more about the decision-making process of the United States Supreme Court.

The best-known member of the Supreme Court is Sandra Day O'Connor, the only female to be appointed to the court in its 200 year history. Yet, only 23% of the people surveyed mentioned Justice O'Connor. Chief Justice Rehnquist was named by only 9% of the respondents, while Justice Stevens ranked at the bottom of the list, recognized by a mere one percent.

These figures are from 1989, a little more than a year after the historic hearings held concerning the nomination of Robert Bork as Supreme Court justice.

In many ways the nine justices are more powerful than the president of the United States. A majority can rule that the president has violated the Constitution or the laws of the land. A single justice, however, can have substantial power, especially if he or she is "undecided" on a particular issue, and the other justices are deadlocked. The recent abortion decisions of the court have been decided by narrow margins, so narrow, in fact, that the newest justice may be the one to decide whether women will retain the right to have an abortion. That is an issue on which the president of the United States has very little influence.

Job for Life

Supreme Court justices are powerful because they have the last word on major policy matters, they are given lifetime jobs by the Constitution and they can be removed only by impeachment. No Supreme Court justice has ever been impeached. There have only been

104 justices (if confirmed Judge Souter will be the 105th justice) on the court over its 200-year history. The average justice, including those still sitting on the court, has served for 18 years, more than twice the maximum time a president can serve.

Lifetime tenure has its advantages, most important of which is independence. Many of the justices in this book surprised the presidents who appointed them by turning out to be "different" than anticipated. In addition to Justice Brennan's surprising Eisenhower, Justice White, appointed by John F. Kennedy in 1962, will go down in history as one of the court's more conservative jurists. On the other hand, Justice Marshall, appointed by Lyndon Johnson as the court's first and only black justice, has been as liberal as predicted.

Justice Blackmun was appointed by Richard Nixon in 1969. Initially, commentators called him, along with fellow Minnesotan, former Chief Justice Burger, the "Minnesota Twins." Blackmun later broke away from his "twin" to become one of the Court's most liberal members.

Similarly, Justice John Paul Stevens, appointed by Gerald Ford, has turned out to be much more liberal than his appointer intended. The latest appointees named by Ronald Reagan, Sandra Day O'Connor, Antonin Scalia and Anthony Kennedy, have generally voted together on the conservative side; however, there are some very interesting differences among them.

The justices are all individuals and vote independently. They meet weekly at a conference to decide various issues, including which cases will be heard and how argued cases will be decided. At votes, the least senior judge votes first so that his or her vote will not be influenced by the more experienced jurists.

Many commentators have said that there are five conservatives and four liberals on the Court now. This is inaccurate. On various issues, the Court lines up differently. During the last term of the court, about one-fifth of the court's decisions were made by 5-4 votes. The majorities in those 32 cases were made up on ten different voting blocks. Twenty majorities included the most conservative five justices: Rehnquist, White, O'Connor, Scalia and Kennedy. Justices Kennedy and Rehnquist both were in the majority in 29 of the 32 cases, Scalia and White 26, O'Connor 25, Blackmun 10, Stevens and Marshall five and Brennan four. No two justices agreed on all of these close cases. This demonstrates that all of the justices think independently, without fear of disagreeing with their colleagues on specific issues. These voting patterns also demonstrate that there are no easy ways to predict how the Court will rule on a particular issue.

From Left to Right

The justices sit in order of seniority, with the Chief Justice on the left, followed by the most senior justice and so on until the rookie justice is on the far right. This book will be organized following the same pattern. The next chapter will be about Chief Justice William Rehnquist. Each chapter is written by one journalist/lawyer, who is identified in the chapter. Supreme Court justices are very private individuals, not publicity-seeking politicians like Congressmen or Senators. Because of this, interviews with justices are very rare. However, a majority of the court was interviewed for this book. The authors have attempted to convey the personalities of the justices, as well as their views on legal matters.

Legal Jargon

Unfortunately, you will have to learn a few legal catch phrases to understand the nation's High Court. The Court has a Rule of Four, which means that any four of the nine justices are needed to vote to hear a case. If the "liberal" faction is reduced to three members, it will be prevented from putting cases on the Court's agenda. About 4,000 cases are submitted to the Court every year, and it agrees to hear only about 150 of them. When four members vote to hear a case it grants the "petition for a writ of certiorari." This means that the parties to the case will have to file briefs and present oral argument to the Court.

When a case has been decided by the Court, it will issue written opinions. Some of the decisions are unanimous, so there will only be one opinion for all of the justices. Most of the time, there will be the majority opinion and a dissenting opinion. Sometimes, less than five members of the Court will agree on any opinion, so there will be a plurality opinion and several dissenting opinions.

You will hear the names of many theories on how the Constitution should be interpreted, including "plain meaning," "original intent" and "strict construction." The original intent doctrine attempts to read the minds of the Founding Fathers, who wrote the Constitution, to determine what they really meant by the words they used. "Plain meaning" gives deference to the actual words without embellishment by intent. "Strict construction" is similar to plain meaning, but all three of these theories mean different things to different people.

The Bill of Rights is the first ten amendments to the Constitution, including the First Amendment (free speech and freedom of religion) and the Fourth

Amendment (freedom from unreasonable searches and seizures). These two amendments are mentioned throughout the book.

A Few General Observations

The current Supreme Court is one of the best educated High Courts in its 200-year history: four justices graduated Harvard Law, one Yale and two Stanford. The Court is more Catholic than ever (three) and more Western. Two justices lived most of their lives in Arizona, one is from California and one is from Colorado. Most previous Courts were much more East Coast oriented. Only justices Brennan, Marshall and Scalia are from the East Coast. Justices Stevens and Blackmun are from the midwest. With the exception of Justice Scalia, the Easterners are liberals, the midwestern justices are moderate to liberal and the Western justices are conservative.

There are three "firsts" sitting on the court: the first woman (O'Connor), the first black (Marshall) and the first Italian (Scalia). During most of the twentieth century, there has been a Jewish justice, though there is not one now.

These general observations are merely a glimpse at the icing on top of the cake. The real cake is underneath and can only be savored by reading about how the justices make their decisions, and what their actual decisions are.

Chapter Two

The Chief Justice

by Warren Weaver, Jr.

Warren Weaver, Jr. was a reporter for the New York Times for more than 40 years before his retirement in 1989. A member of the bar of the District of Columbia and New York, he covered the Supreme Court, national politics and Congress during 25 years as a member of the Times Washington Bureau. He is currently writing a novel on the mysterious death of a national political figure.

William Rehnquist is regarded by many of his passionate critics as the most political judge of our era. But if the consumate politician is one who anticipates shifts in public opinion and accommodates to them early and effortlessly, then the 16th Chief Justice of the United States is not guilty as charged. Throughout his legal and judicial career, Rehnquist has stood resolutely for some of the most unpopular causes and ideas of the day and rarely, if ever, changed his stand on any of them.

When the Supreme Court barred racial segregation

in the American public schools, he was defending the practice as an exercise of individual freedom. When his fellow-clerks at the Supreme Court welcomed opportunities for the Court to erect new barriers to racial and religious discrimination, he denounced "this pathological search for discrimination" that he found popular at the Eastern law schools. When the voters were turning against Barry Goldwater in record numbers as an extremist, he was strenuously campaigning to make him president. When national opposition to the Vietnam War crested and protestors swept through Washington, he called them "the new barbarians" and urged more government police power to curb their demonstrations. When the Court found a right to privacy in the Constitution that permitted women to choose abortion over pregnancy, he was one of only two dissenters, denouncing the decision as an unjustified intrusion into legislative authority.

Over the years, in fact, Rehnquist has stood solidly for a set of very conservative principles that often put him in the minority of his classmates, his colleagues and the American people, from his college days through his apprenticeship as an associate justice on the Burger Court. Undaunted by bitter opposition and frequent defeat, he has refused to come about to put the more favorable winds of majority public opinion in his sails. Instead, he has rarely missed an opportunity to state his unyeilding positions loud and clear, in a stream of Supreme Court dissents, supplemented by outside speeches that have been criticized on at least one occasion as pressing the boundries of judicial propriety.

At the time he was nominated for Chief Justice, Rehnquist had filed 54 solitary dissenting opinions, views in which not one of his eight colleagues was willing to join him, an historic record for the Court. Describing Rehnquist's lack of concern whether his views were fashionable or popular, one of his early law partners observed: "If other people thought it was odd, too bad for them. He did it because he felt it was the way things ought to be done."

Had he made his career in the executive or legislative branches of government, Rehnquist would very likely have been swept away by the voters years ago. But through a combination of intelligence, skill and considerable good fortune, he wound up in the judicial branch, sheltered by the Constitution from the slings and arrows of popular opinion. Not answerable to the public, but only to his own convictions, Rehnquist has been able to persevere until the resurgence of conservatism, political pressure on two Republican presidents and the luck of the draw shifted the cast of players on the high court. Now Rehnquist seems to have become, for the first time in his life, not only a member, but the leader of an emerging, albeit fragile majority.

The Philosophy of a Conservative

In his early years on the Court, Rehnquist was virtually unchallenged in his ideological position at the extreme right end of the bench, a kind of self-imposed isolation that earned him considerable prominence. He filed so many dissents, often solitary, that his clerks presented him with a small statue of the Lone Ranger, which he displayed with pride. Then, as the complexion of the Court began to move to the right with the appointment of Sandra Day O'Connor and later Antonin Scalia and Anthony Kennedy, Rehnquist seemed to become more of a centrist force. As recently as 1985, Rehnquist insisted that he had not changed over the previous dozen years. So, if the perception of his increasing centrality is correct, it may be because the court has shifted to the right behind him.

Rehnquist is not reluctant to describe where he's coming from philosophically as long as the terms of reference are general. "If you think of a judicial conservative as one who generally inclines against broad interpretations of Constitutional provisions," he said five years ago, "I think I am a judicial conservative." Asked to classify himself politically rather than judicially, he replied: "I'm a stong believer in pluralism. Don't concentrate all the power in one place. And, you know, this is partly, I think what the framers also conceived. So it is a kind of line where political philosophy joins or at least borders judicial philosophy. You don't want all the power in the government as opposed to the people. You don't want all the power in the federal government, as opposed to the states."

The justice maintains that he is an advocate of "judicial restraint," rather than an activist with conservative goals "We're carrying out a Constitutional function that is a very delicate one," he said in his last interview in 1985. "Every time that we say a law of Congress is unconstitutional, that a state law is unconstitutional, we are overriding a democratically reached decision. Now the Constitution requires us to do that, but it requires us to do it only with great caution and circumspection." The court is a "thoroughly undemocratic" institution, he recognized, and must accordingly exercise great care to avoid error.

On the issue of judicial activism, more significant now that he is the Court's leader, Rehnquist continued: "I don't know that a court should really have a sense

SIR JOSEPH GOLD MEMORIAL SERIES
International Financial & Economic Law
Vol. 6

EUROPEAN BANKING LAW
POLICY AND PROGRAMME CONSTRUCTION

INTERNATIONAL FINANCIAL LAW SERIES

In cooperation with the SMU Dedman School of Law Institute of International Banking and Finance and the Center for Commercial Law Studies, Queen Mary, University of London

EUROPEAN BANKING LAW

POLICY AND PROGRAMME CONSTRUCTION

George Alexander Walker

British Institute of International and Comparative Law

Published and Distributed by
The British Institute of International and Comparative Law
Charles Clore House, 17 Russell Square, London WC1B 5JP

British Library Cataloguing in Publication Data
A Catalogue record of this book is available from the British Library

ISBN 0–903067–78–1

Typeset by Cambrian Typesetters
Frimley, Surrey
Printed in Great Britain by Biddles Ltd,
King's Lynn

TO MY FATHER ALEXANDER 'SANDY' WALKER

We will never forget your kindness, your care and your limitless generosity. We will never forget your constant good nature, good conduct and good manners. We will never forget your exceptional taste, great humour and great company. Thank you for everything that you did for us. Thank you for everything that you have given us and thank you for everything that you have left us. We will always miss you. We will always remember you. We will never forget you. God Bless.

Foreword

I have known Professor George Walker for over 15 years and I long have been impressed by his scholarship in the banking and financial law area. This current work-product on *European Banking Law* is most probably his best effort to date: this volume is truly an exceptional piece of legal scholarship. Professor Walker has been able to draw together, in a single text and in a masterfully and coherent manner, an enormous amount of complex historical, economic, policy, political, market practice and legal material in developing this substantial piece of analytical work. In my view, this first of two volumes by Professor Walker will come to be considered a seminal work in the European banking and financial area. In any event, this text should assist experienced European law practitioners, policymakers and academics as well as new entrants in this area.

The author uses the first chapter to reduce European law and European integration into five sets of key ideas. These are essentially concerned with banking and financial integration, policy and programme structure and content, legislative adoption and operation, European integration more generally and longer term development law issues. In so doing, a number of fundamental difficulties are identified, including what the author characterizes as a core 'access and control conflict,' underlying policy vacuum and control gap, integration damage or default and the potential for regional contagion, crisis and collapse without any meaningful compensatory control arrangement.

In Chapter 2, Professor Walker explores the proper meaning, importance and nature of financial integration within the European environment more specifically. It is astonishing that this has never been attempted before in any comparable study. The historical background to Europe and European integration is explained in terms of its underlying functionalism and consequent staged Treaty development. The nature of economic integration is examined more specifically. Integration advantages and disadvantages, along with assessment and review, are considered separately in an attempt to understand the importance of integration in a regional trading experiment. Other global and regional models are examined including the GATS, NAFTA and MERCUSOR. The unique nature of the economic and legal order created within the European model is nevertheless highlighted and its supporting institutional structure explained.

The remainder of the book is principally concerned with identifying the key contribution of the European Court of Justice, the Commission, the Council and the European Parliament in constructing an effective banking and financial policy including the production of a series of relevant judicial principles and supporting secondary programme rules to secure proper integration within and among the European markets.

The contribution of the Court is examined in terms of the larger law of free movement including goods, establishment and services (and workers) as well as the more specific decisions produced in the financial area (Chapters 3 and 4). The development of the secondary programme of measures constructed in the banking and financial area is considered separately (Chapter 5).

Chapter 3 provides an original re-examination of the law for free movement beginning with goods and then moving to establishment, services and workers. To my knowledge, Chapter 4 contains the first comprehensive analysis of all of the relevant decisions of the European Court of Justice in the banking and financial area. The case law discussion in Chapter 3 is substantial and original. The author's use of historical sources and secondary comment is commendable. The text blends all of the main decisions and supporting expert commentary in this area together into a single examination of the law on the subject. All of the main textbook and journal discussion and commentary by all of the leading authorities in this area is drawn together and reconciled. There is no need to refer to any other separate discussion.

The remaining challenge for the author is then to explain the meaning, nature and effect of 'mutual recognition' as the core integration doctrine adopted within Europe and to make suggestions for its future revision and refinement. Again, this is achieved in a wholly original and often inspired manner. By itself, this separate analysis of mutual recognition provides a fundamentally new and original examination of the proper origin, validity, meaning, content and operation of this fundamental integration doctrine.

In considering the meaning of mutual recognition in further detail, the author identifies five separate possible uses of the term in the existing writing. Separate internal (directive) and external (essential measures) uses of mutual recognition are also noted. Five separate processes are then identified in connection with the operation of mutual recognition in practice. These include definition and identification, mutual review or pre-review, standards measurement, regulatory adjustment or disapplication, and systems review and validation.

All of this is drawn together in Chapters 7 and 8. These concluding sections summarize the relevant judicial principles identified earlier and the supporting secondary programme rules constructed; explain the link between the two sets of policy provisions in terms of mutual recognition with its limitations being restated; and propose a new integration strategy to draw together all of the separate aspects of this as still incomplete policy in the banking and financial area. This strategy is constructed around such notions as policy correction, policy restatement, continuing policy review, mutual review and corrective action, policy support and institutional revision as well as the adoption and application of the revised core integration doctrine of mutual or functional convergence and equivalence.

The author provides a useful restatement of his final recommendations in Chapter 8. The new integration strategy or framework to be adopted is essentially based on 'mutual convergence' or 'functional convergence.' The common test to be applied in both essential (programme) and non-essential (judicial) areas is 'functional equivalence' with the degree of convergence or approximation being assessed under a continuing process of 'functional adjustment.' This would be supplemented by policy revision in both the judicial and programme areas and supported by an appropriate institutional and legislative framework and revised corrective action procedure to deal with continuing imbalance and distortion in practice. The author concludes that it should be possible to reactivate and complete the integration process already underway in the financial and other areas through the adoption and application of a revised framework of measures based on these new core integration doctrines or devices.

Whether one fully agrees with all of the conclusions drawn and reform proposals put forward, it is a remarkable achievement for Professor Walker to have been able to identify all of the core challenges and difficulties involved so clearly and with all of the continuing weaknesses in the existing policy content and framework. In undertaking this study, the author has been able to identify all of the key components of a successful regional response and, in so doing, create a new language of regional integration and integration law.

The text makes full use of all available primary and secondary sources and constructs the most complete and detailed picture of the development of banking and financial law in Europe to date and of market integration more generally. A number of powerful perspectives are incorporated (including underlying conflicts, policy vacuums, omission theories, ordoliberal contribution and free and social market balance). The author also expertly reconciles all of the existing writing and authorities especially with his initial market and consequent internal regulatory distinction, effects and discrimination test differentiation, discriminatory effect doctrine and combined test and reclassification proviso. Significant new insights are provided in to the origin and meaning as well as legal validity and operation of mutual recognition with a new integration framework and strategy constructed to deal with the limitations identified. The writing is always engaging and informed. The analysis is always controlled and original.

It must be accepted that this is a substantial achievement. After 50 years of European reconstruction and development on the basis of the EEC Treaty and subsequent Treaty amendments, the author has been able to draw together all of the nuances of the European integration process and of the importance and relevance of banking and financial law within this larger initiative. This is indeed a major—arguably seminal—contribution to the better understanding of European banking and financial law specifically and of its position within the history of European integration more generally.

JJ NORTON

Preface

This text is concerned with the nature and content of the underlying policy that has been developed within Europe in the banking and financial law area. While banking and financial markets constitute essential commercial sectors within Europe in their own right, as well as provide a number of fundamental support services within any national economy, this is an area that has been given little dedicated attention until now. Only recently, have the importance of financial markets and financial integration within Europe (and elsewhere) been properly and fully realized.

The dominant doctrine referred to in any discussion of European integration more generally and financial integration specifically has been mutual recognition. Despite the common use and apparently clear meaning and significance of the term, this has again been subject to little separate examination and assessment. A number of difficulties remain with regard to the proper meaning, origin, and legal validity of mutual recognition as well as with its operational effectiveness and value. One of the main purposes of this text is to begin to attempt to understand the origin and evolution of this core doctrine within European law as well as its importance and contribution within the financial area and financial integration more generally.

In so doing, the basic policy issues that arise in attempting to examine the nature of banking and financial integration within Europe are initially examined (Chapter 1). This includes a number of specific problems that relate solely to banking and financial markets although a number of other related policy issues are also highlighted with regard to European law and European integration more generally. It is hoped that this will be of use, in particular, to non-European law experts by creating a structural framework within which European law more generally can be understood. The nature of financial integration is then considered in further detail in an attempt to explain its nature and potential contribution to the larger integration initiatives currently being undertaken within Europe (Chapter 2). This includes its proper meaning, relative advantage and disadvantage as well as possible measurement and assessment. It will become clear that financial integration is not as simple and clear a concept or objective as it appears (as with banking and financial policy and mutual recognition within Europe) more generally.

The nature of the underlying policy developed in the banking and financial area is then considered in further detail. The principal difficulty that arises is that this is partly made up of underlying Treaty rights as interpreted and applied by the European Court of Justice as well as their subsequent incorporation and clarification through the specific secondary programme measures adopted by the Council of Ministers and European Parliament. Policy is accordingly made up of both judicial and programme components with little attempt having been made to understand how these two have developed independently and then how they relate to one another. A number of complex issues arise in attempting to understand, explain and reconcile these essential policy components within Europe. This can, in particular, be most easily achieved by distinguishing between non-essential (judicial) and essential (legislative) areas of integration competence and activity and by then examining the nature and effectiveness of the separate contributions made in terms of judicial (Chapters 3 and 4) and programme policy construction (Chapter 5). This distinction between essential and non-essential accordingly defines the areas of integration activity identified by the Court as requiring legislative intervention at the European level (essential) and those that can be left to be controlled through its jurisprudence (non-essential). It will be seen that this underlines the operation of the system of mutual recognition that forms the basis of the new integration initiative still being constructed in Europe.

Despite the adoption of a large number of particular directives in the financial area, significant difficulties remain in attempting to complete the creation of a single banking and financial market. These partly relate to the structure and content of the particular measures adopted (and larger secondary programme of which they form part) as well as more particular deficiencies in their consequent adoption and implementation at the national level. It must be accepted that substantial successes have been achieved to date although a number of significant difficulties have still to be overcome to create a fully effective and efficient single financial and capital market within Europe.

Despite the problems identified, further progress is still possible through the construction of a new more complete and effective integration policy and framework within Europe. While mutual recognition suffers from a number of inherent policy and technical limitations (principally linked to is assumed pre-convergence or consequent harmonizing or converging effects), this remains a useful integration device. In attempting to secure any deeper or more complete level of integration, however, mutual recognition must be supplemented by a new doctrine of mutual convergence or functional convergence or equivalence (Chapters 6 and 7). Rather than simply assume that markets are already at an appropriate level of convergence or that they will naturally coalesce over time, more specific initiatives must be undertaken to ensure that a consequent level of appropriate policy effect and control is secured in all cases. Functional convergence or equivalence should then be considered as a common or, at least, parallel standard or test in both essential (legislative) and non-essential (judicial) areas. This new standard must then be supported by an appropriate adjustment and ongoing review and enforcement process as well as an effective institutional apparatus within Europe (Chapter 8).

While it was originally intended that the first edition of this book would include a more detailed historical examination of the development of banking, insurance and securities directives within Europe, it has not been possible to include all of this material in the space available. It had also become clear that the main policy issues that arose did not relate to the content of particular early draft directives or other support measures but with the scope and content of the underlying Treaty and judicial principles on which these were based and which were slowly being clarified and amplified through the jurisprudence of the European Court of Justice. The emphasis of this research accordingly shifted at an early stage from an examination of particular programme measures and the content of their detailed specific articles and regulatory provisions to the proper scope and meaning of the underlying Treaty and judicial rights and obligations that existed under European law, in particular, in the banking and financial area. The work then moved from being regulatory to policy content based.

Some of the insights obtained into the historical development of the Commission's policy in this area have nevertheless being retained (principally at the beginning of Chapter 5) by way of background to the secondary programme measures adopted in the banking and financial area. The original (and until now unseen) draft (first) Banking Directive in 1972 is referred to. This is significant in that it represented an attempt to produce a first fully consolidated and comprehensive directive in 1972 for European banking markets although its discussion could not proceed further due to the opposition of a number of Member States including, in particular, the United Kingdom which acceded to the then European Economic Community (EEC) in 1973. The Commission would not be able to produce an equivalent substantially consolidated directive until 2000 and then this still does not include a number of key elements including revised capital provisions as well as competition and merger policy for banking groups.

It was originally proposed to include separate chapters on each of the main financial directives including, in particular, in the banking, securities and insurance sectors. While draft chapters were prepared during the course of the research, it became clear that the most important issues that arose were concerned with more general policy content and evolution rather than with the detailed regulatory obligations imposed under particular programme articles. The immediate focus is accordingly on the nature and content of the underlying policy itself rather than with consequent specific regulatory provisions that were agreed to attempt to give effect to this policy in practice. Many of core provisions adopted are nevertheless referred to, in particular, in Chapter 5 in an attempt to understand the value and effectiveness of the final programme constructed.

It must also be stressed that two further difficulties necessarily arise in attempting to examine the content of individual directives alone. Many of the original provisions adopted were only based on the most minimum level of initial common agreement and understanding. The result of this was that almost all of the early measures only contained the most basic or absolute minimum level of core regulatory provision all of which would have to be revised and extended subsequently. Even where some reasonably substantial direction was provided (such as under the main banking capital measures adopted in 1988 and 1989 to support the Second Banking Directive), these would have to be revised subsequently to reflect more fundamental underlying changes in banking and financial market structure and practice. Banking and financial markets have undergone a number of significant changes in recent years all of which have had to be reflected in current supervisory and regulatory practice. While almost 50 years have passed since the coming into effect of the original free movement provisions contained in the EEC Treaty in 1958, all of the core measures necessary in the financial area are only now either being adopted for the first time or revised to create a meaningful single market in banking and financial services.

It must also be stressed that this still evolving programme of secondary measures is necessarily subject to the rights and obligations created under the underlying European Treaties (as subsequently revised and extended). Directives and other secondary measures only clarify the application and operation of underlying Treaty rights. They do not create (or remove) them as such. It is accordingly necessary to understand these underlying legal rights and obligations in attempting to interpret and apply the individual secondary measures subsequently adopted. The secondary programme is only ancillary to or clarificatory of these underlying core rights and obligations. This then becomes of particular importance where either a directive does not cover a specific activity or the scope of any residual rights of national (host country) control and intervention are unclear. In such cases, the secondary measure must be considered in light of the underlying Treaty provisions on which they are based with the rights and obligations of all respective parties (including financial institutions and the home and host regulatory authorities) only being properly understood in these terms.

European banking and financial law must then begin with a proper understanding of the scope and operation of the underlying Treaty provisions that apply including all available rights of action and redress. These should then be read with the particular regulatory and other obligations imposed under specific secondary programme measures agreed. All of the most important recent key directives adopted in the financial area are referred to in the text although some of these are still either incomplete (without all of the supporting rules having yet been issued by the particular sector committees concerned) or are only in a draft form even at this late stage of the European integration initiative. The measures noted nevertheless include all of the main provisions that will govern the structure and operation of European financial markets in the years to come.

The related issue that could have been given some further attention in this edition is the revised institutional and constitutional framework that has been set up within Europe. Ensuring that an effective institutional structure is in place is essential to ensure that all necessary measures are adopted and brought into effect in a timely manner. This is of fundamental importance both with regard to the construction of an effective legislative environment as well as larger accountability and control framework within Europe. One of the key defects identified in the European integration process has been the institutional conflicts and deficiencies that have arisen and persisted over time. These are principally concerned with extended bureaucratic control, interference and possible distortion, consequent legislative and substantive relevance, content and technical accuracy, additional cost and administrative and legislative delay as well as associated problems of underlying policy consistency and effectiveness. Many of these issues were most clearly and articulately identified in the financial area under the Lamfalussy Committee Report. While specifically directed at capital market reform, the Lamfalussy study revealed a number of considerably more significant underlying problems with the current institutional and legislative structure within Europe. A number of initiatives have subsequently been undertaken to attempt to correct these both within the capital market and other more general financial areas. While the first edition of this book has not retained the earlier material on the structure and evolution of the general institutional framework within Europe, comments and recommendations are made with regard to securing further improvements in this area especially with regard to banking and financial market reform.

The final point to stress is that much, if not almost all, of the issues and more specific legal measures and programme difficulties identified are still evolving. Financial integration is a complex, continuous and inherently dynamic and evolving process. It is accordingly impossible to capture all detail and nuance in any single fixed text. The objective has accordingly been to attempt to identify the most significant issues and key trends that have occurred to date. Hopefully, this will then provide some further insight into the nature and complexity as well as direction and possible outcome of the underlying integration process still under development and construction. While considerable progress has already been achieved, a significant amount of further work must still be undertaken. We may nevertheless still be able to arrive at some substantial and effective final outcome despite all of the difficulties and problems that have yet to be overcome.

While this is simply an opening text or draft which begins to examine some of these core issues, much of this will be taken forward in a more substantial subsequent book.

Contents

PART II FINANCIAL INTEGRATION

PART III JUDICIAL POLICY CONSTRUCTION

Acknowledgements

The author would like to thank each of the following for their considerable time and assistance. No attribution or validation of any form is nevertheless intended. The opinions expressed are solely those of the author.

I must initially thank Professor Derek Wyatt of St Edmund Hall, Oxford and Professor Stephen Weatherill of Somerville College, Oxford for their inspiration and direction as well as great patience, indulgence and support over a number of years. This book could not have been completed without their exceptional kindness and generosity.

I must also thank Avril Cameron, the Warden of Keble College, Ed Peel and the great Professor Jim Harris at Keble College. Living and writing in Oxford was a wonderful experience and a great privilege. Jim Harris is unfortunately no longer with us and we must again extend our most sincere condolences and best wishes to his family and friends. He was an exceptional Professor and both an inspired and inspiring individual.

I am also greatly indebted to Professor Hal Scott for allowing me to conduct large parts of this work as a research associate at Harvard University. Being in Cambridge, Massachusetts was a great experience and inspiration. I must also thank Professor Howell Jackson at Harvard University for all of his considerable time and assistance.

I am separately greatly indebted to Paolo Clarotti, former Head of Banking and Financial Services within the European Commission, and Georges Zavvos formerly with DG XV and now with the Commission Legal Service. I have spent many highly enjoyable hours with Paolo and Georges discussing key events and stories over lunch, dinner, and drinks and have never ceased to be impressed by the depth of their knowledge and understanding of European and global financial law issues as well as by their great humour, patience, and generosity.

I must also thank all of my former lecturers and colleagues at the College of Europe, Bruges, Belgium. I would, in particular, thank Professor Paul Lenearts, Professor Paul Demaret, Professor van Horn, Professor Valentine Korah, and Marc Siragusa. I would also thank and extend my best wishes to all of my former associates within the Christopher Columbus promotion at the College and, in particular, the intellectually exceptional Gerhard Grill.

I would also thank all of my colleagues at the International Monetary Fund, including, in particular, Sean Hagan, General Counsel, and Ross Lekow, Head of Technical Assistance, as well as Françoise Gianviti and Bill Holder who have since retired although not without leaving their very considerable mark on the Fund and its operations. Working with the Fund (as well as with the World Bank and the Asian Development Bank) has allowed me to develop many new perspectives and insights into international, regional and cross-border financial integration and law reform. This has greatly assisted the development of many of the core ideas in this book.

I am also greatly indebted to Professor Noreen Burrell and Professor Balekijan formerly within the European Law Department at Glasgow University for their early inspiration and direction (and lots of very bad jokes before we began any real discussion of current European law issues on a weekly basis). I will also always be indebted to Professor David Walker at Glasgow University for his exceptional example and inspiration as well as for allowing me to begin my first year of legal studies one term late (after a somewhat extended non-recreational visit over the summer to a public general hospital following a rather unfortunate incident with a motorcycle and another considerably larger eight-wheeled vehicle).

I also owe a more general indebtedness to all of my current colleagues at the Centre for Commercial Law Studies in London including, in particular, Professor Janet Dine our new Director and Professor Takis Tridimas, Head of the International Financial Law Unit within the Centre. I must welcome Professor Takis Tridimas again and look forward very much to working with him, in particular, on European Law and European financial integration issues over the coming years.

I would especially like to thank Professor Joseph Norton for his great assistance and great company over many years. Hopefully Joe will be able to stay on at the Centre in an Emeritus position following his standing down as Head of the International Financial Law Unit after many years. His control and balance as well as kindness and support will be greatly missed. Thank you also to Professor Mads Andenas, former Director at the British Institute of International and Comparative Law and now with the University of Leicester. Hopefully, we will be able to take forward, at least, some of the exciting ideas and proposed projects that we have been discussing.

I would also like to express my continuing gratitude to Andrew Mills-Baker, Jonathan Bayliss, and Grania Baird at Farrer & Co, Solicitors, London with whom I have very much enjoyed working over a number of years.

I must also as always thank my family whom I adore. Congratulations, in particular, to Jamie for getting into one of the best schools in Edinburgh. Well done.

Biography of the Author

GEORGE ALEXANDER WALKER
BA, LLB (HONS), DIPLP (Glasgow), DAES (Bruges), LLM (London), PHD (London), DPhil (Oxford)

George Walker is a Barrister and Member of the Honourable Society of Inner Temple in London. He is a Member of the New York Bar and was previously a Solicitor in Scotland and England and Wales. He has been a Legal Consultant with Farrer & Co, Solicitors, London and was formerly a Solicitor in Edinburgh and with various major City of London law firms.

He is a Professor in Law at the Centre for Commercial Law Studies, Queen Mary, University of London. He is Deputy Head of the International Financial Law Unit and Head of the Banking and Finance division. He was formerly Acting Head of Unit between 2002 and 2004.

He is a former Affiliate Lecturer in Law at Cambridge University and held a visiting research position at Harvard University for two years and subsequently at Georgetown University, Washington, D.C. He is an external examiner at Hong Kong University and has been a Visiting Academic Scholar at the Law School, University of Tokyo, Japan. He has been the Senior Examiner for the Securities and Investments Institute (formerly the London Stock Exchange) in Financial Regulation and Compliance (Financial Services Law) since 2000.

He is Legal Consultant with the International Monetary Fund, Washington, DC and has spent a number of summers working at their head office in Washington. He has acted on a number of significant international law reform projects including with the Fund, the World Bank, the EBRD as well as with the Asia Development Bank and with various national governments. He has worked on thirty separate country law projects to date including in Eastern Europe, South America, Africa, Asia and China (including on Chinese financial conglomerates and bank insolvency). He has also assisted a separate Working Group on Japanese Financial Conglomerates.

He is author of the leading reference texts *International Banking Regulation—Law, Policy and Practice* (Kluwer Law 2001) and *European Banking Law—Policy and Programme Construction* (British Institute of International Comparative and Commercial Law (BIICL), 2006).

He is co-author of the leading UK texts on *Banking and Financial Services Regulation* (Butterworths 3rd edn 2002) and of *Blackstone's Guide to the Financial Services and Markets Act* (Blackstones 2001). He is an

Assistant Editor of the *Encyclopaedia of Banking Law* (Butterworths 5 vols Looseleaf) and of the monthly online *Banking Law Update*. He is also an Assistant Editor of *Butterworths Financial Regulation Services* (Butterworths 7 vols Looseleaf).

He is co-author and co-editor of the new leading UK texts with Michael Blair QC, former General Counsel Financial Services Authority, London (FSA), on *Financial Services Law* (OUP 2006) and *Financial Markets and Exchanges Law* (OUP 2006).

He was formerly Executive Editor of the Financial Times, *Financial Regulation Report* and now Informa, *Financial Regulation International*. He is co-editor of various book series. He has published a large number of other refereed and journal articles as well as made numerous chapter and conference contributions.

He is a Senior Fellow in Banking Law at the London Institute of International Banking, Finance and Development Law and a Professorial Fellow at the Asian Institute of International Financial Law, University of Hong Kong and the Institute for International Banking and Finance Law, Dallas, Texas.

Introduction

The purpose of this book is to examine the nature and content of the judicial and programme policy adopted within the European Community in the banking and financial area. While a nominally clear and substantial framework has been constructed, a number of significant difficulties remain in terms of policy content and effect and, in particular, with regard to the meaning, validity and consistency of the main judicial principles involved and the structure, operation and coherence of the underlying secondary programme constructed.

The core difficulty that has to be overcome within any regional trading system is that an essential conflict necessarily arises between the need to promote enhanced market access at the same time as secure proper market control. (This is referred to as a fundamental 'access and control conflict' in the text.) This becomes of particular significance in the banking and financial area in light of the importance of the key functions discharged (savings, credit and payment) and the inherently unstable nature of the markets (due, in particular, to maturity transformation and the associated risk of institutional closure, contagion and systemic collapse). Despite this and the importance of banking and financial markets as independent commercial sectors, a fundamental 'policy vacuum' (and related 'control gap') remain within Europe in this area.

Following the failure of the Commission's earlier efforts to correct this omission through a general process of full harmonization within each industrial and commercial sector, a new approach was adopted based on mutual recognition, minimum harmonization, and home country control. This was, in turn, constructed on the basis of a number of separate principles developed by the European Court of Justice. Despite the apparent validity and clarity of each of these policy components, their meaning, relationship, and relevance are still far from clear. Significant difficulties also remain in connection with a number of key aspects of the underlying jurisprudence of the Court from which these new integration devices are derived. Significant problems also remain with regard to the structure and content of the supporting secondary programme constructed.

The evolution and content of the emerging (but still incomplete) policy adopted in the banking and financial area are accordingly examined in the text. In so doing, the contributions of the European Court and the Commission are considered and the structure and content of the final programme of secondary measures constructed assessed. Conclusions are drawn with regard to the coherence and effectiveness of the policy position arrived at to date with a number of separate recommendations being made for its further revision and reform.

In considering the particular issues that arise in the banking and financial area within the larger European integration initiative, a number of particular themes or key ideas can be identified. These are variously referred to as integration conflicts, doctrines, or principles or integration processes or sub-processes in the text. These are then used as short form references to cover more complex underlying sets of ideas within the larger integration agenda still under construction.

The two main initial ideas identified are the underlying policy vacuum that was left in the terms of the original European Economic Community (EEC) Treaty in the banking and financial area and the essential conflict that necessarily exists in attempting to secure some form of automatic or privileged market access within a regional trading system as well as an appropriate level of market control.[1] The cause or reason for the underlying policy[2] vacuum identified may be understood in terms of a number of omission theories that can be developed. These include a 'Relevance or Treaty Theory', a 'Sensitivity or Damage Theory', a 'Programme or Evolution Theory', a 'Revision or Integration (or Capital Market) Theory', and an 'Amendment or Correction Theory'. Each of these is explained further in the text and used to attempt to understand the underlying objectives of the original Treaty draftsman in the banking and financial area.[3]

The related problem that arises is attempting to secure an appropriate balance between market access and market control within a regional system. The underlying purpose or dynamic of any regional trading system is to allow market operators from one country automatic, mandatory or privileged rights of access to the markets of all other participating territories. To the extent that the local (or host) regulatory or other administrative or technical requirements (that would otherwise apply) have to be removed or, at least, adjusted or diluted, the stability of the local or host market may be undermined. A fundamental access and control conflict accordingly arises within any regional trading or service initiative.[4]

[1] Ch 1, section B (1) and (2).

[2] On the nature of banking and financial policy, see Ch 6, section B (1). On the definition of bank supervision and regulation, see Ch 1 (n 2).

[3] Ch 1, section B (1) and (n 36); and Ch 2, section J and (nn 170 and 173–5).

[4] Ch 1, section B (2). For the purposes of this text, regional will generally be used to refer to any collection of countries operating within a particular geographic area (such as Europe) or with some other common connection rather than to particular areas or sub-areas within countries as the term is often used within the EU. Regional institutions and bodies then refer to the cross-border or inter-governmental agencies set up to manage particular economic, political, legal, or administrative relations or other social or cultural matters at the new collective (non-national) level.

To the extent that regulatory provisions are generally enforced at the national level through local or domestic rather than regional agencies, a further 'control gap' is created.[5] This will arise where no central regional agencies have been created in any particular sector (such as in the banking, securities, or insurance areas). In the event of 'regulatory failure or default' (with no harmonized or minimum provisions having been agreed at the regional level), market control will remain to be governed and enforced at the local level. Even where appropriate regional standards have been agreed, they are often still enforced through national regulatory and administrative systems and agencies (under the principle of 'subsidiarity'). An essential control gap accordingly arises in both non-harmonized and harmonized areas. This then creates further problems in terms of effective and consistent enforcement and sanction.

Separate difficulties arise where the underlying access and control policy used is unclear and market or commercial operators are unable to understand the scope and limits of the rights and obligations conferred. This uncertainty may of itself increase the risk or danger of regional contagion. To the extent that such market participants are not able to understand the precise content of the new regional rights and obligations created, they will not be able to rely on them but continue to conduct their business in accordance with relevant domestic entitlements. This policy confusion will then result in a further 'integration default' to the extent that private parties (as well as governments or government agencies) are not able or prepared to rely on and enforce otherwise legitimate rights and entitlements.[6] Policy confusion (in addition to the original policy vacuum) will then further undermine the integration effect or success of the regional trading system which uncertainty may also increase the risk of intra and inter-market contagion and exposure.

The further problem that this creates is one of 'regional contagion' rather than solely national or domestic crisis.[7] Where a particular institution or set of institutions experience financial difficulties, this exposure may spread to other entities either through direct or perceived credit risk. In the event that this contagion is sufficiently severe, the stability of the particular market or sub-market will be threatened. This contagion may then spread within the domestic financial system and economy as a whole. The additional difficulty created within a regional cross-border trading system with privileged or mandatory rights of access is that this contagion can pass across the whole of the regional area rather than remain solely within the domestic financial system. Regional contagion may then arise as an immediate and direct effect or threat from the establishment of the underlying cross-border access system itself.

5 Ch 1, section B (3).

6 Ch 1, section B (4).

7 Ch 1, section B (5).

A series of core problems accordingly arise within European financial integration including, in particular, policy vacuum, access and control conflict and control gap as well as possible integration damage or default and the ultimate threat of regional contagion and collapse. It is for this reason essential that an effective policy and supporting programme of rights and obligations are constructed to ensure that all of these potential difficulties and threats are properly managed and controlled. This is one of the core challenges of the European financial integration initiative.

A number of further problems can also be identified within any larger integration process such as that under construction within Europe. These can be summarized in terms of financial and programme default, related legislative adoption and implementation deficiencies as well as larger systems problems and more general development issues.[8]

With regard to policy and programme structure and content, particular difficulties arise with regard to Treaty base, judicial policy coherence and consistency, programme content, legislative function and institutional support.[9] In connection with legislative adoption and programme operation, further problems arise in terms of possible implementation and adoption failures or default, interpretation consistency and the need for effective continuing review as well as securing a proper degree of regulatory equivalence and the provision of proper market support.[10]

In relation to the larger European integration process, separate issues arise with regard to the evolving role and contribution of the European Court of Justice, related scope of EU law, the nature of the underlying law of free movement, policy balance (free or social market) and the most appropriate institutional or integration theory to be adopted and applied.[11] A number of additional longer term development issues must also be considered including enlargement effects, constitutional balance and revision, financial and budgetary support as well as external and global relations, and further technical revision or correction and financial innovation adjustments.[12]

Each of these issues is considered in further detail in Chapter 1.

The key doctrine within European integration is mutual recognition. This has been the main operational or policy solution adopted with regard to many of the more difficult particular issues identified. Despite its importance, the origin, meaning and legal validity as well as content and operation of this core integration device are still far from clear.

[8] Ch 1, sections C–F.
[9] Ch 1, section C.
[10] Ch 1, section D.
[11] Ch 1, section E.
[12] Ch 1, section F.

Rather than have any clear Treaty or judicial base, it would appear that mutual recognition was only an executive or administrative policy construct.[13] Mutual recognition was not referred to expressly by the European Court of Justice in the leading case of *Cassis de Dijon* in 1979[14] and any issue of comparability or equivalence was strictly *obiter* as the Court had already decided the case on the basis of the inadequacy of the German Government's arguments.[15] Comparability and equivalence would then only be raised subsequently in such cases as *Fietje* (which involved product labelling) and similar decisions.[16]

Mutual recognition was first expressly referred to by the Commission in its 1985 White Paper[17] although some of the ideas on which it was based were set out in an earlier commentary on the importance of the decision in *Cassis* in 1980.[18]

Problems also apply with regard to its meaning and usage with, at least, five possible different applications being identifiable.[19] Mutual recognition can be used most specifically to refer to the judicial examination of the sufficiency of national protective measures within a particular free movement case before the European Court of Justice or as an internal act of mutual acceptance or validation within a European legislative measure. These generally correspond with its use in non-essential (judicially determined) and essential (legislatively governed) areas. It can also be used as a separate free-standing legal principle of comparability and equivalence (as under the Commission's 1980 Communication on the decision in *Cassis de Dijon*) or to refer to the Commission's *New Approach* to integration (as announced in its 1985 White Paper). It may also be used more generically to refer to any act of conditional recognition.[20]

Further difficulties arise in attempting to identify the proper functions (and sub-functions) of mutual recognition[21] with the meaning of the related doctrines or principles of minimum harmonization and home country control also being unclear and their relationship with mutual recognition unspecified.[22]

13 While mutual recognition has some partial Treaty base (with regard to diplomas, certificates and formal qualifications (Art 47(ex 57)) and companies (Art 293 (ex 220))), it is assumed in each case that there will be some process of prior identification, negotiation and common agreement. Mutual recognition in these cases will not then operate through the Treaty directly but only though the secondary programme measures subsequently adopted. Ch 6, section C (1).

14 Case 120/78 *Rewe-Zentral AG v Bundesmonopolverwaltung fur Branntwein* [1979] ECR 649 [1979] 3 CMLR 494. Ch 3, section C (3) and Ch 6, section C (1).

15 Ch 3, section C (3) and Ch 6, section C (1).

16 Case 27/80 *Fietje* [1980] ECR 3839, [1981] 3 CMLR. Ch 1 (n 72). For further discussion, see Ch 3, section C (3).

17 Commission, *Completing the Internal Market—White Paper from the Commission to the European Council* (Milan 18–29 June 1985), COM(85) 310 final (14 June 1985).

18 Ch 3, section C (3).

19 Ch 6, section D (1).

20 Ch 6, section D (1).

21 Ch 6, section C.

22 Ch 6, section D.

Rather than operate in a single almost static manner, mutual recognition can also be considered as involving up to five separate stages or processes (or sub-processes). These include definition or identification, mutual review (or pre-review), measurement or assessment, regulatory adjustment or disapplication and possible systems review or validation.[23]

Considerable care must accordingly be exercised in attempting to understand and use this core integration device despite its assumed or apparent operational simplicity and validity.

All of the issues identified (including with regard to mutual recognition) must be taken into account in attempting to construct any final or total policy and programme solution in the banking and financial area. Each of these will have a major impact on the success or otherwise of the integration initiative constructed within Europe or elsewhere.

While it is not possible to consider all of these issues in a single text in detail, an attempt can be made to begin to understand the nature and content of the underlying essential (access and control) policy developed in the banking and financial area specifically and to assess its role and importance within the larger integration processes still under construction. Policy in this area is necessarily affected by many of the issues referred to while the solutions and resolutions adopted will be of relevance and value elsewhere.

Many of these ideas will be taken forward in a more substantial subsequent book which will examine each of the main directives adopted in further detail although it is hoped that this more provisional study is of value and assistance at this stage.

The structure of the book is as follows. The importance of banking and financial markets and the nature of banking and financial policy are initially reviewed.[24] The main difficulties that arise with regard to integration more generally and banking and financial integration more specifically are noted. This includes the policy and programme, legislative, European, and development issues already referred to.

The nature of the European Community, European Union, and European and economic integration are then considered in further detail.[25] This includes the perceived advantages and disadvantages of integration as well as a review of some of the main assessment and measurement exercises conducted to date. The nature of other comparable global and regional integration systems are considered including, in particular, the GATS and NAFTA. The nature of the more specific new economic and legal orders created within the EU are noted and appropriate institutional structures referred to. The background to financial integration more specifically and

[23] Ch 6, section E. [24] Ch 1; and Ch 6. [25] Ch 2.

capital and monetary and economic policy within Europe are then reviewed. This is essential to understand the background to the drafting of the original economic and financial provisions in the Treaty of Rome and the subsequent changes that have taken place in this area.

The contribution of the European Court of Justice in the construction of a new law of free movement is then examined in further detail.[26] The background to the emerging principles developed is noted, in particular, with regard to the evolution of the case law in the area of the free movement of goods. This considers specifically the early key cases on duties, charges, and taxes as well as the leading decisions of *Dassonville*, *Cassis de Dijon*, and *Keck* as well as more recent post-*Keck* restatements. The comparable provisions in the establishment and services area are examined including, in particular, the significance of the decisions in *Gebhard* and *Säger* (and *Gouda*).

The assistance provided by the more recent decisions issued in the financial area are examined separately.[27] This includes *Commission v Germany* (Co-insurance), *Schindler* (sales rules), *Alpine Investments* (marketing restrictions), *Reiseburo Broede* (licensing requirements) and *Parodi* (licensing reconsidered). The assistance or otherwise that these decisions provide in clarifying the applicable provisions in the financial area with regard to restrictive effect and possible derogation is assessed.

Other more recent finance related decisions are also referred to including *Bank fur Arbeit* (access to documents), *Paul der Weduwe* (bank secrecy), *Greece v Commission* (state aids), *Caixa-Bank France* (interest on sight accounts) and *Vereinsbank v Commission* (price fixing). These are of interest although they are concerned with more specific technical and procedural matters. More significant policy issues are nevertheless raised in *Germany v European Parliament and Council* in 1997 (deposit protection) and *Peter Paul* in 2004 (regulatory immunity) and are examined in further detail. These consider *inter alia* the scope of the harmonization set up under the main banking and financial directives and the extent to which individual rights of action are conferred under the Directives as opposed to the Treaty. Reference is also made to the House of Lords decision in the UK in *Three Rivers v Bank of England* (misfeasance in public office) which also commented on the purpose of the main early banking measures and the extent to which individual rights were created.

The historical development and basic structure of the final programme of secondary measures adopted in the financial area are then reviewed.[28] This includes a note of each of the principal directives in the main financial sectors as well as a more specific examination of the recent work undertaken by the Commission to attempt to complete this programme by the 2005 and 2010 deadlines respectively. The recent consolidation efforts and

[26] Ch 3. [27] Ch 4. [28] Ch 5.

completion work announced are also considered with provisional conclusions being drawn with regard to the coherence and effectiveness of the agreed and proposed secondary programme still under construction.

A more general assessment is then made of the effectiveness of the overall banking and financial policy adopted to date.[29] This includes a re-examination of the nature of the underlying policy concerned as well as a more specific re-consideration of the nature of mutual recognition as the principal integration doctrine or device adopted and its component elements and operations (and sub-operations). The relationship between mutual recognition and the related principles of minimum harmonization and home country control (as well as 'host country control' and the general good) are also reviewed. The objective is to try to understand more fully the origin, validity, and value of these new integration devices.

A series of recommendations are finally made with a view to the possible revision and further refinement and expansion of the structure, content and operation of the financial policy still under development.[30] For this purpose, a new or, at least, revised or adjusted integration strategy and framework are constructed. The objective is not to replace the existing mutual recognition based approach outright but to attempt to clarify and improve its policy base and the underlying doctrinal assumptions made. A number of revisions or corrections can then be made with regard to the improvement of the operation and effectiveness of the policy and programme solutions adopted and applied in the banking and financial area.

[29] Ch 6. [30] Chs 7 and 8.

PART ONE

Financial Policy

1

European Banking and Financial Law—Policy Content and General Development Issues

An extended and complex programme of measures has been constructed within the European Community[1] over the last five decades in connection with the supervision and regulation of banking and financial markets.[2] The financial regime set up within Europe now constitutes a core and essential

[1] The European Union (EU) was created under Art A of the Maastricht Treaty (MT). The EU is stated to be founded on the European Communities including the European Community, the European Coal and Steel Community and the European Atomic Energy Community (Art A, para 3). Additional powers were conferred on the EU in respect of Common Foreign and Security Policy (Art J) and Home Affairs and Justice Policy (Art K). All references to the European Economic Community Treaty (EEC Treaty) and to the European Economic Community were replaced by references to the European Community Treaty (or EC Treaty) and European Community under Art G.A(1) of the Maastricht Treaty.

Earlier Treaty amendments were subsequently consolidated under the Treaty of Amsterdam which was adopted on 18 June 1997 and came into effect in May 1999. A consolidated copy of the Treaty establishing the European Community was issued in 1997 (OJ C 340, 10 Nov 1997, 173–308). The Amsterdam Treaty also provided for central and eastern European expansion and further work on European citizenship. The Treaty of Nice was signed in December 2000 and was generally concerned with amending the composition of the institutions, voting procedures, enlargement and promoting enhanced cooperation. A full possible European Constitution was produced in July 2003 although not fully ratified within dates set, section F(2) and (nn 91–3). On the EURATOM Treaty (n 33). For general historical background on main Treaties, Ch 2 (nn 7–11).

As the core provisions with regard to European banking and financial services remain within the renamed EC Treaty, the correct legal source of rights and obligations is the EC Treaty rather than Maastrict Treaty although references will generally be made in this text either to the European Community and EC Treaty or to the European Union or Maastrict Treaty more generally depending upon the degree of specificity intended.

[2] For the purposes of this text, unless otherwise indicated, the term regulation is used to refer to the legal rules and regulations or administrative requirements established by financial authorities or by market participants (self-regulatory systems) to limit or control the risks assumed by banks and other financial institutions. Supervision is understood to refer to the associated or complimentary process of monitoring the operation of financial markets more generally or with the overseeing or reviewing of compliance by financial institutions with any regulatory provisions imposed. Regulation then involves a control or governance function while supervision is concerned with oversight or compliance. GA Walker *International Banking Regulation—Law, Policy and Practice* (Kluwer Law International London 2001), Introduction (n 1). With regard to the proper justifications for or theories of financial regulation (n 22). On the correspondence between market access, regulation and supervision with mutual recognition, minimum harmonization and home country control, Ch 6, section C (3).

part of the largest regional trading, industrial and commercial market place in the world.

The significance of the European single or internal market[3] in contrast with other similar initiatives is that it includes both an automatic or mandatory right of market entry and access as well as a still evolving supporting control system. The underlying purpose of any regional trading system must be to provide full cross-border access for all relevant parties at the same time as ensure a necessary degree of cross-border market control within the new integrated market place created. As market access and control will necessarily conflict to the extent that local national technical standards and regulatory provisions have to be reduced or dis-applied with regard to incoming firms from other participating territories, the success or otherwise of the final integrated market constructed will be dependent on the extent to which these two core objectives can be properly and effectively balanced.[4]

The European Community and larger Union are also unique in that they consist of a number of distinct overlapping levels of economic, monetary and social integration rather than constitute any single cooperation or coordination initiative or framework.[5] The European Community is essentially based on a free trade area (FTA) and a customs union (CU) which also operate on the basis of a common market (CM) within which the full free movement of all factors of production are secured (including labour, capital and enterprise).[6] The European Union also incorporates a (combined) economic

[3] The internal market is stated to comprise an area without internal frontiers in which the free movement of goods, persons, services and capital is to be ensured (Art 14(2) EC Treaty). As such, the internal market constitutes a more limited form of the original common market to be established under Art 2 EC Treaty. The internal market was to be progressively established by 31 Dec 1992 in accordance with Arts 15, 26, 47(2), 49, 80, 93 and 95 but without prejudice to the other provisions of the Treaty (Art 14(1) (ex 7a)). Commission, *Completing the Internal Market—White Paper from the Commission to the European Council (Milan 18–29 June 1985)*, COM (85) 310 final (14 June 1985). This followed the Commission's 'Programme of Commission for 1985' presented to the European Parliament on 6 Mar and endorsed by the European Council on 29 and 30 Mar 1985. For further comment, Ch 2 (nn 9, 50 and 140), Ch 3 (nn 83, 94 and 95) and Ch 6, section C(2) and (nn 41–43).

[4] This creates a basic access and control conflict within any regional trading system. Preface and Ch 1, section B (2). On the related problems of policy vacuum, control gap, integration damage or default and regional contagion, crisis and collapse, sections B(1), (3), (4) and (5). On the difference between regional and global systems (n 23). On the related access and support conflict that arises in the absence of any central lender of last resort support mechanism within Europe, Ch 5 (n 167). On European institutional or committee revision in the financial area, Ch 1 (nn 45 and 55).

[5] See, eg, J Viner *The Customs Union Issue* (Carnegie Endowment for International Peace New York 1950); J Tinbergen *International Economic Integration* (Elsevier London 1954); and B Balassa *The Theory of Economic Integration* (Allen & Unwin London 1961). See also F McDonald and S Dearden *European Economic Integration* (3rd edn Longman New York 1999), Ch 2, 34.

[6] A free trade area involves the removal of customs duties, tariffs and quotas on inter-state trade. A customs union involves the establishment of a common external as well as internal

and monetary union (EMU)[7] with some continuing latent aspiration to ultimate full political union (FPU).[8]

The dominant characteristic of post-War European history more generally has been the use of economic functionalism as the main integration mechanism.[9] This involves the pursuit of narrowly defined initiatives in particular economic areas of common interest from which larger integration successes are expected to follow. The assumption is that more general cooperation and closer integration will naturally result from the achievements realised through the pursuit of the more immediate and limited functionally specific economic activity or activities selected. The history of the European Union can then be understood in terms of a continuing process of closer contact and cooperation between the participating nations at any particular time. While this was initially limited to the common pooling and

tariff. A common market consists of a free trade area and a customs union as well as full free movement of production factors (labour, capital and enterprise). Ch 2 (nn 28–30). See generally W Molle *The Economics of European Integration—Theory, Practice and Policy* (3rd edn Ashgate Hants 1997). See also McDonald and Dearden (n 5).

[7] An economic union involves the establishment of common economic policies (including possibly market regulation, competition and industrial structure as well as macro-economic and monetary policy). Monetary union either requires the irrevocable fixing of exchange rates or the introduction of a single currency. Full political union would constitute the last integration stage which would generally operate through shared legislative and executive functions for all participating countries. Ch 2 (nn 33–35). See also Molle (n 6); and McDonald and Dearden (n 5).

[8] On European history generally, K Wilson *The History of the Idea of Europe* (Routledge London 1995); T Salmon and Sir Nicholl William *Building European Union—A Documentary History and Analysis* (Manchester University Press Manchester 1997); W Lipgens *A History of European Integration*, vol I: The Formation of the European Unity Movement 1945–1947 (Clarendon Oxford 1982); Lipgens *Documents on the History of the European Integration*, vols 1–3 (De Gruyter Berlin 1986); Lipgens and W Lath *Documents on the History of European Integration*, vol 4 (De Gruyter Berlin 1991); Katherine Savage *The History of the Common Market* (Longman & Harlow 1969); Max Jansen *History of European Integration 1945–1975* (University of Amsterdam Amsterdam 1975); Fritz Machlup *A History of Thought on Economic Integration* (Macmillan London 1977); D Spierenburg and R Poidevin *The History of the High Authority of the European Coal and Steel Community: Supra nationality in Operation* (Weidenfeld and Nicolson London 1994); and M McCormick *Origins of the European Economy* (Cambridge University Press Cambridge 2001). See also Benjamin Angel and Jacques Lafitte *L'Europe: Petite histoire d'une grande idée* (Paris Gallimard 2004); Marie-Thérèse Bitsch *Histoire de la construction européenne de 1945 à nos jours* (Bruxelles Éd Complexe 2004); Christophe Réveillard *Les dates-clefs de la construction européenne: Histoire, institutions, traités, politiques communes, union économique et monétaire, élargissements, perspectives* (Paris Ellipses 2000); and Charles Zorgbibe *Histoire de l'Union Européenne* (Paris Albin Michel Fondation Robert Schuman 2005). On the internal market see, Michel Ayral *Le marché intérieur de l'Union européenne: les Règles du Jeu*. Paris: (Documentation Française 1998); Jean-Marc Favre *Droit du Marché intérieur* (Gualino ed 2001); and Joël Molinier *Le Droit du Marché Intérieur Européen* (Paris LGDJ 1995). See also Boulouis (et al) *Les Grands Arrêts de la Jurisprudence Communautaire. Tome 2, Droit Communautaire des Affaires. Marché Intérieur. Politiques Communautaires* (Dalloz 2002). See also Ch 2 (n 4). On European legal history, Maurizio Lupoi, *The Origins of the European Legal Order* (CUP Cambridge 1999).

[9] Molle (n 6); and McDonald and Dearden (n 5). See also section E (5) and authorities cited (n 87). For further discussion, Ch 2, section A and (nn 12–19).

management of the main industrial energy (coal) and production (steel) factors,[10] this was extended at an early stage to include atomic energy and more general goods and services[11] and then more recently economic and monetary matters as well as further common provisions on justice and home affairs and defence.[12]

Banking and financial markets have always operated as core elements or components within these larger functional initiatives although rarely identified and examined separately until now.[13] One of the underlying purposes of this text is then to begin to consider the historical importance and relevance of financial markets and financial integration[14] within the larger integration process under construction more generally as well as to assess the nature and content of the specific policy and programme response developed to date.

A. BANKING AND FINANCIAL MARKETS

The banking and financial component of the single market within Europe is of particular importance both in terms of the underlying economic value of the principal sectors concerned[15] as well as the core support functions

[10] Treaty establishing the European Coal and Steel Community 1950 (the Treaty of Paris) (n 1).

[11] Treaty establishing the European Economic Community 1957 (the Treaty of Rome); and Treaty establishing the European Atomic Energy Community 1957 (n 1).

[12] Treaty on European Union (Maastricht Treaty) 1992 (n 1).

[13] The absence of further Treaty direction is considered further below. This can partly be understood in terms of number of omission theories. (n 36) and Ch 2 (nn 169–70 and 173–5).

[14] Integration may be defined as the gradual elimination of economic frontiers between independent states. Molle (6). Financial integration then relates more specifically to the removal of barriers or other obstacles to the integration of each of the main financial sectors on a European basis as well as the further approximation or harmonization of supporting monetary and economic policies. This will include the provision of banking and other financial services by financial intermediaries on a European wide basis as well as the integration of capital matters and cooperation in related areas of monetary and economic policy (n 7). On integration, Ch 2, sections B, C and D. On banking and financial policy, Ch 2, section J and on the banking and financial programme, Ch 5. On mutual recognition, Ch 6. On policy and programme revision, Chs 7 and 8.

[15] The overall increase in consumer surplus for the European economy due to the single market in financial services was estimated to be between 11 billion and 33 billion ECU (£7.7 and £23.1 billion) of which the banking sector made up between 8 and 22 billion. In terms of relative value, financial services (including banking and insurance) were considered to represent approximately 6 per cent of EU GDP. They also provide 2.45 per cent of employment and constitute one of the sectors where Europe has the greatest potential for employment expansion under the Commission's Employment Rates Report. COM (98) 572. See also Ch 2, sections C and D and Ch 5, section D(5).

The original assessment of the potential benefits of integration had been carried out by Paolo Cecchini. P Cecchini *The European Challenge: 1992 The Benefits of a Single Market* (Wildwood House Aldershot 1988). See also Commission *The Impact and Effectiveness of the Single Market: Communication from the Commission to the European Parliament and*

that financial markets and financial intermediaries carry out in any modern economy. In terms of economic function, banking and other financial institutions provide a number of essential intermediation services without which any market based economy could not operate. These include deposit (or savings) and loan (credit) facilities as well as necessary supporting clearing and settlement (payment) systems. Without these core functions, it would be impossible to borrow short or longer term funds for business or individual (consumer) purposes as well as to make any form of payment in settlement (discharge) of financial transactions and legal obligations other than through some barter arrangement.[16]

Related capital markets also provide a range of transferable security based funding and investment mechanisms that are essential to the longer term growth and expansion of any developed economy. Insurance (and re-insurance) markets make available essential fixed (life) and contingent (non-life) risk management services that assist ensure an enhanced degree of financial and commercial predictability in business and personal relations. An increasingly wide range of alternative investment and hedging facilities

Council (Office for Official Publications of the European Communities, Luxembourg 1996); Commission *The Single Market Review* (1996, Office for Official Publications of the European Communities, Luxembourg), 38 Reports; and European Economy, *Economic Valuation of the Internal Market* (1996), Reports and Studies No 4. For comment, Molle (n 6); M Emerson, M Aujean, M Catinat, P Goybet and A Jacquemin 'The Economics of 1992' (OUP Oxford 1988); E Davies, J Kay and C Smales *1992: Myths and Realities* (London Business School London 1989); T Cutler, C Halsem, J Williams and K Williams '1992—The Struggle for Europe (Berg Oxford 1989); J Grahl and P Teague *1992: The Big Market* (Lawrence & Wishart London 1992). See also A Smith and A Venables 'The Costs of Non-Europe: An assessment based on a forward model of imperfect competition and economies of scale' (Commission of European Communities 1988), *Research on the Costs of Non-Europe, Basic Findings* (vol 2); and D Dyker (ed) *The European Economy* (Longman London 1992). For discussion and comment, Ch 2, sections C and D.

The earlier estimates produced were re-examined by the Commission in 1996. European Economy *Economic Valuation of the Internal Market* (1996), Reports and Studies No 4. See also Commission *The Single Market Review* (Office for Official Publications of the European Communities Luxembourg 1996), 38 Reports; Commission 'The Impact and Effectiveness of the Single Market', Communication from the Commission to the European Parliament and Council; and Commission 'Action Plan for the Single Market' (1996), Communication from the Commission to the European Council. For comment, M Monti *The Single Market and Tomorrow's Europe* (Office for Official Publications of the European Communities, Luxembourg 1996).

It has been separately estimated that financial integration could add between 5 per cent and 7 per cent annually to EU GDP which would be equal to 43 billion euro on an annual basis. Report to the European Financial Services Round Table *The Benefits of a Working European Retail Market for Financial Services* (2002) available on http://www.zew.de/erfstudyresults/.

[16] On financial institutions and financial intermediation, see, eg, Lewis and Davis *Domestic and International Banking* (Philip Allan Deddington 1987), Ch 1; PGA Howells and K Bains *Financial Markets and Institutions* (Longman London 1990), Ch 1; and J Gilbody *The UK Monetary & Financial System* (Routledge London 1991), Part II. See also D J Goacher *The Monetary and Financial System* (Bankers' Books London 1990), 35–44; S Valdez *An Introduction to Western Financial Markets* (Macmillan Business Basingstoke 1993), Ch 1; and A Page and R Ferguson *Investor Protection* (Weidenfeld & Nicolson London 1992) Ch 1.

are also provided through other types of financial instruments and markets including currency,[17] derivatives[18] and commodity related products.[19] It must be accepted that the fundamental structure and operation of almost any modern economy is affected, if not largely determined, by the underlying financial framework and systems in place including, in particular, the structure, range and variety of the financial markets and financial instruments and supporting intermediation services and facilities available.[20]

As well as contribute separately to economic value and act as essential service components within the normal operation of any market system, sound banking and financial institutions are necessary to ensure the stability of the particular sub-markets involved and of the local and regional economic system as a whole. The difficulty that arises is that financial institutions and banks, in particular, are inherently vulnerable and prone to collapse in light of the underlying funding risks involved in financing medium and long term loan and other credit commitments through sight or demand deposits.[21] It is for this reason that special statutory or adminis-

[17] See, eg, C Tygier *Basic Handbook of Foreign Exchange* (Euromoney London 1988). Foreign exchange related risks include foreign exchange (FX) settlement risk, FX credit risk, FX liquidity risk, FX market risk, FX replacement risk and FX operational risk. See also Committee on Payment Systems *Settlement Risk in Foreign Exchange Transactions* (CPSS Basel Mar 1996), 4.

[18] See generally Global Derivatives Study Group *Derivatives: Practices and Principles* (Group of 30 July 1993). See also Basel Committee and Technical Committee of IOSCO *Framework for Supervisory Information* (July 1995); *Public Disclosure of the Trading and Derivatives Activities of Banks and Securities Firms* (Nov 1995); and *Survey of Disclosures of the Trading and Derivatives Activities of Banks and Securities Firms* (Nov 1996). In relation to the historical development of swaps, P Goris *The Legal Aspect of Swaps—An Analysis Based on Economic Substance* (Graham & Trotman London 1994), Ch 2. For discussion of main issues which arise from a regulatory perspective and the content of the basic control response constructed at the international level, GA Walker 'Financial Derivatives—Global Regulatory Developments' [1996] JBL Jan 66. In connection with the main private law issues which arise and the nature of the systems of control adopted in the UK, W Blair, A Allen, K Palmer, P Richards-Carpenter and GA Walker *Banking and Financial Services Regulation* (3rd edn 2002 Butterworths London), ch 16.

[19] On commodity risk (including directional risk, basis risk, interest rate risk and forward gap risk), Basel Committee 'Amendment to the Capital Accord to Incorporate Market Risks' (Jan 1996) 27. On revised international capital framework, Basel Committee *The New Basel Capital Accord* (June 2004). For comment, Walker (n 2), ch 8.

[20] While all of these create distinct sets of legal relations with regard to which different aspects of law and regulation apply, they can still be considered to constitute a single class of alternative or competing savings and investment media. See, for example, Page and Ferguson *Investor Protection* (n 16) 10.

[21] The particular difficulty that arises is with regard to banking markets in that banking institutions are inherently unstable in light of the funding (liquidity) risks that arise with maturity transformation. To the extent that banks borrow short through the acceptance of sight or demand deposits which funds are then pooled and on-lent on a medium to long term basis, bank reserves may be easily exhausted in the event of un-anticipated withdrawal demands being made. If a single bank then collapses as a result of such withdrawals, the integrity of other immediate and more removed institutions may be threatened. Through such contagion, the stability of the market itself may be undermined. The final result may in such circum-

trative measures are adopted to protect the stability of the banking (and financial) markets and the interests of all parties affected including, in particular, those of depositors, investors and other policy holders.[22]

stances be systems or systemic collapse. On the nature of this risk and the difference between banking, securities and insurance markets, GA Walker, 'The Law of Financial Conglomerates: The Next Generation' The International Lawyer (vol 30, no 1, Spring 1996), 57–96; and Walker (n 2) Ch 3 and (n 61). See also Ch 6 (n 13).

[22] In terms of regulatory theory, the most commonly referred to justifications for financial regulation are market stability and consumer protection. See generally, DL Llewellyn *The Regulation and Supervision of Financial Institutions* (Institute of Bankers London 1986), The Gilbart Lectures on Banking 9; EP Gardener *Theory and Practice in Banking Supervision: Some Reflections* (Institute of European Finance University of North Wales 1986) 1; and Gardener, *UK Banking Supervision: Evolution, Practice and Issues* (Allen & Unwin London 1986), Ch 2. These justifications can also be understood in terms of proper recognised interests. On relevant interests, Llewllyn.

In historical terms, the main argument for financial regulation has been that government intervention in particular sectors of the economy is required to protect the public interest in these areas. This concept of public interest was most substantially developed in the US during the first half of last century. See generally, AE Kahn *The Economics of Regulation—Principles and Institutions*, (1989). This argument was subsequently reassessed by 'capture' (corrupted public interest) and then 'public choice' theorists who criticised the relevance and validity of public interest arguments in relation to all forms of public utility regulation from the 1950s onwards. This followed the massive increase in the volume of federal regulation that occurred in the US between the late 1930s and 1960s and 1970s. Public choice writers, in particular, questioned whether it was possible to define welfare and efficiency gains with sufficient precision to allow any public interest assessment to be undertaken. See, eg, G Stigler 'The Theory of Economic Regulation' subsequently reproduced in Stigler *The Citizen and the State: Essays on Regulation* (University of Chicago Press Chicago and London 1975) 115; S Peltzman 'Toward a More General Theory of Regulation' (1976) 19 JL Law & Con 211; RA Posner 'Theories of Economic Regulation' (1974) 5 Yale Journal of Economics and Management Science 335 at 347 and 352; EJ Kane 'Good Intentions and Unintended Evil: The Case against selective credit allocation' (1977) 9 JMCB 55; 'Accelerating Inflation, Technological Innovation, and the decreasing effectiveness on banking regulation' (1981) 36, JS 355, at 358; 'Policy Implications of Structural Changes in Financial Markets' (May 1983), 73:2 Am E Con R 96; 'Micro Economic and Macro Economic Origins of Financial Innovation' in Federal Reserve Bank of St Louis *Financial Innovations: Their Impact on Monetary Policy and Financial Markets* (1984).

In light of this criticism, more specific arguments have subsequently been developed in connection with particular aspects of modern financial market inefficiency and possible failure or collapse. A number of 'reformulated' or 'revised' public interest arguments (author's reference) can be constructed to justify market intervention (although these are not based on public interest theory as such). These consist of individual bank failure, contagion and systemic collapse; information asymmetries (arising as a result of inherent information imbalances in connection with the provision and receipt of financial services); and natural monopolies (arising from the natural tendency of financial institutions to move towards monopoly or oligopolositic positions due to increasing returns to scale). See, eg, C Goodhart *Money, Information and Uncertainty* (Macmillan London 1989) Ch IX; and E Baltensperger and J Dermine 'European Banking: Prudential and Regulatory Issues' in Dermine (ed) *European Banking in the 1990s* (Blackwell Oxford 1990), Ch 1. See also D Llewellyn *The Regulation and Supervision of Financial Institutions* (1986) n 2; A Gowland *The Regulation of Financial Markets in the 1990s* (Elgar Aldershot 1990); S Breyer *Regulation and its Reform* (Harvard University Press Camb Mass 1982); and A Ogus *Regulation: Legal Form and Economic Theory* (OUP Oxford 1994). See also C Goodhart, P Hartmann, D Llewellyn, L Rojas-Suarez and S Weisbrod *Financial Regulation—Why, how and where now?* (Routledge London 1998).

The specific danger that arises with the inherently unstable nature of banking and financial markets is that individual institutional collapse may lead to intra-sector contagion and systemic threats at the national level. This local or national instability may then spread through a larger process of regional contagion into other connected cross-border markets. The ultimate result may be national systems closure at the same time as more general regional crisis and collapse. It is for this reason that appropriate control systems must be established to ensure the stability and continued safe operation of the domestic and cross-border markets involved within any regional market structure.[23]

In terms of the scope and content of the European financial programme and the development of an effective response to these challenges, the European Commission initially focused, in particular, on insurance under-

While natural monopolies can be dealt with through cartel and dominant position law and information asymmetries can, at least, be partially corrected through disclosure or other more specific forms of consumer protection requirement (and conduct of business rules), the most serious danger that remains is potential contagion and systemic collapse. The risk of possible collapse in banking markets arises, in particular, from the maturity transformation or mismatching difficulties created through banking institutions funding long term loan positions through short term deposits (n 21). Unlike natural monopolies and information asymmetries, the inherent vulnerability in maturity mismatch and transformation cannot be removed through any particular policy response or corrective action. This is dealt with in practice through financial regulation in a pre-crisis situation and the provision of emergency central bank financial (lender of last resort) support in the event of a significant threat to the stability of the banking and financial system arising. Walker (n 2) Ch 3, section 4.1 and (n 61).

[23] It might also be noted that more modern statutory reformulations of the proper objectives of financial regulation have extended even this market inefficiency based examination to include such other purposes as consumer education and financial awareness as well as market competition, efficiency and innovation and with ensuring that financial institutions carry out a significant role in combating financial crime. This is, in particular, reflected in the statutory objectives and additional 'supervisory principles' set out in s 2(2) and (3) of the Financial Services and Markets Act 2000 in the UK. This represents a new sophistication in modern financial regulation which is, in particular, associated with the emergence of single regulatory systems in many counties which combine banking, securities and insurance oversight and control within a single institutional or statutory model. For further comment, Walker 'Bank Regulation' in R Mansfield et al (eds) *Banking Law Guide* (Butterworths London 2006) paras 1.2–1.6. See also Walker 'Financial Services Authority' in M Blair QC and GA Walker *Financial Services Law* (OUP Oxford OUP), Ch 1, paras 1.47–1.55. On single regulation, Walker 'United Kingdom Regulatory Reform: A New Beginning in Policy and Programme Construction' in D Arner and S Gou (eds) *Tawian Financial Reform* (Kluwer Law 2004).

On the more general issues that arise with regard to international or global market supervision and regulation, Walker (n 2), Introduction and Ch 6. An essential single global market and local control conflict necessarily arises at the international level, in particular, due to traditional doctrines of the sovereign autonomy of the nation state and the legal or jurisdictional exclusivity that this creates under Public International Law. Walker (n 2), Introduction and Ch 1. The main difference that arises between global and regional structures or trading systems is the additional difficulty created by the automatic internal rights of market access provided within the single regional integrated market place constructed. (n 4) and section B (2).

takings from an early stage and then banking institutions.[24] This harmonization work has since been extended to include securities and other more complex financial areas and activities subsequently.[25] The more recent work of the Commission has then included ecommerce, efinance and emoney.[26] The further significant difficulties created by the emergence of increasingly complex financial groups (or conglomerates) that provide services on a cross-sector (banking, securities and insurance) and a cross-border basis have also since been included.[27] The final programme of measures adopted as part of the most recent Financial Services Action Plan

[24] The work of the Commission was initially concerned with the development of harmonised provisions in the insurance area during the 1960s. It was considered that some pre-harmonization would be required before the underlying Treaty rights of services and establishment could be given effect under directives adopted under the original General Programmes in 1961 and 1962 (n 30). Similar pre-harmonization was not considered necessary in the banking area although this view changed following the work conducted by a Commission advisory group between 1966 and 1968 and a subsequent more formally established committee of experts between 1968 and 1972. On the work of these advisory and working groups, Ch 5 (n 9).

[25] Securities were not included within the 1985 White Paper which formed the basis of the Commission's 1992 Single Market Programme (n 3). Reference was only made to banking and insurance with some further provision concerning collective investment schemes and listing. Ch 5, section B. Securities were also not referred to directly in the original terms of the Treaty of Rome. On the banking and insurance references (n 32). The reason for this was that early financial expansion, especially during the late 1950s and 1960s and then in the 1970s, was bank led. Walker (n 2), Ch 1, section 1. Securities firms only began to expand on a cross-border basis during the 1980s with the further technological improvements that had occurred during that period especially with regard to telecommunications and computer software and hardware support. While securities would become a core aspect of the Commission's subsequent Financial Services Action Plan (FSAP), capital market integration would also be specifically considered under the Lamfalussy Report. Although the more general FSAP was to be completed by 2005, the separate capital market proposals were to come fully into effect during 2003. Commission Communication *Financial Services: Building a Framework for Action* COM (1998) 625 final of 28 Oct 1998; Initial Report of the Committee of Wise Men *The Regulation of European Securities Markets* (9 Nov 2000); and Final Report of the Committee of Wise Men *The Regulation of European Securities Markets* (15 Feb 2001). For further discussion, Ch 5, section D. On revised committee structure (n 55). On European securities law generally, N Moloney *EC Securities Regulation* (OUP Oxford 2002).

[26] Council Decision introducing a communication network community programme on trade electronic data interchange system (OJ 1987 L285/1) and following decision (OJ 1991 L208/1). See also Commission of the European Communities, *Proposal for a European Parliament and Council Directive on certain legal aspects of electronic commerce in the internal market* COM (98) 586 (OJ 1999 C30/4).

[27] Proposal for a Directive of the European Parliament and of the Council on the supplementary supervision of credit institutions, insurance undertakings and investment firms in a financial conglomerate and amending Council Directives 73/239/EEC, 79/267/EEC, 92/49/EEC, 92/96/EEC, 93/6/EEC and 93/22/EEC and Directives 98/78/EC and 2000/12/EC of the European Parliament and the Council (2001/0095 (COD)). See also Commission Proposal of 24 Apr 2001, COM (2001) 213 final. Ch 3, section B and (nn 50–2). On the nature and risks that arise with regard to the supervision and regulation of financial conglomerates, see generally, Walker 'The Law of Financial Conglomerates: The Next Generation' (n 21); and Walker (n 2), Ch 3.

(FSAP)[28] has been consequently extended to cover all major areas of domestic and cross-border financial services and market regulation and supervision. The system of privileged market access and supervisory and regulatory control set up within the Community now constitutes the most sophisticated and complex cross-border regime of its type in operation in the world at the present time.

The more general evolution of this programme can also be understood on the basis of a number of separately identifiable historical periods.[29] Within this, the underlying policy adopted has generally moved from being based on an early approach dominated by the attempted full harmonization of all relevant measures to one based on the mutual recognition of agreed standards within a more limited area of selected key provisions. Following the difficulties that arose in attempting to agree complete sets of common standards (full harmonization) in all of the areas set out in the General Programmes issued under the original EEC Treaty,[30] work has since focused on the production of more limited framework measures that only contain common minimum agreed standards in essential technical, regulatory and other public interest areas under the mutual recognition approach constructed to European integration.

During this period, further significant changes in relevant policy have also taken place. While a number of the basic components involved and control mechanisms to be adopted were identified at an early stage, the structure and content of the final programme was only confirmed as part of the negotiations undertaken in connection with the 1992 Single Market programme and then more recent action plan and FSAP work.[31]

Despite the apparent simplicity and success of the European financial programme, a number of difficulties remain both with regard to its origin and development, structure and content as well as completion and final result or effect. A range of distinct issues have then to be taken into account

[28] Communication of the Commission to the European Council *Action Plan for the Single Market* CSE (97) 1 final) of 4 June 1997. See also Commission Communication *Financial Services: Building a Framework for Action* (n 25); Commission *Financial Services: Implementing the Framework for Financial Markets: Action Plan,* COM(1999) 232, 11 May 1999; and Lamfalussy Committee Report (n 25). Ch 5, sections B and D.

[29] This may be structured as follows: Early Policy Development (1958–1967); Bank Harmonization and the 1972 Draft Directive (1968–1972); New Framework Approach (1973–1984); Mutual Recognition and the Single Market (1985–1992); Programme Completion (1993–2003). For further discussion, Ch 5, sections A and B.

[30] General Programme for the abolition of restrictions on freedom of establishment (OJ No 2 15 Jan 1962, 36/62); and General Programme for the abolition of restrictions on freedom to provide services (OJ No 2 15 Jan 1962, 36/62).

[31] (n 25). Commission of the European Communities *Completing the Internal Market,* White Paper, of Mar 1985 COM(85) 310 (n 3) and (nn 25 and 28). See also Ch 5, sections B and D.

in attempting to understand and appreciate the content and effect of the European financial initiative more fully. Without this, any overall or total assessment can only be selective and partial in its value, relevance and accuracy.

In attempting to understand and assess the significance and value of the European financial framework, a number of general integration issues as well as more specific financial and programme issues, related adoption and operational problems as well as larger systems and more general development considerations have to be taken into account. These are considered next. The nature and background to European integration more generally and the banking and financial programme in particular are examined in the following chapter.

B. BANKING AND FINANCIAL INTEGRATION

With regard to European trade and financial integration specifically, particular problems initially arise with regard to policy vacuum, policy conflict and continuing control gap as well as larger integration default and the possibility of regional rather than purely national market contagion and collapse. These are in addition to the more general policy importance, relevance and instability issues already referred to in the introductory section.

(1) POLICY VACUUM

One of the early difficulties created by the absence of any specific provisions with regard to banks and banking within the Treaty of Rome was that an essential policy vacuum arises in the supervision and regulation of banking and financial markets within Europe.[32] Financial market supervision is a complex and delicate process and while specific direction was provided in the EEC and EURATOM Treaties with regard to the development of particular policies in such areas as competition, agricultural policy and the development and utilization of atomic energy resources, no specific guidance was provided in the financial area.[33] A number of general principles can be

[32] The only references to banking in the terms of the original Treaty were that necessary measures had to be adopted on a unanimous basis and that developments in this area had to proceed in line with the liberalization of capital movements (Art 51(2) (ex 61)). The requirement for a unanimous vote was replaced by qualified majority voting under the Single Act 1986. Ch 5, section A. On capital policy, Ch 2, sections H and I.

[33] At the time of negotiation of the two Treaties of Rome, the German Government was concerned to ensure that the French markets, in particular, were open to free competition through a sound European-wide competition policy. On the separate EEC and EURATOM Treaties signed in Rome on 25 Mar 1957, Ch 2 (n 7). The maintenance of an effective competition regime was, in particular, considered necessary under German Ordo-liberal theory which

inferred from the underlying objectives and key provisions of the Treaty[34] although, of themselves, these provide little assistance in the construction of a detailed programme of measures for the supervision and regulation of financial markets.

While it may have been unfortunate that more specific guidance was not provided, it has to be accepted that this was almost certainly the deliberate policy of the Treaty draftsmen. In light of the importance of banking and financial markets in national political and monetary terms, this may have been considered too sensitive and difficult an aspect of market integration to deal with at that stage in the European evolutionary process. Again, the importance of the sector may simply not have been fully appreciated and properly considered during the 1950s especially having regard to the state of development of national and international financial markets on the Continent at that time.[35]

A number of particular omission or development theories can be constructed to attempt to understand the absence of any confirmed policy in the banking and financial area within the Treaty. These include a trade theory as well as a sensitivity, programme, revision (or capital) and correction theory.[36] Despite the assistance that such theories may provide

sought to establish a free market based economy protected through an economic constitution which included appropriate controls on both private and government interference or distortion with the operation of the market system. On Ordo-liberal theory, section D (d) and (n 78). The French Government was, in contrast, concerned to protect the stability of farming prices through the adoption of a formalised Common Agricultural Policy (CAP) and with the separate development of nuclear resources under the provisions which were transferred to the EURATOM Treaty. This was partly intended to create an energy independence not conditional on the supply and price of international crude oil. The early drafting selections made can then be, at least, partly understood in terms of an initial compromise or balance between the then dominant Ordo-liberal (and liberal internationalism) and social market policies in place. For further discussion, section E (4) and (nn 76–78 and 86). On the CAP and budgetary reform, section F(3) and (n 94).

[34] These include open markets, free competition, minimum regulatory interference and consumer protection. The original purposes and objectives of the Community are set out in Part I of the Treaty. More general principles of European law can also be considered to include the principles of equality, proportionality and legal certainty and protection of legitimate expectations as well as certain fundamental rights, fair hearing, effective remedies and administrative liabilities. See, eg, T Tridimas *The General Principles of EC Law* (OUP Oxford 1999). See also Lord Justice Schiemann 'The Application of General Principles of Community Law by English Courts' in M Andenas and F Jacobs *European Community Law in the English Courts* (Clarendon Press Oxford 1998), Ch 9. Although of importance, these provide little direct guidance in terms of the construction of a detailed supervisory and regulatory policy in this area. On the nature of financial supervision and regulation (n 2).

[35] Post-War currency convertibility was only restored in 1958, the same year in which the Treaty of Rome came into effect. See generally, AF Bakker *The Liberalization of Capital Movements in Europe—The Monetary Committee and Financial Integration 1958–1994* (Kluwer Dordrecht and London 1996), Ch 2, 11–14.

[36] *Relevance or Trade Theory*. The omission can possibly be most simply understood in terms of the specific scope of the original Treaty objectives. To the extent that the Treaty was concerned to establish a free trade area and customs union with free movement and certain

in understanding the relevant issues involved, the most likely explanation is that the original EEC was constructed on the basis of the then existing international trade theory and, in particular, the post-War international monetary and financial arrangements set up under the Bretton Woods managed currency regime which included strict capital controls and fixed (but adjustable) currencies.[37] It was for this reason that capital movements

common commercial policies, any further financial integration may have been considered irrelevant or unnecessary. The draftsman may then have deliberately omitted financial regulation to the extent that it did not fall within a narrowly defined range of immediate regional trading objectives.

Sensitivity or Damage Theory. The absence of any specific regulatory policy in the financial area may also be explained in terms of the underlying sensitivity of banking and financial markets and the difficulty that would necessarily have arisen in attempting to agree any comprehensive provisions in this regard. Although the importance of financial regulation may have been recognised, it may have been thought that its negotiation could have delayed, if not wholly obstructed and undermined, the conclusion of any agreement on the other more specific trade related policies identified.

Programme Evolution or Negotiation. It may have been considered sufficient to include banks and other financial institutions within the General Programmes to be set up under the free movement provisions of the Treaty (n 30). Financial activities would then be immediately or initially subject to free movement with any related regulatory or supervisory issues being considered during the course of the subsequent negotiations to be set up in the particular sector under the General Programmes agreed. Regulation may then have been treated as an ancillary or peripheral issue to be discussed and considered as an adjunct to core free movement at a subsequent negotiation phase.

Revision, Integration or Capital Theory. More generally, it may have been assumed that to the extent that some supporting or supplementary policy was necessary in this area, this could be developed under the basic provisions set out in the Treaty. Such an evolutionary or continuum explanation reflects the *traité cadre* nature of the main European constitutional documents. The need for an agreement on an appropriate policy would naturally develop within the larger integration process to be pursued under the Treaty and related *acquis communautaire*. This could also be understood in terms of a related but more specific *Capital Theory* to the extent that progress in the banking and financial area was postponed or, at least, contingent or conditional upon necessary progress having been secured in the area of the free movement of goods and then capital. Ch 2, section I. See also (n 40) on the possible use of a combined *Trade* or *Capital Assumption* theory.

Amendment or Correction Theory. To the extent necessary, further measures (regulations, directives or decisions) could be adopted to give effect to any necessary policy in the regulatory area. Ultimately, a Treaty amendment could be affected if necessary. This would obviously depend upon the relevant perceived importance of the need for an appropriate policy in the financial area at any particular stage in the development of the Community. On the main Treaties (n 1) and Ch 2 (nn 7–11). On the nature and content of the original capital regime set up under the Treaty, Ch 2, sections H and I.

[37] The Bretton Woods Agreement had been signed at a conference in New Hampshire from 1 to 22 July, 1944.This provided for the creation of a revised system of managed exchange rates based on the value of the United States dollar which would replace the earlier orderly market for foreign exchange that had existed under the gold standard and gold exchange standard. The Conference also provided for the establishment of the International Monetary Fund (IMF) and the International Bank for Reconstruction and Development (the World Bank) as well as for the adoption of the General Agreement on Tariffs and Trade (GATT). While it was not possible to agree the creation of a World Trade Organization (WTO) at the original Bretton Woods meetings, this would subsequently be set up on 1 Jan 1995. Walker (n 2), Ch 1, section 2. See, eg, R Fraser and C Long *The World Financial System* (Longman Harlow

were not given the same prominence in the original Treaty rules with only a 'dual' approach being adopted in terms of which capital controls were brought within the overall scope and competence of the EEC but with national sovereignty in this area being preserved and protected.[38] Liberalization in the banking and financial area was also expressly stated only to take place in parallel with progress in the capital area.[39]

The essential reason for the decision not to include any developed capital and financial provisions in the Treaty was accordingly that the original EEC had been established as part of a larger pre-determined international financial system within which trade and capital theory and capital mobility were substantially circumscribed. It was only with the significant reforms and liberalization that subsequently took place during the 1970s and 1980s in these areas that the earlier constraints were removed and the Community was able fully to begin to realise the potential economic benefits and advantages available.[40]

(2) Policy Conflict

The further significant difficulty that arises in attempting to correct this policy vacuum, is that the Commission was obliged to promote full market integration under the terms of the original Treaty of Rome. The integration

1992), Chs 4, 36, sections 1 and 37, section 1; and RW Edwards *International Monetary Collaboration* (Transnational Publishers New York 1985), Chs 1 and Ch 2, 44.

The system of managed exchange rates set up under Bretton Woods lasted until 1971 and 1973. Floating currencies were adopted in place of the earlier fixed system in 1973 following US President Richard Nixon's announcement on 15 Aug 1971 of the closure of the 'Gold Window' and that the United States would consequently no longer allow other governments to present dollars for conversion into gold at US $35 per ounce. Walker (n 2), Ch 1, section 2. See generally J Williamson *The Failure of World Monetary Reform, 1971–74* (Nelson Sunbury-on-Thames 1977); KW Dam *The Rules of the Game: Reform and Evolution in the International Monetary System* (University of Chicago Press Chicago and London 1982); AW Hooke *The International Monetary Fund—Its Evolution, Organisation and Activities* (IMF Pamphlet Series No 37 1982); M Moffit *The World's Money: International Banking from Bretton Woods to the Brink of Insolvency* (1984); J Cavanagh, D Wysham and M Arruda (eds) *Beyond Bretton Woods: Alternatives to the Global Economic Order* (Pluto Press London 1994); and C Geisst *Exchange Rate Chaos-Twenty-Five Years of Finance and Consumer Democracy* (Routledge London 1995).

[38] AF Bakke, *The Liberalization of Capital Movements in Europe* (n 35). See also JA Usher *The Law of Money and Financial Services in the EU* (2nd edn Oxford University Press England 2000), Ch 2; and S Mohammed *European Community Law on the Free Movement of Capital and the EMU* (Kluwer USA and Canada 1999).

[39] (n 32). Art 51(2) (ex 61). This can be expressed in terms of a *Capital Omission* theory in (n 36), para 4.

[40] This might then be referred to as a combined *Trade* or *Capital Assumption* theory under (n 36). On the historical development of free movement of capital and the change that took place, in particular, in the French position during the early 1980s, Ch 2, sections H and I.

and local or regional control conflict that this creates[41] may then operate at two separate levels.

In the first place, in so far as governments have adopted extensive national policies to protect the stability and efficient operation of domestic markets,[42] the effectiveness of these measures will be undermined through the adoption of an aggressive or dominant integration policy without due consideration to the inherent instabilities of banking and financial markets and the need for appropriate government control.[43] If the Commission had only attempted to remove all obstacles to the freedom of establishment and provision of services at the national level, many of the complex local supervisory and regulatory sets of requirements that would otherwise have applied would necessarily have been affected, if not, wholly undermined.

The challenge for the Commission has then been to attempt to remove all unnecessary restraints on trade in financial services throughout the Community without undermining the stability of the markets and the protection of all legitimate interests including depositors, investors and other policy holders.[44] This essential access and control relationship must then be properly and carefully balanced.

(3) Control Gap

The related difficulty that arises concerns the decision to proceed, at least, at this stage in the financial evolutionary process, by retaining the full operation of all of the separate systems of national supervision and domestic supervisory agencies in place rather than attempt to establish any central Community authority or control procedure.[45] This then creates a supporting or related

[41] (n 4). [42] (nn 8 and 9).

[43] (nn 2 and 21). [44] (n 4).

[45] Provision was included in the Maastrict Treaty for the European Central Bank (ECB) to assume a more direct role in the area of bank supervision and regulation (Art 105(6)). This was referred to as the 'Enabling Clause.' It is nevertheless questionable to what the extent the ECB may exercise this power. The Bank is primarily charged with responsibility for the management of monetary policy and already monitors and contributes to the development of prudential supervision through its Supervisory Sub-Committee (formerly the European System of Central Bankers' Supervisory Sub-Committee or the 'Quinn' Committee). The other more significant operational problems that arise are with regard to subsidiarity and home country control. Home country control assigns primary responsibility in respect of the supervision of the activities of banks to their Member State of authorization. Ch 5, section B. Having adopted this primary supervisory principle as the basis for all of the key directives in this area, it could be argued that it would be theoretically inconsistent, almost operationally impossible and consequently politically insensitive for all banks then to be supervised directly on a central basis. This would also be inconsistent with the general principle of subsidiarity which will assign responsibility for particular tasks to the Member States only and unless they can otherwise be dealt with more effectively at the European level. Ch 5 (n 167) and authorities cited. On market support, section D(5) and (n 65). On the revised technical committee structure within Europe, Ch 1 (n 55) and Ch 2 (n 111).

control gap in financial supervision and control within Europe. In the absence of any central control function or mechanism, considerable inconsistencies will inevitably arise in the operation of national systems. This problem will be particularly severe if large amounts of discretion are left to Members States and national agencies in implementing relevant Community rules in this area.

Two further related issues then arise with regard to integration damage or default and regional contagion, crisis and collapse in addition to the core problems of the access and control conflict, policy vacuum and control gap referred to.

(4) Integration Damage or Default

The absence of any clear policy response to the problems that arise in the banking and financial area and additional confusion created through the absence of any coherent regulatory or enforcement regime will necessarily act as a significant disincentive for market operators to attempt to rely on their rights of access and cross-border service provision. Policy omission and confusion as well as regulatory and administrative default will then undermine the value of the core rights created within the regional trading system. The effectiveness of the integration initiative itself and the degree of market integration achieved will consequently be undermined.[46] This remains a continuing problem that must be corrected within any regional trading arrangement.

(5) Regional Contagion, Crisis, and Collapse

In addition to this problem of essential integration default, heightened problems of inter-regional rather than purely domestic contagion, crisis and collapse will also be created.[47] This arises from the automatic or mandatory rights of access created and the consequent need to dis-apply or, at least, adjust or dilute local regulatory apparatus with regard to incoming firms from other participating territories. In the absence of some new common or co-ordinated control system, the risk of market instability will be increased which exposure may be further compounded in the absence of any effective cross-border financial support mechanism.[48]

An effective banking and financial policy must be able to deal with each of these problems of access and control conflict, policy vacuum and control gap as well as integration damage or default and the threat of regional

[46] For the purposes of this paper, this might be referred to as 'integration damage or default.' Preface and Introduction.
[47] (n 21).
[48] (nn 4 and 46) and section D (5). See also Ch 5, section E (5).

contagion and collapse. This is in addition to the underlying more general issues of policy importance, relevance and instability. In the event that these problems are not properly identified and managed, consequent immediate integration damage or default may result with the possibility of ultimate regional contagion and collapse ensuing in the most extreme of cases.

C. POLICY AND PROGRAMME STRUCTURE AND CONTENT

In connection with policy and programme structure and content, separate difficulties arise with regard to Treaty base, judicial coherence and consistency, programme content, continuing legislative function and institutional support.

(1) Treaty Base

The Treaty basis for the law in this area remains the provisions concerning freedom of establishment and the free provision of services as well as the more general emerging law of free movement under European Law. The financial policy constructed to date is nevertheless based partly on the still emerging jurisprudence of the European Court of Justice as well as the secondary programme of measures adopted by the Council and Parliament. A number of difficulties still arise in interpreting these provisions especially with regard to the scope of relevant prohibition and supporting derogation. Whether a more limited discrimination (both direct and indirect) or a full market restriction or effects doctrine should be adopted in applying the core prohibitions on obstacles to free movement is still unclear. The relevant scope of the supporting permitted derogations either provided for expressly under the Treaty or judicially confirmed by the Court also remains uncertain.[49]

(2) Judicial Coherence and Consistency

Whether a consistent jurisprudence has been constructed in the area of establishment and services as well as goods, workers and capital is also far from clear. The essential coherence and consistency problems that arise then create further significant difficulties in terms of legal certainty and predictability which necessarily undermine the application and operation of the law in this area. This, in turn, restricts the ability of commercial operators to rely on the availability of clear and consistent rights which necessarily undermines their

[49] Section E (3) and (n 74). These problems are discussed in further detail in Ch 3, sections C and D; and Ch 4.

ability to exercise these entitlements in practice. All of this uncertainty then again impedes or damages the larger integration process still under construction.[50]

(3) Programme Content

Separate problems arise in connection with the content and operation of the secondary programme of measures constructed to date. Banking and financial market regulation is a complex and sensitive process. Significant difficulties have necessarily arisen in attempting to harmonise or, at least, construct certain common minimum provisions applicable and acceptable to all Member States.

Underlying national financial market regulation remains dependent upon a complex mix of historical and cultural traditions as well as the relative degree of market sophistication and local institutional support. This is also necessarily affected by prevailing market and social protection ideologies that will have a further impact on the degree and content of market regulation (or deregulation) and competition in place.

While the ultimate benefits of the creation of a single banking and financial market are generally accepted,[51] significant difficulties have necessarily arisen in attempting to create an acceptable degree of common provision in this area. An impressive catalogue of secondary measures has been constructed although this still suffers from a number of continuing limitations especially in terms of scope of access, regulatory content, operational supervision, programme completion and institutional revision.[52]

(4) Legislative Function

Some of the most difficult problems in terms of programme evolution and construction have arisen as a result of the complicated and cumbersome European legislative process that has historically become characterised by obstruction, unnecessary and excessive negotiation and detail and consequent delay.[53] This legislative function is, in particular, prone to a high level of unnecessary and often irrelevant political and administrative interference

[50] Section B(4) and (nn 4 and 46). On the different approaches adopted with regard to the law of free movement and, in particular, Art 28 (ex 30), Ch 1, section E(3) and (n 74) and Ch 3 (nn 122–6, 128 and 129). On establishment and services, Chapter 3, section D(1)–(4). On the relationship between free movement of goods, establishment, services and workers, Ch 3, section D(5). On the distinction between more general free market and social market theories and resultant policy balance, section E(4).

[51] Ch 2, sections C and D. See also Cecchini Report and other authorities cited (n 15) and Ch 5, section D(4).

[52] Ch 5, section E and Chs 6 and 7.

[53] Lamfalussy Committee Report (n 25) and Ch 5 (n 132).

(and potential abuse) to the extent that Member States can use negotiating positions to produce overtly localised protective effects within the same, related or even wholly distinct policy areas. The consequence of this is that ill considered and distorted measures may be adopted that are insufficient and inadequate to deal with the specific underlying problems concerned.

This may create particularly undesirable results in the banking and financial area especially in light of the complexity, sensitivity and importance (as well as underlying potential instability) of the markets involved. These problems may be further compounded by the speed of change of market structure and market practice as well as the underlying financial risks and exposures created.

While democratic involvement and accountability have to be respected, legislative systems should be as efficient and as technically specific and relevant as possible which may have to include some degree of immunity from extraneous or unnecessary and irrelevant political or administrative interference.[54]

(5) Institutional Support

The related issue that arises is ensuring that an effective institutional support system is in place to draft or advise on the preparation of technical texts or other implementation or operational issues in each of the main financial sectors.[55] To ensure as relevant and as technically informed and productive a result as possible, this could be most easily achieved through the use of a specialist technical committee structure that would provide more general policy as well as specific operational or administrative support.[56]

[54] Ch 5 (nn 134–138). Specialist technical (politically neutral) and streamlined (fast track) procedures should accordingly be considered in so far as possible in such key areas. Chs 6, 7 and 8.

[55] The financial services committees now consist of the European Banking Committee (EBC) and Committee of European Banking Supervisors (CEBS), the European Insurance and Occupational Pensions Committee (EIOPC) and Committee of European Insurance and Occupational Pensions Supervisors (CEIOPS) as well as the European Securities Committee (ESC) and Committee of European Securities Regulators (CESR). The Council had invited the Commission in Dec 2002 to extend the committee structure applied in the securities sector post-Lamfalussy to banking, insurance and investment funds (n 25). See also 'Financial Services: Commission presents measures to improve regulation of banking, securities and investment funds' (IP/03/1507 of 6 Nov 2003). On the new European financial Committee structure set up following the Lamfalussy Committee recommendations in the capital market area, Ch 2 (n 111). On market support section D(5) and (n 65). On the difficulties that arise with cross-border EU support and the role and function of the European Central Bank (nn 45 and 65) and Ch 5 (nn 154 and 167). For institutional comment, Ch 2 (n 108).

[56] (n 55). This committee system must be staffed in so far as possible by official representatives in each relevant sector area able to provide the necessary professional and technical input. Chs 6 and 7. On market support, section D (5) and (n 65) and Ch 5, section E (5) and 167).

D. LEGISLATIVE ADOPTION AND OPERATION

In terms of policy and programme adoption and operation, further problems arise with regard to national implementation and application, consistency in the interpretation and application of agreed common provisions as well as continuing review and systems effect and support.[57]

(1) Implementation and Application

The main operational problems that arise are concerned with ensuring effective local adoption and implementation of each of the main financial measures at the Member State level. Significant difficulties have continued to arise with regard to adoption or transposition (fragmentation) levels. It is generally accepted that these must be reduced and default levels lowered to ensure any longer term meaningful results.[58]

(2) Interpretation Consistency

Separate difficulties arise in terms of ensuring consistent interpretation of all relevant provisions at the national level. This partly arises as a natural consequence of the use of directives as the main legislative instrument in this field. While this facilitates adjustment and transposition at the national level (through the inclusion of a significant degree of discretion in the implementation and application of relevant measures), this may also result in minor or more substantial differences in interpretation and application with consequent operational divergence arising in practice.

(3) Continuing Review

In light of these dangers, it is necessary to provide for the establishment of some continuing review mechanism at the European level. This must be considered to ensure that all relevant measures are properly implemented and that a sufficient degree of consistency is achieved.[59] The Commission has attempted historically to carry out this role more generally although significant difficulties have arisen in terms of its resources, information support and necessary expertise in many more specific areas including banking and financial services.

[57] Lamfalussy Committee Report (n 25).

[58] Ch 5 (nn131–134). Concerns have been expressed with regard to the gap that has arisen between the political commitment for financial reform and the pace of adoption and implementation. For comment, 'A meeting of minds on markets—views are converging on EU financial services', *Financial Times*, 28 Nov 2002 (editorial). See also Ch 5, section D.

[59] Ch 5 (nn 134 and 139). Ch 7, sections D(4) and E(3); and Ch 8, sections A(5) and D.

(4) Regulatory Equivalence

In addition to basic technical commonality and consistency, the principal consideration or test that should apply in assessing the adequacy of national implementation measures should be whether a necessary and sufficient degree of regulatory or technical equivalence has been secured in practice in each case.

With the adoption of a new integration approach or philosophy based on mutual recognition and minimum harmonization, the underlying assumption made was that a necessary or appropriate degree of equivalence would naturally arise or develop over time. Unfortunately, this expected operational equivalence has simply not materialised in many areas which has resulted in significant differences and disparities arising in terms of uneven regulatory cover and effect.[60]

An appropriate continuing review and assessment mechanism must accordingly be set up that would extend to include implementation consistency and effect. The common test or standard to be applied should then be regulatory or functional equivalence.[61] This must also be supported by an appropriate revision or adjustment mechanism as well as, to the extent

[60] Mutual recognition is generally based on an assumption of initial or consequent regulatory convergence that either simply never existed or has not subsequently materialised as expected in many cases. Resolving this problem of non-materialised regulatory (functional or technical) equivalence is crucial to the longer term success of the European financial programme and European integration more generally. Ch 7, section D(3). 'Functional convergence' or 'functional equivalence' should be considered as a supplement or even replacement for mutual recognition as an immediate but more complete and substantive form of integration mechanism. Ch 8, sections A(5), B, C and D.

This has already begun to occur (although more incidentally rather than by deliberate policy or intent) with the preparation of more detailed regulatory rules under level 2 of the Lamfalussy process. (n 25) and Ch 5, section D(4). This work is carried out by the new sector committees set up post-Lamfalussy (n 55). This expands, extends and supports the more general framework principles set out in the new generation of main financial directives. Ch 5 (nn 136 and 137). With this, European legislative processes have also begun to move back towards a more full harmonization rather than solely mutual recognition based policy approach. Ch 1, Introduction and Ch 5, section A.

The key to any meaningful longer term integration must be to secure an effective degree of legal and regulatory equivalence in practice between all participating territories based on continuing review and adjustment and not just on an assumed result or effect. Ch 8, sections B, C and D. It can clearly be argued that laws, regulations and administrative provisions should not simply be expected to converge naturally over time as many political, legislative, administrative, market and social and cultural as well as more operational and other external or simply practical factors may interfere with this result. It may only be possible to secure the most substantial and desirable degree of convergence through the adoption of a more controlled and managed set of processes that operate in accordance with clear rules and procedures. The need for the adoption of functional convergence or equivalence as a supplementary or replacement core integration doctrine is considered in further detail in Chs 7 and 8.

This more interventionist approach to regulatory convergence parallels the debate that arises with regard to whether markets themselves should be allowed to operate in a wholly uncontrolled or managed basis. Section E(4).

[61] Ch 7, sections D(3) and E(3) and Ch 8, sections B, C and D.

necessary, an effective system of sanctions and penalties especially against significant or persistent breaches.

(5) Market Support

In the event of a financial crisis arising, some form of credible and properly funded market support mechanism must be considered (in addition to harmonised depositor and investor protection schemes).[62] Whether the full details of the operation of such a mechanism are made publicly available or not (for moral hazard reasons),[63] this has to involve the construction of some form of central or co-ordinated national lender of last resort operation.[64] The establishment of some form of European wide market support mechanism unfortunately remains a difficult and largely unresolved issue.[65]

E. EUROPEAN INTEGRATION

In addition to these banking and financial policy specific difficulties, a number of more general issues arise in connection with the larger integra-

[62] See also (n 21). Ch 5, section E(5) and (nn 155 and 170).

[63] This is often considered necessary to limit unnecessary 'moral hazard' problems arising with depositors and investors not exercising any continuing review and discipline over financial intermediaries and relying on either some more general 'lender of last resort' support being provided by the local central bank or recovery being made available under the relevant local compensation scheme. Walker (n 2), Ch 3 (n 61). See also H Thornton *An Enquiry into the Nature and Effects of the Paper Credit System of Great Britain* (1802); and W Bagehot *Lombard Street* (Henry S King & Co London 1873). See also TM Humphrey 'Lender of Last Resort: the Concept in History' 75:2 Fed Res B Richmond Econ Rev 8 (Mar/Apr 1989)

[64] Ch 5, section E (5) and Ch 6 (n 13). Walker (n 2) Ch 3 (n 61). See also M Andenas and L Panourgias 'Applied Monetary Policy and Bank Supervision by the ECB', Section 4. Ch 6, section C.

[65] K Lanoo 'Supervising the European Financial System' (May 2002) Financial Markets Group, Special Paper No 137. See also Commission 'Report on Financial Stability' (May 2000) prepared by ad hoc working group of the Economic and Financial Committee, Economic Papers, No 143; and Commission, 'Report on financial crisis management' (July 2001). See also European Shadow Financial Regulatory Committee, 'EMU, the ECB and financial supervision' (Oct 1998, Statement No 2); K Lanoo 'Financial Supervision in EMU' *Yearbook of International Financial and Economic Law* (1998) 145; C Hadjiemmanuil and M Andenas 'Banking Supervision and European Monetary Union' JIIB (nol 1, no 2) 84; T Padoa-Schioppa 'EMU and Banking Supervision' Lecture to LSE, Financial Markets Group, 24 Feb 1999 (reproduced *International Finance* vol 2, no 2, 295–308); Lanoo 'Does Europe need an SEC?' (1999), European Capital Markets Institute, Occasional Paper No 1; Lanoo 'Challenges to the structure of financial supervision in the EU' (July 2000) CEPS Working Party report; Lanoo 'EU Securities Market Regulation—Adapting to the needs of an integrated capital market' (Mar 2001) CEPS Working Party Report. See also Padoa-Schioppa 'Towards a European Banking Regulatory Framework' Speech at Conference on 'New equilibria between financial intermediaries, savings and firms' organized by Impresa Magazine, Milan, 23 Oct 1987; and Padoa-Schioppa, 'Self vs Public Discipline in the Financial Field' (July 2002) Financial Markets Group, Special Paper No 142. See also (n 45).

tion process still under construction within Europe. In terms of more general systems or institutional issues, the nature of judicial policy contribution and the evolving role of the European Court of Justice must be taken into account with the consequent expansion or contraction in the scope of EU law. The content of this emerging law of free movement must be reviewed to ensure a clear and consistent policy basis. Consideration must also be given to the proper degree of underlying social or free market balance to be achieved within Europe and the most effective institutional structure or set of relations to be set up more generally.

(1) Judicial Policy Contribution

The problems in developing a complete, coherent and effective law of free movement have already been referred to.[66] This has caused considerable difficulties for the Court especially in light of the degree of discretion (and consequent responsibility) left in interpreting and applying many Treaty or secondary programme provisions as well as in correcting specific legislative or substantive legal or policy gaps. This has, in particular, allowed the Court considerable flexibility in the development of the content and effect of the emerging law of free movement.[67]

Historically, the Court considered itself obliged, in particular, to adopt a strong interventionist policy during the early stages of European expansion especially following the apparent harmonization failures at the end of the original transitional period on 31 December 1969. This resulted in the Court *inter alia* confirming the legal indenity and supremacy of European law and the direct effect of a number of key Treaty provisions especially in connection with goods, establishment and services at the same time as generally discuss and issue its decisions in as liberal and expansionary a manner as possible.[68] The legislative failures of the Council that had arisen were to a significant extent only corrected by the assumption of this more activist (*de facto* policy construction) role by the Court.

As some of these early failures were subsequently resolved, the Court has accepted (re-assumed) a more passive or balanced and supportive role within the European institutional infrastructure.[69] The Court nevertheless

[66] Section C (1) and (2).

[67] Ch 3, sections A, B, C and D. On 'judicial policy deficit' Ch 4 (n 6).

[68] For comment, MP Maduro *We the Court* (Hart Publishing Oxford, 1998). See also Lord Slynn 'Critics of the Court: a Reconsideration' in Andenas and Jacobs (n 14) Ch 1.

[69] Ch 3, sections B and C. A Arnull *The European Union and its Court of Justice* (OUP Oxford 1999); R Dehousse *The European Court of Justice* (Macmillan Basingstoke 1998); KPE Lasok *The European Court of Justice: Practice and Procedure* (Butterworths London 1984); LN Brown *The European Court of Justice* (Sweet & Maxwell London 1983); and M Schapiro 'The European Court of Justice', Ch 9 of P Craig and G de Burca (eds) *The Evolution of EU Law* (OUP Oxford 1999). See also AM Arnull, AA Dashwood, MG Ross and DA Wyatt

remains a key and influential institution in the expansion, clarification and application of European law.

(2) Scope of EU Law

The decisions taken by the Court in determining the application of European provisions have, in particular, either extended or constrained the scope of application of relevant European law. This has, in turn, either contracted or expanded the authority and jurisdiction of the Court. The content and scope of coverage of European law are necessarily affected by the decisions taken by the Court in interpreting the more specific law of free movement. This has also had a consequent impact on the role and relationship of the Court with national courts and court systems.[70] The degree of activism or otherwise adopted by the Court has further significant implications on the constitutional relationship between the main institutions within the Community and their relationship with national governments and relevant domestic authorities.

(3) Law of Free Movement

These issues of policy correction and scope of systems or legal coverage are reflected in the different approaches that have emerged with regard to the nature and content of the European market programme and, in particular, the law for free movement within the Community.[71]

A number of theories can be developed with regard to the meaning and operation of the core free movement provisions contained in the EC Treaty including, in particular, art 28 (*ex* 30). The main distinction drawn is essentially between trade restriction and discriminatory intent[72] although some writers have also attempted to construct more complex differentiations.[73] Many of these nevertheless only confuse the scope of initial restriction with possible consequent derogation.

The simplest distinction possibly remains between the adoption of either a market effect (or trade restriction) or a discrimination (or national protec-

European Union Law (4rd edn Sweet & Maxwell London 2000), ch. 9 ; S Weatherhill and P Beaumont *EU Law* (3rd edn Penguin London 1999), ch 6; and P Craig and G de Búrca, *EU Law* (3rd edn OUP Oxford 2002), ch 2.

70 Arnull (n 69), ch 5.

71 Section C(2) and Ch 3, section C(5) and (nn 43, 106 and 117, 118 and 122–124). For comment and reconciliation, Ch 3 (nn 125, 126, 128 and 129).

72 On the early approaches developed, Ch 3 (n 43).

73 Maduro, eg, attempts to distinguish between a discrimination (protectionist) test, a typological (or rules) test (including between product and sales or marketing requirements) and a combined (restriction and possible justification) test. P Maduro *We The Court* (n 68) Ch 2. For discussion, Ch 3 (n 122).

tion) based test although discrimination may still be extended to include direct and indirect forms as well as possible simple discriminatory effects in the most extreme cases.[74]

The relevant balance to be achieved has necessarily varied in particular sectors and areas as well as over time as the Community and Union have evolved. Achieving an effective policy reconciliation in this regard nevertheless remains essential to the longer term success of the European integration initiative.

(4) Market or Social Policy Balance

The scope and content of EU law and the law of free movement specifically have also been affected by the more general approaches adopted with regard to free trade and market support or direction within the Community. This can generally be examined on either a free market or social market basis. With this, a core distinction is drawn between the adoption of an essentially free trade approach to integration (in which all national obstacles to cross-border commerce are removed and open markets promoted) or a more social or market managed approach in which other welfare policies are also taken into account.[75]

[74] Section C (1) and Ch 3, section C(5) and (nn 125, 126, 128 and 129). On the earlier decisions in this area, Ch3 (nn 43, 106 and 117, 118 and 122–4). In practice, the Court may simply select between the two major tests whichever is considered necessary or most appropriate in the particular case. Discrimination will be used where it is present as it is easy to identify and quantify. Where there is no clear discriminatory intent (either direct or indirect), the Court can still use the trade effect of a measure to bring it within the scope of relevant Treaty prohibition. Ch 3 (n 129). On indirect discrimination, Ch 3 (n 32).

Historically, the confusion that has arisen can be most simply explained in terms of the distinction drawn between immediate market entry restrictions and subsequent internal regulatory measures as adopted under the original GATT rules. Ch 3 (nn 35, 36 and 46). Entry rules were subject to an effects test and regulatory provisions to a discrimination based examination. Unfortunately, this apparently clear distinction was not transferred to the original EEC Treaty with the European Court of Justice being left to determine which test to apply in each key area subsequently. Ch 3, section C(1), (2) and (3).

Theoretically, the two main doctrines can still be reconciled through the use of a supplementary test or theory which might be referred to as 'discriminately effect.' The free movement restrictions will then apply in any case where either direct or indirect discrimination is present or there is otherwise a discriminatory effect. Ch 3 (nn 124, 126 and 127). On establishment and services, Ch 3, sections 3 (D)(1), (2), (3) and (4). On the relationship between goods, establishment, services and workers, Ch 3, section 3 (D)(5).

Operationally, the application of the two alternative approaches can also still be incorporated within a single three stage examination process. Market entry rules would be subject to a full effects test and internal regulatory measures to a discrimination based assessment (direct or indirect) but subject to a 'reclassification proviso'. Where an essentially non-discriminatory internal condition still had some discriminatory effect, it would be reclassified as a market entry rule and become subject to a full trade impact or effect treatment and consequent prohibition. Ch 3 (nn 122, 125 and 129).

[75] This can also be understood in terms of the distinction between a competition and intervention based approach to economic integration. Integration by competition relies on individ-

A free market approach generally corresponds with neo-liberal ideas of an open market economy.[76] These generally promote the creation of unrestricted open trade or exchange arrangements with the degree of public

ual action and choice within an open market system to achieve a natural integrative result. This will include institutional competition and might be referred to more generally as market competition. Integration by intervention relies on the achievement of specific policy objectives through direct market intervention. ME Striet and W Mussler 'Evolution of the economic constitution of the European Union' *The New Palgrave Dictionary of Economics and the Law* (1999) 98–110.

[76] Economic liberalism refers to the theory of political economy based on the work of the Scottish Enlightenment writer Adam Smith and subsequent nineteenth and early twentieth century free market theories (n 78). Adam Smith *Theory of Moral Sentiments* (1772); and Smith *The Wealth of Nations* (1776). Economic liberalism directs that government intervention should be kept to an absolute minimum and that free and open markets should prevail insofar as possible. In terms of inter-state relations, free trade should be promoted with government involvement being restricted to issues concerning state security. For discussion, see, eg, Graham Evans and Jeffery Newnham, *International Relations* (Penguin 1998) 140–141; and John Baylis and Steve Smith, *The Globalization of World Politics* (2nd edn Oxford 2001), ch 8.

Other writers in the Scottish Enlightenment included, for example, Lord Kames (Henry Home), David Hume, Adam Ferguson, William Robertson and Thomas Read. The origins of many modern areas of study in the natural sciences and social sciences including philosophy, economics, law, government and medicine were all developed during the period between 1720 and 1780 in the main Scottish Universities. See, eg, Adam Ferguson *An Essay on the History of Civil Society* (1767); David Hume *A Treatise of Human Nature* (1739); Hume *Political Discourses* (1752); Hume *History of England* (1755); Hume *Dialogues Concerning Natural Religion* (1779); Francis Hutcheson *An Inquiry into the Original of Our Ideas of Beauty and Virtue* (1725); Hutcheson *Essay on the Nature and Conduct of the Passions and Affections* (1728); and Hutcheson *The System of Moral Philosophy*. For discussion of the legal relevance of these writers, Peter Stein 'Scottish Enlightenment and the Law' *The New Palgrave Dictionary of Economics and the Law* (Macmillan London 1999). On the Scottish Enlightenment generally, A Broadie *The Scottish Enlightenment* (Birlinn Edinburgh 2001); and A Herman *The Scottish Enlightenment* (Fourth Estate London 2001).

Liberalism in international relations more generally can be considered to date from John Locke (1632–1704). This liberalism is concerned with the promotion of peaceful international relations, balance of interests, the rule of law and formal dispute resolution and collective security (including both interventionist and non-interventionist liberal approaches). (n 86) and Evans and Newnham 304–6.

Other more recent variants of liberal analysis include commercial liberalism (linking free trade and peace), republican liberalism (which stresses democracy and peace) and sociological liberalism (in international integration). All of these sub-theories can be considered to fall within neo-liberalism (or neo-liberal institutionalism). Neo-liberal approaches to international relations stress the importance of cooperative behaviour and institution building within a new decentralised international world order. This allows for the adoption of a multi-polar or 'mixed actor' model which includes international institutions and organizations and transnational agencies in addition to sovereign states. Multiple objectives are also stressed beyond state security alone including wealth and welfare gains from cross-border trade and commerce. Evans and Newnham 360–2. See also Baylis and Smith ch 9.

The antithesis of neo-liberalism is neo-realism (or new or structural realism) which is concerned with the international order within which state relations are constrained rather with the states themselves. See, eg, KN Waltz *Theory of International Politics* (1979). Waltz, in particular, describes the international system as operating like a market place. For comment, Evans and Newnham 364–5. On the idea of order (or *Ordnung*) within a closed economic system (n 78). On realism (n 86). See also Baylis and Smith ch 7.

(and private) interference and intervention being curtailed in so far as possible. The objective is the establishment of an economic system within which open and unrestricted markets operate without obstruction with all of the (potential) consequent welfare gains that this should generate.

Such liberal (and neo-liberal) ideas are not, however, solely based on the maintenance of wholly unrestricted markets and full *laissex faire* market economics. The inclusion of necessary corrective elements was originally recognised by Adam Smith writing in the immediate pre-industrial revolution period as well as by such later writers as John Maynard Keynes.[77] The importance of setting up an appropriate control framework within an 'economic constitution' was also highlighted by the German Freiburg (or *Ordo-liberal*) school of writers in the late 1930s and 1940s in Germany.[78]

[77] A more corrective or compensatory form of liberalism emerged during the mid 20th century which called on increased government intervention to remove persistent inequalities within markets. This 'Keynesian liberalism' has been described as representing a new heterodoxy within modern liberalism. Evans and Newnham (n 76) 141. Keynesian economics has nevertheless been subject to significant criticism subsequently. On liberal internationalism (n 86).

[78] This liberal or open market approach to market operations reflects the Ordo-liberal theories that formed the basis of early integrationist and constitutional design ideas in Europe. Ordo-liberal writings promoted the creation of free markets and an open liberal economy with a necessary degree of proper constitutional protection. Private autonomy was to be enhanced, contracts protected and private competition safeguarded. Public (and private) intervention were to be limited through the laws on free movement and competition. The original EEC Treaty can be considered as creating a form of early economic constitution which established an underlying market place based on free movement and open competition. These ideas support a pure open market philosophy in which individual rights of action are promoted and state intervention and other private forms of market distortion limited (n 76).

Ordo-liberalism began in the 1930s with the economists Walter Eucken (1891–1950) and Franz Bohm (1895–1977) and the lawyer Hans Grossmann-Doerth (1894–1944). Second generation writers included Friedrich Lutz, Paul Hensel, Hans Otto Lenel and Ernst-Joachim Mestmacker. Relevant publications included *Ordnung der Wirschaft* (a series of papers on the Order of the Economy) in 1937 and a yearbook *ORDO* beginning in 1948. These ideas were formative in the construction of the post-war social market economy in Germany. Viktor J Vanberg, 'Freiburg school of law and economics' in *Palgrave Dictionary of Money and Finance* (1992) 172–9. Although clearly influential, other writers have questioned the extent to which these ideas were reflected in the original drafting of the EEC Treaty. For comment, Maduro (n 68) 159. See also Maduro (n 68) 126–31.

Eucken and Bohm were originally concerned with the constitutional foundations of a free economy and society. This challenged the earlier atheoretical approach of the dominant 'Historical School' of Gustav von Schmoller and other writers and attempted to examine all practical political–legal and politico-economic issues in terms of the economic constitution with the link between law and economics being considered essential. Eucken and Bohm highlighted the importance of *Ordnung* (order) as the rules on which economies and economic systems are based (referred to as 'the rules of the game') and *Wirtschaftsordnung* (the consequent economic order that they created). The economic constitution then consisted of the formal legal and institutional and informal conventions and traditions that governed the economic system. The most desirable *Wirtschaftsverfassungspolitik* (constitutional economic policy) would then be used to reform the economic order indirectly (by changing the rules of the game) rather than by direct policy intervention. Participants within the system would be able to pursue their own economic interests at the same time as improve the common interest more generally.

The objective is not then to allow markets to evolve and operate in an exclusively natural and uncontrolled manner but to manage these processes to ensure that they achieve the most desirable consequences both in terms of economic growth and expansion and consequent welfare benefit.

These market based ideas are generally contrasted with (supposedly) more politically responsible social market or welfare based programmes.

Collective political choice would determine the structure and operation of the economic system. While this had often evolved naturally, it was still possible to reform it through human design and political choice. The self-regulating character of markets and *lasissez faire* liberalism were rejected (with the idea of the 'spontaneous emergence' of a natural order) in favour of a more controlled and directed collective order. The successful operation of the free market economy was specifically conditioned on open competition which allowed voluntary exchange and contract to be possible between economic actors on an equal basis. The market economy was then a product of a private law or civil law society rather than feudal society due to the equality guaranteed and removal of earlier sovereign rights and trade and industrial privileges. Free trade and freedom of contract (with the proper enforcement of property rights) had then to be protected against unnecessary direct government intervention and private interference with the market system as well as other potential indirect interest (or pressure) group distortion.

Under these ideas, setting up a market economy still represented a positive constitutional choice. This would allow freedom of decision taking and private action to operate at the sub-constitutional level. This was, in turn, dependent on effective contract and property law as well as employment, bankruptcy and administrative laws. The economic constitution was essentially constructed on the basis of and then maintained using what could now be referred to as commercial law or financial law. Eucken *Staatliche Strukturwandlungen und die Krise des Kapitalismus* (1932), *Grundlagen der Nationalokonomie* (1940) and *Grundsatze der Wirtschaftspolitik* (1952). See also C Joerges *The Market Without the State?—States Without a Market?:Two Essays on the Law of the European Economy* (EUI Florence 1996), Working Paper LAW No 96/2, 6. See also Hayek *The Road to Serfdom* (London ARK 1986 (first published 1944)), 172; Hayek *Law—Legislation and Liberty* (Routledge and Keagan Paul London 1973), 2; DJ Gerber 'Constitutionalising the Economy: German Neo-liberalism, Competition Law and the 'New' Europe' (1988) 42 American Journal of Comparative Law, 25 at 44; JM Buchanan 'Europe's Constitutional Opportunity' in *Europe's Constitutional Future* (London Institute of Economic Affairs Readings 33 1990), 11; S Voigt 'European Political Union—an Appropriate for Applying Constitutional Economics to Real-Life Problems?' (1994) 45 ORDO 273; Peacock and Willgerodt 'Overall View of the German Liberal Movement' in *Germany's Social Market: Origins and Evolution* (London Macmillan 1989), 10; EJ Mestmacker 'On the Legitimacy of European Law', Rabels Z (1994), 617; and EU Petersmann 'Proposals for a new Constitution for the European Union: Building-blocks for a Constitutional Theory and Constitutional Law of the EU' (1995) 32 CMLR 1123. On the nature of the EU economic system, see Striet and Mussler (n 75).

Other writers in this field included Wilhelm Röpke who attempted to develop a philosophical basis for modern capitalism in terms of ordo-liberal ideas. W Ropke *International Order and Economic Integration* (Dordrecht-Holland D Reidel Publishing Company 1959), 24. See also Röpke 'Die Lehre von der Wirtschaft' (13th edn Bern Haupt 1994); *Jenseits von Angebot und Nachfrage* (5th edn Bern Haupt 1979); *Civitas Humana* (4th edn Bern Haupt 1979). See also V J Vanberg 'Ordnungstheorie' as Constitutional Economics The German Conception of a 'Social Market Economy' (ORDO vol 39 1988 ss 17–31); Wohlgemuth 'The present relevance of 'Ordnungstheorie' for the politics and the economics of the social order' in Agnes Labrousse and Jean-Daniel Weisz (Hrsg) *Institutional Economics in France and Germany*; and 'German Ordoliberalism versus the French Regulation School' (Berlin Heidelberg New York 2001 Springer 200–43).

Various forms of socialism can again be distinguished with the most theoretical extremes being Marxism and Leninism.[79] While free and social market theories are often still held out as diametrically opposing forms of socio-political or socio-economic organization, these two policy positions (dogmas) have to a significant extent converged over time with the main differences remaining in terms of the degree of proper market correction or welfare support to be achieved. The issue is then one of mutual policy balance and support rather than absolute conflict or exclusion.

The dominant ideas prevalent at the time that the Treaty of Rome was being drafted can be considered to have included more general market based liberalism (or early forms of neo-liberal institutionalism and liberal internationalism) as well as economic constitution directed Ordo-liberalism and other more directly interventionist social market and planned economic approaches in particular policy areas.[80] The underlying integration objective adopted also had to be achieved within the larger functionalist experiment under construction within Europe as that time[81] as well as operate within the then applicable international trade theory based world order of fixed currencies and capital controls.[82] The original European agenda was then affected by a complex mix of liberal, ordo-liberal, social market, functional and prevalent trade theory related ideas.

The Treaty of Rome can accordingly be considered to have represented a carefully crafted or structured compromise between all of these potentially conflicting and exclusionary objectives or forces and policy approaches. It is to the credit, and indeed genius, of the original Treaty draftsmen that they were able to produce a new dynamic legal, economic

[79] Modern liberalism was considered to have been unable to deal with the protectionist tendencies of Imperial Germany and the United States at the end of the 19th and beginning of the 20th centuries. JA Hobson, in particular, criticised the imperialist potential of liberalism. Imperialism is generally understood to have mainly developed between 1492 and 1763 with Europe assuming control of the Americas and Asia and then with the subjugation of Africa and the Far East between 1870 and 1914. Hobson explained imperialism in terms of the emerging capitalist societies' need for raw materials and cheap labour as well as new markets and investment capability. See Hobson *Imperialism* (1902). These ideas were restated in Vladimir Il'ich Lenin *Imperialism: The Highest State of Capitalism* (1916). See also Karl Max *Das Kapital* (Swan & Sonnenshein & Co London 1896 translated from German third edition by S Moore and E Aveling).

Marxism is essentially concerned with the ideas of class struggle, welfare imbalance, consequent conflict (between the bourgeoisie and the proletariat), the use of war to reinforce and protect capitalism and the need for revolution. Leninism criticises the defects (decay) in capitalism including monopoly structures, unfair competition and competition for resources. Much of this is based on Hobson. For comment, Evans and Newnham (n 76) 317–18. See also Baylis and Smith (n 76) Ch 10.

[80] On early German and French priorities (n 33). On neo-liberalism (n 76). On ordo-liberalism (n 78). On liberal internationalism (nn 76 and 86).

[81] On functionalism Ch 1, introduction and Ch 2, section A and (n 7).

[82] On post-War trade theory section B (1) and (n 36) and Ch 2, sections H and I.

and political model within which all of these different market, social and political objectives, preferences and aspirations could be achieved.[83]

The challenge for Europe is now to attempt to ensure that the most appropriate policy balance is capable of being achieved in light of the more recent equally significant pressures created. These include proposed further enlargement and potential institutional paralysis within an ever extended membership system as well as the greater financial and budgetary pressures imposed especially through further changes in net contribution commitments and welfare expectations across the EU.[84]

This has also to be re-assessed as Europe is forced to respond to the additional competitive challenges that exist within an ever more integrated global trading environment. Separate pressures are imposed through continued financial innovation including with the significant increases experienced in the use of the internet and other digital or electronic communication and delivery mechanisms that further break down traditional geographic as well as legal and regulatory boundaries and barriers.[85]

Any new market and social policy balance secured within Europe will have to be able to respond purposely and effectively to all of these challenges.

(5) INSTITUTIONAL AND RELATIONSHIP THEORIES

The development of banking and financial policy has to a lesser extent been affected by the more general approaches adopted with regard to institutional and state relations within Europe.[86]

[83] (nn 33, 76 and 78). For an economic analysis of this mixed economic constitutional model and its evolution within the EU, Striet and Mussler (n 75).

[84] On longer term core development issues, section F (1), (2) and (3).

[85] On international trade reform and financial innovation, section F (4) and (5).

[86] Early liberal internationalism was reflected in Keynes *The Economic Consequences of The Peace* (1919) which questioned the motives of the allies in setting the terms of settlement following the First World War. The League of Nations was set up in 1920 to attempt to resolve international disputes and conflicts through formal procedures operating through a Council, Assembly and Secretariat. The Locarno Treaties were signed in 1926 which confirmed the German borders and cooperative relations between the main powers. The Treaty of Paris (the Kellogg-Briand Non-Aggression Pact) was entered into in 1928. This general Treaty for the Renunciation of War was initially signed by 15 countries although this was subsequently extended to 68. The Treaty distinguished between wars of aggression and self-defence in an attempt to correct continuing uncertainty left under the Leagues' rules. All signatories were required to renounce war as an instrument of national policy and to agree to have all disputes settled through peaceful means. Evans and Newnham (n 76) 292.

The credibility of liberal internationalism was undermined by the support shown to the development of fascist ideologies during the 1930s and the perceived lack of authority of the League of Nations. Brown notes that the liberal slogan 'law not war' effectively became 'only law through war.' Chris Brown *Understanding International Relations* (2001 2nd edn Palgrave) 27. Writers such as Reinhold Niabuhr questioned the underlying moral stance of liberal internationalism and highlighted the aggressive and acquisitive nature of collective

In terms of international relations theory, European integration can be considered having regard to a number of more general theories or doctrines including functionalism (and neo-functionalism), neo-realism (or liberal inter-governmentalism), neo-federalism and new institutionalism or multi-level governance.[87] Each of these attempts to explain the underlying integration process in terms of the relationship between the various political, institutional and market interests involved.

These theories are of assistance in understanding the underlying processes concerned especially in historical terms. The common assumption made, however, is the importance of underlying functionalism in achieving the longer-term political or social objectives set through more functionally limited immediate goals such as creating a common and then internal market place which are, in turn, based on an efficient law of free movement and (an assumed) effective and stable banking and financial system.

action. Niabuhr *Moral Man and Immoral Society* (Scribner New York 1932). The different levels of resources and capability between states (the 'haves' and the 'have nots') were also highlighted by EH Carr. Carr *The Twenty Years Crisis* (Macmillan London 1939). With Carr's work, earlier liberal international thought was renamed 'utopianism' (or 'idealism') with a new post-1945 war synthesis emerging based on these early realist ideas. Major works included Martin Wight *Power Politics* (1946), Nicholas Spykman *America's Strategy in World Politics* (Harcourt Brace New York 1942); George Kennan *American Diplomacy* (New American Library New York 1952); and Hans J Morgenthau *Politics Among Nations: The Struggle for Power and Peace* (Alfred P Knopf New York 1948). With Morgenthau, Carr's focus on scarcity is replaced by human sin while realism is also formalised or systematised with the production of a series of numbered rules, principles or policies. For Morgenthau, international relations was characterised by states pursuing interests defined in terms of power. For comment, Brown 30–4.

Earlier free trade ideas were subsequently replaced by more modern 'complex interdependence' theories. Complex interdependence was, in particular, developed by Keohane and Nye in 1977 as part of their attack on realism. Keohane and Nye questioned the coherence and dominance of state action and the effectiveness and precedence of force as a policy instrument. Societies can operate through a number of contact channels while no clear hierarchy exists with the use of force being significantly downgraded. Robert Keohane and Joseph Nye (eds) *Transnational Relations and World Politics* (Harvard University Press, Cambridge MA, 1971). Realism is concerned with explaining international relations in terms of state systems driven by power politics based interests (n 76). International politics is considered to involve a 'struggle for power' between states motivated by survival and protectionist instincts. International relations is then characterised as an anarchic state system involving conflict, dominance and self-help. Earlier realist ideas were contained in Machiavelli *The Prince* (1513) and Hobbes *Leviathan* (1651). Earlier writers included EH Carr, R Neibuhr, J Herz, HJ Morgenthau, G Schwarzenberger, M Wight, N Spykman, and GS Kennan. Later writers included R Aron, H Bull, H Kissinger, RA Osgood, R Rosecranche, KW Thompson, RW Tucker, KN Waltz, and A Woolfers. See generally, Evans and Newnham (n 76); and Baylis and Smith (n 76).

87 For discussion, P Craig 'The Nature of the Community' in Craig and de Burca (n 65) Ch 1, section 1 and authorites cited. See also K Armstrong 'The New Institutionalism', in P Craig and C Harlow (eds) *Law making in the European Union* (Kluwer 1998). Giandomenico Majone 'International Regulator Co-operation: A neo-institutional approach' in George A Bermann, Mathias Herdegen and Peter L Lindseth, *Transatlantic Regulatory Co-operation* (OUP Oxford 2000) 119–45.

F. DEVELOPMENT ISSUES

In terms of longer-term development, consideration must also be given to the effects of continued enlargement and further geographic expansion, possible consequent constitutional revision and institutional balance, global relevance and relations, e-finance and other technological correction as well as the final or ultimate political and social objectives to be achieved.

(1) ENLARGEMENT

The separate difficulties that arise with the impact of continued enlargement must be taken into account.[88] It has to be accepted that the single financial market place may eventually extend to over thirty participating countries including the ten new accession states and other residual EEA and linked territories. [89] The particular challenge that this creates (in addition to the essential institutional difficulties that enlargement necessarily creates)[90] is ensuring that the new extended market place created is prop-

[88] The Czech Republic, Estonia, Cyprus, Latvia, Lithuania, Hungary, Malta, Poland, Slovenia and Slovakia were admitted to the EU in May 2004. Treaty of Accession, 16 Apr available http://europa.eu.int/comm/enlargement/negotiations/treatyofaccession.html. Enlargement with central and eastern European countries was agreed at the Copenhagen European Council meeting in 1993 with the original membership criteria being set at that stage. Candidate countries had to have achieved stability of institutions guaranteeing democracy, the rule of law, human rights and respect, the existence of a functioning market economy as well as the capacity to cope with the competitive pressures and market forces within the EU and the ability to take on the obligations of membership involved including adherence to the aims of political, economic and monetary union. It was also agreed at the Madrid European Council in December 1995 that each country had to create the necessary conditions for its integration through the adjustment of its administrative and judicial structures to ensure effective implementation of all EU laws.

The European Council decided at its Luxembourg summit in Dec 1997 that the enlargement process should include a European Conference launched on 12 Mar 1998 to bring ten central European countries together with Cyprus and Turkey within a multilateral framework and with an accession process beginning on 30 Mar 1998 with the central European countries and Cyprus. Malta's application was re-activated in Oct 1996 having been suspended in 1996. 2007 was set as an indicative date for accession by Bulgaria and Romania. Pre-accession negotiations continue with Croatia and Turkey. See http://europa.eu.int/comm/enlargement/index_en.html

[89] See, eg, Commission *Preparation of the Associated Countries of Central and Eastern Europe for Integration into the Internal Market of the Union* COM(95) 163 final, 10 May 1995; and Decision of the Council and Commission of 13 December 1993 on the conclusion of the Europe Agreement between the European Communities and their Member States and the Republic of Poland (OJ L 348/1). The effect of this expansion is to extend considerably the relevance of Community provisions in the banking and finance area which will also then act as a major global rather than purely regional model for market integration and control. For recent comment see, for example, DW Green 'Harmonization and Integration: Regulation of EU Cross-border Financial Integration,' CEPR Economic Policy Roundtable, Brussels, 8 Nov 2002.

[90] Commission *For the European Union: Peace, Freedom and Solidarity—Communication of the Commission on the Institutional Architecture* COM(2002) 728 final/2.

erly supervised and regulated at all times despite the underlying intra-market trading and access privileges provided. A considerable amount of work will be required in this regard at both the European and national levels. This is in addition to the separate institutional, budgetary and adoption difficulties that continued enlargement necessarily creates.

(2) CONSTITUTIONAL BALANCE AND REVISION

The changes that have taken place in the nature of the relations between the main European institutions and more significant developments in the larger integration process were to have been reflected in the new European Constitution produced in July 2003.[91] Although stated by some only to give effect to previous amendments already agreed within the Treaty revision process, the adoption and ratification of the new Constitution would have had a significant longer term impact on the speed and direction or, at least, depth of European integration.[92] Whether the Constitution will ever receive all of the necessary national referenda approval and support is still unclear.[93]

91 The proposed European Constitution was to replace all exiting Treaty and related amending provisions. Reference would then be made to the single consolidating 'Treaty establishing a Constitution for Europe.' The existing separate European Communities and European Union would be merged into a single 'European Union' (n 1). The new integrated European Union was to be given legal personality including express power to enter into international treaties and conventions directly.

92 The draft Constitution document was produced in 18 July 2003 and provided for the inclusion of the Charter for Fundamental Rights within the text and an express confirmation of the primacy of EU law. The EU was to be committed to the progressive development of a common defence policy and common rules on asylum and immigration. Majority voting was to be extended with regard to a number of technical matters although national vetoes were to be preserved in certain key areas including budgetary matters and financing, direct taxation and foreign and defence policy.

The roles of the main institutions were clarified and co-decision (between the Parliament and Council) extended to 95 per cent of all European laws. The Constitution document referred to the use of the principle of 'inter-institutional programming' with regard to Commission functions. Commission composition was to remain on a one Commissioner per Member State basis until 2014 and then be reduced to two thirds of the number of countries with appointments being made on rotational basis. The European Council (as distinct from Council of Ministers) was to be given formal institutional status with a President appointed on a two and half year term basis. A new Union Minister of Foreign Affairs was also to be appointed.

'Double majority' voting was to be introduced in other areas (with decisions requiring a 55 per cent of countries represented and 65 per cent of the total EU population). The maximum number of seats in the European Parliament would be increased to 750 with allocation being determined in accordance with the principle of 'degressive proportionality' and an agreed minimum number of 6 and maximum of 96 seats. Countries were to be given an express right to be able to withdraw from membership of the European Union. For further information on the proposed Convention, http://european-convention.eu.int and http://europa.eu.int/constitution/index_en.htm. For comment, http://news.bbc.co.uk/1/hi/world/europe/2950276.stm. On the future of Europe debate, http://europa.eu.int/constitution/futurum/index_en.htm.

93 The Convention had to be ratified by all Member States with ten initially having announced that they would hold national referenda (Belgium, the Czech Republic, Denmark, Luxembourg, the Netherlands, Poland, Portugal, Spain and the UK) with France subsequently confirm that it would also follow. The referenda in Poland and the UK were to be held last due

Even if fully ratified, its immediate effects in the financial area would have been limited and not affected the main policy and institutional issues considered in this text although this does raise larger integration issues that have still to be resolved within Europe.

(3) Financial and Budgetary Support

Enlargement and the creation of a further extended membership base will also place increasing pressure on the EU's financial and budgetary system. This will become particularly apparent as changes in net contribution commitments take effect and as welfare expectations of new accession territories materialise. This could place almost irreconcilable pressures on Member State relations and good will over time. This will not have an impact on the nature and operation of the single banking and financial market programme directly although it could have potentially significant effects on associated institutional reforms, regional programme successes, Member State relations and wider integration progress.[94]

to the sensitivity of a possible no vote. While the Constitutional Convention cannot come into effect without full ratification, if there was substantial support follow-up referenda may be considered in no opinion countries or possible pressure placed on them to withdraw from the EU. If a majority rejected the Constitution, the concern was that a formal integrationist and non-integration division may have emerged across Europe which could destabilise the Union as a whole. For comment see, for example, 'A difficult birth' *The Economist* (June 26 2004) 41. The French subsequently rejected the Constitution on 29 May 2005 and the Netherlands on 1 June 2005. It was accordingly decided at the European Council meeting on 16 and 17 June 2005 that the date initially planned for a report on ratification of the Treaty (by 1 Nov 2006) would be put back as it was accepted that those countries that had not yet ratified the Treaty would be unable to do so before mid-2007. The process was effectively put on indefinite hold with this being referred to as a 'period of reflection, explanation and discussion.'

[94] The previous seven year budget was agreed at the Berlin Summit on March 1999. This was referred to as Agenda 2000. This included reforms to the Common Agricultural Policy (CAP), the Structural and Cohesion Funds and the pre-accession aid programmes for the new accession territories. This also provided for a revised Inter-institutional Agreement which establishes the procedures for the creation of the annual budget. Under the Agreement, the Council and the European Parliament are made the Community's Budgetary Authority with joint responsibility for deciding the budget on the basis of proposals from the Commission. The projected budget for the following period of 2007–2013 was to be between 875 to 1000 billion euros. 871 billion euros represents 1.06 per cent of EU gross domestic product with the six largest net contributors wishing to cap expenditure at around 1 per cent.

The difficulty that arises is that over 40 per cent of the budget was to be allocated to farming and rural subsidies which only account for about 4 per cent of employment and output. France also, in particular, received approximately 7 billion euros each year which both distorts (reduces) its net contribution to the budget as well as acts a significant disincentive for necessary farming reforms. New accession countries were further not to be entitled to receive the same proportionate amounts under the CAP. Only half of regional support funds were to be made available to accession territories with the balance being allocated to less developed areas within the existing member countries. Subsequent proposals suggested that monies that would otherwise have been allocated to 'competitiveness' investments (including transport and research as well as security and foreign policy) were to be cut to support cohesion fund

(4) GLOBAL RELATIONS

The existence of various other trading, cooperation and association agreements currently in place and the relationship between the Community and other regional and global trading arrangements must also be fully taken into account.[95] The success (or otherwise) of the Community as a trading and capital market will have significant consequences on global and other regional trade initiatives. The application and operation of the revised General Agreement on Trade in Services (GATS) rules may have particular consequences on the operation of the banking and financial services markets within Europe.[96] It is essential that the Community continues to participate closely in the development and operation of the new global trading (and services) framework under construction especially within the Doha and subsequent negotiations within the revised WTO arrangements.

commitments. The effect to of this could have been to reduce substantially the ability of the EU to secure its 2010 Lisbon Agenda objectives in favour of supporting anti-competitive and arguably distortive and unequal support programmes. This debate clearly reflects the more general free or social market choices already highlighted (nn 75–83) although the budget debate is compounded by the problems of securing a fair allocation of the support funds already agreed between the member counties of the EU.

Agreement was eventually secured on the new 'Financial Perspective' at the European Council meeting on 15–16 Dec 2005 during the UK Presidency. An overall budget was agreed of 1.045 billion euros which was higher than the original proposal the UK Presidency had put forward but still lower than the original Luxembourg proposal. Following extended negotiations, the UK agreed to surrender up to 10.5 bn euros (£7bn) or 20 per cent of its rebate while France accepted a more general budget review in 2008–2009 which could lead to subsequent cuts in farm subsidies. In the press conference following the summit meeting, Tony Blair claimed that the UK rebate had remained in full effect on all spending other than the funding for economic development in the new accession territories countries. On the final outcome, see the UK Presidency website http://www.eu2005.gov.uk. For comment, http://news.bbc.co.uk/1/hi/world/europe/4536894.stm.

95 On regional integration more generally, Ch 2, section E. On the relationship between the EU and global free trade, N Emiliou and D O'Keeffe *The European Union and World Trade Law* (John Wiley & Sons USA 1996); P Aeckhoute *The European Internal Market and International Trade* (Clarendon Press Oxford 1994); T Walsh *The Customs Code of the European Union* (Butterworths London 1997); D Lasok *The Trade and Customs Law of the European Union* (Kluwer Law London 1998); F Snyder *International Trade and Customs Law of the European Union* (Butterworths London 1998); A Mayss and A Reed *European Business Litigation* (Ashgate Dartmouth 1998). See also Fraser and Long *The World Financial System* (n 37), Ch 38, section 1. On global relations and globalization more generally, David Held, Anthony McGrew, David Goldbatt and Jonathan Perraton *Global Transformations: Politics, Economics and Culture* (Polity 2001); Paul Hirst and Grahame Tompson *Globalisation in Question* (2nd edn Polity 2003). For more critical studies, Peter Singer *One World: The ethics of globalisation* (Yale Nota Bene 2nd edn 2004); Martin Woolf, *Why Globalisation Works: the Case for the Global Market Economy* (Yale University Press 2004); and Jagdish Bhagwati *In Defence of Globalisation* (OUP Oxford 2004).

96 For comment, W Dobson and P Jacquet *Financial Services Liberalisation in the WTO* (June 1998), Institute for International Economics 73; and R Snape and M Bosworth 'Advancing Services Negotiations' (1996), paper presented at Institute for International Economics Conference *The World Trading Systems: Challenges Ahead* (24–25 June, 1996). On the results of the December 2005 Hong Kong negotiations http://www.wto.org.

(5) Digital and Financial Innovation

As well as respond to the additional supervisory and regulatory challenges created by the establishment of an extended regional financial market place, a number of more specific technical difficulties will have to be dealt with concerning the transfer of many financial activities into internet, digital or other electronic delivery formats. While many of the same basic principles developed to date at the regional and international levels may be reapplied in these new digital environments, certain additional issues will necessarily arise especially with regard to such matters as transparency (including, in particular, access location and identification), relevant law (and jurisdiction) and the nature and content of the relationships to be set up between market operators and market regulators (and between national authorities themselves).[97]

The related issue that arises is then ensuring that the European systems are capable more generally of dealing with other continuing developments in financial innovation and financial engineering (or re-engineering) over time. Apart from in terms of continued risk identification and internal risk management within financial firms,[98] it is, in particular, in connection with the development of new electronic trading systems (ATSs) or platforms (ATPs) that a significant amount of financial innovation is expected to take

[97] On relevant European papers (n 26). See also OECD *Electronic Commerce: Opportunities and Challenges for Government* (1997) (The Sacher Report); OECD *A Borderless World: Realising the Potential for Global Electronic Commerce* (Oct 1998); and OECD *Guidelines for Consumer Protection in the Context of Electronic Commerce* (1999) http:\\www.oecd.org/dsti/sti/it/consumer/ prod/guidelines.htm. For comment, G Ferne *Electronic Commerce: A New Economic and Policy Area* available http:\\www. arraydev.com/commerce/JIBC/9704-08.htm. On the development of the internet, D Kristula *The History of the* Internet (Mar 1997) available www.davesite.com\wabstation\net-history.shtml; and H Walt *The Brief History of the Internet,* www.delphi.com\navnet\fag\ history.html. On the emerging regulatory response, see, in particular, Basel Committee Electronic Banking Group [EBG] *Electronic Banking Group Initiatives and White Papers* (Oct 2000) incorporating EBG White Paper *Cross-Border Electronic Banking Issues for Bank Supervisors* (Sept 2000) and EBG White Paper *Electronic Banking Risk Management Issues for Bank Supervisors* (Oct 2000) available http:\\www.bis.org. On electronic money, see BIS *Implications for Central Banks of the Development of Electronic Money* (Oct 1996) available http:\\www.bis.org; CPSS, *Security of Electronic Money* (1996) http:\\www.bis.org/ publ.htm.; G10 *Electronic Money: Consumer Protection, Law Enforcement, Supervisory and Cross-Border Issues* (Apr 1997) http:\\www.bis.org.htm and authorities referred to; and Basel Committee *Risk Management for Electronic Banking and Electronic Money Activities* (Mar 1998).

[98] See, for example, J Bessis *Risk Management in Banking* (2nd edn John Wiley & Sons Chichester 2002), Ch 1. On financial risk modelling, see Basel Committee,'Amendment to the Capital Accord to Incorporate Market Risks' (Jan 1996). On the most recent proposed amendments to the Basel capital requirements, Basel Committee *The New Basel Capital Accord* (January 2001); *The New Basel Capital Accord: an explanatory note* (2001); *Overview of The New Basel Capital Accord* (2001); *The Standardised Approach to Credit Risk, The Internal Ratings-Based Approach* (2001), *Asset Securitisation* (2001), *Operational Risk* (2001), *Pillar*

place.[99] It is possible that a number of these new arrangements may within a short period of time replace many of the existing formal stock markets and exchanges across Europe at the same time as a significant amount of new financing will be transferred from bank based credit to securitised forms of transferable bond, equity and other security or capital market related formats.[100]

While some of the difficulties that arise with electronic trading and exchange systems were being considered as part of the Commission's review of the 1993 Investment Services Directive and subsequent adoption of the Markets in Financial Instruments Directive (MIFID) in 2004, it is still unclear how many of these issues will be managed and resolved.

G. POLICY EXAMINATION AND POLICY CONTRIBUTION

A number of difficulties accordingly arise in attempting to consider and understand the nature of the integration process still under construction within Europe and especially in the banking and financial arena.

It is not possible to consider all of the separate operational, programme, institutional and constitutional as well as more general development issues identified in a single text in any detail. The nature of the underlying core policy options and solutions available can nevertheless be highlighted and examined to attempt to understand how these problems have been overcome in the banking and financial area.

It has to be accepted that regional integration is a difficult and complex process and especially in the financial area. Rather than provide any fixed or final understanding or interpretation, the objective of this book is to try to make some contribution to the possible clarification and revision of all

2 (Supervisory Review Process) (2001), *Principles for the Management and Supervision of Interest Rate Risk* (2001) and *Pillar 3 (Market Discipline)* (2001). For discussion, Walker (n 2), Ch 8. In relation to development and operation of asset and liability management, see, eg, J Revell *The British Financial System* (Macmillan London and Basingstoke 1973), Ch 1; and E P Gardener (ed) *UK Banking Supervision and Evolution, Practice and Issues* (Allen & Unwin London 1986), Ch 1. See also J W Bitner *Successful Bank Asset/Liability Management* (Wiley, 1992); and FJ Fabozzi and A Konishi (eds) *The Handbook of Asset/Liability Management* (Irwin Chicago and London 1996).

99 M Blair and G A Walker (eds) *Markets and Exchanges Law* (OUP Oxford 2006). See also Financial Services Authority *Infrastructure Service Providers* (FSA London 2000) available http:\\.www.fsa.gov.uk.

100 Blair and Walker (n 99). See generally, Organization for Economic Co-operation and Development (OECD) *The Internationalisation of Banking: The Policy Issues* (1983) (the Pecchioli Report); OECD *Banking and Electronic Fund Transfers* (1983); OECD *International Trade in Services: Banking* (1984); OECD *Trends in Banking in OECD Countries* (1985); OECD *Banking and Monetary Policy* (1985); OECD *Competition in Banking* (1989) (the Broker Report); and OECD *Banks Under Stress* (1992); OECD *Transformation of the Banking System: Portfolio Restructuring, Privatisation and the Payment System* (1993).

of the relevant policy challenges and choices available. This may then be of consequent value in developing more complete integration models and policy responses in other commercial and industrial sector areas more generally.

PART TWO

Financial Integration

2

European Banking and Financial Integration—Historical Background, Content, and Policy Basis

The European Community constitutes the most sophisticated regional trading arrangement in the world. Various global and regional systems have been established during the post-War period although nothing has been attempted on the same scope and depth. Insofar as any comparable arrangements have been set up such as in Latin America, South Africa or Asia, these have often adopted a European or simplified European model.

The European Community is generally based on a free trade area and customs union which secure the full free movement of goods within the internal market established as well as a common framework of controls for products from outside the extended internal market place created. This is supplemented by full free movement of all factors of production including workers (employed and self-employed) and capital and payment. Full free movement of all products and production factors is accordingly secured. This is supplemented by the adoption of common policies in a number of areas and supported by an extended single institutional structure and legal framework. The effect of this has been to create new parallel economic and legal orders within a single regional trading or market arrangement.

One of the most original and important components within this trading system has been the creation of a single integrated market in banking and financial services. This is important both as an individual service sector which forms a significant part of GDP in most Member States as well as in providing the necessary underlying economic and financial framework on which the rest of the Community is based. Banks and related financial institutions carry out a number of core savings, credit and payment functions within any economy which are essential to its continued effective and stable operation. Banking and financial markets are accordingly significant in their own terms as well as core components within the larger political, industrial and commercial operations of the Community.

The particular difficulty that arises in the banking and financial area is that a basic conflict necessarily arises between the desire to facilitate market access within the new single trading system created and the need to secure proper market stability at both the local or national and regional levels.

Financial markets are inherently unstable due to the underlying intermediation and transformation functions discharged. It is this vulnerability or instability (with the importance of the core economic functions that they discharge) that requires that financial markets are subject to proper supervision and control. This becomes even more difficult within a regional financial system to the extent that the existing national regulatory systems in place may be undermined by the privileged or preferred access is to be provided to institutions from foreign territories. Unfortunately, no specific guidance or direction was provided under the Treaty as to how this was to be achieved in practice.

The European Commission has consequently had to attempt to develop an effective policy that can secure both of the objectives of access and control in a balanced and effective manner. In so doing, the Commission has historically moved from an earlier full harmonization policy to a new approach based on mutual recognition and minimum harmonization. At the same time as develop this new approach in connection with goods and services more generally, the Commission has had to reconsider its specific relevance and application in the financial area which has, in particular, included the adoption of the parallel principle of home country control. Whether this new combined approach can secure an appropriate balance between access and control in the financial area remains to be seen.

While the Commission has attempted to develop an effective policy on which to construct the programme of secondary measures developed, the European Court of Justice has had to interpret the underlying Treaty provisions and develop an appropriate range of judicial principles to apply in the general area of free movement and to banking and financial services in particular. The Court has consequently developed a number of core rules over a considerable period of time that are generally based on such doctrines as direct applicability as well as non-discrimination or cross-border effect. As these principles were not constructed for specific application in the banking and financial area, their relevance and operation has had to be reconsidered as appropriate issues for judicial determination have arisen and such cases have come before the Court.

The purpose of this Chapter is to consider the nature and core components of European integration on which the Treaty of Rome is based. The nature of European integration is initially examined and the perceived benefits of economic integration identified and the success achieved in securing them within Europe to date assessed. The structure and content of comparable regional frameworks are referred to and the unique nature of the Community highlighted. The separate economic and legal orders underlying the Community and their Treaty base are identified and their operation and value considered. The related but considerably more ambitious objective of securing financial integration within Europe is then examined in further detail. The nature of integration in the financial area and the obstacles that arise are referred to and the partial resolution achieved noted. Specific reference is made to the progress that was possible in designing and implementing an effective free movement of capital policy across Europe and the success achieved in other related areas of monetary and economic cooperation and coordination. The importance of adopting an appropriate and effective policy in the banking and financial area is considered and the nature and value of the emerging response constructed to date assessed. The more detailed evolution and content of the judicial policy and secondary programme developed in this area and the success or otherwise of the overall result achieved to date are considered in the following chapters.

A. EUROPE AND EUROPEAN INTEGRATION

The general political and economic history of Europe has been subject to extensive examination.[1] In addition to its obvious geological origins and pre-history, this has included the main stages of its socio-political evolution including early and late classicism,[2] the middle ages,[3] renaissance, reformation, absolutism, post-enlightenment revisionism, humanism, capitalism and industrialization, scientific enquiry and the birth of the nation-state.[4]

[1] See generally HAL Fisher *A History of Europe* (Eyre & Spottiswood London 1936); Eugene Weber *A Modern History of Europe* (Norton New York and London 1971); Norman Davies *Europe—A History* (Pimlico London 1997); W Alison Phillipps *Modern Europe, 1815–99* (Rivingtons London 1908); J Merriman *A History of Modern Europe* (Norton New York and London 1997). See also *The New Cambridge Medieval History* (Vols I–VII); Will and Ariel Durrant *The Story of Civilzsation* (11 Vols, 1939–1975). See also Michael Salewski *Geschichte Europas: Staaten und Nationen von der Antike bis zur Gegenwart* (2nd ed Munich Beck 2004). On EU history (n 6). On economic history (nn 39 and 40).

[2] Ancient history can be considered to include the origins of man, the paleolithic and neolithic ages and appearance of the first civilizations. This was followed by the Mesopotamian (3500–539 BC), early Egyptian (3100–30 BC), Hebrew (2000–70 BC) and Greek (3000–336 BC) Civilizations, the Roman Republic and Roman Empire (509–44 BC and 44–476 BC) and the growth of early Christianity (29 BC–529 AD). The Byzatine Empire (325–678) is often placed in the medieval period (n 3) although this can also be considered to stretch until the middle of the 15th century. Strict divisions are nevertheless difficult to confirm and writers vary.

[3] Medieval history can be considered to include the Byzatine Empire (325–678), the growth of Islam (570–1258), the Carolingian Empire (768–814), monasticism, manoralism and feudalism, the Crusades (1096–1291) and Papal reform (910–1215). The revival of learning and the growth of scholasticism then began during the early eleventh century (1050–1300). On early English legal history and the development of the Common Law, GA Walker, 'Bank Recovery—the Development of Judicial and Arbitral Redress under English Law' *Annual Review of Banking Law* (Boston University Boston Mass Spring 2000).

[4] See, eg, Peter Green *Alexander to Actium—the Historical Evolution of the Hellenistic Age* (Thames and Hudson London 1990); Chester G Starr *A History of the Ancient World* (1991); Edward Gibbon *Decline and Fall of the Roman Empire* (Vols I–VI); MP Charlesworth *The Roman Empire* (OUP Oxford 1964); Warren Treadgold *A History of the Byzantine State*

Within the study of history itself, we have also generally moved from structuralism to deconstructionalism and now to a new period of post-modernist examination and debate.[5]

The history of European integration and, in particular, the background to and construction of the original European Communities have been subject to separate critical study.[6] The underlying objective of post-War

and Society (Stanford University Press Stanford 1997); JJ Norwich *Byzantium* (Viking London 3 vols (1998, 2000 and 2001); S Ozment *The Age of Reform 1250–1556* (Newhaven 1980); TA Brady, HA Oderman and JA Tracy *Handbook of European History 1400–1600* (Brill Leiden 1995, 2 vols); Peter Burke *The European Renaissance* (Blackwell Oxford 1998); Andrew Pettegree *The Reformation World* (Routledge London 2000); A Pettegree *Europe in the Sixteenth Century* (Blackwell Oxford 2002); David Hume *The History of England* (Talboys and Wheeler Oxford 1778, vols I–VI, repr 1983); Peter Gray *The Enlightenment—The Rise of Modern Paganism* (Weidenfeld and Nicolson London 1966); and P Gray *The Enlightenment—The Science of Creation* (Weidenfeld and Nicolson London 1969); T Israel *Radical Enlightenment* (OUP Oxford 2001); A Broadie *The Scottish Enlightenment* (Birlinn Edinburgh 2001); JM Thomson *The French Revolution* (Blackwell Oxford 1943); Simon Schama *Citizens—A Chronicle of the French Revolution* (Knopf New York 1989); AJP Taylor *The Course of German History* (Hamish Hamilton London 1962); James J Sheehan *German History 1770–1866* (Clarendon Oxford 1989); Hajo Holborn *A History of Modern Germany 1840–1945* (1969); Mary Fulbrook (ed) *German History Since 1800* (Arnold Loneon 1997); D Urwin *The Community of Europe: A History of European Integration* (Longmann 2nd edn 1995); Denis Judd *Empire* (Harper Collins London 1996); N Canny *The Origin of Empire* (OUP Oxford 1998 4 vols); and S Schama *A History of Britain* (BBC London 2 vols 2000, 2001). See also Hans-Ulrich Wehler *Deutsche Gesellschaftsgeschichte* (4 vols 1987–2003); Nipperdey *Deutsche Geschichte, 1866–1918* (2 vols) and *Deutsche Geschichte 1800–1866* (6th edn 1994).

[5] Post-modernism questions both the accepted canons of historical knowledge and the principles of conventional methodology. Norman Davies *Europe—A History* (Pimlico London 1997), Introduction. See also Gertrude Himmelfarb 'Telling It As You Like It: Post-Modernist History and the Flight From Fact', *TLS* (16 Oct 1992), 12–15 cited in Davies *Introduction* n 24. See also Georg G Iggers *New Directions in European Historiography* (Methuen London 1984); Ernst Breisach *Historiography—Ancient, Medieval and Modern* (University of Chicago Chicago 2nd edn 1994); Iggers *Historiography in the Twentieth Century* (Hanover London 1997); and Keith Jenkins *Why History—Ethics and Postmodernity* (Routledge New York 1999).

[6] See, eg, Kevin Wilson *The History of the Idea of Europe* (Routledge London 1995); Trevor Salmon and Sir Nicholl William *Building European Union—A Documentary History and Analysis* (Manchester University Press Manchester 1997); Horst Ungerer *A Concise History of European Monetary Integration from EPU to EMU* (Quorum London 1997); Walter Lipgens, *A History of European Integration*, vol I: *The Formation of the European Unity Movement 1945–1947* (Clarendon Oxford 1982); Walter Lipgens *Documents on the History of the European Integration*, vols 1–3 (De Gruyter Berlin 1986); Walter Lipgens and Wilfried Lath *Documents on the History of European Integration* vol 4 (De Gruyter Berlin 1991); Katherine Savage *The History of the Common Market* (Longman & Harlow 1969); Max Jansen *History of European Integration, 1945–1975* (University of Amsterdam Amsterdam 1975); Fritz Machlup *A History of Thought on Economic Integration* (Macmillan London 1977); Dirk Spierenburg and Raymond Poidevin *The History of the High Authority of the European Coal and Steel Community: Supra Nationality in Operation* (Weidenfeld and Nicolson London 1994); and Michael McCormick *Origins of the European Economy* (Cambridge University Press Cambridge 2001). See also Benjamin Angel and Jacques Lafitte *L'Europe: Petite histoire d'une grande idée* (Paris Gallimard 2004); Marie-Thérèse Bitsch *Histoire de la construction européenne de 1945 à nos jours* (Bruxelles Éd Complexe 2004); Christophe Réveillard *Les dates-clefs de la construction européenne: Histoire, institutions, traités, politiques communes, union économique et monétaire, élargissements, perspectives* (Paris Ellipses 2000); and Charles Zorgbibe *Histoire de*

European efforts has generally been to develop a series of functionally determined economic and trading arrangements designed to promote closer cooperation between European states and in so doing prevent the continued resolution of disputes through military intervention and territorial attachment, accession or aggrandisement. This new functionalism involves the establishment of agreed integration programmes on the basis of identifiable areas of common interest and possible cooperation and mutual benefit. The advantage is that more general cooperative or integrative progress may arise out of the initial functionally limited specific activity or activities undertaken. The disadvantage of functionalism is that the larger goals or objectives to be achieved may never be clearly stated, agreed or understood with the result that no final end result may ever be secured.

Post-War European history can then generally be understood in terms of the attempt to promote closer unity among nations through initial agreement on the common pooling and management of the principal industrial energy (coal) and production (steel) factors which early initiatives were subsequently extended to include atomic energy and more general goods and services.[7] Despite early difficulties and the economic problems of the late 1970s and early 1980s, further progress was possible with the work undertaken to complete the creation of an *Internal Market* by the end of 1992.[8] Exchange rate fluctuations were also stabilized and inflation rate

l'Union Européenne (Paris Albin Michel Fondation Robert Schuman 2005). On European legal history, Maurizio Lupoi, *The Origins of the European Legal Order* (CUP Cambridge 1999).

[7] Post-War functional efforts began with the establishment of the European Coal and Steel Community (the ECSC) under the Treaty of Paris in 1950. The ECSC had been set up at the instigation of Jean Monnet and Robert Schuman. Following this success, JW Beyen, the Dutch Foreign Affairs Minister, proposed the extension of this to create a common market and customs union in 1953. The separate proposal to set up a European Defence Community was rejected (postponed sine die) by the French Assembly on 30 August 1954 which prevented any more general political initiatives from being considered further at that stage.

Following the Messina Conference on 1 and 2 June 1955, an Intergovernmental Committee was appointed under Paul-Henri Spaak, the Belgium Minister for Foreign Affairs, to consider the possibility of the progressive integration of European markets. The Spaak Report was adopted by the Ministers of Foreign Affairs at their Venice meeting in May 1956. Following a further Intergovernmental Conference, the European Economic Community (EEC) and EURATOM were set up under two Treaties of Rome which were signed in March 1957 at Campodiglio in Rome. The Treaties came into effect on 1 Jan 1958.

The UK had sent observers to act as representatives on the Spaak Committee. Its involvement was terminated with the decision to move towards the establishment of new institutional structures and wider economic integration across Europe. The UK then focused on the establishment of the European Free Trade Association (EFTA) with Austria, Denmark, Norway, Portugal, Sweden and Switzerland. EFTA was set up in 1960.

[8] This was generally based on the decision of the European Court of Justice in *Cassis de Dijon* decision in 1979 which allowed the Commission to reinvigorate the application of the underlying Treaty provisions on the free movement of goods. Care must, however, be taken in understanding the proper meaning and relevance of this judgement. This is considered in further detail in Ch 3 with the secondary programme of measures adopted in the banking and financial area in Ch 5.

convergence promoted with the establishment of the *European Monetary System* (EMS) in 1979. More substantial progress has recently been possible with the establishment of economic and monetary union[9] between a majority of nations[10] while the number of participating countries in these functional exercises has continued to expand through a series of enlargements and possible further expansions.[11]

The development of European integration can be considered in terms of a number of more general doctrines including functionalism, neo-functionalism,[12] neo-realism[13] (or liberal inter-governmentalism),[14] neo-federalism

[9] The Solemn Declaration of European Union was issued following the 1983 Stuttgart Summit. A draft Treaty on European Union was issued by the European Parliament in 1984. The Adonnino and Dooge Committees were set up at the Fontainebleau Summit in 1984. The Dooge Committee, in particular, recommended the creation of the Internal Market. This was followed by the 1985 White Paper on the Completion of the Internal Market which recommended the completion of the Internal Market by end 1992. An Inter-governmental Conference was set up at the Milan Summit in 1985 which led to the adoption of the Single European Act in 1986. This involved amending the Treaty of Rome to provide for the creation of the internal market and for majority voting in related legislative areas. The Single European Act represented both a restatement of the original Treaty objective of creating a single market in the form of a Common Market but also a compromise on further European integration. Chapter 6, (n 41). While certain countries including, in particular, France and Germany wanted to enter into a new Treaty on European Union, others including the UK and Denmark only wanted to secure the establishment of a full Internal Market (n 139).

[10] Following two Inter-governmental Conferences (IGCs) on Economic and Monetary Union and on Political Union, the Maastricht Treaty was signed in February 1992. This followed a report by the Delors Committee on Economic and Monetary Union in 1989. (n 165).

[11] The original European Economic Community was enlarged in 1973 with the accession of the UK, Denmark and Ireland. This followed an extended negotiation period at a time of considerable global instability especially with the collapse of the Bretton Woods systems of managed exchange arrangements in 1973/1974. Despite the recessionary difficulties of the 1970s, a second enlargement followed in 1981 with the accession of Greece, Spain and Portugal in 1986. With the success of European Monetary Union, a third enlargement was completed in May 2004 with the accession of ten Central European countries. Chapter 1, Section F (1) and (n 88).

[12] EB Haas *Beyond the Nation State* (Stanford University Press 1964). See also E Haas *The Uniting of Europe: Political, Social and Economic Forces 1950–57* (Stanford University Press 1958); L Lindberg *The Political Dynamics of European Economic Integration* (Stanford University Press 1963); L Lindberg and S Scheingold *Europe's Would-be Polity: Patterns of Change in the European Community* (Prentice-Hall Englewood Cliffs NJ 1970); L Lindberg and S Scheingold *Regional Integration* (Harvard University Press 1970). For discussion, Paul Craig 'The Nature of the Community' in Craig and de Burca *The Evolution of EU Law* (OUP Oxford 1999), ch 1, s 1. On integration theories, Ch 1 (n 36) and section E (5).

[13] R Keohane *Neo-Realism and Its Critics* (Columbia University Press New York 1986).

[14] A Moravcisk 'Preference and Power in the European Community: A Liberal Intergovernmental Approach' (1993) 31 JCMS, 473. See also Moravcisk *National Preference Formation and Interstate Bargaining in the European Community, 1955–86* (Harvard University Press Cambridge MA 1992); and A Moravcisk 'Negotiating the Single European Act: National Interests and Conventional Statecraft in the European Community' (1991) 41 International Organization 19. See also Craig (n 12) section 2. See also W Sandholtz and J Zysman '1992: Recasting the European Bargain' (1989) 42 World Politics 1; and G Garrett 'International Co-operation and Institutional Choice: The European Community's Internal Market' (1992) 46 International Organization 533.

and new institutionalism[15] or multi-level governance analysis.[16] While functionalism is generally concerned with the promotion of cooperation through specific economic activity,[17] neo-functionalists allow for the existence of competitive economic and political elites as central players in the integration process.[18] Neo-realists replace national governments as the principal instigators of integration rather than supra-national institutions with the promotion of national interest and protection of existing authority becoming dominant.[19] Since the end of the 1980s, neo-functionalism and neo-realism have been succeeded by a more specific examination of the various political and institutional entities in existence and how they are governed and relate.

These sets of theories have been of value in explaining many of the underlying trends on which more specific integrationist activity has been constructed.[20] Whichever set or sets of integration theories are adopted within Europe, they all accept the underlying functional objective of the original Treaty draftsmen. The changing focus has then been on the interest (or self-interest) of the Member States and scope of their residual

[15] K Armstrong 'The New Institutionalism', in P Craig and C Harlow (eds) *Law Making in the European Union* (Kluwer Law London 1998) (n 87). Giandomenico Majone, 'International Regulator Co-operation: A neo-institutional approach' in George A Bermann, Matthias Herdegen and Peter L Lindseth *Transatlantic Regulatory Co-operation* (OUP Oxford 2000) 119–45.

[16] G Marks 'Structural Policy and Multi-Level Governance in the European Community' in A Cafruny and G Rosenthal (eds) *The State of the European Community* (Longmann Harlow 1993); M Jachtenfuchs 'Theoretical Perspectives on European Governance' (1995) 1 ELJ 115; G Marks, L Hooghe and K Blank 'European Integration since the 1980s: State-centric Versus Multi-level Governance' (1996) 34 JCMS 341. See also K Armstrong and S Bulmer *The Governance of the Single European Market* (Manchester University Press Manchester, 1998); T Risse-Kappen 'Exploring the Nature of the Beast: International Relations Theory and Comparative Policy Analysis Meet the European Union' (1996) 34 JCMS 53; J Caporas 'The European Union and Forms of State: Westphalian, Regulatory or Post-Modern' (1996) 34 JCMS 29; S Scharpf 'The Problem Solving Capacity of Multi-Level Governance' (1997) 4 JEPP 520; and G Marks, F Sharpf, P Schmitter, and W Streeck 'Governance in the European Union' (Sage London 1996). See also Craig and de Bùrca (n 12) s 16.

[17] The underlying premise or assumption is that war can be avoided positively (rather than negatively) through cooperative activity directed by non-political agencies in non-contentious areas. For discussion, J Lodge *The European Community and the Challenge of the Future* (Pinter London 1993) Introduction.

[18] Integration then arises from the 'spill-over' from non-controversial technical functionalism into other more important political areas with a consequent gradual reduction in the power of national governments and a corresponding increase in the ability of the new centre to deal with sensitive and politically important issues. Lodge (n 17).

[19] Neo-realism begins with the ascendancy of inter-governmentalism at the beginning of the 1970s following the lack of progress achieved under the 1950s and 1960s functionalist directed efforts. This is characterized by the 'Luxembourg veto' and the subsequent Single European Act and 1992 initiatives during the 1980s and Intergovernmental Conferences (IGCs) during the 1990s.

[20] This considers the contribution made by all national, supranational, sub-national, infranational, public and private sector participants. Armstrong 'The New Institutionalism' (n 15).

authority and then on the increasingly more complex institutional structures created within which layers of legislative and administrative function are discharged. These are all of value in understanding the operational and political complexity of the European Community and European Union.[21]

European history has traditionally then been dominated by ideas of political and military conflict or preventative negotiation and agreement with consequent territorial division, attachment or assimilation. This has most often then been secured through essentially non-democratic means. In contrast, the new post-War European movement has been characterized by the use of economic and consensual processes directed at a range of functionally specific initiatives. With this, the underlying philosophy has shifted from domination or aggregation and assimilation to integration. The essence of the new Europe is then of a continuous but still expanding process of deepening economic and functional integration supported by a shared institutional structure which is itself moving towards more complete democratic inclusion and accountability.

B. ECONOMIC INTEGRATION

Integration is generally concerned with the removal of obstacles or barriers to the common or linked pursuit of any activity.[22] Economic integration can then be referred to as the removal of any barriers or restraints to economic function and the consequent assimilation or, at least, closer approximation of relevant activity. This can also either be carried out within a single territory or between countries.[23] Economic integration can also be understood to refer to a condition or process of change which is designed to achieve certain other objectives such as increased economic welfare or other political goals.[24] It is best then considered as means or mechanism to secure certain objectives rather than an end in itself.

[21] Grainne de Búrca 'The Institutional Development of the EU: A Constitutional Analysis', in Craig and de Búrca (n 13), ch 2; and Deirdre Curtin and Ije Dekker 'The EU as a "Layered" International Organization: Institutional Unity in Disguise' in Craig and de Búrca (n 12) ch 3.

[22] Integration may be defined as the gradual elimination of economic frontiers between independent states. Willem Molle *The Economics of European Integration—Theory, Practice and Policy* (3rd edn Ashgate London 1997). For further discussion (n 114) and Chapter 1 (n 14).

[23] A distinction may be drawn between the static removal of barriers between the national components within a larger economy and the dynamic gradual elimination of economic frontiers between countries through the removal of national discrimination. Molle (n 22) 8. This would appear to be simply concerned with the distinct scope of coverage of the original activities to be integrated. Both inter and intra-territorial integration may be conducted in a single (fixed) stage or a more gradual and dynamic manner. The meaning and use of discrimination as a test within Europe is considered further in Ch 3 section C (5).

[24] Other goals include more general political union or peace, democratic or human rights gains. Molle (n 22) 8.

Economic integration can most clearly be understood in terms of a number of distinct levels or layers of connected or overlapping relations or activity.[25] These generally consist of a free trade area, a customs union, a common market, economic union, monetary union (and economic and monetary union) as well as full political union. The first three mechanisms might be considered to relate to trade or market specific objectives while the latter three are concerned with more general policy objectives.[26] The first three might alternatively be considered to be trade specific, the second two finance related and the last political.[27]

Goods and services are initially dealt with through the establishment of a free trade area and customs union. Free trade refers to the unrestricted passage of goods and services within a regional arrangement with the removal of all quotas, tariffs or measures of equivalent effect.[28] Under a customs union, a common external tariff is fixed to deal with goods and services entering from third countries on an equal basis.[29] With a common market, the free movement of production factors (labour, capital and enterprise) is secured.[30] It must nevertheless be stressed that free movement will

[25] See, eg, J Viner *The Customs Union Issue* (Carnegie Endowment for International Peace New York 1950); J Tinbergen, *International Economic Integration* (1954, Elsevier, London); and B Balassa *The Theory of Economic Integration* (1961, Allen & Unwin, London). See also Frank McDonald and Stephen Dearden *European Economic Integration* (3rd edn Longman New York 1999), 34.

[26] This reflects the approach adopted by Molle. Molle (n 22) 10 and 10–12.

[27] This is the approach adopted in the text as it allows a clear distinction to be drawn between finance and other integration related activities. On the development of financial integration in Europe, see section H.

[28] A *free trade area* involves the removal of customs duties, tariffs and quotas on inter-state trade. McDonald and Dearden (n 25). All internal trade is free from restriction although countries will apply their own rules with regard to goods from third countries. This may then give rise to 'trade deflection' where goods attempt to enter through the lowest internal tariff. To avoid this, goods are assigned 'certificates of origin' which allow internal frontier officials to determine whether they should be permitted automatic free trade (coming from another trading partner) or subject to an additional duty (coming from outside). Molle (n 22) 10.

[29] A *customs union* involves the establishment of a common external as well as internal tariff. Members accordingly agree a common level of duties, tariffs and quotas on goods entering any territory from outside the customs union. Under an incomplete or imperfect customs union, some goods or services but not all are subject to a common external tariff. Molle (n 22) 10–11. See also (nn 46 and 96).

[30] A *common market* consists of a free trade area and a customs union as well as full free movement of production factors (comprising labour, capital and enterprise). Full free movement is secured both by the removal of quotas and pecuniary duties and tariffs as well as any measures with equivalent effect that would otherwise obstruct trade. Free movement of products and production is accordingly provided for.

Molle notes that a common market may treat capital and labour coming from third countries differently. A free trade area in products is accordingly created but not necessarily a production customs union. Various combinations of treatment on either a common or national basis are possible. This may be referred to as an incomplete or partial common market. Molle (n 22) 11.

A full common market is only created when there is full free movement of products (goods and services) and production (capital and labour) as well as common external regulation of products and production elements from third countries.

generally be more easily secured with regard to goods and services rather than establishment due to the higher levels of local protection maintained.[31] Separate policies will also have to be adopted to ensure full free movement of production components including, in particular, capital although this will only be possible if sufficient political commitment is also present.[32]

Economic and social policies can also be harmonized within an Economic Union which would improve effective free movement and the avoidance of trade distortions.[33] The creation of a fixed or almost fixed exchange rate system would also avoid conversion costs within a monetary union although the value of this may be questioned.[34] Political union can be regarded as being a separate supplementary objective distinct from the underlying economic integration to be established.[35]

European integration can then be understood in terms of a number of distinct stages of economic and monetary relations or mutual dependencies. The initial objective of establishing the European Economic Community can be understood in terms of creating a single trading market through a free trade area (with a customs union) and with full free movement of production factors (a common market) and certain supporting economic policies. This was the original and immediate goal of the Treaty of Rome and reflected in the discussions that supported the adoption of the Single Act in 1986.[36] Since then, economic and monetary union have been taken forward under the Maastricht Treaty with further political integration still being discussed by certain interested parties although possibly not with the same force and support as before.

It must be stressed that other common policies have also been adopted within Europe especially with regard to agriculture and transport and with competition rules to ensure fair market structures and practices. Rather

[31] Molle (n 22), ch 7.

[32] On free movement of capital, see section I.

[33] An *economic union* involves the establishment of common economic policies (Art 4 (*ex* 3a)). Relevant economic policy may include market regulation, competition and industrial structure as well as macro-economic and monetary policy. This may also include such other factors as redistribution, social and environmental policies. Common policies will also generally be established with regard to third countries including trade, production, economic sectors and possible monetary stability. Molle (n 22) 11.

[34] *Monetary union* either requires the irrevocable fixing of exchange rates or the introduction of a single currency. Free movement of capital should be secured. Molle (n 22) 11. Participating countries should also adopt a single monetary and exchange rate policy (Art 4(2) (ex 3a(2)). The EMU consists of both an *economic union* and *monetary union*. Currency risk would generally be removed although conversion costs would remain. See section I.

[35] The last integration stage would be the establishment of full *political union* (or FPU). This would generally operate through the establishment of shared legislative and executive competences for all participating countries. This may take a number of forms depending, in particular, on the extent to which local political and legislative competences were retained such as on a federal or confederal model. Full union may only be attained with the establishment of a single common legislative and political function.

[36] (n 139).

than adopt a full market based policy with regard to the allocation of resources, the Community has generally adopted a more social market based approach which has been influenced by prevailing and subsequent Continental practice.[37] The pure economic advantages to be derived from the various integration layers set up are then qualified (or possibly supported) by further redistributive or social policies. The additional adjustments that these policies give rise to must be taken into account in understanding and assessing the real economic nature of the Community.

The other distinguishing feature of the Community is the institutional apparatus that has been set up to secure the effective implementation of the economic and social policies set.[38] This is supported by the parallel legal and economic orders constructed. Whether such a complex institutional structure was necessary to secure the more limited original trading objectives intended must be questioned. This possibly confirms the larger integrationist and ultimately political objectives underlying the original initiatives adopted.

European history more generally can also be understood in terms of various stages of economic integration.[39] It must be stressed that such integration has until recently generally only been the accidental result or by-product of more general technological and industrial change.[40] Only in the post-War period has planned economic integration and functionalism been used as deliberate mechanisms for greater economic interdependence and benefit with closer political union. The related issue of financial integration is considered further below.[41]

[37] On the Ordo-Liberal origins of the Community, Ch 1, section E (4) and (n 78).

[38] This is considered in further detail in section G.

[39] European economic history can generally be divided into five identifiable periods: (a) limited post-mediaeval cross-border trade and investment until the beginning of the industrial revolution (pre-1815); (b) substantially improved free trade after the industrial revolution until the rise of protectionism and the modern nation state (1815–1870); (c) pre-war stagnation, depression and protectionism (1880–1914); (d) inter-war financial disintegration (1914–1945); and (e) post-War reconstruction and new cross-European functional integration (1945 to date). See, eg, Molle (n 22), ch 3. See also authorities cited (nn 1–6).

[40] After the French Revolution, traditional closed feudal economic structures were replaced by new open systems and the establishment of national rather than local or regional economies. Technological advances broke down many of the remaining vestiges of agrarian dependence and practices as new industrial techniques emerged that resulted in massive cost savings and improvements in production capacity, quantity and quality. Open national and international trade was also promoted. See Smith (n 4). See also, Ricardo and Mill. Related improvements in carriage and transport and communications also increased the extent and depth of this new shared economic benefit and connection. See generally, Molle (n 22) n 35.

[41] Sections H and I. See also Chapter 1 (n 14).

C. ADVANTAGE AND DISADVANTAGE

The development of economic integration[42] across Europe can be justified in terms of a number of economic and consequent social advantages. These are essentially concerned with reduced transactions costs, increased growth and competition with consequent higher earnings and investment and related social benefits in terms of higher employment and improved standards of living.[43] Different sets of relative advantage and disadvantage will necessarily arise with each integration step adopted while the total result will be dependent upon the final degree of correction achieved and mix of open and social market policies adopted.[44]

A number of attempts have been made to understand and explain the potential results or benefits of increased economic integration.[45] Such studies have examined both the static and dynamic effects of free movement. Static analysis is concerned with examining the effects where factors of production, technology and competition are constant[46] while dynamic

[42] Section B and (n 22).

[43] These might be summarized in terms of increased choice and lower costs for consumers. Product producers will benefit from increased competition with consequent improvements in domestic innovation, moderrnization, possible specialization and concentration as well as improved international opportunity and competition. More generally, new savings and investment channels will be created with improved allocation of resources at the same time as returns are increased and borrowing and liquidity costs reduced. See generally, Dominique Servais *The Single Financial Market* (Luxembourg 1988).

[44] On customs union theory generally, Molle (22), Ch 5. On free movement of goods and services, Chs 6 and 7. On common market theory and the benefits of free movement of labour and capital, Molle (22), chs 8, 9 and 10. On the need for adjustment policies including with regard to allocation, stabilization, redistribution and external relations, Molle (22), chs 16, 17, 18 and 19. On market balance, Ch 1 section E (4) and (n 76).

[45] See, eg, J Viner *The Customs Union Issue* (n 25); JE Meade *The Theory of Customs Unions* (North Holland Amsterdam 1955); and RG Lipsey *The Theory of Customs Unions: General Equilibrium Analysis* (Weidenfeld & Nicolson London 1970).

[46] The establishment of a customs union may not necessarily have beneficial effects either internally (between the members of the regional group) or externally (between the group and third countries). The net effect of the customs union will depend upon the distribution of low and high cost producer countries within the regional grouping and globally. Viner distinguishes between 'trade creation' and 'trade diversion'. Despite the creation of the common external tariff, import and export volumes will vary with local production capacity. If the lowest cost producer is within the customs union, global markets will benefit. This results in Viner's 'trade creation' with trade moving to the most economic area. If the least cost producer is outside the customs union, the effect of the common external tariff is to divert trade to higher cost areas. Viner refers to this in terms of 'trade diversion'. Trade creation results in resources being allocated solely in terms of comparative advantage. The net effect of the customs union is beneficial if trade creation effects exceed trade diversion. This will occur where the customs union includes low rather than high cost producers and if the external tariff is set at a low level or the most substantial reductions are made available to all countries under a most favoured nation arrangement. See Viner (n 25). See also DH Hansen and J Neilsen *An Economic Analysis of the EU* (McGraw-Hill London 1997). For further discussion McDonald and Dearden *European Economic Integration* (n 25).

studies assess the results of changes in such factors and their relationships inter se.[47] Free movement can be considered generally to increase efficiency, earnings and investment and competition. Against this, adjustment costs may be significant within the regional trading arrangement while the creation of the common external tariff may damage global trade patterns more generally.[48] Adjustment costs and changes in the distribution of income may also require express redistributive policies to be adopted for political reasons and welfare. Uneven benefits will require corrective economic and investment policies to be applied.

The potential benefits of regional economic integration must still be set against the financial and social costs that may arise. The separate trade, economic and political objectives that are also relevant to varying degrees with any such initiatives must be taken into account.

Care must also be taken to ensure that an unnecessary obstructive or inconsistent body of regulations and directives are not adopted which could undermine the achievement of the economic advantages identified. One of the particular difficulties that arises in Europe is avoiding conflicts through the pursuit of an inconsistent or incoherent social market programme as against a more open market policy.[49]

The general objective of a regional trading arrangement should be to approximate the creation of a real single market within which transaction costs are reduced insofar as possible and the other economic benefits of free movement within the single market are fully achieved. The creation of the European Community and its early common market and subsequent internal market can be distinguished from such full single markets as nation states or federal territories including the United States. The main differences between the European Community and the United States include the social rather than open market approach adopted with regard to internal market operations.[50] The United States has also historically operated within an

[47] Regional economic integration may also have dynamic effects through reductions in monopoly power or levels of 'ex-inefficiency' (overmanning, excessive holdings of stocks and other poor management practice) as well as improve economies of scale and learning effects. An increase in sources of supply will reduce monopoly power leading to lower prices and increased output as well as better quality products (non-price competition). Internal economies of scale may arise from the integration of fragmented markets especially with improved use of old plant. External economies of scale may also arise as a result of 'clustering' of specialist producers. Free movement may then increase efficiency (with the reduction of ex-inefficiency and better use of existing capital and labour) and increase investment (with increased income and savings). McDonald and Dearden (n 25).

[48] Adjustment costs may be significant if labour and capital mobility are constrained although this should not persist due to the natural relocation of the factors of production. (n 46).

[49] On social and free market polices, Chapter 1 section E (4) and (nn 76–79).

[50] The European Community has attempted to harmonize such matters as relevant technical regulations, public procurement and state aid policies and taxation. Technical harmonization is now dealt with under the New Approach announced in the 1985 White Paper based on

economic and monetary union which was not in place in Europe until recently. The existence of a real single market does not, however, require the harmonization of all matters including technical and regulatory standards and general and sales taxes. The maintenance of distinct banking and insurance regulations at the state levels as well as residual Blue Sky securities laws more specifically does not prevent the operation of the single market in the United States. Economic efficiency is nevertheless improved where transaction costs[51] are reduced insofar as possible and the static and dynamic potential benefits of free movement secured.

The creation of a single market should accordingly reduce transaction costs between participating countries. Where countries already operate with low costs before entry, the imposition of new cost structures may increase costs while the adoption of further regulations may increase relevant transaction costs further. The constant adoption of complex and often contradictory rules within Europe will then further increase transactions costs and reduce the benefits of market integration.[52] Differences in implementation and failure to implement will also create further divergence across Europe.[53] Fragmentation as a result of additional cultural differences and institutional conflicts must also be taken into account to the extent that they will increase legal and regulatory uncertainty and transaction costs.[54]

minimum harmonization and mutual recognition (n 140). Although the United States constitutes a real single market, a number of legal, regulatory and fiscal inconsistencies still apply. Under the federal system, different state laws regulate the production and sale of goods and services in each state including relevant sales taxes. Technical and environmental standards as well as taxation systems also vary across states. Federal laws prohibit discrimination on the basis of state of origin and anti-competitive practices. There are, however, no federal controls on public procurement or state aids. McDonald and Dearden (n 25). See generally J Pelkmans and M van Heukelen *The Internal Markets of North America, Fragmentation and Integration in the US and Canada* (1988), Research on the costs of non-Europe, Basic Findings (vol 16), (Office for Official Publications of the European Communities Luxembourg 1988).

[51] Transaction costs are concerned with charges imposed on the production, marketing and sale of goods or services. These relate to compliance with local legal and regulatory requirements. They may also be affected by relevant macro-economic policies (including exchange rate risk and currency conversion costs as well as the effects of different inflation and growth rates). The existence of fragmentation across markets also requires further adjustments in product and marketing policies to reflect local conditions which again increase transaction costs. McDonald and Dearden (n 25).

[52] D Mayes, *The Evolution of the Single European Market* (Edward Elgar Cheltenham 1997).

[53] Commission, *The Impact and Effectiveness of the Single Market: Communication from the Commission to the European Parliament and Council* (Luxembourg 1996). See also Commission *The Single Market Review* (Luxembourg 1996), 38 Reports.

[54] Chapter 1, section D (a). The existence of different and often conflicting institutional structures at the Member State level has been recognized as a significant potential difficulty. Local institutional frameworks arise from relevant historical and cultural development. Institutional frameworks are created by legal and governmental action having regard to local cultural and social conditions. Effective frameworks reduce uncertainty and transaction costs while ineffective or contradictory structures increase them. D North *Institutions, Institutional Change and Economic Performance* (CUP Cambridge 1990). It is, in particular, as a result of

D. ASSESSMENT AND REVIEW

The potential advantages of the creation of a single market within Europe have been considered in a number of studies. The most important early report produced was by Paulo Cecchini in 1988 on the *Benefits of a Single Market*.[55] The Cecchini Report attempted to construct a predictive model for the assessment of the costs and benefits that would arise in terms of prevailing economic theory. This can be distinguished from other comparative approaches that attempt to assess the effects that would have arisen if a country had not joined a regional integration arrangement with the actual outcome following participation (referred to as the *anti- monde* position).[56] The Cecchini Report attempted to estimate the net benefits that would arise from the single market based on a number of economic models.[57] Previous studies had suggested that the benefits of economic integration arose from the dynamic effects of free movement. Static effects were not significant nor were there strong trade diversion effects.[58]

the continuing cultural differences within Europe that may require that the United States and Europe adopt different single market responses to allow Europe to compete in the global market. A Jacquemin and L Pench *Europe Competing in the Global Economy* (Edward Elgar Cheltenham 1996). For further discussion, McDonald and Dearden (n 25).

[55] P Cecchini *The European Challenge: 1992 The Benefits of a Single Market* (1988). For comment, see also M Emerson, M Aujean, M Catinat, P Goybet and A Jacquemin *The Economics of 1992* (OUP Oxford 1988).

[56] Anti-monde models attempt to estimate the changes to a size and pattern of trade flows before and after liberalization. This is based on predicted alternative effects from actual results. See, eg, D Mayes 'The Effects of Economic Integration on Trade', (1978) 17 Journal of Common Market Studies 1–25; and LA Winters 'Britain in Europe: A Survey of Quantitative Trade Studies' (1987) 25 Journal of Common Market Studies 315–35.

The difficulty that arises with an anti-monde analysis is that it often fails to take into account all of the factors that may affect trade flows such as growth in income levels among trading partners, reductions in barriers to trade not related to the regional economic system and technological and competitive developments. McDonald and Dearden (n 25).

[57] The Cecchini Report, in particular, examined economies of scale and innovation. C Pratten *A Survey of the Economies of Scale* Research on the Costs of non-Europe, Basic Findings, vol 2 (Office for Official Publications of the European Communities Luxembourg 1988); J Schwalbach *Economies of Scale and Intra-Community Trade* Research on the Costs of non-Europe, Basic Findings, vol 2 (Luxembourg 1988); and P Geroski *Competition and Innovation* Research on the Costs of non-Europe, Basic Findings, vol 2 (European Commission Brussels 1988). A number of studies were also conducted by management consultants with regard to particular sectors including financial services. See Price Waterhouse 'The Costs of Non-Europe in Financial Services', *Research on the Costs of Non-Europe, Basic Findings* (vol 9), Office for Official Publications of the European Communities. See also Ernst and Whinney 'The Costs of Non-Europe: An illustration in the Road Haulage sector', *Research on the Costs of Non-Europe, Basic Findings* (vol 4) (European Commission Brussels); J Muller 'The Benefits of Completing the internal market for telecommunications services', *Research on the Costs of Non-Europe, Basic Findings* (vol 10) (European Commission Brussels); and Group MAC 'The Costs of Non-Europe in the Foodstuffs Industry', *Research on the costs of Non-Europe, Basic Findings* (vol 12) (European Commission Brussels).

[58] A number of other country studies have also been conducted. With regard to the customs

The Cecchini Report reclassified the physical, technical and fiscal barriers set out in the 1985 White Paper as tariffs, quotas, cost-increasing barriers, market entry restrictions and government market distorting activities.[59] A four stage approach was used to assess the effects of free movement.[60]

The cost of non-Europe in financial services was, in particular, considered by Price Waterhouse in 1986. In its *Full Report*, Price Waterhouse considered the various methodological issues that arose. These included the definition of financial services and the identification of relevant producers and users (section 2). A macro-economic and sectoral analysis was then conducted (section 3) and an analysis of the then current structure of financial services markets provided (section 4). This included looking at regulatory barriers to trade in establishment in banking, securities and insurance and exchange control restrictions on trade in financial services. Quantification of the effects of regulation was considered (section 5) and an estimation of the economic impact of integration developed (section 6). This included the potential future price changes, key non-price assumptions, base case estimates and results of integration and macro-economic implications as well as final conclusions.

The Cecchini Report generally concluded that the removal of the remaining barriers listed would increase competition and lower costs leading, in turn, to lower prices and increased investment.[61] The single market would

union see, eg, M Kreinin 'Trade creation and diversion by the EEC and EFTA' (1969) 22 Economia Internazionale 1–43; Kreinin 'Effects of the EEC on Imports of Manufactures' (1972) 82 Economic Journal 897–920; SA Resnick and EM Truman 'An empirical examination of bilateral trade in Western Europe' (1971) 3 Journal of International Economics 305–35; J Williamson and A Bottrill 'The impact of customs unions on trade in manufactures', (1971) 23 Oxford Economic Papers 323–51; and B Balassa 'Trade Creation and Diversion in the European Common Market' (1987) XLII(2) The Manchester School 93–125. On balance of payments, see M Featherstone, B Moore, and J Rhodes 'EEC membership and UK Trade in manufactures' (1979) 3 Cambridge Journal of Economics 399–407; D Mayes 'The effects of economic integration on trade' (1978) 17 Journal of Common Market Studies 1–25; and LA Winters (n 56). For comment, McDonald and Dearden (n 25).

[59] While tariffs and quotas had generally been removed, residual charging arose with Voluntary Export Restraints (VERs) on cars and electronic equipment and textile quotas under the Multi Fibre Arrangement (MFA). Cost-increasing barriers were concerned with customs formalities (including VAT and excise duty assessments) and regulatory compliance and verifications. Market entry restrictions were concerned with specific sector barriers and public procurement controls. Market distorting activities related to state aids (subsidies and tax concessions) and other domestic privileges. McDonald and Dearden (n 25).

[60] Stage I considered the benefits from removing barriers affecting trade (frontier controls). Stage II considered the removal of technical and regulatory burdens that increased costs. Stage III considered the benefits of economies of scale. Stage IV estimated gains from increased competition which led to reductions in ex-inefficiency and monopoly rents. Cecchini Report (n 55); and Emerson (n 55).

[61] New market opportunities would increase economies of scale and rationalize artificially segmented markets. Ex-inefficiency and anti-competitive practices would also be reduced. Benefits would further arise from reductions in transaction costs and liberalized services. McDonald and Dearden (n 25).

also generally stimulate the effectiveness of the supply side of the economy which would increase aggregate demand.[62]

Despite the significant amount of work undertaken and the apparent value of the conclusions produced, the Cecchini Report has been criticized on a number of grounds although it did provide an initial assessment of the potential benefits of the European single market policy.[63]

The single market programme was re-considered by the Commission in 1996. This Review attempted to examine the allocation, accumulation and locational effects of the single market.[64] While the Review was still positive,

[62] This would arise from increases in real purchasing power, investment and improved global competitiveness. Public sector benefits would arise from lower costs of public procurement and increased taxation revenues. Government expenditure could then be used for expansionary purposes which would, in particular, assist with local unemployment difficulties. The productive potential of the economy would generally be improved and higher levels of non-inflationary growth made possible. Government led expansion must, however, be coordinated to prevent monetary instability. Macro-economic instability would have a significant effect on the net benefits achieved. Cecchini Report (n 55); and Emerson (n 55).

[63] The criticisms of the Cecchini Report were generally concerned with the failure to take fully into account the potential costs of economic integration. See, eg, E Davies, J Kay, and C Smales *1992: Myths and Realities* (London Business School London 1989); T Cutler, C Halsem, J Williams, and K Williams '1992—The Struggle for Europe in J Grahl and P Teague *1992: The Big Market* (Lawrence & Wishart London 1992). Differences in opinion also arose with regard to the extent to which the Report quantified the effects of increased competition on ex-inefficiency levels. A Smith and A Venables 'The Costs of Non-Europe: An assessment based on a forward model of imperfect competition and economies of scale' in *Research on the Costs of Non-Europe, Basic Findings* vol 2 (1988); and D Dyker (ed) *The European Economy* (Longham London 1992).

[64] The Review was conducted on the basis of a survey of 20,000 enterprises as well as specific industry studies, investigation of particular issues including public procurement, market liberalization, price convergence and market concentration as well as separate studies on the growth and regional development effects of the single market programme. European Economy *Economic Valuation of the Internal Market* Reports and Studies No 4 (1996). See also Commission *The Single Market Review* (1996), 38 reports; Commission, 'The Impact and Effectiveness of the Single Market', Communication from the Commission to the European Parliament and Council; and Commission, 'Action Plan for the Single Market' (1996), Communication from the Commission to the European Council. For comment, M Monti *The Single Market and Tomorrow's Europe* (1996).

Allocation effects are concerned with improvements in efficiency in the use of resources. These arise from both the static effects of trade creation and diversion and dynamic effects of economies of scale and increased competition. Allocation effects were, in particular, considered in terms of the removal of frontier controls, reductions in costs associated with different technical regulations and standards, public procurement liberalization, changes to the level and composition of trade flows and developments in the nature of the competitive environment and price differentials. The review period was, however, restricted to 1987 to 1994 and did not take account of such significant changes as German unification, the transformation of Central and Eastern Europe and recessionary market conditions during the early 1990s. The estimates must accordingly be treated with some caution. European Economy, 'Economic Evaluation of the Internal Market' (1996) *Reports and Studies No. 4*, Office for Official Publications of the European Communities; and McDonald and Dearden (n 25).

The costs of setting up a new VAT and excise duty system across Europe had cost companies ECU 2.3 billion a year. This was considered necessary following the failure to harmonize relevant duties and the continued use of the destination principle with the abolition of fronit failed to support the earlier estimates set out in the Cecchini Report. This confirmed that work was required in other areas including correcting deficiencies in the legislative programme and related policy areas.

Following the 1996 Review, the Commission proposed a number of further measures to attempt to complete the single market programme. These were announced in an Action Plan in 1996. The main recommendations were concerned with improving implementation, removing market distortions and obstacles to integration and improved social conditions.[65] The Action Plan was to be achieved in three stages by 1 January 1999.[66] Much of this follows the earlier Sutherland Report in 1992.[67] Despite the

tier controls on 1 January 1993. These costs were partly compensated for by reduced formalities.

It was expected that the harmonization of technical regulations and standards and use of mutual recognition would lead to significant reductions in compliance costs. This was confirmed in some industries although many enterprises claimed that there had been no significant benefit. This can be understood in terms of delayed harmonization and low acceptance of mutual recognition. Significant difficulties also remained with regard to public procurement especially in the implementation of relevant directives and enforcement of free access in relation to public contracts.

Trade flows were considered in terms of intra-industry trade in products with similar and dissimilar price and quality characteristics. The results found that there had been significant growth in intra-industry trade between products with different price and quality characteristics. This was, however, to be expected between countries with similar levels of development. The adjustments required for less developed countries within a regional trading system were nevertheless significant and took time to achieve.

Market concentration had grown significantly due to national and cross-border mergers and acquisitions although this had not decreased competition.

In terms of accumulation effects, it was estimated that growth of between 1.1 and 1.5 per cent of GDP had been possible with the generation of between 300,000 to 900,000 additional jobs. Supply side improvements had also reduced inflationary pressures. The Review accepts that these estimates were subject to considerable error. This nevertheless represents a significantly lower figure than produced by the Cecchini Report. McDonald and Dearden (n 25).

Locational effects were also inconclusive. There had been some convergence in economic development as a result of intra-industry trade although inter-industry trade was still important even in certain developed countries. Integration did not restrict growth in less developed countries although other historical, geographical, institutional and technological factors appeared to be of more significance.

65 The Action Plan proposed four main strategic targets: (a) making rules more effective by ensuring that legislation is properly implemented and enforced; (b) correcting market distortions through the removal of differences in taxation and anti-competitive actions including state aids; (c) removing obstacles to market integration through the provision of positive policies such as with regard to research and development; and (d) delivering benefits to all citizens by ensuring that consumer rights are guaranteed and protecting the social conditions of workers and their environment from unacceptable damage. Chapter 5, Section D(1).

66 Outstanding legislation with any further measures necessary to achieve effective free movement were to be implemented. Administrative cooperation would also be developed in national governments and EU institutions to support implementation and enforcement. Chapter 1, section D (1); and Chapter 5, section D (2).

67 See Commission *The Internal Market After 1992* (1992). See also Commission *Reinforcing the Effectiveness of the Internal Market* (1993)COM (93) 256 final; and Commission, *Making the Most of the Internal Market* (1993)COM (93) 632 final.

issuance of other strategic documents[68] and continuing deficiencies within the single market programme, political and executive attention has subsequently focused to other more topical areas such as European Monetary Union and then Constitutional reform and enlargement.[69]

E. REGIONAL INTEGRATION

The European Community constitutes one type of regional trading arrangement. The main set of global trading arrangements in place at the time of the establishment of the Community was the GATT which had been set up fourteen years earlier in 1944.[70] Although the Community borrowed some of the underlying ideas and had been inspired to a significant extent by the operation of the GATT, it went considerably further in terms of the nature or content and degree of market integration secured.

Between the establishment of the GATT until the end of 1992, more than 20 regional arrangements were established in addition to 60 preference schemes[71] and association agreements.[72] These have multiplied substan-

[68] See, eg, Commission *Public Procurement in the European Union: Exploring the Way Forward* Green Paper (1996); and Commission *Commercial Communications in the Internal Market* Green Paper (1996).

[69] Chapter 1, sections E (a) and (b).

[70] The GATT was set up following the Conference held at Bretton Woods in New Hampshire on 1 to 22 July 1944. The objective was to set up new trade and monetary arrangements to come into effect after the World War II. An International Trade Organization (ITO) was to have been established at Bretton Woods to remove restraints on trade including tariffs and import controls. The establishment of this body was not subsequently proceeded with due to US reservations although it was agreed that trade reform could be dealt with under the General Agreement on Tariffs and Trade (GATT) itself which was opened for signature on 30 Oct 1947. This is now administered by the World Trade Organization (WTO) which was eventually set up on 1 Jan 1995. R Fraser and C Long *The World Financial System* (Longman Harlow 1992), ch 38, s 1.

It was also agreed that a system of managed exchange rates would be set up to replace the earlier orderly market for foreign exchange that had existed under the gold standard and gold exchange standard. The architects of the system had been John Maynard Keynes from the UK and Harry Dexter White of the US. Keynes and White had produced separate preparatory proposals for an International Clearing Union and a Stabilization Fund. It was White's proposals that were eventually accepted subject to certain revision. It was also agreed at Bretton Woods to set up the International Monetary Fund (IMF) and the International Bank for Reconstruction and Development (the World Bank). GA Walker *International Banking Regulation—Law, Policy and Practice* (Kluwer London 2000), ch 1, s 1.2.

The Conference had been attended by forty four countries with one representative from Denmark. A Final Act embodying the Arts of Agreement of the World Bank and the IMF were signed. These came into effect in Dec 1945. The World Bank commenced operations on 25 June 1946 and the IMF on 1 Mar 1947.

[71] Membership of selected regional trade arrangements includes: Africa—CEAO (1973) Communauté Economique de L'Afrique de l'Ouest (West African Economic Community). Members (7): Bénin, Burkina Faso, Cote d'Ivoire, Mali, Mauritania. Niger and Sènégal; CEPGL (1976) Communauté Economique des Pays des Grands Lacs (Economic Community

tially further since. These arrangements variously consist of free trade areas, customs unions, common markets and economic unions.[73] The growth of regional trading arrangements has generally been accompanied by multilateral and unilateral reductions in trade barriers. This has contributed to the

of the Great Lakes Countries). Members (3): Burundi, Rwanda and Zaire; EAEC (1967) East African Economic Conununity. Members (3): Tanzania, Kenya and Uganda; ECOWAS (1975) Economic Community of West African States. Members (16): Bénin, Burkina Faso, Cape Verde, Cote d'Ivoire, The Gambia, Ghana, Guinea, Guinea-Bissau, Liberia. Mali, Mauritania. Niger, Nigeria, Sénégal, Sierra Leone and Togo (Integrates the members of the CEAO, MRU, Gabon, The Gambia, Ghana, Guinea-Bissau, Nigeria and Togo); IOC (1982) Indian Ocean Commission Members (5): Comoros, France, Madagascar, Mauritius and Seychelles; MRU (1973) Mano River Union Members (3): Guinea (1980), Liberia and Sierra Leone; PTA (1981) Preferential Trade Area for Eastern and Southern Africa. Members (19): Angola, Burundi, Comoros, Djibouti, Ethiopia, Kenya, Lesotho, Malawi, Mauritius, Mozambique, Namibia (1993), Rwanda, Somalia, Sudan, Swaziland, Tanzania, Uganda, Zambia and Zimbabwe; SACU (1910) Southern African Customs Union. Members (4): Botswana, Lesotho, South Africa and Swaziland; UDEAC (1964) Union Douaruère et Economique de 1'Afrique Centrale (Central African Customs and Economic Union). Members (6): Cameroon, Central African Republic, Congo, Gabon, Chad and Equatorial Guinea.

Asia and the Pacific: ANZCERTA (1983) Australia-New Zealand Closer Economic Relations Trade Agreement (Free trade area formed in 1965). Members (2): Australia and New Zealand; ASEAN (1967) Association of South East Asian Nations. Members (6): Brunei (1988), Indonesia, Malaysia, The Philippines, Singapore and Thailand.

Europe: Benelux Union (1948) Belgium-Netherlands-Luxembourg Economic Union. Members (3): Belgium, the Netherlands and Luxembourg; ECSC The European Coal and Steel Community. Members (12): Belgium, France, Germany, Italy and Luxembourg, the Netherlands. EEC and Euratom (1957) The European Economic Community and European Atomic Energy Community. Members (12): Belgium, Denmark (1973), France, Germany, Greece (1981), Ireland (1973), Italy, Luxembourg, the Netherlands. Portugal (1986), Spain (1986) and the UK (1973); EFTA (1960) European Free Trade Association. Members (7): Austria, Finland (1961), Iceland (1970), Liechtenstein (1991), Norway, Sweden and Switzerland.

Middle East: ACM (1964) The Arab Common Market. Members (7): Egypt, Iraq, Jordan, Libya, Mauritania, Syria and Yemen; ECO (1985) Economic Cooperation Organization (formerly the Regional Cooperation for Development). Members (3): Islamic Republic of Iran, Pakistan and Turkey; recently several states of the former Soviet Union and Afghanistan have become members (1992); GCC (1981) Cooperation Council for the Arab States of the Gulf (also known as the Gulf Cooperation Council). Members (6): Bahrain, Kuwait, Oman, Qatar, Saudi Arabia and the United Arab Emirates.

Western Hemisphere: Andean Pact (1969), Andean Subregional Integration Agreement. Members (5): Bolivia, Ecuador, Colombia, Peru and Venezuela (Chile withdrew in 1976); CACM (1960) Central American Common Market. Members (5): Costa Rica (1962), El Salvador, Guatemala, Honduras and Nicaragua; CARICOM (1973), Caribbean Community. Members (13): Antigua and Barbuda, The Bahamas (1983), Barbados, Belize (1974), Dominica (1974), Grenada (1974), Guyana, Jamaica, Montserrat (1974), St Kitts and Nevis, St Lucia (1974), St Vincent and the Grenadines (1974), and Trinidad and Tobago; LAIA (1980) Latin American Integration Association (superseded Latin American Free Trade Association, LAFTA, signed in 1960). Members (11): Mexico and all South American Countries except Guyana, French Guiana, and Suriname.

USA–Canada: FTA (1988) United States-Canada Free Trade Agreement (also known as Canada–US Free Trade Agreement CUSTA). Members (2): The United States and Canada. US–Israel FTA (1975) United States-Israel Free Trade Agreement. Members (2): The United States and Israel.

[72] Preference schemes are non-reciprocal arrangements which are usually only made avail-

further progress achieved in global trade liberalization in the post war period. Against the advantages of tariff reductions, regional arrangements may nevertheless lead to the creation of protectionist trading blocks while any general increase in members' welfare has only tended to occurr in arrangements between industrialized countries rather than developing countries.[74]

The GATT[75] had originally been agreed without the inclusion of trade in services which was added under the General Agreement on Trade and

able to developing countries and generally provide for stated reductions in tariff rates. Association agreements are reciprocal trade arrangements although they are generally limited in the types of commodities covered but available to all countries. Under Art 24 of the GATT, an exception to the general principle of non-discrimination between Contracting Parties is conferred for regional trade arrangements provided that they do not restrict trade with other countries. On the GATS (n 82).

[73] (nn 28–30). Within a free trade area, member countries reduce or abolish intra-area restrictions on trade while maintaining differential protection against non-members (n 28), With a customs union, members also establish a common external tariff in addition to liberalising intra-area trade (n 29). Under a common market, the customs union is extended to factor movements (n 30). National economic policies are further harmonized within a common market to create an economic union (n 33). See also International Monetary Fund, *World Economic Outlook* May 1993, Annex III, pp 106–15.

[74] Earlier initiatives in the establishment of regional trade arrangements included:

Turkey–EFTA (1992)	Free trade area by 1995; subject to discussion
Chile–Mexico (1991)	Free trade area by 1996
Argentina–Brazil–Paraguay–Uruguay (MERCOSUR 1991)	Common market by 1995
Mexico–Central America (1991)	Free trade area by 1996
Colombia—Mexico–Venezuela (1991)	Free trade area by 1995
Southern African Development Community (1992)	Free trade area and sector cooperation; protocol cooperation to be finalized
EFTA Czech Republic (1992) Slovak Republic (1992) Poland (1992) Romania (1992) Hungary (1993)	Bilateral free trade agreements providing for proressive trade liberalization during the next decade
EC–Czechoslovakia Hungary (1991) Poland (1991) Romania (1993) Bulgaria (1993)	Bilateral association agreeements providing for trade liberalization during the next decade

Source: OECD "Regional Trade Agreements:' Annex to *The Implications of Growing Regional Integration* (Paris Sept 1992).

[75] The GATT was established with the IMF and the World Bank at the Bretton Woods Conference in New Hampshire, Massachusetts in July 1944 (n 70). The core objective of the GATT was to liberalize international trade in goods, services and investment through the progressive reduction of tariffs with regard to customs duties and charges having equivalent effect. The GATT was based on national treatment or non-discrimination between overseas territories (n 79). Under the GATT, financial impediments on market access are prohibited outright while internal market regulation measures are subject to non-discrimination (national treatment). Chapter 3, Section C (1).

Services (GATS) in 1994.[76] The objective of GATS was to establish a multilateral regime for trade and services within the general GATT system.[77] The GATS includes most forms of financial service[78] and provides for the introduction of disciplines on barriers to trade and investment in services against overtly discriminatory or protectionist measures. The adoption of the principle of most favoured nation (MFN)[79] is provided for subject to certain exceptions or derogations[80] as well as transparency with regard to the content of any residual restrictive measures.[81] The GATS is accordingly generally based on non-discrimination in the form of both national treatment (NT) and MFN supported by a general transparency doctrine all of which are given effect to through a core agreement and list of commitment schedules.[82] The main difficulty that arises is that the GATS is voluntary

[76] GATS was entered into to bring services within the scope of the activities covered by the WTO which was set up as the new umbrella organization for the GATT following the Uruguay Round. This began with the Punta del Este Declaration in 1986 which was completed on 15 Dec 1993 and signed in Marrakech on 15 Apr 1994.

[77] This includes the provision of greater discipline on national barriers to trade and services and the establishment of cross-linkage mechanisms in respect of liberalization negotiations and dispute resolutions. USTR *Annual Report of the President of the United States on the Trade Agreements Program* (1984–5), Appendix M (US Goals for Trade and Services). See also Uruguay Round Understanding on Rules and Procedures Governing the Settlement of Disputes, Art 22(3)(c).

[78] These might be referred to as cross-border, local receipt or service, foreign presence and overseas receipt. Art 1 of GATS defines trade and services in terms of four delivery modes. These comprise the provision of services from the territory of one country into another, within the territory of one country to a consumer from another, by a service provider of one country through a commercial presence in the territory of another and by a service supplier of one country through the presence of natural persons from that country in the territory of another. This distinction had originally been developed by Sampson and Snape in 1985. Gary Sampson and Richard Snape 'Identifying the Issues in Trade in Services' (1985) 8(2) *The World Economy* 171–182. One difficulty that arose was that the distinction between the four delivery channels was used to allow for the selective opening of markets. For comment, Wendy Dobson and Pierre Jacquet *Financial Services Liberalisation in the WTO* Institute for International Economics (June 1998), 73. The four delivery modes are also generally complimentary and overlapping rather than alternative in practice. Richard Snape and Malcolm Bosworth 'Advancing Services Negotiations' (1996), paper presented at Institute for International Economics Conference *The World Trading Systems: Challenges Ahead* (24–25 June, 1996).

[79] MFN prohibits discrimination in treatment between foreign countries. This is distinct from national treatment which prohibits discrimination between domestic and foreign firms, goods or services.

[80] GATS, Art II.

[81] GATS, Art III.

[82] The core agreement is made up of a preamble, 28 Articles that set out the obligations of the signatories, 8 Annexes, 8 Administerial Declarations and an Understanding (or Memorandum of Agreement) on Commitments in Financial Services. The conditions under which countries may claim exemption from MFN are set out in the first annex with the others setting the dispositions applicable to particular sectors. The specific services covered are listed in the Annex on Financial Services. This is set out in the form of an exhaustive list which includes insurance and insurance related services as well as banking and securities related activities. Institutional arrangements including the establishment of working groups are dealt

and generally operates by confirming the *status quo* with more substantial liberalization only to be discussed subsequently.[83] It is essentially then dependent on the coincidence of mutual trading interests and supporting political good will.

The other most developed regional as opposed to global trading arrangements are the North American Free Trade Agreement (NAFTA)[84] and Mercosur. NAFTA extends the prior United States-Canada Free Trade Agreement to include Mexico[85] and other potential participant countries. Zero tariffs are introduced on intra-zone trade although no common external tariff is provided for. The effect is to create a free trade zone but not a customs union.[86] Services are generally included (Chapter 12) with financial services being specifically dealt with in Chapter 14 and the Annexes.[87]

with under the Ministerial Declarations. The core agreement sets out the general obligations and disciplines applicable to all sectors. These include the prohibition on discrimination between trading partners or MFN (Art II), transparency (Art III) and a commitment to participate in future negotiations under a 'built-in agenda' to secure progressively higher levels of liberalization (Arts IX to XXI). The schedules of commitments are prepared by a country on an individual basis and set out the extent to which they are prepared to provide market access (under Art XVI) and national treatment (Art XVII) with regard to particular services sectors. This includes a 'positive' list of sectors in which the commitments are made and a 'negative' list of derogations from market access and national treatment. The general obligations of MFN, transparency and negotiations apply where a sector is not separately scheduled.

Individual exceptions adopted at the time the WTO agreement came into effect are valid for up to 10 years subject to a review after five years by the Council for Trade and Services. The Council is to examine whether the conditions that created the need for the exception are still applicable. GATS also provides for certain other general exceptions to MFN in connection with bilateral or regional agreements (Art V), public procurement (Art XIII) and national security (Art XIV).

83 Countries are only obliged to liberalize to the extent that a commitment is made which is also subject to the general and specific exceptions claimed. No further guidance is provided with regard to the conduct of subsequent negotiations which effectively only amounts to a statement of intent. Transparency is limited to the publication of measures adopted that will restrict trade and services. The relevant information only has to be made available locally and is not to be reported to the WTO Secretariat with no central list of restrictions being maintained. Dobson and Jacquet (78) 74.

84 NAFTA was entered into between Canada, Mexico and the United States in Dec 1992 (8 and 17 Dec in Washington, 11 and 17 Dec in Ottawa and 14 and 17 Dec in Mexico City). *North American Free Trade Agreement* (reprinted 32 ILM 289 (1993)).

85 *Canada–United States Free Trade Agreement* (27 ILM 281 (1988)).

86 Chapter 1, section A; Chapter, 2, section B (nn 29–30 and 33).

87 NAFTA, United States Schedule Annex I and II. Financial services are defined to include any service of a financial nature and a service incidental or auxiliary to a service of a financial nature. NAFTA, Art 1416. NAFTA requires unconditional national treatment in connection with financial services under national and provincial or state regulation. NAFTA, Art 1405. National treatment applies to financial institutions of another party, investments made by investors of another party in financial institutions and investors themselves and includes establishment, acquisition, expansion, operation or sale. National treatment is unconditional although it is satisfied if equal competitive opportunities are afforded. NAFTA, Art 1405(5).

NAFTA provides for a general right 'to participate widely in a Party's Market' and more specifically to establish a financial institution in the other party's territory. This right of market participation includes the provision of a range of financial services through separate entities as

Mercosur is the third largest trading bloc in the world. Mercosur was established in 1991 between Argentina, Brazil, Paraguay and Uruguay.[88] Mercosur was set up to create a common market by the end of 1994 between the participating territories based on a common external tariff and free movement of goods, services, capital and labour on a progressively liberalising basis.[89]

As with GATS, NAFTA and Mercosur have established important frameworks within which global and regional trade may be facilitated. These are generally based on the abolition of overt discrimination between participating territories and increasingly extended national treatment between home and host products or services. Mercosur is more ambitious than NAFTA although both protect regulatory autonomy at the national level. Market access is facilitated although generally only on a voluntary and qualified basis.

It has not been possible under any of these arrangements to establish any complete framework to balance the desired objectives of full, or at least, improved market access with proper market protection. Little assistance is accordingly provided in resolving the basic access and control conflict that arises within any extended trading arrangement. These other regimes have further not involved the establishment of any new separate economic and legal orders as well as supporting institutional framework. The European Union accordingly remains the most comprehensive and ambitious regional programme or experiment to date.

required by regulation, the right to expand geographically and the right to own financial institutes despite limits on foreign ownership. NAFTA, Art 1403. Barriers to cross-border trade in financial services are to be removed. NAFTA, Art 1404(1).

NAFTA does not provide for any harmonization of financial regulatory requirements or for any form of mutual recognition. Any 'reasonable' prudential measures may be specifically excepted from the disciplines of Chapter 14 of NAFTA which protects the regulatory autonomy of the Agreement signatories. While national treatment and limited market access are provided, regulatory authority is protected.

[88] Treaty Establishing a Common Market (The Treaty of Asuncion), 26 Mar 1991, (30 ILM). Mercosur takes forward a number of initiatives originally established under the Latin American Free Trade Association (LAFTA) and Central America Common Market (CACM). LAFTA was superseded by the Latin American Integration Association (LAIA) in 1980 after it had failed to establish a free trade area within 12 years of its establishment in 1960. The CACM was set up to establish a common external tariff within five years and to develop cooperation in monetary and fiscal policies. It has since become more of a political rather than an economic forum. Tariffs were also to be eliminated and economic policies harmonized under the Andean Pact which was set up in 1979 and the Caribbean Common Market (CARICOM) in 1973. Only limited progress has been possible under each of these initiatives. See, eg, Julio Nogues and Rosalind Quintanilla 'Latin America's integration and the Multilateral Trading System' in Jamie de Melo and Arvind Panagarya *New Dimensions in Regional Integration* (CUP Cambridge 1993).

[89] See generally, Jorge N Guria and Marcelo R Tavarone 'Mercosur: Consolidation Amid Turmoil', in Joseph J Norton (ed) *Yearbook of International Financial and Economic Law* (Kluwer Law International Deventer 1997) 441–56.

F. NEW ECONOMIC AND LEGAL ORDER

The European Union has created a new type of still expanding regional trading arrangement that has gone considerably further in the establishment of more complete inter-territorial integration than under any of the other models or initiatives developed to date.[90] Although initially based on a free trade area and customs union with full free movement of other production factors and certain common policies, an economic and monetary union has since been created under the Maastricht Treaty while further cooperation continues on defence and justice and other social affairs related matters. The progress achieved to date has been based on both a new economic and legal order set up under the various Treaties entered into.

The Union operates through a common market and an economic and monetary union (Article 2 ECT).[91] This is supplemented by a number of common policies and activities (in Articles 3 and 4). This reflects the traditional approach adopted with regard to the legal identity of the European Union (which is confirmed in recent German writing).[92] As such, the Union

[90] This establishes a basic economic framework within which the law of free movement operates (nn 28–30 and 33–4). The nature and structure of the integration arrangements established within Europe in the financial area are considered in further detail in Chs 3, 4, and 5.

[91] OJ C340, 10 Nov 1997, 173–308.

[92] C Koenig and M Pechstein *Die Europäische Union* (Mohr 1995) 5, 20–63 cited in Deirdre M Curtin and Ige F Dekker 'The EU as a "Layered" International Organization: Institutional Unity in Disguise' in Craig and de Búrca (n 12) ch 3, at 84 n 2. See also R Dehousse 'From Community to Union' in Dehousse (ed) *Europe After Maastricht* (Law Books in Europe Munich 1994), 5; HG Schermers and NM Blokker *International Institutional Law* (3rd edn The Hague Martinus Nijhoff 1995), 977. Other writers have argued that the Treaty of Maastricht has established a new international organization with its own structure and competencies which exist as a single legal system within which the three pillars co-exist. O Dorr 'Zur Rechtsnatur der Europaischen Union' (1995) EuR 334–48; A von Bogdandy and M Nettesheim 'Die Europaische Union: Ein Einheitlicher Verband mit eigener Rechtsordnung' (1996) EuR 3–26 cited in Curtin and Dakker. See also RA Wessel 'The International Legal Status of the European Union' (1997) 2 European Foreign Affairs Review 109–29; B De Witte 'The Pillar Structure and the Nature of the European Union: Greek Temple or French Gothic Cathedral?' in T Heukles, NN Blokker and MMTA Brus (eds), *The European Union after Amsterdam—A Legal Analysis* (Kluwer The Hague and London 1998).

More generally, see, J Shaw *Law of the European Union* (Macmillan London 1996) 5–8 and 62–79; AM Arnull, AA Dashwood, MG Ross and DA Wyatt *European Union Law* (4rd ed Sweet & Maxwell London 2000); and Stephen Weatherill and Paul Beaumont *EU Law* (3rd ed Penguin London 1999). See also U Everling 'Reflections on the Structure of the European Union' (1992) 29 CMLRev 1052–77, 1063; DN Curtin 'The Constitutional Structure of the European Union: A Europe of Bits and Pieces' (1993) 30 CMLRev 17–70; JHHWeiler 'Neither Unity nor Three Pillars, The Trinity Structure of the Treaty on European Union' in J Monar et al (eds) *The Maastricht Treaty on European Union, Legal Complexity and Political Dynamic* (European Inter-University Brussels 1993) 49–62; TC Hartley 'Constitutional and Institutional Aspects of the Maastricht Agreement' (1993) 42 ICLQ 213–37; PC Muller-Graff 'The Legal Bases of the Third Pillar and its Position in the Framework of the Union Treaty' (1994) 31 CMLRev 493–510; ID Hendry 'The Third Pillar of Maastricht: Co-operation in the Fields of Justice and Home Affairs' (1993) 36 GYIL 295–324; T Heukels and J de Zwann 'The

represents one highly sophisticated form of regional trading arrangement.[93] Rather than constitute a single type of integration facility, the Union is made up of a number of overlapping devices or mechanisms including a free-trade area, a customs union and a common market as well as an economic and monetary union. The genius of the European Union and European Community within it is that they operate as a complex series of inter-connected integration structures designed to achieve a number of stated objectives[94] and based on a number of common policies or activities.[95]

These layers of economic integration are given effect to under the early parts of the Treaty of Rome (as amended). The basic policies are set out in Part III. Title I provides for the free movement of goods with the establishment of a customs union (Articles 23 (*ex* 9) and 24 (*ex*10) and Chapter 1)[96]

Configuration of the European Union: Community Dimensions of Institutional Interaction' in DN Curtin and T Heukels (eds) *The Institutional Dynamics of European Integration* (Martinus Nijhoff Dordrecht and London 1994) 195–228.

[93] Section E.

[94] The Community shall, in particular, have as its tasks to promote harmonious, balanced and sustainable development of economic activities, a high level of employment and social protection, equality between men and women, sustainable and non-inflationary growth, a high degree of competitiveness and convergence of economic performance, a high level of protection and improvement of the quality of the environment, the raising of the standard of living and quality of life and economic and social cohesion and solidarity among Member States. Art 2 (ex 2).

[95] The activities of the Community include: (a) the prohibition of customs duties and quantitative restrictions on the import and export of goods and of all other measures having equivalent effect; (b) a common commercial policy; (c) an internal market characterized by the abolition as between Member States of obstacles to the free movement of goods, persons, services and capital; (d) measures concerning the entry and movement of persons as provided for in Title IV (Visas, asylum, immigration and other policies related to the free movement of persons); (e) a common policy in the sphere of agriculture and fisheries; (f) a common policy in the sphere of transport; (g) a system ensuring that competition in the internal market is not distorted; (h) the approximation of the laws of Member States to the extent required for the functioning of the common market; (i) the promotion of coordination between employment policies of the Member States with a view to enhancing their effectiveness by developing a coordinated strategy for employment; (j) a policy in the social sphere comprising a European Social Fund; (k) the strengthening of economic and social cohesion; (l) a policy in the sphere of the environment; (m) the strengthening of the competitiveness of Community industry; (n) the promotion of research and technological development; (o) encouragement of the establishment and development of trans-European networks; (p) a contribution to the attainment of a high level of health protection; (q) a contribution to education and training of quality and to the flowering of the cultures of the Member States; (r) a policy in the sphere of development cooperation; (s) association with other overseas countries and territories in order to increase trade and promote jointly economic and social development; (t) a contribution to the strengthening of consumer protection; and (u) measures in the spheres of energy, civil protection and tourism (Art 3) (1) (*ex* 3). In all of these activities, the Community is to aim to eliminate inequalities and to promote equality between men and women (Art 3(2)).

[96] The Community is to be based on a customs union which is to apply to all trade and goods and involves the prohibition between Member States of customs duties on imports and exports and of all charges having equivalent effect and the adoption of a common customs tariff in their relations with third countries (Art 23 (ex 9)). (n 29) and Ch 3, section C.

and for the removal of quantitative restrictions and measures having equivalent effect (Articles 28 (*ex* Article 30) and 29 (*ex* Article 34)).[97] Title III of Part 3 provides for the free movement of persons, services and capital. Chapters 1 and 2 of Title III are concerned with workers[98] and establishment.[99] Chapter 3 extends the provisions against obstacles to free movement

Products from third countries are to be considered to be in free circulation where necessary formalities have been complied with and any duties or charges paid (Art 24 (ex 10)). The prohibition of customs duties, establishment of the common customs tariff and related functions of the Commission are developed in Arts 25, 26, and 27 (ex 12, 28, and 29). Before the Treaty on European Union, the provisions on free movement of goods were set out in Part II under the Title 'Foundations of the Community'. Part II is now concerned with 'Citizen of the Union' with Part III being renamed 'Community Policies'.

[97] Art 28 (ex 30) prohibits the maintenance of any quantitative restrictions on imports and all measures having equivalent effect between Member States. Art 29 (ex 34) prohibits quantitative restrictions and measures having equivalent effect with regard to exports. A number of Treaty exemptions from these prohibitions are provided for under Art 30 (ex 36) provided that they do not constitute a means of arbitrary discrimination or disguized restriction on trade. These consist of (a) public morality, public policy or public securities; (b) the protection of health and life of humans, animals and plants; (c) the protection of national treasures possessing artistic, historic or archaeological value; and (d) the protection of industrial and commercial property. For discussion, Stephen Weatherhill and Paul Beaumont *EU Law* (n 92), Ch 16; and AM Arnull, AA Dashwood, MG Ross, and DA Wyatt *European Union Law* (n 92), 345–351; Paul Craig and Grainne de Bùrca *EU Law* (2nd edn OUP Oxford 1998), 594–604. Ch 3, section C.

[98] Free movement of workers is secured under Art 39 (ex Art 48). This is to involve the abolition of any discrimination based on nationality between workers of Member States as regards employment, remuneration and other conditions of work and employment. It is, in particular, to include the right to accept offers of employment, move freely, stay in employment or remain after employment subject to any limitations on the basis of public policy, public security or public health (Art 39(1)(2) and (3) (ex 48(1)(2) and (3)). Implementation directives or regulations are to be adopted under Art 40 (ex 49). Member States are to encourage exchange of young workers and adopt appropriate supporting social security arrangements (Arts 41 and 42 (ex 50 and 52).

[99] Restrictions on freedom of establishment of nationals of a Member State in the territory of another Member State are to be prohibited. This includes restrictions on the setting up of agencies, branches or subsidiaries by nationals (Art 43 (ex 52)), para 1. Freedom of establishment is to include the right to take up and pursue activities as self-employed persons and to set up and manage undertakings, in particular, companies or firms (within the meaning of Art 48, para 2) under the conditions laid down for nationals of the law of the country where the establishment is effected. This is only subject to the provisions of Chapter 4 on 'Capital and Payments' (Art 43 (ex 52), para 2). Section I. Ch 3, section D.

Directives are to be adopted under Art 44 (ex 54). Activities connected with the exercise of official authority may be excluded (Art 45 (ex 55)) with further derogations being possible on the grounds of public policy, public security or public health (Art 46 (ex 56)). The Council is to issue directives providing for the mutual recognition of diplomas, certificates and other evidence of formal qualifications to assist the taking up and pursuit of activities by self-employed persons (Art 47 (ex 57)). Companies or firms formed in accordance with the law of a particular Member State within which they have their registered office, central administration or principal place of business within the Community are to be treated in the same way as natural persons. Companies or firms mean companies or firms constituted under civil or commercial law including cooperative societies and other legal persons governed by public or private law except for non-profit making bodies (Art 48 (ex 58)).

to include services.[100] The remaining factor of production capital is dealt with under Chapter 4.[101] The provisions concerning persons are supplemented by further new or extended rules with regard to visas, asylum, immigration and other policies in Title IV (*ex* Title III(a)). The Common Policies of the Community include agriculture (Title II) and transport (Title V (*ex* Title IV)).[102]

The objective of these core Treaty provisions is to secure the full free movement of goods and free movement of labour, capital and enterprise. The movement of goods within the Community is secured through the removal of all quotas and pecuniary charges as well as any other measures of equivalent effect. With this, consumer choice is to be increased and market competition improved. Goods coming from outside the Community are subject to a single tariff regime which prevents any advantage arising in terms of import location. In addition to these demand side enhancements, the production and supply of goods is improved through the free movement of workers (employed and self-employed), companies (enterprises) and capital (including current payments). The underlying objective is to facilitate the optimal allocation of resources across the Community which should lead to maximum economic efficiency and, in turn, wealth creation and more general consequent economic benefit.

[100] Restrictions on freedom to provide services are prohibited in respect of nationals of Member States who are established in a State other than that of the person for whom the services are intended. This may also be extended to nationals of a third country who provide services and are established within the Community (Art 49 (ex 59)). Chapter 3, section D.

This prohibition applies to services which are normally provided for remuneration and not governed by the provisions relating to free movement of goods, capital or persons. Services will, in particular, include activities of an industrial character, a commercial character, craftsmen or any of the professions (Art 50 (ex 60)). Without prejudice to the provisions concerning establishment, the person providing a service may temporarily pursue this activity in the state where the services are provided under the same conditions as are imposed on local nationals (Art 50 (ex 60), para 2).

Liberalization of specific services is to be promoted through directives (Art 52 (ex 63)). The Commission is also to make recommendations to Member States to extend this liberalization where their general economic and specific sector situations permit (Art 53 (ex 64)).

Where restrictions have not been abolished, each Member State must apply any restrictions without distinction on grounds of nationality or residence (Art 54 (ex 65)). The derogations, mutual recognition of qualifications and treatment of company provisions provided for with regard to establishment are extended to services (Art 55 (ex 66)).

[101] All restrictions on the movement of capital and payments between Member States and between States and third countries are prohibited (Art 56 (ex 73b)). Certain transitional provisions are provided for (Art 57 (ex 73c)). The prohibition on restrictions on capital and payment is without prejudice to enforcement actions in connection with taxation or the prudential supervision of financial institutions (Art 58 (ex 73d)). Ch 4 also makes provision for safeguard measures to be taken by the European Central Bank or other necessary measures taken by the Council (Arts 59 and 60 (ex 73f and 73g)).

[102] For further comment, Weatherhill and Beaumont (n 92); Wyatt and Dashwood (n 92); and Craig and de Búrca (n 12).

The effect of the basic free movement rules is to prohibit financial and non-financial restrictions on the movement of goods, workers (and establishment), services and capital. Other obstacles may nevertheless be created in the form of fiscal or other state advantages in favour of local products. Supporting Treaty rules are accordingly adopted with regard to the maintenance of discriminatory tax structures (Articles 90–93 (ex 95–99)) and other forms of state aid (Articles 87–89 (ex 92–94)). Private parties may also distort the operation of the market either through restrictive agreements (cartels) or abuse of a dominant position (in oligopolistic markets). Appropriate rules are accordingly provided for concerning anti-competitive agreements and other structural abuses (Articles 81 and 82 (ex 85 and 86)).

As well as promote integration negatively through prohibitions on obstructions to free movement, the Treaty contains a number of further provisions designed to ensure positive harmonization through the adoption of appropriate common standards in various areas (Article 94 (ex 100)).[103] The integration programme provided for under the Treaty then operates on both a negative or prohibitive as well as positive and legislative basis.

The Community is accordingly based on the simple economic objective of market integration to be achieved through the construction of a series of connected or overlapping trading and service regimes. The drafters of the original Treaty provisions have in this way created a new economic order based on a series of interconnected legal rights and obligations. To that extent, the Community can be seen as an economic function, entity or objective that has been given legal identity and effect under international law. This then operates through a separate but parallel new legal order based on a series of connected trading relationships designed to secure the underlying integration objective set.[104] Europe can in this way be considered to be made

[103] Art 94 (ex 100) provides for the issuance of directives for the approximation of laws, regulations or administrative provisions wherever this directly affects the establishment or functioning of the common market. Special provision is included for completion of the internal market as provided for in Art 14 (ex 7a). This provides that the Community is to adopt measures with the aim of progressively establishing the internal market by 31 Dec 1992. The internal market comprises an area without internal frontiers in which the free movement of goods, persons, services and capital is insured in accordance with the Treaty. Ch 1 (n 3). The Council, acting by qualified majority on a proposal from the Commission, is to determine the guidelines and conditions necessary to ensure balanced progress (Art 14 (ex 7a)).

The Commission may initiate appropriate discussions where Member States' laws distort conditions of competition within the common market. Necessary directives may be issued by the Council. Other appropriate measures may also be taken as provided for in the Treaty (Art 96 (ex 101)). Member States may consult with the Commission where they are concerned that competition may be distorted (Art 97 (ex 102)). Ch 6, section C (2).

[104] In addition to these overlapping levels of integration, Europe has to be considered in terms of a number of constitutional layers, in particular, following the Treaty of Maastricht in 1992 which created the two further pillars of the Common Foreign and Security Policy (CFSP) and cooperation in the fields of Justice and Home Affairs (CJHA). For comment, Deirdrie M Curtin and Ige S Dekker 'The EU as a "layered" international organization: Institution Unity

up of both a new economic and legal order with the underlying integration objectives set being secured through a series of connected or overlapping sub-processes or regimes.

G. INSTITUTIONAL STRUCTURE

The draftsmen of the Treaty of Rome intended to construct a new economic order although one based on clearly defined legal principles that were set out in the original terms of the Treaty. In addition to this core economic and legal base, the Treaty has set up an extended institutional structure which includes a number of formal (and informal) entities.[105] Title I, Chapter 1 of Part V of the Treaty provides, in particular, for the establishment of the European Parliament, the Council, the Commission, Court of Justice and the Court of Auditors.[106] This builds on and then assimilates the original

in Disguise', ch 3 of Craig and de Búrca (n 12). On the origins of the idea of the economic identity of the Community in terms of the writings of the Freiburg School of Ordoliberalism., Chapter 1, section E (4) and (n 78).

105 The European Parliament is set up under Chapter 1 of Title I (189–201 (ex 137–144)). The Council is set up under section 2 (Arts 202–210 (ex 145–154)) and the Commission under section 3 (211–13 (ex Art 155–163)). The Court of Justice is set up under section 4 (Arts 220–245 (ex 164–188)) and the Court of Auditors under section 5 (Art 246) (ex 188(a)).

106 The European Parliament consists of representatives of the peoples of the States brought together to exercise the powers conferred on it by the Treaty (Art 189 (ex 137)). Representatives are appointed for five year terms through direct elections with the country allocations being as set out in the Treaty. These include Germany 99 and France, Italy and the United Kingdom having 87 (Art 190 (ex 138)). The Parliament elects its President and officers from among its Members. Members of the Commission may attend all meetings and may require to be heard. The Commission must reply orally or in writing to questions addressed to it by the Parliament or its Members. Council representation is governed by its Rules of Procedure (Art 197 (ex 140)). Voting is to be by absolute majority with a quorum set out in the Rules of Procedure to be adopted by the Parliament (Arts 198 and 199 (ex 141 and 142). Parliament must discuss the annual general report of the Commission in open session and the Commission may be required to resign as a body on an essential motion of a two-thirds majority of the votes cast following a three day debate (Arts 200 and 201 (ex 143 and 144)).

The Council is to ensure coordination of the general economic policies of the Member States and may take decisions and confer on the Commission implementation powers in respect of any rules adopted (Art 202 (ex 145)). The Council consists of representatives of each Member State at ministerial level authorized to commit the government of the State. The Presidency rotates on a six monthly basis (Art 203 (ex 146)). The Council meets when convened by the President or at the request of one of its members or the Commission (Art 204 (ex 147)). The Council votes by majority although it may act by qualified majority as provided for under the Treaty in accordance with the weighted votes set (Art 205 (ex 148)). Council Members may act on behalf of others for voting purposes (Art 206 (ex 150)). The Council is assisted by its Committee of Permanent Representatives (COREPER) and a General Secretariat. It adopts its own Rules of Procedure (Art 207 (ex 151)). The Council may request the Commission to conduct studies, determine the rules governing committees provided for under the Treaty and set salaries, allowances and pensions for the Commission and Court (Arts 208, 209 and 210 (ex 152, 153 and 154)). On enlargement, Ch 1, section E (1) and (n 88).

The Commission is to ensure that Treaty provisions and measures are applied, formulate

institutional framework set up under the Treaty of Paris in respect of the Economic Coal and Steel Community.[107] The European institutional structure has, of course, developed considerably since and now includes a large number of other institutions and committees not anticipated within the formal framework set up under the Treaty.[108]

This original institutional apparatus set up has, of course, been subject to continuous review to attempt to remove perceived difficulties including legislative delay and inefficiency. Further revision has also been necessary in response to the challenges created by continued enlargement and especially with the admission of ten new member territories on I May 2004.[109] A number of further institutional reforms were also included in the proposed Constitutional Treaty recommendations which were finalized in June 2004 but then subsequently shelved.[110]

recommendations or deliver opinions, assist in the adoption of measures by the Council and European Parliament and exercise implementation powers conferred on it by the Council (Art 211 (ex 155)). The Commission is to publish an annual general report on the activities of the Community within one month of the opening of the European Parliament (Art 212 (ex 156)). The Commission consists of 20 Members selected on the grounds of their general competence and independence with members being separately required to act in the general interest of the Community and in an independent manner. Members are prohibited from engaging in any other office or occupation during their term of office (Art 213 (ex 157)). Members are appointed on five year renewable terms with the President being nominated by common accord and approved by the Parliament (Art 214 (ex 158)). Members' duties end on resignation or compulsory retirement (Art 215 (ex 159)). Commission Members may be removed by the Court when they no longer fulfill the conditions required for the performance of their duties or have been guilty of serious misconduct (Art 216 (ex 160)). The Commission may appoint a Vice-President or two Vice-Presidents from among its Members (Art 217 (ex 161)). The Council and Commission are to consult and settle their methods of cooperation by common accord with the Commission adopting its own Rules and Procedures separately (Art 212 (ex 162)). The Commission is to work under the political guidance of its President. The Commission is to act by majority with meetings being governed by its Rules of Procedure (Art 219 (ex 163)). For discussion, Weatherill and Beaumont (n 92), chs 2, 3 and 4.

107 The two sets of institutional arrangement were merged in 1968.

108 For discussion of the issues that arise in connection with this institutional revision, see, for example, Graine de Bùrca, 'The Institutional Development of the EU: A Constitutional Analysis' in Craig and de Bùrca (n 12), ch 2. De Bùrca argues that the evolution and development of EU institutional practice and the institutional framework more generally have created new difficulties that have still not been fully resolved within the constitution of the EU. These more informal arrangements have created significant challenges within the former constitutional relations and balance set up under the Treaty. De Bùrca recommends that certain fundamental principles of accountability, coherence, openness, fairness and amenability to political or judicial control should be clearly agreed, observed and enforced at all levels and with regard to all aspects of the EU's policy and law-making processes. On recent Constitutional proposals, Ch 1, Section F(b) and (nn 93 and 94). See also (n 111).

109 Commission *For the European Union: Peace, Freedom and Solidarity—Communication of the Commission on the Institutional Architecture* COM (2002) 728 final/2. Ch 1, section F (2) and (n 88).

110 Proposed 'Treaty establishing a Constitution for Europe' available http://europa.eu.in/futurm/index_en.html. Ch 1, section F (2) and (nn 91–93).

The establishment of this institutional structure to service the new economic and legal order created within Europe further distinguishes the Community from any comparable regional trading arrangement. This separation is continued with the inclusion of financial policy specifically within the scope of the integration process and with the creation of an identifiable single market in banking and other financial services.

This financial market work is, in turn, supported by a dedicated technical committee framework the main elements of which were only recently confirmed.[111] The changes that have been given effect were considered necessary following the recommendations made by the Lamfalussy Committee into the action required to complete the creation of a single capital market in Europe.[112] The Lamfalussy Committee had drawn particular attention to the significant legislative and related institutional defects that persisted within Europe and had suggested *inter alia* that two new committees be set up in the securities area with one focusing on policy and the other on more technical implementation related matters. A revised four stage adoption procedure was also recommended based on the initial preparation of general framework principles, the subsequent development of supporting more detailed regulatory rules, enhanced inter-agency cooperation and strengthened implementation review and enforcement. This new institutional and legislative model would subsequently be extended into other financial sectors and then the work of the Commission more generally.

[111] The Council had invited the Commission in Dec 2002 to extend the committee structure applied in the securities sector to banking, insurance and investment funds. One Directive and six Commission decisions were issued on 5 Nov 2003 to establish two specialist committees in each of the areas of banking, insurance (and occupational pensions) and securities (including undertakings in collective investments and transferable securities (UCITS)). 'Financial Services: Commission presents measures to improve regulation of banking, securities and investment funds' (IP/03/1507 of 6 Nov 2003). These partly re-constitute earlier bodies (such as the Banking Advisory Committee, the Insurance Committee and UCITS Contact Committee) as well as create new complementary entities. The objective is to ensure improved supervisory and regulatory cooperation and increase consistent implementation and enforcement. The financial services committees now consist of the European Banking Committee (EBC) and Committee of European Banking Supervisors (CEBS), the European Insurance and Occupational Pensions Committee (EIOPC) and Committee of European Insurance and Occupational Pensions Supervisors (CEIOPS) as well as the European Securities Committee (ESC) and Committee of European Securities Regulators (CESR). Ch 1 (n 55).

[112] Committee of Wise Men, *Initial Report on the Regulation of European Securities Markets* (7 Nov 2000) FINAL (n 57); and Committee of Wise Men *Final Report on the Regulation of European Securities Markets* (15 Feb 2001), FINAL (n 57). The terms of reference of the Committee had been set by the European Union's Economic and Financial Ministers (ECOFIN) on 17 July 2000. Ch 5, section D (4).

H. EUROPEAN FINANCIAL INTEGRATION

Financial integration represents one aspect of the larger integration process under construction within Europe.[113] This relates specifically to the integration of each of the main financial sectors on a European basis as well as the further approximation or harmonization of supporting monetary and economic policies. This includes the provision of banking and other financial services by financial intermediaries as well as currency and capital matters and cooperation in other areas of monetary and economic policy.[114] It is essential that each of these is managed appropriately on an individual country and collective (regional) basis.

Many of the specific advantages of financial integration overlap with those generated under economic integration more generally.[115] This should produce the most efficient allocation of resources within the economy as well as its more general stable and effective operation. Capital and investment should be most efficiently allocated. Transaction costs should be reduced for traders and investors with consequent increases in earnings and returns. Labour costs may also be lower and employment rates higher. Competition and innovation should increase and growth rates be higher. Monetary and economic policy management should also be more accurate and more effective and economic conditions generally more stable.[116]

Although banking and financial market regulatory policy only forms one part of the larger economic system under management, financial intermediaries carry out essential savings, credit and payment functions without which the rest of the economy would not be able to operate. Whatever level of integration is achieved in the intermediate to long term, banking and financial markets will accordingly act both as significant independent sectors within the new regional economy as well as essential support channels and mechanisms within each market or sub-market concerned.

In historical terms, little progress was possible in securing financial integration in Europe during the early stages of the development of the

[113] Section B. See generally Molle *The Economics of European Integration—Theory, Practice and Policy* (n 22).

[114] Financial integration can be understood to refer to the approximation or assimilation of all financial related functions within any trading arrangement. Section B and (n 22). The specific content of this policy is unfortunately more difficult to specify due to the lack of any precise definition and the inconsistent usage often adopted. For the present purposes, financial policy is generally understood to refer to domestic monetary and economic policy, foreign exchange rate policy, capital movements and banking and financial market regulation. Ch 6, section B (1). A number of overlaps as well as necessary dependencies arise between each of these aspects of financial policy although this general five point distinction is adopted for discussion purposes in this text (n 168).

[115] Section C.

[116] See, eg, Molle discussing the potential advantages of economic and monetary union within Europe. Molle (n 22) 400–1.

Community following signature of the Treaty of Rome on 27 March 1957. The post-War period of reconstruction and development had been dominated by investment shortages and the maintenance of extensive controls on currency and financial transactions.[117] While Germany had relaxed restrictions on capital movements at an early stage,[118] strict controls were maintained in almost all other countries. Fixed exchange rates were accepted as a necessary framework within which international trade was to take place. This had been reinforced by the setting up of the Bretton Woods system on managed currency arrangements.[119] Post-War currency convertibility was only re-introduced on 27 December 1958.[120] The Organization of European Economic and Cooperation (OEEC) was set up on 16 April 1948 although any substantive realization of active cooperation in the economic and financial area was limited.[121]

Some early economic recovery did follow which allowed agreement to be reached on the adoption of the first two free movement of capital directives

[117] Negotiations on the Treaty of Rome had been conducted against the background of shortages of official reserves and significant monetary imbalances. Only minimal provisions could then be included it this regard. A compromise had to be accepted. Age F Bakker *The Liberalization of Capital Movements in Europe—The Monetary Committee and Financial Integration 1958–1994* (Luwer Dordrcht and London 1996) 33.

[118] Germany was anxious to open its borders as quickly as possible. Ludwig Erhard, the Minister of Economic Affairs, had decided to follow Wilhelm Ropke who had argued for the free competition of market forces. Germany was able to generate current account surpluses for its official reserves from 1952 onwards and withdrew all restrictions on capital outflows in 1957. Bakker (n 117) 34.

[119] (n 70). The Bretton Woods system had operated by fixing the values of all foreign currencies to the dollar (subject to a formal adjustment mechanism) and the value of the dollar to gold to serve as an anchor currency for the system. The closure of the dollar/gold exchange window effectively ended the operation of the managed exchange rate regime that had been in operation since the end of the War. Walker (n 70). See generally J Williamson *The Failure of World Monetary Reform, 1971–74* (Brighton 1987). See also KW Dam *The Rules of the Game: Reform and Evolution in the International Monetary System* (University of Chicago Press Chicago and London 1982); AW Hooke *The International Monetary Fund—Its Evolution, Organisation and Activities* (IMF Pamphlet Series No 37 Washington 1982); M Moffit *The World's Money: International Banking from Bretton Woods to the Brink of Insolvency* (Joseph London 1984); J Cavanagh, D Wysham and M Arruda (eds) *Beyond Bretton Woods: Alternatives to the Global Economic Order* (1994); and C Geisst *Exchange Rate Chaos—Twenty-Five Years of Finance and Consumer Democracy* (Routledge London 1995).

[120] The European Payments Union had been set up in 1950 to manage the progressive restoration of the external convertibility of the European currencies.

[121] The OEEC was replaced by the Organization for Economic Cooperation and Development (OECD) in 1961 following its expansion to include other non-European industrial countries. The OECD was directed at promoting international trade in goods and services as well as liberalization of capital movements. A *Code of Liberalisation of Capital Movements* was produced in 1961 which set out the obligations assumed with regard to capital transfers. Compliance was monitored through the *Committee on Capital Movements and Invisible Transactions* (CMIT). The IMF has also focused on current account convertibility rather than capital movements under Art VIII of its Article of Agreement. Art VI permits the imposition of capital controls provided that these do not restrict payments for current transactions or transfers in settlement.

in 1960 and 1962 although no further agreement would then be possible for over twenty-five years.[122] The early capital Directives had been agreed after the production of a report by Robert Marjolin in 1959 that had advised that a policy of full relaxation of capital restrictions should be adopted.[123] France did move towards a relaxation of policy at the end of 1966 but this had to be reversed with the unrest experienced in May 1968.[124] An ambitious attempt was made at the Hague Summit in December 1969 to reconsider the possibility of establishing an economic and monetary union within Europe which led to the production of the Werner Report on 8 October 1970. No significant progress on this was nevertheless possible until the late 1980s.[125] The 1960s could accordingly

[122] A draft proposal for a third directive had been produced in August 1963 although no further progress was possible partly due to the draft having been too ambitious and partly the prevailing economic conditions within which countries were reluctant to surrender control over domestic monetary policies and with the threat of capital flight. A revised draft produced in Jan1964 also failed.

Under the 1960 and 1962 Directives, three sets of capital transactions were identified. Certain transactions were to be deregulated unconditionally. These included direct investment, real estate purchases, short and medium term trade credits, personal transactions (including the repatriation of earnings and investments) and the acquisition of quoted stocks by non-residents in the local territory. These were considered to be directly related to the free movement of goods (trade credits), employees and self-employed (personal transactions) and establishment (direct investment and stock acquisition). These items were either placed in a List A or a List B with the former having to be made on the basis of the exchange rate applying to payments in current transactions.

The second group consisted of partly freed transfers including the issuance and placement of listed shares on the stock market of another territory, the acquisition of non-quoted shares by non-residents, shares purchased by investment funds and long term trade credits. These were placed in a List C.

There was no obligation to liberalize imposed on the last category which included short term transactions such as Treasury bonds or other capital stock purchases and the opening of bank accounts by non-residents. These were placed in a List D. Molle (n 22) 220–1; Servais (n 43) 28–31. See generally, Bakker (n 117) ch 5.

[123] European Commission, *La liberation des mouvements de capitaux en application de l'Article 67.1 du Traité de Rome* (1959). Marjolin was the Director General for Economic and Financial Affairs.

[124] France had moved from negative (prohibited) to a positive (permissive) approach with capital transfers being allowed unless excluded. Further liberalization was then halted by the social unrest that erupted during May 1968 (*les evenements de mai*). The disruption that had began in the universities had spread to the labour markets and resulted in the foreign exchange and gold markets being closed and capital restrictions being re-introduced. Bakker (n 117) 102–3.

[125] Mr Pierre Werner, the Premier and Minister of Finance of Luxembourg, was asked to chair an ad hoc group to consider the drafting of a phased plan to set up an economic and monetary union. The failure to achieve any financial integration in Europe had been attributed to the lack of any effective economic coordination. Policy cooperation should be strengthened over two stages with a centre for economic policy decision and a Community system of central banks being set up. The exchange rate stability that would follow would then allow the progressive liberalization of capital flows. While much of the recommendations in the Werner Report were not implemented, at least, immediately in response to the report, a *Decision on the strengthening of cooperation between national central banks* was issued by the Council on 22 Mar 1971. A *Resolution on the attainment of economic and monetary union in stages* was

be considered to have been characterized by lost opportunity and general retrenchment in capital terms.

During the early 1970s, the Commission became concerned to adopt strict controls on global capital flows especially with the large speculative movements out of the US dollar that had occurred. Although it was anxious to try to promote further cooperation and coordination within Europe, the Commission was as protective of the European economic space as many national governments were of their own areas of influence and responsibility. This restrictive approach resulted, in particular, in the adoption of the 1972 European Directive on international capital flows. Further protectionist measures followed with the collapse of Bretton Woods beginning 15 August 1971[126] and with the adoption of floating currency rates and the beginning of the oil crisis in 1973. Europe was then characterized by financial disintegration as countries attempted to follow their own short term protectionist agenda. With economic divergence, it was impossible for any clear Community policy to be pursued. If anything, Commission opinion supported an inward protectionist position even with the setting up of the European Monetary System (EMS) on 13 March 1979.[127]

The restricted insular policies adopted only began to change with the abandonment of exchange controls by the United Kingdom in 1979. Restrictions on outward direct investment were abolished and portfolio investment relaxed on 18 July 1979. The Exchange Control Act 1947 was suspended on 23 October 1979 with the effect that all inward and outward restrictions were removed.[128] With the relative currency stability created under the EMS and the new liberal policy adopted by the United Kingdom as well as in Germany and the Netherlands, pressure was placed on other countries to reconsider their positions with regard to exchange controls and restrictions on the free movement of capital. The reversal of this earlier restrictive and protectionist policy began most significantly in France in

also released. This provided for the narrowing of exchange rate margins as recommended in the Werner Report although it was not possible to give this any effect before the currency turmoil of the early 1970s prevented further work. Bakker (n 117) 110–14.

126 US President, Richard Nixon, had announced on a radio broadcast the closure of the 'Gold Window' as part of his 'New Economic Policy.' The governments of foreign countries would no longer be able to present dollars for conversion into gold (at US $35 per ounce). An attempt was made to develop an alternative managed system between 1971 and 1973 although when this failed, floating rates were generally adopted (n 119 and authorities cited). Walker (n 70).

127 A Council Decision on the attainment of a high degree of convergence of economic polices had been adopted in 1974 although there was no clear enforcement mechanism and no attempt made to develop any supporting policy. National economic performances continued to diverge. It was only with the proposal to set up the EMS in 1978 that any attempt was made to return to some form of cooperative function. The EMS was proposed by the French President Valery Giscard D'Estaing and the German Chancellor Helmut Schmidt. The objective was to establish a monetary stability zone across Europe. Bakker (n 117) 136–7.

128 Japan had also abandoned its exchange controls in 1981.

March 1983 with Mitterand's Socialist government's decision to adopt a more open stability directed package of measures following a further devaluation of the franc.[129] With this change in the French position, it was quickly realized that progress may eventually be possible in Europe in the area of capital liberalization and with financial integration more generally. With these changes in national opinion, the Commission began to seize the new opportunity that was created to develop not only a European financial market place but also to complete the original common market objectives of the Treaty of Rome.[130]

The need for some progress in the area of financial policy and financial integration was highlighted by the Commission in a Communication on Financial Integration in 1983.[131] The Commission noted that despite the progress that had been achieved in other trade related areas, little had been possible in the financial area.[132] In response to this, the Commission recommended greater financial integration through the removal of capital market partitions, the actual provision of financial services on a European wide basis and the establishment of 'genuine financial unity' in Europe. This was

[129] The franc had had to be devalued in Oct 1981 (by 8.5 per cent), June 1982 (10 per cent) and Mar 1983 (8 per cent). The government had tried to follow an expansive reflationary policy against a larger global recession. Capital controls were enforced to try to isolate the national economy while financial institutions were nationalized. The new socialist government under Francois Mitterand, which had come into power in 1981, was forced to reverse its policy in light of the speculative attacks, continuing capital outflows (leakage) and the confidence crisis that ensured. Rather than withdraw from the EMS outright, it was decided to adopt a reformulated financial and industrial strategy and to open up rather than close the markets. This new stability orientated policy was largely engineered by the then Finance Minster Jacques Delors who would become the President of the Community in 1985. Bakker (n 117) 152–3.

[130] The approach adopted by the Commission had begun to swing back in favour of capital liberalization and some increased level of financial integration. While the Commission had originally supported the adoption of the first capital directive in 1961 and 1962, by the early 1970s it had become concerned to try to insulate the European financial markets from larger global pressures. The Commission would adopt a more liberal approach during the early 1980s although this was initially only directed at improving internal financial stability at the same time as continue to isolate the European market place. Molle (n 22) 154–6.

[131] Commission of the European Communities, *Financial Integration* COM(83) 207 final, (Communication from the Commission to the Council). For comment, Servais (n 43).

[132] The Commission contrasted what had been achieved with regard to goods as against the 'sluggishness of European progress in the area of finance.' The process of financial integration involved the mobilization, circulation and allocation of financial resources within the Community. Barriers operating through exchange regulations and differences in taxation and financial regulation should be removed. The Commission stated that Europe should seek to establish an open, single, homogeneous market within which operators could optimize the return on their investments by freely buying, selling and trading in financial assets with maximum mobility of capital within the financial sector. There should also be necessary mechanisms for the efficient mobilization of Community savings and their allocation to productive investment. The Commission considered that it was a significant disadvantage that Europe was not an integrated financial area and that this was a serious obstacle to reinforcing the common market, restructuring the Community economy and to stabilising the international financial system. *Financial Integration* (n 131) 7.

accompanied by measures to liberalize capital transfers and strengthen the then ecu (euro) as well as adoption of appropriate secondary measures, in particular, in the insurance, securities and banking areas. Although capital liberalization was an element of this programme, this was mainly only concerned with ecu (euro) related transfers and with supporting the use and strength of the ecu (euro).[133]

The issues raised in the 1983 paper were expanded in two further Communications in 1986[134] and 1987,[135] the second of which was accompanied by the recommendation by the Commission to proceed to the full liberalization of capital movements across Europe.[136] Progress on capital liberalization then coincided with the decision to re-launch the completion of the original free movement objectives of the Treaty with the Internal Market programme in 1985. The proposal for the completion of the Internal Market had been taken by ECOFIN in 1982[137] although it was not

133 Bakker notes that the Commission effectively sided with the French position in requiring the simultaneous strengthening of EMS mechanisms and improved procedures to secure economic convergence. Increased exchange rate stability and closer convergence would permit the sequencing of the removal of capital restraints. The Commission's 'leitmotiv was not yet capital liberalization per se, but rather the promotion of its pet child the ECU.' Bakker (n 117) 155. The Commission did not support the Monetary Committee's view that all capital restrictions should be removed. The related difficulty that had arisen was that Germany was reluctant to promote the ecu without a common monetary policy while the UK and the Netherlands would not accept any attempt to use positive discrimination of the ecu to shield Europe from the rest of the world. The Monetary Committee had been set up under Art 105(2) to promote coordination of monetary policy between the Member States (nn 155 and 157). Section I.

134 Commission of the European Communities, *Programme for the Liberalization of Capital Movement in the Community* COM(86) 292 final (Communication from the Commission to the Council). Since the 1983 Communication, capital liberalization had become one of the Community's 'top priorities' due to the new requirements of financial integration created by the adoption of the Single Act and the supposed close link between the EMS and free movement of capital. The 1986 Single Act was considered to have affirmed the need for the internal market to assume a full financial dimension since the objective of free movement by 1992 also applied to capital and financial services. The Communication distinguished between different degrees of capital liberalization (capital operations, securities related transactions and financial credits as well as money market instruments) and recommended that this be pursued in two stages. Financial integration was also considered to require parallel work in the areas of cohesion (including financial regulation and effective payment systems) and monetary policy.

135 Commission of the European Communities, *Creation of a European financial area* COM(87) 550 final, (Communication from the Commission). The 1987 Communication argued for the full liberalization of capital and had attached a draft directive as well as two further measures intended to amend the 1972 Directive on international capital flows and create a new regulation to provide medium-term balance of payment assistance. The Communication also considered the related issues of the harmonization of supervisory and prudential rules, taxation and the relationship between capital liberalization and the EMS.

136 Section I.

137 A decision had been taken in 1982 to devote a special session of the Council of Economic and Finance Ministers (ECOFIN) to deal with Internal Market matters which subsequently became referred to as the 'Jumble Council'. This brought together Ministers of the various Departments interested with Internal Market affairs. The meeting was held in Nov 1982 and led to the subsequent establishment of a new Internal Market Council which held its first meeting in Feb 1982. The new Council made little impact in developing its remit which was the

until a new Commission team had been assembled under the incoming President Jacques Delors that substantial progress was possible.[138] The objective was to ensure that all of the measures required to secure full free movement of goods and services (a customs union) and factors of production (a common market) were in place. Appropriate Treaty revisions especially with regard to decision taking and some institutional reform were given effect to under the Single Act 1986.[139] This new initiative would then

'Completion of the Internal Market' and the matter was only referred to in brief terms under the title dealing with the 'Development of Community Policies' in the Solemn Declaration on European Union signed at Stuttgart on 19 June 1983 by the Heads of Government and the Foreign Secretaries of the Member States. The attainment of the Internal Market was also removed from the agenda of the European Council meeting in Fontainebleau in June 1984. Lord Cockfield *The European Union—Creating The Single Market* (1994) 22–24.

[138] For comment, Ethan B Kapstein *Governing the Global Economy—International Finance and the State* (Harvard University Press Cambridge Mass and London 1994) 40. With the appointment of Jacques Delors to the Presidency of the European Commission in 1985, a new and impressive group of Commissioners was assembled to take forward the re-launching of the Community which had begun a few years earlier. Delors was recognized for being responsible for engineering the 'Big Bang' in French financial markets with his banking legalization bill receiving a unanimous vote in the National Assembly (n 129). Delors' new team included the appointment of Lord Arthur Cockfield as his Internal Market Commissioner (n 140).

[139] An intergovernmental conference was agreed at the Milan Summit on 28 and 29 June 1985 and the Single Act was subsequently adopted by the European Council in Luxembourg in December 1985 and signed in February 1986. The Act came into effect on 1 July 1987. This was referred to as the Single Act as the objective was to bring together in one piece of legislation all of the measures necessary to amend the Community Treaties with a view to completing the Internal Market and strengthening European political cooperation. Servais (n 43) 14–17. Art 1 refers to the objective of the European Communities and European political cooperation as being to make concrete progress towards European unity.

The major institutional success achieved was that qualified majority voting would apply to measures for the approximation of provisions laid down by law, regulation or administrative action with the objective of the completion (establishment and functioning) of the internal market (Art 100a). The Council was also entitled to use either directives (as before) or regulations for this purpose (Art 100a). These provisions supported the adoption of mutual recognition as the governing integration principle. Chapter 6, section D (1) and (2). It was, however, also provided that proposals concerning health, safety, environmental protection and consumer protection would be set at a high level of protection. A restricted safeguard measure was introduced with Member States being able to apply for national provisions to be maintained for the purposes of 'major needs' (including public morality, public order or protection of health) provided that they did not constitute arbitrary discrimination or a disguised restriction. Harmonization measures would also allow territories to take temporary exceptional measures in the event of particular difficulty.

Under Art 8a, the internal market would be achieved 'over a period expiring on 31 Dec 1992' (equal to two Commission terms). The Commission had proposed that the internal market be defined as an area without internal frontiers in which the free movement of goods, services and capital would be ensured under the same conditions as in a Member State. Ch 1 (n 3). This would have approximated the Community to a full single market such as in the United States. One of the reasons for this extended definition was indirectly to include free movement of capital as a full unqualified Treaty freedom. Following wide national objection, the reference was revised to 'in accordance with the provisions of this Treaty.' It was only agreed with regard to capital movements that the highest possible degree of liberalization was to be attained with unanimity being required to re-introduce any capital restrictions (Art 70). One of the difficulties that had arisen was that the Commission had tried to circumvent the

principally be taken forward by Jacques Delors and the UK Commissioner Lord Cockfield. Jacques Delors had been instrumental in bringing about the French 'Big Bang' which had secured capital liberalization while Margaret Thatcher and Lord Cockfield were anxious to ensure that the potential benefits that would arise with the completion of the single market in Europe were fully realized.[140]

usual negotiation procedures by not confirming relevant matters with the ECOFIN Council or the Monetary Committee in advance. Bakker (n 117) 162–3.

No progress had been possible with regard to monetary matters. It was rather confirmed that future developments in the fields of economic and monetary policy would require Treaty amendment for which unanimity would be necessary (Art 102a). The Monetary Committee and Committee of Central Bank Governors would also have to be consulted. Germany had, in particular, objected to any ill-conceived measures to confer a monetary competence on the Community that would undermine the independence of the Bundesbank. This would later be reconsidered under the Delors Committee Report in 1989. Agreement would then be possible as more time would be provided for and Ministers of Finance directly involved in the drafting (n 165).

[140] Following a dinner at 10 Downing Street in Oct 1984, Jacques Delors agreed with the British Prime Minister Margaret Thatcher that Lord Cockfield would be appointed the Commissioner responsible for the Internal Market. The scope of Cockfield's portfolio was also extended to include the whole of DG III which dealt with industry matters, DGXV financial institutions and company taxation, the Customs Union and indirect taxation which was subsequently merged to form a new DG XXI. Lord Cockfield began to prepare a complete programme for the Internal Market on the model of a British 'White Paper.' It was proposed that the 1992 programme last two Commissions which would end on 31 Dec 1992 (n 139).

In addition to proposing that a complete programme be set within a specific framework, Lord Cockfield wished to create a new 'philosophical' framework and a revised approach distinct from the traditional emphasis on goods, services, people and capital. Rather than focus on free movement directly, it was decided to stress the removal of obstacles or barriers to trade irrespective of the particular area or type of activity involved. It was also decided to treat goods and services on the same terms to attempt to correct the earlier stagnation that had arisen in the services area. To achieve these objectives, it was decided to apply a 'New Approach to Standards' based on establishing essential requirements and mutual recognition following the decision in *Cassis de Dijon* in 1979. Ch 3, section C (3); and Ch 6, section C (1) and (2). Lord Cockfield was particularly concerned to ensure that this New Approach was applied to services and goods on an equal basis.

The New Approach to Standards was set out in a Commission Communication dated 7 May 1985 which was the precursor to the 1985 White Paper. Cockfield (n 137) 39–40. The first test area for the New Approach was the field of pressure vessels in connection with which the proposed Community legislation was reduced from an estimated 500 pages (in 10 directives of 50 pages each) to 5 pages. As the New Approach was based on the removal of existing obstacles, the White Paper was structured on the basis of the treatment of Physical Barriers, Technical Barriers and Fiscal Barriers and with the removal of frontiers becoming the most important part of the new philosophy adopted. The Completion of the Internal Market was then defined as an area without internal frontiers (n 139).

The new Commission began on 6 Jan 1985. Although a meeting was held the following day, the first full meeting of the Commission was on 9 Jan 1985. Following a request by the Heads of Government in Dublin in December 1984 to ask the Council in its appropriate formations to take steps to complete the Internal Market, further meetings were held within the Commission to elaborate the ideas to be developed. Agreement with all of the other Chefs de Cabinet on the terms of the White Paper and its 300 proposals for securing the Internal Market was subsequently secured by Lord Cockfield's Chef de Cabinet Adrian Fortescue. The programme was approved by the Commission at two further meetings and formally endorsed by the Heads of Government in Milan in June 1985. Ch 6, section C (1) and (2).

The political opportunity had accordingly arisen to attempt to construct a new single financial market in Europe at the same time as the initiative was taken to complete the creation of the original common market in goods, services and labour. It must be accepted that these two parallel events or objectives were intimately connected and that the final success achieve required substantial progress on both.

I. CAPITAL AND MONETARY POLICY

Despite the importance of the New Approach advanced under the 1985 White Paper, it was not possible to make any significant progress in this area until substantial free movement of capital had been secured across Europe. This could not, in turn, be achieved until national and Commission opinion with regard to the need to maintain protective exchange control and related administrative regulations had been reassessed and a more open and liberal capital and supporting financial policy was possible.

The Treaty of Rome had only included minimal provision with regard to finance and capital related matters.[141] While more specific provision may have been discussed at drafting meetings, it was not possible to agree anything of any substance. It was then decided that while the Treaty would not provide for the further integration of such policies, it would not prevent this. An open progressive approach to capital and financial integration was accordingly adopted.[142] This policy was adopted in light of the traditional approach that governed international trade and domestic monetary and economic policy during the early 1950s. Monetary policy at that time was conducted through direct measures supported by restrictions on capital withdrawal.[143] This allowed an internal low interest rate policy to be followed with capital flight to obtain higher yields being prevented through

141 Member Sates were generally only to ensure equilibrium in their overall balance of payments, confidence in the currency, a high level of employment and stable prices (Art 104). These objectives were to be achieved through the coordination of national economic policies (Art 105) and especially cyclical polices (Art 103), stabilization of exchange rates (Art 107) and, to the extent necessary, assistance with balance of payments difficulties.

142 The only matter that was prohibited was budgetary policy under Art 199. The budget of the Community had to balance with any short falls being made up by Member State contributions. The Community was not to be permitted to raise money through taxes or capital market borrowing. Molle (n 22) 404.

143 Capital restrictions could generally be imposed either through: (a) administrative controls on cross-border capital movement; (b) a dual or multiple exchange rate system (with a separate 'financial rate' for capital and certain current account transactions); (c) imposition of additional tax charges on financial flows or income on external investments; and (d) other indirect restrictions or regulations such as limitations on interest payments on deposit accounts held by non-residents, provisions on the net external positions of commercial banks or equivalent provision. Bakker (n 117), ch 2, 11–14.

exchange controls.[144] It was generally accepted that it was impossible to balance a fixed exchange rate policy, monetary autonomy and free movement of capital.[145] Capital measures and an active control policy were accordingly considered necessary which policy was reflected in the original Treaty drafting.

The Treaty included a number of provisions on capital and current payments as well as exchange rate policies, economic policy and balance of payments. The general objective was to create a framework for consultation and cooperation with necessary corrective action being possible in appropriate circumstances. This was nevertheless to be achieved without undermining the sovereign autonomy of the Member States in these areas. The Treaty basis for the free movement of capital was Article 67(1) which provided for the progressive abolition of restrictions but only to the extent necessary to ensure the proper functioning of the common market.[146] Supporting provisions were included with regard to capital markets and credit systems, progressive liberalization, a general standstill, reporting of third country transfers and a corrective action clause (both with and without Commission approval).[147] Current payments were dealt with under

[144] Artificially low interest rates could be imposed supported by other direct controls on banks' assets and liabilities. Capital outflows to secure higher returns would then have to be prevented. Credit ceilings could also be imposed with restrictions on capital inflows to prevent avoidance. Direct monetary controls and capital restrictions were considered to be mutually inter-dependent and self-sustaining. Bakker (n 117) 3.

[145] This was variously referred to as the 'incompatible triangle'. This idea was associated with optimum currency theory in the 1960s. Bakker (n 117) 4. See also McDonald and Dearden (n 25); and Servais (n 43).

[146] Art 67(1) provides that Member States shall to the extent necessary to ensure the proper functioning of the common market progressively abolish between themselves all restrictions on the movement of capital belonging to persons resident in Member States and any discrimination based on the nationality or on the place of residence of the parties or the place where such capital is invested. This is subject to the common market proviso referred to, only applies with regard to intra-market transfers, may be complied with at any stage during the transitional period and includes an extended discrimination test in addition to the basic prohibition.

[147] Where capital restrictions apply to domestic rules governing the capital market and credit system, these must be applied in a non-discriminatory manner (Art 68(2)). The progressive liberalization of capital is to be given effect to through directives adopted following consultation with the Monetary Committee (Art 69).

Member States are to endeavour to avoid introducing any new exchange restrictions on the movement of capital and current payments nor make such rules more restrictive (Art 71, para 1). They also declare their readiness to go further than the degree of liberalization of capital provided for under the Treaty to the extent that their economic situations especially with regard to their balance of payments may permit (Art 71, para 2). The Commission may make recommendations in this regard after consulting with the Monetary Committee (Art 71, para 3).

The Commission is to be informed of any movements of capital to and from third countries (Art 72). The Commission may give its opinion to the Member State or states concerned as it considers appropriate.

The Commission may authorize any Member State to take protective measures in the field of capital where capital movements have led to disturbances in the functioning of its capital market. The Commission must consult with the Monetary Committee although the Council

Articles 67(2) and 106(1)[148] with the difference between current payments and capital movement being that payments related to transfers in consideration of underlying transactions. Separate provisions were included with regard to exchange rate policy,[149] economic policy[150] and balance of payments[151] with an extended corrective action procedure in the event of balance of payment difficulties.[152]

has authority to revoke the authorization or amend any conditions attached by qualified majority (Art 73(1)). Member States may take any such measures on their own initiative where this is necessary on the grounds of secrecy or urgency. The Commission and the other Member States should be informed with the Commission being able to decide after consulting with the Monetary Committee whether the measures adopted should be amended or abolished (Art 73(2)).

148 Under Art 67(2), current payments connected with the movement of capital between Member States are to be free from all restrictions by the end of the first stage of the transitional period at the latest. Each Member State also undertakes to authorize any payments connected with the movement of goods, services or capital and any transfers of capital and earnings to the extent that the movement of goods, services or capital and persons has been liberalized under the Treaty (Art 106(1), para 1). Member Sates also declare their readiness to go further in so far as their economic situation and balance sheet permit (Art 106(1), para 2).

149 Each Member State is to treat its exchange rate policy as a matter of common concern (Art 107(1)). The Commission may authorize alterations to exchange rates which would otherwise interfere with balance of payments (under Art 104) and distort competition but only for a limited period and subject to such conditions as may be specified (Art 107(2)).

The progressive coordination of exchange rate policies in connection with capital movements between Member States and third countries was to be secured through directives with the Council aiming to achieve the highest possible degree of liberalization (Art 70(1)). Member States were to be as liberal as possible in granting exchange authorizations (Art 68(1)). Member States were also to endeavour to avoid introducing any new exchange restrictions on the movement of capital and current payments nor make such rules more restrictive (Art 71, para 1).

150 Each Member State is to pursue the economic policy needed to ensure the equilibrium of its overall balance of payments and to maintain confidence in its currency while taking care to ensure a high level of employment and stable level of prices (Art 104). For this purpose, Member States are to coordinate their economic policies and for this purpose provide for cooperation between their appropriate administrative departments and their central banks (Art 105(1)). The Commission is to make recommendations to the Council on how this should be achieved.

151 Member States are to pursue the economic policy needed to ensure the equilibrium of its overall balance of payments (Art 104).

152 The Commission is to investigate the position of any Member State in difficulties or threatened with difficulties concerning its balance of payments where such difficulties may jeopardize the functioning of the common market or the progressive implementation of the common commercial policy. The Commission is to state which measures it recommends the State to take (Art 108(1), para 1). The Commission may recommend that the Council grant mutual assistance where the measures suggested are insufficient and after consulting with the Monetary Committee (Art 108(1), para 2). Mutual assistance is to be provided by directive or decision with such conditions as may be considered necessary (Art 108(1)). If this assistance is still insufficient, the Commission may authorize the Member State to take protective measures on such conditions as may be specified (Art 108(3)).

Where a sudden crisis in the balance of payments occurs and a decision is not immediately taken by the Council as provided for under Art 108(2), the Member State may take necessary protective measures provided that these cause the least possible disturbance to the functioning of the common market and are not wider in scope than strictly necessary to remedy the diffi-

The effect of these measures was to bring financial policy within the scope of competence of the Community but without undermining the original authority of the Member States with regard to their management and control. The Treaty had accordingly adopted a 'dualist' approach with regard to capital and financial matters. Exchange rate, economic and monetary policy were made issues of 'common concern' although national sovereign autonomy was preserved. Financial policy was brought within the general scope of Community activity but without imposing any automatic obligations on Member State governments in this regard. The same cautious approach has been adopted by the European Court of Justice in its decisions concerning capital and financial policy.[153] The Commission would also adopt a permissive approach to the exercise of safeguard clauses by a number of Member States to protect national interests although it became increasingly clear that these were of little use in practice.[154]

To deal with the institutional gap that was left with regard to monetary and economic policy, the Treaty provided for the establishment of a Monetary Policy Committee.[155] Other committees and sub-committees were set up although none had the same formal Treaty status as the Monetary Committee.[156] The original functions of the Monetary

culties that have arisen (Art 109(1)). The Commission and other Member States are to be informed and the Commission may recommend to the Council that mutual assistance is provided under Art 108 (Art 109(2)). The Council may by qualified majority decide that the State amend, suspend or abolish the protective measures adopted following receipt of an opinion from the Commission and after the Monetary Committee has been consulted (Art 109(3)).

[153] See, eg, Case 7/78 *Thompson* (financial, real and monetary capital distinguished); Case 203/80 (Art 67 did not have direct effect); Case 286/82 and 26/83 *Luisi & Carbone* (capital and current payments distinguished); and Case 157/85 *Brugnoni & Ruffinengo* (administrative restrictions to be removed with regard to liberalized transactions).

[154] (nn 161 and 162).

[155] The Monetary Committee was set up under Art 105(2). This provides for the establishment of a committee to promote coordination of the policies of the Member States 'in the monetary field to the full extent needed for the functioning of the common market.'

[156] A Committee on Short-Term Economic Trends was set up in 1960 to coordinate economic policy. A Committee on Budget Policy and a Medium-Term Economic Policy Committee were established in 1964. The three committees were subsequently merged into a single Economic Policy Committee although this operated through three sub-committees in each of the relevant areas. Council Decision of 18 Feb 1974. The only other two committees provided for expressly under the Treaty were the Transport Committee (Art 83) and the Economic and Social Committee (Art 193).

The Committee of Central Bank Governors (CCBG) was set up separately in 1964 (Art 105(1)) to promote further cooperation and to consider monetary policy issues from a central bank perspective. This overlapped with the meetings of central bank governors conducted through the Bank for International Settlements in Basel. Walker (n 70), ch 1, section 4. The CCBG could to some extent be considered to have formed an European sub-group of the larger BIS operation. The CCBG and the Monetary Committee were then included within Art 102A by the Single Act 1986 with the effect that both had to be consulted on institutional changes in the monetary area. The CCBG was replaced by the European Monetary Institute (EMI) under Maastricht Treaty. The EMI was subsequently transformed into the European Central Bank (ECB). (nn 164 and 165).

Committee were to review relevant monetary and financial matters and report regularly as well as provide opinions on its own initiative or as requested.[157] These have been considerably extended subsequently. While the functions with regard to monetary policy specifically have since been removed under the Maastricht Treaty arrangements, the Committee still carries out a number of key tasks.[158] Despite its importance, the Committee is unique both in terms of its composition and operation.[159] It was largely due to the high level of understanding and cooperation possible through the confidential nature of the Committee's proceedings that substantial progress was possible initially in the area of capital movement and then economic and monetary union.[160]

The traditional consensus that fixed exchange and capital controls were necessary to protect national monetary and economic policy also changed during the late 1970s and early 1980s. While Germany had adopted an open capital regime since the 1950s, some exchange controls were relaxed in the United Kingdom early 1979 and then completely abolished in late 1979. This was followed by France in 1983. By this time, it had become increasingly clear that capital controls were substantially ineffective while the most efficient allocation of resources was distorted and competition and innovation restricted. Foreign investment was inhibited while the national bureaucratic systems necessary to operate the controls were costly to maintain and open to abuse.[161] It was accordingly generally accepted that countries

157 The Monetary Committee was to keep under review the monetary and financial situation of the Member States and of the Community and the general payments system of the Member States and report regularly to the Council and the Commission. It was also to deliver opinions at the request of the Council or Commission or on its own initiative (Art 105(2)).

158 The Statutes of the Monetary Committee were approved by the ECOFIN Council on 25 Feb 1958. Further functions were assigned at that time as well as under subsequent secondary measures. The Committee's early functions included preparation of multilateral surveillance of economic policies, oversight of economic convergence programmes, examination of economic consequences of the Common Agricultural Policy, surveillance of credit facilities and international relations. Its other tasks included a *tour d'horizon* of recent policy measures and economic developments, preparation of a biannual statement to the Interim Committee on behalf of the Community, and bilateral discussions with prospective Member States. Bakker (n 117) 61–5.

159 The Member States and the Commission each appointed two members to the Monetary Committee (Art 105(2), para 2).

160 The Monetary Committee would, in particular, assume the lead in developing financial cooperation and financial related initiatives during the 1980s. Between 1979 and 1981, the work of the Committee focused on preparations for the establishment of an European Monetary Fund which was to come into operation within two years of the setting up of the EMS. This did not come to anything and the Committee focused on financing balance of payments deficits after the second oil crisis in 1979. Beginning in 1982, the Committee would assume the primary role in promoting capital liberalization. Bakker (n 117), ch 7.

161 Capital controls increasingly demonstrated a low degree of effectiveness in operation, were considered to undermine economic discipline, restricted the international development of local financial centres and appeared to involve substantial unjustifiable costs to administer. Bakker (n 117) 3 and 22–4.

should move toward a more liberal capital position with monetary and related functions being carried on through open market operations and other indirect rather than direct forms of control.

With this shift in capital policy, the Commission was able to propose extensions to the original 1960 and 1962 Capital Directives in 1986 and then the full liberalization of capital movement in 1987.[162] This new liberalization policy was given effect to under the 1988 Capital Directive.[163] Full free movement of capital was then eventually achieved in 1990 although some Member States were permitted to operate under an extended transitional period and with Greece ensuring full free movement by May 1994.

With this major obstacle to financial integration having been removed, it was possible to consider further initiatives. It was accordingly recommended that further work was undertaken with regard to economic and

[162] The approach of the Commission had also changed by 1984 and 1985. Until then, the Commission had adopted a permissive policy with regard to the use of capital safeguard clauses which contributed to the continued fragmentation of the European market place. The Commission had also become aware that the policy to promote the ecu through positive discrimination would also be insufficient. This discrimination policy was severely criticized by Germany, Denmark, the Netherlands and the United Kingdom during the Monetary Committee's meetings in 1983 and 1984. These discussions began in Venice in Autumn 1983. Any measures designed only to promote the ecu in isolation or enlarge financing mechanisms without progress on capital movements and monetary and financial convergence were rejected. A package deal was then gradually put together which would 'trade-off' EMS improvements as against larger capital and financial integration. Following Denmark's decision to remove all remaining capital restrictions on I Jan 1984, the Commission agreed to enter into discussions with France, Italy and Ireland on their continued reliance on the safeguard measures. Bakker (n 117) 156–8.

The issues of economic convergence, financial integration and the strengthening of the EMS were discussed at the ECOFIN meeting in Rambouillet on 12 May 1984. The Monetary Committee considered a report in Sept 1984 by its Alternates under Jean-Jacques Rey from the Belgium National Bank. Under Michel Camdessus, the Monetary Committee agreed that a policy of 'active gradualism' would be adopted with regard to the removal of capital restrictions while measures would be adopted to strengthen the EMS. This was accepted at the ECOFIN Meeting at Dromoland Castle in Ireland in Oct 1984. More detailed proposals to strengthen the operation of the EMS rather than simply follow a policy of positive discrimination were to be taken forward by the Committee of Central Bank Governors (CCBG).

Capital restrictions were examined by the Monetary Committee in Dec 1984 although a disagreement developed between the Committee and the Commission as to the scope of the review. This was the first time that the restrictions had been examined by the Committee since 1965. The Commission had tried to argue that the Committee could only consider the possibility of liberalization but not the safeguards as such. It was agreed that both would in future monitor the safeguards more strictly. It was also agreed that the remaining French controls would be removed within two years and those in Ireland and Italy within three years. Bakker (n 117) 160–2.

[163] Council Directive 88/361 OJ 1988 L 178/5. For discussion, John Usher *The Law of Money and Financial Services in the EU* (2nd edn Oxford 2000); and Usher 'Financial Services, Taxation and Monetary Movements' in Mads Andenas and Wulf-Henning Roth *Services and Free Movement in EU Law* (OUP 2002), ch 14. See also Weatherill and Beaumont (n 92), ch 21; and Jan Dalhuisen 'Financial Liberalisation and Re-regulation' in Andenas and Roth, ch 10.

monetary union beginning late 1987.[164] Following a report by Jacques Delors and two inter-governmental conferences later,[165] the Maastricht Treaty was signed on 7 February 1992 with Economic and Monetary Union coming into effect on 2000 and the full replacement of original national coinage with the Euro on 1 January 2001.

J. BANKING AND FINANCIAL PROGRAMME

The creation of a single market in banking and financial services has generally been dealt with separately from the work undertaken with regard to free movement of capital and financial policy more generally. These functions have been managed within separate Directorates and distinct teams in the Commission. It must nevertheless be accepted that it would not have been possible to secure the full free movement of financial services until capital liberalization had been achieved. As noted, a soft dualist approach had been adopted in this area which meant that Member States were never under any Treaty obligation to liberate their capital and related financial policies. This was then strengthened through the 'active gradualism' adopted in the capital area.[166] While the banking and capital programmes were being developed separately from the capital negotiations that, in particular, took place within the Monetary Committee, it must be accepted that it was only when full free movement of capital was agreed that it was

[164] The French government had proposed monetary convergence and the establishment of a European Central Bank in 1987. A 'pact' was entered into with Germany at the end of June 1988 for further study of the possible stages for the establishment of the new central bank. The idea had been advanced by the French Finance Minister Balladur and received with interest by Hans-Dietrich Genscher, the German Minister of Foreign Affairs. See, for example, lecture by Balladur in Frankfurt on 2 July 1987 reproduced in *Auszuge aus Presseartikeln*, Deutsche Bundesbank, 3 July 1987. The French position had changed from proposing further reform of the EMS system which would always be qualified by the independence of the Bundesbank to placing monetary policy under common management through the establishment of a new central bank. Genscher also recognized the larger political advantage of monetary unification. Bakker (n 117) 228.

[165] It was agreed at the European Council Meeting in Hanover on 27 and 28 June 1988 that a committee of central bank governors and independent experts would be set up to take concrete steps towards the establishment of economic and monetary union. The Committee was to be chaired by Jacques Delors. The report was presented in June 1989 at the European Council Meeting in Madrid. The need for further economic policy coordination was stressed and the success already achieved with capital liberalization and the integration of banking and financial markets. The report recommended that an independent system of central bank governors was set up to ensure price stability of the new currency. The report was partially accepted at the Madrid meeting and it was agreed that the first stage would begin on 1 July 1990. Two inter-governmental conferences (IGCs) were convened to consider European Monetary Union and European Political Union. The IGCs were conducted under the Luxembourg and Dutch presidencies. The final reports were produced in 1991 and final text agreed at Maastricht on 7 Feb 1992.

[166] Section I.

possible to begin to complete the work necessary to secure full free movement of banking and financial services.

Banking and financial activities are dealt with under the general Treaty provisions governing establishment and services. Banking and some other services were included in the General Programmes adopted under Treaty. The only reference in the original Treaty provisions to banking, however, was in Article 61(1) and the original version of Article 57(2) which provided that harmonization in the field of banking would take place with the progressive liberalization of capital movements within the Community.[167]

The effect of these limited references was to leave a policy vacuum in the banking and financial area.[168] Banking and financial services did not appear to have been expressly or specifically considered in the negotiation and adoption of the various decisions, conference resolutions and treaties creating the new structure created. This means that the access and regulatory policy followed cannot be dealt with only in terms of the directives adopted in this area but must also be considered in terms of the whole body of Community law and relevant governing principles.

A number of omission or gap theories can be developed to attempt to explain the underlying policy vacuum left in the Treaty of Rome in the banking and financial area. These can generally be considered in terms of a relevance or trade theory, a sensitivity (or damage), a programme (evolution or negotiation) theory, a revision (integration or capital) theory or an amendment (or correction) theory.[169] The reason for the omission is unclear and undocumented. In the light of the importance of the effective operation of banking and financial markets as independent commercial sectors and as key supporting facilities within the economy, the absence of any express provision in this regard is particularly significant.

The absence of any specific provision is possibly best understood in terms of a combination or partial combination of each theory. The importance of banking and financial markets was possibly not fully understood during the early and mid-1950s. The focus was then on traditional trade theory with fixed interest rates and direct monetary controls supported by restrictions on capital movements. Market regulation was not considered to be as important, in particular, to the extent that the activities of banks on

[167] Section A. Ch 1 (n 32).

[168] For the purposes of this text, banking or banking and financial policy is concerned with the measures adopted with regard to the supervision and regulation of banks and other financial intermediaries. On the meaning of the terms supervision and regulation, chapter 1 (n 2). Financial policy by itself refers to all of the related polices that may be adopted in the financial area including exchange rate and monetary policy and any sub-polices within these more general headings (n 114). Ch 6, section B (1).

[169] Ch 1, section B (1) (n 36).

the European continent were already substantially constrained.[170] To the extent that their activities were not directly controlled, the focus was on preventing market inefficiency from arising through competition and dominant position law. Appropriate provision was included in this regard in the Treaty, in particular, at the insistence of German government representatives.[171]

With regard to international financial markets, it has to be accepted that the substantial expansion of the Eurodollar markets did not begin in London until the late-1950s and early-1960s. No attempt would also then be made to agree any cross-border supervisory or regulatory measures until the mid-1970s with the establishment of the Basel Committee on Banking Supervision by the Governors of the Central Banks of the G10 in December 1974.[172] At the national level, banking and financial markets were important although their operation and potential volatility was restricted through direct monetary controls. Market regulation would then have been considered an ancillary aspect of economic and financial management. The need for a specific policy in this regard may then not have been recognized or only treated as an aspect of larger monetary and financial cooperation.

It must also have been recognized that banking and financial market control was a sensitive and difficult area. Attempting to agree any formal provision in this regard would have led to protracted negotiations that could have delayed or obstructed any agreement on other important policy matters.[173] Rather than deal with the matter expressly, it would have been preferable only to include more general provision and leave the issue for subsequent reconsideration and negotiation over time.[174] Free movement would initially have been secured between banks and financial institutions. Any anti-competitive practices would be controlled through competition law and more general monetary or financial cooperation could be dealt with over time at Council level.

The draftsmen may also have recognized that if the need for an express or substantial regulatory policy became necessary, this could be adopted through the use of any of the main legislative measures available (regulations,

[170] Under a Relevance or Trade Theory, the draftsman may then have deliberately omitted financial regulation to the extent that it did not fall within a narrowly defined range of regional trading objectives with any further rules on more complex financial integration having been considered irrelevant or unnecessary. Ch 1 (n 36).

[171] This was important under German Ordo-liberal theory (n 104). Ch 1 (n 78).

[172] Walker (n 70), Chs 1 and 2.

[173] With a Sensitivity or Damage Theory, concerns may have arisen that attempting to agree any more complete set of rules on banking and financial markets may have delayed or prevented the successful conclusion of agreement on other trade related matters. Ch 1 (n 36).

[174] It may simply have been considered sufficient to include banks and other financial institutions within the General Programmes provided for under Treaty with regulatory or supervisory issues being examined during the course of the later negotiations in each particular area. This may be referred to as a Programme (Evolution or Negotiation) Theory. Ch 1 (n 36).

directives or decisions)[175] or through subsequent Treaty amendment.[176] This would again reflect the fundamental *traité cadre* and dynamic nature of the European integration process.

Despite the absence of clear Treaty direction, banking and financial markets are important as significant commercial sectors and in terms of the essential support functions provided. The other trade related objectives of the original free trade area and customs union would not have been possible without effective savings, credit and payment services across Europe. The intended single market in services would also have been incomplete without the inclusion of banking and other financial intermediaries. Although possibly not fully recognized at the time of signature, the stability of the new economy created was also to a large extent dependent upon the stable and effective operation of each of the separate local markets (and sub-markets) involved and of the regional trading system as a whole. It was accordingly necessary for all of these reasons that a clear, complete and effective policy was created over time. The development and content of this policy is considered in further detail in the following chapters.

[175] Under a Revision Theory, any further measures could be agreed and adopted over time as necessary. With a more specific Capital Theory, any immediate progress in the banking and financial area would not be necessary due to the assumed capital restrictions that prevailed. Relevant measures could then be adopted subsequently once a sufficient degree of liberalization had been secured in this area. Section I and Chapter 1 (n 36).

[176] Necessary policy including any additional legal authority or formal powers could alternatively be provided through Treaty Amendment or Correction.

PART THREE

Judicial Policy Construction

3

European Court of Justice—Judicial Policy Construction and Effect

In initially considering the evolution of policy in the banking and financial area, it is necessary to assess the nature and importance of the contribution of the European Court of Justice. Despite the continuing efforts of the Commission and the Council of Ministers since the establishment of the original European Economic Community in 1958, it was not possible to develop any clear or coherent policy and programme of supporting secondary measures certainly before the end of the transitional period on 31 December 1969. It was only following the limited progress that was possible during this period that the Court began to assume a more dominant role in the development of many of the most important provisions in the Treaty especially in the law of free movement. Banking and financial services were then not considered separately by the Court during the early stages of this judicial revisionism or reform although all of the original general principles developed are capable of equal application while some more recent specific guidance has been provided in these areas. It is accordingly necessary to attempt to assess the assistance provided by the more general case law in this area as well as the more recent particular financial matters that the Court has commented on.

In considering the contribution of the Court, two related sets of issues have to be taken into account in connection with its constitutional function and role within the European institutional system set up under the Treaty of Rome and with regard to the content of the emerging substantive law still under construction.

In connection with its constitutional role, the contribution of the Court has been significant although the inherent limitations that arise within any judicial function more generally and within the specific operational procedures adopted by the European Court cannot be ignored. The judicial function within any modern legal system is necessarily limited to the extent that laws are enacted by the legislator which the courts will then only interpret and apply. Even where courts have historically been able to make some more substantial and original contribution to the development of relevant legal principle, this has tended to be based on existing customary rules or other accepted standards of behaviour or more general commercial or mercantile practice. Despite this traditional position, the European

Court of Justice has been able to a significant extent to assume a unique original policy role within the European legal system although the nature and limits of its function cannot be ignored.

The specific operational procedures adopted by the Court have also necessarily limited its potential contribution in certain important respects. The need for consensus, confidentiality and the production of a single composite decision have meant that the judicial function within Europe has been fundamentally opaque at the same time as the absence of any system of formal precedence means that obvious inconsistencies and disparities have arisen which adds further incoherence on to an already essentially non-transparent system. The fundamentally selective or accidental nature of the court process more generally also means that the total body of European law constructed will necessarily always be incomplete at any particular time. Each of these factors have to be taken into account in attempting to understand the contribution of the Court in this area.

With regard to substantive law, the two further issues that arise are concerned with the evolving nature of the Court's jurisprudence and the consequently amended policy base for the secondary legislative programmes adopted. While a number of more general and specific principles have been confirmed by the Court in the development of the law of free movement, problems continue to arise in determining the limits of many of the core concepts created. The main issue that has still not been confirmed is whether a discrimination (direct and indirect) or effects based test should be adopted in determining the scope of the underlying prohibitions set out in the Treaty of Rome in the area of free movement. In practice, a sort of combined or double test or approach is often applied although the limits of this are still not clear. Related problems then arise in confirming the nature and content of the parallel judicial derogation that has also been constructed. This will, in particular, necessarily vary with the scope of the underlying Treaty restrictions imposed. Whether an identical or, at least, equivalent approach should be adopted in each of the sub-areas of the law of free movement (goods, workers, establishment, services and capital) is also still not clear. Further difficulties then arise in relating these judicial principles fully and consistently with the separate policy components or more general doctrines and design rules developed by the Commission and Council in constructing the secondary legislative programmes adopted (including, in particular, mutual recognition, minimum harmonization and home country control).

Each of these issues has to be taken into account in attempting to understand and assess the significance and value of the judicial contribution to policy construction within the law of free movement more generally and in the banking and financial area specifically.

The structure of this chapter is as follows. The composition and function of the European Court of Justice is initially noted including the Treaty base for its powers of judicial intervention. Some of the more important constitutional decisions of the Court are referred to which confirm or, at least, anticipate the significance of the overall or total contribution made by the Court in many core areas of European integration policy. The nature and content of the law of free movement is then examined in further detail. The law relating to goods is considered by way of background to the development of the parallel principles adopted in the areas of establishment and services. Reference is also made to related developments in the area of workers. The objective is to identify the key principles underlying the more general law of free movement and to assess their relevance and application in the area of banking and financial services. Some provisional conclusions are drawn with regard to the contribution of the Court in the construction of some form of more complete or coherent policy in this area.

The Commission's restatement of relevant principles of Community law in the banking area with its 1987 Interpretative Communication and the more recent particular cases in which the Court has been able to consider particular aspects of modern banking and financial practice are examined in the following Chapter.

A. JUDICIAL FUNCTION

The essential function of the European Court of Justice is to ensure that the law is observed in the interpretation and application of the Treaty.[1] The Court now consists of over twenty-five Judges and is assisted by a number of Advocates General.[2] The Court generally sits in plenary (full) session

[1] Art 220 (ex Art 164). For discussion, S Weatherill and P Beaumont *EU Law* (3rd edn Penguin London 1999), ch 6; AM Arnull, AA Dashwood, MG Ross and DA Wyatt *European Union Law* (4rd edn Sweet & Maxwell London 2000); P Craig and G de Burca *EU Law* (3rd edn OUP Oxford 2002). See also L Neville Brown and Tom Kennedy *The Court of Justice of the European Communities* (5th edn London Sweet & Maxwell 2000); Anthony Arnull *The European Union and its Court of Justice* (OUP Oxford 1999); TC Hartley *The Foundations of European Community Law* (OUP 4th edn 1998); and T Tridimas *The General Principles of EC Law* (OUP Oxford 1999).

[2] Art 221 (ex 165), para 1 and Art 222 (ex 166), para 1. The functions of the Advocate General are to provide reasoned submissions in open court on cases brought before the Court to assist it in the performance of its functions of interpreting and applying the Treaty. Advocates General must act with complete impartiality and independence. The number may be increased by the Council (acting unanimously) at the request of the Court. Art 222 (ex 166), paras 2 and 3. The number of judges was increased from fifteen to twenty-five following the most recent enlargement. Ch 1, section F(1).

although chambers may be set up consisting of three, five or seven Judges.[3] The Court appoints its own Registrar and rules governing service.[4]

The main Court is supported by a Court of First Instance which was established to hear and determine certain specific classes of action or proceeding.[5] Appointment qualifications are more relaxed for the Court of First Instance although Judges again act on six year renewable terms with half being replaced or re-appointed every three years.[6]

In addition to its general functions of ensuring that the law is observed in the interpretation and application of the Treaty, the Court hears a number of specific remedial actions provided for in the Treaty. These include actions against a Member State for failing to fulfil an obligation under the Treaty[7] and actions by Member States against other States[8] with the Court being able to direct the State concerned to take necessary measures to comply with the judgment issued.[9] The Court may be given

[3] Art 221 (ex 165), para 2. Chambers are used either to undertake certain preparatory enquiries or to adjudicate on particular categories of cases in accordance with the rules laid down for these purposes. The Court must sit in plenary session when a Member State or a Community institution is a party and so requests (para 3). The number of Judges may be increased by the Council acting unanimously at the request of the Court (para 4). A ninth Advocate General was appointed between 1 Jan 1995 and 6 Oct 2000. On enlargement (n 2) and Ch 1, section E (1).

The Judges and Advocates General are chosen from persons whose independence is beyond doubt and who possess the requisite qualifications for appointment to the highest judicial offices in their countries or are jurisconsults of recognized competence. Appointments are for six years with half being replaced every three years. Art 223 (ex 167), paras 1 and 2. Eight and seven Judges are replaced alternatively every three years. Advocates General are also replaced every three years with four being changed on each. Judges and Advocates General are eligible for re-appointment. Art 223 (ex 167), para 3.

The President of the Court is appointed by the judges from among their own members for a three year term subject to re-election. Art 223 (ex 167), para 4.

[4] Art 224 (ex 168).

[5] The Council determines the classes of action or proceeding to be considered before the Court of First Instance on the request of the Court and after consulting the European Parliament and Commission. The Council must act unanimously. The Council will also determine the composition of the Court and adopt necessary adjustments and additional provisions to the Statute of the Court of Justice. Art 225 (ex 168a), para 2. Actions before the Court of First Instance are always subject to appeal on points of law to the Court. Art 225 (ex 168a), para 1. The Court of First Instance has established its own Rules of Procedure in agreement with the Court (subject to unanimous approval by the Council). Art 225 (ex 168a), para 4.

[6] Art 225 (ex 168a), para 3.

[7] The Commission is required to deliver a reasoned opinion where it considers that a Member State has failed to fulfil an obligation under the Treaty after giving the State the opportunity to submit observations. If the State does not comply with the opinion within the period laid down by the Commission, the matter may be brought before the Court. Art 226 (ex 169).

[8] A Member State which considers that another State has failed to fulfil an obligation under the Treaty may bring the matter before the Court. The matter must initially have been brought before the Commission which is to deliver a reasoned opinion after which the State is given the opportunity to submit its case and observations either orally or in writing. The absence of any opinion by the Commission for three months does not prevent the matter from being brought before the Court. Art 226 (ex 170).

[9] Art 228 (ex 171). If the Commission considers that a State has not taken any necessary

unlimited jurisdiction with regard to penalties under regulations adopted by the Parliament and the Council.[10] The Court is to review the legality of acts adopted by the Parliament and Council or acts of the Council, the Commission and European Central Bank as well as acts of the Parliament intended to produce legal effect with regard to third parties.[11] Where the Parliament, Council or Commission has failed to act, an action may be brought before the Court by any Member State or other institution.[12] When an institution's act has been declared void or the institution has failed to act, it will be required to take necessary measures.[13]

The Court may issue preliminary rulings on the interpretation of the Treaty, the validity and interpretation of acts of any institution and interpretation of the statutes of bodies established by the Council.[14] The Court also has jurisdiction in actions for damages, staff matters and European Investment Bank issues.

In discharging its functions especially with regard to the consideration of preliminary rulings, the Court has been required to comment on the nature of the European legal system as well as determine a number of significant constitutional and other substantive law issues.[15] The substantive work of

measures, the reasoned opinion procedure will apply again with the Commission bringing the matter before the Court in the event that no action is taken within the time limit set. The Commission will specify the amount or lump sum or penalty payment that it considers appropriate with the Court determining which sum may be imposed. Art 228 (ex Art 171), para. 2.

[10] Art 229 (ex 172).

[11] Art 230 (ex 173). For this purpose, the Court is to have jurisdiction in actions brought by the Member States, the Council or the Commission on grounds of lack of competence, infringement of an essential procedural requirement, infringement of the Treaty or of any rule of law relating to its application or misuse of powers. The Court has the same jurisdiction in actions brought by the Parliament, the Court of Auditors or by the European Central Bank for the purpose of protecting their prerogatives. Any natural or legal person may institute proceedings against a decision addressed to them or which is otherwise of direct and individual concern. Proceedings must be instituted within two months of the publication of the measure or its notification failing which the day on which it came to the knowledge of the person concerned. Art 230 (ex Art 173), paras 2, 3, 4 and 5. If the action is well-founded, the Court is to declare the act concerned to be void although it may declare certain effects of a regulation to be considered as definitive. Art 231 (ex Art 174).

[12] Art 232 (ex 175). The institution concerned must first be called to act. The institution will have two months to define its position failing which action may be commenced within a further two months. Natural or legal persons may complain to the Court that a Community institution has failed to address to that person any act (other than a recommendation or an opinion). The Court has equivalent jurisdiction in proceedings brought by the European Central Bank in actions falling within its competence and actions or proceedings against it. Art 232 (ex Art 175), paras 2, 3 and 4.

[13] Art 233 (ex 176),

[14] Art 234 (ex 177), para 1. Where a question has been raised before any court or tribunal in a Member State and it considers that a decision on the question is necessary to enable it to give judgement, the European Court may be requested to provide a ruling thereon. If the question is raised in a case from which there is no judicial remedy under national law, the court or tribunal must bring the matter before the Court. Art 234 (ex 177), paras 2 and 3.

[15] Section B.

the Court has, in particular, included considering the two core issues that arise within any integration system of securing effective market access at the same time as ensure a proper degree of market regulation although not in these express terms.[16]

In attempting to define the scope of relevant prohibition within its jurisprudence, the Court has developed a number of concepts including direct and indirect discrimination (or distinctly and indistinctly applicable measures). These were partly based on borrowed international provisions and especially those used in connection with the General Agreement on Tariffs and Trade (GATT).[17] It has also had to construct its own series of supporting derogations where measures have been held to be restrictive of inter-state trade and fall outside the Treaty exceptions provided but still require judicial sanction or approval. Unfortunately, the limits of these judicial constructs have still not been fully determined.

Related problems have arisen in attempting to construct a coherent body of jurisprudence across all of the separate areas of law involved including goods, establishment and services, workers and capital. The policy construction process involved has also raised related constitutional issues with regard to the validity and supremacy of European law and institutional matters in terms of securing a proper balance between the respective competencies of each of the formal agencies established under the founding Treaties and between Community and national institutions.

B. LEGAL IDENTITY, SUPREMACY, AND DIRECT EFFECT

The most significant early contributions of the European Court of Justice were made in creating or, at least, confirming the legal or constitutional character and identity of the Community especially in terms of the doctrines of supremacy and direct effect in 1963 and 1964. It had been assumed until that time that the legal effect of the original Treaty of Rome as an international agreement would be governed by the constitutional law of each Member State.[18] Subsequent supremacy would then be determined in accordance with the application of ordinary conflict laws within the national legal order. While international treaties on domestic transforma-

[16] Ch 1 (n 4) and section B (2).

[17] Section C(1) and (2).

[18] The dominant approach was based on 'Dualism' which prescribed that national legal orders were separate and that international treaties only had effect at the domestic level through recognition and national law. Under the 'Monist' approach, national legal orders were creatures of international law and therefore directly subject to them. For discussion, B de Witte 'Direct Effect, Supremacy and the Nature of the Legal Order' in Paul Craig and Grainne de Búrca *The Evolution of EU Law* (OUP Oxford 1999), ch 5, 178–180. See also P Maduro *We The Court* (Oxford Hart Publishing 1998) ch 1.

tion would supersede all earlier provision, they would themselves be overruled by later legislative enactment.

The significance of the decision by the Court in *Van Gend en Loos* in 1963 was to confirm the separate identity of the new European legal order with the parties to this new jurisdiction including individuals as well as their governments and Community institutions. The provisions of the Treaty could also have direct effect and that it was for the Court to determine which specific measures would be covered.[19] The Court separately confirmed in *Costa v ENEL* in 1964 the primacy or supremacy of Community law as against any contravening national law.[20]

[19] Case 26/62, *Van Gend en Loos v Nederlandse Administraitie der Belastingen* [1963] ECR 1, [1963] CMLR 105. Van Gend en Loos had argued that an increase in the duty on the import of chemicals from Germany into the Netherlands since the coming into force of the Treaty was contrary to Art 12. The Dutch Tariefcommissie referred two questions to the European Court of Justice the first of which asked whether Art 12 was capable of direct application and whether nationals acquired individual rights that must be protected. The Belgian, German and Netherlands governments were supported by Advocate General Roemer who considered that the question was inadmissible. The Belgian and Netherlands governments had argued that the reference related to the application rather than interpretation of the Treaty and that it was for national courts to determine the effect of an international treaty that was not intended to have domestic impact. It was claimed that the concept of direct effect would contradict the intentions of the Treaty's signatories.

The Court rejected these submissions and stated that the objective of the Treaty in establishing a Common Market implied that it was more than an agreement to create mutual obligations between contracting states. The reference to peoples as well as governments in the preambles, the establishment of institutions with sovereign rights effecting citizens and the involvement of nationals through the European Parliament confirmed this approach.

The Court accordingly concluded that the Community constituted a new legal order of international law for the benefit of which states had limited their sovereign rights (within limited fields) and the subjects of which comprised the Member States and their nationals. Community law therefore imposed obligations on individuals but also conferred rights independently of national legislation. These rights arose where they were expressly granted by the Treaty but also by reason of the obligations that the Treaty imposed in a clearly defined way upon individuals as well as the Member States and upon the institutions of the Community. For comment, see for example, de Witte (n 18).

[20] Case 6/64, *Costa (Flaminio) v ENEL* [1964] ECR 585, [1964] CMLR 425. In this case, Mr Costa had refused to pay bills to the newly created national electricity corporation and had claimed that the act of nationalising the corporation was contrary to the Treaty. In a subsequent reference, the Court confirmed that Community law prevailed over contrary national provisions. This was based on the argument that the Treaty had created its own legal order which had become an integral part of the legal systems of the Member States. With Member States having limited their sovereign rights to that extent, it was impossible for domestic provision to have primacy over European law. The obligations undertaken were also unconditional and not contingent with the direct applicability of regulations otherwise being made meaningless. For comment, Craig and de Bùrca (n 18) 258–60.

The effect of the ruling was confirmed in subsequent decisions which dismissed any examination of the nature of domestic law including constitutional provisions and stated that Community law had to be given immediate and direct effect. This extends to setting aside national rules that bar domestic courts from providing interim relief. Case 11/70, *Internationale Handelstesellschaft mbH v Einfuhr-und Vorratsstelle für Getreide und Futtermittel* [1970] ECR 1125, [1972] CMLR 255; and Case 106/727, *Amministrazione delle Finanze dello Stato v Simmenthal SpA* [1978] ECR 629, [1978] 3 CMLR 263; Case C-213/89,

The effect of these rulings was to establish the constitutional identity and effective operational supremacy of the new Community legal order as well as the directly enforceable nature of many core Treaty provisions by individuals.[21]

In terms of substantive legal development, the Court has also had to assume a direct role in the development of the Community economic order based on the four fundamental freedoms. In the absence of an effective body of supporting secondary legislative measures as intended and provided for under the Treaty, the Court has had to construct an almost wholly original new law of free movement by initially confirming the direct applicability of the core provisions in each functional area (goods, workers, services and establishment and capital) and then interpreting them to extend the scope of the prohibition to include discriminatory as well as not overtly discriminatory but still restrictive provisions. In so doing, the Court has had to confirm the limits of the restrictive doctrines set out in the Treaty as well develop its own judicial derogation to support its extended interpretation of these core prohibitions. Difficulties have subsequently arisen in arriving at a coherent and consistent jurisprudence in each area as well as in establishing some unity of comparability across the separate sectors involved.

The importance of this in the banking and financial area is that the activities of banks and related institutions are subject to the full jurisprudence of the Court in connection with activities not covered by the secondary measures adopted. Although a substantial programme of supporting legislative provision has been agreed,[22] significant gaps remain at the same time as a large degree of uncertainty arises with regard to the meaning and application of these measures in many respects. The nature of the judicial principles developed by the Court are considered in the remainder of this and the following Chapter and the content and value of the parallel secondary programme of measures constructed in the subsequent Chapter.

R v Secretary of State for Transport, Ex parte Factortame Ltd and others [1990] ECR I-2433, [1990] 3 CMLR 1. For comment on some of the main decisions by the House of Lords in the UK, Ch 4, section D(2) (n 177).

Despite the apparent absolutism demonstrated by the Court in this regard, the effectiveness of this doctrine is still strictly dependent upon national acceptance and application (n 18). For further discussion, J Weiler 'The Community System: The Dual Character of Supranationalism' (1981) 1 YBEL 267. See also de Witte (n 18).

[21] Despite this, the precise nature of the Community is still far from clear in more general theoretical terms. On relevant international law approaches (n 18). On market and social balance Ch 1, section E (4) and (nn 75–8). On the distinct theories attached to the development of European integration including functionalism, neo-functionalism, neo-realism (or liberal intergovernmentalism), neo-federalism and new institutionalism (or multi-level governance analysis), Ch 1, section E (5) and (n 87) and Ch 2, section A and (nn 12–20). On the new economic and legal order created, Ch 2, section F.

[22] Ch 5.

C. LAW OF FREE MOVEMENT OF GOODS

In examining the emerging law of free movement, it is necessary to consider each of the constituent areas involved separately in light of their distinct underlying Treaty base as well as factual relevance and possible effect. Goods, services and establishment (as well as workers and capital) must nevertheless also be examined together to the extent that they create a single body of law. Although the Court may have adopted a slightly different approach in each area, it has generally applied the same underlying principles at the same time as try to develop the law on as consistent and uniform a basis as possible.

In developing its jurisprudence on the free movement of goods, the Court has had to deal with the underlying difficulty that arises in attempting to secure effective market access across Europe at the same time as allow a proper degree of national regulatory control to be maintained. This corresponds with the basic access and control conflict identified.[23]

Market access has been promoted by interpreting the relevant Treaty provisions to prohibit national measures that restrict entry by overseas products into local markets. The main difficulty that the Court has had to deal with in this regard is to determine whether this should be subject to a discrimination or effects based test.

The maintenance of a proper degree of local market regulation or control has been achieved by the development of a parallel judicial derogation (or derogations) based on the ideas of reasonableness, mandatory requirement and public interest (as well as the general good in the financial area)[24] in addition to the strict exemptions already provided for under the Treaty (Article 30, ex 36). To the extent that financial regulation, in particular, does not fall within any of the express Treaty exceptions provided for, it has to be assessed having regard to the emerging concept of public interest or the general good. The evolution of the Court's policy in determining the scope of relevant judicial derogation has then been concerned with the identification and refinement of the relevant conditions to be applied in each case.

23 Ch 1 (n 4) and section B (2).

24 Financial regulation as such is considered to constitute an essential area within which some legislative integration is required. Ch 5. The relevant rights and obligations of parties are then set out in directives or other measures adopted by the Council and Parliament under the Treaty. Ch 6. While this generally operates on a home country control basis, a degree of intervention is reserved to the host territory which is either defined expressly under the measure concerned or the more general judicially recognized concept of public interest or general good (n 60). Financial market regulation is one of the areas that would fall within the legitimate scope of protected activity of the host Member State. Regulation is accordingly not then subject to the general good as such but forms part of it. Ch 6, section D (4).

The evolution and general development of the Court's approach in the area of goods can be divided into five main periods.

(1) Treaty Duties, Charges, and Taxes—*Commission v Italy* (1968) and Statistical Levy (1969)

The free movement of goods is initially secured under the Treaty[25] by the creation of a customs union and the prohibition of customs duties on imports and exports and charges having equivalent effect.[26] This prohibition was applied by the Court on an effects rather than purpose basis in *Commission v Italy* in 1968 which concerned a tax imposed on the export of artistic, historical and archaeology items.[27] Any other charges having an equivalent effect were also prohibited *ab initio*.[28] Charges may be permitted where they constituted a payment for a legitimate service[29] or mandatory inspections under Community law.[30]

[25] Six general levels of integration can be identified within any regional system including a free trade area, a customs union, a common market, economic union, monetary union (and economic and monetary union) as well as full political union. Ch 1 (nn 6 and 7) and Ch 2 (nn 28–30).

[26] The customs union is set up under Art 23(1) (ex Art 9(1)). Customs duties on imports and exports and charges having equivalent effect as well as duties of a fiscal nature are prohibited under Art 25 (ex 12). The former Art 13 obliged Member States to abolish existing duties within the transitional period with the original Art 16 prohibiting duties on exports. These provisions have since been repealed.

[27] Case 7/68, *Commission v Italy* [1968] ECR 423 in which Italy had imposed a tax on the export of artistic, historical and archaeology items. Art 16 prohibited the imposition of any customs duty on exports or of any charge having equivalent effect. The same result is now secured under Art 25. The provision made no distinction based on the purpose of the duty and charge concerned. It was held that the disputed tax fell within Art 16 by reason of the fact that export trade in the goods in question was hindered by the pecuniary burden that was imposed on the price of the exported articles. See also Cases 2 and 3/69, *Sociaal Fonds voor de Diamantarbeiders v SA Ch Brachfeld & Sons* [1969] ECR 211, [1969] CMLR 335 which was concerned with the rejection of a Belgian charge of 0.33 per cent on the value of imported diamonds to support a social fund for industry workers.

[28] Case 24/68, *Commission v Italy* [1969], ECR 193, [1971] CMLR 611 which involved an Italian export levy imposed for the collection of statistical material for use to determine trade patterns. The Court held that any pecuniary charge, however small and whatever its designation and mode of application, which is imposed unilaterally on domestic or foreign goods by reason of the fact that they cross a frontier, constitutes a charge having equivalent effect even if it is not imposed for the benefit of the State, it is not discriminatory or protective in effect and if the product on which the charge is imposed is not in competition with any domestic product (para 9). The prohibition on new customs duties or charges having equivalent effect with the principle of free movement of goods constituted a fundamental rule which, without prejudice to the other provisions of the Treaty, did not permit of any exceptions (para 10). See also Cases 2 and 3/69, *Diamantarbeiders* (n 27).

[29] Case 87/75, *Bresciani v Amministrazione Italiana delle Finanze* [1976] ECR 129, [1976] 2 CMLR 62 (Italian charge imposed on compulsory veterinary and public health inspections on imported cowhides).

[30] Case 18/87, *Commission v Germany* [1988] ECR 5427 (1990) 1 CMLR 561 (German regional authority charge on live imported animals under Directive 81/389 was permitted).

The Treaty also prohibits the imposition of discriminatory internal taxation (under Articles 90/93 (ex 95/99)) which has the same effect as a customs duty or charge. The Treaty does not require Member States to adopt any particular internal taxation regime but only that the system set up is not applied in a discriminatory manner.[31] Indirect discrimination may also be prohibited.[32] A discrimination based test is then applied to internal taxation related measures although this is extended to cover direct and indirect nationality related restrictions. While the taxation provisions contain no equivalent with regard to the Treaty exceptions in Article 30 (ex 36), indirect measures may be capable of objective justification.[33]

The significance of the decision by the Court to adopt a pure effects test with regard to pecuniary charges in *Commission v Italy* was that this followed the equivalent approach adopted under Article XI of the GATT.[34] Under the GATT rules, an effects or obstacle based prohibition was applied with regard to point of entry financial charges (duties and charges of equivalent effect) as well as unauthorized quantitative restrictions (quotas) and measures of the same effect.[35] Where market access was denied or restricted, an absolute effects doctrine was adopted. With regard to internal regulatory measures (including taxes or other legislative administrative requirements), a discrimination based test was applied. Market and regulatory provisions were both subject to the 'General Exceptions' provided for under Article XX.[36]

[31] Case 21/79, *Commission v Italy* [1980] ECR 1, [1980] 2 CMLR 613 (Italy charged lower taxes on regenerated oil); and Case 148/77 *H Hansenv Hauptzollamt Flensburg* [1978] ECR 1787 [1979] 1 CMLR 604 (German tax relief was only made available to spirits made from fruit by small business and collective farms).

[32] Case 112/84, *Humblot v Directeur des Services Fiscaux* [1985] ECR 1367, [1986] 2 CMLR 338 (French car tax based on power rating was held contrary to Art 95 where the only cars covered were imported). Indirect discrimination generally refers to the application of any condition other than nationality which has the same effect of distinguishing between national and non-national products, firms, services or workers. Case 153/73 *Sotgiu v Deutsche Bundespost* [1974] ECR 153 in relation to Art 49 (ex 59). Less clear is the extent to which this requires some discriminatory intent. For further discussion (nn 125 and 126). See also Wyatt and Dashwood (n 1) 446–7. On trade discrimination and national treatment (nn 46 and 135).

[33] Case 140/79, *Chemial Farmaceutici v DAF SpA* [1981] ECR 1, [1981] 3 CMLR 350 (differential Italian tax with regard to synthetic and fermented ethyl alcohol). The Court would accordingly recognize an underlying environment protection objective. This is now further strengthened with the inclusion of environmental concerns within the Treaty, Art 3(l) and Art 6 (ex Art 3(c)).

[34] Ch 2 (n 70).

[35] The term 'quantitative restriction' was used in the comparable GATT provisions. Under Art XI, quantitative restrictions generally include quotas, import and export licences or other measures. The GATT did not use the term 'measures of equivalent effect' as such although in light of the breadth of quantitative restriction it could be argued that a narrow meaning should be adopted to measures of equivalent effect. For comment, GA Bermann, Roger J Goebel, WJ Davey and EM Fox *European Community Law* (1993) 341.

[36] Art XX provides that, subject to the requirement that such measures are not applied in a manner that would constitute a means of arbitrary or unjustifiable discrimination between

Within the European Community, it was nevertheless unclear until the decision in *Dassonville* in 1974[37] whether an effects or discrimination based approach would be adopted with regard to non-financial rather than financial measures of equivalent effect as in *Commission v Italy*.[38]

Before the decision by the Court in *Dassonville*, the Commission confirmed that it considered that measures having equivalent effect applied to those that operated with or without distinction between domestic and imported products. This was, in particular, stated in the Commission's answers to Parliamentary questions in 1966 and 1967[39] and subsequently confirmed in Directives 70/32/EEC and 70/50/EEC.[40] Directive 70/50, in particular, prohibited measures that applied to domestic or imported products (Article 2) and to distinctly applicable measures (Article 3).[41] Directive

countries where the same conditions prevail or amount to a disguised restriction on international trade, nothing in the Agreement is to be construed to prevent the adoption or enforcement by any contracting party of measures: (a) necessary to protect public morals; (b) necessary to protect human, animal or plant life or health; (c) relating to the importations or exportations of gold or silver; (d) necessary to secure compliance with laws or regulations that are not inconsistent with the provisions of the Agreement (including those relating to customs enforcement, the enforcement of monopolies (under para 4 of Art II and Art XVII), the protection of patents, trademarks and copyrights and the prevention of deceptive practices); (e) relating to the products of prison labour; (f) imposed for the protection of national treasures of artistic, historic or archaeological value; (g) relating to the conservation of exhaustible natural resources if such measures are made effective in conjunction with restrictions on domestic production or consumption.

[37] Case 8/74, *Procureur du Roi v Dassonville* [1974] ECR 837, [1974] 2 CMLR 436. Section C (2).

[38] The Court would confirm that the prohibition on quantitative restrictions covers measures which amount to a total or partial restraint of (according to the circumstances) imports, exports or goods in transit. Case 2/73 *Geddo v Ente Nazionale Risi* [1973] ECR 865, [1974] 1 CMLR 13. See also Case 7/61 *Commission v Italy* [1961] ECR 317, [1962] CMLR 39 (Italian suspension of imports from other Member States in June 1960); and Case 34/79 *R v Henn and Darby* [1979] ECR 3795, [1980] 1 CMLR 246 (UK statutory prohibition on import of pornographic material subject to possible justification); and Case 118/78 *Meijer* [1979] ECR 1387, [1979] 2 CMLR 398 (UK restriction on import of main crop potatoes).

[39] These were in response to Parliamentary questions of Mr Deringer, No 118 of 8 Dec 66 (OJ 122 and 301/1967) and No 64 of 11 May 66 (OJ 1967, 169/11) cited in Rene Barents, 'New Developments in Measures Having Equivalent Effect' CMLR, 271 at 272.

[40] Directive 70/32/EEC of 17 Dec 69 (OJ 1970, L 13/1); and Directive 70/50/EEC of 22 Dec 69 (OJ 1970, L 13/29). These had been adopted after three earlier measures under Art 33(7), Directive 64/486/EEC of 28 July 64 (OJ 2253/64 of 20.8.64); Directive 66/682/EEC of 7/11/66 (OJ 3745/66 of 30 Nov 66); and Directive 66/683/EEC of 7 Nov 66 (OJ 3748/66 of 30 Nov 66).

[41] Art 2(1) prohibited measures, other than those applicable equally to domestic or imported products, that hindered imports that could otherwise take place including those that were more difficult or costly than domestic production. Art 2(2) provides that measures having equivalent effect include those that make imports or their disposal, at any marketing stage, of imported products subject to a condition (other than a formality) that is required in respect of imported products only or a condition differing from that required from domestic products and more difficult to satisfy. A number of examples of measures having equivalent effect are listed in Art 2(3) which include: minimum or maximum prices; less favourable prices; reductions in intrinsic value or increased costs; payment conditions; other conditions with regard to

70/50 was partly based on certain earlier Commission decisions on the legitimacy of indistinctly applicable measures (such as with regard to Belgium nitrogen requirements in 1966 and French blanket sizes in 1968)[42] although it was not until *Dassonville* that the Court was able to rule on the matter directly.

Whether Directive 70/50 resulted in measures having equivalent effect being subject to an extended discrimination or full effects test was accordingly left unclear and whether such a more extensive effects test should be adopted more generally was subject to dispute for some time. The opinion of informed commentators on the issue differed with a narrow, intermediate or liberal approach being adopted.[43] The more restrictive views argued

packaging, composition, identification, size and weight that only apply to imported products or that are more difficult to satisfy; purchase preferences or hindrances; publicity limitations; stocking requirements; and local agency requirements. See, eg, Case 74/76, *Iannelli & Volpi Spa v Bitta Paola Meroni* [1977] ECR 557, [1977] 2 CMLR 688.

Art 3 applied to measures governing the marketing of products that dealt, in particular, with the presentation or identification of products and which applied equally to domestic and imported products but where the restrictive effects of such measures on the free movement of goods exceeded the effects intrinsic to trade rules. This would then apply where the restrictive effects on the free movement of goods were considered out of proportion to their purpose or where the same objective could be achieved by other means that were less of an obstacle to trade. Case 75/81, *Joseph Henri Thomas Blesgen v Belgian State* [1982] ECR 1211, [1983] 1 CMLR 431. The result was that overtly discriminately provisions were prohibited automatically with a presumption that indistinctly applicable measures were compatible rather than incompatible subject to the restrictive effects test. For comment, P Oliver *Free Movement of Goods in the EEC* (1988), para 6.35 et seq.

42 The Commission had required the Belgium government to repeal a 1961 requirement that only ammonium nitrate containing, at least, 22 per cent nitrogen could be sold in Belgium (when the usual Community nitrogen content was 20.5 per cent). The effect (and perceived intent) was to prefer local production. Written Question 118/66 [1966] JO 901, 903. The Commission also required that a 1968 French Ministerial Decree be repealed which prohibited the sale of blankets in France unless they were of certain sizes (not used anywhere else) with the effect that imported products were significantly disadvantaged (having to be adjusted for local sale). Directive 70/50 was drafted having regard *inter alia* to these decisions. Oliver (n 41) para 6.35.

43 The restrictive view was defended by such writers as Meier, Seidel, Marx and Graf. Barents (n 39) and authorities cited. Other commentators such as van Themaat and Waelbroeck argued that all state measures with the effect of restricting inter-state trade were prohibited, at least, insofar as they were not regulated by other Treaty provisions. The determinant was then the restrictive effect rather than the discriminatory nature. Other writers such as Beraud, Dona-Viscardini, Ehlermann and Ulmer expressed intermediate opinions.

For a review of the various positions adopted, see Ehlermann in Groeben, Boeckh and Thiesing, *Kommentar zum EWG-Vertrag* (1974), vol 1, 263 (since revised); Waelbroeck, *Les réglementations nationals de prix et le droit communautaire* (1975), 23; Meiji and Winter, 'Measures having an equivalent effect to quantitative restrictions' [1976] CMLR 79; Gerven, 'The Recent Case Law of the Court of Justice concerning Arts 30 and 36 of the EEC Treaty' [1977] CMLR 5; Ehlermann 'Das Verbot der Massnahmen gleicher Wirkung in der Rechtsprechung des Gerichtshofes' in *Feschrift fure Ipsen* (1977), 579; Veelken, 'Massnahmen gleicher Wirkung wie mengenmaesige Beschraenkungen' [1977] EuR 311; van Themaat, 'De artikelen 30–6 van het EEC-Verdrag' *R.M. Themis* 4/5, 378.

In referring to the same authorities, Oliver qualifies the inclusion of Meier in the narrow

that only distinctly applicable measures were caught (on various bases). The intermediate positions tended either to support the general approach adopted by the Commission in Directive 70/50 or to apply the Article 3 test (excessive restrictive effect) to all measures. The most extensive interpretations argued that all restrictions were caught that did not fall within Article 36 or any other Treaty provision. This was based, in particular, on the absence of any reference to discrimination in Article 28 (ex 30). The issue was then considered expressly by the Court in 1974 in *Dassonville*.

(2) TRADE RESTRICTIONS AND REASONABLE MEASURES—*DASSONVILLE* (1974)

The decision in *Dassonville* was concerned with the validity of a Belgian requirement that goods bearing a destination of origin could only be imported if they were accompanied by a certificate from the government of the exporting country confirming their right to the designation applied. *Dassonville* had imported Scotch whisky from France into Belgium without the required certificate. The European Court held that the requirement of a certificate of authenticity, which was less easily obtainable by importers of an authentic product that had been put into free circulation in a regular

camp and notes that Ulmer and Steindorff were particularly critical of Directive 70/50. Oliver also notes that Advocate General Capotorti in *Cassis de Dijon* had adopted a liberal approach rejecting the Commission's caution ('attitude of prudence') in Directive 70/50. The Advocate General had also extended Art 36 (30) to include consumer protection although the claim was not made out on the basis of the facts in the case. Oliver concludes that the proper test is not whether the measure discriminates against imports but whether it restricts them. Oliver (n 41) para 6.45. For more recent discussion and comment (n 122) and (nn 123, 124, 125 and 126 and 128).

See also Seidel 'Der EWG-rechtliche Begriff der "Massnahmen gleicher Wirkung wie eine mengenmassige Beschrankung"'[1976] NJW 2081; Graf *Der Begriff 'Massnahmen gleicher Wirkung wie mengenmaessige Einfuhrbeschrankungen' im EWG-Vertrag* (1972), 25; Marx *Funktion und Grenzen der Rechtsangleichung nach Art 100 EWG-Vertrag* (1976), 84; Ehle and Meier *EWG-Warenverkehr* (1971), 158; Beraud 'Les measures d'effet equivalent au sens des articles 30 et suivants du Traité be Rome' [1968] RTDE 265; Dona 'Les measures d'effet equivalent a des restrictions quantitatives' [1973] RMC 224; Mattera 'Libre circulation des marchanises et articles 30 a 36 du Traité CEE' [1976] RMC 500; Steindorff *Dienstfreiheit und Versicherungsaufsicht Markt* (1971), 79; and Ulmer 'Zum Verbot mittelbarer Einfuhrbeschrenkungen im EWG-Vertrag' [1973] GRURI, 502. For further discussion, Oliver (n 41) paras 6.36–6.40.

The position of the Commission, in particular, under Directive 70/80 would appear to have been intermediate. Despite the application of Art 3 to equally applicable measures, the tenth recital refers to imported products either being precluded or their disposal being made more difficult or costly than domestic production. This suggests that the Commission had adopted a discrimination based approach although this included both express and indirect forms of discrimination (n 32). Wyatt nevertheless argues that even restrictions considered by the Court not to involve any form of discrimination (direct or indirect) could be thought to be indirectly discriminatory. Wyatt and Dashwood (n 1) 321 and 329.

manner in another Member State than by importers of the same product directly from the country of origin, constituted a measure of equivalent effect.[44]

With regard to the scope of the prohibition to be imposed, the Court stated in the judgement that:

> All trading rules enacted by Member States which are capable of hindering, directly or indirectly, actually or potentially, intra-Community trade are to be considered as measures having an effect equivalent to quantitative restrictions. (paragraph 5)

This would subsequently be relied on as the core statement of the Court with regard to the determination of the scope of national measures restricting trade in goods prohibited under Article 28 (ex 30) of the Treaty. Although the Court could have adopted a discrimination based test with regard to national provisions (other than market entry barriers) as under the GATT,[45] the Court decided to adopt a more absolute obstacle (or full effects) doctrine. In so doing, financial and non-financial barriers to trade were to be treated in an identical manner.

The problem that had arisen was that the Treaty had not expressly stated which test was to be applied to non-market entry related (non-financial) restrictions. Under the GATT rules, entry restrictions had been subject to an absolute prohibition while internal regulatory measures had only to be non-discriminatory. The Treaty of Rome did distinguish between market entry financial restrictions (customs duties and charges having an equivalent effect) and internal measures (taxation under Article 95), although the same clear distinction was not adopted with regard to non-pecuniary restrictions. The opportunity accordingly arose in *Dassonville* for the Court to correct this gap by applying the same test to both types of non-pecuniary measures.[46] Non-specificity within the Treaty had then allowed the Court the opportunity to determine whether a discriminatory or a non-discriminatory based test should be applied.

[44] Para 19 of the judgement. For comment, D Chalmers 'Free Movement of Goods within the European Community: an Unhealthy Addiction to Scotch Whisky?' (1993) 42 ICLQ 26 and Wils 'The Search for the Rule in Art 30 EEC: much ado about nothing?' (1993) 18 ELRev 475.

[45] (n 35) and Ch 2 (n 70).

[46] Weiler notes that the Court then 'conflated' the GATT market access and national regulatory restrictions and applied the same test based on unjustified obstacle whether or not discriminatory or protectionist. Weiler (n 20) 359. While *Commission v Italy* (Statistical Levy) had followed the GATT precedence with regard to pecuniary restrictions to which an absolute no '*de minimus*' and strict (non-discriminatory or protectionist) prohibition was applied, in *Dassonville* the Court did not follow general trade law practise which would have applied a discriminatory (national treatment) test to other non-pecuniary national regulatory measures as well internal taxes.

In light of the apparent clarity of the GATT arrangements, it can only be assumed that this drafting omission (or anomaly) within the Treaty of Rome had been deliberate. Rather than provide for a more restrictive discrimination only based internal regulatory doctrine, it was decided to leave the issue open for subsequent development or confirmation. By the time that the Court was able to consider the matter in 1974, it was decided that as extensive or expansive an interpretation as possible would be adopted to promote free trade. The fact that the Court had to wait until then can only be explained in terms of the accidental nature of the litigious process.[47] The language of the judgement was, however, not without precedence.[48]

The longer term importance of *Dassonville* cannot be questioned in terms of judicial policy construction although its immediate impact was limited. The decision was initially only applied in the agricultural sector and it was not until *Cassis de Dijon* in 1979 and subsequently that the full significance of the open or liberal approach adopted with regard to the scope of relevant Treaty prohibition was fully recognized. With *Cassis*, the Court would then be able to rule on the extended application of Article 28 (ex 30) in connection with all industrial products and goods in a similar manner.[49]

[47] For further comment, Introduction and see Weiler (n 20).

[48] The basic language in the main para 5 statement was used in Cases 56 and 58/64 *Consten SARL & Grundig-Verkaufs GmbH v Commission* [1966] ECR 299 (1966) CMLR 418 and in Case 56/65 *STM/MBU* [1966] ECR 235; Case 5/69 *Volk v Vervaecke* [1969] ECR 295. While the free movement rules are concerned with the removal of restrictions imposed by Member States' government and public authorities, the competition measures apply with regard to agreements entered into between private parties or as a result of market restructuring positions. In developing a common or parallel approach, the Court would appear to be following or promoting the principle of the unity of the common market. For further discussion, Barents (n 39) 274.

Barents also notes that the inclusion of the words *actually or potentially* suggest that the Court had rejected the inclusion of the discriminatory character of a state measure as constituting a decisive element in the Art 30 (28) prohibition. This may, however, have ignored the importance of indirect rather than directly discriminatory measures. Barents (n 39) 277. The language with regard to *capable of hindering* is in line with judgments concerning the prohibition on charges having equivalent effect. See, for example, Case 34/73 *Variola v Amministrazione dell Finanze* [1973] ECR 981.

Although the judgement refers to *directly or indirectly*, there is no express reference to measures that do or do not apply equally to domestic and imported products with the decisive element being the restrictive effect on trade. Barents notes that it was not until Case 13/77 *GB-INNO v ATAB* that indistinctly applicable measures were covered by Art 30 (28). In Case 190/73 *Van Haaster* and Case 111/76 *Van den Hazel* breach of a Community regulation was also involved. The effects based nature of the test was then again confirmed in Case 82/77 *van Tiggele*.

[49] Barents (n 39) 277. The use of a destination of origin with regard to Sekt and Weinbrand was considered by the Court in 1974 although this was under Directive 70/50 rather than Art 28 (ex 30). In *Commision v Germany* Case 12/74 [1975] ECR 181, [1975] 1 CMLR 340, the Court had held that a 1971 German law could not prevent the use of Sekt and Weinbrand with regard to imported products (which were required to use the designations 'Schaumwein' and

Care must nevertheless be taken in reading the judgement in *Dassonville*. It can clearly be argued that the general statement on trade restrictions (paragraph 5) was strictly *obiter* to the extent that the certification requirement in question had placed one group of importers (from the country into which the original goods had already been imported) at a disadvantage as against other importers (directly from the country of origin).[50] Secondary importation was then indirectly disadvantaged or discriminated against certainly to the extent that the national rules were not applied equally to imported and domestic products and to imported products from the country of origin and other countries.[51] The facts accordingly confirm that the issue concerned was one of discrimination although the Court took the opportunity to set out the applicable doctrine in as wide a manner as possible without any express reference to discrimination. It was possibly, at least partly, for this reason that the full implications of the decision were not immediately apparent.

The main significance of the decision was in confirming how wide the scope of the underlying Treaty prohibition may extend as well as in providing judicial recognition of the entitlement of national governments to maintain some restrictions on imported goods. In *Dassonville*, this emerging judicially created derogation was defined simply in terms of reasonableness.[52] The precise scope of this judicial exception was then left unspecified at the time[53] with the importance to which the Court might attach to it

'Branntwein aus Wein' respectively). The German government had claimed that the restrictions were justified as appellations of origin (on the same basis as French Champagne and cognac). The Court rejected this on the basis *inter alia* that the grapes used may be of indeterminate origin and that the area of origin referred to (the whole of the Federal Republic of Germany and Austria) did not demonstrate any homogeneous natural features not found in adjacent areas. There was also nothing in the method of production used that created a product with distinct quality and characteristics that made them peculiarly German.

50 Para 9.

51 The Court states that even without having to examine whether such measures are covered by Art 36, they must not, in any case, constitute a means of arbitrary discrimination or a disguised restriction on trade between Member States (para 7). The Court continues that that may be the case with formalities required by a Member State for the purpose of proving the origin of a product which only direct importers are in a position to satisfy without facing serious difficulties (para 8). The Court concludes from this that a certification requirement that is less easily obtainable by certain importers constitutes a measure of equivalent effect (para 9). It is unclear whether the Court considered the requirement to constitute a means of 'arbitrary discrimination' or 'disguised restriction' (para 7) although this would appear to amount to indirect discrimination. For similar comment, Wyatt and Dashwood (n 1) 322. See also Wyatt (n 1) 321 and 329.

52 The Court states that in the absence of a Community system guaranteeing for consumers the authenticity of a product's designation of origin, if a Member States takes measures to prevent unfair practices, it is subject to the condition that these measures should be reasonable and that the means of proof required should not act as a hindrance to trade between territories and should, in consequence, be accessible to all Community nationals (para 6). This has been referred to as a 'rule of reason' the meaning of which was developed subsequently. (n 76).

53 The Court only referred to these measures as being 'reasonable' although it added the

being uncertain and undeveloped. It was not until *Cassis de Dyjon* in 1979 that the Court would be able to clarify both the scope of underlying prohibition and judicial derogation further.

(3) TRADE EFFECTS AND MANDATORY REQUIREMENTS—*CASSIS DE DIJON* (1979)

By the late 1970s, the precise scope of application of Article 30 (28) was still far from clear. Directive 70/50 had suggested that measures of equivalent effect would include distinctly as well as indistinctly applicable requirements (subject to a restrictive effects qualification) while the general terms of *Dassonville* (paragraph 5) indicated the adoption of a pure effects doctrine. This was not, however, supported by the facts in *Dassonville* although the subsequent decisions in Case 13/77 *GB-INNO-ATAB*[54] and Case 82/77 *Van Tiggele*[55] did suggest the adoption of an extended view. The matter was not then placed beyond doubt until the decision of the Court *Cassis de Dijon* on 20 February 1979.[56]

In *Cassis de Dijon,* Rewe-Zentrale had intended to import the fruit based liqueur *Cassis* from France into Germany and had applied for the relevant authorization from the Federal Monopoly Administration for spirits (*Bundesmonopolverwaltung für Branntwein*). It was advised that spirits could not be sold in Germany with an alcohol content of less than 32 per cent.[57] It is reported that Rewe-Zentrale had requested an equivalent excep-

double further test that it should still not act as a restriction and be accessible to all Community nationals. This would then appear to apply both an effects and discrimination qualifier to the original reasonableness condition.

54 Case 13/77 *GB-INNO v ATAB* [1977] ECR.

55 Case 82/77 *Van Tiggele* [1978] ECR was concerned with the criminal proceedings against a licensed victualler who sold alcohol (new Holland gin) at a price below the minimum fixed under a 1975 Dutch Royal Decree. The Court restated para 5 of *Dassonville* (para 12) and concluded that the minimum retail price requirement was a measure of equivalent effect where it had an adverse effect on marketing on imported products even though it was indistinctly applicable (paras 18 and 21).

56 Case 120/78 *Rewe-Zentrale AG v Bundesmonopolverwaltung für Branntwein* [1979] ECR 649 [1979] 3 CMLR 494. See generally Dehousse '1992 and Beyond: The Institutional Dimension of the Internal Market Programme' [1989/1] LIEI 109; McGee and Weatherill 'The Evolution of the Single Market—Harmonisation or Liberalisation?' (1990) 53 MLR 578; and Reich 'Protection of Diffuse Interests in the EEC and the Perspective of Progressively Establishing an Internal Market' (1988) 11 JCP 395. See also R Bieber, R Dehousse, J Pinder, and J Weiler (eds) *1992: One European Market?* (Nomos 1988).

57 Rewe-Zentrale had applied for authorization on 14 Sept 1976. It was advised on 17 Sept 1976 that authorization under the Law on the Monopoly and Spirits of 8 April 1922 had been granted by notice on 8 Apr 1976 with regard to the importation of spirits. Art 100(3) of the Law, however, provided that only potable spirits having a wine spirit content of, at least, 32 per cent could be marketed subject to the exceptions set out in the Regulation on the Minimum Wine-Spirit Content of Potable Spirits of 28 Feb 1958. As Cassis only contained an alcohol volume of between 15 and 20 per cent it was not covered by the regulation and individual

tion to that granted earlier in connection with *Anisette* following an agreement between the Commission and Germany on the settlement of a previous infringement action.[58] The plaintiffs then brought an action against the decision which was referred to the *Hassisches Finanzgericht* on 27 December 1976. It is significant that the Commission was not directly involved with the action at any stage before submissions.[59]

In considering the reference for a ruling, the Court recognized the residual (original) authority of Member States to regulate matters relating to the production and marketing of goods where there was no equivalent European provision. The Court stated that:

> In the absence of common rules relating to the production and marketing of alcohol—a proposal for a regulation submitted to the Council by the Commission on 7 December 1976 (Official Journal C309, p 2) not yet having received the Council's approval—it is for the Member States to regulate all matters relating to the production and marketing of alcohol and alcoholic beverages on their own territory. (paragraph 8)

This residual authority was nevertheless subject to the condition that any restriction imposed was justified having regard to certain 'mandatory requirements' (*exigences imperatives* or imperative state or necessary public interests)[60] recognized under Community law. Any possible restrictive effect

derogations were not granted. The plaintiffs brought an action against the decision which was referred to the *Hessisches Finanzgericht* on 27 Dec 1976. The *Finanzgericht* referred two questions to the Court on 28 Apr 1978 with regard to the scope of application of the concept of measures having equivalent effect and whether alcohol content rules may constitute discrimination regarding the conditions under which goods are produced and marketed between nationals of Member States under Art 37 of the Treaty. The Court rejected the application of Art 37 which was concerned with state monopolies of a commercial character and assessed the matter under Art 28 (ex 30).

[58] The Commission had challenged the same German law in 1974 in identical proceedings. The Commission had agreed not to continue after political agreement to allow Anisette into the German market although the law remained in full effect. On the earlier proceedings, Commission Document 373 (17 July 1975). On the approach followed with regard to Sekt and Weinbrand (n 49).

[59] This is confirmed by Karen Alter and Sophie Meunier-Aitsahalia following interviews with many of the parties to the proceedings. Alter and Meunier-Aitsahalia 'Judicial Politics in the European Communion—European Integration and the Path breaking *Cassis de Dijon* Decision' *Comparative Political Studies* (Jan 1994), nol 26, no 4, 535 (n 1). It is significant that the Commission did not bring the action in *Cassis* especially as it had already allowed the German law to remain in effect following the arguably inappropriate settlement in the Anisette proceedings (n 58). This permissive and non-confrontational approach contrasts significantly with the aggressive and activist policy adopted following the decision in *Cassis*.

[60] A better translation of the original French reference to *exigences imperatives* would possibly be 'compelling state interests' or even 'necessary public interests.' The German reference is to *zwingende Erfordernisse* and Italian to *esigenze imperative*. Weatherhill notes that 'compelling' is better than compulsory, mandatory or imperative. Weatherill (n 1) 575, n 35. Bermann, Geobel, Davey and Fox prefer 'imperative state interests.' Bermann et al, *Cases and Materials in European Community Law* (West Group St Paul MN 1993), 356, n 2.

had to be justified having regard to recognized public interests. The Court then went further than in *Dassonville* and identified four such possible interests:

> Obstacles to movement within the Community resulting from disparities between the national laws relating to the marketing of the products in question must be accepted insofar as those provisions may be recognized as being necessary in order to satisfy mandatory requirements relating in particular to the effectiveness of fiscal supervision, the protection of public health, the fairness of commercial transactions and the defence of the consumer. (paragraph 8)

The Court rejected the arguments put forward by the German Government to justify the imposition of the import prohibition. These arguments had generally been based on public health (to prevent alcoholism)[61] and unfair commercial practice (due to the competitive advantage that arises from the lower tax rate applicable).[62] The mandatory fixing of minimum alcohol content was not considered an essential guarantee of the fairness of commercial transactions. Suitable information could be conveyed to the purchaser simply by requiring the display on the product packaging of an indication of origin and the alcohol content.[63] The Court accordingly considered that the requirements imposed did not serve a purpose that was in the general interest and such as to take precedence over the requirements of the free movement of goods.

The Court concluded:

> There is therefore no valid reason why, provided that they have been lawfully produced and marketed in one of the Member States, alcoholic beverages should not be introduced into any other Member State; the sale of such products may not be subject to a legal prohibition on the marketing of beverages with an alcohol content lower than the limit set by the national rules. (paragraph 14)

The decision in *Cassis* was important in confirming the application of Article 28 (ex 30) to indistinctly applicable measures. The decision supported the right of Member States to impose national regulations in the

[61] The French Government used the same argument of combating alcoholism in *Commission v France* Case 152/78 [1980] ECR 2299. Wine and beer (produced locally and imported) were not subject to any advertising restrictions. Brandy, calvados and other fruit based liquors (generally of domestic production) were partially restricted. The advertising of whisky, gin, and vodka (all imported) was fully prohibited.

[62] Paras 9–13.

[63] ibid.

absence of relevant Community provision.[64] Before considering possible justifications, the Court restated its earlier reasonableness requirement in *Dassonville* as mandatory requirements (imperative state interests or necessary public interests) with the four specific instances provided (paragraph 8).[65] The Court looked again to the effect of the restriction on trade rather than to its purpose or intent.[66] In addition, the Court added that provided that the beverages had been lawfully produced and marketed in one Member State, there was no valid reason why they should not be introduced into any other Member State (paragraph 14).

Cassis accordingly confirmed the indistinctly applicable operation of the definition of measures having an equivalent effect and further clarified the nature of the judicial derogation originally introduced under *Dassonville*. The decision also contained the further statement with regard to lawful production and marketing (paragraph 14). While *Dassonville* was concerned with the nature of the underlying restriction or prohibition contained in the Treaty, *Cassis* moved to consider the equivalence of the protection provided by the country of origin rules.[67] The focus then shifts from prohibition to permission with market entry becoming conditional on compliance with the home state rules with regard to initial production and sale. This would subsequently be referred to as mutual recognition or possibly, more accurately, as regulatory or even functional equivalence.[68]

The most significant element of the judgment was the insertion of the new conditional (or dependent) clause with regard to prior lawful production and

[64] Para 8 of the judgment.

[65] (n 95). These are generally considered to be non-exclusive. For discussion, Weatherill and Beaumont (n 1) ch 16. Although mandatory requirements are referred to in para 8, the Court subsequently used the term 'general interest' in para 14. Having assessed the arguments put forward by the German Government, the Court stated that it was clear that the requirements relating to the minimum alcohol content did not serve a purpose which was in the general interest and such as to take precedence over the requirements of the free movement of goods.

[66] The Court concluded that the principal effect of the alcohol content requirements was to promote beverages having a high alcohol content by excluding from the national market products of other Member States that did not conform with that description (para 14). The unilateral requirement imposed therefore constituted an obstacle to trade which was incompatible with Art 30 of the Treaty.

[67] While *Cassis* followed the same logic or methodology as *Dassonville* of looking at relevant rules or regulations (Community or otherwise), justification (if they were nationally applied) and restrictive effect, *Cassis* adds the element of equivalence. This idea of equivalence or functional equivalence was arguably implied in *Dassonville*. Although both cases were directly concerned with sales restrictions, the certification of origin constituted a form of additional or ancillary condition attached to the sale as such while the alcohol content rule was more concerned with initial product production. *Dassonville* also involved a distinctly applicable requirement which had a (direct) discriminatory result. *Cassis* was indistinctly applicable with an (indirectly) discriminatory consequence. *Dassonville* looked to the restrictive effect of the host rule while *Cassis* considered the positive effect of home compliance. The idea of equivalence was nevertheless strictly *obiter* (n 70) and Ch 6, section C (1).

[68] The reference to 'mutual trust' is also used in some texts although this is clearly less precise. See, eg, Berman, Geobel, Davey and Fox (n 60), n 90.

marketing (paragraph 14). The Court had already considered the arguments advanced in justification of the restrictive effect of the national provision and had rejected them (principally on the basis of disproportionality). The Court did not expressly refer to *Dassonville* although it effectively applied its extended scope of prohibition subject to reasonable justification *ratio*. The additional statement in paragraph 14 was then unnecessary and strictly *obiter* as (as in *Dassonville*) this did not fall within the scope of the facts revealed by the judgement.[69] The opportunity was nevertheless taken to allow the Court to introduce the idea of prior compliance or equivalence albeit outside the strict scope of the relevant facts and the decision required.[70]

The validity of the decision in *Cassis* was initially confirmed in Case 788/79 *Gilli and Andres*, the judgement in respect of which was issued on 26 June 1980.[71] In *Gilli*, an Italian prohibition on the sale of non-wine vinegar was held to be contrary to the Treaty in a criminal prosecution against importers of apple vinegar from Germany. Of possibly more relevance was then Case 27/80 *Fietje* in which the issue of equivalence was more clearly considered with regard to product labelling. The preliminary ruling was issued on 16 December 1980.[72] The decision in *Cassis* was then

[69] The most important and original element of the actual *ratio* was arguably not the separate dependent clause but the balancing of the new justifications (fiscal supervision, public health, commercial fairness and consumer protection) against the law of free movement.

[70] The judgement does not refer to equivalence or mutual equivalence as such. This is nevertheless implied in the idea of prior-compliance that prevents a Member State from applying its corresponding provisions with regard to the production or marketing of any particular goods. (n 75) and Ch 6, section C (1) and (n 28). See also, eg, Alter and Meunier-Aitsahalia (n 59) 539. The possibility of derogation was, however, introduced under *Dassonville*. This may accordingly be better regarded as a re-formulation rather than original statement of policy. Contrast Alter and Meunier-Aitsahalia, 539–540 commenting on the true legal contribution of the rule of reason in *Cassis*. Rather than consider *Cassis* as an extension of *Dassonville*, this could be more accurately referred to as a restriction, or at least, clarification with the expansion of specific mandatory requirements to be recognized that would fall within the reasonableness formulation introduced under *Dassonville*. See also Barrents (n 39); LW Gormley 'Actually or potentially, directly or indirectly? Obstacles to the free movement of goods', *Yearbook of European Law* (1989), 9, 197–208; and J-C Masclet 'Les articles 30, 36 et 100 du traité Cee à la lumiere de l'arret *Cassis de Dijon*', *Revue de Droit Européenne* (1980), 611–34.

[71] Case 788/79 *Criminal Proceedings against Herbert Gilli and Paul Andres* [1980] ACR 1071, [1981] 1 CMLR 146.

[72] Case 27/80 *Criminal Procedings against Anton Adriaan Fietje* [1980] ECR 3839, [1981] 3 CMLR. The case was concerned with a Dutch requirement to include a statement confirming the nature of goods on their labels (in that case 'liqueur'). The Court recognized the authority of the Member Sate to act in the absence of any common Community rules (para 7). The Court accepted that a labelling requirement could be justified on consumer protection grounds (para 11) although it then stated that, '[t]here was no longer any need for such protection if the details given on the original label of the imported product have as their content information on the nature of the product and that content includes at least the same information and is just as capable of being understood by the consumers in the importing State as the description prescribed by the rules of that State.' (para 12). The Court then expressly compared the degree of protection secured under the home and host rules. *Cassis* had not raised the issue of comparability directly as there was no equivalent French requirement concerned.

upheld in a large number of cases subsequently both with regard to sales restrictions specifically[73] and more generally.[74] Some care must nevertheless be taken not to overstate this as a number of separate elements formed part of the original *Cassis* decision[75] while other inconsistencies or anomalies have arisen in the Court's jurisprudence.[76]

Although the full importance of the judgement may not have been immediately apparent, both the Commission and the German Government were surprised by the wide terms in which the Court's decision was

[73] Case 120/78 *Gilli and Andres* (wine vinegar); Case 193/80 *Commission v Italy* [1981] ECR 3019 (cider vinegar); Case 53/80 *Officier van Justitie v Koninklijke Kaasfabriek Eyssen BV* [1981] ECR 409 [1982] 2 CMLR 20 (prohibited additives (nisin) in cheese); Case 30/80 *Kelderman* [1981] ECR 517 (dry matter content of bread); Case 272/80 *Frans-Nederlandse Maatschappij voor Biologische Producten* [1981] ECR 3277 (plant protection products); and Case 6/81 *Industrie Diensten Groep v Beele* [1982] ECR 707 (imitated products). For further discussion, see Oliver (n 41) paras 7.52–58.

[74] These include Case 27/80 *Fietje* (n 72); and Case 94/82 *De Kikvorsch* [1983] ECR 947, [1984] 2 CMLR 323 (labelling requirements); Case C-358/95 *Tommaso Morellato v Unita Sanitairia Locale (USL) No 11 di Prodenone* [1997] ECR 1-1431 (moisture content of bread) and Case C-17/93 *Van der Veldt* [1994] ECR I-3537, [1995] 1 CMLR 621 (salt content of bread); Case 220/81 *Robertson* [1982] ECR 2349, [1983] 1 CMLR 556 (Hall-marking of silver products) (see also Case C-293/93 *Houtwipper* [1994] ECR I-4249); Case 261/81 *Rau* [1982] ECR 3961, [1983] 2 CMLR 496 (margarine to be sold in cube-shaped packets); Case 286/81 *Oosthoek's* [1982] ECR 4575. [1983] 3 CMLR 428 (advertising restrictions or prohibitions); Case 207/83 *Commission v United Kingdom* [1985] ECR 1201, [1985] 2 CMLR 259 (country of origin requirement); Case 178/84 *Commission v Germany* [1987] ECR 1227, [1988] 1 CMLR 780 (prohibition on beer additives); Case 407/85 *Drei Glocken GmbH* [1988] ECR 4233 (wheat flour content of pasta products); Case 298/87 *Smanor SA* [1988] ECR 4489 (prohibition on sale of deep frozen yoghurt as fresh yoghurt); and Case 286/86 *Deserbais* [1988] ECR 4907 (minimum fat content requirements of Edam cheese).

[75] The decision in *Cassis* was made up of a number of separate elements which can be considered to include: (a) the recognition of residual national authority (para 8), (b) the identification of certain new *exigences imperatives* (para 8), (c) an assessment and rejection of possible justifications (paras 9–13), (d) conclusion in favour of free movement (para 14) and (e) the separate lawful production and marketing statement (para 14). Elements of this would be confirmed in later decisions although it is important to consider which. The core *ratio* was then limited to assessing the new derogations listed as against the core Treaty prohibitions designed to protect the full free movement of goods. For further comment and implied principles of pre-compliance and pre-review in *Cassis* see Ch 6 (nn 26 and 28). See also (n 168).

[76] Compare *Cassis* with Case 155/80 *Oebel* [1981] ECR 3147 (night bread delivery) and Case 75/81 *Blesgen* [1982] ECR 1211 (alcohol sale). In both decisions, the measures were held not to be incompatible as they were indistinctly applicable. See also Case 148/85 *Directeur Général des Impôts v Forest* [1988] 2 CMLR 577 (flour milling quotas). *Blesgen* is generally understood to give rise to a 'rule of reason' in that restrictions will not be caught where their effects are so tenuous as to fall outside Art 28 (ex 30). For discussion, L Gormley *Prohibiting Restrictions on Trade within the EC* (1985), 252; and A Dashwood 'The Cassis de Dijon line of authority' in *In Memoriam JDB Mitchell* (1983), 145 at 152. For comment, see Oliver (n 41) para 6.44, n 120. Weatherill explains the rule of reason in terms of the need to interpret strict Treaty prohibitions in a flexible and pragmatic manner. See Weathreill and Beaumont (n 1) 575–6 and 818. The Court can more generally be seen to have developed a narrow restrictive approach in *Oebel* and subsequent cases following *Oebel* (such as *Blesgen* and *Quietlynn*) and then a more inclusive policy in *Oosthoek* and related decisions (*Buet*, *GB-INNO*). For discussion, see, for example, KV Kole and A D'Amato *European Union Law Anthology* (1998), 107–16.

expressed.[77] Despite its initial hesitation to become involved, the Commission also then quickly recognized the potential value of the decision as a means of re-activating its integration policy within Europe.

The adoption of a new more general harmonization policy was subsequently announced by Monsieur Etienne Davignon, the Internal Market Commissioner, in October 1979 before the European Parliament.[78] A separate communication was produced by the Commission in October 1980[79] which followed an earlier communication that had been sent to the Parliament, the Council and the Member States.[80] The Commission's further statement was reproduced in the Official Journal on 3 October 1980.[81] In this statement, the Commission noted that it had decided to use the judgement of the Court in *Cassis* to revive its efforts to promote the integration of European markets. New measures would accordingly be proposed to the Council to supplement specifically the 1969 General Programme on the Removal of Technical Barriers to Trade in goods.[82]

The objective of the Commission's 1980 Communication on *Cassis* was to develop new policy guidelines on the basis of the Court's ruling. In the Communication, the Commission summarized the effect of *Cassis* on technical and commercial rules (paragraphs 5–6), drew a number of general and more specific conclusions (paragraph 6) and issued certain guidelines (paragraph 8).[83]

[77] It is reported that the German Government expected that its law would be held invalid although the breadth and scope of the judgement could not have been anticipated. Alter and Meunier-Aitsahalia (n 59) 540.

[78] *Debates of the European Parliament* (22 Oct 1979), OJ CE No C183/57, 21 July 1980.

[79] OJ No C256, 3 Oct 80, 2.

[80] Document COM (1980) 30 DEF, 24 Jan 80.

[81] OJ No C256, 3 Oct 80, 2. An earlier Communication had been sent to the European Parliament (n 80). A report was produced by the Economic and Monetary Committee of the Parliament which was presented on 1 Oct 1980 (Document 1-440/80). The Commission's intention to send the letter to Member States as part of its new strategy was announced at a press conference by Commissioner Davignon in July. See *Agence Europe* 18 July 80, 11.

[82] OJ C 76 of 17 June 69. The growing number of restrictive measures that affected movement of goods was referred to by the Commission in its earlier communication of 6 Nov 1970 (safeguarding free trade within the Community). See also Bulletin of the EC, No 7/8, 1980, n 1.3.2.

[83] The Commission considered that the decision in *Cassis* was important in confirming the scope of its earlier *Dassonville* based definition of measures of equivalent effect in connection with technical and commercial rules (paras 4 and 5). The Commission immediately set out the Court's statement in para 14 (that any product lawfully produced and marketed in one Member State must, in principle, be admitted to the market of any other Member State) (para 5). Rather than re-state the Court's recognition of national regulatory authority (where there was no comparable Community provision), the validity of the justifications provided and restrictive effect of the measure, the Commission immediately focused on the additional statement with regard to lawful production and sale. While this cannot be questioned from a political or policy perspective, its legal basis is unsound. The Commission effectively extracts the

The most significant element of the 1980 Communication was the adoption by the Commission of the conditional or dependent clause introduced in *Cassis* as an independent legal principle (paragraph 14). In its original decision, the Court had not referred to equivalence or mutual equivalence (and recognition) as such although it was considered implied that Member States must take into full account any requirements imposed by other territories. The

new conditional or dependent clause and re-states it as an independent and free standing legal principle. For earlier criticism Barents (n 39) 296–9.

The Commission continued that technical and commercial rules (even those equally applicable to national and imported products) may create barriers to trade but only where those rules were necessary to satisfy mandatory requirements and to serve a purpose which is in the general interest and for which they were an essential guarantee. This purpose must be such as to take precedence over the requirement of the free movement of goods which constituted one of the fundamental rules of the Community (para 6).

In its conclusions, the Commission attempted to develop the implications of the additional statement in para 14 of *Cassis* further (paras 7–14). Any product imported from another Member State must in principle be admitted to the territory of another State if it has been lawfully produced (that is conforms to rules and processes of manufacture that are customarily and traditionally accepted in the exporting country) and marketed in that territory (para 9). Member States may not take an exclusively national viewpoint in developing commercial or technical rules and must give consideration to the legitimate requirements of other Member States (para 10). Barriers to trade will only be accepted on strict conditions (para 11). The rules must be necessary—that is appropriate and not excessive in satisfying the mandatory requirements defined; serve a purpose in the general interest (although of itself this is repetitive) which justifies an exception to the fundamental rule of free movement; and be essential for the purpose to be attained (relevant and not disproportionate although this is again repetitive).

The Commission's additional 'guidelines' then attempt to set out the obligations that it considers apply to Member States as a result of the judgement (paras 15–22). The Commission states that the principles deduced by the Court imply that a Member State may not in principle prohibit the sale in its territory of a product lawfully produced and marketed in another even if the product complies with technical or quality requirements that are different from those imposed on domestic products. Where a product 'suitably and satisfactorily' fulfils the legitimate objective of a Member State's own rules (including public safety or protection of the consumer or environment), the importing country cannot justify prohibiting its sale on the basis that 'the way it fulfils the objective is different from that imposed on domestic products'. In such a case, an absolute sales prohibition could not be considered 'necessary' to satisfy a 'mandatory requirement' as it would not be an 'essential guarantee' in the sense defined by the Court. The Commission will therefore take action ('tackle') commercial rules that are inadmissible according to the Court's criteria (including rules with regard to composition, designation, presentation and packaging of products as well as rules requiring compliance with certain technical standards) at the same time as its harmonization work will focus on national laws that impact the functioning of the common market but are admissible under the criteria set (paras 19 and 20).

The Commission accordingly distinguishes between national rules that fall within derogations permitted under the decision and other inadmissible rules (paras 16–19). It states that its function will be to focus on the admissible rules (para 20). The intention is to leave Member States to remove local restrictions that conflict with the ruling in *Cassis* while it focuses its efforts on harmonising residual measures through secondary legislation. This corresponds with the distinction later adopted between essential and non-essential areas with legislative intervention being required with regard to essential matters and other non-essential issues being dealt with through mutual recognition as developed in the jurisprudence of the Court (n 97). These ideas would be restated and expanded in the 1985 White Paper and more specifically with regard to the new approach developed towards technical harmonization. Ch 6, section C (1) and (2) and (nn 26 and 28).

Communication nevertheless noted that restrictions would only be enforceable where they were justified on the basis of necessity (appropriate and not excessive), their purpose was in the general interest and they were essential (appropriate (again) and proportionate). The effect of the scope of the judicial prohibition imposed under *Cassis* then meant that the Commission's harmonization work could subsequently be focused on measures that fell within these exceptions. This approach would form the basis of the new integration policy to be adopted post-*Cassis* which would be further developed in the Commission's subsequent 1985 White Paper.[84]

The 1980 Communication was accordingly important in restating the implications of the decision in *Cassis* from a more general free trade perspective.[85] This is based, however, on the assumption that the additional lawful production and marketing statement (paragraph 14) was part of the full *ratio decidendi* of the original ruling. The effect of this is to treat the additional language (in paragraph 14) as a separate or free-standing condition as against which national measures are to be assessed. Whether this was the intention of the Court is unclear.[86] The Commission's purpose was nevertheless to take the decision in *Cassis* and use it to validate the adoption of a more general integrationist policy based on mutual recognition and to re-invigorate its work in this area.

The decision in *Cassis* and the Commission's Communication nevertheless attracted a considerable amount of criticism at the time. Many Member States were concerned with Germany that the result may be to undermine necessary product standards. France and Italy supported the view that unnecessary standardization would lower safety and quality controls. The British Government is also understood to have expressed certain reservations despite its pro-market and anti-excessive regulatory and over interventionist philosophy.[87] Significant concerns were also expressed by consumer and other interest groups. While they welcomed the possibility of lower prices and increased choice, this had to be balanced against the need

[84] Commission, *Completing the Internal Market—White Paper from the Commission to the European Council (Milan 18–29 June 1985)*, COM (85) 310 final (14 June 1985).

[85] This represented the first use of an interpretative communication. This constitutes the most formal statement of interpretation of policy below a directive. Only ten interpretative communications were issued between 1980 and 1994. These are modelled on national provisions where a law is not clear. Alter and Meunier-Aitsahalia (n 59) 3.

The issuance of the communication was separately explained by its draftsman Mattera within one month of it being issued. Mattera notes that the *Cassis* ruling had allowed the Commission to develop a new approach to harmonization which would end internal protectionism and safeguard the *acquis communautaire*. A Mattera ' "*Cassis de Dijon*": Une nouvelle approche pour la realization et le bon fonctionnement du marché interieur', *Revue du Marcat Commun* (1980), 505–13.

[86] Barents (n 39) 298.

[87] Alter and Meunier-Aitsahalia (n 59) 542.

to protect the health, safety and economic interests of consumers.[88] A number of consumer and trade groups, however, took the opportunity subsequently to develop new business and lobby strategies to attempt to take full advantage of the potential benefits of the *Cassis* ruling.[89] A number of conferences and seminars were held by legal and business associations across Europe during 1980 and 1981 and the full implications of the decision in *Cassis* and the Commission's Communication examined in considerable detail by legal scholars and commentators.[90]

It should also be stressed that the Council of Ministers had separately asked its Legal Service to examine the judgement in *Cassis* and the legal validity of the Commission's interpretation. This led to the production of a counter-interpretation that concluded that almost nothing had changed under *Cassis*.[91]

The main significance of both the decision of the Court in *Cassis* in 1979 and the Commission's 1980 Interpretative Communication was that neither referred to recognition or mutual recognition as such. Equivalence was only implied and national authorities required to take into account marketing or composition rules already imposed in the country of origin. A more clear and substantial policy was only developed in this regard as part of the Commission's subsequent creation of its new approach to technical standards. This would then be further expanded in connection with the Commission's 1985 White Paper which attempted to remove all remaining physical, technical and fiscal barriers to free trade.[92] This provided, in particular, for the completion of a fully unified internal market by 1992 on the basis of a programme and timetable to be produced by the

[88] Opinion of the Consumers Consultative Committee on the consequences of the judgement in the *Cassis de Dijon* case (1981) reported House of Lords, 13 July 1982. See also Report of the Select Committee on the Internal Market Memorandum on the Implications of *Cassis de Dijon* by the Food and Drink Industries Council to the House of Lords, 24 Feb 1982.

[89] Alter and Meunier-Aitsahalia (n 59), 544–5.

[90] See, eg, Barents (n 39); Masclet (n 70); and Gormley '*Cassis de Dijon* and the Communication from the Commission', *European Law Review* (1981) 6, 454; F Capelli 'Les Malentendus Provoques Par L'arret sur le Cassis de Dijon', *Revue du Marche Commun* (1981) 421–35.

[91] While the definition of the measures covered by Art 30 (28) differed from those listed under Directive 70/50/EEC and more specific guidelines were provided under which national measures could be examined, the criteria remained the same as under the earlier directive. (*Service Juridique du Conseil des Communautés Européenes* 10690/80). The Commission's generalization of the para 14 statement was also considered excessive with compatibility of national measures having to be examined on a case by case basis under the criteria set out in Directive 70/50/EEC.

[92] Commission *Completing the Internal Market—White Paper from the Commission to the European Council (Milan 18–29 June 1985)*, COM (85) 310 final (14 June 1985) (n 84). This followed the Commission's 'Programme of Commission for 1985' presented to the European Parliament on 6 March and endorsed by the European Council on 29 and 30 Mar 1985 (n 94). Ch 6, section C (2).

Commission.[93] The idea of mutual recognition as such would then only more slowly emerge over the five-year period between the decision in *Cassis* and the 1985 White Paper.

By 1985, the Commission would be able to propose in its White Paper the adoption of a new approach in connection with the removal of technical barriers based on 'essential equivalence and mutual recognition.' In introducing this new integration approach, the Commission was careful not to state that existing Community law provided for mutual recognition as such but only that equivalence and recognition should be adopted as a core general principle.[94] The Commission notes that although public interest controls may take different forms, they were essentially the same which meant that they could generally be accorded equal recognition in all Member States.[95] The essential equivalence of the objectives of national legislation recognized by the Council then meant that mutual recognition could be adopted as an effective integration strategy.[96]

A new strategy would then be developed based on the use of mutual recognition in non-essential integration areas and legislative harmonization in essential areas with a further adjusted or combined process (in essential

[93] Paras 1 and 2. The Heads of State and Government at the European Council meeting in Copenhagen in 1982 had pledged themselves to the completion of the internal market as a high priority. This was repeated at Fontainebleau in June 1984 and Dublin in December 1984 and in Brussels in March 1985. The internal market would draw together the ten (and then twelve, fifteen and twenty-five) individual markets into a single market of 320 million people, ensure that it was expanding and not static and that it was flexible to allow all resources (people, materials and capital) to be able to flow to the areas of greatest economic advantage. To achieve this first objective, the Commission had developed a programme for the removal of all physical, technical and fiscal barriers. Para 10. This followed a Consolidation Programme submitted by the Commission that had identified a series of proposals to be adopted by the Council during 1984 and 1985. COM(84) 305 final (13 June 1984). The 1985 White Paper would develop the Consolidation Programme further by focusing on the essential items identified.

[94] The Commission states that subject to certain important constraints (para 65), 'the general principle should be approved that, if a product is lawfully manufactured and marketed in one Member State, there is no reason why it should not be sold freely throughout the Community' (para 58). In Part II of the White Paper (The Removal of Technical Barriers), the Commission develops the need for a new strategy (paras 61–4), the chosen strategy (paras 65–6), harmonization as a new approach (paras 67–73), preventing the creation of new obstacles (paras 74–6) and mutual recognition (paras 77–9).

[95] The Commission states that although the rules and controls developed to achieve the protection of human health and life and of the environment may take different forms, they were essentially the same. They should generally be accorded recognition in all Member States allowing for the possibility of cooperation between national authorities (para 58). The Commission was fully aware that this strategy implied a change in habits and in traditional ways of thinking but argued that a radical change of attitude would lead to new and innovative solutions to the elimination of all border controls (para 59).

[96] Conclusions on Standardization, 16 July 1984. The essential equivalence of the objectives of national legislation recognized by the Council meant that mutual recognition could be adopted as an effective strategy (para 63).

areas where harmonization had not yet been achieved).[97] An outline timetable for the removal of all technical barriers as well as physical and fiscal barriers was set out in the tables contained in the Annex to the White Paper.

This new approach based on essential legislative harmonization and non-essential mutual recognition would be extended in the financial area to include the adoption of the three principles of mutual recognition, minimal harmonization and home country control.[98] The inclusion of home country control was considered necessary, in particular, to deal with the additional difficulties that arise with the need to supervise financial institutions on a continuing basis after their initial market entry although this was not expressed in the While Paper in these terms.[99] The core integration devices of mutual recognition, minimum harmonization and home country control were accordingly adopted as the basis for future secondary programme construction through the political and institutional endorsement of the Commission's 1985 White Paper proposals.[100]

[97] The chosen strategy would be based on three principles: (a) a distinction would be drawn between essential internal market initiatives that had to be harmonized and those that may be left to mutual recognition of national regulations and standards; (b) legislative harmonization (under Art 100) would be restricted to laying down essential health and safety requirements which would be obligatory in all Member States; and (c) where harmonization had not been achieved, mutual recognition would still be applied subject to agreed procedures to prevent unnecessary barriers to trade being maintained (para 65).

The legislative harmonization of standards would be confined to agreeing essential requirements with the assessment of whether technical specifications were in conformity being delegated to various standards bodies (para 68). The creation of new barriers would be governed by Directive 83/189/EEC which provided for Commission notification of all draft regulations and standards with regard to technical specifications. The new information procedure with a standstill arrangement allowing the Commission and other Member States to comment came into effect on 1 January 1985 (paras 75 and 75). Ch 6, section C (1) and (2).

The European Parliament and the Dooge Committee had separately stressed that goods lawfully manufactured and marketed in one Member State must be allowed free entry into other Member States. Where the harmonization of supporting regulations and standards was not considered essential, immediate and full recognition should be the rule. There was no obligation on the buyer to prove equivalence nor to submit a product to additional technical testing nor certification procedures. The Commission would use all powers available under the Treaty, in particular, under Arts 30–6 to reinforce this principle of mutual recognition (para 77). Ch 6 (n 42).

[98] Paras 102 and 103. For further discussion, Ch 6, section C.

[99] Ch 6, section D (3) and (5).

[100] While it remains questionable to what extent these principles were based on underlying Treaty or judicial provision or precedent, they were adopted by the Council as the basis for all relevant secondary programmes. Although this legitimates their use for the specific purpose of directive drafting and adoption, the validity of the underlying principles on which the policy is based remain unsupported as separate and independent *acquis communautaire*. The difficulty that arises is then not in assessing the validity of any of the secondary measures agreed but the extent to which they properly and fully give effect to the underlying Treaty and judicial principles on which they are based. For further discussion, Ch 6, section C.

Whether the Court fully supported the extended interpretation developed by the Commission of its ruling in *Cassis* at the time is unclear. Attention nevertheless quickly attached to the possible use of the decisions in *Dassonville* and *Cassis* to challenge all forms of national commercial or technical rules on the basis of Article 28 (ex 30) which led to a significant increase in the number of references being made to the Court from national courts. The Court had then to reconsider the application of the extended terms of its general statements in *Dassonville* (paragraph 5) and *Cassis* (paragraph 14). Unfortunately, a number of inconsistencies arose,[101] in particular, with the Court also having increasingly to consider whether less intentionally protectionist measures should be prohibited under Article 28 (ex 30) at the same time as confirm the scope of the new judicial derogations first introduced under *Dassonville* and expanded in *Cassis*.[102]

In re-considering this jurisprudence, many of the post-*Cassis* decisions that arose can either be understood in terms of those that imposed a dual or equal burden on the imported product or importer. A dual burden is created where the country of origin and import both impose requirements with regard to, for example, product composition. The obligation of the importing (or host) territory will then be judged having regard to the protection already provided by the country of origin rule. An equal burden arises where the country of import imposes a requirement on all goods irrespective of origin and with no underlying protection or discriminatory purpose.[103] A separate approach is followed with regard to export restrictions.[104]

[101] Contrast *Cassis* with, for example, *Oebel* Case 155/80 [1981] ECR 3147 (prohibition on the delivery of bread at night) and *Blesgen* Case 75/81 [1982] ECR 1211, [1983] 1 CMLR 431 (holding spirits for sale on adjoining premises). For comment Oliver (n 41) para 6.44. *Blesgen* can also be understood to include a rule on remoteness. Dashwood 'The Cassis de Dijon line of authority' in *In Memoriam JDB Mitchell* (1983), 145; and Gormley *Prohibiting Restricitons on Trade within the EEC* (1985), 252.

[102] For discussion, Weatherill and Beaumont (n 1) 532–5; and Craig and de Burca (n 1) 608–10.

[103] The Court held in certain cases that Art 28 (ex 30) did not apply such as with regard to restrictions on the sale of strong spirits for consumption on premises in all places open to the public (see Case 75/81 *Blesgen* [1982] ECR 1211, [1983] 1 CMLR 431) and the sale of lawful sex articles from unlicensed sex establishments (Case C-23/89 *Quietlynn* [1990] ECR I-3059, [1990] 3 CMLR 55). The Court has also distinguished rules prohibiting the delivery of bakery products to consumers and retailers as opposed to wholesalers at night (Case 155/80 *Oebell* [1981] ECR 1993, [1983] 1 CMLR 390) and quotas for the milling of flour for human consumption (Case 148/85 *Direction Générale des Impôts and Procureur de la République v Forest* [1986] ECR 3449, [1988] 2 CMLR 577).

Other decisions of the Court did not, however, appear to follow this strict division. In *Cinetheque* it was held that a French ban on the sale or hire of videos of films during the first year after the film's release was not covered by Art 30 (28). In reaching this decision, the Court had noted that the rule applied equally to domestic and imported videos (para 21) but that it could still have a restrictive effect due to 'the disparities between the systems operated in different Member States and between the conditions for the release of cinomatographic works in the

These difficulties culminated, in particular, in the United Kingdom Sunday Trading restrictions considered in *Torfaen* and *Marchandise*.[105] Rather than attempt to place proper limits on the scope of the underlying Treaty prohibition and disapply its application in sensitive areas of national

cinemas of those States' (para 22). The Court continued, '[i]n those circumstances a prohibition of exploitation laid down by such a system is not compatible with the principle of free movement of goods provided for in the Treaty unless any obstacle to intra-Community trade thereby created does not exceed that which is necessary in order to insure the attainment of the objective in view and unless that objective is justified with regard to Community law' (para 22). The Court accepted the need to encourage the creation of cinematographic works irrespective of their origin as a proper justification (para 23) and accordingly ruled that the requirement did not constitute a measure of equivalent effect (para 24). The Court accordingly arrived at the same result as in the above cases (following the same argument structure or methodology as in *Dassonville* or *Cassis*) although it initially held that the rule did restrict trade and then only after approving its purpose did the Court rule on its validity.

The Advocate General Slynn had argued in *Cinéthèque* that Art 30 (28) did not apply as the measure was not specifically directed at imports, it did not discriminate against imports, it did not make it any more difficult for an importer to sell products and provided no protection to domestic producers. Cases 60 and 61/84 *Cinéthèque* [1985] ECR 2605 at 2611. The Advocate General had defined Art 30 (28) as applying to import restrictions, discriminatory barriers to trade and indistinctly applicable rules that required the producer or distributor to take additional steps that would not normally be required. Similar difficulties again arose in *Torfaen* (n 105).

[104] The Court's treatment of exported goods under Art 29 (ex 34) is distinct and is only applied where there is some element of discrimination. Case 15/79 *PB Groenveld BV v Produktschap voor Vee en Vlees* [1979] ECR 3409, [1981] 1 CMLR 207 (Dutch prohibition on stocking or processing horse meat did not infringe Art 34(29)). The can be understood in terms of the equal burden of the obligation imposed although this may be revised with regard to establishment and services. For further discussion, Craig and de Burca (n 1) Ch 17. See also Case 237/82 *Jongeneel Kaas v The State (Netherlands) and Stichting Centraal Organ Zuivelcontrole* [1984] ECR 483, [1985] 2 CMLR 53; and Case 98/86 *Ministère Public v Mathot* [1987] ECR 809.

[105] The Court followed the same extensive approach in *Torfaen* as in *Cinéthèque*. B&Q had been prosecuted for a violation of Sunday trading laws that prohibited retail shops from selling a number of products subject to certain exceptions on Sundays. The Court referred to its decision in *Cinéthèque* (para 12) and to its decision in *Oeboel* that national rules governing hours of work, delivery and sale in the bread and confectionery industry constituted a legitimate part of economic and social policy consistent with the objectives of public interest pursued under the Treaty (para 13). The same considerations must apply as regards national rules governing the opening hours of retail premises which reflect certain political and economic choices (para 14). The Court then referred to Art 3 of Directive 70/50 which prohibited national measures governing the marketing of products where the restrictive effects of such measures on the free movement of goods exceeded the effects intrinsic to trade rules (para 15). Unfortunately, the Court referred the determination as to whether the national rules remain within that limit back to the national court (para 16). The Court had accordingly held that Art 28 (ex 30) applied although this was subject to reasonable justification the assessment of which was reserved to the national court. The difficulty that arose was that a number of courts within the UK subsequently applied the test established by the Court in an inconsistent manner. *Stoke City Council v B&Q plc* [1990] 3 CMLR 31; *Wellingborough BC v Payless* [1990] 1 CMLR 773; *B&Q plc v Shrewsbury BC* [1990] 3 CMLR 535; *Payless v Peterborough CC* [1990] 2 CMLR 577. For comment, see A Arnull 'What Shall We Do On Sunday?' (1991) 16 EL Rev 112. See also, Weatherill and Beaumont (n 1) 603–10; and Wyatt and Dashwood (n 1) 237–328.

In light of the confusion that arose, the Court decided to assess itself whether restrictions

market regulation, the Court continued to adopt an extended scope rule until the decision in *Keck and Mithouard* in November 1993.[106]

It was not then until *Keck* that the Court was able to begin to place some limits on the scope of *Dassonville* and *Cassis*. Even with this, significant difficulties arise in understanding the proper limits of the new formulation adopted and in fully reconciling this with the still emerging jurisprudence of the Court in this and related areas.

(4) PRODUCT AND SALES RULES—*KECK* (1993)

The need to impose some limits on a full effects doctrine was eventually accepted by the Court in its judgement on *Keck and Mithouard*.[107] The case concerned the prosecution of Messrs Bernard Keck and Daniel Mithouard for resale at a loss under relevant French law.[108]

were justified in a number of subsequent cases. Sunday employment restrictions were accordingly held not to create disproportionate effects to their objectives with Sunday trading rules also being held proportionate and lawful. Case C-312/89 *Union Departement des Syndicats CGT de l'Aisne v SIDEF Conforama* [1991] ECR I-997; Case C-332/89 *Ministère Public v Marchandise* [1991] ECR I-1027; and (with regard to Sunday trading) Cases C-306/88, 304/90 and 169/91 *Stoke-on-Trent CC v B&Q plc* [1992] ECR I-6457, 6493 and 6635, [1993] 1 CMLR 426; and Cases C-418–421, 460–462 and 464/93, 9–11, 14–15, 23–24 & 332/94 *Semeraro Casa Uno Srl v Sindaco del Commune di Erbusco* [1996] ECR I-2975, [1996] 3 CMLR 648.

[106] Commentators still consider that the Court had not clearly and consistently established a proper limit to Art 28 (ex 30). In response to *Torfaen*, White (a member of the Commission's Legal Service) argued that a distinction had to be drawn between product characteristics and rules governing their subsequent sale or usage. *Cassis* had established that the term 'characteristics' referred to the composition, size, shape and weight of goods as well as their presentation, denomination and labelling. Member States were not entitled to require that imported products have the same characteristics as domestic products unless this was strictly necessary for the protection of some legitimate interest. This is distinct from other rules concerning the manner in which goods are sold or used in the importing territory. Provided that goods enjoy equal access to the market, they are not deprived of any other advantage that they would otherwise have been entitled to. White, 'In Search of the Limits of Art 30 of the EEC Treaty' (1989) 26 CMLRev 235, 246–7.

See also J Stiner 'Drawing the Line: Uses and Abuses of Art 30 EEC' (1992) 29 CMLRev 749; and K Mortelmans 'Art 30 of the EEC Treaty and Legislation Relating to Market Circumstances: Time to Consider a New Definition' (1991) 28 CMLRev 115. While Stiner generally focuses on whether the rules constitute a restriction to trade, Mortelmans draws a similar distinction as White between characteristics and rules relating to market circumstances including in particular the terms in which goods are sold.

The Court's maintenance of an extended doctrine of restrictive effect was also criticised by Advocate General Walter van Gerven, in particular, in *Torfaen* and similar cases. The Advocate General adopted a similar approach to Sir Gordon Slynn in *Cinéthèque* (n 103).

[107] Cases C-267 and 268/91 *Criminal Proceedings Against Keck and Mithouard* [1993] ECR I-6097 [1995] 1 CMLR 101.

[108] Keck and Mithouard were charged with reselling products in an unaltered state at prices lower than their actual purchase price contrary to Art 1 of French Law No 63/628 of 2 July 1963 (as amended by Art 32 of Order No 86/1243 of 1 Dec 1986). The Tribunal de Grande Instance in Strasbourg referred two preliminary questions to the Court concerning the compat-

In its judgment on 24 November 1993, the Court focused on the compatibility of the prohibition on resale at a loss with the law of free movement of goods.[109] The Court referred to its *Dassonville* definition of a measure having equivalent effect (paragraph 11). The Court noted the purpose of the legislation (paragraph 12) and accepted that although it may restrict the volume of sales it had to assess whether that possibility was sufficient to characterize the legislation as a measure of equivalent effect (paragraph 13).

The Court then stated that it had considered it necessary to re-examine and clarify the relevance of Article 28 (ex Article 30) in light of the implied abuses that had taken place.[110] The decision in *Cassis* was restated (paragraph 15).[111] The Court then added:

> However, contrary to what has previously been decided, the application to products from other Member States of national provisions restricting or prohibiting certain selling arrangements is not such as to hinder directly or indirectly, actually or potentially, trade between Member States within the meaning of the *Dassonville* judgement (Case 8/074 [1974] ECR 837), provided that those provisions apply to all affected traders operating within the national territory and provided that they affect in the same manner, in law and in fact, the marketing of domestic products and of those from other Member States. (paragraph 16).

In *Keck*, the Court distinguished selling arrangements subject to a dual discrimination (equal application) and effects (in law and fact) test. The

ibility of the prohibition with the law on the free movement of goods, services and capital and free competition. The questions referred were specifically concerned with the anomaly that arose with local manufacturers being able to sell at a loss and the distortive effects on competition between traders on the basis of nationality and place of establishment.

109 The Court distinguished free movement of persons, services and capital as the prohibition was concerned with the marketing of goods (para 6). The Court stated that there was no discrimination under Art 7 as the legislation applied without reference to nationality (citing Case 308/86 *Ministère Public v Lambert* [1988] ECR 4369) (para 8). The competition aspects were also dismissed on procedural grounds, in particular, as the request only referred to Art 3 and none of the other Treaty rules on competition (para 9).

110 The Court stated that in view of the increasing tendency of traders to invoke Art 30 (28) as a means of challenging any rules the effect of which was to limit their commercial freedom (even where they were not aimed at products from other Member States), the Court considered it necessary to re-examine and clarify its case law on the matter (para 14).

111 In '*Cassis de Dijon* . . . it was held that, in the absence of harmonization of legislation measures of equivalent effect prohibited by Art 30 include obstacles to the free movement of goods where they are the consequence of applying rules that lay down requirements to be met by such goods (such as requirements as to designation, form, size, weight, composition, presentation, labelling, packaging) to goods from other Member States where they are lawfully manufactured and marketed, even if those rules apply without distinction to all products unless an application can be justified by a public interest objective taking precedence over the free movement of goods' (para 15).

basis for this was that market access was not prevented or restricted more than that for domestic products. The Court stated that where these conditions (as set out in paragraph 16) are fulfilled, the application of such rules to the sale of products from another Member State is not by its nature such as to prevent their access to the market or to impede access any more than it impedes the access of domestic products. Such rules therefore fall outside the scope of Article 30 of the Treaty (paragraph 17). The effect of this is to separate composition and sales rules with the latter being excluded from the scope of prohibition (subject to the conditions stated).

The decision is accordingly important in attempting to place some proper limits on the unrestricted effects of the *Dassonville* formulation. A number of difficulties nevertheless still arise with regard to the meaning[112] and effect[113] as well as the importance of the decision more generally. Much of this has been examined as part of a larger revision of the law in this area.

(5) POST-*KECK* EFFECT AND MARKET IMPACT

The basic distinction drawn in *Keck* between product and sales rules has been applied in a number of cases subsequently.[114] While some provisions

[112] The specific meaning of the term in law is unclear although this will presumably include all overtly discriminatory legal provisions. This would then retain a discrimination related element within the new *Keck* approach. This is supported by the reference immediately before the 'in law and in fact' proviso (in para 16) to measures being equally applicable to all traders. The provisions must accordingly not be discriminatory either in terms of application or content. The result of this is that both a discriminatory and effects based component is included within the *Keck* proviso.

[113] Quality in fact may be much more difficult to determine in practice. This will require an examination of the result or impact of the measure in the particular circumstances. Dual burden rules would clearly be caught. Equal burden rules such as in the Sunday trading cases would be excluded to the extent that they were applied in the same manner in fact. Weatherill notes that equal burden rules would satisfy the *Keck* test (n 1 at 613). This may nevertheless still be subject to a further effects' assessment. See, eg, *Familiapress* (n 115) and *Gourmet* (n 116).

[114] Cases C-401 and 402/92 *Criminal Proceedings Against Tankstation 't Heukske vof and JBE Boermans* [1994] ECR I-2199, [1995] 3 CMLR 501 (rules providing for the compulsory closing of shops and petrol stations fell outside Art 30(28)); Cases C-69 and 258/93 *Punto Casa SpA v Sindaco del Commune di Capena* [1994] ECR I-2355 (Italian rules on the closure of retail outlets on Sundays fell outside Art 28 (ex Art 30)); Case C-292/92 *Ruth Hünermund and others v Landesapothekerkammer Baden-Württemberg* [1993] ECR I-6787 (advertising by pharmacists outside the pharmacy of quasi-pharmaceutical products); Case C-412/93 *Société d'Importation Édouard Leclerc-siplec* [1995] ECR I-179, [1995] 3 CMLR 422 (prohibitions on television advertising in particular sectors although Advocate General Jacobs was critical of the reasoning in *Keck*); Case C-391/92 *Commission v Greece* [1995] ECR I-1621, [1996] 1 CMLR 359 and [1995] All ER (EC) 802 (Greek prohibition on the sale of processed milk for infants other than through pharmacies); Case C-387/93 *Banchero* [1995] ECR I-4663, [1996] 1 CMLR 829 (national rules confining tobacco sales to authorized retailers); Case C-162/97 *Gunnar Nilsson* [1998] ECR I-7477 (national rules requiring authorization for the distribution of bovine semen); Cases 140-142/94 *Dip Spa v Commune di Bassano del Grappa* [1995] ECR I-3257, [1996] 4 CMLR 157 (licensing requirement on shop opening); Joined Cases C-34–36/95 *Konsumentonbudsmannen (KO) v de Agostini (Svenska) Forleg AB*

have been accepted as to constitute selling arrangements and held not to be restrictive, the Court has still been prepared to consider certain measures prohibited in appropriate cases such as in *Familiapress*[115] or *Gourmet*.[116]

While the Court has been rather restrictive in its use of *Keck*, it has still continued to follow this analysis where it considers it appropriate despite the criticism that it has received[117] (including from within its own offices).[118] The result of this is that it is still possible to distinguish between

[1997] ECR I-3843 (outright ban on advertising aimed at children less than 12 years of age and misleading advertising). In Case C-320/93 *Lucien Ortscheit GmbH* [1994] ECR I-5243, [1995] 2 CMLR 242 it was held that a rule prohibiting advertisements containing offers to obtain medicinal products by individual importation fell within Art 28 (ex 30) as it applied only to foreign medicinal products. For further discussion of the post-*Keck* decisions of the Court, MP Maduro 'Harmony and Dissonance in Free Movement' Ch 3 of Mads Andenas and Wulf-Henning Roth *Services and Free Movement in EU Law* (Oxford OUP 2002).

115 The Court may in appropriate cases consider that certain promotional restrictions are so intimately connected with the product itself that they relate to composition rather than sales. Case C-368/95 *Vereinigte Familiapress Zeitungsverlags-und Vertriebs GmbH v Heinrich Bauer Verlag* [1997] 3 CMLR 1329 in which *Keck* was distinguished and an Austrian prohibition on the inclusion of prize competitions in newspapers was caught by Art 30(28) on the basis that it required publishers to alter the contents of their periodicals with the effect of impairing access to intra-State trade.

116 Case C-405/98 *Konsumentombudsmannen (KO) v Gourmet International Products AB (GIP)* Judgement of the Court (6th Chamber), 8 Mar 2001 (Swedish prohibition on the marketing of alcoholic beverages on radio and television as well as in periodicals or other publications). The Court noted that a prohibition on all advertising would impede market access by products from other States as against products with which consumers were familiar, in particular, as a result of traditional social practices and local habits and customs (para 21). The reference in para 17 of *Keck* (that the restriction must not prevent or impede access) was applied. With regard to services, the Court also considered that the prohibition on advertising constituted a restriction on the free provision of services as it had a particular effect on the cross-border supply of advertising space even though it was applied in a non-discriminatory manner (para 39 following *Alpine Investments*). Advocate General Jacobs had issued a concurrent opinion on 14 Dec 2000 (n 171). For further discussion, Maduro (nn 18 and 122).

117 Stiner and Mortelmans (n 106). See also N Reich 'The "November Revolution" of the European Court of Justice: *Keck*, *Meng* and *Audi* Revisited' (1994) 31 CMLRev 459; D Chalmers 'Repackaging the Internal Market—The Ramifications of the *Keck* Judgement' (1994) 19 ELRev 385; P Maduro '*Keck*: The end? The beginning of the end? or just the end of the beginning?' (1994) I Irish Journal of EurLaw 33; L Gormley 'Reasoning Renounced? The Remarkable Judgement in *Keck & Mitouard*' (1994) EBLRev 63; and Gormley 'Two Years After *Keck*' (1996) 19 Fordham International Law Journal; S Weatherill 'After *Keck*: Some Thoughts on how to Clarify the Clarification' (1996) 33 CMLRev 885; N Bernard 'Discrimination and Free Movement in EC Law' (1996) ICLQ 82; Freidbacher 'Motive Unmasked: The European Court of Justice, The Free Movement of Goods and the Search for Legitimacy' (1996) 2 ELJ 226. See also L Gormley 'Assent and respect for judgements: *Uncommunautaire* reasoning in the European Court of Justice' in Cramer, Micklitz and Tonner (eds) *Law and Diffuse Interests in the European Legal Order*; and P Maduro *We, The Court* (n 18) Ch 3.

118 Advocate General Jacobs rejected the strict distinction between product and sales rules adopted in *Keck* and in *Leclerc* suggested the adoption of a substantial restriction test similar to that adopted under competition law. Where a measure affects goods directly, there is a presumption of a substantial impact with the measure being prohibited unless justified. When the measure is concerned with selling arrangements (and not otherwise discriminatory), it would be subject to an effects test having regard to the range of goods concerned, the nature

two basic tests either based on discrimination (direct or indirect)[119] and a pure post-*Dassonville* effects test. The refinement of the effects doctrine is to look at substantial impact or restriction.[120] The difficulty that arises with even this clarified effects test is that this requires an examination of the specific impact of the measures on cross-border trade in a similar manner as conducted in a competition case.[121] With *Keck*, the Court had arrived at a compromise position whereby a general (but not exclusive) distinction was drawn between product and sales rules with the former being subject to a traditional post-*Dassonville* effects test and the latter being presumed to be non-restrictive subject to the in law and fact equality test.

The result is unfortunately (operationally) confusing and arguably (intellectually) unsound. While the two main tests or doctrines developed are clear (discrimination or effect), their relationship and application in particular cases are still difficult to determine.[122] There are clear limitations to a

of the restriction, whether the impact was direct or indirect and the extent to which other selling arrangements were available. Jacobs in Case 412/93. See also opinion of the Advocate General in Case C-384/93 *Alpine Investments* (n 171). See also Advocate General Lenz in Case C-391/92 *Commission v Greece*.

[119] As supported, for example, by Wyatt. Wyatt and Dashwood (n 43).

[120] AG Jacobs (n 118).

[121] Certain commentators criticize this as being unworkable in light of the expensive and specialist expertise required. See, for example, Craig and de Búrca (n 1) 626. Craig and de Burca also question the meaning of the market access element of the effects test and whether any real distinction can be drawn between measures that prohibit market access or only limit trading volumes. (n 1) 624–625.

[122] (nn 43, 106 and 117 and 118). Some writers have attempted to summarize the debate in terms of three main sets of theories: a discrimination test, a typological test and a combined test. See Maduro (18) Ch 2.

A discrimination approach is essentially concerned with limiting the protectionist intervention by Member State governments. For this purpose, discrimination may be considered to take one of a number of forms. Marenco, for example, defines discrimination to include: (a) express or formal discrimination; (b) material or *de facto* discrimination (indistinctly applicable provisions intended to prefer local products); and (c) excessive or disproportionate provisions (indistinctly applicable measures imposing unnecessary additional regulatory burdens on overseas products). G Marenco 'Pour une interpretation de la notion de measure d'effet equivalent a une restriction quantative' (1984) CDE 291. See also Marenco 'The Notion of Restriction on the Freedom of Establishment and Provision of Services in the Case-law of the Court' (1991) YEL 111 (and 'La notion de restriction aux libertes d'etablissement et de la prestation de services dans la jurisprudence de la Cour' (1992) *Gazette du Palais* 317); and L Defaque 'Le concept de dirimination en matiere de libre circulation des merchandise' (1987) 23 CDE 741 and 5481. Discrimination will then involve some intentional protectionist element. See also N Burrows, *Free Movement in Europnea Community Law* (Oxford Clarendon Press 1987), 54.

The term 'typological' has also been used to refer to tests based on particular types of rules. This would include the distinction drawn by White between product and marketing rules (n 106) and the Court's product and sales rule reformulation in *Keck* (nn 107–113). This would also include Mortelman's locational and territorial refinement (qualifying the types of marketing rules excluded) as well as Van Gerven's 'partitioning effect' doctrine and Stiner's 'single market' test. Mortelmans (n 106), Van Gerven (106) and Stiner (n 106). All of these theories then look at the scope of effect of the particular restriction concerned although with different results. On indirect discrimination (n 32).

discrimination based rule although this does depend upon how discrimination is defined.[123] A full effect or market impact analysis may also be considered excessive and unnecessary in many cases.[124]

One possible compromise solution may to be develop a combined or progressive approach that would look initially to overt and then indirect discrimination on a traditional nationality basis but still retain the possibility of subjecting more complex cases to an effects test where some damage may still result to intra-territory trade (through the use of a reclassification

Reference may also be made to a 'balance' or 'cost benefit' test which is concerned with the relative value of the national restriction concerned having regard to the obligation and trade effects created. Maduro (18) 49. This, however, generally confuses the initial scope of restriction and subsequent determination of possible validity under the public interest or general good tests developed by the Court. No attempt is then made to confirm either the scope of basic restriction or supporting derogation.

The current debate can possibly best be summarized in terms of a clarified discrimination test (including direct and indirect discrimination irrespective of protectionist intent) and market access or effect. A more useful distinction may then be drawn having regard to whether the restriction is directed to market access or internal regulation with either an effects or discrimination being adopted in each case (n 46). In more complex situations, however, a further reclassification proviso may have to be applied where an apparently legitimate internal regulatory provision may still have a significant market effect (nn 125, 128, and 129).

123 The adoption of a discrimination based test can be supported on the basis of Court experience (both European and national) and familiarity. See, for example, Wyatt and Dashwood (n 1) at 328–9. Courts are already familiar with examining restrictions on the basis of overt or covert discrimination. They are less familiar with more general policy assessments of legitimate justification for market impact restrictions.

Against this, it could be argued that courts are already familiar with examining market effects in the context of competition law. A distinction could then be drawn in the free movement of goods situation between restrictive effect (under Art 28) and judicial derogation (public interest or general good). Again it could be argued that an established market access theory does not yet exist as under cartel or dominant position law. Even then, this would involve more complex and costly market examination with a consequential detrimental effect on Court workload and the speed and cost of litigation. See, eg, Craig and de Búrca (n 1) 66 and 67.

The advantage of the alternative substantial impact doctrine is that the emphasis would then return to inter-state trade effect or effects. The artificial distinction between product and sales rules would be removed and any measure caught where it had an identifiable impact or effect on market access and trade. On the meaning and scope of discrimination (nn 32 and 136).

124 The Court's position in *Keck* would appear to represent a compromise with sales related rules being presumed to be non-restrictive subject to the revised discrimination proviso (in law and fact). The pre-*Keck* product cases are then not affected. They continue to be subject to a post-*Dassonville* effects test. Pre-*Keck* sales cases have now to be revised in light of the new presumption against restrictive effect created.

The residual issue to be determined is whether the revised discrimination and refined effects doctrines can be reconciled. It has to be accepted that in determining whether indirect discrimination exists, the effect of the measure has to be examined and assessed. The degree and relative sophistication of the examination conducted will depend upon the nature of the restriction imposed. In a complex situation, this will necessarily approximate with the full impact type of examination conducted under an effects test. It is possible that the two approaches will then converge in practice depending upon the complexity of the case and, in particular, the degree of increasingly marginal effect on trade involved (nn 126, 128 and 129).

proviso).[125] The result may then be that the discrimination and effects based approaches may converge in the most difficult of cases.[126]

The doctrine of the unity of the Community still requires that a consistent approach should be adopted across all areas of law insofar as possible.[127] That does not necessarily mean that a more complex competition based examination must be conducted in every free movement case. This may nevertheless be considered necessary in appropriate situations. The final resolution may then relate more to the adoption of an informed and balanced methodology (or procedure) rather than a single intellectually coherent juridical formula.[128]

[125] While *Keck* reflects one possible intermediate solution, this is still somewhat confused and contrived. A simpler resolution may be to adopt a combined or layered approach with a three stage test based on the existence of express discrimination (essentially in law), indirect discrimination (in fact) and (then) market (or discriminatory) effect. While a basic direct and indirect discrimination based test will be appropriate in most cases, only in more difficult situations will a full effects examination be required. This would then represent a practical and operational compromise that would avoid the need to consider the costs and delay involved with a full effects test in all cases. This could also reconcile a number of the separate approaches or theories developed to date including Marenco, Mortelmans, Van Gerven and Stiner as well as White (nn 106 and 122) and the earlier writers referred to (n 43).

[126] The issue that arises from a theoretical perspective is to what extent any difference remains between indirect discrimination (n 32) and market impact or effect in the more complex situation (n 124). The answer is probably none provided that the concept of identifiable effect is equated with indirect discriminatory result. The confusion that may arise is between the separate purpose or function of the restrictions being examined where they have some other essentially non-discriminatory social, industrial or other public good function. That does not, however, prevent them from having a restrictive effect within an extended concept of indirect discrimination.

This more complex examination of market impact in particular cases may be referred to as 'discriminatory effect.' The revised test could then still be discrimination based although this would involve the three elements of direct and indirect discrimination as well as 'discriminatory effect' in more complex cases (nn 125 and 129).

The adoption of an extended concept of indirect discrimination is, for example, supported by the Court's decisions on national price restrictions where this may place the importer at a disadvantage. See, for example, Case 65/75 *Tasca* [1977] ECR 291, [1977] 2 CMLR 183; Cases 88–90/75 *SADAM* [1976] ECR 323, [1977] 2 CMLR 183; Case 5/79 *Hans Buys* [1979] ECR 3203, [1980] 2 CMLR 493; and Cases 16–20/79 *Danis* [1979] ECR 3327, 3 CMLR 492. Restrictions in the area of workers may also be examined in the same manner. See, for example, Case C-57/96 *H. Meints* [1997] ECR I-6689, [1998] 1 CMLR 1159. Contrast Case *Generics BV v Smith Kline and French Laboratories Ltd* [1997] ECR I-7231, [1998] 1 CMLR 1 (use of patent to prevent market authorization on basis of manufactured samples); and Case C-473/98 *Toolex* [2000] (general prohibition on product use). For discussion, see Wyatt and Dashwood (n 1) 328–30.

[127] Section D (5). Barents (n 39).

[128] As discussed in (nn 125 and 126), an appropriate solution or reconciliation may be based on the adoption of a three stage methodology of direct and indirect discrimination and then 'discriminatory effect'. A full quasi-competition law market effects examination would only be required in more exceptional cases. Otherwise, judicial efficiency at the national and European levels would be protected (promoted) through the use of a simpler revised discrimination based approach. This would also reconcile market entry and post-entry market control or regulation on a GATT trade model (nn 35 and 46).

In practice, it may simply be that the Court will initially look for discrimination, failing which consider whether any separate restriction on inter-state trade exits. A combined or double test may then be applied. While this may not have great theoretical consistency or value, it is practical and effective in allowing it to consider the nature and extent and then justification of any particular restriction under European Law.[129]

The result of any detailed examination of the jurisprudence of the Court in the goods area is that the precise rules applicable to non-secondary legislation based activities are still unclear. Activities or functions that fall outside the scope of the financial directives will have to be examined in practice in accordance with the case law of the Court. The difficulty that arises is that the precise limits of restrictive effect and judicial derogation are still unclear. The further confusion that has arisen as a result of *Keck* and the post-*Keck* sales discussion is of particular relevance in the financial area in light of the need for institutions to promote established and new products. The limited decisions that have been provided in this area are considered in the next Chapter following a review of the more general decisions on establishment and services.

129 The conclusion that may have to be drawn is that the Court may simply select between, or even combine, the two major tests wherever this is considered necessary or appropriate. Discrimination will generally be used where this is present as it is relatively easy to identify and quantify. Where there is no significant discriminatory element (either direct or indirect), the Court can still assess the trade effect of the measure. If a trade restriction is present, the law of free movement will apply. The Court will then be able to assess the relative advantage and disadvantage of the measure and its possible justification.

This is consistent with the theoretical reconciliation and alternative three stage methodology suggested above (nn 122, 124, 125, 126, and 128). A full (*Dassonville*) effects doctrine should continue to be applied to identifiable restrictions on market entry. A discrimination test would be used for other more regulatory intended internal measures (which would operate on both a direct (express) and indirect basis). Where an internal measure was not discriminatory and, in particular, had some obvious or apparent social, industrial or other public good function, this could still be caught where there was a significant (residual) effect on trade. This could be explained in terms of the measure being reclassified as an entry restriction and made subject to a full effects test (nn 122 and 128).

This is consistent with the approach adopted under the GATT and GATS (nn 46 and 128) and reconciles the separate approaches applied by the Court to initial market access or entry and subsequent internal regulatory restriction (nn 43 and 122). It also provides a more substantial theoretical basis for the possibly more practical or pragmatic approach followed by the Court in its decision making.

This is further supported by the parallel extension of the case law of the Court in the establishment, services and workers area. Section D. Certainly in the area of workers, it is possible that post-*Kraus* and *Bosman* (nn 187–188), any effect on trade will be considered sufficient to bring a national measure within the scope of relevant restriction. The Court will use discrimination if available. If not, the Court will simply rely on trade effect to allow it to move on to assess possible derogation and justification.

D. LAW OF ESTABLISHMENT AND SERVICES

The creation of an effective internal market requires both free movement of the results of the production process (goods and more recently services) as well as the original factors of production (labour, enterprise and capital). Movement of production factors is secured within Europe through the creation of express Treaty rights in respect of persons (employed and self-employed including companies), establishment (and services) and capital. The relevant provisions are included in Title III of the revised Treaty on the free movement of workers,[130] establishment, services[131] and capital.[132] Further provisions have also been added concerning visas, asylum and immigration.[133]

The objective of these provisions is to ensure that a proper open market for the production of goods and provision of services is created between all participating territories.[134] In connection with this, the Court has developed a number of further judicial precedents in addition to the basic underlying Treaty rights provided. While each of these is generally based on the principle of non-discrimination as set out in Article 12 (ex 6), the Court has extended the application and content of these rights beyond the traditional scope of the underlying idea of national treatment at the same time as continue to develop an extended mechanism of judicial derogation.[135]

This accordingly represents another area in which the Court has exercised considerable formative powers in the construction of a new *acquis communautaire*. Equivalent, if not more significant, difficulties nevertheless arise in attempting to determine the proper limits of these extended principles of Treaty prohibition and supporting judicial derogation or exemption. The main reason for this is the considerably more complex nature of the relationship between the person exercising the rights concerned (establishment or services) and the host territory that will attempt to invoke or

[130] Section D (5).

[131] Sections D (1), (2) and (3).

[132] All restrictions on the movement of capital and payments between States and between States and third countries are prohibited within the framework of the Treaty (Art 56(1) (ex 73(b)). This is without prejudice to the application to third countries of any restrictions on capital movements or direct investment in effect on 31 Dec 1993 (Art 57 (ex 73(c)) and domestic tax law (Arts 58 (ex 73(d)). A special procedure is also provided for action to be taken in exceptional circumstances where capital movements to or from third countries may cause or threaten serious difficulties with regard to economic and monetary union (Art 59 (ex 73(f)). For historical comment, Ch 2, section I.

[133] Title IV (ex Title IIIa) Visas, Asylum, Immigration and other Policies related to Free Movement of Persons. For comment, Weatherill and Beaumont (n 1) Ch 18; Wyatt and Dashwood (n 1) Chs 14 and 16; and Craig and de Búrca (n 1) Ch 16.

[134] The Commission has proposed a new Directive on Services although this is disapplied in the financial area. Proposed Directive of the European Parliament and of the Council on Services in the Internal Market of 5 Mar 2004 (COM (2004) 2 final/3).

[135] Section C (1) in connection with the work of the Court in the area of goods. On discrimination and national treatment (nn 32 and 46). See also (nn 138 and 163).

impose its local regulatory requirements. With regard to establishment, in particular, the local measures will operate at both a form of pre-production (business set ups) and continuing post-production stage while establishment and services regulation will potentially include both initial market entry and other continuing or on-going compliance conditions or obligations.[136] The law in this area then becomes more difficult and further confused with regard to banking and financial markets due to the limited number of directly relevant decisions produced. Considerable problems of legal certainty and predictability necessarily arise that limit the production of a consistent and coherent body of law in this area which further impedes reliance and consequent market integration.[137]

The purpose of this section is to attempt to understand the limits of the Court's current jurisprudence in the establishment and services areas and to anticipate possible future developments. The main decisions on establishment and services are initially reviewed with the associated parallel developments that have taken place in connection with the extension of these provisions to apply to distinctly and indistinctly applicable measures. The specific issue of legitimate local (host) regulatory activity is referred to and the continuing problems that arise in determining the legitimate scope of national intervention assessed.

The position with regard to workers is also referred to in an attempt to understand whether the Court has yet been able to construct a consistent and coherent jurisprudence in the law of free movement especially with regard to resolving the basic conflict that arises in promoting enhanced market access at the same time as ensure proper and legitimate market control. The content of the limited but significant jurisprudence that is beginning to emerge in the financial area is examined in further detail in the following chapter.

136 While establishment and services are often discussed together, establishment is, of its nature, more concerned with the setting up of an initial production process or capability while services represent the result (or product) of that process. Establishment can then be considered to constitute a factor of production and services a production consequence or product. The provision of services is consequently economically more analogous to the sale of goods which inherent economic correspondence does not apply with regard to establishment. While the same general principles may be applied to each right, different results or consequences may necessarily follow in practice. This is reflected in some of the apparently more inconsistent decisions of the Court. This distinction is also relevant in the financial area although possibly of less importance to the extent that a financial institution will generally have to comply with the local territory's regulatory system in any case where it conducts a relevant regulated activity in that country. This will then apply whether full establishment is to be sought or only more limited services provided in the local territory. The relevant regulatory prohibitions and licensing requirements will apply in both cases although some concessions may be available where only local marketing is involved. Section D (3) and (n 164).

137 This is referred to as integration damage or default. Ch 1, section B (4).

(1) ESTABLISHMENT AND SERVICES

Restrictions on the freedom of establishment of nationals of a Member State in the territory of another State are prohibited within the framework of the provisions set out in the Treaty (Article 43 (ex 52), paragraph 1). This prohibition extends to restrictions on the setting up of agencies, branches or subsidiaries by nationals of any State established in the territory of another State. Establishment includes both the right to take up and pursue activities as self-employed persons and to set up and manage undertakings (Article 43 (ex 52), paragraph 2).[138]

Restrictions on the freedom to provide services within the Community are prohibited in respect of all nationals of Member States who are established in a State other than that of the person for whom the services are intended subject to the provisions of the Treaty.[139] The right to provide

[138] Freedom of establishment includes the right to take up and pursue activities as self-employed persons and to set up and manage undertakings, in particular, companies or firms (within the meaning of the second paragraph of Art 48 (ex 58)) under the conditions laid down for nationals by the law of the country where such establishment is effected but subject to the provisions relating to capital and payments (Art 43 (ex 52), para 2). On the still emerging law of free movement of companies, Case C-208/00 *Uberseering BV v Nordic Construction Company Baumanagement GmbH* of Nov 5 2002. For comment, Mads Andenas 'Free Movement of Companies' (2003) 119 LQR 221. See also the earlier decision in *Centros Ltd v Erhvervs- og Selskabsstyrelsen* [1999] ECR I-1459; and Henning Roth, 'Case Note' (2000) 37 CMLR 147.

The right of establishment includes both the right of a natural or legal person to establish in a Member State as well as, once established, to set up agencies or branches in other Member States. Art 43 (ex 52). For comment, Wyatt and Dashwood (n 1) 430. This separate right of 're-establishment' includes the right to move a primary establishment or set up a secondary establishment in another Member State, the right to have more than one place of business and the right to carry on business under the same conditions as local nationals (national treatment).

The rules on establishment do not apply to activities connected with the exercise of official authority even if only occasionally (Art 45 (ex 55)) and national laws, regulations or administrative action may treat foreign nationals differently on grounds of public policy, public security or public health (Art 46 (ex 56)). To assist taking up and pursuing activities as self-employed persons, directives are to be issued under the Treaty for the mutual recognition of diplomas, certificates and other evidence of formal qualifications and for the coordination of other provisions concerning the taking up and pursuit of such activities (Art 47(1) and (2) (ex 57)).

Companies or firms are to be treated in the same manner as natural persons provided only that they are formed in accordance with the law of a Member State and have their registered office, central administration or principal place of business within the Community. Companies or firms mean any company or firm constituted under civil commercial law including cooperative societies and other legal persons governed by public or private law except for those that are non-profit making (Art 48 (ex 58)).

[139] These rights may be extended by the Council to nationals of third countries (Art 49 (ex 59)). Services are defined as those normally provided for remuneration on condition that they are not governed by the provisions relating to goods, capital or persons. Services will, in particular, include activities of an industrial character, a commercial character, craftsmen or the professions. Without prejudice to the right of establishment, the service provider may temporarily pursue the activity in a State where the service is provided under the same conditions as are imposed on nationals (Art 50 (ex 60)).

services extends to the provision of services from the home to the recipient in the host State and where the provider either moves to the host State to provide the service or the recipient moves to the home territory. The provider may offer the services in another State other than that of original establishment.

The Treaty provides that freedom of establishment and services with regard to particular activities may be secured through directives (Articles 44 and 52 (ex 54 and 63)) in response to which two General Programmes were issued in 1961 and 1962.[140] Some measures were subsequently adopted[141] although early progress was slow.[142] In light of the delays that arose, the Court took the opportunity in 1974 to confirm in *Reyners* and *Van Binsbergen* that both Articles 52 and 59 (43 and 49) were directly effective without the need for further secondary legislation.[143] This paralleled its activist intervention with *Dassonville* in the area of goods.[144]

The liberalization of banking and insurance services connected with movements of capital was to be effected in parallel with the liberalization of capital (Art 51(2) (ex 61)). Ch 2, sections H and I. Directives were to be adopted to secure the liberalization of specific services (Art 52 (ex 63)). Member States also declared their readiness to liberalize services (on the recommendation of the Commission) beyond the directives provided for where their general economic situation and the economic sector permitted (Art 53 (ex 64)). To the extent that the free movement of services has not been established, each State must apply any residual restrictions without distinction on grounds of nationality or residence (Art 54 (ex 65)). Arts 45 to 48 apply equally to services as establishment (Art 55 (ex 66)).

[140] OJ Sp Edn (Second Series) IX, p 7; and OJ Sp Ed (Second Series) IX, 3. These did not constitute legislation as such but may be used by the Court as an aid to interpretation. For comment, Weatherill and Beaumont (n 1) 697; and Wyatt and Dashwood (n 1) 439–43. These provisions were subsequently deleted under the Treaty of Amsterdam. See also Ch 5 (n 1).

[141] Directive 73/148 created a general right of entry and residence and Directive 75/34 a right to remain in the territory of a Member State. These measures parallel Directives 68/360 and Regulation 1251/70 in the field of workers. Equality in employment had then been judicially secured rather than through legislation such as under Regulation 1612/68 for workers. See, eg, Case 197/84 *Steinhauser v City of Biarritz* [1985] ECR 1819 (the local municipality only rented lock-ups for business purposes to French nationals and not a German resident artist); and Case 63/85 *Commission v Italy* (1988) ECR 29, [1989] 2 CMLR 601 (only Italian nationals had access to publicly funded housing and reduced rate mortgage loans). A number of other directives have since been adopted in specific areas such as under Directives 77/249, 89/48 and 98/5 in respect of lawyers.

[142] A Arnull *The European Union and its Court of Justice* (OUP Oxford 1999), ch 9. Arnull notes, in particular, that this was required in light of the Council's failure to implement the General Programmes by the end of the transitional period on 31 Dec 1969 which was, in part, caused by the adoption of the *Luxembourg Compromise* in 1966 which required consensus rather than majority voting. Arnull 335.

[143] Case 2/74 *Reyners v Belgian State* [1974] ECR 631, [1974] 2 CMLR 305 (A Dutch national was denied admission as *avocat* to the Belgian Bar although he was resident in Belgium and held the relevant Belgian legal qualification); and Case 33/74 *Van Binsbergen v Bestuur van de Bedrijfsvereniging voor de Metaalnijverheid* [1974] ECR 1299, (1975) 1 CMLR 298 (Netherlands requirement that only locally established persons could act as legal representatives or advisers before the social service courts could not be applied to a Dutch national who had since transferred his residence to Belgium).

In *Reyners*, the Court rejected any argument that the effectiveness of Art 43 (ex 52) was

Whether establishment or services is involved in any particular case would subsequently be determined in accordance with the tests set out in *Gebhard* in 1994.[145] This depends, in particular, upon whether the activity is conducted on a 'stable and continuing basis' or only on a 'temporary basis' with the temporary nature of the activity being assessed having regard to its 'periodicity, continuity and regularity.'

The Court has also extended Article 43 (ex 52) to apply with regard to nationals returning to their home Member State[146] although neither Articles 43 nor 49 apply exclusively to national activity with no cross-border element.[147] In *Gebhard*, the Court nevertheless added that any

dependent on the adoption of directives regulating the professions under Arts 44(1) and 48(1) (ex 54(2) and 57(1)). Art 43 (ex 52) was stated to be a specific implementation of the principle of non-discrimination set out in Art 12 (ex 6).

In *Van Binsbergen*, the Court considered that any requirement of a linkage between the place of permanent establishment and the place where services were provided would have the effect of turning the right to provide services into a mere right of establishment. The Court nevertheless accepted that the rule may be objectively justified by the need to ensure observance of professional rules of conduct connected, in particular, with the administration of justice and with respect for professional ethics (para 14). Whether the requirement was justified in the particular case was referred to the national court. In making its assessment, the Court had to consider whether the objective could have been achieved by alternative and more proportionate means. Section D.4.

144 Section C (2).

145 Case C-55/94, *Reinhard Gebhard v Consiglio dell 'Ordine degli Avvocati e Procuratori di Milano* [1995] ECR I-4165, [1996] 1 CMLR 603, paras 25, 26 and 27. The case concerned a German national authorized to practice as an *Rechtsanwalt* in his Member State of origin who had sought to use the title *Avvocato* in Italy as his Member State of establishment without joining the local bar.

146 Art 43 (ex 52) is ambiguous with regard to whether the scope of prohibition applies to returning nationals. In Case 136/78 *Ministère Public v Auer* [1979] ECR 437: [1979] 2 CMLR 373, the Court held that an Austrian national who had become naturalized in France could not rely on the direct effect of Art 47(1) (ex 57(1)) to use his Italian veterinary qualifications to practice in France. Art 43 (ex 52) was restricted to providing national treatment and could therefore only be relied on by nationals of one Member State in another with local restrictions on free movement only being removed by mutual recognition directives. The decision was confirmed in Case 115/78 *Knoors v Secretary of State for Economic Affairs* [1979] ECR 399, [1979] 2 CMLR 357 in which a Dutch national residing in Belgium was able to exercise rights to work as a plumber conferred by a directive issued under Art 44 (ex 54). It was held in Case 107/83 *Ordre des Avocats v Klopp* [1984] ECR 2971 that a Member State could not deny a national from another State the right to enter and exercise the profession of advocate solely on the ground that he maintained local chambers even where the national rules applied without discrimination on the basis of nationality (n 150). Member States of origin are also prohibited from hindering the establishment of their own nationals or locally incorporated companies in other States. Case 81/87 *R v HM Treasury and Commissions of Inland Revenue, ex p Daily Mail and General Trust plc* [1988] ECR 5483, [1988] 3 CMLR 713, para 16. These rights may be extended to apply to spouses although only where some disadvantage can be established. Case C-370/90 *R v Immigration and Appeal Tribunal and Surinder Singh, ex p Secretary of State for the Home Department* [1992] I-4265 (a spouse might enjoy, at least, the same rights of entry and residence as would be granted under Community law if his or her spouse chose to enter and reside in another Member State).

147 On the development of the application of the freedom of establishment rules to apply to nationals relying on domestic measure, see *Knoors, Auer*, and *Bouchoucha* (French national

provision that was sufficiently obstructive to constitute a hindrance to the freedom of establishment would fall within the scope of Article 43 (ex 52) and require justification (at paragraph 37).

(2) DISCRIMINATION AND EFFECT

While the early decisions of the Court on establishment and services involved some element of discrimination, this would later be extended to include non-discriminatory and indistinctly applicable measures in certain cases.[148]

Article 43 (ex 52) is ambiguous as to whether it should apply on a discriminatory or non-discriminatory basis. The Court had initially followed a discrimination based formulation in *Reyners*[149] which approach was continued in such later cases as Case 221/85 *Commission v Belgium.*[150] The inclusion of indistinctly applicable measures with regard to social security exemptions for self-employed persons was recognized in Cases 154–155/87 *RSVZ v Wolf*[151] and the adoption of a more complete

had obtained an osteopathy diploma in the UK but was prosecuted in France for not holding the relevant qualification). For comment, P Stanley (1996) 33 CMLRev 713, 719–21. Some Community element must still be present. See, for example, Cases 54 and 91/88 and 14/89 *Nino and others* [1990] ECR 3537, [1992] 1 CMLR 83 (prosecution of four Italian nationals practising pranotherapy and biotherapy without medical licenses); and Case C-112/91 *Werner-Finanzamt Aachen-Innenstadt* [1993] ECR I-429 (failed challenge to national tax provisions that favour residents over non-residents).

148 Disagreement nevertheless exists on the meaning and scope of discrimination and the relationship between this and the other tests adopted by the Court (nn 32, 46, 122, 125, 126, 128 and 129). Contrast also the different approaches adopted by the writers in Andenas and Roth (n 161). For further discussion (n 161).

149 (n 143). On indirect discrimination (nn 32, 124, 126, 158, and 188).

150 [1987] ECR 719, [1988] 1 CMLR 620. The case concerned the imposition of restrictions on the provision of clinical biology services by laboratories. See also Case 182/83 *Robert Fearon and Co Ltd v The Irish Land Commission* [1984] ECR 3677, [1985] 2 CMLR 228 which involved an Irish exemption for the compulsory purchase of land conditional on members and shareholders residing on the relevant land. This narrow discrimination based approach was extended in Case 107/83 *Ordre des Avocats v Klopp* [1984] ECR 2971, [1985] 1 CMLR 99 in which a German lawyer had been refused admission to the Paris Bar on the basis that he had failed to maintain a single office within the district of the court where he was admitted (n 146). While this may have been understood as meaning that all indistinctly applicable rules may be caught by Art 43 (ex 52), a more restrictive view is that a non-discriminatory rule may not be used to prevent the exercise of secondary establishment across the Community. For comment, Craig and de Búrca (n 1) 745. The earlier narrow approach was then further extended again in Case C 19/92 *Dieter Kraus v Land Baden, Wurtemberg* [1993] ECR I-1663. (nn 153 and 187).

151 [1988] ECR 3897; Case 143/87 *Stanton v Inasti* [1988] ECR 3877, [1987] 3 CMLR 761; and C-53/95 *Inasti v Kemmler* [1996] ECR I-704. This was further extended in Case 292/86 *Gullung v Conseil de 'l 'ordre des Avocats* [1988] ECR 111, [1988] 2 CMLR 57 (indistinctly applicable requirement that all practising lawyers must be registered at the local bar and be objectively justified); and Case 271/82 *Auer v Ministère Public* [1983] ECR 2727, [1985] 1 CMLR 123 (company registration requirement justified on the basis of need to ensure the observance of moral and ethical principles and the disciplinary control of the relevant activity).

effects test confirmed in *Gebhard* in 1995.[152] In *Gebhard*, the Court did not refer to direct or indirect discrimination as such but rather to all national measures that are 'liable to hinder or make less attractive the exercise of [the] fundamental freedoms guaranteed by the Treaty' subject to the four possible justification conditions set.[153]

An equivalent early discrimination based approach was adopted by the Court in connection with Article 49 (ex 59) beginning with *Van Binsbergen* in 1974. The extension of Article 49 (ex 59) to apply to discriminatory and non-discriminatory provisions was anticipated in Case 427/85 *Commission v Germany*.[154] This was then confirmed in *Säger* 1991 in which the Court referred to the elimination of all discrimination on the grounds of nationality and 'the abolition of any [other] restriction, even if it applies without distinction to national providers of services and to those of other Member States, when it is liable to prohibit or otherwise impede the activities of a provider of services established in another Member State where he lawfully provides similar services.'[155]

The effect of *Säger* (as with *Gebhard* in connection with establishment) would appear to have been to abandon discrimination as the sole basis of proper Treaty prohibition in favour of a more general non-discriminatory (indistinctly applicable) test.[156] The necessary further consequence of this is

[152] Case C-55/94 *Gebhard v Consiglio dell 'Ordine degli Avvocati e Procuratori di Milano* [1995] ECR I-4156. For discussion, Wyatt and Dashwood (n 1) 431–9. See also Weatherill and Beaumont (n 1) 672–9 and 679–91.

[153] *Gebhard* confirmed that restrictive measures may be exempted provided that: (a) they are applied in a non-discriminatory manner; (b) they are justified by imperative requirements in the general interest; (c) they are suitable for securing the attainment of the objective which they pursue; and (d) they do not go beyond what is necessary in order to attain it. This was on the basis of Case C-19/92 *Dieter Kraus v Land Baden, Württemberg* [1993] ECR I-1663 (n 150); Case 115/78 *Knoors v Secretary of State for Economic Affairs* [1979] ECR 399, [1979] 2 CMLR 357; Case 107/83 *Ordre des Avocats au Barreau de Paris v Klopp* [1984] ECR 297 (n 150); Case C-370/90 *R v Immigration and Appeal Tribunal and Surinder Singh, ex p Secretary of State for the Home Department* [1992] ECR I-4265; Cases C-154/89, C-180/89 and C-198/89 *Commission v France, Italy and Greece* [1991] ECR I-659, 709 and 727 (a licensing requirements on tour guide operators could not be justified on the basis of securing the effective dissemination of knowledge); and Case C-76/90 *Manfred Säger v Dennemeyer & Co Ltd* [1991] ECR I-4221. For discussion, Commission, *Commission Interpretative Communication concerning the free movement of services across frontiers* (OJ 1993/C334/3).

[154] [1988] ECR 1123, [1989] 2 CMLR 677. The decision concerned the implementation of Directive 77/249 in Germany on the exercise by lawyers of the freedom to provide services. The approach was supported by Advocate General Jacobs in *Säger* (pp 4234–5) which opinion was repeated in *Alpine Investments*. The same formulation was not adopted by the Court although it generally followed the extended approach recommended by Advocate General Jacobs in *Säger* and *Alpine*. Case C-384/93 *Alpine Investments* [1995] ECR I-1141, paras 35–8 (n 171). Ch 4, section A (3).

[155] Case C-76/90 *Manfred Säger v Dennemeyer & Co Ltd* [1991] ECR I-422, [1993] 3 CMLR 639, para 12. The Court ruled that a German requirement that the provision of patent renewal services required a license in Germany was invalid.

[156] Section C (3). For general discussion of the parallel development of the Court's approach

that a significant number of national measures that would otherwise have fallen outside the scope of Articles 49 (and 43) will now be covered and subject to an assessment of objective justification and proportionality. The result is considerably to extend the scope of prohibition and the authority of the European Court in determining proper justification in this area again.[157]

Despite the apparent extension of the scope of Article 43 (ex 52), in particular, to include equally applicable measures, this may still be understood in terms of indirect discrimination where an additional burden is imposed on non-nationals as opposed to nationals.[158] Such an examination is, for example, supported by the establishment decisions concerning taxation issues in which the Court has treated the registered office, central administration or principal place of business of a company as equivalent to the nationality of an individual[159] although not all decisions are consistent with this approach.[160]

with regard to establishment and services, Jesper L Hansen 'Full Circle: Freedom of Establishment and to Provide Services' ch 7 in Andenas and Roth (n 114).

[157] Introduction and Ch 1, section E (2).

[158] G Marenco 'The Notion of a Restriction on the Freedom of Establishment and the Provision of Services in the Case Law of the ECJ' (1991) 11 YBEL, 111. This applies to both 'Clinical Biology Services' and *Fearon* as well as *Klopp* and *Stanton, Kemmler and Wolf*. Even *Kraus* (Art 43 (ex 52)) and *Gebhard* (Art 43 (ex 52)) can be understood in terms of indirect discrimination. In *Kraus*, a greater number of non-nationals than nationals will necessarily possess foreign academic qualifications while in *Gebhard* the rules of the Milan Bar will necessarily create more obstacles to non-nationals than Italian nationals. For comment, Wyatt (n 43). On the decisions in *Kraus* and *Bosman* (nn 187 and 188). (n 149).

[159] See, eg, Case C-3/88 *Commission v Italy* [1989] ECR 4035, [1991] 2 CMLR 115 (Italian law required that only companies in which all or a majority of the shares were directly or indirectly in public or state ownership may enter into agreements for the development of data-processing systems for public authorities). Wyatt (n 1) 446–7. See also Case 270/83 *Commission v France* [1986] ECR 273, [1987] 1 CMLR 401 (invalidity of distinct treatment of taxation of companies with registered office in France and branches in France of companies with registered office in other countries); Case C-1/93 *Halliburton Services v Staatssecretaris van Financién* [1994] ECR I-1137 (invalidity of Netherlands property transfer tax in connection with transfer from German subsidiary of US company to Netherlands subsidiary); Case C-330/91 *R v Inland Revenue Commissioners, ex p Commerzank AG* [1993] ECR I-4017, [1993] 3 CMLR 457 (invalidity of denial of repayment supplement on overpaid tax following repayment under double tax convention); and Case C-80/94 *Wielockx v Inspecteur de Directe Belastingen* [1995] ECR I-2493 (invalidity of deductions from taxable income business profits allocated to a pension reserve); and Case C-107/94 *PH Asscher v Staatssecretaris van Financién* [1994] ECR I-1137, [1996] 3 CMLR 61 (validity of Netherlands higher rates for non-residents to offset avoidance of progressive taxation). See also Case C-204/90 *Bachmann v Belgian State* [1992] ECR I-249, [1993] 1 CMLR 785 (validity of non-deductibility of sickness and insurance payments under Belgian law with regard to German national on basis of the need to preserve the cohesion of the tax system); Case C-279/93 *Finanzamt Köln-Alstadt v Schumacker* (1995) ECR I-225, [1996] 2 CMLR 450 (validity of denial to non-residents of tax benefits where a major part of income is generated in the State of residence); Case C-264/96 *ICI v Colmer (Her Majesty's Inspector of Taxes)* [1998] ECR I-4695, [1998] CMLR 293 (invalidity of consortium relief conditional on requirement that a holding company's business consist wholly or mainly in the holding of shares and subsidiaries that have their seat in

While the initial judgments of the Court were then based on an express discrimination based test, this was subsequently extended to include indirect discriminatory provisions (with an unequal burden being imposed on non-national individuals or firms). It would also appear that the Court has been prepared in appropriate circumstances to extend this to include a more general effects doctrine such as in *Gebhard* and *Säger* and similar cases. As in the area of goods, achieving any clear consistency in the judgments is difficult.[161] It could nevertheless be argued that the Court would appear to

local States); Case C-250/95 *Futura Participations SA v Administration des Contributions* [1997] ECR I-2471, [1997] 3 CMLR 483 (validity of Luxembourg restriction on the carrying forward of tax losses in respect of profits and losses arising from Luxembourg activities for non-residents); Case C-307/97 *Compagnie de Saint-Gobain v Finanzamt Aachen-Innenstadt* [1999] ECR I-6161 (invalidity of German tax concession entitlements only being enjoyed by German registered companies). For discussion, Wyatt and Dashwood (n 1) 447–456. Although these cases raise taxation issues, they were considered in terms of the extent to which they imposed a restriction on freedom of establishment. The Court accordingly treated the registered office, central administration or principal place of business of a company as equivalent to the nationality of an individual and held any restrictions to be incompatible with the Treaty where they directly or indirectly discriminated against such companies subject to possible justification (including on the basis of the preservation of the cohesion of the tax system). This then parallels the more general discussion on the scope of proper prohibition conducted in connection with the law of free movement. See also the decision in *Centros* (n 177).

[160] See, eg, Case C-70/95 *Sodemare SA v Regione Lombardia* [1997] ECR I-3395, [1998] 4 CMLR 667 (restrictions on the activities of non-profit making organizations held to restrict the right of establishment but capable of justification); Case C-255/97 *Pfeiffer Großhandel GmbH v Löwa Warenhandel GmbH* [1999] ECR I-2835 (a restraining order preventing Austrian subsidiary of a Germany company from operating discount stores under the trading name 'Plus' would constitute an impediment to the realization of a uniform advertising concept across the Community). Wyatt and Dashwood (n 1) 458–9. See also Joined Cases C-418/93 *Semeraro Casa Uno Srl v Sindaco de Commune di Erbusco* [1996] ECR I-2975 (the effect of a prohibition on retail shops opening on Sundays and public holidays was considered to be uncertain and indirect).

[161] Opinion and interpretations still differ on the evolution and resultant consequent position of the Court in the services and establishment area. See, for example, the contributing authors to Andenas and Roth (n 114). Roth argues that the Court had only adopted a discrimination based test in the area of services and that *Keck* was not necessary although he qualifies this by accepting that restrictions on the market access of the provider of the service are also caught. The Court has then continued generally to adopt a discrimination test and only a 'restriction test' in specific cases. Roth 'The European Court of Justice's Case Law on Freedom to Provide Services: Is Keck Relevant?' in Andenas and Roth (n 114), Ch 1.

Maduro argues that the Court has been developing separate tests based on either double burden or restriction on market access. The double burden approach is associated with a general concept of discrimination with additional costs being placed on non-national service providers. Discrimination can nevertheless be confused with simple lack of harmonization in any particular area. Difficult definitional and assessment problems also arise with the market access test. Maduro suggests that a more consistent approach is possible by re-applying in the services and establishment area the 'representative malfunction' test that he has constructed in relation to goods (Maduro n 18). This attempts to justify Court 'activism' only in cases where the interests of nationals in other Member States have not been properly protected and intervention is justified despite the necessary limitations on the Court's resources. Maduro, 'Harmony and Dissonance in Free Movement' in Andenas and Roth (n 114), Ch 3. This, however, confuses more general judicial function and balance theories with the more specific

have generally applied a discriminatory (direct and indirect) test to national regulatory measures and an outright prohibition on obstacles to market entry (an effects test). This is consistent with the underlying GATT policy adopted in connection with entry and regulatory measures. While this does create a certain theoretical consistency, it is unfortunate that the Court has not been as clear or express in all of its judgements.[162]

(3) MARKET ENTRY AND REGULATION

One of the main difficulties that has arisen in the areas of establishment and services is that the Treaty expressly recognizes the power of Member States to regulate the carrying on of activities in local territories.[163] The issue of permitted derogation then becomes of particular importance in the financial services area where Member States will necessarily attempt to impose

objectives of the law of free movement which is only to create a meaningful single market in goods, establishment, services and workers. For comment, Roth (8–10).

Snell and Andenas consider that the Court has applied a market test in the areas of services and workers irrespective of whether a multiple burden is created or discrimination is involved (following *Alpine* and *Bosman*). This market access component can then be understood either in terms of a sufficient impact (*de minimis*) or cross-border condition. A *de minimis* requirement is dismissed on the basis of difficulty in application and consequent uncertainty. The cross-border impact interpretation is preferred although the more general approach of the Court is criticized on the basis of inconsistency, relevance, vagueness and conflict with the corresponding decisions on export restrictions under Art 29 (ex 34). Jukka Snell and Mads Andenas 'Exploring the Outer Limits: Restrictions on Free Movement' in Andenas and Roth (n 114), Ch 4, 117–27. While the Court has also only applied a discrimination test with regard to export restrictions in relation to goods, Roth argues that it has gone further in applying a full restriction trigger in the area of services in *Alpine Investments* (21–4). Snell and Andenas conclude that the Court has been moving towards a more general market access test although they question its centralising effects and lack of coherence and clarity with the wide variations in its use and application and lack of supporting reasoning.

Jarass distinguishes between obstacles to free movement based on discrimination, factual or material disadvantage (double burden) and core restrictions (market access) restrictions. Where restrictions exist, they may be justified on either a textual (Treaty) or general good basis. The common factor considered to apply in each case is 'proportionality' which is considered to consist of suitability, necessity and reasonableness. The final determination of the Court in any particular case will nevertheless also be affected by the intensity of the judicial examination conducted. Hans D Jarass 'A Unified Approach to the Fundamental Freedoms' in Andenas and Roth (n 114), Ch 5. See also writers referred to in (n 184).

162 For discussion on the more general difficulties that arise in this area, see, for example, Wyatt and Dashwood (n 1), 456–60, Weatherill and Beaumont (n 1) 679–96. See also Siofra O'Leary 'The Free Movement of Persons and Services' in Craig and de Bùrca (n 18) Ch 11. See also discussion (n 161).

163 Arts 53(2) and 50(3) (ex Arts 52(2) and 60(3)) refer to the rights of establishment and services being exercised under the conditions laid down by States for their own nationals. This accordingly applies the principle of national treatment within the establishment and services area. As such, the maintenance and application of national regulatory provisions on a continuing basis are given express Treaty recognition. Section D (1). On GATT origins, Ch 2, section E and (n 75).

national regulatory requirements on banks and other financial intermediaries.[164]

National governments are considered to retain authority to regulate the conduct of industrial, commercial and professional activity within their territories. Treaty derogations were provided for although these only related to discriminatory provision and were strictly applied.[165] While the Court has clearly established that non-discriminatory restrictions were prohibited,[166] it has had to exercise more caution in its examination of non-discriminatory and indistinctly applicable measures.[167]

In light of the significant restriction that national regulatory measures may place on the functioning of the single market, the Court has adopted a wide approach to restrictive effect at the same time as develop an equally liberal policy to possible justification. An equivalent combined prohibition (*Dassonville*) and exemption (*Dassonville* (reasonableness) and *Cassis* (mandatory requirement)) style approach has since been developed in the establishment and services areas. The Court will initially look to the restrictive effect of any national measure and then consider its possible justification. This combined effects and derogation approach dates from *Van*

[164] Although this applies both to establishment and services, more significant difficulties arise with regard to establishment where this involves the application of all of the various authorization, supervision and enforcement provisions set out under local laws for the regulation of any particular financial sector. The more permanent nature of the relationship to be set up between the financial institution and the local territory will also have to be taken into account. The provision of services will then trigger the operation of the local 'general prohibitions' in each sector (which restrict the carrying of unlicensed or unregulated financial activities) although some marketing related concessions may be available in such situations. Any separate promotions and marketing restrictions and conditions will then also apply with regard to services, in particular, in addition to the underlying authorization requirement. (n 136).

[165] Arts 45, 46 and 55 (ex 55, 56 and 66). These parallel the relevant provisions applicable to workers under Arts 39(3) and (4) (ex 48(3) and (4)). It was, in particular, confirmed in *Reyners* that the public service exception had to be construed narrowly and would not apply to the whole of the legal profession. There had to be a direct and specific connection with the exercise of official authority. Case 2/74, para 54.

[166] Case 2/74 *Reyners* and Case 33/74 *Van Binsbergen*. See also Case C-246/89 *Commission v United Kingdom* [1991] ECR I-4585, [1991] 3 CMLR (United Kingdom requirement that the legal and beneficial owners of registered fishing vessels had to be British nationals or United Kingdom incorporated companies with, at least, 75 per cent of the shares held by British nationals (or by companies fulfilling the same requirement) and 75 per cent of the directors being British nationals).

[167] Case 71/76 *Thieffry v Conseil de L'Ordre des Avocats* [1977] ECR 765 [1977] 2 CMLR 373 (Paris Bar rejection of application by a Belgian national holding a Belgian doctorate in law was held incompatible with Art 43 (ex Art 52) but only because the University of Paris I recognized the Belgian qualification as equivalent); and Case 136/78 *Ministère Public v Auer* [1979] ECR 437 (Italian vet not entitled to practise in France without recognition of equivalence of relevant veterinary medical qualification). See also Case 11/77 *Patrick v Ministre des Affaires Culturelles* [1977] ECR 1199; Case C-61/89 *Bouchoucha* [1990] ECR I-3551; and Case C-319/92 *Salmone Haim v KVN* [1994] ECR I-425.

Binsbergen[168] although the Court has subsequently added the concept of equivalence and functional recognition in later cases.[169] At the same time as the Court has developed this idea of equivalence in the establishment and services areas, the more general concept of mutual recognition was used as part of the Commission's 'New Approach' to the adoption of secondary legislation, in particular, with regard to the mutual recognition of educational and professional qualifications under the 1992 Single Market Programme.[170]

The Court has had the opportunity more recently to consider certain aspects of services and establishment law in the financial services area. These decisions have confirmed the general rules referred to with regard to direct and indirect discrimination as well as the need to consider the protective contribution of home country authorization and supervisory systems, in particular, in non-programme areas. The Court has not, however, been as anxious to narrow the scope of restrictive effect in these cases as it has in the connection with goods. It is then possible that the Court will continue to adopt an expansive interpretation of Treaty prohibition outside the *Keck* rules in the financial area.

168 The approach adopted in *Van Binsbergen* with regard to restrictive effect and judicial derogation would appear to have been more particular than in *Dassonville*. Section C (2). The significance of *Cassis* was that it added the concept of equivalence and deemed compliance where the rules of the exporting territory had already been satisfied. This is to some extent implied in the idea of alternative means suggested in *Van Binsbergen* although not properly developed until later. The concept of equivalence was considered in *Thieffry* although on a strict recognition basis. The Court only looked to determine whether the territory in which the activity was conducted expressly recognized the equivalence of the qualification in question. There was no examination (or consideration) as to whether the relevant degrees were in substance comparable and equivalent without the external admission of equivalence. This idea would then be more strictly applied in such other cases as *Auer* (n 151). See also (nn 67 and 70).

169 The provision of insurance services on a cross-border basis was considered in *Coenen* although only from a residence requirement. Case 39/75 *Coenen* [1975] ECR 1547 (Belgian rules prevented provision of insurance broker services to Dutch non-resident). The quality of the supervision conducted by the Home State was recognized in *Webb* in 1981. Case 279/80 *Webb* [1981] ECR 3305, [1982] 1 CMLR 719 (Netherlands law prevented a British national from supplying temporary staff to local firms without licence). The need to consider the degree of protection already secured by the authorization and supervision established in a home territory was then examined in further detail in the German Insurance case. Case 205/84 *Commission v Germany* [1986] ECR 3755, [1987] 1 CMLR 69. This was one of four cases in which the validity of the maintenance of local controls on the provision of insurance services in national territories was examined by the Court. Although it considered that some conditions including a local establishment requirement were invalid, other protective measures were recognized. Ch 4, section A (1).

170 See, for example, Directive 89/48 in connection with professionals (OJ 1989 L 19/16). This provided for the adoption of a system of mutual recognition in connection with the conduct of professional activities based on certain agreed standards. The general right created was to have higher degrees recognized where they were of, at least, three years duration subject to evidence requirements and in certain cases an adaptation period or aptitude test. These rights were extended under Directive 92/51 to shorter degrees and other professional and education training requirements (OJ 1992 L 209/25). See also Ch 6, section D(1).

In *Schindler*, the Court, for example, considered that the United Kingdom restrictions on lotteries fell within the scope of the *Säger* prohibition and were accordingly subject to justification and proportionality.[171] If the earlier pre-*Säger* approach had been applied, the rules would have been considered to be non-discriminatory and therefore not subject to further consideration under Article 49 (ex 59). Having extended the scope of legitimate prohibition, the Court also expanded the supporting derogation to include moral, religious and cultural issues as well as the risk of crime and fraud. Rather than apply an objective test, the Court allowed Member States themselves to assess whether lotteries should be restricted and the nature of the restrictions to be imposed. A subjective rather than objective approach was accordingly adopted.[172]

In *Alpine Investments*, the Court adopted a more generous post-*Keck* type approach and considered that a prohibition on unsolicited telephone calls to potential clients directly affected access to the market and services and was therefore capable of hindering intra-Community trade.[173] The Netherlands and United Kingdom had argued that such restrictions were non-discriminatory and should not fall under Article 49 (ex 59) on a simple *Keck* analogy.

A number of these cases are, however, unusual in their own terms and it is unclear to what extent they confirm or correct the more general law of establishment and free movement outside their financial field of application. The main cases in the financial area are considered in further detail in the following Chapter.[174]

(4) JUDICIAL DEROGATION AND THE GENERAL GOOD

Continuing uncertainty consequently arises specifically with regard to the scope of permitted derogation in connection with both establishment and services. Treaty exceptions are available with regard to official authority[175]

[171] Case C-275/92 *Her Majesty's Customs and Excise v Schindler & Schindler*. For discussion, Ch 4, section A (2).

[172] For comment, Wyatt and Dashwood (n 1) 478.

[173] Case C-384/93 *Alpine Investments Bv v Minister van Financien* [1995] ECR I-1141: [1995] 2 CMLR 209; [1995] All ER [EC] 543, para 38. Ch 4, section A (3).

[174] Ch 4, section A.

[175] Art 45 (ex 55) provides that the provisions on establishment shall not apply insofar as any Member State is concerned with the exercise, even occasionally, of official authority (n 138). This also applies to services under Art 55 (ex 66). As Treaty exceptions, these derogations must nevertheless be construed strictly. In *Reyners v Belgian State*, the Court held that Art 45 (ex 55) only applied to those activities which, taken on their own, involved a direct and specific connection with the exercise of official authority (n 143). This would not include professional representation in Court as an *avocat*. It was held in *Commission v Belgium* that this would involve the exercise of powers conferred by public law and duties designed to safeguard the general interests of a State. Case 149/79 [1980] ECR 3881, [1981] 2 CMLR 413 in which it was held that acting as a traffic accident expert did not involve the exercise of official authority. This would also only apply to restrictions on admission to certain activities rather than to discrimination following

and public policy[176] although more difficult issues arise with regard to the further non-discriminatory judicially determined exemptions that may be made available in a particular case.

Derogation on the basis of objective justification is available in connection with establishment[177] although this is now generally subject to the *Gebhard* conditions. Professional rules justified by the general good were initially recognized in *Van Binsbergen* as being permissible as with regard to services.[178] This would be extended in *Gouda*[179] to permit restrictions

appointment. Case 152/73 *Sotgui v Deutsche Bundespost* [1974] ECR 153 (application of Art 7 of Regulation 1612/68 with regard to employees in German postal service).

In *Van Wesemael*, it was held that a Member State could not impose a licensing requirement on an employment agency established in another Member State where it was supervised and licensed in the home State unless the requirement was justified by the need to ensure observance with professional rules of conduct or the protection of the entertainers placed by the agency. Joint Cases 110–111/78 *Ministère Public and 'Chambre Syndicale des Agents Aartistiques et Impresarii de Belgique' ASBL v Willy van Wesemael and others* [1979] ECR 35, [1979] 3 CMLR 87. This was extended in *Commission v Germany* to require that any local requirements may only be imposed if the provisions were justified in the public interest even where this was not safeguarded by the requirements of the Member State of establishment. Case 205/85 *Commission v Germany* [1988] ECR 3755: [1987] 2 CMLR 69. The effect was that access to service providers from another Member State could only be restricted where there were objective grounds to do so. Wyatt notes that this is indistinguishable from the approach adopted with regard to goods in *Cassis* although properly constructed within the analytical framework of discrimination. For comment, Wyatt and Dashwood (n 1) 473–6.

176 Arts 46 (ex 56) and 55 (ex 66) permit applicability of provisions providing for special treatment of foreign nationals on grounds of public policy, public security and public health (n 138). These exceptions will again be interpreted strictly and will generally only apply to entry and residence rather than post-appointment terms and conditions. *Sotgui* (n 175). Art 39(3) (ex 48(3)) and Art 46 (ex 56) are given effect to under Directive 64/221. This applies to any national of a Member State who resides in or travels to another Member State either in order to pursue an activity as an employed or self-employed person or as a recipient of services.

177 Case 107/83 *Ordre des Avocats au Barreau de Paris v Klopp* [1983] ECR 2971, [1985] 1 CMLR 99; Case 143/87 *Stanton v Inasti* [1988] ECR 3877, [1989] 3 CMLR 761; Case C-53/95 *Inasti v Kemmler* [1996] ECR I-704; and Case C-212/97 *Centros Ltd v Erhvervs-og Selskabsstyrelsen* [1999] ECR I-1459, [1992] 2 CMLR 551 (Danish authorities were not entitled to refuse to register a branch of an English company on the basis that it failed to satisfy minimum local capital requirements as the interest of public creditors could be achieved by less restrictive alternative means). (n 138).

178 These related, in particular, to organization, qualifications, professional ethics, supervision and liability which were binding on any person established in the State in which the service was provided, where the person providing the service would escape from the ambit of those rules by being established in another Member State. *Van Binsbergen*, para 12 (n 143). In *Van Binsbergen*, the restriction had to be adopted in pursuance of a legitimate public interest that was not incompatible with the Community's aims, be equally applicable to persons established in that State and objectively justified by the need to observe the legitimate professional rules in question. Craig and de Bùrca (n 1) 775–776. A Member State could also require auditors to maintain an establishment in a national territory to secure the application of national rules in the public interest designed to uphold the integrity and independence of those practising the profession. Case C-106/91, *Ramrath v Ministère de la Jusice and l'Institut des Reviseurs de'entreprises* [1992] ECR I-3351; [1992] 3 CMLR 173.

179 Case C-288/89 *Stichting collective Antennevoorziening Gouda and others v Commissariaat voor de Media* [1991] ECR I-4007.

justified by overriding reasons relating to the public interest or where the requirements had already been satisfied by the rules of the country of establishment and the measures were appropriate and proportionate. The Court listed a number of possible overriding reasons in *Gouda*[180] which would be extended to include social and cultural features to maintain order in society,[181] the reputation of the financial sector[182] and debt recovery.[183]

The fundamental problem that remains is attempting to determine in which circumstances possible derogation may or may not be available.[184] The uncertainty that this creates undermines legal predictability and consequent reliance which must necessarily be considered to restrict market integration. This difficulty is then further compounded by the apparent absence of any coherent jurisprudence in the establishment and services as well as other free movement areas. Some clarification of the main rules that apply in the financial area has been provided under the Commission's Interpretative Communication[185] although a number of residual inconsistencies still remain.

(5) Goods, Establishment, Services, and Workers

A similar approach to restrictive effect has been followed by the Court with regard to workers. Article 39(1) (ex 48(1)) provides that freedom of movement for workers is to be secured within the Community.[186] This involves

[180] Joined Cases 110–111/78 *Van Wesemael* [1979] ECR 35, [1979] 3 CMLR 87, para 28 (professional rules intended to protect recipients of services); Case 62/79 *Coditel* [1980] ECR 881, [1981] 2 CMLR 362 (protection of intellectual property rights); Case 279/80 *Webb* [1981] ECR 35505 [1982] 1 CMLR 719, para 19; joined Cases 62/63/81 *Seco v EVI* [1982] ECR 223, para 14; and Case C-113/89 *Rush Portuguesa* [1990] ECR I-1417, [1991] 2 CMLR 818, para 18 (protection of workers); Case 220/83 *Commission v France* [1986] ECR 3663, para 20 and others (consumer protection); Case C-180/89 *Commission v Italy* [1991] ECR I-709, para 20 (conservation of national historic and artistic heritage); Case 220/83 *Commission v France*, para 20; and C-198/89 *Commission v Greece* [1991] ECR I-727, para 21 (archaeology, historical and artistic heritage of a country and the widest possible dissemination of knowledge of artistic and cultural heritage).

[181] Case C-275/92 *Schindler*. See also Case C-124/97 *Läärä* [1999] ECR I-60007; and Case C-67/98 *Zenatti* [1999] ECR I-7289.

[182] Case C-384/93 *Alpine Investments*, Ch 4, section A (3).

[183] Case C-3/95 *Sandker*, Ch 4, section A (4).

[184] For more recent discussion, Siofra O'Leary and Jose M Fernandez-Martin 'Judicially Created Exceptions to the Free Movement of Services' Ch 6 in Andenas and Roth (n 114); and Michel Tison 'Unravelling the General Good Exception: the Case of Financial Services' Ch 12 in Andenas and Roth (n 114). See also Hansen 'Full Circle: Freedom of Establishment and to Provide Services' Ch 7 in Andenas and Roth (n 114) 204–7, see also (n 161).

[185] Commission Interpretative Communication, Freedom to provide services and the interests of the general good in the Second Banking Directive (97/C 219/04). Ch 4, section B. For comment, Wyatt and Dashwood (n 1) 488–91. See also Craig and de Bùrca (n 1) 774–80.

[186] This is to include the right (subject to public policy, public security or public health limitations): (a) to accept offers of employment actually made; (b) to move freely within the territory of Member States for this purpose; (c) to stay in a Member State for the purpose of

the abolition of any discrimination based on nationality between workers as regards employment, remuneration and other conditions of work and employment (Article 39(2) (ex 48(2)). In this area again, the Court has extended the scope of relevant prohibition considerably beyond simple discrimination[187] especially in such more recent decisions as *Kraus* and *Bosman*.[188]

In these cases, a distinction can again be drawn between access and regulation and the law interpreted as imposing an absolute (effects) prohibition on market access restrictions and a discriminatory (direct or indirect) test on internal regulatory measures imposed after market entry has been secured. While some of the more recent decisions can still be understood in terms of indirect discrimination, other rulings including *Bosman* and *Kraus* suggest that the Court may apply a full access test in the area of workers

employment (in accordance with the provisions governing the employment of nationals of that State as laid down by law, regulation or administrative action); and (d) to remain in the territory of a Member State after having been employed in that territory (subject to conditions to be set out in the implementing regulations (Art 39(3), (ex 48(3))). The provisions of Art 39 are not to apply to employment in the public service (Art 39(4), (ex 48(4))). Directives or regulations to secure the free movement of workers are provided for under Art 40, (ex 49)). Territories are to encourage the exchange of young workers within the framework of a joint programme (Art 41 (ex 50)) while measures are to be adopted in the field of social security to support the free movement of workers (Art 42 (ex 51)).

[187] Art 39(1) and (2) (ex 48) expressly prohibits discrimination on the basis of nationality although the freedom may also be considered to extend to non-discriminatory restrictions. The right to entry and residence is developed in Directive 68/360 (1968 JO L257/13, 1968 OJ Spec Ed (II), 485) and equality of treatment under Regulation 1612/68 (1968 JO L257/2). The right of free movement has been held to apply to discriminatory and non-discriminatory provisions. Case C-19/92 *Dieter Kraus v Land Baden-Wuerttenberg* [1993] ECR I-1663 (a German authorization condition on the recognition of a Scottish academic title (LL.M. at Edinburgh University) was held to be incompatible with Art 39 (ex Art 48) even though it applied without discrimination on the grounds of nationality); Case C-415/93 *Union Royale Belge des Société de Football Association ASBL v Jean-Marc Bosman* [1995] ECR I-4921, [1996] 1 CMLR 645 (a sporting association's requirement that a football club pay to another a transfer, training or development fee in respect of the move of a professional footballer constituted an obstacle to the free movement of workers even though it was non-discriminatory); and Case C-18/95 *FC Terhoeve v Inspecteur van de Belastingdienst Particulieren/Ondernemingen Buitenland* [1999] ECR I-345 (the imposition of heavier social security requirements on migrant workers was contrary to Art 48 (ex Art 39)).

[188] (n 187). The test developed in *Kraus* was based on whether the restriction was liable to hamper or render less attractive the exercise by Community nationals of the fundamental freedoms provided by the Treaty. Craig and de Bùrca note that the case could be considered to have involved an element of indirect indiscrimination although the decision would appear to suggest that it would apply whether any element of disadvantage was involved or not. Craig and de Bùrca (n 1) 747–8. The Court accepted in *Bosman* that the requirement was non-discriminatory and, while it applied to transfers within States on the same basis, it still directly affected players' access to the employment market in other Member States and was therefore capable of impeding the free movement of workers (para 103). In *Terhoeve*, the Court considered the deterrent effect that the higher social security costs would have on the movement of workers. The restriction accordingly constituted an obstacle to the free movement of workers with it being unnecessary to consider whether there was indirect discrimination on the grounds of nationality under Regulation 16/12/68 (para 41).

wherever necessary. *Pfeiffer* can also be understood either as permitting the use of 'a uniform advertising concept' across Europe or 'more restrictively' that firms should not be prevented from using a title or trade name available in the home State as this would otherwise restrict access to the market of the host State. *Semeraro* indicates that a *Keck* type analysis may be adopted with regard to Article 43 (ex 52) (paragraph 32) although the application of the same general principles in connection with distinct rights of free movement may still lead to different rights in practice.[189]

In applying these measures, it is nevertheless significant that the Court has adopted the same general principles with regard to persons (including workers and establishment) and services.[190] While different results may be produced in particular situations, the Court has generally been consistent in its development of Articles 39, 43 and 49 (ex Articles 48, 52 and 59) and to a lesser extent these provisions and Article 28 (ex Article 30). The Court has stated that a comparison between Articles 39 (ex 48), 43 (ex 52) and 49 (ex 59) shows that they are based on the same principles both insofar as they concern the entry into and residence in the territory of Member States of persons covered by Community law and the prohibition of all discrimination between them on the grounds of nationality.[191] It is, however, in the areas beyond overt discrimination and in determining possible justification or derogation that more difficult issues arise.

While the same general principles apply in both the establishment and services area and between goods, establishment and services, their operation in specific factual situations and having regard to the particular freedom involved can create different results. The Court appears nevertheless to be moving towards a consistent jurisprudence based on *Keck*, *Bosman*, *Gebhard* and *Alpine* although this process is still some way from completion. Even with the use of common principles, it has to be expected that distinct results may follow in applying separate Treaty rights to different

[189] For comment, Wyatt and Dashwood (n 1) 456–60.

[190] The Court has been more likely to hold a requirement restrictive of trade in connection with services and establishment where the more permanent nature of the relationship between the entity and the host State may justify a more restrictive approach (nn 136 and 164). See also Weatherill and Beaumont (n 1) 680–1.

[191] Case 48/75 *Procureur du Roi v Royer* [1976] ECR 497: [1976] 2 CMLR 619. The case concerned a preliminary ruling as to whether the proceedings fell within the provisions concerning workers, establishment or services. See also Case 188/75 *Watson & Belmann* [1976] ECR 1185, [1976] 2 CMLR 552. The Court has adopted the same approach with regard to Arts 39 (ex 48) and 43 (ex 52) in Case C-106/91 *Ramrath v Ministère de la Justice* [1992] ECR I-3351, [1992] 3 CMLR 173 [1995] 2 CMLR 187 at para 17; and Case C-107/94 *P. H. Asscher v Staatssecretaris van Financiën* [1994] ECR I-1137, at para 29. Care must nevertheless be exercised in considering the effects of the application of these principles in each case. Results will vary depending upon the particular freedom concerned and underlying facts. Wyatt and Dashwood (n 1) 445–6 and 456–60.

factual circumstances. Although understandable in theoretical terms, this again creates further difficulties with regard to legal certainty, predictability and consistency that have to be resolved over time before an effective law can be created based on the free movement of all relevant economic factors.

The general effect of *Keck, Bosman, Gebhard* and *Alpine* would accordingly appear to be that the Court is attempting to develop a unified jurisprudence although full internal consistency has not yet been achieved. The omission of a full *Keck* qualification in the services area can possibly be explained in terms of the Court's increased concern to ensure that market access is in no way restricted in such cases. Although many of the earlier and more recent cases can be understood in terms of indirect discrimination, the Court would still appear to have adopted a full effects test, at least, where market entry is obstructed. While this is in line with the original market entry and internal regulation distinction adopted under the GATT, further clarification of the Court's jurisprudence is required.[192]

E. EMERGING LAW OF FREE MOVEMENT—MARKET ENTRY, DISCRIMINATION, EFFECT, AND DEROGATION

The law of free movement has been constructed within the Community further than in any comparable regional or global trading system. This has involved extending traditional prohibitions on tariffs and quotas to include all other measures having equivalent effect. These then operate on a mandatory (rather than voluntary or agreed) basis with the creation of any new restrictions being prohibited under law. Secondary programmes have also been adopted in particular areas to reduce or remove from them the operation and effect of existing restrictions.

The underlying policy gap or omission that arose under the terms of the original Treaty of Rome in connection with goods was in confirming whether a discrimination or effects based test should apply to the removal of these restrictions. The effect of this was to allow the Community either to adopt a full discrimination or effects (or combined) test. Under a combined approach, an effects doctrine could be adopted with regard to initial market access or entry restrictions and discrimination applied to subsequent market control, regulation or other administrative practice.

One of the most significant early contributions of the European Court of Justice was to adopt a full effects doctrine under *Dassonville* with regard to measures impeding trade in any way subject only to a general (unspecified) reasonableness test. This was then developed and clarified under *Cassis*

[192] (n 129).

which also included an anticipatory doctrine of equivalence. Under this principle of equivalence (or regulatory or functional equivalence), national authorities would not be allowed to subject products to additional requirements where they had already satisfied the relevant conditions in the country of origin.

The Court has subsequently extended Article 28 (ex 30) to apply to a range of distinctly (discriminatory) and indistinctly (non-discriminatory) measures although it would attempt to place some limits on the extended scope of the doctrine adopted. This would subsequently be restated under *Keck* in terms of which selling arrangements are distinguished subject to an in law and fact proviso. This, however, suffers from its own limitations especially with regard to scope of application and the inconsistencies inherent in the new double proviso attached.

The Court has expanded the law on establishment and services in a similar manner to include both discriminatory (direct and indirect) and non-discriminatory measures. The scope of prohibition and permitted derogation in the establishment area were combined in *Gebhard* in 1995 to include any restriction except where it was non-discriminatory, justified, suitable and necessary. The Court had adopted an equivalent approach to *Cassis* in connection with services in *Säger* four years earlier. Parallel extensions have also since been adopted with regard to permitted mandatory requirements such as in *Ramrath*, *Seco* and *Gouda*.

Difficulties nevertheless remain in determining the proper scope of permitted derogation in connection with both establishment and services and especially in the banking and financial services area. It is particularly unclear whether an objective or subjective test will be adopted in all cases (such as in *Schindler*). Uncertainties also arise with regard to possible continued extensions (such as under *Alpine*) and with regard to the underlying quality of the judgement or assessment exercised in particularly specialist cases (such as in *Parodi*). These issues are considered in further detail in the following chapter.

4

Banking and Financial Services—Judicial Policy Development and Correction

The two main issues that the European Court of Justice has had to consider are concerned with the proper scope of European law and the limits of the permitted derogations to be recognized. The issue of scope has principally arisen in connection with determining whether various national rules have breached the Treaty provisions protecting the free movement of services and establishment (as well as goods, workers and capital). A liberal interpretation of the free movement rules clearly extends the scope of application of European law and restricts national law. By adopting an open policy in this regard especially with the maintenance of a discriminatory (distinctly applicable) and non-discriminatory (indistinctly applicable) test or trigger, the Court has confirmed the extended application of the European law restrictions.

The related issue that arises is the proper scope of judicial exemption or derogation to be permitted. This has, in particular, arisen in connection with the Court's discussion of the concept of public interest or the general good which had to be developed as a judicial balance or counter weight to the non-discriminatory application of the core free movement rules.[1] Although it may have been expected that the Court would have adopted a restrictive approach to the evolution of judicial derogation (as with the statutory exemptions provided for under the Treaty which have traditionally been interpreted in a narrow manner), a generous approach has been followed that has extended rather than constrained the limits of these judicially recognized exemptions. While this may conflict with the approach that would have been expected in connection with the scope of application of discriminatory exemptions, this can be understood in terms of the need to extend the limits of the general good to compensate for the extended application of the underlying free movement rules.

While the general principles developed by the Court are capable of equal application in the banking and financial area, it is unfortunate that more finance related decisions have not yet been issued. This necessarily reflects the selective and partial nature of the litigious process and slow and non-uniform nature of judicial decision making as a policy construction rather than purely enforcement instrument. Some important decisions have nevertheless been

[1] Ch 3, section C.

issued that have indicated the type of particular approach that the Court will follow in such cases. A number of more general conclusions can also be drawn with regard to the potential significance and value of the contribution of the Court in this area.

The Commission has separately attempted to set out its understanding of the meaning and application of certain key Treaty and programme provisions through the issuance of interpretative communications including in the banking and financial area.[2] The 1997 Communication in connection with banking comments specifically on the nature and scope of the right to provide services on a cross-border basis and the meaning and operation of the general good exemption as set out in the Second Banking Directive (and now the Banking Consolidation Directive).[3] Although limited in terms of scope and legal validity and value, this provides a useful restatement of a number of core provisions in this area. An increasingly substantial financial law is accordingly beginning to emerge especially with the assistance of this restatement of general free movement rules as well as the emerging body of finance related decisions being produced by the Court.

The Court has subsequently had to consider a number of more recent specific banking and financial issues since the production of the Commission's Communication in 1997. Many of these later decisions have been concerned with more technical rather than general or substantive policy matters. Some assistance has been provided in confirming the nature and operation of the European single market in banking and financial services although their more general policy contribution has been limited. The Court has most recently been able to rule on the extent to which individual rights are conferred on depositors under the European Deposit Guarantee Directive and general banking directives including in *Peter Paul* in October 2004.[4] This also confirmed that measures governing the regulatory liability of national supervisory agencies were only to be dealt with at the Member State level and that this was not regarded as being an essential part of the scheme to create a single banking and financial market across

[2] Commission Interpretative Communication, Freedom to provide services and the interests of the general good in the Second Banking Directive (97/C 219/04). See also Commission Communication on 'Upgrading the Investment Services Directive' on 16 Nov 2000 (COM(2000) 729; and Commission Communication on 16 Nov 2000 on the application of 'conduct of business rules' to investment firms.

[3] Second Council Directive 89/646/EEC on the coordination of laws, regulations and administrative provisions relating to the taking up and pursuit of the business of credit institutions of 15 Dec 1998 (OJ L 386, 30 Dec 89, p 1); and Directive 2000/12/EC of the European Parliament and Council of 20 Mar 2000 relating to the taking up and pursuit of the business of credit institutions. Ch 5, section B and (n 22).

[4] Case C-222/02 *Peter Paul, Cornelia Sonnen-Lütte and Christel Mörkens v Bundesrepublik Deutschland*. Reference for a preliminary ruling under Art 234 EC of 12 Oct 2004. Section D (3). See also *Germany v Parliament and Council*, section B (1).

Europe based on mutual recognition and home prudential supervision. The decision is accordingly of importance in clarifying both the scope and content of the European single market initiative in this area.

The purpose of this Chapter is to consider the value and importance of the early decisions of the Court in banking and financial matters and the extent to which they have assisted (or confused) the construction of a more complete and coherent jurisprudence in this area. The importance of the Commission's 1997 Interpretative Communication is noted and the difficulties that arose in attempting to by-pass proper legislative procedures through the use of the communication device. The further clarification provided in the more recent technical decisions in this area is then considered in further detail. The scope of the right to depositor (or investor) protection and the issue of regulatory liability under Community and national law are examined separately. Provisional conclusions are drawn with regard to the current state of development of judicial policy construction in the banking and financial area.

A. FINANCIAL POLICY CONSTRUCTION

A number of issues that arise in the banking and financial area have been considered by the Court and by national judges on various occasions. Advice in this area is nevertheless generally dependent upon the application of the general case law constructed, in particular, in connection with services and establishment although this has to a significant extent been effected by parallel developments in the area of goods.[5]

The particular difficulty that arises at the European level is that only a relatively limited number of banking and finance related matters have arisen for judicial determination. The Court's examination of this particular area of law has accordingly been selective and partial until recently. This necessarily reflects one of the fundamental difficulties that arises in relying on the judicial process for policy construction purposes.[6]

In addition to the European Court of Justice, some issues have been considered at the national level.[7] Although not strictly authoritative in

[5] Ch 3, section C.

[6] This might be referred to as a 'judicial policy deficit.' Ch 1, section E(1); and Ch 3, Introduction.

[7] The meaning and effect of a number of the provisions contained in the First Banking Directive were, for example, examined by the House of Lords in the UK in its rulings on the validity of the claims made by the depositors of BCCI against the Bank of England. *Three Rivers District Council v Governor and Company of the Bank of England* was presented to the House on 22 Mar 2001 ([2001] UKHL 16). The case was heard before Lord Steyn, Lord Hope of Craighead, Lord Hutton, Lord Hobhouse of Woodborough and Lord Millett. Lord Neill of Bladen, QC, Mr Richard Sheldon, QC, Mr Robin Dicker, QC, Mr Dominic Dowley

terms of their interpretation of European law, they assist in clarifying and understanding certain specific matters that the Court has not had the opportunity to comment on until now. Despite their limited value in terms of European law validity, national dicta can be of assistance in beginning to construct a larger corpus of European judicial analysis in the banking and financial area. This is an area that will require further examination and attention over time.

The early Court decisions in the banking and financial area are examined in the following section with the extent to which they provide clarification on the structure and operation of the single market in banking and financial services. The content and value of the Commission's Interpretative Communication is considered in the following section. Some of the more recent technical decisions that have been issued are then examined. The scope of individual rights to depositor or investor protection and the liability of national regulatory agencies are considered separately.[8]

(1) ESTABLISHMENT AND AUTHORIZATION CONDITIONS—*CO-INSURANCE* (1986)

The first main examination of the issues that arise in the financial area was conducted by the Court in the *Co-insurance Cases* in December 1986.[9] The Commission had brought actions against four Member States for alleged infringements of Community law in the co-insurance area.[10] Each of the

and Mr Barry Isaacs acted for the depositors. Mr Nicholas Stadlen, QC, Mr Mark Phillips, QC, Mr Bankim Thank; and Mr Ben Valentin acted for the Bank of England. The action was on appeal from an order for dismissal by the Court of Appeal under Lord Justice Hirst and Lord Justice Robert Walker with Lord Justice Auld dissenting (*The Times*, 10 Dec 1998; (2000) 2 WLR 15). The decision had already been on appeal from an order by Mr Justice Clarke of 2 Oct 1997. The House of Lords also considered the constituent elements and scope of the tort of misfeasance in public office (*The Times*, 19 May 2000; (2000) 2 WLR 1220). The case was subsequently abandoned on 2 Nov 2005. (n 170)

[8] Section D.

[9] Case 220/83 *Commission v French Republic* [1986] ECR 3663; Case 252/83 *Commission v Kingdom of Denmark* [1976] ECR 3713; Case 205/84 *Commission v Federal Republic of Germany* [1986] ECR 3755; and Case 206/84 *Commission v Ireland* [1986] ECR 3817. The Opinion of the Advocate General Sir Gordon Slynn was delivered on 20 Mar 1986 with the Judgement of the Court in the four cases being issued on 4 Dec 1986.

[10] Co-insurance relates to the insurance of a single risk by a number of co-insurers each of which is only liable for a proportion of the risk covered. While one insurer will act as the lead party and negotiate contract terms and conditions, the liability of all of the co-insurers is several as opposed to joint and several. Co-insurance is distinct from re-insurance under which the insurer will pass part of the risk on to other counter-parties but remain liable to the original insured party for the whole amount covered. See Opinion of Sir Gordon Slynn, *Commission v France*, 3685. The cases are generally concerned with direct insurance other than transport insurance or compulsory insurance (including life assurance). Co-insurance was considered under the second and third heads of claim. Judgment of the Court in *Commission v Germany*, para 11–17.

cases was concerned with different national legislation although as the same general sector was being considered, the Opinions of the Advocate General Sir Gordon Slynn and the Court were issued together.[11] The first two cases *Commission v France* Case 220/83 and *Commission v Denmark* Case 252/83 and *Commission v Ireland* Case 206/84 were generally concerned with services although *Commission v Germany* Case 205/84 also raised further issues with regard to the legality of local authorization and establishment requirements applicable to any service provider in the insurance sector. In light of the importance of the proceedings, a total of eight (out of the then ten) Member States were involved in the proceedings with the Netherlands and the United Kingdom intervening in support of the Commission with Belgium and Italy in support of the defendant States.

The actions were generally concerned with breach of Arts 59 (49) and 60 (50) by requiring undertakings from other Member States to be locally established or authorized or otherwise prevented from participating in local co-insurance transactions. In so doing, the defendant States had also ignored the direct effect and primacy of Community Law. A number of arguments were raised with regard to the admissibility of the claims although these were quickly dismissed by the Court on the general basis that the relevant European provisions and supporting directives raised questions of interpretation that had to be dealt with in the substance of the cases.[12]

On the main issue of whether a local authorization and establishment requirement was contrary to the provisions on services, the main judgement was issued in *Commission v Germany*.[13] With regard to the scope of application of Articles 49 (ex 59) and 50 (ex 60), the Court noted that they had become directly applicable on the expiry of the transitional period which applicability was not conditional on the further harmonization or coordination of relevant national laws. These provisions accordingly required the removal of any discriminatory provision on the grounds of nationality as well as all restrictions on the freedom to provide services imposed by reason of the fact that a person is established in a Member State other than that in

[11] (n 9).

[12] The Irish Government had, for example, claimed that in bringing the actions, the Commission was pre-empting Council action under Art 57(2) (47) as the issues covered were dealt with under the proposed Second Directive concerning Direct Insurance other than Life Insurance that was currently under discussion (OJ 1976, C32, 2). The Court stated that even if the proposed measure on adoption would have terminated the alleged infringements, the Commission was still entitled to proceed under Art 169 (226). The French and Irish Governments had also argued that the Commission was, in effect, challenging the legality of Directive 78/473/EEC of 30 May 1978 on the coordination of laws, regulations and administrative provisions relating to Community Co-insurance (OJ 1978, L151, 25). This was also dismissed.

[13] The Court refers generally to its decision in *Commission v Germany* in each of the other *Co-insurance* Cases.

which the service is to be provided.[14] From *Van Wesemael* and *Webb*, specific requirements imposed on the provider of services may not be considered to be incompatible with the Treaty where they have as their purpose the application of rules governing such activities although the freedom to provide services may only be restricted by provisions justified by the general good and which are applied to all persons (or undertakings) insofar as the interest is not safeguarded by the provisions to which the provider is subject in its State of establishment. Such requirements had also to be objectively justified by the need to ensure that professional rules of conduct are complied with and that the interests which such rules are designed to safeguard are protected.[15] The Court considered that the requirement of a local permanent establishment and separate authorization constituted restrictions on the freedom to provide services.[16] The basis for this was supposedly the increased cost in the local territory especially where the insurer only conducts business occasionally.[17]

[14] *Commission v Germany* (n 9) para 25. Certain government parties including Germany claimed that the third paragraph of Art 60 (50) allowed the State of the person insured to apply its supervisory legislation to insurers from other Member States. The Court had, however, confirmed in Case 279/80 *Webb* that the aim of the paragraph was to allow the provider of the service to pursue the activity without discrimination but that it did not follow that all national legislation applicable to nationals of that State and usually applied to the permanent activities of undertakings established there may be similarly applied in their entirety to the temporary activities of undertakings established in other Member States (para 26).

[15] Para 27. See generally Michel Tison 'Unravelling the General Good Exception: the Case of Financial Services' Ch 12 in Mads Andenas and Wulf-Henning Roth *Services and Free Movement in EU Law* (OUP Oxford 2002). See also Siofra O'Leary and Jose M Fernandez-Martin 'Judicially Created Exceptions to the Free Movement of Services' Ch 6 in Andenas and Roth.

[16] Para 28.

[17] The reference to a cost argument alone is questionable. The initial reference to 'the cost of such services' may have suggested that the Court was concerned with the burden to the consumer. Increased costs would, by implication, mean less choice. From the further reference to the insurer's conduct of 'business in that State only occasionally' it would appear that the Court was concerned with the cost to the service provider and not the consumer. Although not expressly stated, the effect of this may be to limit the possibility of cross-border expansion through service provision. Trade would then be restricted through opportunity loss and financial disincentive. In light of the importance of the basis on which the requirements under examination constitute a restriction, the Court's reasoning is surprisingly short in this regard.

Sir Gordon Slynn explained that the cost to the service provider, in particular, in *Commission v. Germany* may be substantial. This case was distinct in that the branch had to be an independent working unit with separate accounts and not merely a branch or agency of the insurer's head office. The number of staff required to man and the cost of running such an independent branch would have been substantial whether or not the Commission's estimate of, at least, 30 staff and annual running costs of DM 1.8 million were correct. The effect would have been substantially to rule out the possibility of an insurer from another Member State taking part in any occasional co-insurance business in Germany. Opinion of the Advocate General, *Commission v Germany*, para 3785.

With regard to authorization, Sir Gordon Slynn did not accept that this was justified especially where policy holders were likely to be large commercial or industrial concerns and that policies would be 'tailor-made' for the particular and often exceptional risk involved.

Having considered that the establishment and authorization requirements were contrary to the freedom to provide services, the Court examined possible imperative reasons relating to the 'public interest' that could justify this. The Court considered the issue in terms of relevant interest, existing protection and necessity or least restrictive effect. The Court accepted that there were imperative reasons justifying restrictions in light of the nature of the service and the size of the market.[18] With regard to the protection provided by the rules of the State of establishment, national rules concerning technical reserves and the condition of insurance may be maintained provided that they did not exceed what is necessary to protect policyholders and insured persons.[19] With regard to necessity, the Court accepted that an establishment requirement for direct insurance business (other than transport insurance) through salesman, representatives, agents or other intermediaries was not necessary although that did not extend to compulsory insurance and insurance for which the insurer either maintained a permanent presence equivalent to an agency or a branch or

Authorization would clearly require a detailed examination of many matters. The Advocate General noted that the aim was supposedly to achieve 'transparency' with the terms offered by various insurers being as uniform as possible. Although this latter argument is questionable, the burden involved in having to require separate authorization would be substantial. The Advocate General concluded that the Commission was entitled to its declaration under Arts 59 and 60.

18 All parties agreed that the insurance sector was a particularly sensitive area in terms of consumer protection both where a person acted as a policy holder and as an insured person. This sensitivity was considered to arise, in particular, because of the nature of the service provided in which the occurrence or timing of future events was uncertain at the time the contract was concluded. An insured person would then be in a precarious position where they did not receive payment after a relevant event. It was also difficult for consumers to judge whether they would receive payment having regard to the future development of the insurer's financial position and the contract terms which were usually imposed by the insurer. Although the drafting could possibly have been improved, the definition of relevant risk is accurate (para 30). The German Government had also noted that insurance had become a mass phenomenon in certain fields with contracts being concluded in such numbers that the protection of the interests of insured persons and injured third parties affected virtually the whole of the population (para 31).

It was for these reasons that Member States had sought to introduce legislation to make insurance undertakings subject to mandatory rules both with regard to the financial position and conditions of insurers and to permanent supervision to ensure that those rules were complied with (para 32). This then sets out the basis for insurance regulation both in terms of relevant regulatory requirements (mandatory rules including capital adequacy and other financial conditions) and continuing supervision (ongoing compliance) as well as review of contractual terms and private agreements (consumer protection). Ch 1 (n 2).

19 The Court noted that the first coordination Directives 73/239 and 79/267 were only designed to facilitate the setting-up of branches or agencies in other States. Although they were not directed at services, they were nevertheless of assistance in determining whether conditions were sufficiently equivalent and supervision sufficiently effective having regard to the restrictions imposed by the States in which the services are provided (para 36). The two Directives, however, only applied capital resources and not technical reserves nor conditions of insurance. National legislatures could accordingly apply their own requirements in these respects provided that they were necessary (para 41).

directed the business entirely or principally towards the host territory.[20] The need for a permanent establishment was not justified[21] although authorization as opposed to an establishment requirement could be permitted, at least, with regard to certain types of insurance. The Court also upheld the Commission's second claim that Germany had breached the Treaty and Directive 78/483 in requiring leading insurers to be authorized and established.[22] The Commission's third head of claim with regard to the existence of threshold levels was held inadmissible and considered to fail.[23]

[20] The Court dismissed the Commission's first head of claim with regard to authorization (para 57). It accepted the German Government's argument that authorization was necessary to provide an effective means of ensuring supervision which was justified on policyholder and insured person consumer protection reasons. Art 6 of the First Coordination Directive required States to make the taking-up of the business of insurance in its territory subject to official authorization. This was also to be retained in the proposed Second Directive although this would generally be provided by the State of establishment following consultation with the State in which the services were to be provided. This would be supported by permanent (continuing) cooperation between the two sets of supervisory authorities.

As such a system could only be set up by legislation, it had to be acknowledged that, at that stage, it was for the State in which the service was to be provided to grant and withdraw authorization (para 46). That authorization must nevertheless be granted to any undertaking that satisfied the relevant conditions (non-discrimination), that those conditions did not duplicate equivalent statutory provisions in the State of establishment (duplication) and that the local authorities took into account the supervision and verifications already carried out in the State of establishment (equivalence). Some difference in treatment may still have to be retained with regard to distinct types of insurance such as commercial insurance but the Court was not in a position to determine whether in individual cases the needs of protection did not justify the requirement for authorization (para 50).

With regard to establishment, this was a restriction on the provision of services following Case 39/75 *Coenen* and Case 76/81 *Minister of Public Works*. Ch 3, section D. Administrative considerations did now, however, justify derogation from rules of Community law following Case 29/82 *Van Luipen*. The Court accordingly rejected the German Government's argument that an establishment requirement facilitated verifications *in situ* and continuous monitoring.

[21] Paras 52–7.

[22] Directive 78/473 was ambiguous as to whether the lead insurer had to be authorized in the State of establishment or the territory where the service was provided. It only referred to the lead insurer being 'authorized in accordance with the conditions laid down in the first coordination directive' which did not confirm which set of regulatory requirements applied. Under Case 218/82 *Commission v Council* [1983] ECR 4063 when the wording of secondary Community law was open to more than one interpretation, preference had to be given to that which rendered the provision consistent with the Treaty. As the Court had already held that a general establishment requirement was incompatible with Arts 59 (49) and 60 (50), it only examined further the issue of authorization with regard to the lead insurer. The Court noted that Directive 78/473 generally only applied to insurance taken out by large undertakings or groups of undertakings that were in a position to assess and negotiate the policies proposed to them. Consumer protection arguments were then not as strong as with other forms of insurance. An authorization requirement could also not be imposed where equivalent conditions had already been satisfied in the State of establishment. A difference in treatment between the lead insurer and other co-insurers could further not be objectively justified. The Court accordingly concluded that neither an authorization nor establishment requirement could be applied with regard to lead insurers (paras 58–68).

[23] The Commission had complained that the Federal Insurance Supervision Office had maintained excessively high thresholds in respect of risks arising in connection with fire insur-

In *Commission v France* and *Commission v Denmark*, the Court held that the local establishment and authorization requirements were contrary to Community Law. In *Commission v Ireland*, the requirement for the lead insurer to be authorized and established was held to be contrary to Community law. The claim, in each case, that the defendant government had also failed to observe the direct effect of Articles 59 (49) and 60 (50) was dismissed on the basis that this did not constitute a separate infringement.[24]

The *Co-insurance Cases* were of value in confirming the direct applicability of the services provisions with regard to financial activities and that they extended to both discriminatory and non-discriminatory restrictions.[25] Although certain restrictions may be permitted following *Van Wesemael* and *Webb*, these had to be justified on the basis of the general good.[26] These provisions could include relevant regulatory requirements as well as other controls on contract terms. While the existence of such imperative reasons were recognized, in particular, in the insurance area, these had still to be justified on the basis of no dual burden and necessity.[27] States had to consider the extent of the supervision already effected in other territories where this was governed by relevant European provisions. This would certainly apply to capital resources in the insurance area although not technical reserves nor contract conditions.[28] Rather than hold that the country of service must consider the extent of the supervision effected by the State of establishment also in non-harmonized areas, the Court assumes that this is not sufficient and entitles the local territory to apply its own rules subject to necessity. This effectively equates the rules of the State of establishment condition referred to with no prior harmonization.

In considering necessity, at least, with regard to authorization, the Court again appears to ignore the extent of the supervision effected by the State of establishment. In *Commission v Germany*, it simply accepts the German Government's argument that an authorization requirement is necessary to ensure effective supervision despite the fact that the insurance undertaking would already be authorized in its State of establishment. The Court considered that the creation of a 'home' based authorization system required secondary legislation which meant that until adoption of the Second Coordination directive, the host territory could impose its own

ance, civil liability aircraft insurance and general civil liability insurance with the effect that co-insurance was excluded for risks below those thresholds. As the head of claim was wider than that set out in the application, it was inadmissible. The Commission was complaining about the existence rather than the level of the thresholds as such (paras 69–71).

24 Opinion of Sir Gordon Slynn, *Commission v France* (n 29) 3701.

25 See, eg, judgment of the Court in *Commission v France*, para 16.

26 Para 17.

27 *Commission v Germany* (n 9) paras 34–57.

28 Paras 34–41.

authorization requirement. This was the same effect as under the First Banking Directive until the adoption of the Second Directive. Home country control is then made conditional upon the adoption of necessary secondary legislation despite the direct applicability of the underlying Treaty provisions. The absence of prior harmonization also meant that any considerations of dual burden and necessity were reduced to questions of prior-harmonization.

The decision of the Court with regard to the limits of mutual recognition have to be accepted although some difficulties do arise with regard to the supporting discussion of the general good. The necessary link maintained between the restrictive effect and its possible justification also causes some confusion between the effect of the rights created under the secondary legislation in the financial area and the residual scope of the general good recognized under these measures.

(2) EQUAL BURDEN SALES RULES—*SCHINDLER & SCHINDLER* (1994)

The Court considered the issue of the sending of mailshots in connection with large-scale lotteries to residents of other Member States in *Schindler and Schindler* in March 1994.[29] Gerhart Schindler and Jorge Schindler were independent agents of the German public lottery body SKL[30] and had sent mailshots from the Netherlands to United Kingdom nationals inviting them to participate in the 87th issue of the SKL. The envelope containing application forms and pre-printed reply envelopes were intercepted and confiscated by the Commissioners of Customs and Excize at Dover Postal Depot in breach of relevant United Kingdom legislation.[31] In an action brought by the Commissioners against the defendants, it was claimed that the United Kingdom legislation was incompatible with Article 28 (ex 30) or (in the alternative) Article 49 (ex 59). The High Court of Justice stayed the proceedings and made a preliminary ruling to the Court under Article 234 (ex 177).[32]

[29] Case C-275/92 *Her Majesty's Customs and Excise v. Schindler & Schindler.*

[30] *Suddeutscha Klassenlotterie* (SKL) was a public body responsible for organized 'class' lotteries on behalf of Lander of the Federal Republic of Germany.

[31] Section 1(ii) of the Revenue Act 1898 prohibited the importation of any advertisement or other notice relating to the drawing of any lottery in or any act relating to lotteries. Section 1 of the Lotteries and Amusement Act 1976 prohibited lotteries that do not constitute gaming within the meaning of the relevant legislation including, in particular, the Gaming Act 1968 which applied to the distribution of winnings in money or monies' worth on the basis of chance where money had been staked by players. Small-scale lotteries for charitable and similar purposes were exempt. It was also an offence under s 2 of the 1976 Act to bring any advertisement of a non-exempt lottery into Great Britain, send out of Great Britain any document recording the sale or distribution or identity of the holder of any ticket of such a lottery or cause or procure any person to do any of the above or attempt to do so.

[32] The High Court referred six questions: (1) did the tickets or advertisements constitute goods for the purposes of Art 28 (ex 30); (2) if so, did Art 28 (ex 30) apply to the UK prohi-

On the issue of whether the Treaty provisions concerning goods or services applied, the Court considered that the activities involved constituted services for the purposes of the Treaty.[33] The sending of advertisements and application forms could not be considered independently of the operation of the lottery as a whole. The importation and distribution of 'objects' were not ends in themselves and lotteries were not activities relating to goods as such and therefore fell within the Treaty provisions governing services.[34]

The Court then had to determine whether the restrictions constituted an obstacle to provide services and whether that restriction could be justified on grounds of social policy and the prevention of fraud. With regard to restrictive effect, the Court considered that the United Kingdom prohibition on the holding of lotteries (subject to specified exceptions) was an obstacle to the freedom to provide services. Although the Court could have stated that the restriction amounted to indirect discrimination,[35] it held the provisions to be indistinctly applicable and applied *Säger*.[36] In so doing, the

bition on the importation of such tickets or advertisements even if they were applied without discrimination and irrespective of whether the law was organized from outside or within the UK; (3) if so, did UK social policy reasons justify the restriction; (4) (in the alternative) did the provision of tickets or sending of advertisements for a lottery constitute services for the purposes of Art 49 (ex 59); (5) did this apply to the prohibition; and (6) if so, were the restrictions justified in the present case (para 12).

33 A number of Member States had claimed that the operation of lotteries did not constitute an 'economic activity' and that they fell outside the scope of the Treaty. The Court confirmed that the importation of goods or the provision of services for remuneration had to be regarded as 'economic activities.' Case 13/76 *Donà v Mantero* [1976] ECR 1333, at para 12; and Case 196/87 *Steymann v Staatsecretarias van Justitie* [1988] ECR 6159, at para 10 (para 19).

34 Although the defendants had claimed that the advertisements and application forms were goods within the meaning of the Treaty, this was not considered sufficient to reduce the activity to one of exportation or importation (paras 18 and 23).

The services at issue were those provided by the operator to enable purchasers of tickets to participate in the game of chance by arranging for stakes to be collected, draws to be organized and prizes or winnings to be confirmed and paid out (para 27). Such services were normally provided for remuneration constituted by the price of the ticket (para 28). The services were cross-border in nature (para 29) and could not be treated as illegal or involving illegal products even if the laws in certain Member States treated gaming contracts as void. Case 294/82 *Einberger v Hauptzollamt Freiburg* [1984] ECR 117 (drugs); and Case 159/90 *Society for the Protection of the Unborn Child v Grogan* [1991] ECR I-4685

The element of chance inherent in a lottery and allocation of winnings did not further prevent the transaction from having an economic nature (paras 33 and 35). Its recreational use also did not prevent it from constituting a service (para 34). The failure to refer to lotteries in Directive 75/368 of 16 June 1975 (to facilitate the effective exercise of freedom of establishment and services in respect of certain activities) was irrelevant. To the extent that the promotional activities concerned did not constitute goods, the Court dismissed the second and third questions.

35 The Commission and defendants argued that the legislation was, in fact, discriminatory (para 40).

36 The Spanish, French, Greek, and UK Governments had accepted that the legislation may restrict services even though it was applied without distinction. Belgium and Luxembourg had claimed that there was no restriction as the legislation had been indistinctly applicable (para 41).

Court followed Advocate General Gulmann.[37] It could possibly have been argued that the Court could have applied its *Keck* reformulation in *Schindler*, in particular, as the judgement had only been issued four months earlier. It could be claimed that the prohibition on mailshots amounted to a 'selling arrangement' that imposed an equal burden on domestic and foreign service providers.[38] It is possible in *Schindler* that the Court looked to the fact that the effect of the legislation was to prevent the sale of all large-scale lotteries in the United Kingdom, in particular, where these were permitted elsewhere or on a more limited scale within the United Kingdom.[39] It is nevertheless unfortunate that the Court did not refer to its *Keck* ruling directly.

[37] Advocate General Gulmann considered the issues of restriction and derogation together. He noted that the Court had always stressed that the Treaty rules on services primarily prohibited overt and covert discrimination but that the prohibition may also effect restrictions other than those stemming from discriminatory rules. The Court had held in *Van Wesemael* in 1979 and *Webb* in 1981 that the rules may also limit the possibility for Member States to apply non-discriminatory rules to foreign services. This was then stated even more clearly in the 1986 *Co-insurance* cases which related to non-discriminatory requirements regarding establishment and authorization in the insurance sector (n 49). This was further reiterated in the 1991 'Tourist Guide Cases' and in *Säger* in 1991 (para 54).

In summarising the Court's case law, Advocate General Gulmann noted that while all discriminatory measures were caught, some, but not necessarily all, other measures that restrict the activities of foreign service providers in the host country may be caught (para 57). The Advocate General dismissed *Société Générale Alsacienne de Banque* (Case 15/78 [1978] ECR 1971) (Stock exchange time-bargains carried out by banks for customers) and *Debauve* (Case 52/59 [1980] ECR 833) (Belgium prohibition on the transmission on cable television of foreign advertisements). The Advocate General noted that the UK Government had confirmed that its legislation would be changed to allow the establishment of a national lottery subsequently (para 63).

[38] For comment, M Andenas and J Snell 'Keck and Free Movement of Services' ABLR (1998). See also M Bjorklend 'The Scope of the General Good Notion in the Second EC Banking Directive According to Recent Case Law' *European Business Law Review* (July/August) 1998, 227 at 235. For discussion on *Keck*, Ch 3, section C (4) and (5).

[39] The mailshots would clearly appear to constitute 'selling arrangements' that were prohibited by the UK legislation. They also imposed an equal burden on national and foreign service providers. In the absence of any unequal restrictive effect, it is arguable that the measure ought not to have been caught by the restrictions on free movement. The Court could then have further limited the extended application of *Cassis* at the same time as clarify the meaning of its new post-*Keck* sales rules exclusions.

Advocate General Gulmann did consider whether the UK rules were substantively discriminatory (paras 65–70) although without referring to *Keck* and concluded that they were not. The regulations had to be regarded as a legitimate manifestation of the legislature's views on how the gambling market should be organized. The fact that the legislation treated different forms of gambling in distinct ways did not of itself signify covert discrimination. The fact that traders would then effectively have been treated in the same manner 'in law and in fact' supports the view that the Court could have applied *Keck* to exclude the application of services rules.

The Court noted that the legislation did treat small and large scale lotteries differently but accepted that there were still distinctions between their objects, rules and methods of operation as against the large public lotteries in other Member States before enactment of the National Lottery Act 1993. The legislation was accordingly considered not to be discriminatory (para 50).

Having considered that the legislation constituted an obstacle to the freedom to provide services, the Court examined its possible justification. The Court acknowledged some of the consumer protection and public order exceptions that it had already recognized in justifying restrictions on the freedom to provide services.[40] Having recognized the stated objectives of the United Kingdom legislation,[41] the Court referred to a number of other factors that it considered justified the imposition of restrictions on the sale and operation of lotteries.[42] The Court itself then extends the scope of legitimate derogation especially in terms of social policy and the prevention of fraud at the same time as it allows the nature of the public interest arguments recognized of themselves to mean that no further consideration has to be given with regard to such issues as proportionality, equivalence or necessity. The Court appears to assume either that these tests are already satisfied or that they are not necessary in the particular case.

The effect of the decision is to confirm the application of the services rules to non-discriminatory restrictions but at the same time extend the range of derogations recognized to justify the restrictive effects in the particular case. Both the examination of Treaty prohibition and possible derogation are, however, not fully developed and of questionable content and value.

(3) EXPORT MARKETING RESTRICTIONS—*ALPINE INVESTMENTS* (1995)

The Court had the opportunity to consider telephone 'cold calling' one year later in *Alpine Investments*.[43] The Dutch Securities Transactions Law of 30

[40] The Court cited *Wesemael*, para 28; Case 220/83 *Commission v France*, para 20; and Case 15/78 *Koestler*, para 5.

[41] The legislation was designed: (a) to prevent crime and to ensure that gamblers would be treated honestly; (b) to avoid stimulating demand in the gambling sector which has damaging social consequences when taken to excess; and (c) to ensure that lotteries could not be operated for personal and commercial profit but solely for charitable, sporting or cultural purposes (para 57).

[42] (a) It was not possible to disregard the moral, religious or cultural aspects of lotteries with other types of gambling in all Member States. The general tendency of Member States was to restrict or even prohibit the practice of gambling and to prevent it from being a source of private profit. (b) Lotteries involved a high risk of crime or fraud given the size of the amounts that can be staked and the winnings that could be earned. (c) They were an incitement to spend which may have damaging individual and social consequences. (d) Although it could not of itself be regarded as an objective justification, lotteries made a significant contribution to the financing of benevolent or public interest activities such as social and charitable works as well as sport and culture (para 60). These factors were considered to justify national authorities having a sufficient degree of latitude to determine what is required to protect players and, more generally, to maintain order in society. It was accordingly for them to assess whether it was necessary to restrict lotteries or even prohibit them outright provided that this was not effected in a discriminatory manner (para 61).

[43] Case C-384/93 *Alpine Investments BV v Minister van Financiën* [1995] ECR I-1141: [1995] 2 CMLR 209; [1995] All ER [EC] 543, para 38. For general discussion and comment, JL Vilaca 'On the Application of Keck in the Field of Free Provision of Services' Ch 2 in Andenas and Roth (n 15); and J Snell and M Andenas 'Exploring the Outer Limits: Restrictions on Free Movement' Ch 4 in Andenas and Roth (n 15).

October 1985 had the effect *inter alia* of prohibiting locally established firms from approaching prospective clients in other Member States through telephone marketing.[44] Alpine Investments claimed that the prohibition on cold calling was a restriction on their freedom to provide services not justified on the grounds of public policy, public security or public health to the extent that it prevented the company from approaching potential clients in other Member States. Three questions were referred by the Administrative Court to the European Court of Justice in connection with the compatibility of the restriction with Article 49 (ex 59).[45]

The Court ruled that Article 59 (ex 59) applied to the offer of services by telephone to persons in other Member States without moving from the territory in which the provider was established.[46] With regard to whether the prohibition on cold calling amounted to a restriction within Article 59 (ex 59), the Court distinguished *Keck* on the basis that the provision in that case did not prevent access of products to the market of the Member State of importation or impede access more than it impeded access by domestic products.[47] The prohibition in this case was imposed by the State of establishment and affected both addressees in that State and other Member States and therefore directly affected access to the market and services in other Member States and was therefore capable of hindering intra-Community

[44] Alpine Investments provided financial services and, in particular, acted as an 'introducing broker' in connection with commodities futures trading. The firm provided 'managed accounts' services (discretionary), 'semi-managed accounts' (subject to confirmation) and 'non-managed accounts' (execution only). The Minister of Finance had granted Alpine Investments an exemption on 6 Sept 1991 under the 1985 Securities Transactions Law from the prohibition to act as a securities intermediary without a license (Arts 6(1)) and 8(1)). This allowed the firm to place orders with Merrill Lynch Inc although it was prohibited by a decision of 12 Nov 1991 under Art 8(2) of the Law from cold calling (defined as approaching prospective clients by telephone or in person unless they had already expressly agreed in writing to be approached in such a manner and for so long as that agreement had not been revoked by registered letter). Following administrative objection, the firms' exemption was withdrawn although a further exemption was granted to place orders with Rodman & Renshaw Inc. although this was also subject to an equivalent restriction on cold calling. Following rejection of Alpine's administrative objection, the matter was referred to the Administrative Court for Trade and Industry. Advocate General Jacobs noted that the Finance Minister had decided to impose the cold calling restrictions on all exemptions after a number of complaints had been received from the public. This had been confirmed by a press release dated 1 Oct 1991.

[45] The Court was asked: (a) to confirm whether Art 59 (49) applied to the services in question; (b) whether the conditions involved amounted to a restriction for the purposes of Art 59 (49); and (3) whether the restriction was justified in the public interest (3(a)) and necessary and proportionate (3(b)).

[46] The Court considered that the freedom to provide services would become illusory if national rules were at liberty to restrict offers of services. Para 19 of the judgement of the Court dated 10 May 1995. The prior existence of an identifiable recipient was not a pre-condition to the provision of services. There was also a provision of services from the express terms of Art 59 (49) where the offer was made by a provider established in one Member State to the potential recipient in another (para 21).

[47] Para 37.

trade and services.[48] The Court accordingly took the opportunity to clarify *Keck*. Although cold calling could clearly be classified as a selling arrangement or sales rule, its effect in this case was considered to impact (restrict) the provision of services in other territories and therefore limit intra-state trade. *Keck* had to be distinguished on that basis. The Court's rejection of *Keck* was strongly supported by AG Jacobs.[49]

The other difficulty that arose with regard to the restrictive effect of the cold calling arrangements was whether they were considered consistent with the established case law on Article 29 (ex 34) which prohibited quantitative restrictions and measures of equivalent effect on exports. The Court recognized that a prohibition would not constitute a restriction on the provision of services only where another Member State applied less strict rules to the same service (referring to *Peralta*).[50] Such a prohibition, however, deprived the home operators of a useful technique for marketing services in other Member States.[51] It could be claimed that such other cases

[48] Para 38. The Court had earlier stated that three points had to be considered in determining whether the conditions imposed constituted a restriction. These related to the relevance of the fact that (a) service providers in other Member States were not subject to the same restriction, (b) the condition was imposed by the Member State of establishment and (c) it falls outside Art 59 as a selling arrangement permitted under *Keck*.

With regard to the first point, the Court noted that the prohibition would not constitute a restriction solely on the basis that other territories applied less strict rules (under Case C3-379/92 *Peralta* [1994] ECR I-3453, at para 48). It can nevertheless constitute a restriction where it deprives the operators concerned of a rapid and direct technique for marketing and for contacting potential clients in other Member States (para 28).

On the second point, the Court noted that the first paragraph of Art 59 (49) applied to restrictions in general irrespective of whether they were imposed by the State of destination or origin. The right to provide services may then be relied on by undertakings against their own State and other Member States (on the basis of Case C-18/93 *Corsica Ferries Italia v Corpo de Piloti del Porto di Genova* [1993] ECR I-1783 at para 30; *Peralta* para 40; and Case C-381/93 *Commission v. France* [1994] ECR I-5145, para 14).

With regard to *Keck*, the Dutch and UK Government had claimed that the service was an analogous non-discriminatory measure and therefore fell outside Art 59 (49). As noted in the text, the Court distinguished *Keck* on the basis that it did not prevent access while the restriction on cold calling in this case did (paras 33, 37 and 38).

[49] The Advocate General distinguished between the importing rules considered in *Keck* and exporting restrictions in the present case in that they affected both the provision of services in the local territory as well as in other Member States. Para 60 of the opinion of Advocate General Jacobs of 26 Jan 1995. The freedom to provide services would also become nugatory if both exportation and importation rules were held to fall outside Art 59 (49) as export would then have to comply with both sets of provisions even if they were not objectively justified and if they imposed contradictory requirements (para 61 of the Opinion).

Advocate General Jacobs also noted that there were difficulties in determining the effect of *Keck* even with regard to Art 30 (28) citing his Opinion in Case C-412/93 *Leclerc-Siplec* [1995] ECR I-179 (para 59 of the Opinion). The Advocate General added that, 'even if one were to accept that some analogy with *Keck* might be appropriate' in the case of *Alpine Investments* which confirms that opinion on the validity and value of *Keck* within the Court was far from consistent. See Ch 3, section 5 C (4) and (5).

[50] Para 27.

[51] Para 28.

as *Groenveld*, *Obel* and *Sulzer*[52] contradicted this. AG Jacobs distinguished these cases on the basis that it was unclear whether they would apply to rules of the exporting State concerning the marketing of goods. The State could prohibit traders from using techniques to sell their products in the local territory in a particular way. It could not, however, restrict them from marketing goods in other States otherwise permitted in the host territory.[53] Whatever the decision with regard to goods under Article 34 (29), a restriction on the marketing of services in another State must be seen as a restriction on the freedom to provide services.[54] The Advocate General also distinguished *Peralta* on the basis that the Italian prohibition on the discharge of harmful substances in other territorial waters was not concerned with either the provision or marketing of services with any effect on the freedom to provide services being so remote, tenuous and indirect as not to constitute a restriction under Article 59 (49).[55] While the limitation of export rules to discriminatory rather than non-discriminatory measures is understandable from a policy perspective,[56] the extension of such provisions with the effect that they result in interference with the provision of services in another Member State is sufficient to obstruct intra-Community trade in services.

Having decided that Article 59 (49) applied and that the prohibition in question constituted a relevant restriction, the Court considered whether this could be justified. The Court accepted the Netherlands Government argument that the prohibition on cold calling in off-market commodities

[52] Case 15/79 *Groenveld v. Produktsechap voor nen Vles* (1979) ECR 3409; Case 155/80 *Obel* (1981) ECR 1993; and Case C-339/89 *Alsthom Atlantique SA v Sulzar SA* (1991) ECR I-107.

[53] Para 55 of the Opinion.

[54] Para 56.

[55] Para 57.

[56] *Cassis* was considered not to apply to non-discriminatory export restrictions. See, for example, Weatherill and Beaumont, *EC Law* (3rd edn 1999), 604–7. The Court had held in *Groenveld* that Art 29 (ex 34) was exclusively concerned with, 'the establishment of a difference in treatment between the domestic trade of a Member State and its export trade' and was therefore inapplicable where there was no discrimination (para 7). This view was confirmed in Case 237/82 *Jongeneel Kaas* [1984] ECR 483, [1985] 2 CMLR. The approach is understandable to the extent that no 'dual burden' is imposed as the domestic and export goods are subject to the same requirements. The comments are, however, restricted to where the rules in question relate to the production process rather than subsequent marketing.

The direct market access doctrine used by the Court is also questionable to the extent that it is contrary to the policy of mutual recognition (that one set of rules is recognized not that no rules apply at all) and that such rules may be a legitimate expression of national preference (businesses can relocate or lobby for change in legislation if they are not satisfied). For comment, M Bjorkland 'The Scope of the General Good Notion of the Second EC Banking Directive According to Recent Case Law' EBLR (July/August 1999) 227 at 236. This, however, ignores the fact that the restriction in question applied to both the marketing of services in both the local and host territories and therefore had an effect on cross-border provisions. For further discussion, M Andenas and J Snell '*Keck* and the Free Movement of Services', EBLR (1998).

futures trading safeguarded the reputation of the financial markets and protected the investing public. The Court accordingly extended the range of imperative reasons of public interest to include the good reputation of the national financial sector.[57]

It could be argued that the proper justification was investor or consumer protection although the Court appeared to be concerned to base the decision on market reputation to allow it to extend the scope of the restriction to protect consumers in another Member State.[58] Market reputation may accordingly only be considered as a device to allow the Court to extend the scope of consumers covered by the relevant protection.

The main point that arises in this case is that the decision is concerned with the sale of complex financial products potentially to inexperienced investors outside the territory in which the service provider is located and regulated. The Court accepts this point subsequently with regard to proportionality.[59] This is not, however, simply an issue of proportionality but an essential part of the need for protection to be provided in the particular case. Investors in other Member States were to be safeguarded from the aggressive 'tele-selling' of complex contracts. In the absence of harmonized provisions, this was best secured by the territory in which the service provider was established. The reputation of the Dutch financial system was accordingly almost irrelevant, in particular, as the location of the telephone caller may not even have been disclosed. It was the location of the underlying trading company (ultimately Rodman & Renshaw Inc) that was important. As the Advocate Generate noted, the Commission was at that time working on the proposed Directive in respect of Distance Selling.[60] It was accordingly recognized that harmonized controls on cold calling were necessary although none had yet been adopted. The Court then anticipates the subsequent measures to be adopted which is essentially a consumer protection measure.

[57] Para 44. The Netherlands Government had argued that financial markets played an important role in the financing of economic operators and, given the speculative nature and the complexity of commodities futures contracts, the smooth operation of financial markets was largely contingent on the confidence they inspired in investors. That confidence, in turn, was dependent, in particular, on the existence of professional regulations that served to ensure the competence and trustworthiness of the financial intermediaries on whom investors were particularly reliant (para 42).

[58] The Court stated that although the protection of consumers in other Member States was not, as such, a matter for the Netherlands authorities, the nature and extent of that protection did have a direct effect on the good reputation of Netherlands financial services (para 43).

[59] For similar discussion, V Hatzopoulos 'Case C-384/93 *Alpine Investments BV v Minister van Financiën*, Judgement of 10 May 1999, NYR (1995)' 32 *CMLR* 1427.

[60] COM (93) 396, OJ 1993 C 308, 18. The initial proposal was COM (92) 11, OJ 1992 C 156, 14. Paras 21–23 of the Opinion. The Advocate General had already reviewed the Investment Services Directive 93/22/EEC (OJ 1993 L 141, 27) and Directive 85/577/EEC concerning the protection of consumers in respect of contracts negotiated away from business premises (OJ 1985 L 372, 31). Paras 12–20 of the Opinion.

The reference to market reputation can accordingly be best understood solely in terms of the need to extend the scope of the restriction to consumers in other territories for which the Netherlands authorities were not responsible. The longer term validity of the decision must then be questioned both in terms of its relevance (with the subsequent adoption of the Distance Selling Directive) and its underlying rationale. This simply reflects the Court's perceived need and willingness to uphold a measure considered to be inappropriate in advance of relevant Community provision. The Court, of course, quickly disposed of any arguments concerning the restriction not being proportionate, appropriate or necessary.[61]

In assessing *Alpine Investments*, the decision was important in initially distinguishing *Keck* with regard to export sales restrictions that had an impact on intra-Community trade and services. *Keck* only applies with regard to selling arrangements within a particular territory. Non-discriminatory export provisions could nevertheless be caught by the Treaty. The relevant goods case law had to be distinguished where there was again an effect on intra-Community trade. Public interest imperative reasons were also extended to include market reputation although this has to be understood in light of the unusual circumstances of the particular case. The Court was generally concerned with consumer protection issues but would appear to have been constrained to define this in terms of market reputation to allow one territory effectively to protect the interests of consumers in another. From a policy perspective, this can be understood in terms of the generally recognized need to control cold calling especially in connection with complex high risk contracts which anticipated the Distance Selling Directive. Although useful in the particular circumstances, of itself this may be of essentially limited value and relevance elsewhere. It is in the pre-

[61] The Court stated that it was well settled that requirements had to be appropriate to ensure the achievement of the intended aim and must not go beyond what was necessary to achieve that objective (Case C-288/89 *Collective Antennevoorziening Gouda and Others v Commissariat voor de media* [1991] ECR I-4007, para 15). The Court rejected Alpine Investments' argument that message recipients were best protected in their local territory. Even if the receiving State wished to prohibit cold calling or to subject it to conditions, it would not be in a position to prevent or control telephone calls from another Member State without cooperation with the home authorities. The prohibition was accordingly considered to be appropriate (on the basis of securing the integrity of those markets).

The prohibition was also considered to be necessary. The Advocate General noted that the fact that less strict rules were imposed in one territory than another did not mean that they were necessarily disproportionate. Alpine Investments had claimed that it would have been sufficient to record unsolicited calls (the practice adopted in the UK by the Securities and Futures Authority) at the time.

Any argument with regard to the prohibition constituting an unnecessary burden was also rejected. Limiting the prohibition may not be sufficient to achieve the objective of restoring and maintaining investor confidence in the national securities markets in general (para 53). The rules were also limited in scope being restricted to non-agreed telephone approaches, only potential and non-existing clients and were limited to the commodities futures market within which previous abuses had occurred (para 54).

disposition of the Court to extend relevant derogation to include new interests or policy considerations that *Alpine* is particularly significant.

(4) LICENSING REQUIREMENTS—*REISEBÜRO BROEDE* (1996)

The separate issue of local licensing was considered by the Court ten months later in *Reisebüro Broede*.[62] Ms Ramthun, the managing director of INC Consulting SARL, had been prevented from enforcing a debt against Mr Sandker in Germany on the basis that debt collection undertakings were prohibited from representing their creditor clients in legal proceedings under the relevant legislation.[63]

The Court dismissed any objection by the German Government and the Commission that the action was inadmissible as no cross-border issue had been raised. It had been claimed that the Treaty would not apply where all of the relevant elements were confined within a single Member State which was a question of fact for the national court to determine.[64] The Court noted that Reisebüro Broede had, in this case, given power of attorney to INC Consulting based in France which had, in turn, granted Ms Ramthun the power of attorney in Germany. The case clearly raised a cross-border issue.[65]

The Court then ruled that the relevant Treaty provisions were those concerning services rather than establishment.[66] The prohibition of debt collection within Germany without the involvement of a lawyer would

[62] Case C-3/95 *Reisebüro Broede v Gerd Sandker.*

[63] Reisebüro Broede was a travel agency in Cologne that had obtained an order against Mr Sandker who resided in Dortmund. INC Consulting was a debt collection and corporate consultancy service established in France which had been given full authority to recover the debt. INC Consulting gave its managing director, Ms Ramthun, who resided in Germany, power of attorney to enforce the debt. Having applied to the court in Dortmund for the issue of an attachment order, the application was dismissed on the ground that Ms Ramthun had lacked the requisite legal capacity under the German Law on Legal Advice of 17 Dec 1935. (The Code of Civil Procedure of 30 Jan 1877 permitted persons to act directly or through an intermediary in cases not before a *Landgericht* or any higher court.) On appeal to the *Landgericht Dortmund*, the court referred two questions to the European Court of Justice asking whether the requirement for a local license would be prohibited under Art 59 (49) and whether only German law was applicable as both parties were resident in the same State and the debt enforceable in that State.

[64] Case C-23/93 *TV 10 v Commissariaat voor de Media* [1994] ECR I-4795, para 14.

[65] Paras 13–16 of judgment of the Court (5th chamber) of 12 Dec 1996.

[66] The German Government and the Commission had argued that INC Consulting may have been able to establish a permanent residence in Germany on account of Ms Ramthun's residence. Having noted that services were subordinate to establishment and referring to the tests set out in *Gebhard*, the Court felt constrained to assume for the purposes of answering the questions referred that Art 59 (49) applied. It is was for the national court to determine whether the activity pursued was of a temporary nature having regard to its duration, regularity, periodicity and continuity. The Court added that INC Consulting had undertaken debt collection work in France and Germany for French and other French clients and had only acted for Reisebüro Broede on six occasions between February and May 1994 (paras 17–24).

restrict services as it made it impossible for those services to be provided in Germany by non-qualified persons even where the activities were of a purely occasional nature.[67]

Following *Gebhard*, the Court considered whether the restriction was non-discriminatory, justified, suitable and proportionate. The Court noted that the prohibition was inherently non-discriminatory and applied without distinction to service providers from other Member States.[68] The purpose was to protect recipients of the service from any harm suffered as a result of legal advice given to them by persons who did not possess the necessary professional or personal qualifications as well as to safeguard the proper administration of justice.[69]

More difficult issues arose with regard to suitability and necessity. The Commission and Reisebüro Broede had claimed that the necessary protection could be provided by alternative means.[70] The Commission had also claimed that the measures were not concerned with the protection of creditors or officials as the Code of Civil Procedure permitted parties to act without the assistance of a lawyer. This was distinguished on the basis that exemption was only available to natural persons and those who acted on their own behalf and not where litigation services were provided on a professional basis. The purpose of the Law on Legal Advice was to ensure

[67] It had been confirmed in Case C-272/94 *Guiot* [1996] ECR I-1905 that Art 59 (49) applied to discriminatory provisions as well as to any indistinctly applicable restriction that was liable to prohibit, impede or render less advantageous the activities of a provider of services established in another Member State where he lawfully provides similar services (para 25). Advocate General Fennelly added that German law effectively imposed two separate restrictions on debt collection: debt collectors had to be authorized by the competent regional authorities to carry out extra-judicial activities; and were prohibited from seeking judicial enforcement of debts unless the services of a lawyer were retained. The Advocate General referred to *Säger* in which an equivalent professional qualification requirement was imposed for patent monitoring services under the same Article of the Law on Legal Advice. The restriction accordingly fell within Art 59 (49). Although as it was non-discriminatory, it was necessary to consider whether it was justified. Paras 18 and 19 of the Opinion of Advocate General Fennelly of 27 June 1996.

[68] Para 30.

[69] *Säger* and *van Binsbergen*. The decisions in these cases were discussed by the Advocate General at paras 30 and 33 of the Opinion. He noted that Advocate General Jacobs had stated in *Säger* that the justification required would depend on the nature of the services and restrictions. The relevant law had the dual purpose of protecting members of the public against damage and protecting lawyers against unfair competition from unqualified persons not subject to the constraints of a regulated profession. To these, Advocate General Fennelly added the need to protect the proper functioning of the legal system. He added that the services concerned in the particular case were also of an unusual or specialized nature and unlike the more general essentially routine services provided in *Säger* (para 30). *Van Binsbergen* was distinguished on the basis that the present case did not require a residence requirement as such but only that the services of lawyers were engaged in undertaking judicial debt collection work (para 34).

[70] The German authorities could have accepted a certificate of integrity or solvency issued by the competent authorities of the home territory or could have required an election of domicile in the host State for the purposes of receiving legal documentation.

that such services were only provided by lawyers who were answerable personally to the courts.[71] The Court added that Member States were free to regulate the exercise of their own legal professions in the absence of relevant Community rules[72] and that the professional rules relating to lawyers (such as organization, qualifications, professional ethics, supervision and liability) were designed to ensure that the consumers of legal services and the sound administration of justice were provided with necessary guarantees in relation to integrity and experience.[73] It was accordingly for Member States to assess whether it was necessary to place restrictions on the professional recovery of debts by way of judicial proceedings. Although the activity was not reserved to lawyers in other territories, Germany was still entitled to consider that its objectives would not be attained by less restrictive means.[74] Following *Alpine Investments*, the fact that debt collection agencies were not subject to legal regulation in France did not make the German rules disproportionate.[75]

A *Keck* analysis could not have been adopted in this case as it related to the qualifications of the service providers. This has to be equated with composition or product rather than sales rules. Although non-discriminatory, the effect of the requirement for debt collection to be carried out by lawyers (other than in personal actions) did restrict trade and services. To that extent, the judgement is faultless. Whether the restriction was justified is more questionable. It could be argued that the requirement was clearly discriminatory as between legally and non-legally qualified service providers. The provision of unqualified legal advice is certainly of concern in any territory and would justify protection. Debt collection, and in particular, enforcement of an already obtained order, however, does not constitute the provision of legal advice or a legal service as such (although it does have legal effect). Debt enforcement in many Member States can be carried out through court officers or externally trained recovery agents or bailiffs. This is then concerned with the final enforcement of a court order through the physical seizure and collection of assets. Unfortunately, the different stages in the enforcement process (court order, order for enforcement and asset recovery or seizure) were not considered directly in the judgement.

From the information available, Ms Ramthun had only applied for an attachment order. No further information is provided as to how that order would subsequently have been effected. Rather than protect the recipient of any nominal service, the effect of the judgement only then appears to be to

[71] Paras 34 and 35.
[72] Case 107/83 *Ordre des Avocats du Burreau de Paris v Klopp* [1984] ECR 2971, para 17.
[73] Case 292/86 *Gullung v Conseills de l'Ordre des Avocats du Burreau de Colmar et de Saverne* [1988] ECR 111; and *Van Binsbergen*.
[74] Para 41.
[75] Para 42.

confirm the monopoly rights of lawyers before the courts in Germany. The arguments raised by the Commission and Reisebüro Broede with regard to less restrictive measures being available should also have been given more consideration. It can be easily argued that the requirement for costly legal representation in connection with simple debt enforcement was discriminatory, unnecessary and disproportionate. There would also then be no more general Community interest in allowing the decision such as in *Alpine Investments*.

While the effect of *Reisebüro Broede* was to confirm the natural limits to *Keck* with regard to qualification requirements and the restrictive effects of local authorization regimes, the generous and uncritical approach that the Court adopted with regard to the application of the mandatory requirements tests must be questioned. The scope of judicial derogation must be extended as the consequences of the adoption of a non-discriminatory policy with regard to restrictive effects are recognized. Any extension of the general good tests must, however, be considered, appropriate, properly justified and consistent. *Reisebüro Broede* was possibly not detrimental to the extent that it did not change the relevant rules as such but arguably regressive in the manner in which it applied the established tests. The overall effect may also have been to extend the scope of the meaning of legal services across the Community in an unnecessary and uncritical manner. The result of this is that local restrictive practices will be more easily upheld with the consequent additional costs, burden and potential delays that this may impose on potential litigants.

(5) National Authorization Reconsidered—*Parodi* (1997)

The court had to re-consider the effects of a local licensing requirement in July 1997 in *Parodi*.[76] The Dutch de Barry Bank had granted a mortgage loan to Parodi, a French real property company, in November 1984.[77] After the case had been dismissed by the Regional Court and Appeal Court,[78] the *Cour de Cassation* asked the European Court to confirm whether national legislation requiring authorization to supply banking services in the local territory was contrary to Articles 59 (49) and 61(2) (51) of the Treaty.[79]

[76] Case C-222/95 *Societe Civile Immobilière Parodi v Banque H Albert de Bary*.

[77] Six years later, Parodi sought to have the loan declared void on the ground that de Barry Bank had not been authorized under Law No 84/46 of 24 Jan 1984 on the activity and supervision of credit institutions.

[78] The *Tribune de Grande Instance* (Regional Court) dismissed Parodi's claim on 12 June 1991. The *Cour d'Appel* (Appeal Court) upheld the decision on 15 June 1993 *inter alia* on the ground that the bank enjoyed freedom of establishment and freedom to provide services under the then EEC Treaty and Directive 73/183/EEC of 28 June 1973 (OJ 1973 L 194, p. 1).

[79] Art 61(2) (51(2)) provided that: 'The liberalization of banking and insurance services connected with movements of capital shall be effected in step with the progressive liberalization of movement of capital.'

The Court considered that the provision of mortgage loans was not prevented by the rules then in force concerning capital movements from being subject to the Treaty requirements governing the provision of services.[80] With regard to Articles 59 (49) and 60 (50), the Court restated that they applied to discriminatory and other provisions that inhibited, impeded or rendered less advantageous service activities citing *Reisebüro Broede*. The need to obtain additional authorization from the supervisory authorities in the State of destination made it more difficult for credit institutions to provide services on a cross-border basis and therefore created a restriction on the freedom to provide services.[81] The Court accordingly ruled again that the prohibition on rules restricting the free provision of services was easily satisfied. To the extent that authorization had to be equated with manufacturing or composition, the sales rules exemption provided for under *Keck* was inapplicable.

The Court restates the derogation tests although in slightly different terms.[82] The Court recognizes that the banking sector is particularly sensitive

[80] The effect of Art 61(2) (51(2)) of the Treaty was to allow Member States to retain measures designed to restrict capital movements (where there had been no European liberalization) without any challenge being possible under Arts 59 (49) or 60 (50) that they constituted direct obstacles to the free provision of services (para 9 of the judgment of 9 July 1997). The services rules did not then apply to banking where capital restrictions were in place as permitted under Community law.

Free movement of capital had not become directly applicable from the end of the transitional period and had to be effected under Council directives adopted on the basis of Art 69 (Case 203/80 *Casati* [1981] ECR 1595, paras 8–13 and Case C-484/93 *Svensson and Gustavsson v Ministre du Logrment et de l'Urbaniseme* [1995] ECR I-3055, para 5.

At the time the loan was granted, it fell within Heading VIII.A of Annex II of the Second Council Directive 63/21/EEC of 18 Dec 1962 (OJ, English Special Edition 1963–1964, 5). The First Council Directive for the implementation of Arts 67 of the Treaty had been adopted on 11 May 1960 (OJ, English Special Edition 1959/1962, 49). Under Art 3(1) of the First Directive, Member States were required to issue necessary foreign exchange authorizations with regard to the capital movements set out in List C of Annex I except where this might form an obstacle to the achievement of its economic policy objectives under Art 3(2). Although the French Government had exercised derogation under Art 3(2), this only applied to transactions over FF 50 million and therefore did not effect the loan in question (paras 8–16).

[81] Para 19.

[82] The Court stated that freedom to provide services may be limited only by rules that are justified by imperative reasons relating to the public interest and which apply to all persons or undertakings pursuing an activity in the State of destination insofar as that interest is not protected by the rules to which the person providing the service is subject in the Member State in which it is established. This then immediately restates the no duplication test without first referring to the absence of any discrimination. The reference to imperative reasons is also stated to be a fundamental principle of the Treaty. This judicial derogation is, however, distinct from the strict exceptions provided for under the Treaty in connection with discriminatory restrictions.

The Court then continues by requiring those requirements to be objectively necessary in order to ensure compliance with professional rules and to guarantee the protection of the recipient of services as well as not exceed what is necessary to obtain those objectives. This restates the necessary requirement, capable function and proportionality tests. As before, the Court refers to Case 279/80 *Webb*, Case 205/84 *Commission v Germany* and Case C-76/90 *Säger* (para 21).

although apparently only with regard to consumer protection.[83] The Court notes that some progress was made with the First Banking Directive 77/780/EEC of 12 December 1977 although full mutual recognition in the banking area was not secured until the Second Banking Directive 89/646/EEC of 15 December 1989.[84] The Court does accept that authorization was subject to certain minimum requirements under the First Banking Directive (Article 3(1)) although this was without prejudice to other conditions of general application laid down by national laws (under Article 3(2)). The Court accordingly concluded from this that there were within the banking sector imperative reasons relating to the public interest capable of justifying the imposition by the State of destination of conditions regarding the activities of credit institutions and their supervision that went

[83] The Court adds that it is necessary to protect consumers against the harm that they would suffer through banking transactions effected by institutions not complying with the requirements relating to solvency and whose managers do not have the necessary professional qualifications or integrity (para 22). This, however, appears to confuse private law consumer protection issues with regulatory solvency and financial stability.

The reference to transactions (in para 22) suggests that the Court is concerned with such traditional consumer protection issues as full disclosure and avoidance of conflicts of interest. Disclosure of terms and interest rates is dealt with through other Community measures while almost no other banker customer relationship requirements have been adopted at the Community level.

Having referred to individual banking transactions, solvency related requirements and the suitability type conditions imposed on management then appear to be confused. The purpose of solvency regulations is to protect the stability of the bank in the event that it suffers unexpected loss. This is not, however, the main financial requirement with the principal obligation in practice tending to relate to liquidity and reserve requirements (which require banks to match their funding and lending commitments and hold sufficient reserves to cover all expected withdrawal demands). The reference to solvency with individual transactions would accordingly appear to be confused. The separate reference to suitability (necessary professional qualifications and integrity) is also unclear. Suitability is important to ensure that the managers of the bank are capable of managing its assets and liabilities effectively as a whole. This will require ensuring that all loans are generally entered into in appropriate terms and that all consequent credit commitments are covered by the banks' source of funds (its deposit base or available inter-bank borrowing facilities).

Relevant consumer protection (essentially private law) and regulatory (bank and market stability) issues would appear to have been confused. It is possible that the Court was not properly advised as to the nature and risks inherent in the banking market.

[84] The references again appear confused. The Court refers to, 'those needs which are specific to the banking sector' (referring to the issues referred to in n 83) as having led to the adoption of the First Banking Directive. The Directive had no specific consumer protection objective. It was adopted to facilitate the establishment of banks from one Member State in other territories although still subject to the authorization requirements of the host territory. It anticipated the subsequent adoption a home country control rule although at that stage not clearly on the basis of mutual recognition. The Directive introduced a number of initial minimum requirements (including requiring banks to be managed by, at least, two directors of sufficient repute) and abolish local endowment capital requirements. The Directive was adopted after a fully consolidated first proposed measure in this area had to be abandoned by the Commission in 1972. The proposal for the Directive was issued in 1974 as part of the Commission's new evolving framework approach to banking harmonization. For further discussion, section D (2); and Ch 5, sections B and C and (nn 9–12 and 24).

beyond the minimum requirements set out in the First Banking Directive and already implemented in the State of origin.[85] The Court then implies a general good exemption into the terms of the First Banking Directive although no express reference was made in the secondary legislation until the Second Banking Directive and then only at the insistence of certain Member States. While it had to be accepted that host territories retained a significant amount of residual authority under the First Banking Directive, this was not, certainly at that time, to be understood in terms of specific general good considerations. It was simply that it had not been possible, despite the earlier work of the Commission, to agree harmonized provisions in many key areas of bank regulation. The significance of this is that the Court then equates the scope of the general good doctrine that it would subsequently recognize with the scope of original host country control in all areas where harmonized provisions had not been adopted despite the fact that the Treaty anticipated their use.[86]

Rather than determine whether the French legislation contained any such additional conditions, the Court stated that this was for the national court to determine. The Court agreed with Advocate General Elmer that insufficient information had been provided as to the exact purpose served by the authorization requirement imposed or as to the authorities' practice with regard to banks established in other Member States. The Court's reference to this purpose being unclear would appear simply to be misinformed. The objective of banking regulation is to ensure that individual institutions are managed effectively to prevent their collapse and to protect the stability of other banking institutions and the market as a whole (as well as their depositors). The Court does, however, admit (in the same paragraph) that the national provisions do not appear to be designed specifically to protect borrowers but rather to give effect to prudential rules tended to guarantee that the banks are solvent with regard to savers.[87] This would appear to correct some of the earlier confusion referred to (under paragraph 22). The Court draws a further distinction between the nature of the banking activity and the risks incurred by their counterparties. It adds that the need to

[85] Paras 25 and 26.

[86] Art 52(1) (*ex* 63) provides for directives to be adopted to give effect to the freedoms of establishment and provision of services under the earlier General Programmes. The Treaty accordingly appeared to make the exercise of the rights of establishment and services conditional upon appropriate recognition directives being adopted. Even with the amendments adopted under the Single Act and the removal of the unanimity requirement in this regard, the Treaty regime still assumed implementing measures being applied in practice. The effect of the Second Banking Directive was then to provide for the full mutual recognition of national licenses across all Member States on the basis of the agreed minimum harmonization provisions set out in the First and Second Directives and on the continuing supervision effected by the home territories under the principle of home country controls. Ch 5, sections B and C and (n 22); and Ch 6, section C.

[87] Paras 27 and 28.

protect the borrower will accordingly vary with the nature of the transaction with no protection possibly being required in certain cases.[88]

The Court generally followed Advocate General Elmer who issued an unfortunately short opinion. The AG concluded that the local authorization requirement was likely to hinder or impede loans by credit institutions lawfully established in other Member States on the basis of *Van Binsbergen*. This may, however, be justified on the basis of *Webb* and the *Co-insurance* cases. It is noted that ensuring consumer protection can justify restrictions on the freedom to provide services following *Schindler* although the AG then focuses on the definition of consumer and the relationship between consumer protection and the free movement of capital. There is again no clear examination of the nature and purpose of bank regulation and the relationship between regulatory requirements and other banker customer relationship connected consumer protection issues.

The Court finally notes that the legislation required an establishment requirement in addition to local authorization. The Court dealt with this point quickly by confirming that, if the requirement of authorization constituted a restriction on the freedom to provide services, a permanent establishment requirement would be the very negation of that freedom. It would then have the effect of depriving Article 59 (49) of all effectiveness.[89]

The decision in *Parodi* was of interest in confirming the effectiveness of host authorization conditions in the banking area. A local authorization requirement clearly amounted to a dual burden and created an obstacle to intra-Community trade. Banking markets are of fundamental importance to any society and financial system. It is then not difficult to advance imperative reasons why local conditions should be permitted. On any proper examination of the nature of banking and the operation of banking markets, however, the principal justification is market stability rather than consumer protection. The Court's discussion is possibly then often confused and apparently misinformed. Some of the earlier errors, however, are to some extent corrected subsequently although this may only further confirm the difficulty with collegiate and confidential decisions.

Of particular interest is the Court's equation of general good considerations with the scope of the authority of the host State. Rather than consider this purely in terms of an area in which only limited harmonization had been achieved, the Court looked immediately to the restrictive effect of

[88] This would anticipate the adoption of different levels of rules having regard to whether counterparties were retail, experienced or professional. This is the general principle adopted in many national systems such as in the UK. This was also suggested in *Commission v Germany* in which only professional counterparties were involved (para 29).

[89] Having stated that, however, the Court still admitted that such a requirement may be accepted if it could be shown that it constituted a condition that was indispensable for obtaining the objective pursued. *Commission v Germany* and Case C-101/94 *Commission v Italy* [1996] ECR I-2691, para 31.

national regulations and then possible justification. The original Treaty provisions were conditional upon necessary secondary measures being adopted although once the core rights of establishment and services had been held to be directly applicable all national regulations became subject to Community law to the extent that they constituted an obstacle to cross-border trade. In so far as they were then further indistinctly applicable, it became necessary to consider their possible justification.

Apart from some of the confused discussion, the most unfortunate aspect of the judgment is possibly the Court's reluctance to uphold the need for a national banking system. This would appear to be the opposite of the over-generous approach adopted in *Reisebüro Broede* and possibly *Alpine*. The need for national bank regulation is arguably more important than protecting the rights of debt collectors or restricting those of cold callers. The Court's reluctance to assist further may be partly explained due to the connected requirement of a local establishment as well as authorization condition. Rather than decide the case on the basis of possible depositor (consumer) protection considerations, the Court could have a created a new market stability related derogation. This would then have partly followed *Alpine Investments* although it would have been considerably more intellectually and theoretically sound.

If *Parodi* had to be re-considered after the adoption of the Second Banking Directive, the local authorization condition in France would have to have been immediately dismissed in light of the effect of the mutual recognition provided for (principally under Article 18(1) of the Directive). National territories are not allowed to require the separate authorization of banks from other Community territories. There is express reference to the possibility of general good conditions being imposed although not with regard to authorization as such and the other harmonized minimum conditions listed.

B. COMMISSION POLICY RESTATEMENT

The Commission attempted to confirm or, at least, re-state certain provisions governing the application of the Community freedoms in the banking area with the publication of an Interpretative Communication in 1997. This followed an earlier Draft Communication in 1995.[90] The purpose was 'to explain and

[90] Draft Commission Communication, 'Freedom to provide services and the interests of the general good in the Second Banking Directive' (OJ No C291, 4 Nov 1995, p. 7) (n 2). The intention of the draft communication was to begin consultation on the issues that arose in exercising the rights provided under the Second Banking Directive especially with regard to services and the interest of the general good. The Commission had received numerous contributions from various parties including Member States, professional associations, credit insti-

clarify the Community rules'[91] with regard to services and the general good having regard to underlying Treaty provisions and secondary measures as well as the supporting jurisprudence of the European Court of Justice.[92]

The Communication constitutes a restatement of relevant Community provisions and case law as it may apply in the banking area. In so doing, it reviews the principles developed by the Court and sets out the Commission's position on outstanding issues. The Communication does not impose any obligations on Member States and cannot prejudice the Court's interpretation. Difficulties had earlier arisen when the Commission had attempted to use the device of an interpretative communication to impose a series of new obligations on Member States. This was considered by the Court to constitute a legislative measure with the Commission being prohibited from attempting to by-pass prescribed Council and Parliamentary channels.[93] The Court added that the purpose of directives in relation to directly applicable Treaty provisions was to limit the discretionary powers of Member States depending upon the degree of specific direction provided in the Treaty.[94]

tutions, consumer organizations and lawyers. Hearings had been held with all of the parties that had taken part in the written consultation. Member States had contributed through the Banking Advisory Committee and the Working Group on the Interpretation of the Banking Directive which had been set up to identify and consider relevant issues. The Second Banking Directive had been adopted in 1989 and came into effect in 1992. Second Council Directive 89/646/EEC of 25 Dec 1989 on the coordination of laws, regulations and administrative provisions relating to the taking-up and pursuit of the business of credit institutions and amending Directive 77/780/EEC (OJ No L386, 30 Dec 1989, 1) as amended by Directive 92/30/EEC (OJ No L110, 28 Apr 1992, 52). Ch 5, sections B and C. This has since been replaced by the Banking Consolidating Directive 2000/12/EC (n 3).

91 Commission Interpretative Communication (n 2), para 6. The Communication would provide a reference document defining the legal framework within which (in its view) banking activities benefiting from mutual recognition should be pursued.

92 The Communication would not cover all of the problems identified but merely the most frequent or most likely to arise. From the Commission's discussions, these were concerned with the scope and nature of services provided and the operation of the general good.

93 *French Republic v Commission of the European Communities* [1997] ECR I-1627. The French Government had challenged a draft communication issued by the Commission on the freedom of management and investment of funds held by institutions for retirement provision. Draft Communication on an internal market for pension funds (OJ 1994, C360–7). The complaint was based on lack of competence, infringement of Art 190 of the Treaty and for lack of legal certainty. The Court annulled the communication as it contained the same general provisions as set out in the Commission's proposal for a Pension Funds Directive in 1991 (OJ 1991, C312–3). The communication accordingly attempted to impose new obligations on Member States that could only be effected through a directive that had been adopted by the Council in accordance with relevant Treaty provisions. The issuance of interpretative communications was not *ultra vires* as such but the Commission could not supplant the proper legislative role of the Council. For comment, M Andenas 'The Interplay Between the Commission and the ECJ in Giving Effect to the Right to Provide Financial Services' in Craig and Harlow (eds) *Law Making in the European Union* (1998); Andenas 'Current Developments' (1994) 43 ICLQ 731; and (1996) 45 ICLQ 230 at 234–5.

94 In *France v Commission* (n 93), the Court considered the relationship between directives

The Commission stated that the Communication was issued to promote the exercise of the free movement rights provided[95] as well as to facilitate information provision and electronic commerce.[96] The Communication considers each of the two main sets of issues dealt with in connection with the relationship between services and establishment and the nature of the general good in turn. The Communication initially examines the nature of the notification procedures created, the relationship between services and establishment and the commencement rules.[97] While the notification procedures are considered first, the most interesting issues possibly arise with regard to the relationship between services and establishment. The common element is the distinct nature of the treatment (if any) permissible where the banking institution is not to be established in another territory. With regard to the general good, the Communication considers the difficulties that had arisen in practice in connection with the operation of the notification procedure, the relevant rules and private international law implications.[98]

The Communication is important in reviewing and restating relevant Community provisions in certain core residual areas of uncertainty that had

and communications. With regard to the doctrine of direct effect, where Treaty provisions were not directly effective directives translate the basic Treaty obligations imposed into rules that can be transposed into Member State law. Where provisions are directly effective, directives may be used to limit the wide discretionary powers left to Member States depending upon the degree of specific direction provided in the Treaty. Where a directive does not fully implement a Treaty obligation, the Treaty will take precedence and the directive interpreted by the Court in a consistent manner. The directive is distinct from a communication in that it can impose obligations on Member States by limiting their discretion which a communication cannot. Communications should only be used to clarify existing rather than create new obligations. For further discussion, Andenas 'Rules of Conduct under the Principle of Subsidiarity' (1994) 14 Co Law 61; and Andenas 'The Financial Market and Commission as Legislators' (1999) 19 Co Law 98.

95 The Commission had considered that the continuing uncertainty that had arisen, in particular, regarding the interpretation of such basic concepts as freedom to provide services and the interests of the general good had deterred institutions from exercising the freedoms promoted under the Second Banking Directive and consequently limit the free movement of banking within Europe. Communication, para 4. This is referred to as 'integration damage or default' for the purposes of this text. Ch 1, section B (4) and (n 46).

96 The Commission also confirms that the Communication was issued as part of Community policy regarding the information society which was aimed at promoting the growth and movement of information society services between Member States and, in particular, electronic commerce. Communication, para 8. See also Council Resolution on new policy priorities regarding the information society, adopted on 8 Oct 1996; Commission Communication to the European Council: 'Putting services to work': CSE (1996) 6 final of 27 Nov 1996; Communication to the European Parliament, The Council of the European Union and the Economic and Social Committee, 'Regulatory Transparency in the single market for information society services'; Proposal for a European Parliament and Council Directive amending for the third time Directive 83/189/EEC laying down a procedure for the provision of information in the field of technical standards and regulations (COM(96) 392 final of 30 Aug 1996; OJ No C307, 15 Oct 1996, p. 11).

97 Interpretative Communication, paras 7–13.

98 Interpretative Communication, paras 13–22.

arisen in the banking area. This restatement is then supplemented by the Commission's expressed interpretation of certain points. Following the consultations conducted, the Communication represents a reformulated expression of the main difficulties that had arisen in practice. This then provides a useful restatement of relevant Community decisions in this area.

The Commission's Interpretative Communication is accordingly of value in confirming the application of Community law in the banking area and, in particular, in identifying certain residual areas of uncertainty and the most probable interpretation to be adopted in each case with reference to the case law of the Court. The discussion with regard to services is of particular use to the extent that it is essentially involved with clarifying the distinction between services and establishment in particular areas. Some of the discussion especially with regard to the operation of the notification procedure is more technical although still of interest in highlighting the respective rights and obligations of the parties concerned. The notification rules will probably become redundant in time especially with the continued expansion of electronic banking services. The most difficult residual areas at this stage appear to be independent intermediaries and such electronic devices as ATMs although the Commission has clearly and intelligently attempted to clarify the relevant principles to be applied in each case. It has to be expected that these will be further reviewed as market structure and practice develop although the guidance provided in the Communication should still be of assistance. The Communication also contains important clarification with regard to the combined exercise of the rights of establishment and services and for secondary branch exercise of the right to provide services in third countries.

The separate discussion of the general good is informed although possibly still unclear on some points. The clarification of the general good objectives recognized to date is of assistance and the discussion of the applicable conditions insightful. Particular difficulties, however, continue to arise with regard to the more general nature and operation of some of these conditions especially with regard to the need to include a separate general good objective test, the country of origin rule, capability and proportionality. Residual difficulties arise with regard to the scope of the pre-harmonization exclusion and validity of the country of origin rules. Problems also arise with regard to the relationship between the capability and proportionality tests.[99] It is unfortunate that the Commission did not consider these issues further especially in light of the volume of the comments received as part of the extended consultation exercise conducted.

This is nevertheless a sensitive and difficult area and the Commission has provided an important service through the publication of the

[99] Ch 6, section D (4).

Communication. It also appears to have accepted the lessons from its earlier attempt to use a communication to avoid complying with existing legislative and adoption procedures. To the extent that these can clarify and improve understanding of the underlying Treaty and judicial provisions concerned, communications are clearly a useful device.

It has to be assumed that additional and separate comment has already or since been received by the Commission on the application and operation of the banking and financial directives especially through the banking advisory committees and the original Interpretation Working Group. Opinion will also have been received on the Banking Consolidation Directive and more recent proposed and finalized measures.[100] In light of the volume of the comments (and criticisms) received, some further amending measure (*refonte*) may have been more appropriate than a non-binding statement of interpretation although this could only have been effected through the normal legislative channels. It is understood that the Commission was working on such a *refonte* in the banking area although this had to be delayed due to the consolidation work undertaken under the SLIM (Simpler Legislation for the Internal Market) programme[101] and the more recent efforts carried out on the completion of the Single Market.[102]

The original 1997 Communication accordingly remains a useful although essentially limited tool. It only provides guidance on the Commission's understanding of some relevant law and its application and operation in practice. The Communication has no direct legal effect and is limited both in terms of scope and content. For any more authoritative direction with regard to the law in this area, it is necessary to refer directly to the judgements issued by the European Court of Justice on both more general and on financial related matters. The more recent cases considered in the banking and financial area are considered next.

C. FINANCIAL POLICY REVISION

The European Court of Justice has had the opportunity to consider a number of further issues in the banking and financial areas since the late 1990s. Many of these have been more specific or technical in nature although this has still allowed the Court to provide some further clarification on the scope and content of the law of free movement in the financial area.

[100] Ch 5, section B.

[101] SLIM was an 'Inter-institutional Agreement' on an accelerated method for the production of an official codification of legislative texts concluded on 20 Dec 1994 by the European Parliament, the Council and the Commission. The first phase was completed in November 1996 (SMN no. 6, 1996). Ch 5, section C (nn 58–60).

[102] Communication of the Commission to the European Council, *Action Plan for the Single Market* CSE (97) 1 final) of 4 June 1997. Ch 5, section D (1).

It would generally appear that more references are being made to the Court although under a number of separate Treaty bases. These include free movement of services[103] and establishment[104] as well as capital[105] and competition law,[106] taxation,[107] state aids,[108] commercial policy, common foreign and security[109] and the law governing the institutions[110] and

[103] Case C-445/03 *Commission v Grand Duchy of Luxemburg* [2004] ECR I-10191; Case C-334/02 *Commission v French Republic* [2004] ECR I-02229; Case C-153/00 *Criminal Proceedings against Paul Der Weduwe* [2002] ECR I-11319; Case C-283/99 *Commission v Italy* of 15 February 2001; Case C-51/96 and C-191/97 *Christelle Deliege v Ligue Francophone de judo et Disciplines Associées ASBL, Union Européenne de judo* (C-51/96) and *Francois Pacquée* (C-191/97), [2000] ECR I-02549; and Case C-366/97 *Criminal Proceedings against Massimo Romanelli and Paolo Romanelli*, [1999] ECR I-00855.

[104] Case C-222/02 *Peter Paul, Cornelia Sonnen-Lütte and Christel Mörkens v Bundesrepublik Deutschland*, [2004] ECR I-09425; Case C-442/02 *CaixaBank France v Ministère de l'Économie, des Finances et de l'Industrie*, [2004] ECR I-08961; Case C-463/00 *Commission v Kingdom of Spain*, [2003] ECR I-04581; Case C-324/00 *Lankhorst-Hohorst GmbH v Finanzamt Steinfurt*, [2002] ECR I-11779.

[105] Case C-367/98 *Commission v Portuguese Republic*, [2002] ECR I-04731; and the Opinion in C-478/98 *Commission v Kingdom of Belgium*, [2000] ECR I-07587.

[106] Case T-56/02 *Bayerische Hypo- und Vereinsbank AG v Commission*, [2004] ECR 00000; T-158/00 *ARD v Commission*, [2003] ECR II-03825; C-340/99 *TNT Traco SpA v Poste Italiane SpA and Others*, [2001] ECR I-04109; C-147/97 and C-148/97 *Deutsche Post AG v Gesellschaft für Zahlungssysteme mbH (GZS) (C-147/97 and Citicorp Kartenservice GmbH (c-148/97)*, [2000] ECR I-00825. See also case T-213/01 R *Osterreichische Postsparkasse AG v Commission*, [2001] ECR II-03963; Case T-214/01 R *Bank für Arbeit und Wirtschaft AG v Commission*, [2001] ECR II-03993; Case T-216/01 R *Reisebank AG v Commission*, [2001] ECR II-03481; Case T-219/01 *Commerzbank AG v Commission*, [2003] ECR II-02843; and Case C-335/99 PCR *HFB Holding für Fernwarmetechnik Beteilligung Sgesellschaft mbH & Co KG and Others v Commission*, [1999] ECR 1-08705. See also Opinions Case C-309/99 *Wouters*, [2002] ECR I-01577; Cases C-115/97 and C117/97 *Brentjens' Handelsonderneming BV v Stichting Bedrijfspensionenfonds voor de Handel in Bouwmaterialien*, [1999] ECR I-06025; Case C-219/97 *Maatschappij Drijvende Bokken BV v Stichting Pensioenfonds voor de Vervoren Havenbedrijven*, {1999] ECR I-06121; and Case C-67/96 *Albany International BV v Atichting Bedrijfspensioenfonds Textielindustrie*, [1999] ECR I-05751.

[107] Case C-8/03 *Banque Bruxelles Lambert SA (BBL) v Belgian State*, [2004] ECR I-10157; Case C-187/01 and C-7/02 *Gemeente Leusden (C-187/01) and Holin Groep BV Cs (C-7/02) v Staatssecretaris van Financiën*, [2004] ECR I-05337; Case C-8/01 *Assurander-Societetet et v Skatteministeriet*, [2003] ECR I-13711; Case C-294/99 *Athinaiki Zythopoiia AE v Elleniko Dimosio*, [2001] ECR I-06797; Case C-240/99 *Forsakringsaktiebolaget Skandia* [2001] ECR-I01951; Case C-136/99 *Ministre du Budget and Ministre d L'Économie et des Finances v Société Monte Dei Paschi Di Siena* [2000] ECR I-06109.

[108] C-278/00 *Hellenic Republic v Commission*, [2004] ECR I-03997; Case C-457/00 *Kingdom of Belgium v Commission*, [2003] ECR I-06931; Case T-228/99 and T-233/99 *Westdeutsche Landesbank Girozentrale and Land Nordhein-Westfalen v Commission*, [2003] ECR II-00435; Case C-209/00 *Commission v Federal Republic of Germany*, [2002] ECR I-11695; Case C-482/99 *French Republic v Commission*, [2002] ECR I-04397; Case C-288/96 *Fedeal Republic of Germany v Commission*, [2000] ECR I-08237; Cases T-204/97 and T-270/97 *EPAC—Empresa para a Agroalimentaçäo e Cereais SA v Commission*, [2000] ECR I-02267. See also Orders T-195/01 R and T-207/01 R *Government of Gibraltar v Commission*, [2001] ECR II-03915.

[109] Case T-306/01 R *Abdirisak Aden, Abdulaziz Akli, Ahmed Yusuf and Al Barakaat International Foundation v Council of the European Union and Commission*, [2002] ECR II-02387.

[110] Case C-167/99 *European Parliament v d'aménagement et d'équipement de la region de*

customs union.[111] Some further decisions have been issued in the areas of the law relating to undertakings,[112] European citizenship,[113] environment and consumers[114] and intellectual property.[115] The general effect has been to provide additional clarification on the application of European law more generally in the banking and financial area.

In terms of interpretation of the Second Banking Directive (now the Banking Consolidation Directive)[116] the Court confirmed in *Romanelli* that other repayable funds within the definition of a credit institution will include any instruments subject to a contractual agreement to repay the funds paid.[117] The Court has also issued some interesting decisions in *Bank*

Strasbourg and Ville de Strasburg, [2003] ECR I-03269; Case T-195/00 *Travelex Global and Financial Services Ltd, formerly Thomas Cook Group Ltd and Interpayment Services Ltd v Commission*, [2003] ECR II-01677. See also Opinions C-11/00 *Commission v European Central Bank*, [2003] ECR I-07147; and case C-15/00 *Commission v European Investment Bank*, [2002] ECR I-07281.

111 Cases T-186/97, T-187/97, T-190/97, to T-192/97, T-210/97, T-211/97, T-216/97, T-217/97, T-218/97, T-279/97, T-280/97, T-293/97 and T-147/99 *Kaufring KG and Others v Commission*, [2001] ECR II-01337.

112 Case C-306/99 *Banque Internationale pour L'Afrique Occidentale SA (BIAO) v Finanzamt für Großunternehmen in Hamburg*, [2003] ECR 1-00001; and Opinion in Cases C-223/99 and C-260/99 *Agorà Srl and Excelsior Snc di Pedrotti Bruga & C v Ente Autonoma Fiera Internazionale di Milano and Ciffat Soc Coop Air*, [2001] ECR I-03605.

113 Opinion in C-224/02 *Heikki Antero Pusa v Osuuspankkien Keskinäinen Vakuutusyhtiö*, [2003] ECR I-05763.

114 Opinion in C-473/00 *Cofidis SA v jean-Louis Fredout*, [2002] ECR I-10375; and Order Case T-331/99 *Mitsubishi HiTec Paper Bielefeld GmbH v Office for Hamonisation in the Internal Market (Trade Marks and Designs) (OHIM)*, [2001] ECR II-00433.

115 Case T-87/00 *Bank für Arbeit und Wirtschaft AG v Office for Hamonisation in the Internal Market (Trade Marks and Designs) (OHIM)*, [2001] ECR II-01259; and case T-331/99 *Mitsubishi HiTec Paper Bielefeld GmbH v Office for Hamonisation in the Internal Market (Trade Marks and Designs) (OHIM)*, [2001] ECR II-00433.

116 Ch 5, sections B and C.

117 Case C-366/97 *Criminal Proceedings against Massimo Romanelli and Paolo Romanelli*, [1999] ECR I-00855. The decision concerned a reference to the Court for a preliminary ruling from the *Tribunale Civile e Penale*, Florence. Maximo Romanelli and Paulo Romanelli had been issuing trust securities and debenture warrants between 1994 and 1995 which was considered contrary to Legislative Decree No 385 of 1 Sept 1993. This prohibited undertakings other than banks from taking savings from the public (Art 11(2)) which included the acquisition of funds accompanied by an obligation of reimbursement in the form of deposits or otherwise (Art 11(2)). The taking of savings from the public was also an offence under Art 130. Dispute arose as to whether the taking of savings under Decree 385 should be interpreted in a narrow manner which would only cover financial instruments which embodied the repayment obligation rather than where the requirement of repayability was dependent on separate contractual provision. The trust securities were described as involving the sale to third parties of an instrument representing an amount receivable and the immediate re-purchase thereof at a price which incorporated the agreed interest (para 5 of the judgment). The defendants had claimed that the banking law directives only applied to protect credit capital including certificates of deposit and bonds and not risk capital such as company shares which are not invested on the basis of a guarantee of repayment but with the aim of making speculative gains. The Commission argued that a wide interpretation had to be adopted with the support of the Belgium, Austrian and Finnish Governments. The Advocate General had argued that a narrow interpretation would undermine the objective of protecting consumers. The Court referred to

für Arbeit (access to documents),[118] *Paul Der Weduwe* (validity of national restrictions on bank secrecy),[119] *Greece v Commission* (State aids),[120] *Caixa-Bank France* (interest on sight account)[121] and *Vereinsbank v Commission* (currency exchange charges).[122] An important Opinion was issued by Advocate General Jacobs in *Commission v Belgium* (on Eurobond Sales).[123]

The more important issues raised in these cases are considered below. The separate problems of deposit protection and regulatory liability are examined in the following section.

(1) Access to Documents—*Bank für Arbeit* (2001)

The Court considered the issue of interim measures and the right of access to documents in a competition case in *Bank für Arbeit und Wirtschaft AG v Commission.*[124] This involved an application for suspension of a decision[125] closing an earlier procedure relating to the transmission of a statement of objections and supplementary statement of objections relating to the conclusion of anti-competitive agreements against eight Austrian banks (including the applicant) in connection with bank fees for exchanging currencies for Euros contrary to Article 81 EC. The Commission had originally initiated proceedings against the applicant and seven other Austrian banks having become aware of a document (referred to as 'Lombard 8.5.') A copy of the document had also been sent by the *Freiheitliche Partei Osterreichs* (the FPO) as a user of bank services requesting the Commission to commence proceedings. A dispute subsequently arose with regard to the access by the FPO to the statement of objections and supplementary statement of objections produced by the Commission.

Parodi and the underlying purpose of the First and Second Banking Directives and concluded that the restriction in Art 3 against the carrying on of an unauthorized credit institution business had to be understood to extend to include financial instruments in which the requirement of repayability derived from a contractual provision (para 15). While the ruling related to the reference to other repayable funds within the restriction on unauthorized business in Article 3 of Directive 89/646, this must also be understood to be equally applicable to the words contained in the definition of credit institution within Article 1 of Directive 77/780.

118 Case T-214/01 R *Bank für Arbeit und Wirtschaft AG v Commission*, [2001] ECR II-03993. Section C (2).

119 Case C-153/00 *Criminal Proceedings against Paul der Weduwe*, [2002] ECR I-11319. See Opinion of Advocate General Philippe Leger of 23 Apr 2002. Section C (1).

120 C-278/00 *Hellenic Republic v Commission*, [2004] ECR I-03997. Section C (2).

121 Case C-442/02 *Caixa-Bank France v Ministére de l'Économie, des Finances et de l'Industrie*, [2004] ECR I-08961. Section C (5).

122 Case T-56/02 *Baverische Hypo- und Vereinsbank AG v Commission*, [2004] ECR 00000. Section C (4).

123 Case C-478/98 *Commission v Kingdom of Belgium*, [2000]ECR II-03993.

124 Case T-214/01R *Bank für Arbeit und Wirtschaft AG v Commission*, [2001] ECR II-03993.

125 COM P/D-1/36. 571 of 25 July 2001.

The President of the Court of First Instance dismissed the application for interim measures. The application was held admissible on the basis that the contested decision constituted an act open to challenge (paragraph 46) in that the earlier correspondence exchanged had constituted preparatory acts while the contested decision contained prima facie the Commission's definitive decision with regard to the transmission of non-confidential versions of the statement of objections.[126] While the applicant then claimed that implementation of the decision would cause it serious and irreparable damage, it was considered that this had not been established with a sufficient degree of probability[127] and that even if such damage could arise the balancing of interests favoured dismissal. The Community interest in placing third parties whom the Commission had recognized as having a legitimate interest took priority over the applicant's desire to delay transmission of the statement of objections.

The decision was of interest in raising the issue of an interim application for annulment against disclosure of statements of objection in a competition action against a group of national banks. The underlying cause of action related to alleged anti-competitive practices in relation to the fixing of exchange rate fees. While the issue of admissibility was quickly decided in favour of the applicant, urgency and the balancing of interest claims were rejected. This specifically included the possibility of reputational damage and liability under a related US class action.

(2) Bank Secrecy—*Paul der Weduwe* (2002)

The Court had to consider the issue of national bank secrecy in connection with the canvassing activities of a bank employee in Belgium in *Paul der Weduwe* in December 2002. Mr der Weduwe was a Netherlands national living in Luxemburg who had been employed by two Luxemburg banks (Banque UCL and Rabobank) to canvass clients in Belgium with a view to placing money in deposits or negotiable instruments with the banks. Mr der Weduwe allegedly received money from Belgian clients and collected coupons relating to negotiable securities which were taken to Luxemburg.

[126] Case T-90/96 *Peugeot v Commission* [1997] ECR II 663, paras 34 and 36.

[127] The applicant contended that implementation of the decision would result in the FPO making targeted disclosure of the complaints contained in the objections for political purposes. It was claimed that the FPO and its leading members had in the past attempted systematically to bring legal proceedings against political opponents. Targeted disclosure would encourage the public to condemn the applicant and its board of directors, causing considerable reputational harm and irreparable financial damage. A large number of US citizens were also claiming damages from several European banks, including the applicant and its subsidiary, in a class action before the District Court of the Southern District of New York for compensation for allegedly excessive fees charged in respect of foreign exchange transactions. Information contained in the statement of objections could accordingly be made available to support the US proceedings (paras 49–53).

A judicial investigation was subsequently conducted concerning forgery, use of forged documents, fiscal forgery, use of forged tax returns, money laundering and failure to declare income under the Belgium income tax law. Mr der Weduwe and Mr Marc Troch, an employee of Banque UCL, were questioned in connection with the manner in which clients were canvassed and the negotiable securities transferred to Luxemburg. Mr der Weduwe and Mr Troch refused to answer questions on the basis of professional secrecy under Luxemburg law. The Belgian court considered that the extra-territorial application of Luxemburg law on bank secrecy may constitute an unreasonable impediment to cross-border banking activities.[128] A series of questions were accordingly referred to the European Court of Justice.[129]

The Court noted that Article 458 of the Belgian Criminal Code provides that breach of professional secrecy is a criminal offence although this is disapplied in the banking sector. Breach of professional secrecy under Article 458 of the Luxemburg Criminal Code is, in contrast, specifically applied to the banking sector by Article 41 of the Luxemburg Law of 5 April 1999 (paragraph 16). The extra-territorial scope of the Luxemburg laws may then constitute an impediment to the collection of evidence in the main proceedings in Belgium (paragraph 17). This also creates unequal treatment of banks and their clients according to nationality and place of establishment (paragraph 19). The admissibility of the reference was questioned by Mr der Weduwe on the basis that inadequate factual and legal information had been provided to allow the Court to give a useful answer (paragraph 22). The Luxemburg Government also questioned the admissibility on the basis that the questions raised were based on a hypothetical interpretation of Luxemburg law (paragraph 28).[130]

The Court noted that it was settled case law that it was for the national court to determine the need for a preliminary ruling and the relevance of the questions submitted.[131] The Court may still in exceptional circumstances

[128] Para 12. It was established in Case C-384/93 *Alpine Investments* that Art 59 (49) required that Member States may not maintain national rules that impede trade in services between territories unless that rule satisfies all the conditions necessary for it to be deemed to be in the public interest. Section A (3).

[129] The first and second questions related to whether Art 49 precludes the criminal law and criminal procedural law of a second Member State from requiring employees of banks carrying on services in another territory from giving evidence or authorizes them to disclose the necessary information (paras 13 and 14). The third and fourth questions relate to whether Art 49 prevents the criminal law of the first Member State precluding such employees from breaching banking secrecy where they are heard as witnesses or defendants in proceedings brought in the second Member State (paras 13 and 15).

[130] The Luxemburg Government submitted in hearing before the Court that it considered that the Luxemburg bank secrecy law did have extra-territorial scope although the exemption from criminal liability for witnesses providing evidence in judicial proceedings also operated extra-territorially (para 30).

[131] Case C-415/93 *Bosman* [1995] ECR I-4921, para 59; Case C-379/98 *Preussen Elektra* [2001] ECR I-2099, para 38; and Case C-390/99 *Canal Satélite Digital* [2002] ECR I-607, para 18.

examine the conditions under which the case was referred to determine its jurisdiction.[132] The Court may then decline to rule where, for example, the problem is hypothetical or the Court has insufficient factual or legal material (paragraph 33). With regard to the third and fourth questions, Advocate General Philippe Leger had argued that the interpretation selected by the national court was hypothetical with the issue not having been confirmed under Luxemburg law.[133] As this was not the only possible explanation and as insufficient information had been provided with regard to the interpretation selected, the Court ruled that the questions were inadmissible (paragraph 39). The Court also ruled that the first and second questions were inadmissible on the basis that no specific reasoning had been provided as to why the court asks whether Article 49 must be interpreted as precluding the application of the Belgian Criminal Code and Code of Criminal Procedure (paragraph 40).

The decision was of interest in questioning whether national bank secrecy laws (and their supporting derogations) could operate as an impediment to the cross-border provision of services (and potentially establishment). It is clear from *Alpine Investments* that national rules may impede trade and services unless justified in the public interest which could potentially cover bank secrecy requirements. Rather than comment on the underlying substance of the issue raised, the Advocate General and the Court chose to dismiss the application on the basis of the selective interpretation adopted by the Belgian court as to the scope and effect of Luxemburg law in this area. It remains to be seen whether a further reference may be made to the Court in the event that an equivalent issue arises under either Luxemburg law or the law of another Member State.

(3) STATE AIDS—*GREECE v COMMISSION* (2004)

The Court had to rule on the validity of state aids provided by the Greek Government to certain agricultural cooperatives which included the settlement of debts and re-organization.[134] The Commission had determined that the Greek laws concerning the reorganization of cooperatives constituted a state aid that did not satisfy the requirements of the rules governing aid to cover damage caused by natural disasters or exceptional occurrences nor the rules governing restructuring aid for undertakings. Both sets of aid schemes were considered incompatible with the Common Market. The Greek authorities were accordingly required to take all measures necessary to recover the unlawful aids made available to the recipients and to report

132 *Preussen Elektra*, para 39; and *Canal Satélite Digital*, para 19.
133 Opinion of the Advocate General, para 49.
134 C-278/00 *Greece v Commission* of 29 Apr 2004.

to the Commission on the action taken within two months. The Greek Government asked the Court to declare its application for annulment admissible and to annul the contested decision in its entirety or, at least, the recovery requirement.

The Court ruled that the application should be dismissed. The Commission was not at fault in not examining each individual aid granted under the relevant Greek laws. The Commission had rightly classified the laws as a non-notified new aid scheme. The schemes were not affected by a Council decision validating certain previous aid measures. There had accordingly been no breach of Article 88 EC nor the rule in *Lorenz.*[135] The Court also ruled that there had been no infringement of Article 87(1), 87(2)(b), 87(3)(a) nor 87(3)(c). The sixth plea of alleged infringement of the principles of proportionality and protection of legitimate expectations were also rejected with the seventh plea of inability to recover the aid provided.

Hellenic Republic v Commission was of importance in confirming the general application of the laws concerning state aids to cooperatives. National governments must exercise care in providing aid in the forms of debt settlement or debt re-organization. In the event that the Commission considers that any relevant concessions have not been complied with, the aids will be ruled unlawful and have to be recovered from the relevant recipients. The case may clearly be of wider relevance with regard to operation and the restructuring of financial cooperatives or mutual funds and other financial institutions more generally.

(4) INTEREST ON SIGHT ACCOUNTS—*CAIXA-BANK FRANCE* (2004)

The Court considered the validity of national rules that prohibited credit institutions which were subsidiaries from companies from another territory from paying interest on sight accounts in Euros in 2004. The case concerned a reference for a preliminary ruling in an action by *Caixa-Bank France v Ministère de l'Economie, des Finances et de l'Industrie.*[136] Under French law, credit institutions were prohibited from paying remuneration on sight accounts including Euro accounts opened by residents in France whatever their nationality.[137] The Caixa-Bank France nevertheless

[135] Case 120/73 *Lorenz* [1973] ECR 1471 which established that a preliminary examination had to be conducted within two months of notification.

[136] Case C-442/02 of 5 Oct 2004.

[137] Art L.312–3 of the *Code Monétaire et Financier* (Monetary and Financial Code) prohibits payment of remuneration on sight accounts or accounts for less than five years as fixed by regulation of the *Comité de la Reglementation Bancaire et Financière* (Committee for Banking and Financial Regulation). Regulation No 83–13 of the Committee prohibited the payment of any remuneration on sight accounts which was approved by decree of the *Ministre de l'Economie et des Finances* (Minister for Economic and Financial Affairs) of 14 May 1986 (JORF, 15 May 1986, 6330).

marketed a sight account remunerated at the rate of 2 per cent per annum on balances of, at least, 1,500 Euros from 18 February 2002. Caixa-Bank France was a subsidiary of Caixa Holding in Spain. Caixa-Bank was prohibited from concluding new contracts with French residents relating to such accounts by decision of the *Comité Bancaire et Financière* of 16 April 2002. Caixa-Bank appealed against the decision to the *Conseil d'Etat* which referred a preliminary ruling to the European Court of Justice on whether the restriction on remuneration on sight accounts constituted an obstacle to freedom of establishment and any available possible public interest justifications that may be used to support this.

The Court noted that the Banking Consolidation Directive 2000/12 EC was not applicable as it did not refer to restrictions on the establishment of subsidiary companies in other Member States (paragraph 7). The questions referred essentially then related to whether Article 43 EC precluded national legislation which prohibited subsidiary credit institutions from another Member State from paying such remuneration to local residents (paragraph 8). The Court considered that the prohibition could constitute a serious obstacle to the pursuit of the activities of a subsidiary bank from another Member State within Article 43.[138] The Court also examined whether the restriction could be justified on the basis that it served overriding requirements relating to the public interest, was suitable to secure the attainment of the objectives pursued and did not go beyond what was necessary to attain those objectives.[139] The French Government's arguments that the restriction supported consumer protection and the encouragement of medium- and long-term saving were rejected.[140] The restriction was accordingly considered contrary to Article 43 and non-justifiable in the circumstances.[141]

138 Art 43 includes the right to take up and pursue all types of self-employed activity in the territory of another Member State, to set up and manage undertakings and to set up agencies, branches or subsidiaries. Case C-255/97 *Pfeiffer* [1999] ECR I-2835, para 18. This applied to natural and legal persons under Art 48. All measures which prohibit, impede or render less attractive the exercise of the freedom of establishment must be eliminated. Case C-55/94 *Gebhard* [1995] ECR I-4165, para 37; Case C-108/96 *Macquen and others* [2001] ECR I-837, para 26; and Case C-79/01 *Payroll and others* [2002] ECR I-8923, para 26.

139 Case C-424–97 *Haim* [2000] ECR I-5123, para 57; *MacQuen*, para 26; and Case C-439/99 *Commission v Italy* [2002] ECR I-305, para 23.

140 The French Government's consumer protection and savings arguments were both rejected as going beyond what was necessary to attain their aims. Consumers could, for example, be given the choice between an unremunerated sight account with certain banking services remaining free of charge and a remunerated sight account with charges being imposed for such additional services as cheque issuance (para 22). Prohibiting remuneration on sight accounts was justifiable on the basis of encouraging medium and long term saving although it again went beyond what was necessary to obtain that objective (para 23).

141 The Advocate General and Court had come to the same conclusions. Opinion of the Advocate General Tizzano of 25 Mar 2004.

The decision confirmed again the potential wide scope of application of Article 43 and the Court's concern to ensure that no restrictions impeded the freedom of establishment. This applied specifically to subsidiaries rather than branches otherwise covered by the main banking directives. Presumably the same result would have arisen if Caixa-Bank had been a Spanish subsidiary operating in any other Member State. The Court was clearly concerned to promote market access and competition through rate benefits (paragraph 14). This was particularly necessary against more traditionally established groups with extensive branch networks in France (paragraph 13). The reference to 'raising capital' from the public appears to be somewhat confused in pure banking terms (paragraphs 13 and 15) although the general policy of assisting foreign subsidiaries compete with locally established banks is commendable. The willingness of the Court to consider such more detailed operational issues as charges for bank services is also to be supported. It has to be expected that further decisions may follow in this area.

(5) PRICE FIXING—*VEREINSBANK v COMMISSION* (2004)

Another application for annulment of a Commission decision relating to Article 81 proceedings against German banks in connection with charges for exchanging Euro zone currencies was raised in *Bayerische Hypo-und Vereinsbank AG v Commission* in October 2004.[142] The Commission had commenced an investigation in 1999 against 150 banks in Belgium, Germany, Ireland, the Netherlands, Austria, Portugal and Finland in connection with the fixing of their prices of currency exchange services during the transitional period to the introduction of the Euro. The Commission subsequently issued a decision stating that it considered that a number of identified German banks had entered into an agreement in Frankfurt-an-main on 15 October 1997 with a view to fixing the charges for the exchange of in-currency banknotes (percentage commission) and a target price level of approximately 3 per cent (to achieve 90 per cent exchange margin income recovery) for a four year period beginning on 1 January 1999. A range of fines were imposed from 28 million Euro to 2.8 million. The banks concerned included the applicant which subsequently applied for annulment of the contested decision or annulment of the fine imposed or a reduction in the amount fixed.

The application raised a number of issues of law relating to breaches of the rights of defence during administrative procedures, infringement of Article 81 due to errors of law and fact, participation, imputability of the

[142] Case T-56/02 *Bayerische Hypo- und Vereinsbank AG v Commission*, [2004] ECR 00000. See also section C (1).

infringement, reasons for the contested decision, misuse of powers and determination of the amount of the fines. In examining the facts and arguments presented, the Court considered that the Commission had failed to establish to the requisite legal standard that there was an agreement on the manner of charging for currency exchange services (paragraph 77). The Court concluded that on the evidence provided, the Commission had not adduced to the relevant standard proof of the existence of the agreement relating both to the fixing of the prices for currency exchange services and the manner in which those prices were charged (paragraph 119). The contested decision was accordingly annulled with costs (paragraphs 120 and 121).

D. DEPOSIT PROTECTION AND REGULATORY LIABILITY

The European Court of Justice has been able to issue a number of decisions that raise specific issues in the banking and financial area. Within this, however, only a more limited number of cases have raised important policy considerations. This necessarily reflects the selective or accidental nature of the litigious process and the inability of the Court to make any more substantial policy contribution in the absence of national reference or relevant Treaty dispute.

The early cases that arose were principally concerned with confirming the direct applicability of Articles 52 (43) and 59 (49) as well as the natural tendency of the Court to construe the scope of relevant restriction widely to allow it then to determine the content of the supporting derogations to be applied in each case. The need for local permanent establishment and separate authorization conditions in the insurance area was subject to an imperative reason and necessity test in *German Insurance*. The sale of lottery tickets was brought within Article 49 (ex 59) in *Schindler* although justified on the basis of social policy and the prevention of fraud. Unsolicited calls on a cross-border basis were caught in *Alpine Investments* with the Court then having to rely on an overseas market reputation test to justify the restrictions imposed (in advance of the Distance Selling Directive). The provision of professional legal services was then confused with enforcement procedures in *Reisebüro Broede* with an increasingly unsatisfactory re-use of the *Gebhard* tests. The pre-single market effects of local licensing requirements under the First Banking Directive were also considered in *Parodi*.

These decisions are of value in confirming the wide scope of application of the core underlying restrictions on freedom of services and establishment as well as the general good conditions. The Court's analysis is, however, more suspect in such decisions as *Reisebüro Broede* with a less than sound understanding of the operation of banking and financial markets being displayed on occasion both in the reasoning of the Court and the Advocates General. The continued extension of the scope of judicial derogation is also to be expected although a clear and consistent application of the underlying tests would have been of value. The inclusion of overseas market reputation in *Alpine Investments* was clearly surprising although arguably necessary from a policy perspective. The danger that this creates is nevertheless that legal certainty and predictability are undermined to the extent that the proper scope of Treaty restriction and judicial derogation remain correspondingly unclear and unpredictable. Legal certainty may often then be sacrificed in favour of immediate perceived policy result at times.

The Court was able to confirm a number of more specific technical or procedural points in its more recent decisions. These include interim measures (*Bank für Arbeit*), the validity of national bank secrecy restrictions (*Paul der Weduwe*), State Aids (*Greece v Commission*), interest payments on sight accounts (*Caixa-Bank France*) and Euro currency exchange charges (*Vereinsbank*).[143] The effect has been to clarify the operation and application of a number of procedural areas of European law which raise banking and financial market related issues. The contribution in terms of more general policy construction has nevertheless been limited.

One area in which the Court has been able to make an arguably more substantial impact has been in connection with national deposit protection schemes and corresponding agency and regulatory liability issues. Three specific sets of issues have been raised in connection with the scope and validity of Community deposit protection rules, the extent to which individual rights have been conferred on depositors under the Community deposit protection and more general banking and financial directives and whether national regulatory liability rules are subject to Community law restrictions. Two further related issues also arise with regard to the underlying nature and purpose of the European banking and financial regulatory regime and the availability of residual compensatory remedies in favour of individual depositors under Member State laws. Fundamental policy problems have accordingly been raised the successful resolution or reconciliation of which are essential to the construction of any effective financial regulatory regime within Europe.

The European Court of Justice was able to rule on the validity of European wide deposit protection rules in its judgement in *Germany v European Parliament and Council* in 1997[144] in which it decided that a 'no export' clause was valid until the end of the transitional period assigned under Directive 94/19. The Court was then able to consider the proper

[143] Section C.
[144] Case C-233/94 of 13 May 1997. Section D (1).

purpose and scope of protection provided by both Directive 94/19 in the area of deposit guarantee schemes as well as the banking directives more generally in *Peter Paul* in 2004.[145] The Court concluded that no individual rights were available and consequently that no supporting compensatory remedies were available under European law.

National courts have also been able to consider the extent to which relevant heads of liability exist under domestic law in some important recent cases.[146] The scope of the banking directives and the extent to which individual rights of protection or recovery were conferred was considered by the House of Lords in the UK in one of the preliminary rulings in the *Three Rivers v Bank of England* case in 2000.[147] While the decision of the House of Lords in *Three Rivers* was supported by the European Court of Justice in *Peter Paul* to the extent that no individual depositor rights of action arose, the availability of a separate right of action under misfeasance in public office was confirmed despite the statutory immunity conferred on bank regulators (under s 1 of the Banking Act 1987 and now Schedule 1, paragraph 19 (1) of the Financial Services and Markets Act). The Court confirmed in *Peter Paul* that European law did not undermine the immunity from damages conferred on national supervisory authorities under domestic law. This did not, however, preclude the application of alternative means of recovery such as under tort or administrative law more generally. The Court added that the coordination of national rules on liability of national authorities in respect of depositors in the event of defective supervision did not fall within the essential objectives of the European banking directives.[148] The issue of compensatory immunity was accordingly supported although the issue of alternative compensatory redress left open.

The purpose of this section is to consider the basis on which the no-export clause was ruled to be valid under Directive 94/19 in *Germany v European Parliament and Council*. The examination by the House of Lords in the UK into the nature of compensatory relief under European law and the extent to which individual rights of action were conferred under the banking directives in *Three Rivers* is also considered. The House of Lords'

145 Case C-222/02 of 12 Oct 2004. Section D (3).

146 Section D (2).

147 *Three Rivers District Council and others v Bank of England*, HL (Lord Steyn, Lord Hope of Craighead, Lord Hutton, Lord Hobhouse of Woodborough and Lord Millett) of 18 May 2000 (nn 7 and 170). The decision considered the extent to which individual depositors had a right of action against the Bank of England following the collapse of the Bank of Credit and Commerce International (BCCI) in July 1995. The issue was raised as a possible alternative right to recovery under Community law rather than under the tort of misfeasance in public office under English law. The House of Lords examined the relevant European law on recovery in damages under direct effect and state liability and the detailed provisions contained in the European banking directives. Their Lordships concluded that no individual rights of recovery arose. Section D(2).

148 Paras 42 and 43 of the judgment.

rulings on the possible liability of regulatory agencies to aggrieved depositors under English law are also referred to. The content and importance of the European Court's judgement in *Peter Paul* is reviewed separately. Some general observations are made with regard to the extent of possible additional liability on the part of regulatory agencies under UK, French and German law.

(1) EU Deposit Protection—*Germany v European Parliament and Council* (1997)

The main issues raised by *Germany v Parliament* were concerned with the proper Treaty and policy basis for the establishment of a common deposit protection regime across Europe and the appropriate degree of harmonization to be achieved.[149] The case was accordingly concerned both with policy basis and policy content. The decision seven years later in *Peter Paul* raised the further issues of the extent to which individual rights were conferred on depositors under the common deposit guarantee scheme and the banking and financial directives more generally as well as whether any rights to compensation arose under European law for defective supervision and regulation or whether this was simply left to the vagaries of Member State laws to determine.

The European Commission had issued a recommendation on deposit protection in 1986. This required all Member States to adopt some form of deposit insurance although without any obligations being imposed with regard to the minimum or maximum coverage available.[150] The Recommendation was generally based on a host country control or territorial approach to ensure competitive equality between banks operating in a single state.

A proposal was then issued for the adoption of a Council Directive on deposit guarantee schemes on 14 April 1992. This was accepted by the Parliament subject to certain amendments (including an increase in the level of cover provided) on 10 March 1993. A revised proposal was submitted to the Council on 7 June 1993 with a common position being arrived at on 25 October 1993. A number of further amendments were proposed by the Parliament under the co-decision procedure under Article 189b on 9 March

[149] (n 144). See generally Mads Andenas 'Directive on Deposit Guarantee Schemes Challenged' (1995) 16 Co Lawyer 18; Andenas 'Deposit Guarantee Schemes and Home Country Control' in Ross Cranston (ed) *The Single Market and the Law of Banking* (LLP 1995) 105; Landsmeer and Van Empel 'The Directive on Deposit Guarantee Schemes and the Directive on Investor Compensation in View of Case C-233/94' [1998] EFSL 143; and Roth 'Case C-233/94, Federal Republic of Germany v European Parliament and Council of the European Union' (1998) 35 CMLR 495.

[150] Commission Recommendation 87/63/EEC.

1994. After further disagreement and reference to a Conciliation Committee, a joint text for Directive 94/19 was agreed on 30 May 1994.

Directive 94/19/EC is generally based on home country control, mandatory minimum cover[151] (initially 15 ECU subsequently raised to 20,000 Euros), an optional host country 'top-up' clause[152] and a home 'no export' clause[153] with all additional matters (including funding and pricing) being left to local Member State discretion.

The purpose was accordingly to establish a mandatory minimum cover protection scheme across Europe (of 20,000 Euros) with a voluntary host top-up (to allow overseas banks to supplement their deposit cover) but with a mandatory no export clause (to avoid banks from territories that offer higher protection gaining any competitive advantage over host institutions). The general allocation policy had shifted from host to home country control although qualified through the operation of the no export obligation imposed. All other operational aspects are left to Member State determination. These included private or public sector management as well as pricing and funding.[154]

151 Each Member State was to ensure that within its territory one or more deposit guarantee schemes are introduced and officially recognized with no credit institution authorized in that Member State being permitted to take deposits unless it is a member of such a scheme (Art 3(1)). Credit institutions may be exempt where they belong to a scheme that protects the credit institution itself and, in particular, ensures its liquidity and solvency and guarantees the protection of depositors, at least, equivalent to that provided by a deposit guarantee scheme. Any relevant exemptions are to be notified to the Commission. Credit institutions may continue to take deposits where they are excluded from a deposit guarantee scheme under national law and subject to the express consent of the local competent authorities, provided that it has made alternative guarantee arrangements that ensure that depositors enjoy a level and scope of protection, at least, equivalent to that offered by the officially recognized scheme (Art 3(4)).

Deposit guarantee schemes are to stipulate that the aggregate deposits of each depositor must be covered up to 20,000 Euros in the event of deposits being unavailable (Art 7(1)) although this does not preclude the retention or adoption of provisions that offer a higher or more comprehensive cover for deposits (Art 7(3)).

Credit institutions are required to inform depositors about the relevant deposit guarantee scheme available (Art 9) with payments having to be made under relevant schemes within three months of deposits becoming unavailable (Art 10).

152 Where the level or scope (including percentage) of cover offered by the host Member State guarantee schemes exceeds that of the Member State in which a credit institution is authorized, the host territory is to ensure that there is an officially recognized deposit guarantee scheme within its territory which a branch may join voluntarily to supplement the guarantee that its depositors already enjoy by virtue of membership of the home Member State scheme (Art 4(2)).

153 Deposit guarantee schemes introduced and officially recognized in a Member State under Art 3(1) shall cover the depositors at branches set up by credit institutions in other Member States. Neither the level nor scope (including percentage) of cover are nevertheless to exceed the maximum level or scope offered by the corresponding guarantee within the territory of the host Member State until 31 December 1999 with the Commission preparing a report for the possible continuation of this restriction after that date (Art 4(1)).

154 A Landsmeer and M Van Empel 'The Directive on deposit-guarantee schemes and the Directive on investor compensation schemes in view of Case C-233/94' (n 149). See also Richard Dale, 'Deposit Insurance: Policy Clash over EC and US Reforms' 13–16 May 1993 (unpublished paper presented at London School of Economics).

The objective of Directive 94/19 was accordingly to create a parallel common deposit protection requirement across Europe in addition to the underlying single passport rights established under the banking directives. As with the other measures adopted, this would be on the basis of mutual recognition, minimum harmonization and home country control. The difficulty that arose, however, was that a number of different and almost incompatible schemes existed across the Member States in this area. A compromise had accordingly to be agreed both in setting the relevant level of cover (including permitting local top-up where the host cover was higher than in the country of origin) and in restricting the export of higher cover on a home country control basis.

The significance of the regulatory compromise agreed was that it clearly illustrated the difficulties of using mutual recognition, minimum harmonization and home country control in such a complex area. It is often in practice only possible to agree a minimum level of protection and then only in a select number of core supervisory and regulatory areas. While local requirements may be raised to that minimum, this will only apply where common European standards are imposed. In agreed minimum and non-agreed minimum areas, local territories may still be able to provide additional levels of protection for local depositors although they will not be able to export this into other countries. Depositor protection will then be undermined in harmonized areas where the level of protection imposed is lower in other territories and in non-harmonized areas where no common standards are agreed at all. Common levels of depositor protection are then sacrificed in favour of the creation of a single licence (mutual recognition). The severity of this in the deposit protection area is further aggravated by the absence of any individual rights and common provisions with regard to compensation in the event of defective supervision or regulation.

The difficulties that arise where a lower forced level of depositor protection is imposed on Member States was most apparent in Germany which had the highest level of compensation across Europe. Full deposit cover was effectively available under the Federal Association of German Banks' deposit guarantee fund which had been set up in 1976. Parallel schemes also applied to cooperative and savings and other banks. Although voluntary, almost all banks in Germany were subject to a guarantee scheme (with only five institutions not being members in October 1993). Where a credit institution did not belong to an authorized deposit guarantee body, it was required to inform customers before an account was opened. National authorities may prohibit a credit institution from receiving payments if it does not belong to a guarantee scheme and is threatened with insolvency. The deposit guarantee fund can obtain all necessary information from the supervisory authorities and the central bank to allow it to confirm the information provided. It also has access to company documents and rights of inspection and verification.[155]

The German Government decided to challenge the legality of Directive 94/19 insofar as it undermined the operation of the German deposit guarantee schemes and the higher level of protection made available to depositors and consumers. The Directive was challenged on the basis that Article 57(2) had provided an inadequate legal basis and that the reasons on which it was adopted were not stated as required under Article 190 of the Treaty. In the event that this was unsuccessful, Germany applied for annulment of the three specific provisions imposing compulsory participation (Article 3(1)), the host top-up obligation (Article 4(2)) and the no export clause (Article 4(1)). This application was rejected by the Court on 13 May 1997 following the recommendation of Advocate General Leger on 10 December 1996.

With regard to the application for annulment of the Directive, the Court ruled that the Directive had been adopted on the correct legal basis and that the Parliament and Council had not failed to state reasons as required under Article 190. The Parliament and the Council were entitled to adopt the Directive solely on the basis of Article 57(2) which authorizes the Community to eliminate obstacles to the taking-up and pursuit of activities of self-employed persons through the coordination of the provisions laid down by law, regulation or administrative action taking into account the public interest of the Member States and adopting a level of protection that seems acceptable to the Community (paragraph 8).[156] Advocate General

[155] Opinion of Advocate General Leger on Case C-233/94 of 10 Dec 1996, paras 17–24.

[156] The German Government had argued that the purpose of the Directive was primarily to increase protection for depositors in addition to regulating banking operations (para 9). The Directive should accordingly have been adopted under Art 235 of the Treaty which requires unanimity (para 11). The Court noted that the choice of legal basis for a measure must be based on objective factors that are amenable to judicial review which factors, in particular, include the aim and content of the measure. Case C-268/94 *Portugal v Council* [1996] ECR I-6177, para 22. Art 3(c) of the Treaty provides that the Community's activities are to include the creation of an internal market characterized by the abolition of obstacles to the free movement of goods, persons, services and capital as between the Member States. Art 7a then provides that the Community is to adopt measures with the aim of establishing an internal market in accordance, in particular, with Art 57(2) of the Treaty. Member States may nevertheless impose national measures pursuing a legitimate aim that is compatible with the Treaty and is justified on overriding public interest grounds which include the protection of consumers. Case 205/84 *Commission v Germany* [1986] ECR 3755. Member States may consequently adopt or maintain measures that constitute an obstacle to free movement within Art 57(2) authorising the Community to eliminate such obstacles by coordinating the provisions laid down by law, regulation or administrative action (para 17). In so doing, the Community is to have regard to the public interest aims of the various Member States and to adopt a level of protection that seems acceptable to the Community (para 17). The effect of the machinery established under the Directive is to prevent Member States from invoking depositor protection in order to impede the activities of credit institutions authorized in other Member States. It is accordingly clear that the Directive abolishes obstacles to the right of

Leger had considered that if a second legal basis was required, Article 129A(1) would have been appropriate rather than Article 235.[157] With regard to the alleged failure to give reasons, while the Parliament and Council had not expressly referred to the principle of subsidiarity in Directive 94/19 they had provided reasons under Article 190 insofar as they had explained that they considered that their action was in conformity with that principle by stating that the objective to be sought could best be achieved at Community and not at the Member States' level (paragraph 10). An express reference to the principle of subsidiarity was not required (paragraph 28). The plea of infringement of the obligation to state reasons was accordingly unfounded in fact and was rejected (paragraph 29).[158]

establishment and the freedom to provide services (para 19). The Parliament and Council consequently correctly adopted the Directive on the basis of Art 57(2) and were not required to use any other legal basis (para 20).

[157] Advocate General Leger had noted that Art 129a(1)(b) had allowed the adoption of binding provisions that would have provided a lawful second legal basis for the contested Directive (para 64 of the Advocate General's Opinion). Since the Art 189b procedure used to adopt the Directive is the same as under Art 129a, the omission of any reference to the latter amounts to a purely formal defect that cannot render the contested measure null and void. While consultation with the Economic and Social Committee is obligatory under Art 129a, there was no dispute that such consultation took place (para 65). Art 235 is only an enabling provision of last resort and applies in the absence of any other legal basis (para 66). The Advocate General had earlier noted that the Directive had the dual objectives of harmonization of freedom of establishment and services in the banking sector and stability of the banking system and protection of savers (para 35). The Advocate General reviewed the provisions of the Directive and concluded that harmonization should be considered paramount rather than secondary (para 39).

[158] The German Government had claimed that the Parliament and Council had failed to explain how the Directive was compatible with the principle of subsidiarity enshrined in Art 3b, para 2 of the Treaty. The German Government claimed that as the principle limited the powers of the Community and as the Court had power to examine whether the Community legislature had exceeded its powers, the principle must be subject to review by the Court (para 22). The claim was accordingly not that the principle of subsidiarity had been breached, but only that the grounds to substantiate the compatibility had not been specified (para 24). Art 190 required that a statement of reasons was provided to allow the Court to exercise its power of review and to allow national governments to determine the conditions under which the Community institutions had applied the Treaty. Case C-41/93 *France v Commission* [1994] ECRI-1829, para 34. The Court then referred to the second, third, and fifth recitals of the Directive which highlight the cross-border effects of the closure of an individual credit institution (para 26). The failure of the earlier Recommendation to achieve the desired results was also noted (para 27). The Court concluded that it was apparent on any view that the Parliament and Council had explained why they considered that their action was in conformity with the principle of subsidiarity and had accordingly complied with the obligation to state reasons (para 28).

The Advocate General had noted that the Community was acting not under subsidiary powers but in clear accordance with its exclusive powers with the effect that the Community authorities were not required to demonstrate that the conditions laid down in the second paragraph of Art 3b were satisfied (para 86). The principle of subsidiarity was set out in the Treaty on European Union as a basic principle of Community Law in accordance with the positions adopted at the Edinburgh European Council (Bulletin of the European Communities, No12, 1992, Annex 1 to Part A, para I.15, p14). In the inter-institutional Declaration on Democracy,

The Court then considered the arguments in the alternative for annulment of the three specific provisions concerning the export prohibition, host top-up and mandatory participation. The Court ruled that the no export clause (Article 4(1)) was lawful in that adequate reasons had been given,[159] it did not infringe Article 57(2),[160] it did not fail to achieve a sufficiently high level of consumer protection[161] and it did not breach the

Transparency and Subsidiarity, the Community authorities had concluded that each institution must show that this principle had been observed (para 88). It does not then seem excessive to expect the Community institutions in future systematically to state reasons for their decisions in view of the principle of subsidiarity (para 89). All measures adopted by the Community should, therefore, indicate either implicitly or explicitly but in any event clearly on what basis the authority concerned is acting—even if only to state, where this is the case, that the principle of subsidiarity does not come into play (para 90).

[159] The German Government had claimed that the 14th recital had failed to provide an adequate statement of reasons and, in particular, as to why the Council and Parliament had taken the view that it was necessary that the level and scope of the guarantee should not become an instrument of competition (para 35). The Court considered that adequate reasons had been provided (paras 37 and 38). Market disturbances could be caused by branches of credit institutions offering levels of cover higher than those offered by institutions authorized in the host country. The level and scope of cover should not become an instrument of competition. It was accordingly decided that the level and scope of cover should not exceed the maximum provided by the host territory, at least, during an initial period (para 36).

[160] The German Government had argued that requiring branches to reduce the amount of their guarantee made it more difficult and even impossible for them to pursue their activities in the host territory and was accordingly contrary to Art 57(2) which was concerned to facilitate the taking-up and pursuit of activities of self-employed persons (para 39). It was also noted that the Italian, Danish and French schemes all provided a higher level of protection than the minimum included within the Directive (para 40). The Court noted that the purpose of Art 57(2) was to allow the Parliament and Council to issue directives to abolish obstacles to the right of establishment and provision of services (para 41). Where harmonization takes place, traders in one Member State may inevitably lose the advantage of national legislation which was particularly favourable to them. The export prohibition cannot be considered contrary to Art 57(2) solely on the basis that some disadvantage was created for branches of credit institutions authorized in one particular Member State (para 42). While the export prohibition was an exception to the minimum harmonization and mutual recognition that the Directive generally sought to achieve, the Parliament and Council were empowered to achieve the necessary harmonization progressively in view of the complexity of the matter and the differences between the legislation in the Member States (para 43). Case C-193/94 *Skanavi and Chryssanthakopoulos* [1996] ECRI-929, para 27. The imposition of a minimum €20,000 obligation was considered much less onerous than having to comply with the different schemes in every Member State. Art 41 accordingly facilitated the taking-up and pursuit of banking business in other Member States even in regard to branches of credit institutions authorized in Germany (para 44).

[161] The German Government argued that the export prohibition was to the disadvantage of savers in low protection countries as well as savers in high protection territories who wished to transfer funds to another State with lower deposit protection (para 47). The restriction was accordingly contrary to the consumer protection objectives of the Treaty (paras 46 and 47). The Court dismissed this on the basis that consumer protection was not the sole objective of the Community and that the Community legislature was not required to adopt the highest level of protection that could be found in any particular Member State. The reduction in the level of protection that may arise in certain cases under Art 4(1) of the Directive did not call into question the general result that the Directive sought to achieve, which was a considerable improvement in the protection of depositors within the Community (para 48).

principle of proportionality.[162] The Court ruled that the host top-up (Article 4(2)) was not contrary to the principle of home country control[163] and to the principle of proportionality.[164] The Court also rejected the claim

[162] The German Government argued that the export prohibition was contrary to Art 52 in that it restricted the right of establishment with branches being deprived of an element of competition as against national banks of the host Member State to such an extent that financial institutions may be forced to refrain from establishing a network of branches in another Member State (para 51). The export prohibition was also not considered necessary to achieve the objective of the Directive which was to prevent the market disturbances that arise if customers withdraw their deposits from their national credit institutions to transfer them to the branches of approved credit institutions in other Member States (para 52). An effective protective provision could have been inserted for the benefit of credit institutions in Member States where the protection of depositors is less extensive authorising intervention only where a disturbance in a Member State is imminent (paras 52 and 53). The Court has held that it must be ascertained whether the means which a measure employs are suitable for the purpose of achieving its desired objectives and whether they do not go beyond what is necessary to achieve them in considering whether a provision complies with the principle of proportionality (para 54). Case C-84/94 *United Kingdom v Council* [1996] ECR I-5755, para 57. The Community legislator was seeking to regulate an economically complex situation with many different deposit protection schemes in place (para 55) with the Court not being able to substitute its own assessment for that of the legislature (para 56). The Court could only find fault with the legislative choice made if it appeared manifestly incorrect or if the resultant disadvantages for certain economic operators were wholly disproportionate to the advantages otherwise offered (para 56). Under the 14th recital, the Parliament and Council had stated that they had chosen to avoid from the beginning any market disturbance resulting from the offer by branches of some credit institutions of higher cover than that offered by institutions authorized by the host Member State (para 57). Since the possibility of such a disturbance could not be wholly ruled out, it followed that the legislature had shown to the requisite legal standard that it was pursuing a legitimate objective and that the restriction imposed under the export prohibition was not manifestly disproportionate (para 57).

[163] The German Government argued that Art 4(2) infringed the principle of supervision by the home Member State. This principle had definitively been laid down under the Second Banking Directive which came into effect on 1 Jan 1993 and had earlier been designated in the Commission's 'White Book' (White Paper) in 1985 as an essential means of harmonization and coordination of national provisions in the field of financial services. The White Paper had been expressly approved by the European Council in 1985 (para 61). The effect of the use of the supplementary guarantee under Art 4(2) infringed the principle of home country supervision (para 62). The supervision of banks, the power of audit and the guarantee of deposits become shared competences although the host deposit scheme is prevented by the Second Banking Directive from adequately reviewing the liquid assets and solvency of the branch in bearing the risk of the branch's insolvency (para 62). The German Government added that according to the case law of the Court, the Community legislature may not, when exercising its powers, depart from its previous practice without stating reasons (para 63). The Court held that it had not been established that the Community legislature had laid down the principle of home State supervision in the sphere of banking law with the intention of systematically subordinating all other rules in that sphere to that principle. As it was not a principle laid down by the Treaty, the legislature could depart from it provided that it did not infringe the legitimate expectations of the persons concerned with no expectations having yet been created as it had not acted with regard to deposit guarantees previously (para 64).

[164] The German Government argued that Art 4(2) was contrary to the principle of proportionality as the measure was not indispensable to the attainment of the objective pursued (para 66). The host scheme should assume responsibility for the difference between the lower cover provided in the home territory and the higher cover granted in the host state and even, in certain cases, for the entire guarantee (para 67). The host scheme therefore faced considerable

that Article 3(1) was contrary to Article 3b, third paragraph of the Treaty[165] and to the general principle of proportionality. The Advocate General had concluded that the action instituted by the Federal Republic of Germany was without foundation.[166] On the contrary, it appeared that the Directive pursued the harmonization of banking laws by seeking a high degree of alignment between the laws of the Member States while allowing a respite for those States that do not yet have a deposit guarantee scheme or whose guarantee scheme does not yet offer an adequate level of protection all in compliance with Community rules.

The decision in *Germany v Parliament and Council* accordingly established that Article 57 was a sufficient basis for harmonization in the banking and financial area and that none of its provisions could be annulled on the basis of lack of reasons, consumer protection and proportionality or the principle of home country control. Despite this confirmation of legal validity, the Directive nevertheless remains an awkward compromise of underlying conflicting policy objectives in the deposit protection area. Schemes that provide almost full cover (such as in Germany) with the objective of protecting systemic stability co-exist with more limited consumer protection models (such as in the UK) where only partial cover is provided. This is confirmed with the optional 10 per cent co-insurance provision to be applied at State discretion. The Community has then avoided rather than

risks as it was required to compensate depositors even though it was no longer in the position adequately to supervise the liquid assets and solvency of the branch and therefore to foresee or prevent the possible insolvency of a branch of a foreign institution (para 68). The provision of a supplementary guarantee through the home scheme would have been a less radical solution (para 69) with the risk of solvency and therefore the obligation to compensate depositors remaining with the home State and not being transferred to the host territory (para 69). The Court considered that it would appear reasonable to set the harmonized minimum at €20,000 and agreed with the Advocate General (in points 136 to 146 of his Opinion) that the obligation on the host State was subject to various conditions to ease its task including contribution and information (paras 70–2). It followed from these provisions that Art 4(2) did not have the effect of causing an excessive burden for the guarantee schemes of host Member States (para 72).

165 The German Government argued that the Community had to endeavour to take account of well established national practices in adopting legislative measures and offer alternative solutions to Member States to achieve the objectives pursued (para 76). It was claimed that the German scheme was not taken into account (para 77) and, in particular, that a voluntary option was not provided (para 78). The membership obligation imposed under the Directive was also claimed to create an excessive burden on credit institutions (para 79). The Court noted that the Community could not respect all national practices, Germany was the only State with voluntary membership, it was not unreasonable to impose a mandatory requirement in some territories where there was no deposit guarantee scheme and only five out of 300 credit institutions would be affected in Germany as of Oct 1993 (paras 80–3). The legislature could not accordingly be criticized for having failed to provide an alternative approach to compulsory membership which could have ensured a harmonized minimum level of guarantee for all deposits (para 84). The application for annulment of Art 3(1) was accordingly rejected (para 85).

166 Opinion, para 162.

resolved the problem of identifying the proper policy content for deposit protection. The related omission that arises is with regard to moral hazard with no attempt having being made to limit the dangers that arose, in particular, in the US with the provision of *de facto* full deposit guarantee cover.[167] Specific difficulties have arisen with regard to funding and pricing of relevant risks to limit the moral hazard assumed by the banks concerned as opposed to underlying depositors. While the US has attempted a number of initiatives in this area and especially with regard to the use of risk related premia, the problems of depositor and bank moral hazard have simply been ignored within Europe. The overall effects of the top-up and no export clauses are also to create competitive equality within national markets but at the expense of inequality across the single market as a whole. Cross-border inequality is then sacrificed in favour of inter-branch domestic equality.

This is nevertheless a complex area and it has to be accepted that the Community did adopt a reasonable compromise position that attempted to reconcile the various conflicting objectives involved. Where clear solutions on all relevant issues were possibly not achievable at that stage (such as with regard to pricing and funding) this could be left to market practice, pressure and development with the overall operation of the system still being subject to continuing Commission review.

Rather than consider Directive 94/19 and the arguments raised by the German Government in isolation, however, this is possibly of more significance in again confirming the underlying difficulties that arise with regard to the use of a mutual recognition, minimum harmonization and home country control integration model. Minimum harmonization is necessarily selective and partial with supervisory and regulatory gaps being left to national agency discretion or correction. Even within harmonized functions, significant disparities can arise and consequently different levels of depositor and investor protection secured. An uneven single market is accordingly created with significant variations remaining in terms of the coverage, content and quality of the supervision and regulation effected. The most unique or original element of Directive 94/19 was the imposition of the no-export obligation. Rather than resolve differences in national depositor and investor protection, this only served to highlight the disparities that arose. The further problems that have to be taken into account

[167] Hal Scott and Philip Wellons *International Financial Casebook* (7th edn Foundation Press Westbury New York), 337–8. Scott and Wellons also note that depositors in US branches of foreign banks that took retail deposits had to be insured until 1991. After then, retail deposit branches were prohibited with retail deposits only being receivable through subsidiaries. The policy reason for abolition of retail insured foreign bank branches was that of concern that the host state would have to pay for the supervisory failures of the foreign country. Scott and Wellons, 338.

with regard to the absence of individual rights and harmonized provisions concerning regulatory liability would be considered by the European Court of Justice subsequently in *Peter Paul* in 2004.[168]

(2) UK FINANCIAL LIABILITY—*THREE RIVERS v BANK OF ENGLAND* (2000 AND 2001)

The extent to which the European banking directives conferred individual rights on depositors was examined by the House of Lords in the UK in one of the pre-trial judgements in *Three Rivers District Council v Governor and Company of the Bank of England* on 18 May 2000.[169] The action related to the claim by the former depositors of the Bank of Credit and Commerce International SA (BCCI) against the Bank of England for failing to supervize BCCI effectively and to close it down at an earlier stage. The House of Lords subsequently allowed the action to proceed to trial on 22 March 2001 although only after extensive argument.[170]

The result of the March 2001 judgment by the House of Lords was that the claimants were given permission to proceed to trial against the Bank of

[168] Section D(3).

[169] *The Times*, May 19, 2000; (2000) to WLR 1220.

[170] [2001] UK HL 16. The action was originally commenced in 1993 with a writ of summons being issued on 24 May 1993. Clarke J made an order on 19 July 1995 for certain preliminary issues to be considered. These included whether the defendants were capable of being liable for the tort of misfeasance in public office, whether the losses were caused in law by the acts or omissions of the defendant and whether the plaintiffs were entitled to recover for the tort as existing or potential depositors. The claimants were given leave to amend their pleadings on 19 July 1995 and a re-amended statement of claim was lodged on 21 Aug 1995. Judgement on the preliminary issues was produced on 1 Apr 1996 and 10 May 1996 ([1996] 3 All ER 558 and 634). The claimants applied for leave to re-re-amend the claim with arguments being heard in Nov and Dec 1996. A series of further amendments were proposed and an eighth draft statement of claim produced on 6 Jan 1997. Following a further hearing in Apr 1997, Clarke J concluded that the claim was bound to fail on the basis of the evidence available. There was no real possibility that the claimants would obtain evidence in the future which might enable them to succeed and that it would be an abuse of process and vexatious or oppressive to allow the action to proceed. Application to re-re-amend was refused and the action struck out on 3 July 1997. The order of Clarke J was upheld by the Court of Appeal ([2000] 2 WLR 15) although leave to appeal to the House of Lords was granted on 21 Jan 1999. The requirements of the tort of misfeasance in public office and the rights of depositors under European law were considered by the House of Lords in January 2000 with judgement on 18 May 2000. The claimants had been given leave to appeal against the refusal of leave to re-re-amend the statement of claim on 12 May 1999. Following a further procedural hearing on 27 June 2000, the claimants served new draft particulars on the Bank of England on 17 July 2000. The House of Lords considered whether the appeal should be allowed on 22 Mar 2001 ([2001] UK HL 16). Walker 'Regulatory Comment' and 'Three Rivers v Bank of England' in *Farrer's Financial Services Quarterly Bulletin* (Summer 2001). The action was subsequently abandoned on 2 Nov 2005. G A Walker 'Regulatory Review' FRI (Informa) and Walker 'Regulatory Review'. The Bank was later awarded costs on an indemnity basis of £81 million on 31 Jan 2006. Walker 'BCCI Closure but not without Cost' *Financial Regulation International* (Informa Feb 2006).

England for over £1 billion (£550 million plus another £500 million worth of accrued interest over 10 years) and legal costs. The action was led by Deloitte & Touche on behalf of Three Rivers District Council, Hertfordshire as well as almost 6,000 other former BCCI depositors. BCCI was closed in July 1991 following the production of a report by PriceWaterhouse which confirmed that fraud had been conducted within BCCI. A coordinated closure of the bank's global operations had been organized by the Bank of England with the assistance of *inter alia* the supervising authorities in the US, Luxemburg and Cayman Islands. The BCCI scandal has been referred to as the biggest fraud in history, with depositors and investors losing in excess of $5 billion but with total losses possibly exceeding £20 billion.[171] The report produced by PriceWaterhouse under s 41 of the Banking Act 1987 confirmed the existence of fraud and prevented the possibility of any rescue of BCCI. While the Bank of England had known about the possibility of fraud for some time, it considered that it did not have sufficient grounds and that it would not have been in the best interests of depositors (present and future) to close the bank until the s 41 report had been produced in July 1991.

The action against the Bank was based on the ancient tort of misfeasance in public office. The claimants had to rely on this tort in light of the statutory immunity from liability in damages for negligence conferred under s 1 of the Banking Act 1987 (now paragraph 19 of Schedule 1 of the Financial Services and Markets Act 2000) and the difficulty of recovering more general economic loss in tort under English law. The constituent elements of the tort of misfeasance in public office were restated by the House of Lords in May 2000 following a hearing on 24–27 January 2000.[172] The ruling was issued by Lord Steyn, Lord Hope of Craighead, Lord Hutton, Lord Hophouse of Woodborough and Lord Millett. The tort was consid-

[171] BCCI had originally been set up by Agha Hassan Abedi and Suraleh Naquvi in Pakistan as an international bank to serve Muslim and Third World borrowers that had not been properly serviced by Western banks. BCCI's capital grew from $2.3 million to $23 billion between 1972 and 1991 by which time it had 420 offices in over 70 countries. BCCI had 45 branches in the UK by 1978 having originally been licensed in 1973. BCCI's expansion was facilitated by the rapid increase in oil prices during 1973 and 1974 although substantial losses were suffered due to mis-management and poor credit quality. Many of these losses were initially hidden through a Cayman Islands subsidiary (referred to as 'the dustbin'). BCCI's corporate structure was deliberately used to avoid effective oversight with its registered office in Luxemburg and headquarters in London. $849 million were lost between 1982 and 1986 at which time Abedi began to service Latin American drug operators. BCCI acted for General Manuel Noriega in Panama following the death of the President in 1981. Extensive drug money laundering operations were developed across Latin America and into Hong Kong and Abu Dhabi. The bank's criminal culture was confirmed following a sting operation in Miami in 1987. Despite this, the Bank of England maintained that it was not able to close the bank down until confirmed evidence of fraud in the UK was produced in July 1991.

[172] [2000] 2 WLR 1220. See also *Yuen Kun-Yeuv AG of Hong Kong* [1987] 2 All ER 705, [1988] AC 175; and *Davis v Radcliffe* [1990] to All ER 538, [1990] 1 WLR 81.

ered to be based on a number of earlier decisions by electors against denial of the right to vote by a returning officer.[173] While the tort was denied by the Court of Appeal in 1907, it was recognized by the Privy Counsel in 1981 and then further developed by the Court of Appeal in 1985.[174] The House of Lords confirmed that a remedy was available where a public power had been exercised for an improper purpose with the specific intent of injuring a person or persons or a public officer had acted in knowledge that he had no power to carry on the act complained of and that it would cause probable injury to the claimant.[175]

Having identified the main elements of the tort in May 2000, the House of Lords had to consider in March 2001 whether the action should be allowed to proceed to trial on the basis of the evidence available or whether that would amount to an abuse of process or be vexatious and oppressive (under the new CPR Rule 24.2). The two main issues that arose were whether the amended pleadings were sufficient in their terms to substantiate the claim and whether the claim should be struck out on the basis that it had no reasonable prospects of success. Lords Steyn, Hope and Hutton considered that the pleadings were sufficient and that the bank's application to dismiss should be rejected. The main judgment was given by Lord Hope. Lord Millett, however, explained in an eloquent and succinct judgement why the pleadings were still defective while both Lord Millett and Lord Hobhouse considered that it would be an abuse of process to allow the action to proceed.[176]

The issue of whether the European banking directives created rights in favour of individual depositors was considered as part of the January 2000 hearing and in the May 2000 judgment. The issue was examined, in particular, by Lord Hope and Lord Millett. In considering the European law issues that arose, Lord Hope noted that the plaintiffs had argued that the First Banking Directive 77/780 had imposed certain well-defined Community law obligations on the competent authorities of Member States in relation to the authorization and supervision of banks and that it conferred on depositors and potential depositors corresponding Community law rights against the competent authorities to have these

[173] *Turner v Sterling* (1671) to Vent 24, 86 BR 287; and *Ashby v White* (1703) 3 LD Raym 320.

[174] Contrast *Davis v BromleyCorp* [1908] 1 KB 170; *Dunlop v Woollahara Municipal Council* [1981] 1 All ER 1202, [1982] AC 158; and *Bourgoin SA v Ministry of Agriculture, Fisheries and Food* [1985] 3 All ER 585, [1986] QB 716.

[175] Lord Steyn identified the six ingredients of the tort as: (a) the defendant must be a public officer; (b) the conduct must be in the exercise of a public function; (c) there had to be targeted malice or abuse; and (d) probable injury; (e) there had to be a duty to the plaintiff and causation; and (f) sufficiently foreseeable damage. The ingredients of the tort were also commented on by Lord Hutton and Lord Hobhouse.

[176] ([2001] UK HL 16). Walker (n 170).

obligations fulfilled. These Community law rights must then prevail over the requirement in national law to prove bad faith or dishonesty under the tort of misfeasance in public office under the English Common Law and the Bank of England's right to seek exemption from liability under s 1(4) of the 1987 Banking Act.

Lord Hope reviewed the conditions of liability for damages by a state or an emanation of a state under Community law. Having distinguished between direct effect (*Becker*) and state (*Francovich*) liability,[177] Lord Hope

[177] Little dispute had arisen between the parties concerning the conditions of liability which were considered by the majority of the Court of Appeal ([1999] 4 All ER 800 N, [2000] to WLR 15 at 70–80) and the judgment of Auld LJ (at 106–10). Lord Hope distinguished between two distinct routes to claim damages under European law. The purpose of the right to claim damages was to ensure that provisions of Community law prevail over national provisions with the full effectiveness of Community law being impaired if individuals were unable to obtain redress in national courts where their rights were infringed by breach of Community law. *Brasserie du Pecheur SA v Germany, Rv Secretary of State for Transport,* ex *P Factortame Ltd* Joined cases C-46/93 and C-48/93 [1996] All ER (EC) 301 at 361, [1996] ECR I-1029 at 1142 (para 20). Damages against a state or an emanation of a state could then be available under the principle of direct effect or of state liability.

With regard to direct effect, Lord Hope referred to the decision in *NV Algemene Transporten Expeditie Onderneming van Gend & Loos v Nederlandse Belastingadministratie* Case 26/62 [1963] ECR 1. The European Court of Justice held that Art 12 (25) of the EC Treaty was capable of producing direct effects and creating individual rights which national courts had to protect. It was also clear that directives could create direct effects under Art 189 (Art 249) of the Treaty and the case law of the Court. It was specifically confirmed in *Becker v Finanzamt Münster-Innenestadt* Case 8/81 [1982] ECR 53 at 70–1 (paras 22–9) that a Member State cannot rely on its own failure to perform obligations imposed under a directive and that the provisions of a directive may be relied on against national provisions where they are unconditional and sufficiently precise. This *Becker* type liability could then be relied on to nullify a national provision incompatible with the directive or to claim damages for breach of an obligation of Community law.

The existence and scope of the liability of the State for damages resulting from breach of obligations under Community law was considered in *Francovich v Italy* Joined cases C-6/90 and C-9/90 [1991] ECR I-5357. While *Francovich* raised the issue of *Becker* direct effect liability, it also raised the separate issue of state liability. Lord Slynn of Hadley summarized the conditions for state liability in *RV Secretary of State for Transport, ex p Factortame Ltd* [1999] 4 All ER 906 at 916, [1999] 3 WLR 1062 at 1072 as requiring that there be a grant of right to individuals by the directive, the content of these rights is clear and the loss suffered is shown to be caused by the failure to implement. The European Court of Justice then re-stated the conditions for state liability under *Francovich* in terms of *Becker* type liability in *Dillenkofer v Germany* Joined cases C-178, 179, 188, 189, and 190/94 [1996] All ER (EC) 917 at 937, [1996] ECR I-4845 at 4878–4879 (paras 20–3).

The dispute that arose between the parties was whether on implementation, a directive is supplanted by rights under national law or whether the directive can continue to be the immediate source of enforceable rights under the *Becker* type principle even if it has been transposed into national law. The majority of the Court of Appeal (at 80) found support in *Norbrook Laboratories Ltd v Ministry of Agriculture, Fisheries and Food* Case C-127/95 [1998] ECR I-1531 that there may be a category of directives in respect of which a Member State's obligation of proper implementation is not restricted to a once-for-all legislative process but also requires a continuing administrative process. In connection with this, Auld L J (at 139) had noted that the precondition of liability for damages of bad faith on the part of the Bank or its officers could have arisen through the mis-implemention of Directive 77/780 (at 139) and that recent decisions including *Norbrook Laboratories Ltd* suggested that the Court was indifferent as to the precise

considered that the relevant conditions were almost identical (under *Dillenkofer)* and proceeded to consider whether Directive 77/780 conferred rights on individual depositors (or potential depositors) and whether the content of those rights was identifiable from the provisions of the Directive. Clarke J had concluded at first instance that Directive 77/780 was not intended to confer rights upon individual savers even though the underlying purpose of the supervision of credit institutions was for their benefit ([1996] 3 All ER 558 at 602 and 614).

While some argument had arisen before the Court of Appeal as to whether the Bank had altered its position, Lord Hope considered that there had been no substantial change. Lord Hope referred to the plaintiff's submission that the proper purpose of the Directive was to protect depositors referring to its legislative background, its terms and relevant case law.[178] He then reviewed all of the main terms of the Directive[179] and

route through which it gives effect to a directive (at 141). Lord Hope concluded that although the plaintiffs' case under Community law is put in different ways and is based on both types of liability (*Becker* and *Francovich*), the conditions to establish damages are so closely analogous as to be the same.

The critical question following *Dillenkofer* was then whether Directive 77/780 entailed the grant of rights to individual depositors and potential depositors and whether the content of those rights was identifiable on the basis of the provisions of the Directive.

[178] Lord Hope did not consider that any of the authorities referred to provided any assistance in confirming that the purpose of the Directive was to protect depositors. The reference to credit and banking profession in Art 56(2) was only illustrative of 'measures concerned with savings.' This did not mean that directives issued under the provision were solely intended to protect individual depositors and potential depositors.

The decision in *Germany v European Parliament* and Directive 94/19/EC was distinguished on the basis of the particular circumstances of the case. The inclusion of a consumer protection objective under that Directive did not undermine its harmonization and promotion of establishment or services purposes.

Consultation with ECOSOC was required under Art 100, second para (Art 94 EC) although this did not advance the plaintiffs' case. The proper purpose of Directive 77/780 was to promote harmonization of regulatory measures and not to confer Community law rights on individual depositors.

This was further confirmed in *Parodi*. Ch 4, section A (5) and (n 76). Under *Parodi*, Member States were entitled to apply their own consumer protection measures in the banking sector pending the entry into force of the Second Council Directive which rendered national provisions otiose. The purpose of Directive 77/780 was to begin the process of harmonization throughout the single market but without weakening or impairing the protection of depositors. The protection of depositors was seen therefore not as a purpose of Directive 77/780 but as a constraint on the provision of banking services to the public which had to be recognized.

In *Romanelli* the Court accepted that it was clear from Directive 77/780 and Directive 89/646 that the protection of savings constituted one of the objectives of the measures taken to coordinate credit institutions (n 117). This nevertheless added little to *Parodi* and that, as a matter of fundamental principle, restrictions on the freedom to provide services must be justified by imperative reasons in the public interest which are objectively necessary to guarantee the protection of the recipient of services and which do not exceed what is necessary to attain those objectives. This provides no support for the argument that a purpose of Directive 77/780 was to promote or protect the interests of individual depositors.

[179] Lord Hope referred to the fifteen recitals and fifteen articles in Directive 77/780 and, in

concluded that its proper purpose was to act as a first step in the process of harmonization of the provisions concerning credit institutions. It confined itself to imposing a number of minimum conditions and prohibitions on Member States as to the authorization and supervision of credit institutions having their head offices in another Member State or having their head offices outside the Community. It was based on an appreciation of the fact

particular, recitals 3, 4, 5, and 12 and Arts 3 (authorization), 6 and 7 (continuous supervision) and 8 (revocation). Lord Hope reviewed the Directive as a whole to consider whether it entailed the grant of rights to individuals, whether the content of those rights were identifiable on the basis of the provisions of the Directive and whether a causal link existed between breach of the State's obligation and the loss and damage suffered by the injured parties under *Dillenkofer.*

In referring to the recitals, Lord Hope considered that they confirmed that the proper purpose of the Directive was not to protect depositors but to begin the process of coordinating the conditions for the supervision of all institutions in successive stages having regard to the need to coordinate measures to protect savings on the one hand and to create equal conditions of competition on the other (recitals 2–5). The eventual aim of the harmonization process was to introduce uniform authorization requirements throughout the Community for comparable types of credit institution with only certain minimum requirements being specified initially (recitals 6–9). The purpose of coordination was to achieve a system whereby credit institutions having their head office in one Member State would be exempt from national authorization requirements in signing up branches in other Member States (recitals 10 and 11). The Directive also aimed at producing a gradual approximation of the systems for monitoring the solvency and liquidity of credit institutions (recital 12). The protection of savings and creation of equal conditions of competition were, nevertheless, still only to be taken into account in harmonising relevant national provision which was the proper purpose of the Directive.

Lord Hope noted that the Directive contained no definition of individuals or consumers which would have been surprising if its purpose was to protect their interests. Lord Hope distinguished *Dillenkofer* and *Rechberger v Austria* Case C-140/97 (1999) Transcript 15 June 1999 which concerned Council Directive 90/314/EEC (OJ 1990 L158, 59) concerning package travel, package holidays and package tours which did define 'consumer.' The Court had held that Art 7 of Directive 90/314 gave consumers a right to be reimbursed or repatriated in the event of the insolvency of the tour operator. No equivalent definitions or rights to reimbursement were included within Directive 77/780.

Lord Hope referred to the *German Environmental Cases* which concerned Germany's failure to implement water and air quality directives. *Commission v Germany* Case C-131/88 [1991] ECR I-825, *Commission v Germany* Case C-298/95 [1996] ECR I-6747. While it was accepted that these did confer rights on individuals and that no relevant definition was included, the cases were distinguished on the basis that environmental and human health issues affected all members of society and that the absence of any specific definition was consequently of no importance.

It was accepted that Art 3 did not apply to BCCI as it was already carrying on business when the Directive came into effect. The fact that BCCI was granted a licence under the Banking Act 1979 was a matter of UK and not of Community law. Lord Hope interpreted Art 10(1) generously to include the legitimate carrying on of business under any system of law in force at the time the Directive came into effect. BCCI was nevertheless still covered by Art 10(4) which allowed competent authorities to require an existing credit institution to become authorized.

The decision in *Wagner Miret v Fondo de Garantia Salarial* Case C-334/92 [1993] ECR I-6911 was distinguished on the basis that the obligation assumed under article 10(4) was voluntary and not obligatory. The voluntary incorporation by a Member State of a provision in a directive under international law which it is not obliged to incorporate under Community law does not give rise to a Community law obligation. While the Court of Justice may assist the

that credit institutions required regulation in order to protect savings with any harmonization measures having to satisfy the twin objectives of protecting savings and creating conditions of equal competition between credit institutions operating in more than one territory. It also placed duties of cooperation on the competent authorities of different States although it stopped short of prescribing any duties of supervision to be performed by the competent authorities within each Member State. It was not then possible to discover provisions that entailed the conferral of rights to individuals as such rights were not necessary to achieve the intended results of the Directive.

Lord Hope was (with the greatest of respect) unable to agree with Auld LJ's conclusions in the Court of Appeal that Directive 77/780 imposed clearly defined obligations on Member States and on their regulatory bodies and that in so doing it gave rise to corresponding Community law rights in favour of depositors to enforce those obligations by an action of damages ([2000] 2 WLR 15 at 102–3). Lord Hope preferred the views of Clarke J

national court in construing the Directive, it does not follow that the obligation is a Community law obligation. *Leur-Bloem v Inspecteur der Belastingdienst/Ondernemingen Amsterdam 2* Case C-28/95 [1997] All ER (EC) 738, 764-765, [1997] ECR I-4161, 4202 (paras 33–4). No obligation was accordingly created under Art 3(1) and even if it was, no individual rights were conferred.

Auld LJ had considered that Arts 6 and 7 had imposed immediate duties of a technical banking nature on regulators to ensure that savings were protected ([2000] 2 WLR 15, 113). Lord Hope nevertheless considered that Art 6 only imposed a duty to formulate structural ratios to facilitate cooperation between national authorities in setting relevant standards or coefficients to ensure the sound management of credit institutions which would be coordinated between Member States in due course. Art 7 only imposed a supporting duty of cooperation and information sharing between supervisory authorities. Neither provision imposed any general duty to supervize. No further assistance was also available from the observations of Advocate General, Sir Gordon Slynn, in *Municipality of Hillegom v Hillenius* Case 110/84 [1985] ECR 3947, 3948 (which only re-states the wording of Art 7, para 1) and *Carbonari v Università degli Studi di Bologna* Case C-131/97 [1999] ECR I-1103 (in which the rights of medical students to remuneration during their training periods were unconditional and sufficiently precise although it was unclear which body was required to bear the obligation imposed). Lord Hope noted that none of the provisions in Arts 6 and 7 of Directive 77/780 define any categories of individual on whom rights were conferred nor do they state in obligatory terms that credit institutions 'shall be subject to appropriate supervision' by the competent authority. Even if such an obligation in general terms could be implied, the absence of even the slightest amount of detail as to the system of supervision required by Community law which was to be adopted and enforced by the national courts would make it impossible to say that, as a matter of Community law, the obligation to supervise was unconditional and sufficiently precise to satisfy the *Becker* type liability test.

Auld LJ had accepted that Art 8 had imposed a duty on competent authorities to withdraw authorization in the circumstances specified ([2000] 2 WLR 15, 114). Lord Hope nevertheless considered that this only laid down a series of provisions with a view to the harmonization of the criteria to be applied to credit institutions having their head office in a Member State and their branches in other Member States. There was nothing surprising in para 1 being permissive and para 2 being obligatory. There was also nothing to suggest that rights were conferred on individuals to insist upon the withdrawal of authorization in the circumstances referred to in para 1.

that the true position was that the Directive was not intended to require the imposition of a duty to supervize on the supervisory authority because, whatever the underlying purpose of the system of supervision, the immediate purpose of the Directive was only to act as a first step towards harmonization of the systems in the Member States which was assumed to and no doubt did exist ([1996] 3 All ER 558 at 616). The position was then similar to *Re International Stock Exchange of the UK and the Republic of Ireland Ltd, exp Else (1982) Ltd, Re International Stock Exchange of the UK and the Republic of Ireland, exp Roberts.*[180] Its purpose was not to lay down a duty to supervize or radically alter the existing systems but, even if it was, it was not to confer rights upon either savers or other creditors. The majority of the Court of Appeal agreed that Directive 77/780 did confer enforceable rights on credit institutions which were to be supervized under its terms. A credit institution which was refused authorization for reasons incompatible with Article 3 or which had its authorization withdrawn for reasons incompatible with Article 8 would (in the event of non-transposition) most probably have had a right to challenge the Bank's decision on the basis that the *Becker* conditions were satisfied. There was not, however, any sufficient clarity or certainty in the position of depositors (or other customers of credit institutions) to create equivalent liability. Lord Hope accordingly agreed with the Court of Appeal subject to having substituted the *Francovich* test as applied in *Dillenkofer* for *Becker* as it was more precise.

Lord Hope noted that neither party had asked for a preliminary reference to the European Court of Justice under Article 234 EC (*ex* 177 EEC). Clarke J would have referred the matter as to the meaning and effect of Directive 77/780 had the parties not requested him to give judgment on the Community law issue without doing so ([1996] 3 All ER 558, 625). While the majority of the Court of Appeal did not consider that the issue concerning the *Becker* liability was *acte clair*, they decided not to make a reference as a matter of discretion having regard, in particular, to the unanimity of the parties in requesting the court not to do so. By the time that the matter had reached the House of Lords, the plaintiffs had decided to request a reference to be made on whether Directive 77/780 conferred individual rights against the competent authorities of member territories. This was on the basis of the observations made in the courts below, the dissenting judgement of Auld LJ in the Court of Appeal and to the apparent change of position by the Bank with regard to the purpose and intent of Directive 77/780. Lord Hope considered that it would not be appropriate for a reference to be made to the European Court of Justice on the basis that the matter was *acte clair* and having regard to the unanimity within their Lordships and the full oral and written submissions made.

[180] [1993] 1 All ER 420, [1993] QB 534.

In reviewing the European law issue, Lord Millett considered that it was clear that Directive 77/780 did not have as one of its objectives the protection of depositors which was the function of national banking laws.[181] In Lord Millet's opinion, the proper objective of the Directive was nevertheless of only marginal relevance as to whether the Directive conferred individual rights. This could only be determined by reference to the particular provisions of the Directive on which the plaintiffs sought to rely.[182] Whether a directive conferred individual rights was also considered secondary to whether the specific provisions referred to had been breached. Lord Millett then referred to the arguments raised with regard to Article 3 (breach of the obligation to withhold initial authorization), Articles 6 and 7 (failure to provide continuous and effective supervision) and Article 8 (failure to revoke authorization).[183]

[181] National banking laws placed restrictions on the freedom to provide banking services which restrictions were inherently anti-competitive and therefore contrary to Art 59 EEC (Art 49 EC) but recognized in the interests of depositors. As these restrictions are imposed by national legislators, they will vary from one Member State to another and inevitably distort the operation of the single market. The objective of Directive 77/780 was then to begin the process of coordination of the national laws in order to remove anti-competitive barriers to the free provision of banking services throughout the single market insofar as this could be achieved without weakening or impairing the protection of depositors. The adequate protection of depositors was therefore not an objective of the Directive but rather operated as a constraint upon the extent to which its objective could be achieved. Lord Millett considered that this was confirmed by the European Court of Justice in the *Parodi* decision Case C-222/95 [1997] All ER (EC) 946, [1997] ECR I-3899. Section A(5) and (n 76).

[182] Lord Millett noted that what was decisive was not the interest which a directive as a whole seeks to protect but the interest sought to be protected by the provisions which were alleged to have been breached. Prechal *Directives in European Community Law: a study of directives and their enforcement in national courts* (1995), 138. Attempting to identify the underlying objective or main objective of a directive and to distinguish it from other subsidiary objective was in Lord Millett's opinion as unprofitable as it was illusory.

[183] Art 3(1) imposed an obligation on Member States to require institutions to obtain authorization before commencing their activities and was not retrospective. BCCI had commenced its activities in the UK before the Directive came into force and therefore Art 3(1) had no application (n 179). Existing institutions are dealt with under Art 10 which deems them to be authorized and subject to modified requirements. Art 10(4) only permits (rather than obliges) competent authorities to require institutions which are legitimately carrying on business without authorization to obtain authorization for the future. The UK could have exempted BCCI but went further than the Directive required by obliging such institutions to obtain authorization. In such circumstances, an unlawful grant of authorization in breach of the provisions of the Banking Act 1979 would amount to a breach of UK but not Community law.

Lord Millett distinguished *Wagner Miret v Fondo de Garantia Salarial* Case C-334/92 [1993] ECR I-6911 which the plaintiffs claimed meant that where a Member State voluntarily assumes obligations laid down by a directive it cannot escape liability by reason of the absence of any Community requirement to assume them (n 179). In the present case, no underlying Community obligation arose.

Lord Millett considered that Arts 6 and 7 imposed obligations of cooperation and the establishment of appropriate financial ratios to be applied subsequently. The obligation to provide 'continuous and effective supervision' was also far too imprecise and left too much discretion to Member States to be capable of conferring individual rights.

With regard to Art 8, Lord Millett considered that this was prohibitory rather than permis-

Lord Millett concluded that the scheme of the Directive made sound regulatory sense. Member States must withhold authorization from institutions wishing to commence business unless the prescribed criteria set out in Article 3(2) were met. The authorities were, however, free to select their own criteria in allowing existing institutions to continue to carry on business after the Directive came into effect. Authorization may only be withdrawn or business prohibited in certain prescribed circumstances. Where those circumstances exist, it is left to the national authorities to have regard to any countervailing considerations in exercising their discretion whether to withdraw authorization or to close down an existing business. The plaintiffs were consequently unable to allege any breach of Article 3 (which did not apply to BCCI) or Article 8 (which did not impose any relevant obligation) while neither Article 6 nor 7 conferred rights on individuals. Lord Millett accordingly considered that the proper purpose of the Directive was to begin the process of coordination or harmonization of national laws. The plaintiffs' case was accordingly dismissed on the basis that the specific articles relied on did not impose a relevant obligation nor confer any enforceable rights.

The judgement of the House of Lords in *Three Rivers* was significant in confirming that Directive 77/780 did not confer individual rights on depositors and certainly in such clear and precise terms that liability could either arise under *Becker* (direct effect) or *Francovich* (state liability). The underlying purpose of the Directive was not to protect depositors specifically but to commence a process of regulatory and supervisory harmonization across Europe. Depositors were to be protected under national laws and not through Community measures as such. To the extent that the Community provisions nevertheless restricted establishment or services, they had to be assessed having regard to legitimate public interests including market stability and the protection of depositors. The Directive only placed duties of cooperation on the competent authorities where a credit institution was operating in more than one Member State other than that in which its head office was situated. It did not, however, prescribe any duties of supervision to be performed by the competent authorities within each Member State. While the decision of the House of Lords stated that no right to compensation arose under European law, it was accepted that liability may still arise under national law and, in particular, on the basis of misfeasance in public office under UK law. The issue of regulatory liability would then have to be determined in accordance with relevant national law.

sive or obligatory. It prevented competent authorities from withdrawing authorization except in prescribed circumstances. Where those conditions exist, the article does not interfere with the power of the authorities to withdraw authorization at their discretion but it does not oblige them to do so without regard to any countervailing considerations.

(3) EU REGULATORY IMMUNITY—*PETER PAUL* (2004)

The European Court of Justice was able to comment further on the content and effects of Directive 94/19/EC and the scope of regulatory liability for defective supervision seven years after *Germany v European Parliament and Council* in *Peter Paul.*[184] The case concerned a reference for a preliminary ruling on the interpretation of Arts 3 and 7 of Directive 94/19 and the First Banking Directive 77/780/EEC and the Second Banking Directive 89/646/EEC. The reference was made in the course of proceedings by Mr Paul, Ms Sonnen-Lutte and Ms Morkens against the German Government for compensation for the belated implementation of Directive 94/19 and the defective supervision by the *Bundesaufsichtsamt für das Kreditwesen* of the *BVH Bank für Verenogensanlagen und Handel AG* (BVH). The decision was of interest in allowing the Court to comment on the scope of the rights created under the Deposit Guarantee Directive and other main banking directives, the possible extent of liability under European law for defective financial supervision and the effect of any exclusion or immunity provision under national law against such liability.

Paul and others had been depositors with the BVH Bank which had been authorized by the *Bundesaufsichtsamt* to carry on banking business in 1987. BVH had unsuccessfully applied for admission to the German deposit guarantee fund run by the *Bundesverband Deutscher Banken ev*. BVH had not satisfied the relevant admission conditions and its application was withdrawn. The *Bundesaufsichtsamt* subsequently revoked the bank's authorization and applied for its bankruptcy on 14 November 1997 following a third examination of its internal operations and affairs. Paul, Sonnen-Lutte and Morkens had opened deposit accounts with the bank on 7 June 1995, 28 February 1994 and 17 June 1993 respectively with almost DEM 300,000 being outstanding at the time of BVH's bankruptcy (DEM 131,455.80, DEM 101,623.51 and DEM 66,976.20).

Proceedings were commenced before the *Landgericht* (Regional Court) in Bonn against the *Bundesrepublik Deutschland* for compensation due to the losses suffered following the non-implementation of Directive 94/19 before 1 July 1995 (art 14(1)).[185] The *Landgericht* ordered compensation to be paid to each plaintiff of DEM 39,450 (equivalent to 20,000 Euro under Art 7(1) of Directive 94/19) plus interest although the *Landgericht* and the *Oberlandesgericht* (Higher Regional Court) Cologne rejected the

[184] Case C-222/02 *Peter Paul, Cornelia Sonnen-Lütte and Christel Mörkens v Bundesrepublik Deutschland* (n 4). Reference for a preliminary ruling under Art 234 EC of 12 Oct 2004.

[185] Directive 94/19 was implemented in Germany under the Law Transposing the EC Deposit Guarantee Schemes Directive and the EC Investor Compensation Schemes Directive of 16 July 1998 (BGBI. 1998 I, 1842) which came into effect on 1 Aug 1998.

claims for any additional recovery on the basis that the *Bundesaufsichtsamt* had exercised its functions only in the public interest under paragraph 6(4) of the *Gesetz uber das Kreditwesen* (Law on Credit Institutions or KWG).[186] In the absence of paragraph 6(4), liability would otherwise have arisen under the German Civil Court and Basic Law.[187] On appeal (Revision) before the *Bundesgerichtshof* (Federal Court of Justice), reference for a preliminary ruling was made to the European Court of Justice.

The core issue that arose was whether paragraph 6(4) of the KWG could validly limit the liability of breach of duty of the *Bundesaufsichtsamt* under paragraph 839 of the German Civil Code (BGB) and the Basic Law (GG).[188] The *Bundesgerichtshof* had noted that if the European banking directives had conferred individual rights on depositors, paragraph 6(4) of the KWG would be ineffective as this refers to supervisory functions only being conducted in the public interest.[189] Three questions were accordingly referred to the European Court.[190] These essentially related to individual rights and possible direct effect or state liability.[191]

[186] Para 6(4) of the KWG provides that the *Bundesaufsichtsamt* shall exercise the functions assigned to it under this Law and other Laws only in the public interest (BGB I. 1998 I, 2776). This is now re-stated under para 4(4) of the *Gesetz uber die Bundesanstalt für Finanzdienstleitungsaufsicht* (Law on the Federal Institution for the Supervision of Financial Services (of 22 April 2002 (BGBI. 2002 I, 1310).)

Para 6(3) of the KWG provides that the *Bundesaufsichtsamt* may, in the context of the functions assigned to it, issue to an institution and its managers orders which are appropriate and necessary in order to prevent or remedy defects within the institution which could jeopardize the security of the assets entrusted to it or affect the proper performance of banking transactions or financial services.

[187] Under para 839(1), first sentence of the *Burgerliches Gesetzbuch* (German Civil Code), if an official wilfully or negligently commits a breach of official duty incumbent upon him as against a third party, he shall compensate the third party for any damage arising therefrom. Art 34, first sentence of the *Grundgesetz* (Basic Law), also provides that if a person infringes, in the exercise of a public office entrusted to him, the obligations incumbent upon him as against a third party, liability therefor shall attach in principle to the State or to the body in whose service he is engaged.

[188] Judgment of the Court, para 20.

[189] Judgment, para 21. Paul and others claimed that the purpose of the banking directives was to protect depositors and that they formed part of an overall scheme of banking supervision which would be denied practical effect if the *Bundesaufsichtsamt* was to exercise its functions only in the public interest under para 6(4) of the KWG. Para 22.

[190] The *Bundesgerichtshof* asked whether Arts 3 and 7 of Directive 94/19 conferred on depositors the right to require competent authorities to exercise the rights available to them against non-participating credit institutions (under Arts 3(2)–(5)) including revocation and whether this included the right to compensation for damages in addition to the minimum amount guaranteed under the Directive.

The second question was concerned with whether the banking directives more generally (either individually or in combination) conferred on savers and investors rights to require competent authorities to take prudential supervisory measures in their interests with corresponding liability for any misconduct or whether Directive 94/19 provided an exhaustive set of rights to compensation in the event of the unavailability of deposits.

In the event that individual rights were conferred, the third question related to whether these rights had direct effect or whether state liability arose in the event of non-implementation and,

While concerns had been expressed with regard to the admissibility of the questions raised, the European Court of Justice considered that their relevance had been established and sufficient legal and factual background information provided.[192] In dealing with the first question, rather than respond directly to the issues raised the Court turned the matter round to examine the problem of the validity of paragraph 6(4) of the KWG as identified by the *Bundesgerichtshof*.[193] The Court noted that the purpose of Directive 94/19 was to ensure that all credit institutions were members of a relevant deposit guarantee scheme (Article 3(2)–(5)) and to specify the minimum conditions of operation of such schemes (paragraph 29). The Court concluded that Article 3(2)–(5) did not confer individual rights on depositors if compensation is insured in the event that their deposits are unavailable (paragraph 30). While this deals with the issue of individual rights raised by the *Bundesgerichtshof* this is strictly not dependent on the availability of compensation (paragraph 30) but the proper purpose of the Directive (paragraph 29). The Court adds that this is supported by the 24th recital[194] (paragraph 31) and concludes that Article 3(2)–(5) cannot be interpreted as precluding a national provision such as paragraph 6(4) of the KWG (paragraph 32). The Court accordingly jumps from proper implementation to no liability under an appropriate national exclusion clause.

The Court's analysis is slightly more developed on the second question. The Court again inverts the specific terms of the question raised to determine whether the main banking directives preclude a national immunity provision (paragraph 33). The Court notes that the proper purpose of the banking directives is to harmonize the relevant laws, regulations and administrative provisions in this area as part of the larger internal market (paragraphs 35 and 36). The degree of essential harmonization to be achieved is nevertheless only that necessary and sufficient to secure the mutual recognition of national authorization and supervisory systems through the provision of a single licence (paragraph 37). The Court accepts that some of the recitals to the directives refer to one of the objectives being to protect depositors (paragraph 38) and that a number of supervisory obligations are imposed on national authorities (paragraph 39). That does not, however, mean that the directives seek to confer rights on individual

if so, whether this constituted a sufficiently serious breach of Community law for liability to arise.

191 Section D (2) and (n 177).

192 Para 24.

193 Paras 21 and 22.

194 The 24th recital to Directive 94/19 provides that the Directive may not result in Member States or their competent authorities being made liable in respect of depositors if they have ensured that one or more schemes guaranteeing deposits or credit institutions themselves and ensuring the compensation or protection of depositors under the conditions prescribed in the Directive have been introduced and officially recognized.

depositors in the event that their deposits are unavailable as a result of defective supervision on the part of competent national authorities (paragraph 40). No express rule is included (paragraph 41) and the essential harmonization secured does not include coordination of the national rules governing the liability of supervisory authorities (paragraphs 42 and 43). The absence of such liability in a number of Member States is noted (paragraph 40)[195] and the minimum deposit protection provided under Directive 94/19 referred to (paragraph 45). The Court concludes from this that the main banking directives cannot be interpreted as conferring individual rights in the event of deposit unavailability following defective supervision (paragraph 46) and therefore that they do not invalidate a national immunity provision (paragraph 47).

The third question is dismissed on the basis that no individual rights to compensation are created in the event of defective supervision (paragraph 50). No liability can therefore arise under Community law.[196] No issue of Community law liability arises as no individual rights are conferred.

The Court is clearly anxious in *Peter Paul* to assist the German Government and the *Bundesgerichtshof* by dismissing any admissibility objections and re-interpreting the questions referred to allow it to rule on the validity of the underlying national law. It must be accepted that it is not the clearest of judgements both in terms of its analysis and the limited scope of the ruling provided. In examining the effects of Directive 94/19, the Court notes its harmonization purpose and the absence of individual rights to take supervisory measures (under Articles 3(2)–(5)) and concludes that this does not invalidate a national immunity clause. The absence of individual rights is nevertheless confused with proper implementation (paragraph 30) rather than left to be dependent on the proper harmonising purpose of the measure (paragraph 29). The reference to proper implementation in the 24th recital is also confused (paragraph 31) as this is

[195] The Court accepted that it was not possible in a number of Member States for the national supervisory authorities to be held liable in respect of defective supervision including in Germany. Such exclusion or immunity rules are based on the complexity of banking supervision and the number (plurality) of interests which include the stability of the financial system and presumably (by implication) in addition to depositor protection (para 44). The issue raised is not directly concerned with the proper purposes or theories of bank regulation but with the need for appropriate limitation of liability provisions. This can correctly be most simply explained in terms of the complexity of bank supervision. This more specifically relates to the sophistication of internal bank risk management and oversight and the need for trained and appropriate supervisory judgement and discretion. The reference to 'plurality of interests' appears to confuse the range of interested parties (including banks themselves, depositors and other creditors and the general public) and more specific objectives (including efficient and stable operation of the banking and financial system and more general depositor or consumer protection).

[196] Joined Cases C-46/93 and C-48/93 *Brasserie du Pêcheur and Factortame* [1996] ECR I-1029, para 51; Joined Cases C-178/94, C-179/94 and C-188/94 to C-190/94 *Dillenkofer and others* [1996] ECR I-4845, para 21; and Case C-63/01 *Evans* [2003] ECR I-0000, para 83.

concerned with not creating any additional regulatory liability in establishing national protection schemes while the case was actually concerned with German non-transposition. The issue raised in *Peter Paul* was whether further regulatory liability could arise in addition to the minimum depositor compensation provided under Directive 94/19.[197] The Court appears to ignore this issue and only considers the validity of the specific exclusion clause concerned.

In considering the second question, the Court notes the nature of the essential harmonization intended under the banking directives (paragraphs 36 and 37). It accepts that one of the objectives included was depositor protection (paragraph 38) and that supervisory obligations are imposed on national authorities (paragraph 39) although the Court considers that this does not confer individual rights in the event of defective supervision (paragraph 40). The more correct provisional observation should possibly have been that no individual rights were conferred with regard to the conduct of the prudential supervision of credit institutions. The Court then jumps directly to defective supervision and closure rather than inadequacies in pre-collapse continuing general supervision. The Court adds that no such express rule is conferred (paragraph 41). It may have been more correct to have noted that no relevant definitions are included and express rights to continuing supervision conferred.[198]

The Court is correct to note that the essential harmonization intended does not include coordination of national liability rules (paragraphs 42 and 43) and that minimum deposit protection was provided under Directive 94/19 (paragraph 45). While the Court accepts the existence of national exclusion rules and confirms their validity (paragraphs 44 and 47), it equates the absence of rights in the event of defective supervision with the validity of national exclusion clauses. As the proper purpose of the directives is only to secure the minimum harmonization necessary in the banking area to facilitate mutual recognition, no individual rights arise in respect of continuing prudential supervision.[199] The separate issue that then arises is whether any right to compensation arises in the event of defective supervision, at least, in addition to Directive 94/19. The issue of depositor protection under Directive 94/19 is

[197] The purpose and effect of recital 24 remains unclear (n 194). This can either be understood (restrictively) to mean that no additional liability will be created on the part of national competent authorities with the establishment of local deposit protection schemes or (more generously) that all heads of liability under national law will be annulled automatically with the coming into effect of the Directive. As the Court admits in *Peter Paul*, the issue of the coordination of national rules on regulatory liability is outside the scope of the essential harmonization intended under the banking directives (para 43). Recital 24 must accordingly be read narrowly only to mean that no additional liability may arise.

[198] Compare Lord Hope's examination of the provisions contained in the First Banking Directive in *Three Rivers*. Section D (2) and (n179). See also Lord Millett's discussion (n 183).

[199] Lord Hope and Millett in *Three Rivers*. Section D (2) and (nn 179 and 183).

then wholly distinct from defective supervision which remains to be governed by national law subject to any permitted exclusion or immunity as provided for under the banking directives.

With regard to the exclusion of liability under Community law, the Court refers to the main directives not conferring rights on depositors in the event that deposits are unavailable as a result of defective supervision but only if the compensation of depositors prescribed by Directive 94/19 is ensured (paragraph 50). The link between the absence of rights to recovery and the existence of Directive 94/19 is unnecessary. The simpler analysis in *Three Rivers* is to be preferred whereby no rights to compensation in respect of either direct effect or state liability arise as no individual rights are conferred under the directives in respect of the continuing supervision of credit institutions.[200]

In addition to the Court's analysis of the issues raised, difficulties also arise with regard to the scope of the ruling provided. While the validity of the German public interest based exclusion is approved, the nature of other exclusion or limitation of liability clauses is not commented on. The possibility of other separate heads of liability arising apart from under the European Banking Directives is also ignored. This may, for example, include other administrative law causes of action including judicial review or liability under tort or misfeasance in the UK.[201] The Court accepts that coordination of regulatory liability at the national level is not within the essential harmonization intended to be achieved (paragraph 43) with the effect that other possible heads of liability are left unaffected. The Court accordingly does not comment on the validity of other causes of action or liability arising apart from under the banking directives and the effect of any other exclusion clauses (apart from a public interest requirement).

Oversight of state and public institutions is generally secured under English law through judicial review (accountability) and tort or misfeasance in public office (liability). Under English administrative law, parties aggrieved with the decision of a public body can either rely on one of the three prerogative orders of *certiorari* (quashing), *prohibition* and *mandamus* (direction) or declaration and injunction.[202] While liability may

[200] It is interesting to note that the banking directives referred to did not include the Own Funds Directive but only the Solvency Ratio Directive 89/299. The OFD is usually referred to with the SRD and the SBD. All of these were subsequently re-stated under the Consolidated Banking Directive. Ch 5, sections B and C and (nn 29 and 65).

[201] Section (D) (2).

[202] See, eg, Paul Craig *Administrative Law* (5th edn Sweet & Maxwell London 2003), Ch 22. The earlier prerogative orders are now referred to as quashing, prohibiting and mandatory orders under the Civil Procedure Rules (CPR). It has also been proposed that any Latin references be dropped. Lord Chancellor's Department *The Administrative Court: Proposed Changes to Primary Legislation Following Sir Jeffrey W Bowman's Review of the Crown Office List* (2001), Consultation Paper, para 12.

theoretically arise under tort, difficulties arise in establishing any duty to rescue, recovery for pure economic loss and existence of general public policy Common Law immunity from liability available in addition to the more specific statutory exclusion of liability available in the banking and financial area.[203] Liability may also arise for breach of statutory duty although this requires an inference of legislative intent that the duty creates corresponding private rights and that the breach will be actionable at the instance of right holders.[204]

In light of these difficulties and, in particular, the statutory immunity from suit conferred on financial authorities, liability may generally only arise under the tort of misfeasance in public office, at least, in the absence of express bad faith.[205] This generally requires that a public power has been exercised for an improper purpose with the specific intention of injuring a person or persons (targeted malice) or that a public officer has acted in the knowledge that he had no power to act in the manner complained of and that this would probably injure the claimant (untargeted malice).[206]

In *Three Rivers v Bank of England* in the UK, the House of Lords allowed the case at a second hearing to proceed to trial although insufficient evidence was available under the pleadings to confirm whether any liability arose.[207] The trial subsequently commenced in January 2004 before Mr Justice Thomlinson and was not expected to complete before the end of 2005 or early 2006.[208] A reference was not made by the House of Lords to the European Court of Justice on the issue as to whether the First Banking Directive 77/780 conferred individual rights on depositors and potential depositors as the matter was considered to be *acte clair*. Following *Peter Paul*, the issue that may have to be referred is whether liability under misfeasance in public office could be considered to be no longer relevant following the coming into effect of the European banking regime and the statement of rights conferred. This would presumably be considered to fall outside the essential harmonization intended to be achieved although the

[203] Section D (2). On possible liability in tort see, eg, Christos Hadjiemanuil 'The Question of Liability for Regulatory Decisions', Ch 5 of *Banking Regulation and the Bank of England* (Lloyds of London, 1996).

[204] *Atkinson v Newcastle &Gateshead Waterwork Co* (1877) to Ex D 44.1 (CA).

[205] Section (D) (2).

[206] In the case of untargeted malice, an act performed with indifference to the outcome would be sufficient. Recklessness would nevertheless be assessed on a subjective rather than objective basis. The claimant would therefore have to prove that the public officer acted with the state of mind of reckless indifference as to the illegality of the act involved. If damages for consequential economic loss were to be recovered, the claimant would have to establish that the public officer acted in the knowledge that his act would probably injure the claimant or a person of the class of which the claimant was a member. The public officer would then have to have foreseen the probability of damage or have been reckless as to the harm that would be likely to follow. *Three Rivers v Bank of England* [2000] to WLR1220 (n 7). Section D (2) and Walker (n 170).

[207] [2001] UHL 16. Walker (n 170).

[208] (nn 7 and 170).

effects of the immunity provision contained recital 24 of Directive 94/19 remains unclear.[209]

Under French law, decisions of the *Commission Bancaire* may be challenged before the administrative courts for annulment (*recours pour exces de pouvoir*) or liability (*responsabilité administrative*).[210] In establishing liability, illegal administrative acts will generally be considered to constitute a fault or *faute de service*.[211] While this has generally required a high standard of fault (*faute lourde*), a lower degree (*faute simple*) has been considered appropriate in some recent supervisory cases such as *El Shikh* and *Kechichian*.[212] The administrative courts in France have accordingly

209 (nn 194 and 197).

210 Bank supervision is generally conducted under the Banking Law of 24 Jan 1984 (*Loi Numero* 84/46 of 24 Jan 1984, *Journal Officiel*, 25 Jan 1984, 390 as amended by *Loi Numero* 99–532 of 25 June 1999, *Journal Official* 29 June 1999, 9487. The *Commission Bancaire* is established under Title III, Arts 37–50 of the Banking Law. It was formally referred to as the *Commission de Controle des Banques*. The other main supervisory agencies include the *Comité de la Reglementation Bancaire et Financière* which produces prudential regulations and ratios (Arts 33–6) and the *Comité des Etablissements de Credit et des Enterprises d'Investissements* which provides authorization to commence banking operations (Art 15). See generally, Decoopman, 'Renforcement des Pouvoirs et Coordination des Autorites de Controle du Secteur Financier' [1999] *Revue de Droit Bancaire et de la Bourse* 148. See also Mads Andenas and Duncan Fairgrieve 'To Supervise or to Compensate? A Comparative Study of State Liability for Negligent Banking Supervision' in Andenas and Fairgrieve (eds), *Liber Amicorum* for Lord Slynn of Hadley: Judicial Review in International Perspective (Kluwer Law International London 2000), 17.

Directive 94/19 was implemented in France under an amendment to the Banking Law of 1984 of 8 Aug 1994. Arts 52–1 of the Banking Law, *Comité de la Reglementation Bancaire et Financièr's Reglement* No 95/01 of 21 July 1995 (*Journal Officiel* 28 Sept 1995, 14143–14146). This established a new public administered *fonds de garantie des depots* which replaced the earlier scheme operated by the *Association Francaise des Banques* (AFB). Fairgrieve and K Belloir 'Liability of the French State for Negligent Supervision of Banks' (1999) European Business Law Review 17.

211 Andenas and Fairgrieve (n 208).

212 Liability for failed supervisory acts was originally established in *Achard*. *Conseil d'Etat* 24 Jan 1964, *Achard* [1964] *Recueil des Decisions de Conseil d'Etat* 43. In *Fauvry*, the *Tribunal administrative de Marseille* held that the *Commission Bancaire* had not committed *faute lourde* in failing to close the *Banque Phoceenne* which went into liquidation in 1981 following an earlier inspection which revealed significant internal irregularities in 1977.

The *Cour Administrative d' Appel* has nevertheless subsequently suggested that the lower standard of *faute simple* may be appropriate in supervisory cases. In *El Shikh*, the *Cour Administrative d'Appel de Paris* applied a dual *faute simple* test with regard to the supervisory activities of the *Commission Bancaire* with a higher *faute lourde* test with regard to malpractice in the use of disciplinary powers. The case concerned an action by depositors against the French supervisory authorities for compensation following the collapse of the BCCI branches in France. It was claimed that the *Commission Bancaire* had failed to react appropriately in imposing disciplinary measures following a preliminary investigation into the activities of the bank. The *Comité des Etablissements de Credit* was claimed to have failed to withdraw BCCI's banking licence when it no longer complied with the relevant criteria. It was also argued that the Governor of the Banque de France had failed to require shareholders to provide financial support under Art 52(1) of the Banking Law.

With regard to the *Commission Bancaire's* administrative activities, the Court rejected the plaintiff's arguments on the basis of causality in that the loss primarily arose due to the fraudulent activities of BCCI personnel especially at the principal place of business in London. The claim

relaxed the applicable standards although regulatory liability has still been limited through the use of causality in both the decisions in *El Shikh* and *Kechichian*.

In Germany, potential administrative liability is available under Article 33 of the Basic Law (GG) and Article 839 of the Civil Code (BGB).[213] Article 34 GG provides for the constitutionalization of tort liability for public authorities with Article 839 of the BGB imposing a specific obligation to compensate where an official wilfully or negligently commits a breach of official duty. State liability is then expressed in more general terms without the various public law obstacles that arise under English law.[214] While banking supervision was formerly carried out by the *Bundesaufsichtsamnt fur das Kreditwessen*,[215] responsibility has since been transferred to the new single financial regulator. With regard to liability for defective supervision, the Supreme Court has ruled that the purpose of financial supervision was to protect the interests of the public at large and not individual depositors.[216] The Court then confirmed in 1979 that individual non-deposit bank creditors (*Glaubiger*) represented a public interest.[217] The Supreme Court subsequently held in *Wetterstein* that the

against the Governor was rejected on the basis that no obligation was imposed on shareholders to support the proposed capital injection. Failure to revoke BCCI's licence was also dismissed on the basis that it had not been established that the *Comité des Etablissements* had information that BCCI no longer fulfilled the necessary criteria and that non-compliance was ultimately caused by its final closure. With regard to alleged malpractice on the part of the *Commission Bancaire*, the Court reapplied the *faute lourde* standard but considered that this had not been breached despite the length of time taken to prevent the bank from taking further deposits.

The distinction between *faute lourde* and *faut simple* was reapplied in *Kechichian* in Jan 2000 which concerned action against the *Commission Bancaire* for its alleged defective supervision of United Banking Corporation. While the *Cour Administrative d'Appel de Paris* considered that the Commission had been defective in failing to act more promptly and to improve the financial condition of the failed institution, only 20 per cent of the loss was allocated to the *Commission's* fault. For comment, Andenas and Fairgrieve (n 208).

213 (nn 186 and 187).

214 Mads Andenas and Duncan Fairgrieve 'Sufficiently Serious?' in Andenas (ed) 'English Public Law and the Common Law of Europe' (Key Haven London 1998).

215 The *Bundesaufsichtsamnt* was established under the Banking Act of 1961 (KWG) which reversed the earlier delegation of bank supervision to the *Lander*. CV Szagunn, U Haug, W Ergenzinger, *Gesetz uber das Kreditwesen* (6th edn Stuttgart 1997), 58–63. The purpose of the *Bundesaufsichtsamnt* was to counteract undesirable developments in the banking and financial services sector which may endanger the safety of the assets entrusted to institutions, adversely affect the proper conduct of banking business or financial services or involve serious disadvantages for the national economy (KWG, Art 6). While the objective was to protect depositors against loss of their deposits, this was not expressly included in the list of tasks or functions of the KWG. *Begr Reg* EKWG 1961, AII Para 3, III Para 1. The *Bundesaufsichtsamnt* was required to cooperate closely with the *Bundesbank* including on the exchange of information (KWG, Art 7).

216 F Ossenbuhl *Staatshaftungsrecht* (Munich 1998) 64. BGH Z 54, 96 at 98. This related to the supervision of insurance companies although it was understood that this also applied with regard to banking supervision. Andenas and Fairgrieve (n 208) 26.

217 F Ossenbuhl *Staatshaftungsrecht* (Munich 1998) 63–4.

Banking Act protected individual bank customers and that a failure by the *Bundesaufsichtsamnt* to protect their interests could lead to liability in damages.[218] The Court further confirmed in *Herstatt*[219] that capital adequacy and consolidated supervision requirements were intended to protect the interests of individual bank creditors. The KWG was amended in 1984 to provide that the *Bundesaufsichtsamnt* only acted in the public interest to prevent any incidents of individual liability arising. Ordinary liability rules would nevertheless apply with regard to claims by banks and their management against unlawful administrative acts of the *Bundesaufsichtsamnt.*[220] The constitutionality of the exclusion of liability was challenged at the time of adoption although it was subsequently ruled to be valid.[221] Directive 94/19 was then implemented in 1998[222] although the earlier additional non-statutory cover minima are continued through other voluntary schemes. It is understood that the objective and effect is to continue the earlier high levels of protection provided within Germany and overseas. This could then be contrary to European law and to the judgement in *Germany v European Parliament and Council.*[223]

The European Court's decision in *Peter Paul* was of value in confirming that no individual rights arise with regard to compensation for defective supervision under Directive 94/19 or the other main banking directives and (by prior implication) that no rights arise to benefit from the scheme of continuing prudential supervision set up within the Community. No rights to compensation then arise under Community law for state liability and (by implication) direct effect in the financial area. National limitation of liabil-

[218] The *Bundesaufsichtsamnt* had failed to prevent the company from issuing securities which only licenced banks were allowed to issue despite previous approaches by potential investors in the company. The *Bundesaufsichtsamnt* had refused to provide information on the basis of confidentiality although it had already been in negotiations with the company concerning its activities. The Supreme Court examined the legislative history of the banking system and its function and concluded that the state had a duty to protect individuals from danger and loss and that liability could arise in the event of defective supervision. BGHZ 74, 144 at 147.

[219] It was claimed that the *Bundesaufsichtsamnt* had failed in its duty to supervize Herstatt Bank in failing to identify the significant foreign currency risks that had been incurred. Having confirmed the possible breach of duty to individual depositors and customers, the issue was sent back to the Court of Appeal which held that no breach had occurred in the circumstances. For comment, M Andenas and Fairgrieve (n 208) 26–8. BGHZ 75, 120 at 122.

[220] Andenas and Fairgrieve (n 208) 29.

[221] The *Bundesrat* (Federal Second Chamber) had questioned the withdrawal of the right to remedies under the proposed amendment although the Finance Committee of the Bundestag (First Chamber) ruled that it was constitutional. V Szagunn, U Haug, W Ergenzinger *Gesetz uber das Kreditwesen* (6th edn Stuttgart 1997) 170. See also W R Schenke and J Ruthig 'Amtshaftungsanspruche von Bankkunden bei der verletzung staatlicher Bankenaufsichtsplichten' NJW 1994, 2324.

[222] 1998 BGBl. I,1848.

[223] R Sethe 'Europarectswidrige Kollusion von Gesetzgeber und Bankvirtschaft ?' (1999) ZIP 1461. See also Andenas and Fairgrieve (n 208) (n 151).

ity provisions based on public policy exclusion were approved although the Court did not rule on the validity of other types of exemption or immunity provision and more significantly on other possible heads of regulatory liability under national law. The Court also appeared by implication to approve the split German deposit protection regime based on a mandatory minimum statutory requirement and a voluntary top-up scheme although significant difficulties appear to remain with regard to its validity under European law.

E. FINANCIAL POLICY RESULT—JUDICIAL CONFIRMATION AND CORRECTION

The limited number of cases that have been decided in the financial area have confirmed the general application of the same principles developed with regard to establishment and services in this sector. The *Co-insurance Cases* and *Parodi*, in particular, confirm the pre-Second Banking Directive position. The direct applicability of Articles 59 (49) and 60 (50) was confirmed in *Co-insurance* in which a permanent establishment and separate authorization condition were held to constitute a restriction on the freedom to provide services and establishment subject to justification on the basis of imperative reason and necessity.

In *Schindler*, the Court confirmed that the sale of lotteries was subject to Article 49 (ex 59) although this was justified on the basis of social policy and the prevention of fraud. While the Court could have considered that the restriction was indirectly discriminatory, it ruled that the provisions were indistinctly applicable and applied *Säger*. The Court also ignored *Keck* despite the decision having only been issued four months earlier. *Schindler* supports the application of the services provisions to indistinctly applicable measures but also the competence and willingness of the Court to extend the permissible derogations where necessary.

Keck was distinguished in *Alpine Investments* in connection with unsolicited calls on the basis that market access was affected in that case. While this can be supported (in light of the more significant impact of the restriction on the provision of services rather than circulation of goods), the extension of possible derogation to include market reputation in another Member State must be questioned. The decision is possibly best understood in terms of the Court's concern to support the objectives underlying the (then proposed) Distance Selling Directive.

The extended *Gebhard* formulation was again applied to the licensing requirement for debt collection services in *Reisebüro Broede*. The Court's reasoning with regard to suitability and necessity are, however, questionable, in particular, in light of the Court's apparent failure to understand the nature of the underlying enforcement process involved. The Court would appear to have adopted an over generous approach (if not assumption) that a full legal qualification was required. The case is of value in re-applying *Gebhard* although the reasoning supporting the examination of each of the four tests for justification applied is more doubtful.

The general effect of these decisions is to confirm the adoption of an extended approach with regard to restrictive effect in the financial area. The Court would appear to be concerned to establish a trade restriction in each case which would then allow it to assess possible justification and derogation. To the extent that the scope of restrictive effect is interpreted widely, it has to be expected that a correspondingly generous approach would be followed with regard to possible justification and derogation. The extensions of imperative interest to include, in particular, market reputation in *Alpine* and the uncritical examination adopted in *Reisebüro Broede* are, however, unfortunate. The emphasis of the Court on consumer protection and reputation related ideas as against market effectiveness and market stability is especially regrettable.

In *Parodi,* the Court ruled that the requirement under French banking law that firms had to be authorized to supply banking services was contrary to Articles 59 (40) and 61(2) (51) of the Treaty in a pre-second Banking Directive case. The relevant Treaty articles apply to any discriminatory and other provisions that inhibit, impede or render less advantageous the rights concerned. Some but not all of the restrictions imposed are then justified on the basis of an implied pre-SBD general good examination. Although generally solid, the reasoning is at times suspect (such as in confusing consumer protection with market stability).

The Commission's 1997 Interpretative Communication was of value in reviewing and re-stating certain core Community law provisions in the banking area and attempting to resolve some of the uncertainty and confusion that had arisen especially with regard to the scope of the right to provide services and the interest of the general good under the Second Banking Directive. The Communication is of particular value in distinguishing between services and establishment in the banking area although further problems may still arise with regard to independent financial intermediaries operating on a cross-border basis and such electronic devices as ATMs and internet services provision. The relationship between the banking and electronic commerce measures will also have to be resolved, including, for example, the meaning of country of origin, the use of a host country control rule under the insurance directives and the scope of the general good in such cases. Although informed, the general good discussion will also have to be reconsidered in light of subsequent market developments and financial innovation and the operation and application of the separate tests confirmed (including, in particular,) the capability and proportionality conditions). The Commission should consider the production of a revised Communication following the more recent cases, including, in particular, *Germany v European Parliament and Council* and *Peter Paul* as well as the relationship between the banking and e-commerce and electronic money measures.

The more recent decisions of the Court are also of value in clarifying a number of further more specific points of interpretation, application and procedure. The general prohibition imposed under the banking directives applies to any financial instrument which is inherently repayable or repayable subject to contract (*Romanelli*). Some other interesting although essentially limited insights have been provided under *Bank für Arbeit* (interim measures), *Paul der Weduwe* (the validity of national bank secrecy restrictions), *Greece v Commission* (State Aids), *Caixa-Bank France* (interest payments on sight accounts) and *Vereinsbank* (on Euro currency exchange charges).

In connection with deposit protection and agency or regulatory liability, the Court has ruled on the validity of the no export clause under Directive 94/19 (Deposit Guarantee Schemes). More significantly, it has held that depositors do not have any individual rights of action under either Directive 94/19 or the other banking directives (including the First Banking Directive and Second Banking Directive as reconstituted under the Banking Consolidation Directive). Community law does not prohibit the operation of immunity clauses under national law although the more general issue of state liability under other heads of tort or administrative law have been left open.

More generally, it could be claimed that the later decisions reflect a greater degree of sophistication on the part of the Court with regard to the specific issues concerned and the nature of the underlying banking and financial markets concerned. This may, nevertheless, be simply explained in terms of the more limited nature of the problems raised and the scope of the dicta produced. Despite this, it has to be accepted that the basic nature and purpose of the new European banking law regime has been further clarified. Harmonization is to be limited to that which is essential, necessary and sufficient to secure the mutual recognition of national authorization and continuing supervision and make possible the grant of a single licence recognized throughout the Community (paragraph 42 in *Peter Paul*). This will include imposing minimum common provisions on depositor compensation (including maximum payment levels as in *Germany v European Parliament and Council*) but exclude national rules governing the liability of supervisory agencies in the event of defective supervision. While it also has to be expected that the Court will continue to adopt an expansionary approach with regard to the scope of Treaty restriction, continuing problems may nevertheless arise with regard to the availability and content of supporting judicial derogation.

The most difficult issue then remains the proper scope and content of the general good and host country control. The lack of legal certainty and predictability that this creates will continue to undermine reliance and confidence in the underlying rights of services and establishment created. This will, consequently, increase integration default or defect within the Community system in this particular area as well as undermine more general confidence and credibility in the larger European integration initiative as a whole.

One solution to this continuing uncertainty and omission would be to produce a revised and extended Commission Communication. Further clarification by the Court would also be welcome although this is necessarily dependent on dispute and instruction or reference. A more effective solution may be for the new post-Lamfallussy financial committee structure to be used to consider specific problems of derogation (general good) and host country control within each of the main banking, securities and insurance sectors. While it may not be possible to agree every condition and eventuality, the main Committees may be able to agree a more substantial set of common rules and principles governing the operation of the general good and the scope of host country authority. The Committee of European Banking Supervisors (CEBS) and the European Securities Regulatory Committee (ESRC), in particular, could consult on the scope of each Member State's understanding of their entitlements to impose additional obligations in the interests of the general good and compare the specific regulatory obligations maintained. A more substantial set of draft guidelines and permitted restrictions could then be produced for Commission and market comment. The effect would be to attempt to deal with the problem of derogation scope through the production of agreed harmonized rules on permitted restrictions with further guidance or, at least, some interpretative principles to assist determine the validity of future exceptions. It may also be possible to arrange (or manufacture) an appropriate reference to the Court to comment on the accuracy and validity of the guidance provided.[244]

One of the continuing concerns that arises within this emerging jurisprudence would appear to be a lack of a clear understanding of the nature and operation of financial markets and financial services. This is of particular concern in the judgements of some of the Advocates General. It could, of course, be argued that market stability and prudential issues are dealt with separately under the secondary programme measures adopted although the Court's jurisprudence is still relevant to the extent that particular activities either fall outside the directives agreed or within the scope of the recognized general good and then have to be determined in terms of prohibition and

[224] Chs 7 and 8.

derogation. This financial non-sophistication has possibly to be expected in a unitary court system without any separate commercial or mercantile jurisdiction. The result must nevertheless be of some concern.

The main residual difficulty that arises is then again one of policy predictability and legal certainty. In advising financial institutions on regulatory and private client (as well as conduct of business) matters, the scope of application of the provisions subject to mutual recognition under the financial directives will initially have to be specified. This may not be easy in all cases. Where particular requirements or activities are considered not to fall within the scope of the secondary programme, a further examination will then have to be made to determine whether particular provisions may fall within the extended scope of *Gebhard* or *Säger* and then whether they may (or may not) be justified under *Gebhard* or *Gouda*. The apparent willingness of the Court to consider underlying, if not wholly separate, policy issues and to extend the scope of possible derogation whenever this may considered necessary or appropriate must be considered to create considerable uncertainty at the limits of judicial dicta and the judicial function.

The substantial, continuing and efficient development of an integrated financial services market place within Europe requires that a clear and consistent set of legal rights, obligations and remedies is applied in all cases. This is essential both with regard to the scope of permitted market access to be provided as well as the proper and proportionate degree of regulatory control or restriction to be maintained. While a substantial secondary programme has been constructed and an emerging body of supporting jurisprudence produced, a number of significant difficulties continue to arise both with regard to the content and application of relevant legislative rules and judicial principles as well as particular programme rights and duties. It must be accepted that all of this will continue to act as a significant barrier to ongoing reliance and enforcement and the larger development of a fully integrated financial market place. Residual legal uncertainty in the financial area specifically may then further obstruct the more general objectives and successes of European integration in all other trade, industrial and commercial areas.

PART FOUR

Programme Construction

5

*European Banking and Financial Law—Programme Content, Structure, and Completion**

At the same time as the Court has attempted to develop its more general policy of free movement in the areas of goods, services and establishment (as well as workers and capital), the Commission has been working on the construction of necessary secondary legislative programmes in each of the areas of activity (and sub-activity) set out in the original General Programmes adopted under the Treaty.[1] The objective was to give effect to all of the main provisions necessary to secure the effective operation of the underlying Treaty rights created in each trade, industrial and commercial sector. The General Programmes included specific reference to banking and insurance.

The directives to be adopted under the General Programmes were either intended to give effect directly to the underlying rights of establishment or free provision of services or to establish common provisions that would allow these rights to be exercised in practice. They were accordingly either access or compliance (control) driven or both. Where standards were set, this was initially on an assumed full harmonization basis to the extent that common obligations were to be imposed with regard to all areas of compliance. Pre-compliance with these standards would then entitle the firm to exercise the particular right of establishment or services provided for.

While it had originally been understood that some form of prior harmonization or pre-compliance would only be required in the insurance area, it was subsequently realized that this would also be necessary for banks. The importance of securities markets as independent sectors would be recognized subsequently. The difficulty that arose in connection with each specific financial sector area, however, was that no further guidance was provided in the Treaty with regard to the content and structure of the

* An earlier version of this chapter was reproduced in GA Walker 'European Financial Programme: Content, Structure and Completion' [2004] EBLR 305.

[1] General Programme for the abolition of restrictions on freedom of establishment (OJ No 2 15 Jan 1962, 36/62); and General Programme for the abolition of restrictions on freedom to provide services (OJ No 2 15 Jan 1962, 36/62). See also Commission *Completing the Internal Market—White Paper from the Commission to the European Council (Milan 18–29 June 1985)*, COM(85) 310 final (14 June 1985).

harmonization or pre-compliance to be secured. It was simply assumed that the relevant requirements in each area could and would be harmonized. Once a firm complied with the relevant requirements, it would be entitled to market access on the basis of the underlying Treaty rights of establishment or services provided.

A basic policy vacuum accordingly existed in the Treaty with regard to the content of the new control regimes to be set up in each industrial, commercial and financial sector. It was simply assumed that some from of pre-harmonization and pre-compliance could be agreed in each case. The issue was left to Commission and Council expert and working groups to resolve. The earlier full harmonization regime initially adopted was subsequently replaced by a new mutual recognition based approach developed during the 1980s under which market access would become conditional upon compliance with a more narrowly defined set of common minimum standards in particular core areas of activity. The original policy vacuum referred to had, however, by then become even more acute with the move from full common to selected minimum harmonization. The task for the Commission has subsequently been to resolve the basic access and control conflict that has arisen within the revised policy framework adopted.

The construction of a new banking and financial programme has since proceeded through the adoption of a number of particular legislative measures in each of the main financial sector areas. While these have generally consisted of directives, this has also included some recommendations and other measures such as interpretative communications.[2] The objective of these has generally been to give effect to the underlying rights of establishment and services provided for under the Treaty at the same time as begin to build appropriate supporting supervisory and regulatory systems across Europe.[3] Some substantial progress has been possible in a number of areas. Difficulties have nevertheless arisen in others while adoption and implementation has been disappointing in many cases.

A number of further measures have since been announced more recently to attempt to complete this process of secondary programme construction. This work has, in particular, been undertaken as part of the Commission's larger Action Plan initiative to complete the Single Market which was originally announced at the Amsterdam European Council Summit in 1997.[4] This more general completion initiative includes a financial services specific

[2] Commission Interpretative Communication, Freedom to provide services and the interests of the general good in the Second Banking Directive (97/C 219/04). Ch 4 (n 2) and section B. On the legal effects of interpretative communications, *French Republic v Commission of the European Communities* [1997] ECR I-1627. See Ch 4 (nn 93 and 94).

[3] Commission *Completing the Internal Market—White Paper from the Commission to the European Council* (n 1) paras 101–7.

[4] Communication of the Commission to the European Council *Action Plan for the Single Market* CSE (97) 1 final) of 4 June 1997.

component which makes provision for the adoption of a number of amending measures and new directives in certain key areas. A series of capital market specific recommendations were also issued under the Lamfalussy Committee Report in February 1991.[5] The purpose of each of these efforts was to attempt to complete the original Single Market programme and with it to realize the full potential economic and related benefits that should follow. Whether this could be achieved and within which over all time frame was nevertheless unclear.

The purpose of this chapter is to consider the issues of programme construction, programme structure and programme completion and to assess the most recent work undertaken by the Commission in the banking and financial area. The nature of the original integration policy adopted is noted and subsequent changes considered. The basic structure of the banking and financial programme is reviewed and recent consolidation work referred to. The various components of the more general completion programme subsequently developed are examined in further detail. This includes the background to the Financial Services Action Plan and its basic structure and content as well as the later implementation progress achieved to date. The separate parallel work undertaken in connection with capital markets is noted. Provisional observations are made with regard to the importance and value of this work within the larger European single market initiative.

A. PROGRAMME AND INTEGRATION POLICY

In attempting to understand the nature of the current integration policy applied by the Commission, the historical development of the main approaches adopted may be reconsidered in terms of the two main stages involved. These consist of a full harmonization and a new mutual recognition based approach with an interim framework policy also having to be considered in the financial area. A number of sub-processes or functions can also be identified within each integration phase.

The original approach adopted by the Commission was based on the negotiation of a full set of common standards in each particular area of trade or service activity. Under this full harmonization approach, market integration was to be achieved through the development of agreed common standards in all major areas, pre-compliance with the relevant requirements imposed and then the subsequent withdrawal of corresponding national prohibitions or restrictions on sale, establishment or service provision. Full harmonization accordingly involved common standards, pre-compliance

[5] Committee of Wise Men *Final Report on the Regulation of European Securities Markets* (15 February 2001). See section D (4).

and consequent regulatory withdrawal. Regulatory withdrawal would generally operate through some form of exemption system.[6]

The problem that arose with this approach was that it became difficult from an early stage to agree common standards in all detailed technical areas. With this, countries also became increasingly concerned about the need to maintain protective measures either on the basis of consumer protection or on competition grounds. Substantial delays accordingly arose with the integration timetables set out in the original General Programmes with the result that little progress had been possible in many areas by the end of the transitional period on 31 December 1969.

The particular difficulty that arose in the banking area was that it was initially unclear whether some degree of harmonization (or pre-harmonization) was necessary before the rights of establishment and services conferred under the Treaty could be exercised and, if so, whether it would be possible to agree all of the relevant terms within a single measure. Work in this area was initially carried out through the establishment of an advisory or working group in 1966 and then a more formal Committee of Experts in 1968. As a result of the advice provided by the first working group, it was decided that some harmonization would be required although the Commission would separately produce a draft free movement directive which was adopted in 1973.[7]

Following this preparatory work, the Commission's separate Committee of Experts produced a first draft banking measure on a German–Dutch model in 1972.[8] This was necessary in light of the generally underdeveloped nature of the French laws at that time and unnecessary institutional complexity within the Italian system. A first draft of a first fully consolidated banking directive was produced in July 1972[9] although its consider-

[6] See, eg, preamble 10 of First Council Directive 77/780/EEC on the coordination of laws, regulations and administrative provisions relating to the taking up and pursuit of the business of credit institutions of 12 Dec 1997 (OJ L 322 12 Dec 1997, 30). See also Ch 6, section E (4) and Ch 7, section E (5)

[7] Council Directive 73/183/EEC of 28 June 1973 on the abolition of restrictions on freedom of establishment and freedom to provide services in respect of the self-employed activities of banks and other financial institutions. See further (n 23).

[8] Interview with Paolo Clarotti, former Head of Commission Directorate on Bank, Insurance Institutions and Company Law part of General Directorate, Domestic Markets and Harmonization of Law (XIV).

[9] An initial group of national experts had been asked to advise the Commission on whether measures would have to be harmonized within the banking area between the then six original Member States and on the content of any harmzonized provisions required. The Working Group met between 1966 and 1968. The group consisted of Albert Dondelinger (Luxembourg), Professor Antionne Cavalda (France), Professor Leon Dabin (Belgium), Guido Ruta (Italy), Nachenius de Bgil (the Netherlands) and Professor Ulricht Klug (Germany). The objective was to compare the existing national laws and consider whether any material differences existed and possible grounds of harmonization. The Working Group, in particular, examined licensing, solvency, liquidity, risk concentration and legal form issues (n 8). The group reported at the end of 1967 and beginning of 1968. Interview with Paolo Clarotti.

ation could not proceed further with the accession of the United Kingdom, Ireland and Denmark in 1973.[10] Continuing resistance by France and Italy and the opposition of the new Member States including, in particular, the United Kingdom meant that the 1972 proposal could not proceed further.

The Working Group was replaced by a more formal Committee of Experts which met between the second half of 1969 until the first half of 1971. While the earlier Working Group had only operated on an individual and *ad hoc* basis, its work was taken forward by the more formally constituted Committee of Experts. Members included Albert Dondelinger (Luxembourg), Guido Ruta (Italy) who was replaced by Guisseppe de Vecchie (Italy), Huib Muller (the Netherlands), Professor Jean Lebrun (Belgium) and a number of representatives from France and Germany. The purpose of the Committee of Experts was to make recommendations on the production of a set of harmonized laws for the then existing Member States.

The Committee produced in July 1972 a 'Draft Directive for the coordination of the legal and administrative provisions for the taking up and exercise of the 'independent operator' activities of credit institutions' (XIV/508/72-D, Orig, D). The draft 1972 Directive contained a comprehensive set of measures for the supervision and regulation of credit institutions. The draft consisted of 9 Parts and 41 articles. These included specific provision with regard to definition and lists (Art 1), authorization procedure (Art 2), own funds (Art 3), legal form (Art 4), persons in charge (Arts 5 and 6), domestic, foreign and several branches (Arts 7, 8 and 9), geographical and practical sphere (Arts 10, 11 and 12), mergers and amalgamations (Art 13), own funds (Art 140), reference data for coefficients (Art 15), scale of coefficients (Art 16), coefficients and foreign branches (Art 17), deposit protection (Art 18), credit declarations (Art 19), communication of information (Art 20), monthly and annual returns and accounts (Art 21), secrecy (Art 22), protection of names (Art 23), withdrawal as regards head office (Art 24), consequences of withdrawal (Art 25), closing of branches (Art 26), prohibition on the provision of services (Art 27), authorization of branches of third country institutions (Arts 28, 29, 30, 31 and 32), transitional measures (Arts 33, 34, 35 and 26) and general and final provisions (Arts 37, 38, 39, 40 and 41).

[10] The July 1972 draft was never formally adopted by the Commission. See, eg, 'The European Commission have given up the attempt to coordinate "bank legislation" in the "nine" by a single all-inclusive directive, in view of the impossibility of harmonising the positions of the old and new Member States,' *Europe* (Thursday 10 Jan 1974) 9. Under the consultation procedures in place during the second half of 1972 concerning accession countries, the UK, Denmark and Ireland were included within the negotiations which effectively extended the 1969 Committee to nine. In light of the basic differences of opinion that had arisen between the 'old' and 'new' Member States especially with regard to the absence of any system of 'prior agreement' (authorization), in particular, in the UK and Denmark, no compromise was seen as possible as this affected the basic principles on which the legislation had been drafted. Rather than abandon the establishment of uniform provisions, the Commission would adopt a progressive approach to harmonization under which several separate directives would be adopted. A series of ad hoc measures would then be adopted for different aspects and different types of credit institution with priority being given to harmonization in the least difficult areas. It was expected that the UK would, in particular, move closer to the continental approaches adopted over time. Ibid.

The difficulty of dealing with the non-statutory regime operating in the UK had been commented on separately in the press. It was reported that the Bank of England had been anxious to avoid the inflexibility that could result through legislation and detract from London's standing as an international financial centre. See generally A Rowley 'EEC's laws seen as danger to City banks,' *The Times* (6 June 1973) 24, col E; I Morison 'EEC entry "may pose a threat to City banking"', *The Times* (25 Oct 1972) 23, col H; G Bell 'How will the City fare in Europe?', *The Times* (25 Oct 1972), 25, col D; F Vogl 'Germany sees City as hub of EEC banking,' *The Times* (5 May 1972) 1, col H; I Morison 'The City may have to swallow its pride,' *The Times* (10 May 1972) 25, col A. The Bank nevertheless accepted that its discretionary system of banking controls would have to be changed. See, for example, 'European law

As a partial alternative to this attempted full harmonization within the banking area, the Commission adopted a new framework approach.[11] This involved identifying a number of core regulatory areas within the banking area and developing separate directives in respect to each. As a result of this change in approach, some of the main outline provisions set out in the original 1972 draft were retained within the proposal for the 'First Banking Directive' in 1974 which would later be adopted in 1977.[12] The initial standards contained in the proposal for the First Banking Directive included minimum own funds, the number and suitability of directors, controllers,

problem for the Bank of England,' *The Times* (8 Jan 1972) 24, col D. See also, I Morison 'Regulating banking—The wink and a nod may not be enough,' *The Times* (4 Oct 1972) 19, col A.

The Bank would subsequently decide that a formal regulatory system was appropriate to allow it to continue effectively to supervise the large number of foreign banks that had been established in London. The benefits of this would then outweigh the perceived disadvantages of losing its earlier non-statutory and informal ('moral suasion') based approach to bank supervision. Its original objection to a statutory based regulatory system would then be reversed. GA Walker *International Banking Regulation—Law, Policy and Practice* (Kluwer Law International London 2001), Ch 1, section 4. See also, eg, D Blake 'Government to bring in new code for control of banking,' *The Times* (30 Oct 1975) 19, col A; and 'Supervisory role vital, Bank Governor says,' *The Times* (29 Nov 1975) 19, col D.

[11] A more general directive to remove discrimination in regulatory banking practices was announced by Monsieur Françoise Treppaniers at a Banking Conference in London on 16 January 1974. This preliminary 'umbrella' directive would include basic provisions concerning conditions under which licenses were issued, minimum levels of liquidity, risk and solvency, competition, accounting disclosure requirements, winding-up, banking operations and third country arrangements. Monsieur Treppaniers was speaking on behalf of Monsieur Henri Simonet, Vice-President of the European Commission for Taxation, Financial Institutions and Company Law. The Commission had to reconsider its approach to the whole problem of harmonising banking rules in the Communities and had attempted to separate from the generality of the subject various aspects which would be treated separately. See, eg, 'EEC wants rules on banking harmonized,' *The Times* (16 Jan 1974) 16, col 3. Monsieur Henri Simonet, Vice-President of the European Commission, had expressed the hope in June 1973 that agreement would eventually be reached on the harmonization of European banking controls. 'Banking harmonization,' *The Times* (30 June 1973) 19, col 6.

Robin Hutton, the new Director of Banking, Insurance and Financial Institutions in the Commission, would subsequently announce that a more flexible approach to the regulation of European banking was required. The comprehensive and detailed rules put forward by the Commission as part of the July 1972 draft Directive had formed an 'amalgam of the national systems of control in the original Six but owed most to Germany'. Robin Hutton added that they had run into difficulties with all of the national government negotiators and were acceptable to none of the Member States at that time. The Commission was accordingly working on a new approach to the problem of coordination of regulatory systems across Europe. It was added that it should be possible to isolate a number of crucial points and harmonize them following discussions with central banks and other authorities and with the cooperation and advice of the banks themselves. With regard to implementation, Mr Hutton did not support the creation of a central European authority but would leave power where it should be in the hands of national regulatory authorities. See also M Blanden '"Last chance" to alter EEC banking rules,' *Financial Times* (21 Nov 1973).

[12] First Council Directive 77/780/EEC on the coordination of laws, regulations and administrative provisions relating to the taking up and pursuit of the business of credit institutions of 12 Dec 1997 (nn 6 and 24).

conditions for withdrawal of license, reciprocity and information exchange. The First Banking Directive also anticipated passport rights, home country control and transitional minimum harmonization.

One of the particular problems that had arisen by the early 1970s was that new financial ratios (especially with regard to capital adequacy) had to be developed with the changes that had taken place in banking market structure and practice. In light of the complexity of the issue and underdeveloped nature of each of the national systems at that time, it was decided to undertake a data collection and examination exercise through the Banking Advisory Committee (BAC) which was set up under the Directive.[13] The BAC was accordingly instructed to monitor financial ratios and attempt to develop common standards subsequently which may be acceptable in all national territories.

The new framework approach that was adopted by the Commission accordingly allowed some initial success to be achieved, in particular, with the agreement on the First Banking Directive while related financial ratios were developed through the BAC. The underlying policy was, however, still essentially harmonization determined. The system was then still common standards, pre-compliance and regulatory withdrawal based.[14] The only difference was that harmonization would now be effected through a series of separate measures rather than a single directive.

The underlying integration policy adopted would then be fundamentally changed with the subsequent move to mutual recognition. Following the further delays that had arisen by the early 1980s with the completion of the original Common Market as provided for under the Treaty of Rome, the decision was taken to try to re-launch the integration process with the adoption of a new approach based on the 'mutual recognition' of national laws and regulations. This was derived (although only indirectly) from the

[13] The BAC is distinct from the European Contact Group (*Groupe de Contact*) which had been set up in 1972 to facilitate operational contact and cooperation between national supervisory authorities in the banking field (n 24). The Contact Group had been established on the recommendation of Albert Dondelinger and Huib Muller with the Secretariat being provided by the Bank of England (nn 9 and 24). On revised committee structure, Ch 1 (n 55) and Ch 2 (n 111).

[14] The longer term objective to be attained was to make it possible to exempt, in so far as possible, credit institutions that had already set up a network of branches throughout the Community from the supervision of each of the separate host countries involved while 'making them subject to centralized supervision in the country of origin alone.' Commission, Proposal for a Council Directive on the coordination of laws, regulations and administrative provisions governing the commencement and carrying on of the business of credit institutions, COM(74) 20 10 final (10 Dec 1974), para 4. The seventh recital to the proposal for the First Banking Directive also stated that the final objective of coordination was to introduce a system whereby branches of an undertaking established in a Member State would operate throughout the Community subject to no separate authorization requirement. This would be based on a parallel authorization procedure consisting of uniform requirements, Preamble 5. For discussion, Ch 6, section D (3)

decision of the European Court of Justice in *Cassis de Dijon* in 1979.[15] The principle of mutual recognition would then be developed more fully in the Commission's 1985 White Paper on the *Completion of the Internal Market.*[16]

Mutual recognition is based on the identification of a number of core aspects of control within which certain minimum common standards are established.[17] In the banking and financial area, in particular, the additional principle of home country control also allows for supervisory allocation or division of key functions between the home and host territories.[18] Mutual recognition then requires each set of national authorities to recognize the validity of the license provided by the home country. This includes both the authenticity and sufficiency of the original license and its operational effectiveness within the jurisdiction of the host territory.[19]

The difference between mutual recognition and full harmonization is that mutual recognition is not based on the establishment of a complete set of common standards but only a minimum level of protection on selected pre-agreed issues. In the financial area, pre-compliance is also not sufficient by itself as with full harmonization. Rather continuing compliance is secured through the operation of the supervisory allocation secured under home country control. Continuing rather than prior compliance is also then effected.

The two integration approaches are accordingly different in terms of standards and compliance.[20] Both nevertheless provide for regulatory with-

[15] Case 120/78 *Rewe-Zentrale AG v Bundesmonopolverwaltung für Branntwein* [1979] ECR 649 [1979] 3 CMLR 494. See also Commission Communication on its interpretation of the decision. OJ No C256, 3.10.80, 2. This had followed an earlier communication that had been sent to the Parliament, the Council and the Member States. COM(1980) 30 DEF, 24 Jan 80. Ch 3, section C (3) and (nn 81 and 83 and 85) and Ch 6, section C (1).

[16] Commission, *Completing the Internal Market—White Paper from the Commission to the European Council*, COM(85) 310 final (n 1). Ch 6, section C (2).

[17] Commission, White Paper (n 1), paras 77–80.

[18] Commission, White Paper (n 1), para 103. Ch 6, section D(3). See also Eva Lomnicka 'The Home Country Control Principle in the Financial Services Directive and the Case Law' Ch 11 in Mads Andenas and Wulf-Henning Roth *Services and Free Movement in EU Law* (OUP 2002). For discussion of more general trends in European financial integration, Jan H Dalhuisen 'Financial Liberalization and Re-regulation' Ch 10 in Andenas and Roth.

[19] The scope of mutual recognition extends to the home license and continuing supervision exercised by the home authorities. This corrects the regulatory and operational gaps left under the scope of minimum harmonization set up under the main financial directives.

This new mutual recognition based approach was then used to develop a series of directives in place of the original comprehensive 1972 draft. An original single measure approach was accordingly replaced by a framework or progressive system although this still assumed full harmonization of all relevant requirements. This would, in turn, be replaced by mutual recognition which involves the identification of certain core areas in which minimum standards could be agreed. The validity of each national license would then be recognized on the basis of the minimum protection provided in these areas rather than the full set of underlying common standards agreed. For further discussion (n 152) and Ch 6, sections (C) and (D).

[20] The difficulty that arises with regard to assumed equivalence and the absence of any central implementation or continuing systems review is considered further separately. Ch 6, sections (C) and (D); Ch 7, section (D) (3); and Ch 8, sections (B), (C), and (D).

drawal principally through exemption from the application of the host regulatory requirements and, in particular, the local core prohibition on the (unauthorized) conduct of the particular financial activity concerned. The host requirements are accordingly relaxed (disapplied) in each case and the validity and scope of the license (and authorization) provided by the home country recognized and extended into the local or host territory.

Full and framework harmonization did include an element of mutual recognition to a certain extent. The difference is that the recognition now operates on the basis of reciprocal compliance with agreed minimum standards in certain pre-defined areas rather than with compliance with a full of range of pre-set common standards. In the banking and financial area, this also operates on continuing rather than simple initial market entry basis.

B. PROGRAMME STRUCTURE

In applying this new mutual recognition based integration approach in the banking and financial area, a number of measures have been adopted to attempt to create a full set of relevant access rights. The effect of each of these is to translate the underlying Treaty obligations into regulatory requirements that can be transposed into national law.[21]

The most important of these measures in the banking area was the Second Banking Directive (SBD).[22] This followed an earlier 1973 free movement measure[23] and the 1977 First Banking Directive

[21] For comment on the importance and nature of directives in giving effect to Treaty rights, see dicta of the European Court of Justice in *French Republic v Commission of the European Community* [1997] ECR I-1627 (n 2) and Ch 4 (nn 93 and 94).

[22] Second Council Directive 89/646/EEC on the coordination of laws, regulations and administrative provisions relating to the taking up and pursuit of the business of credit institutions of 15 Dec 1998 (OJ L 386, 30 Dec 89, 1). The Second Banking Directive (SBD) came into effect on 31 Dec 1992. It defined the activities that would be covered by the final banking programme (including the list of permitted activities set out in the Annex to the Directive). It provided for the right of branch establishment and free provision of services across Europe for defined institutions (Art 18(1)), set up a notification procedure (following the outline provisions set out in the earlier 1972 Draft Directive), contained express provision for the general good (Arts 19(4), 21(5) and relevant Preambles) and introduced more sophisticated reciprocity provisions (Arts 8 and 9 replacing Art 9 of the FBD). The Directive contained additional provisions with regard to initial capital, suitability of managers and controllers, restrictions on investments, further provisions with regard to inspections and verifications and disciplinary measures.

[23] Council Directive 73/183/EEC of 28 June 1973 on the abolition of restrictions on freedom of establishment and freedom to provide services in respect of the self-employed activities of banks and other financial institutions (n 7). The Directive had originally been proposed in 1964 although it was not possible to secure agreement on its scope of application until 1973. The Directive only applied with regard to the services listed in Annex I and included banks, savings and loan undertakings, syndicates, intermediaries and certain other stock-

(FBD)[24] which set out a number of framework provisions for subsequent development.

These measures were supported by the 1989 Own Funds Directive (OFD) and the Solvency Ratio Directive (SRD) which created a basic system of credit risk capital cover[25] and a subsequent 1992 Large Exposures

exchanges, financial consultants, clearing houses and trust companies although brokers (including money and stock-brokers) were excluded. The objective was to remove discrimination against incoming firms. The Directive was accordingly based on the principle of national treatment. The Directive was superseded by the decisions in *van Binsbergen* and *Reyners* in which the European Court held that the underlying Treaty provisions were of direct effect from the end of the transitional period. Case 33/74 *Van Binsbergen v Bestuur van de Bedrijfsvereniging voor de Metaalnijverheid* [1974] ECR 1299; and *Reyners v Belgium State* Case 2/74 [1974] ECR 631. Ch 3, section D.

[24] First Council Directive 77/780/EEC on the coordination of laws, regulations and administrative provisions relating to the taking up and pursuit of the business of credit institutions of 12 Dec 1977 (nn 6 and 12). The FBD was intended to develop initial harmonization in certain key areas as well as establish a framework that could be developed through further measures subsequently. The Directive contained specific measures with regard to authorization, host country licensing, banking names, capital measures, supervisory cooperation, withdrawal of authorization and reciprocity. The Directive did not impose any specific financial requirements but provided for the establishment of a number of observation ratios that would be monitored over time. These would later be developed into the capital requirements imposed under the Own Funds Directive and Solvency Ratio Directive (n 25). The Commission considered that one of the most important components was the establishment of the Banking Advisory Committee (BAC). The BAC was set up to assist the Commission in ensuring the proper implementation of the Directive and Council Directive 73/183 (n 23) insofar as it related to credit institutions and carried out the specific tasks prescribed by the First Banking Directive as well as generally assist the Commission in the preparation of new proposals to the Council concerning the further coordination of relevant requirements especially with regard to capital adequacy (Art 11). The BAC was distinct from the Contact Group (*Groupe de Group*) which had been set up in 1972 as a cooperation forum to consider issues that arose with regard to the cross-border supervision of individual banks (n 13).

[25] Council Directive 89/299/EEC on the own funds of credit institutions of 17 April 1989 (OJ L 124, 5 May 1989, p 16) as amended by Directive 91/633/EEC of 3 Dec 1991 (OJ L 339, 11 Dec 1991, 33) and Directive 92/16/EEC of 16 Mar 1992 (OJ L 75, 21 Mar 1992, 48); and Council Directive 89/647/EEC on a solvency ratio for credit institutions of 18 Dec 1989 (OJ L 386, 30 Dec 1989, 14) as amended by Directive 91/31/EEC (OJ L 17, 23 Jan 1991, 20).

The purpose of the Own Funds Directive was to establish certain common standards for the calculation of the own funds (capital) of credit institutions that would be available to ensure the continuity of credit institutions and to protect savings. Preamble 1. The Directive listed a number of items (Art 2 (paras (1)–(8)) and certain deductions (paras (9)–(13)). The capital items generally consisted of paid up capital, reserves and retained profits, revaluation reserves, general funds and value adjustments as well as other items that are freely available to the institution to cover normal banking risks and securities of indeterminate duration subject to certain conditions. Long-term (5 year) subordinated debt was also included. Relevant deductions were set out in Art 6 which secured the same effect as the Basel Committee's requirements in its 1988 Capital Accord. This generally imposed an 8 per cent minimum capital ratio requirement with tier 1 (primary capital) making up 50 per cent of the total (4 per cent) and subordinated debt consisting of up to 50 per cent of tier 2 (secondary) capital (2 per cent in total). Basel Committee, 'International convergence of capital measurement and capital standards' (July 1988) as amended. For discussion and comment, GA Walker *International Banking Regulation—Law, Policy and Practice* (n 10), Capital Postscript.

The Solvency Ratio Directive provided for the calculation of a total risk-adjusted asset

Directive which introduced formal concentration limits.[26] Various other more ancillary measures including a Deposit Guarantee Directive[27] and a Winding-up proposal[28] were also adopted. The main measures in the banking area were then drawn together and restated in a Consolidated Banking Directive in May 2000.[29]

The general effect of these measures was to give effect to the underlying Treaty rights of establishment and cross-border provision of services.[30] These operated within a new general regulatory framework defined in terms of mutual recognition, minimum harmonization and home country control. The underlying objective was to provide for both full market access at the same time as secure proper market control. The supporting control system was generally based on a number of separate regulatory and supervisory provisions. The regulatory requirements imposed principally consist of initial authorization[31] and continuing compliance.[32] These obligations are supplemented by a number of further basic supervisory provisions which are essentially concerned with the monitoring and oversight of credit

figure of a bank (including off-balance sheet items) and imposed the 8 per cent minimum requirement. Risk adjustment generally operated by assigning asset items (loans) to risk buckets (classifications) which were then totalled to produce the aggregate figure. Four risk buckets were used (0 per cent, 20 per cent, 50 per cent and 100 per cent) depending on the perceived credit standing of the borrower (counterparty) within the loan book. These generally provided for OECD countries and central banks borrowing in their own currency (0 per cent) and other currencies (10 per cent or 20 per cent), secured lending (50 per cent) and all other lending (100 per cent). A conversion process was applied with regard to off-balance sheet items to provide on-balance sheet equivalent values which were then subject to the counterparty risk ratios depending upon the particular borrower involved.

The earlier European capital rules set out in the OFD and SRD will be replaced by the Capital Requirements Directive (CRD) which implements the new Basel II capital framework within Europe. Capital Requirements Directive COM(2004) 486 final of 14 July 2004. Walker, Capital Postscript.

26 Concentration limits for credit institutions were introduced under Council Directive 92/121/EEC on the monitoring and control of large exposures of credit institutions of 21 Dec 1992 (OJ L 29, 5 Feb 1993, 1) following an earlier Commission Recommendation 87/62/EEC (OJ L 33, 4 Feb 1987, 10).

27 (n 34).

28 The Winding-up proposal was subsequently adopted in 2001. Directive on the Winding-up and Liquidation of Banks 2001/24/EC adopted 4 Apr 2001. See also Directive on the Reorganization and Winding-up of Insurance Undertakings 2001/17/EC adopted 19 Mar 2001. Section D (5) and (n 144).

29 Directive 2000/12/EC May 2000 relating to the taking up and pursuit of the business of credit institutions (BCD). Section C and (n 65).

30 BCD, Art 18 (formerly SBD, Art 18(1)). (n 22).

31 The initial market entry or authorization is generally based on a minimum capital requirement (Art 5(1)), management and shareholder suitability (Arts 6(1) and 7(2)) and internal controls (Arts 8 and 17).

32 Continuing regulatory compliance includes capital adequacy (under the Own Funds and Solvency Ratio Directives) (BCD, Arts 34–47) and large exposures (Arts 48–50), suitability of controllers (Arts 7 and 16), restrictions on commercial holdings (Art 51), administrative and internal controls (Art 17) and separate requirements on bank and branch disclosure. Compliance is secured through various supervisory procedures imposed (n 33).

institutions to ensure, in particular, that they comply with the basic regulatory obligations imposed.[33] Market exit (as opposed to entry) is partly dealt with through the Deposit Guarantee Directive[34] (liability resolution) and the Winding-Up Directive[35] (asset realization). These essential regulatory and supervisory measures are supported by further specific transactional requirements such as with regard to bank charges and guarantees, consumer protection and payment and settlement.[36]

In addition to these measures, directives have been adopted in the securities and investment services area. The Investment Services Directive (ISD) created an equivalent set of rights for investment firms as credit institutions in 1993.[37] This was supported by the Capital Adequacy Directive (CAD) which set out the minimum capital requirements to be applied to banks and investment firms in respect of securities related market (or position) risk as well as foreign exchange and operational and commodity risks.[38] Following the identification of a number of difficulties with the basic provisions contained in the ISD, a series of papers were issued in connection with its reform which eventually led to the adoption of the Markets in Financial Instruments Directive 2004/39/EC (MIFID) in 2004.[39]

[33] The supervisory framework set up is generally based on consolidated supervision (Arts 52–56), consultation and cooperation between authorities (Art 28), information exchange (Art 30), inspections and verifications (Art 29) and disciplinary measures (Art 32).

[34] Directive 94/19 of 30 May 1994 on deposit guarantee schemes (OJ 1994, L135/5). This followed an earlier Commission Recommendation 87/63 concerning the introduction of deposit guarantee schemes in the Community of 22 Dec 1986 (OJL33/87). For comment, R Dale 'Deposit Insurance: Policy Clash over EC and US Reforms' Financial Markets Group, June 1993. The difficulty that arose in the European Community with regard to protection schemes was in determining whether they should operate on a home or host state basis in respect of deposits made in another country. See, eg, D Schoenmaker 'Home Country Deposit Insurance' Financial Markets Group, June 1992; and Schoenmaker 'A Note on the Proposal for a Council Directive on Deposit Guarantee Schemes' Financial Markets Group, August 1992; and J Le Brun 'The Directive on the Protection of Depositors,' Ch 16 of G Ferrarini (ed) *Prudential Regulation of Banks and Securities Firms* (1995). For judicial discussion, Ch 4, section D (1) and (3).

[35] (n 28).

[36] Section D (5).

[37] Council Directive 93/22/EEC on investment services in the securities field of 10 May 1993 (OJ L 141, 11 May 1993, 27). For comment, E Lomnicka 'The Internal Market and Investment Services,' ch 4 in M Andenas and S Kenyon-Slade (eds) *EC Financial Market Regulation and Company Law* (1992). See also, Niamh Moloney *EC Securities Regulation* (OUP Oxford 2002).

[38] Council Directive 93/6/EEC on the capital adequacy of investment firms and credit institutions of 15 March 1993 (OJ L 141, 11.6.1993, 1 as amended). When a group of financial companies does not include a credit institution, the definition of financial holding company in the Consolidated Supervision Directive (n 49) was amended to include any financial institution the subsidiaries of which are either exclusively or mainly investment firms or other financial institutions at least one of which is an investment firm. (Art 7(3)). Under Art 7(2), the capital adequacy and large exposures requirements imposed by Arts 4 and 5 of the Directive were to be applied on a consolidated basis.

[39] The Commission issued an initial Communication on Upgrading the Investment Services

A number of related provisions have also been adopted with regard to stock exchange listing and public promotions. National conditions with regard to listing were established under the 1979 Admission to Listing Directive, the 1980 Listings Particulars Directive and 1982 Interim Reports

Directive on 16 Nov 2000. This was generally designed to extend the scope of the single passport, in particular, through the removal of continuing disparities with regard to national conduct of business rules as well as to extend the regulatory framework to include new alternative trading systems. The main difficulty that arose was with regard to the perceived dilution of the basic principle of home country control through an extended application of the general good especially with regard to conduct of business rules under Art 11. The effect of this had been to over-regulate many areas of inter-professional and retail business. The Commission issued a separate Communication on 16 Nov 2000 on the application of conduct of business rules to investment firms. The objective of the Communication was to consider whether the general principles set out in Art 11 of the ISD were being respected and whether the FESCO (Forum of European Securities Commissions') definition of professional investor may be more appropriate.

Wide variations had separately arisen with regard to the implementation of core service definitions and the designation of 'regulated markets'. Unprecedented growth in the securities area had rendered many of the basic provisions in the ISD obsolete. The creation of new trading platforms as well as associated electronic clearing and settlements systems as part of a larger development of market-based (capital market) financing had required a re-examination of the basic provisions set out in the ISD. Section D (4). Another key deficiency identified by the Commission was the absence of any mechanism for harmonising national implementation which was subsequently considered by the Committee of Wise Men under Alexandre Lamfalussy. Section D (4) and (nn 129, 138 and 139).

The purpose of the MIFID was to correct such deficiencies but also allow European capital markets to develop further over time in response to continuing changes in market structure and practice. The Directive was adopted on 21 Apr 2004 (OJ 145–30 Apr 2004–1, 44). This creates an effective single passport for investment firms which will allow them to operate throughout the EU on the basis of home country authorization and home country control (IP/04/546). Firms are to be able to process client orders outside regulated exchanges which is not currently possible in all Member States. A high level of protection is to be made available to all investors whenever they use an investment firm located in any territory within the EU. A regulatory framework is set up for the organized execution of investor transactions by exchanges, other trading platforms and investment firms.

The original proposal had been put forward by the Commission in November 2002 and amended by the European Parliament in September 2003. The text was further amended by the Council and negotiations conducted between the Parliament, the Council and the Commission before a second reading in Parliament. The Directive is to be implemented within two years of its Official Journal publication on 30 April 2004.

The draft Directive (ISD II) was originally referred to as the 'Directive on Investment Services and Regulated Markets' (CON (2002) final, 2002/0269 (COD)) although this was subsequently shortened to the Directive on Markets in Financial Instruments. This constitutes the level 1 measure adopted under the Lamfalussy revised legislative procedure. Section D (4) and (n 136). While this sets out the general principles to be applied, necessary implementing measures must still be adopted under level 2.

A number of initial requests were made to the CESR as part of the level 2 implementing process. This includes on such matters as the appropriate list of financial instruments (Art 4 and annex I, section C), the definition of investment advice (Art 44), conduct of business rules (Article 19), the suitability and appropriateness test and execution only business (Art 19), best execution and pre-trade transparency on regulated markets, limit order displays (Art 22), eligible counterparties (Art 24) and other transparency related issues. Subsequent requests were made on Arts 25 and 58 and Arts 13 and 18.

The Commission separately announced during 2005 that it would consider delaying the

Directive[40] as well as the later 1989 Prospectus (Public Offers) Directive.[41] The main Directives relating to listing were subsequently consolidated in May 2001.[42] Further measures were also proposed as part of the Financial Services Action Plan and Lamfalussy Committee Report. These included a new single Prospectuses Directive (based on full mutual recognition which would replace both Directive 80/390/EEC and Directive 89/298/EEC),[43] a revised set of transparency obligations for publicly traded companies[44] and a new directive on Market Abuse that would apply to both insider dealing and market manipulation.[45]

implementation of the MIFID in light of the complexities that had arisen and especially in agreeing all of the relevant level 2 implementing measures. It was then expected that final implementation would be delayed by up to one year beyond the original 2006 date set.

40 Council Directive 79/279/EEC of 5 Mar 1979 coordinating the conditions for the admission of securities to official stock exchange listing (OJ L 66, 16 Mar 1979, 21) as amended by Directive 88/627/EEC (OJ L 348, 17 Dec 1988, 62); Council Directive 80/390/EEC of 17 Mar 1980 coordinating the requirements for the drawing up, scrutiny and distribution of the listing particulars to be published for the admission of securities to listing (OJ L 100, 17 Apr 1980, 1) as amended by Directive 94/18/EC (OJ 135, 31 May 1994, 1); Council Directive 82/121/EEC of 15 Feb 1982 on information to be published on a regular basis by companies the shares of which have been admitted to official stock exchange listing (OJ L 48, 20 Feb 1982, 26). See also Council Directive 88/627/EEC of 12 Dec 1988 on the information to be published when a major holding in a listed company is acquired or disposed of (OJ L 348, 17 Dec 1988, 62).

41 Council Directive 89/298/EEC of 17 Apr 1989 coordinating the requirements for the drawing up, scrutiny and distribution of the prospectus to be published when transferable securities are offered to the public (OJ L 124, 5 May 1989, 8) (n 43).

42 Directive 2001/34/EC of 28 May 2001 on the admission of securities to official stock exchange listing and on information to be published on those securities (OJ L184, 6.7.2001, 1). This consolidated Directives 79/279, 80/390, 82/121 and 99/627 and related amending relevant measures (n 43).

43 Directive 2003/71/EC of the European Parliament and of the Council of 4 Nov 2003 on the prospectus to be published when securities are offered to the public or admitted to trading and amending Directive 2001/34/EC (OJ L 345, 31 Dec 2003 P 0064–0089). The Commission has released a number of implementing measures following advice from the ECSR. See eg Commission Regulation (CE)809/2004 of 29 Apr 2004 implementing Directive 2003/71/EC of the European Parliament and of the Council as regards information contained in prospectuses as well as the format, incorporation by reference and publication of such prospectuses and dissemination of advertisements. A number of meetings were subsequently held on transposition.

44 Directive 2004/109/EC of the European Parliament and of the Council on the harmonization of transparency requirements with regard to information about issuers whose securities are admitted to trading on a regulated market and amending Directive 2001/34/EC (OJ l 390/38, 31 Dec 2004). Advice has been requested from the ECSR on implementing measures.

45 Directive 2003/6/EC of the European Parliament and of the Council of 28 Jan 2003 on insider dealing and market manipulation (OJ L 096,12 Apr 2003 P 0016–0025). The Commission had issued implementing measures following advice from the ECSR. See, eg, Commission Directive 2004/72/EC of 29 Apr 2004 implementing Directive 2003/6/EC of the European Parliament and of the Council as regards accepted market practices, the definition of inside information in relation to derivatives on commodities, the drawing up of lists of insiders, the notification of managers' transactions and the notification of suspicious transactions; Commission Directive 2003/124/EC of 22 Dec 2003 implementing Directive 2003/6/EC of the European Parliament and of the Council as regards the definition and public disclosure of

An equivalent set of rights has also been created for insurance undertakings with three generations of measures having been adopted in the life and non-life areas.[46] The objective of these has generally been to extend the basic right of establishment which initially operated only on a host country control basis to include services on a home basis and ultimately establishment and services on a home rule in respect of both non-life and life business.

All of the main sector Directives were amended by the Prudential Supervision Directive (PSB) which was agreed after some delay on 18 May 1995.[47] This was adopted in response to the collapse of BCCI and revised the core Directives in a number of significant respects including, in particular, with regard to supervisory transparency, place of operations and audit functions.[48]

As well as create a series of core sector measures for individual financial institutions, the Commission has from an early stage been concerned to develop more group based forms of supervision. Consolidated supervision was initially introduced in the banking area in 1983 although this was later

inside information and the definition of market manipulation; Commission Directive 2003/125/EC of 22 Dec 2003 implementing Directive 2003/6/EC of the European Parliament and of the Council as regards the fair presentation of investment recommendations and the disclosure of conflicts of interest; Commission Regulation (EC)2273/2003 of 22 Dec 2003 implementing Directive 2003/6/EC of the European Parliament and of the Council as regards exemptions for buy-back programmes and stabilization of financial instruments.

46 First Life Directive 79/267/EEC of 5 Mar 1979 (OJ No L 63, 13 Mar 1979, 1); Second Non-Life Directive 88/357/EEC of 22 June 1988 (OJ No L 172, 4 July 1988, 1); Second Life Directive 90/619/EEC of 8 Nov 1990 (OJ No L 330, 29 Nov 1990, 50); Third Non-Life Directive 92/49/EEC of 18 June 1992 (OJ No L 228, 11 Aug 1992, 1); and Third Life Directive 92/96/EEC of 10 Nov 1992 (OJ No L 360, 9 Oct 92, 1). For comment Clifford Chance *Insurance Regulation in Europe* (Apr 1993); R Falkner, 'Insurance' in D Campbell (ed) *Financial Services in the New Europe* (Graham & Trotman London 1992); D Ferry 'Insurance Regulation: past, present and future' in EJ Swann (ed) *The Development of the Law of Financial Services* (1993); P Nicholas and R Croy *EC Insurance Law* (Chancery Lane Publishing London 1991); and H Benink *Financial Integration in Europe* (Kluwer The Netherlands 1993), Ch V. On the differences in scope and application between the insurance and other financial directives, Marc Dassesse 'Localization of Financial Services: Regulatory and Tax' Ch 13 in Andenas and Roth (n 18).

47 Council Directive 95/26/EC of 29 June 1995. The adoption of the Directive had been considerably delayed as a result of the new conciliation decision-taking procedure introduced under the Maastrict Treaty, Art G(61) which added a new Art 189b to the European Community Treaty. Although intended to improve the decision-taking processes within the Community by making them more democratic through the introduction of further co-decision with the European Parliament, the effect can be to complicate and delay the adoption process. For comment (nn 130, 133, and 138).

48 The Directive strengthened the powers of authorities with regard to refusal of authorization where a group structure was not sufficiently transparent, required financial institutions to maintain their head and registered offices in the same Member State, provided for additional exchange of information provisions and introduced reporting obligations for external auditors. On BCCI, Ch 4, section D (2).

extended in 1992 to include holding companies and investment firm subsidiaries under the second Consolidated Supervision Directive (CSB).[49]

One of the most important recent measures proposed has been in connection with the supervision of financial conglomerates.[50] In light of the increasing integration that has taken place between the main financial sectors, it is essential that an adequate framework is constructed to supervise the increasingly complex cross-sector financial groups that are emerging. The difficulty that arose within the Community was that delays had occurred in agreeing the Group Insurance Directive. Following agreement on this, it was possible to restart the earlier preparatory work that had been undertaken in connection with conglomerates. A final Directive was produced and adopted in 2002.[51]

This is an important first measure in the conglomerate area although the Commission accepts that it is limited in content and will only begin the larger process of aligning the relevant directives to ensure a minimum degree of equivalence in the treatment of such cross-sector groups. Harmonization is accordingly not the major objective, at least, at this stage. The purpose of the Directive is generally only to introduce relevant definitions, adjusted capital requirements and supplementary supervision for such groups.[52] The focus on capital adequacy in the conglomerate proposal

[49] Council Directive 92/350/EEC on the supervision of credit institutions on a consolidated basis of 6 April 1992 (OJ L 110, 28.4.1992, 52). Under the Directive, consolidated supervision was extended to apply to groups headed by a financial holding company. Art 3(2). A financial holding company is a financial institution the subsidiary undertakings of which are either exclusively, or mainly, credit or financial institutions with at least one subsidiary being a credit institution; Art 1. These provisions are now included in the BCD (nn 29 and 65).

[50] Commission, 'Commission launches consultations on regulation of conglomerates' (19 Dec 2000). See also Proposal for a Directive of the European Parliament and of the Council on the supplementary supervision of credit institutions, insurance undertakings and investment firms in a financial conglomerate (2001/0095 (COD)). Walker (n 10) Ch 3.

[51] Directive 2002/87/EC of the European Parliament and of the Council of 16 Dec 2002 on the supplementary supervision of credit institutions, insurance undertakings and investment firms in a financial conglomerate and amending Council Directives 73/239/EEC, 79/267/EEC, 92/49/EEC, 92/96/EEC, 93/6/EEC and 93/22/EEC, and Directives 98/78/EC and 2000/12/EC of the European Parliament and of the Council (OJ L 035, 11/02/2003). The European Financial Conglomerates Committee (EFCC) has issued general guidance to EU supervisors on supervision in Switzerland and the US. A provisional list of groups has also been produced that are identified as financial conglomerates as defined.

[52] A financial conglomerate is defined under Art 2(13). A financial conglomerate is a group the activities of which mainly consist of providing financial services. These activities are significant if the group includes, at least, one insurance undertaking and a bank or securities firm. Supplementary supervision is mainly conducted through the imposition of alternative capital adequacy calculations (Art 5) and the imposition of controls on intra-group transactions and risk concentrations (Art 6). The capital options are set out in Annex 1 and consist of three methods of 'accounting consolidation', 'deduction and aggregation' and 'deduction'. This follows the recommendations produced by the Joint Forum on Financial Conglomerates.

The measures facilitating supplementary supervision include the appointment of a coordinator (Art 7), functions of the coordinator (Art 8), a cooperation and exchange of information requirement (Art 9) as well additional provisions on internal control mechanisms (Art 10),

(with limited provision only for the calculation of a total group figure under certain options) is also unfortunate although possibly understandable. At this initial stage, the additional provisions included with regard to the conduct of supplementary supervision are nevertheless valuable and will begin to provide for the more effective oversight of such groups which can be extended further over time.

Separate but connected measures have been adopted in connection with the free movement of capital.[53] Any meaningful progress in the banking area was only possible once full free movement of capital had been secured across Europe during the late 1980s and early 1990s.[54] Separate proposals have also been issued in connection with clearing and settlement.[55]

A number of important measures have accordingly been adopted in each of the main financial sector areas (including capital). With these provisions, an attempt has been made to reconcile the basic conflict that arises in attempting to provide full market access with proper market control with in any regional trading system. Substantial progress has been achieved

access to information (Art 11), verification (Art 12), and additional powers of competent authorities (Art 13). The Directive contains further provision with regard to third countries (Arts 14 and 15) and assigns certain powers to the Commission and provides for the establishment of the new 'Financial Conglomerates Committee' (Arts 16 and 17). It is understood that the new Financial Conglomerates Committee was to be given considerably more powers than the existing sector based financial committees to assist the adjustment and development of relevant regulatory provision in this area. On financial conglomerates generally, Walker, *International Banking Regulation—Law, Policy and Practice* (n 10) Ch 3.

[53] Council Directive 85/583/EEC of 20 Dec 1985 amending Directive of May 11 1960 for the implementation of Art 67 of the Treaty (OJ l 372 31 Dec 1985); Council Directive 86/566/EEC of 17 Nov 1986 amending the First Directive of 11 May 1960 for the implementation of Art 67 of the Treaty (OJ l 332 26 Jan 1986); and Council Directive 88/36/EEC of 24 June 1988 on the implementation of Art 67 of the Treaty (OJ L 178 8 July 1988). See also First Directive for implementation of Art 67 of the Treaty of 11 May 1960 (OJ 921/60 12 July 1960); and Second Council Directive 63/21/EEC adding to and amending the First Directive for the implementation of Art 67 of 18 Dec 1962 (OJ 62/63 22 Jan 1963); and Council Directive 63/474/EEC liberalizing transfers in respect of invisible transactions not related to the movements of goods, services capital and persons (OJ 2240/63 17 Aug 1963).

[54] Arts 73b–g. Capital Directives date from 1961 and 1963 although Member States had relied on standstill provisions until further measures were adopted in 1986 and 1988. See generally, Age FP Bakker *The Liberalisation of Capital Movements in Europe—The Monetary Committee and Financial Integration, 1954–1994* (Kluwer Dordrecht and London 1996). Ch 2, sections H and J. See also, John Usher 'Financial Services, Taxation and Monetary Movements' ch 14 in Andenas and Roth (n 18); and Dalhuisen (n 18).

[55] See, eg, Commission, Clearing and Settlement in the European Union—Main policy issues and future challenges COM(2002) 257 (28 May 2002). The Communication was concerned with the removal of barriers to the finalization of individual cross-border transactions through national divergences in technical requirements and market practice, tax procedures and laws applying to securities as well as the removal of competitive distortions or unequal treatment of entities carrying out similar clearing and settlement functions. The meaning and importance of clearing and settlement was considered. Current practices were reviewed and recommendations made for the achievement of the Commission's stated objectives. Current relevant EU legislation is summarized in Annex I with possible action to address market practice and technical barriers being set out in Annex II.

although a number of significant gaps and omissions remain. It is for this reason that the more recent consolidation and completion work of the Commission is of essential importance to the longer term development and ultimate effectiveness of this process.

C. PROGRAMME CONSOLIDATION

The immediate response of the Commission to the lack of progress achieved was to attempt to clarify the content and operation of the main directives, in particular, in the banking area through a programme of legislative consolidation. The Commission had announced in 1997 that a codifying or consolidating directive would be issued to replace nineteen of the then existing banking directives.[56] The intention was to restate seven of the core directives and twelve amending provisions within a single measure which was to constitute a 'new banking code' for Europe.[57]

The consolidating measure was adopted under the SLIM (Simpler Legislation for the Internal Market) scheme.[58] Under the SLIM rules, no substantive amendments were permitted to be made to the codified measures[59] which had only to be restated in a comprehensive and coherent

[56] Commission, *Proposal for a European Parliament and Council Directive* relating to the taking up and pursuit of the business of credit institutions (codified version), 18 Dec 1997 (n 29).

[57] (n 29). The Directives replaced included the First Banking Directive (FBD), the Second Banking Directive (SBD), the Own Funds Directive (OFD), the Solvency Ratio Directive (SRD), the Large Exposures Directive (LED) and the Consolidated Supervision Directive (CSD) and the amending measures (nn 6, 12, 22, 24, 25, 26, and 49). Directives not to be consolidated included the Deposit Guarantee Directive, the Money Laundering Directive, the Capital Adequacy Directive and the accounting measures (nn 34 and 38).

[58] SLIM was an 'Inter-institutional Agreement' on an accelerated working method for the official codification of legislative texts concluded on Dec 20, 1994 by the European Parliament, the Council and the Commission. This involved the establishment of small informal working groups or teams of experts from national administrations, users of the legislation and the Commission to identify problems with existing rules and to make recommendations for their correction. The Commission issued a Communication which was presented to the Internal Market Council on 27 Nov 1997. This contained a summary of measures that the Commission intended to take. The first phase of SLIM was completed in Nov 1996 (SMN no 6, 1996).

[59] The Commission had instructed its staff on 1 Apr 1987 that all legislative measures should be codified after no more than ten amendments although this was only stated to be a minimum requirement with departments to attempt to codify at shorter intervals wherever possible to ensure that Community rules were clear and readily understandable. *Memo to the Commission* reproduced in the draft Consolidation Directive 1. The importance of legislative codification had been stressed at the Edinburgh European Council in Dec 1992. As no changes of substance were to be made to the instruments affected by the legislative codification, the Parliament, Council and Commission agreed under the Inter-institutional Agreement of 20 Dec 1994 that an accelerated procedure would be used to first-track adoption of codification instruments (n 58).

format. In light of the number of amendments that DG XV would have liked to have introduced in the banking area,[60] it had already been decided that a further amendment directive (*refonte*) would be adopted following the Consolidation Directive although this was then postponed with the crisis that arose within the Commission during March and April 1999 and with the subsequent re-allocation of resources required to prepare and give effect to the Financial Services Action Plan.[61]

The Banking Consolidation Directive was adopted in May 2000 and is described as the 'essential instrument for the creation of the internal market in the field of credit institutions.'[62] The approach adopted is stated to be to achieve only the essential harmonization necessary and sufficient to secure the mutual recognition of authorization and prudential systems[63] with supervision generally being conducted on a home Member State basis.[64]

Although stated to be a simplification, the Directive extended to seventy-three preambles, eight Titles and six Annexes.[65] While some of the language

60 In the banking area, the SLIM team concluded that existing problems with the banking legislation did not necessarily arise from the complexity of the measures adopted although it considered that certain aspects of the legislation should be re-examined. Following the team's recommendation, it was announced that the Commission would: (a) propose the abolition of the requirement on credit institutions intending to provide services in another Member State to notify that country's supervisory authority in advance (under Art 20 of the SBD and the ISD); (b) invite all national, EU and international authorities imposing reporting requirements to avoid duplication; (c) examine the functioning of the comitology procedure to ensure that amendments to legislation that were purely technical or resulted from separate international discussions (such as the Basel Committee) could be adopted quickly; (d) examine the inconsistencies or discrepancies that had arisen with the banking directives through the Banking Directives Interpretation Group with a view to proposing amendments; (e) consider the special needs of small banks when proposing legislation for complex supervisory rules; (f) evaluate whether the exemption for banks affiliated to a central bank from certain requirements of the FBD should be extended; (g) examine whether the information procedure on general good rules for cross-border branching should be extended to cross-border services; (h) examine 'well-evidenced' requests to revise the thresholds for calculating market risks under the CAD and, if appropriate, propose revisions; and (i) submit proposals before the end of 1998 to ensure that an up-to-date list of all authorized credit institutions was published regularly in the OJ. For comment, SMN December 1997, 4–5. see also section B (1) and (nn 131–134).

61 (n 60) and Section D.

62 (n 29). Preamble 4.

63 Preamble 8. Section B. On mutual recognition, Ch 6, sections C, D, and E.

64 Preamble 9. Section B and Ch 4.

65 The Banking Consolidation Directive comprises Title I (Definitions and Scope), Title II (Requirements for Access to the Taking-up and Pursuit of the Business of Credit Institutions), Title III (Provisions concerning the Freedom of Establishment and the Freedom to Provide Services), Title IV (Relations with Third Countries), Title V (Principles and Technical Instruments for Prudential Supervision), Title IX (Banking Advisory Committee), Title XII (Powers of Execution), and Title XIII (Transitional and Final Provisions).

Title V (Principles and Technical Instruments for Prudential Supervision) is made up of three Chapters comprising: Ch 1 (Principles of Prudential Supervision), Ch 2 (Technical Instruments of Prudential Supervision) including section 1 (Own funds), section 2 (Solvency ratio), section 3 (Large exposures) and section 4 (Qualifying holdings outside the financial sector), and Ch 3 (Supervision on a Consolidated Basis).

may in places appear awkward in translation,[66] an intelligent and well-structured restatement of the relevant provisions is provided. As so many preambles have had to be used, the inclusion of some headings or sub-headings may have been useful. The separate Title VI on the Banking Advisory Committee is also valuable although it may have been of value to include separate provisions with regard to other European committees such as the then Contact Group and the European Banking Supervision Committee. Any substantial revisions may, however, have required further amendment which would have disapplied the special adoption procedures available. This confirms again that while the consolidation process is of importance of itself, there was a need for further immediate amendment.[67] To the extent that any subsequent *refonte* is to be produced, it must be hoped that this will be issued in a fully revised and consolidated form and not as a separate amending measure.

It is essential that a clear and complete but also transparent and accessible programme of measures is adopted in each major financial sector area. Commercial operators can only rely on underlying Treaty rights and secondary expansions where these are set out in clear and unambiguous terms and in an accessible and useable manner.[68] Whether both of these residual issues of substantive (internal) coherence and transparency (and access) will be fully dealt with under the further completion initiatives under development remains to be seen.

D. PROGRAMME COMPLETION

A number of further steps were subsequently announced to attempt to ensure that an effective banking and financial programme has been constructed within Europe. An original *Action Plan for the Single Market*

The Annexes comprise: Annex I (List of Activities subject to mutual recognition), Annex II (Classification of off-balance-sheet items), Annex III (The treatment of off-balance-sheet items concerning interest rates and foreign-exchange rates), Annex IV (Types of off-balance-sheet items concerning interest rates and foreign-exchange rates), Annex V (Part A Repeal directives and Part B Deadlines for implementation) and Annex VI (Correlation Table).

66 The reference in Title II to 'Requirements for Access to the Taking-up and Pursuit of the Business of Credit Institutions' could have been simplified to 'Authorization Conditions'. In Title III, 'Provisions Concerning the Freedom of Establishment and the Freedom to Provide Services' could have been referred to as, 'Freedom of Establishment and Freedom to Provide Services.' In Title V, 'Principles and Technical Instruments for Prudential Supervision' could more easily have been included as 'Continuing Supervision' while 'Technical Instruments of Prudential Supervision' in Ch 2 could have been referred to as 'Capital Requirements.' 'Supervision on a Consolidated Basis' in Ch 3 of Title V would have been better as 'Consolidated Supervision.'

67 (n 60) and (132–5).

68 On the issues of regulatory transparency, access and reliance and integration default, Ch 1, section B (4).

was proposed at the Amsterdam European Council Summit in 1997 to ensure that all of the directives adopted under the 1985 White Paper had been properly implemented and were effective and that they worked to the greatest advantage of European citizens and businesses.[69]

The original Action Plan was followed by a framework document in the financial area in October 1998.[70] This *Framework for Action* had been requested by the June 1998 Cardiff European Council and was to be presented at the following Vienna Council. The Framework was generally based on the adoption of a number of measures in the area of wholesale and retail markets as well as improved supervisory cooperation and other financial coordination such as in the area of taxation.[71] The Commission was asked to prepare a programme timetable to achieve the objectives set[72] and an implementation paper was subsequently produced in May 1999.[73]

A separate report was prepared in the capital market area by a Committee of 'Wise Men' under Baron Alexandre Lamfalussy. The Committee produced an initial paper in November 2000 and a final report in February 2001.[74] The later report, in particular, recommended the establishment of two further committees in the securities area (a European Securities Committee (ESC) and a European Securities Regulators Committee (ESRC)) and the adoption of a four part approach to European capital market reform.[75] While the Financial Services Action Plan was to be achieved by 2005, an earlier date of 2003 had been set for capital markets.

The objective of these initiatives was to attempt to complete the construction of the European single market in banking and services. This included both a more general financial integration objective to be achieved by 2005 (under the extended Financial Services Action Plan) and a more specific capital market programme by 2003 (under the Lamfalussy recommendations). The Action Plan was, in particular, to include the adoption of 42 specific legislative and other measures to which certain further instru-

[69] Communication of the Commission to the European Council, *Action Plan for the Single Market* CSE (97) 1 final) of 4 June 1997 (n 4).

[70] Commission Communication, *Financial Services: Building a Framework for Action* COM (1998) 625 final of 28 October 1998.

[71] Commission, 'Financial Services Commission proposes Framework for Action' (28 Oct 1998) available http://europa.eu.int/comm/internal_maketen/en/finances/general/fsen.htm.

[72] Commission, 'Financial Services Commission outlines Action Plan for single financial market' (11 May 1998) available http://europa.eu.int/comm/internal_maketen/en/finances/general/action.htm. The request had been made by the European Council, the Presidency of the Council of Ministers and the Legal Affairs and Economic and Monetary Committees of the European Parliament.

[73] Commission, *Financial Services: Implementing the Framework for Financial Markets: Action Plan,* COM(1999) 232, 11 May 1999. Section D (2).

[74] Initial Report of the Committee of Wise Men, *The Regulation of European Securities Markets* (9 Nov 2000); and Final Report of the Committee of Wise Men, *The Regulation of European Securities Markets* (n 5). Section D (4).

[75] Section D (4) and (nn 135–139).

ments were subsequently added in response to later market developments. The intention was to make the EU most competitive economy in the world by 2010.

Each of the main elements of this completion programme are considered in turn.

(1) FINANCIAL SERVICES ACTION PLAN

The Commission issued its initial framework for action in the banking and financial area in October 1998.[76] This followed the adoption of the original *Action Plan for the Single Market* at the Amsterdam European Council Summit in 1997.[77] One of the major targets set out in the plan was for the elimination of the backlog of transposition (or implementation) of all relevant Single Market directives.[78] As a result of work adopted under the Action Plan, the fragmentation factor (the ratio of non-implemented measures in one or more Member States) fell from 35 per cent to 50 per cent between June 1997 and the end of 1998. The Commission recognized, however, that a significant amount of further work had still to be undertaken to secure the completion of the original 1 January 1999 deadline. For this purpose, the Action Plan set out four 'Strategic Targets.' These were generally concerned with making rules more effective, removing market distortions and specific sector obstacles as well as promoting individual benefits.[79] The Plan also made provision for three 'phases' of differentiated

[76] Commission, *Financial Services: Building a Framework for Action* COM(1998) 625 final (n 70).

[77] Communication of the Commission to the European Council, *Action Plan for the Single Market* (n 69).

[78] While the Commission had anticipated that the introduction of the Euro would create a new dynamism within the Single Market integration process by making prices and costs more transparent and by deepening Europe's capital markets, it anticipated that Member States may come under increasing pressure to raise other barriers to the free flow of goods, people, services and capital. Commission *Single Market Scoreboard*, No 3 (Oct 1998, 1).

[79] Strategic Target 1 was concerned with 'Making rules more effective.' Matters already achieved under Target 1 included the submission of transposition timetables by Member States, the establishment of Coordination centres and contact points for businesses and citizens, the provision of information by Member States on enforcement structures and procedures, accelerated investigation of complaints and infringements, the completion of SLIM phases III and IV and the national simplification initiative and the establishment of the European Business Test Panel.

Strategic Target 2 referred to 'Dealing with key market distortions.' While a tax package and guidelines on regional aid had been adopted under Strategic Target 2, difficulties remained with regard to the clarification and codification of state aid procedures and elimination of distortions in indirect taxation.

Strategic Target 3 was concerned with the 'Removal of sectoral obstacles to market integration.' In the financial area, a Green Paper on Pensions Funds had been issued with a proposal for a new Directive on collective investment schemes, a draft directive on late payments and the draft directive on distance selling of financial services. While work continued on a European Company Statute, delays had arisen with regard to the Tenth Company

implementation (Annex 1)[80] and a provisional 'annotated list of priority actions' (Annex 2).[81]

The *Framework for Action* paper was then adopted in the financial area in 1998. This highlighted the continuing importance of financial services within Europe.[82] While substantial progress had been secured in this area, a proper Single Market had still not been achieved. The existing framework of measures was not considered to require any radical revision although a number of recommendations were made in specific areas. While the Communication was principally concerned with capital markets and retail financial services, a number of important initiatives were announced in various other areas.[83]

The Communication was prepared following consultation with representative bodies of financial services users and industry, market practitioners and national administrations. Six main objectives were identified[84] and while a fundamental revision to existing legislation was not considered necessary, 'pragmatic but decisive' action had to be taken to allow the opportunity created by recent market developments to be properly realized. International monetary difficulties were also referred to although effective action had to be taken without any necessary adjustments being further delayed.

The following specific areas were considered by the Commission in the 1998 Communication document:

Law Directive on cross-border mergers and Regulations on European Statutes for cooperations, associations and mutual societies.

Strategic Target 4 was concerned with 'Delivering a Single Market for the benefit of all citizens.' A Directive on supplementary pensions had already been issued and 'dialogue' established although work remained on securing improvements to the EURES service and the directive on the sale of consumer goods and associated guarantees. Delays had also accumulated with regard to the elimination of border controls and communication on the Single Market and the environment. See also (n 107).

80 The three phases consisted of: (a) actions requiring immediate implementation in accordance with Annex 2; (b) the adoption of existing proposals 'by the earliest possible date;' and (c) attain maximum possible agreement on the remaining measures by 1 Jan 1999. Commission, *Action Plan for the Single Market*, Annex 1 (n 69).

81 Commission, *Action Plan for the Single Market* CSE (97) 1 final), Annex 2 (n 69).

82 Commission Communication, *Financial Services: Building a Framework for Action* COM (1998) (n 70), Executive Summary, para 1 (and n 1).

83 The Communication concentrated on the creation of deep and liquid Europe capital markets which served both issuers and investors better and with the removal of the remaining barriers to cross-border provision of retail financial services to ensure consumer choice while maintaining consumer confidence and a high level of consumer protection. Executive Summary, para. 7.

84 The objectives of the Framework were to: (a) equip the EU with a legislative apparatus to meet present and future challenges; (b) eliminate remaining capital market fragmentation to minimize the cost of capital raised on EU markets; (c) make the advantages of open markets available to both users and suppliers of financial services; (d) encourage the closer coordination of supervisory authorities; (e) promote the emergence of an integrated infrastructure at EU level; and (f) reduce barriers to the Single Market resulting from disparities in taxation. 1998 Communication, 1–2.

(a) Regulatory Apparatus

The Communication accepted that the existing framework of measures established must be continually revised to reflect changing market conditions. While the framework of measures adopted was generally considered satisfactory, the legislative structure had to be revised to ensure that it was as speedy, flexible and streamlined as possible.[85]

As well as developing faster response times and improving legislative techniques, the Commission was concerned to make the most of existing rules through better implementation, enforcement and clearer and more uniform interpretation.[86]

To ensure the establishment of a leaner and more effective regulatory apparatus, the Commission would continue to attempt to enforce the timely

[85] The Communication recommended that appropriate methods were adopted to ensure speedier adjustment of legislation and a streamlined approach to drafting prudential requirements. As technology advances and market integration increased, legislative procedures must not create unnecessary delays in adopting appropriate responses. European institutions had already been penalized in terms of market competition, for example, by not being allowed to use sophisticated financial models until recently. While banks were allowed to use such models in 1996, it took two and a half years to introduce the necessary amendments within the Community (n 38 and below). Speeding up the legislative process and the use of comitology procedures would be examined to attempt to agree fast-track adoption mechanisms. Paras 6–8.

The Commission would consider how more qualitative and less quantitative regulatory requirements could be developed to attempt to ensure a better balance between regulatory objectives and specific measures. The Commission was, in particular, concerned that unnecessary detail was included in many measures especially following amendments introduced during negotiations. While the Capital Adequacy Directive (CAD) proposal only contained 26 pages, this was later extended to 79 with 42 pages of annexes which were subsequently amended by another 28-page Directive four years later (CAD II). While the Commission would continue to develop a solid framework of core legislative measures, it would consider how more detailed guidance could be provided in a flexible supplementary form through, for example, communications, recommendations or decisions. Paras 9–10.

[86] The Commission was generally satisfied with the 98.94 per cent transposition rate for banking, insurance and securities measures although it noted that late, incomplete or incorrect implementation had already imposed considerable financial costs on market participants. This had led to distortions and inefficiencies which disrupted the effective functioning of the Single Market. The Commission, in particular, criticised the late implementation of the Investment Services Directive (ISD) which had caused perceived market rigidities as well as a lack of competition and difficult market access (nn 37 and 39). This may, in turn, have meant that investment firms were 'less than optimally prepared' for the re-adjustment benefits and enhanced competition which the introduction of the Euro could bring. Implementing delays should in future be kept to an absolute minimum while Member States should attempt to ensure more effective enforcement of national rules. This may include the creation of some form of self-monitoring mechanism to improve collective discipline. Paras 11–12.

The Commission would continue to attempt to assist with the production of clear and consistent interpretation of legislative measures through interpretative communications although it also recommended that national authorities develop other non-legislative and self-regulatory solutions including the 'bench marking' of best supervisory practise with a view to removing divergencies. Mutual understanding and transparency should, in particular, be secured in the securities area especially through the work of the Forum of European Securities Commissions (FESCO). Paras 12–13. FESCO has since been replaced by the ESRC. Section D (4).

and effective implementation of directives, proceed with the production of interpretative communications to assist national authorities and market participants and present detailed suggestions for discussion on a better approach for further prudential financial services legislation.

(b) Wholesale Markets

The Commission accepted that while the introduction of the Euro would assist in the development of a large and liquid European capital market, this would not, of itself, integrate capital markets. Residual regulatory, administrative and tax obstacles resulted in a high degree of market fragmentation (with other financial and corporate governance distortions) which meant that capital markets were significantly underdeveloped in a number of Member States.[87]

To assist in the creation of integrated wholesale markets across Europe, the Commission recommended that issuers should be able to enjoy easy access to European wide capital markets on competitive terms.[88] Investors should be free to invest their assets without encountering significant legal, administrative or information barriers.[89] Investment service providers should also be able to operate throughout the EU without confronting overlapping sets of legal and administrative formalities.[90] The main recommendations made were accordingly access, investment and compliance driven.

[87] Stock market capitalization within the EU was only 32 per cent of GDP which compared with over 100 per cent in the US. Significant markets were only found in the UK and the Netherlands.

[88] Various steps would be taken to improve the access of all companies to obtain a stock market listing. The Commission would, in particular, propose improvements to the 1989 Listing and Prospectus Directives to ensure the more effective operation and closer cooperation between supervisors (nn 40–4). It would examine whether legal initiatives could assist specialist venture capitalist funds to mobilise capital following the establishment of the EIF Start-Up facility and the SME guarantee facility under the Growth and Employment initiative with the European Investment Fund OJ 302/8 (1 Oct 1998). The Commission would also continue to support public and private sector bodies in their attempt to improve national regulatory frameworks for corporate governance where no single model existed. Para 17.

[89] The Commission was concerned with divergences in accounting and disclosure rules, investment restrictions through currency matching requirements and the creation of a level playing field for fund managers. Action would be taken in each of these areas. The Commission would, in particular, attempt to ensure that accounts were as transparent and comparable as possible, that sensible but sound prudential rules were adopted to allow pension fund managers to optimize their portfolio structures within Europe and create policy coherence in dealing with distinct financial products to ensure enhanced transparency for consumers and effective competition. Para 18.

[90] The Commission would continue to attempt to remove difficulties in the operation of the Investment Services Directive especially in eliminating distortions in the application of host conduct of business rules such as with regard to the operation of fit and proper standards. For this purpose, it would attempt to promote convergence of national approaches with regard to non-professional investors but restrict the application of such rules in respect of professional investors. Paras 19–20.

(c) Retail Markets

Despite efforts to complete a single market in financial services, the direct supplier-to-consumer provision of services remained largely undeveloped on a cross-border basis with divergences in prices for financial products continuing in many areas.[91] In adopting a pragmatic approach to developing a single market in retail financial services, the Commission had attempted to balance the interests of consumers against enhanced competition between financial intermediaries. While the Commission remained committed to the development of an open market through home country control, it was concerned to ensure that consumers were confident that their interests were properly protected.[92] Completion of the single market in this area would accordingly be developed on an incremental and pragmatic basis.[93]

(d) Supervisory Cooperation

The Commission recognized that increased cooperation between supervisory authorities was of crucial importance to the management of institutional and prudential risk. It noted, in particular, the contribution made by the various committees that assisted the Commission[94] and other European bodies.[95]

While the effective supervision of financial institutions on a cross-border and increasingly cross-sector basis had to be ensured, the Commission considered that this was best achieved through increased cooperation between national authorities rather than the creation of any new pan-European arrangements at this stage. For this purpose, increased cooperation was would be promoted between supervisory authorities and between

[91] Cross-border sales of life insurance was almost non-existent in most Member States (Danish companies recorded the highest at 0.14 per cent). Non-life assurance varied between 0.13 per cent in Germany to 4.13 per cent in Belgium. Price differences ranged from three times higher in relation to credit cards to seventeen times higher in respect of some commissions.

[92] See, eg, Commission Communication, *Enhancing Consumer Confident in Financial Services*, COM(97) 319 Final.

[93] The Commission would, in particular: (a) promote a clear and common understanding of the distinction between professional and non-professional users; (b) identify and catalogue substantive differences between legal provisions which were seen to require application of host country rules to improve transparency and proportionality; (c) promote the convergence of national practices towards a high level of consumer protection; and; (d) better coordinate national systems in respect of redress to limit unfair trading practices on a cross-border basis. Paras 28–33.

[94] These included the Banking Advisory Committee, the Insurance Committee, High Level Securities Supervisors, the Accounting Committee and the UCITS Contact Committee (n 13).

[95] These consisted of FESCO (now the ESRC) and the Banking Supervision Committee of the European System of Central Banks (formerly the Banking Supervisory Sub-Committee of the European Central Bank Governors and then the European Monetary Institute).

supervisory and monetary authorities. To assist in the development of enhanced coordination, the Commission would contribute with the elaboration of a 'supervisors' cooperation charter' which would aim to assign clear responsibilities for the performance of different tasks on a cross-border basis at the same time as set up mechanisms to deal with supervisory difficulties that may arise.[96]

At the international level, the Commission would continue to carry out a full and active role in developing international consensus and widespread implementation of best practise and financial regulation.[97]

(e) Wider Efforts

To ensure the creation of an optimal functioning single financial market, the Commission made a number of recommendations in respect of such wider conditions as infrastructure, competition policy (including state aids) and taxation. With regard to infrastructure, the Commission would attempt to close legal loop-holes in payment and security systems and develop effective retail payment systems.[98] The Commission would consider the competition policy implications of increased integration between financial institutions and, in particular, the specific difficulties that arose with regard to the

[96] Paras 34–37. This would appear to amount to the preparation of a common Memorandum of Understanding (MoU) for all national supervisory agencies within Europe. This would define relevant responsibilities and set up appropriate exchange of information and cooperation procedures. The reference to a 'charter' is, however, unfortunate and appears to confuse regulatory (or stability) and consumer protection issues. On MoUs generally, GA Walker 'International Supervisory Cooperation' in W Blair, A Allison, K Palmer, P Richards-Carpenter; and G Walker *Banking and Financial Services Regulation* (2002), ch 21. See also IMF *International Capital Markets: Developments, Prospects, and Policy Issues* (Aug 1995), Annex III, 'Mechanics for International Co-operation in Regulation' 161; IMF *International Capital Markets: Developments, Prospects, and Key Issues* (Sept 1996), Annex IV, 'International Co-operation of Supervision and Regulation of Financial Institutions' Box; Working Party No 4 of the Technical Committee of IOSCO, *Principles for Memorandum of Understanding*, Documents of the XVI Annual Conference IOSCO, No 5, Sept 1991; and Basel Committee *Essential Elements of a Statement of Cooperation between Banking Supervisors* (May 2001). IOSCO has since issued a replacement multilateral MoU which has become the industry model. This provides for the exchange of relevant information and cooperation as well as coordination of action in emergency situations. Available http://www.iosco.org.

[97] Paras 38–9. The Commission would develop supervisory cooperation partly through the GATS and through direct contact with specific countries or groups of countries. A substantial amount of work had, for example, been undertaken with accession candidates in Eastern Europe with the Commission assisting them implement the relevant financial services Directives through supervisory assistance and the construction of effective monitoring and surveillance mechanisms. Paras 40–1. On enlargement Ch 1, section F (1). The Commission would also consider with the Basel Committee amendments to the European bank capital rules under its new Capital Accord of June 2004. Walker (n 10), Capital Supplement. (n 25). It would also cooperate with the Joint Forum in the construction of an effective set of prudential controls in respect of financial conglomerates. Walker (n 10), Ch 3 (nn 51 and 52).

[98] Para 43. (n 55).

provision of state aids in this sector.[99] Action would also be taken to correct various distortions within the financial services area as a result of differences in taxation policy.[100]

A number of useful initiatives were accordingly outlined especially in terms of procedural (and legislative) revision, programme completion and supervisory cooperation. This delayed recognition would nevertheless be insufficient to correct all of the deficiencies identified. The initial programme of proposals would then be supplemented by the production of a structured timetable for implementation, some new agency assistance, a series of more substantial recommendations in the capital market area and separate regular progress reporting.

(2) ACTION PLAN IMPLEMENTATION

The European Council asked the Commission at its Cardiff meeting in June 1998 to table a programme of action to give effect to the main recommendations to be set out in the 1998 framework paper.[101] In response to this, the Commission issued a separate implementation document in May 1999.[103] This identified a number of issues requiring urgent action to ensure the proper functioning of the European financial market (and the 'benefits of the single currency'). It had been stated to be vital 'to translate a clear consensus on the challenges and opportunities that confronted EU financial markets into a concrete and urgent work programme' at the Vienna European Council meeting in December 1998.[103]

Five main areas for reform were highlighted in the 1999 Implementation report. These were generally concerned with legislative revision, capital market correction, rights' access, improved supervisory cooperation and retail infrastructure development.[104] A Financial Services Policy Group

[99] The Commission had prepared a report on 'Services of General Economic Interest in the Banking Sector' following the Amsterdam European Council meeting in 1997 which was to have been submitted to the ECOFIN Council. The Report considered, in particular, whether credit institutions provide services of general economic interest in different Member States, whether this includes the provision of a comprehensive and efficient financial infrastructure, whether an exception under Art 90, para 2 of the EC Treaty was available and whether different Member States' situations were comparable. Particular cases would be dealt with on an individual basis in accordance with the rules agreed. Paras 44–8.

[100] These included tax distortions on the placement of savings, harmful tax competition between financial centres, the taxation of financial service products, tax obstacles to pan-European company structures and the mobility of persons and the divergent tax treatment of debt and equity. Paras 49–54.

[101] European Council, Presidency Conclusions from Cardiff European Council (15/16 June 1998), Pt. 17.

[102] Commission, *Financial Services: Implementing the Framework for Financial Markets: Action Plan* (n 73).

[103] (n 73). Presidency Conclusions from Vienna European Council (11/12 Dec 1998), Pt 51.

[104] The Commission recommended that: (a) the EU should be endowed with a legislative

(FSPG) had been set up to assist the Commission identify relevant priorities in advance of the May 99 ECOFIN Council meeting.[105]

The 1999 Implementation paper sought to confirm the objectives that would guide financial services policy over the following years, assign 'a relative order of priorities and an indicative time-scale for their achievement' and identify a number of mechanisms that would contribute to their realization. It also provided for three priority actions[106] and four strategic objectives.[107] The revised objectives were

apparatus capable of responding to new regulatory challenges; (b) any remaining capital market fragmentation should be eliminated to reduce the cost of capital raised on EU markets; (c) users and suppliers of financial services should be able to exploit freely the commercial opportunities offered by a single financial market at the same time as benefit from a high level of consumer protection; (d) closer coordination of supervisory authority should be encouraged; and (e) an integrated EU infrastructure should be developed to underpin retail and wholesale and financial transactions. 1999 Communication (n 73) 3.

105 Section D (3) and (n 112).

106 Priority one actions required immediate attention. These were considered crucial to realization of the full benefits of the financial services sector. Priority two actions were considered important to the functioning of the single market in financial services through the amendment of existing legislation or adaptation of present structures to meet new challenges. Priority three actions were areas where a clear general consensus existed that new work should be developed with a view to finalising a coherent policy by the end of the Euro-transitional period. 21. (n 80).

107 Strategic objective 1—a single EU wholesale market. A number of measures were proposed: (a) to enable corporate issuers to raise finance on competitive terms on an EU-wide basis; (b) provide investors and intermediaries with access to all markets from any single point-of-entry; (c) allow investment service providers to offer their services on a cross-border basis without encountering unnecessary hindrances or administrative or legal barriers; (d) establish a sound and well integrated prudential framework within which asset managers could put funds at their disposal to the most productive use; and (e) create a climate of legal certainty so that securities trades and settlement were safe from unnecessary counterparty risk. 22–5.

Strategic objective 2—open and secure retail markets. Concerted efforts were required: (a) to equip consumers with the necessary instruments (information) and safeguards (clear rights and effective dispute settlement) to permit their full and active participation in the single financial market; (b) identify and rollback unjustified insistence on non-harmonized consumer-business rules as an obstacle to cross-border provision of services; (c) promote the emergence of effective mechanisms for overcoming faults in the single retail financial market which had their origin in differences in private law; (d) create legal conditions in which new distribution channels and distance technologies could be put to work on a pan-European scale; and (e) encourage the emergence of cost-effective and secure payment systems that enable citizens to effect small-value cross-border payments without incurring exorbitant charges. 26–7.

Strategic objective 3—financial stability and state-of-the-art prudential rules and supervision. Work was required: (a) to eliminate any gaps in the EU prudential framework arising from new forms of financial business or globalization as a matter of urgency; (b) set rigorous and appropriate standards to allow the EU banking sector successfully to manage intensification of competitive pressures; (c) contribute to the development of EU supervisory structures that can sustain stability and confidence in changing market structures and globalization; (d) develop a regulatory and supervisory approach that will serve as the basis for successful enlargement; and (e) enable the EU to assume a key role in setting high global standards for regulation and supervision including with regard to financial conglomerates. 28–30.

General objective—wider conditions for an optimal single financial market. Further work would be undertaken to address disparities in tax treatment and to develop an efficient and transparent legal system for corporate governance. 31. For progress on the achievement of the objectives set, section D (5).

wholesale[108] and retail markets,[109] supervision,[110] and ancillary issue structured.[111] This slightly revises the 1998 formulation with the content of each objective also being clarified further. While the removal of 'regulatory apparatus' from the beginning may appear to have diluted regulatory content, the 1998 reference was more concerned with legislative support than supervisory and regulatory efficiency. Specific obligations are then developed through the recommendations which are essentially corporate (wholesale) or individual (retail) focused and with the separate supervisory discussion being more agency and cooperation directed. The overall emphasis was generally then on market efficiency and economic value as opposed to financial stability as such. Market regulation was not ignored but postponed to economic benefit factors.

(3) FINANCIAL SERVICES POLICY GROUP

The 1999 framework programme had been developed by the Commission with the assistance of the FSPG.[112] The FSPG had been established on the recommendation of the Commission to assist take forward the proposals set out in the 1998 Communication. The group consisted of personal representatives of the national Finance Ministries chaired by a Commission representative.[113]

The specific objectives of the Group were to identify and prioritise actions by June 1999 and to assist the Commission in the collective monitoring of implementation and enforcement of financial services legislation. A separate High Level consultation mechanism was also to be established to ensure that market practitioners and users of financial

108 With regard to wholesale markets, the 1999 Communication refers to: (a) common rules for integrated securities and derivatives markets; (b) raising capital on an EU wide basis; (c) financial reporting; (d) a single market framework for supplementary pensions; (e) collateral; and (f) a secure and transparent environment for cross-border restructuring, 5–9.

109 With regard to retail markets, the 1999 Communication refers to: (a) information and transparency; (b) redress procedures; (c) a balanced application of consumer protection rules; (d) the promotion of ecommerce based retail business; (e) insurance intermediaries; and (f) cross-border retail payments, 9–12.

110 With regard to supervisory structure, the 1999 Communication refers to: (a) clarity of supervisory structures; (b) closer cooperation between securities supervisors; and (c) review of existing arrangements for cross-border banking supervision, 12–15.

111 With regard to general conditions for an efficient EU financial market, the 1999 Communication referred to corporate governance (a new inclusion) and taxation, 15–16 (n 79).

112 The FSPG was made up of representatives of ECOFIN Ministers and the European Central Bank under the Chairmanship of the Commission. The FSPG met three times before the May 1999 ECOFIN Council. This was also supported by a European Parliament Resolution on the Framework for Action, Res PE 229.721 FIN (EP 15 Apr 99). Commission, *Financial Services: Implementing the Framework for Financial Markets: Action Plan* (n 73), 3.

113 Commission, 'Financial Services: Commission proposes framework for Action', 28 Oct 1998 available http:\\europa.eu.int. Section D (1).

services were able to make a full contribution to the formulation of policy in this area.[114]

The Policy Group held a number of meetings with various important policy areas having been considered. While the early meetings focused on more general regulatory issues for prioritization purposes (including governance and accounting and audit as well as retail markets, e-commerce and financial conglomerates),[115] increasingly specialist securities issues were discussed later.[116] The FSPG has separately considered accession issues as well as the Lamfalussy Report and time-tabling and

[114] 1998 Communication (n 70), paras 55–62.

[115] The first meeting was held in Brussels on 28 Jan. It was principally concerned with the identification of immediate priorities, prudential rules, corporate governance and accounting and auditing. In relation to prudential rules, the Group noted that the Banking Advisory Committee (BAC) was attempting to identify and remedy shortcomings in the banking supervisory standards in parallel with the work undertaken at the Basel Committee level. It referred to the work undertaken by the Commission's Insurance Committee especially in relation to non-life business. With regard to financial conglomerates, the Group examined how supervisors could form an overall view of the risks run and ensure that all risks were covered and the potential systemic difficulties created with high concentration levels being kept as low as possible.

The second meeting of the Group was held on 25 and 26 Feb 1999. This considered supplementary pensions funds, expediting legislation for financial markets, completing retail financial markets and economic commerce and financial services. As the Commission noted in its Communication, the Group was particularly critical of the delays that arose in responding to changes in the prudential and risk demands of financial markets. While the Group recognized that the EC Treaty could not be amended directly, it thought that there was scope within existing institutional arrangements for a more rational and streamlined approach to elaborating financial legislation. This would be considered further.

At the third meeting of the Group on 26 March 1999, a range of measures were considered with regard to wholesale markets and to supervisory structures. These developed some of the recommendations contained in the Commission's 1998 Communication. With regard to supervisory structures, the Group noted that a forum had to be established to develop cross-sector cooperation and coordination although this must build on existing structures. Efforts should be continued to set up a securities committee although various difficulties had arisen in this regard (n 137). At the international level, the Commission confirmed its commitment to attempting to develop a common, clear and coherent European view in discussions with the shaping and identification of the activities of nascent new structures for international supervisory cooperation. Commission 'Conclusions of the third meeting of the Financial Services Policy Group, (26 Mar 99)' BIO/99/132–1. See also, the Commission 'Financial Services Policy Group convenes on 26 Mar for third meeting' BIO/99/132.

The following reported meeting was held on 19 Oct 1999. The meeting was chaired by Frits Bolkestein and considered progress on implementation of the Action Plan, the need to adopt a streamlined legislative procedure, progress on pension funds, retail financial services and e-commerce and conglomerate supervision.

[116] The sixth meeting was held on 11 Feb 2000 which considered open and integrated securities markets, market information, company accounts and stability, integrity and investor protection. With regard to open and integrated securities markets, the Group considered how the regulatory and supervisory framework could be reinforced without undermining investor protection or market stability. The Group was particularly concerned to improve capital raising efficiency, develop reliable and cost-efficient exchange and market infrastructure (served by state-of-the-art clearing and settlement systems) at the same time as align securities markets supervision to secure common high levels of market integrity and investor protection.

deadline problems.[117] Subsequent discussions turned to payment charges and capital revision, takeovers and the new Prospectuses Directive.[118]

The policy work of the FSPG was supported through a number of sepa-

[117] The seventh meeting was held on 11 May 2000 which considered progress on the Action Plan, the review of the ISD, e-commerce and the possible development of an assessment process for accession candidate countries. The objective of the assessment exercise would be to develop a form of informal 'peer review' system made up supervisors from EU and accession country authorities to assess the administrative capacity of accession territories in the regulation of their markets. This would not constitute an extra accession condition nor replace the Commission's assessment of country practice and 'preparedness'. The Group did not appear to have considered the possibility of establishing an intra-EU peer review process for current Member States presumably for political reasons although this was proposed for accession candidates. On earlier proposals (n 16)).

The eighth meeting was held on 12 Oct 2000 which considered progress and priorities of the FSAP, financial conglomerates and possible measures to prevent market manipulation.

The ninth meeting was held on 22 Feb 2001 which examined e-commerce and financial services, the Lamfalussy Report and progress on the FSAP. The personal representatives of ECOFIN Ministers present supported the main recommendations of the Lamfalussy Report to establish a faster decision-making procedure on securities legislation although this had to operate within the confines of the present Treaty (nn 135–139). There was support for the need to build on national supervisory and market expertise and the need for gradual convergence of national regulatory structures. The Report was considered to have provided positive contributions to resolve the shortcomings of the present system.

The tenth meeting was held on 24 Apr 2001. The meeting discussed the follow-up work necessary after the Stockholm European Council which reaffirmed the importance of the original 2003 and 2005 deadlines. The meeting examined the Draft Fourth Progress Report on the FSAP, a mid-term report by the Swedish Presidency on progress since the beginning of the year, clearing and settlement and e-commerce and financial services.

[118] The eleventh meeting was held on 19 June 2001 which considered the final report of the Swedish Council Presidency. The main issues that arose were cross-border payment charges, pension funds and capital adequacy. With regard to capital revision, the Group noted the parallel discussions being conducted at the Basel and EU levels and the need for the development of a framework that provided proportionate treatment for global firms and diverse local practice within the EU.

The twelfth meeting on 20 Sept 2001 considered take-over bids, the proposals for regulation on cross-border payments in euro, clearing and settlement, the mid-term report by the Belgian Council Presidency and the implications of enlargement following the European Council in June 2001. The European Council had concluded that enlargement was irreversible and that negotiations with candidate countries that were ready should be completed by end 2002. Ch 1, section F (1).

The thirteenth meeting on 22 Sept 2001 considered the Giovannini Report on clearing and settlement, reports by the Belgian and incoming Spanish Presidency, the draft Fifth Progress Report on the FSAP and the impact of 11 Sept on financial services policy. The general economic impact and effects of the 11 Sept crisis were discussed in some detail. The overall strength of the markets was noted. The need to implement the responses agreed was stressed including, in particular, the political declarations of the European Council and the 16 Oct Finance and Justice Council (MEMO/01/330).

The fourteenth meeting on 26 Feb 2002 considered the draft proposals on prospectuses, pension funds and financial conglomerates, the follow-up to the mid-term review, take-over bids and the report from the Spanish Council Presidency. The fifteenth meeting on 17 May 2002 discussed the Barcelona European Council in Mar 2002 and the informal meeting of Economic and Finance Ministers in Oviedo in Apr 2002. The European Council asked the Council and European Parliament to adopt eight key legislative measures during 2002 on international accounting standards, collateral, distance selling, market abuse, financial

rate 'Forum Groups of Market Experts'.[119] These were set up to assist identify imperfections and practical obstacles to the functioning of specific areas of the single market.[120] Five 'forum groups' were initially established with participants selected with the assistance of European representative organizations. The work of each group was stated to be directed by the 'setting of general lines of debates' although groups were entitled to discuss other issues that they considered relevant to their work.

The Forum Groups were not to produce policy papers as such but develop technical recommendations for subsequent consideration.[121] The function of the groups can accordingly be understood in terms of providing market input at the preparatory rather than negotiation stages of particular measures. This allowed market participants and users to make an important substantive contribution to the overall policy construction process. This also assisted correct any resource or technical limitations within the Commission's internal resources.[122] The various groups set up produced a series of useful papers that have assisted in the development of a number of the secondary measures necessary to complete the Financial Services Action Plan.[123]

conglomerates, insurance intermediaries, pension funds and prospectuses. The intentions of the Danish presidency were also referred to.

119 A number of papers were produced by separate Forum Groups of Market Experts. These included the Forum Group papers on the *ISD Green Paper* (Oct 1999), *Market Manipulation* (Oct 1999), *Cross-Border Use of Collateral* (Oct 1999), *Information* (Oct1999), *Market Obstacles* (Mar 2000) and *Facilitating Cross-Border Corporate Financial Services—Issues Paper* (June 2000) and *Findings* (Oct 2001).

120 Commission, 'Forum Group of Market Experts—Explanatory Note' (Oct 1999).

121 The objective of the technical discussions conducted within the Forum Groups was not to 'negotiate' nor to present 'positions' of EU representative bodies or markets on specific issues. This would be taken forward once the Commission had produced formal draft proposals. Individuals were rather expected to provide 'forward-looking, specific, unbiased, concrete and detailed technical input from a market perspective'. See, for example, Forum Group on Market Manipulation, Issues Paper for the First Meeting of the Group (Oct 1999), 3. While the Commission would chair meetings, this would be as a 'facilitator' of discussions. The Commission would produce issues papers setting out the main themes and possible areas of attention but only by way of general guidance.

122 Significant concerns had arisen with regard to the ability of the Commission to develop all of the necessary measures included as part of the FSAP. The success of the overall initiative would depend on the quality of each of the underlying proposals produced. In light of its limited resources, the Commission has had increasingly to rely on external market and governmental contributions (n 134). For comment, Walker 'Regulatory Review' *International Financial Regulation* (Informa, Dec 2002). The establishment of the Forum Groups of Market Experts can be considered as one way of organizing industry input and further assisting the Commission with the provision of technical advice and comment both of which were to be welcomed as important initiatives.

123 (n 4). The Forum Group on 'Market Manipulation' held its first meeting in Oct 1999. The Group had four meetings and produced its final report in Mar 2000. The main issues considered by the Group were malpractice (limits and innovation), instruments, markets, manipulators, best practices and penalties. The general objective was to assist the preparation of the new Market Abuse Directive (n 45). This would replace the earlier provisions contained

The Commission also set up a separate '2005 Group' to assist in the achievement of the Action Plan deadlines set. The 2005 Group consisted of representatives from the Council and European Parliament. It met regularly to align working schedules and identify problems to avoid delays and assist speed up formal procedures.[124]

While the Financial Services Policy Group and supporting technical fora were only established to assist with the Financial Services Action Plan preparatory work, the Commission had found them of considerable value and has recommended that some more formally constituted equivalent

in the Insider Dealing Directive (ISD) as well as extend this to include other aspects of market manipulation. The result would be to parallel the aspects of market abuse covered by section 118 of the Financial Services and Markets Act 2000 in the UK.

The Forum Group on the 'Cross-Border use of Collateral' met for the first time in Oct 1999. The purpose of the group was to advise the Commission as to the best way of achieving legal certainty as regards the validity and enforceability of collateral provided for cross-border use. The growth and use of collateral was noted by the Group. The two main types of collateral considered included pledge collateral (without transfer of ownership) and title transfer. The contribution of the Settlement Finality Directive (SFD) was noted and other areas in which legal certainty was required identified. A number of continuing problems and uncertainties were identified and action proposed. A copy of the Giovannini Group Mar 1999 Report was attached as an annex to the Forum Group's issues paper.

The Information Forum Group considered the difficulties that arose in ensuring a high degree of consumer protection for retail financial services in the new Internal Market. The barriers that had existed were noted and an attempt made to develop guiding principles for information provision covering the full range of cross-border retail financial services. The three objectives identified by the Forum Group were to facilitate the creation of a single market in retail financial services, provide a high level of protection of purchasers and promote choice for purchasers and competition in the industry. A series of separate 'guiding principles' were developed. The eleven provisional principles identified included requiring that all information should be clear and easily understandable, a key documents feature, each stage of the contract and service relationship should be covered, all product characteristics disclosed and price and payment arrangements made clear (para 4.3 of the Oct 1999 Issues Papers). The Group would identify key products and services for cross-border development and conduct joint work with the Forum Group on Cross-Border Trade.

The Commission produced a subsequent issues paper on 'Retail Financial Services: overcoming remaining barriers—A legal analysis' (20 Mar 2000). This considered the cross-border market for retail financial services, the obstacles that arose from 'marketing rules' and related contract law barriers. A number of provisional conclusions were drawn with the separate tax issues that arose being considered within an annex to the paper.

The Forum Group on 'Cross-Border Corporate Financial Services' considered the legal, administrative and tax obstacles that arose to the cross-border conduct of financial services by large financial institutions including multinationals and other small and medium sized corporate users. The issues considered included coordination between central banks in the offsetting of notionally pooled amounts against banks' consolidated balance sheets, rules concerning joint and several liability guarantees, transfer order revocation, bank account operations and disparities in the taxation treatment of relevant services. The Oct 2000 Findings paper made a number of recommendations with regard to harmonising account opening requirements, cash pooling, electronic signatures, cross-border insolvency and the removal of other regulatory inconsistencies.

[124] Commission, 'Financial Services: Commission calls for quantum leap towards rapid implementation of Action Plan', 8 Nov 2000.

bodies be set up to operate on a continuing basis.[125] The Commission has also recommended that some type of consultation procedure be created to allow more general policy discussions to be conducted with European Parliament representatives from an early stage outside the formal legislative procedures currently in place. These proposals confirm the need for continuing specialist official and market support as well as the separate difficulties that can arise with the complex legislative procedures in operation within the EU. It is essential that effective technical advice and support is provided at the same time as unnecessary political delay or interference avoided in such complex and essential areas as financial market efficiency and stability.

(4) Capital Markets and Lamfalussy Report

The main issues that arose with regard to securities markets integration were considered separately by the Committee of Wise Men chaired by Baron Alexandre Lamfalussy.[126] The Committee produced an Initial Report in November 2000[127] and a Final Report in February 2001.[128] In the 2001 paper, the Committee considered the need for change in the EU and made a number of recommendations for regulatory reform. The Report was subsequently endorsed at the Stockholm European Council meeting in March 2001 and agreement achieved with the European Parliament on the revised legislative procedures to be followed.[129]

[125] 1999 Communication (n 73) 16–17.

[126] The Committee of Wise Men was made up of Alexandre Lamfalussy as Chairman, Cornelius Herkstroter, Luis Angel Rojo, Bengt Ryden, Luigi Spaventa, Norbert Walter and Nigel Wicks. The Rapporteur was David Wright and the Secretary, Pierre Delsaux.

[127] Committee of Wise Men *Initial Report on the Regulation of European Securities Markets* (7 Nov 2000), FINAL (n 74). The terms of reference of the Committee had been set by the EU's Economic and Financial Ministers (ECOFIN) on 17 July 2000.

[128] Committee of Wise Men *Final Report on the Regulation of European Securities Markets* (15 Feb 2001), FINAL (nn 5 and 74). The Committee had been asked to produce the report by February 2001 under the ECOFIN Conclusions of 26/27 Nov 2000 in advance of the Stockholm European Council of Heads of State and Government on 23 and 24 Mar 2001. For comment, Lamfalussy 'Regulation under Strain' *Financial Times* (8 Feb 2000); and Lamfalussy 'Reflections on the Regulation of European Securities Markets' (SUERF Studies, Vienna, 2001). See also ESFRC 'The Regulation of European Securities Markets: the Lamfalussy Report' (26 Mar 2001), Statement no 10 (available http://www.ceps.be); Report of a CEPS Task Force (Alfred Steinherr, Chairman) 'EU Securities Market Regulation—Adapting to the Needs of a Single Capital Market' (Mar 2001); G Thieffry 'After the Lamfalussy Report: the First Steps towards a European Securities Commission (ESC)?' in M Andenas and Y Avreginos (eds) 'Financial Market Supervision in Europe: Towards a Single Regulator' (Kluwer Law London 2001).

[129] The European Parliament agreed on 5 Feb 2002 a series of measures to ensure the effective operation of the recommendations by the Lamfalussy Committee. Discussions had been conducted within the Committee on Constitutional Affairs, the Committee on Economic and Monetary Affairs and the Committee on Legal Affairs and the Internal Markets. The Parliament subsequently agreed to limit the duration of the delegation of executive powers to

The Committee agreed that considerable economic benefits would be gained from an integrated financial market.[130] Despite the potential advantages available, a number of significant obstacles continued to restrict European integration in this area.[131] In addition to the legislative,[132] regulatory and implementation difficulties referred to, other more general factors constrained longer-term growth. These included underlying differences in legal and taxation systems as well as other trade, political and cultural barriers.[133] The Committee identified significant areas of legislative

the Commission to four years from the entry into force of each directive subject to an extension proposed by the Commission and accepted by the Parliament and Council. A report was subsequently produced by Karl von Wogau. The Parliament would have three months from the first transmission of each measure to examine its content and provide an opinion. Full transparency would be facilitated. Press Announcement, 5 Feb 2002.

This compromise position was only arrived at after the resolution of the dispute that arose between the Parliament and the Council and Commission concerning the extent of the Parliament's 'call back' power. Press Release of the European Parliament of 23 Mar 2001 and 2 May 2001 and letter of response from Frits Bolkstein dated 2 May 2001 (incorporated in the May release). For comment, Federal Trust, 'Reaction to the Wise Men's Final Report' (13 Mar 2001).

130 The Committee identified a number of 'micro' and 'macro' benefits. Micro economic benefits included more rational allocation of capital, greater liquidity benefiting all companies and, in particular, small and medium sized enterprises (SMEs), lower cost of capital, higher net yields for consumers and cheaper cross-border clearing and settlement. Macro economic benefits included increased productivity of capital and labour as well as stronger growth and employment. Open, competitive and innovative financial markets would benefit all Members States. The Committee noted that the capitalization of European insurance, investment (UCITS) and pensions funds alone was equivalent to 10 trillion Euros which equalled the size of European GDP. Although the Euro bond market was 40 per cent larger than the US Treasury market, European stock exchanges were still only approximately half the size of those in the United States. 9–10.

131 The Committee identified five core barriers: (a) the absence of any clear European-wide regulation on a number of important issues including prospectuses, cross-border collateral, market abuse and investment service provision; (b) an inefficient regulatory system (with over 40 separate agencies involved); (c) inconsistent implementation partly due to interpretation differences; (d) the large number of transaction and clearing and settlement systems maintained that fragmented liquidity and increased costs; and (e) the inadequate development of funded pension schemes in most Member States. 10.

132 Legislative gaps or difficulties included: (a) a lack of commonly agreed guiding principles for financial services legislation; (b) failure to apply mutual recognition in the wholesale, retail, market and capital areas; (c) outdated rules on listing requirements (including no distinction between admission to listing and trading and lack of a definition of public offer); (d) ambiguity over the scope and application of the ISD conduct of business rules and definition of a professional investor; (e) no appropriate rules on alternative trading systems; (f) inconsistencies between the E-commerce Directive and financial services directives; (g) no comprehensive market abuse regime; (h) no cross-border collateral arrangements; (i) no common accepted international accounting standards; (j) outdated investment rules for UCITS and pension funds; (k) unresolved public policy issues concerning clearing and settlement; (l) no agreed take-over rules; (m) no high and equivalent levels of consumer protection; and (n) no efficient methods for resolving cross-border consumer disputes.

133 The Committee referred in particular to: (a) differences in legal systems (including bankruptcy proceedings and effective judicial procedures); (b) taxation (withholding taxes, stamp duty and different rates on equity and government bonds); (c) external trade barriers (such as

'blockage' at the European level.[134] The system was generally considered to be too slow and rigid. It involved too much ambiguity and failed to distinguish between core and essential framework principles and day-to-day implementing rules. The Committee concluded that the basic legislation was not in place, there was insufficient prioritization, the then current legislative and regulatory system did not work effectively while implementation was erratic.

In response to these difficulties, the Committee produced a series of general principles for securities regulation[135] and recommended that a new four level approach was adopted for regulatory reform in the capital market area. The new approach to be followed generally involved only having framework principles produced at the European level within the existing legislative procedures available (Level 1).[136] More detailed implementing rules would then be developed through two new specialist committees consisting of the ESC and ESRC (Level 2).[137] Enhanced cooperation in

the non-authorization of EU trading schemes in the US); (d) political barriers (creative protectionism to favour local markets or products); and (e) cultural barriers (including different approaches to corporate governance, competition policy, market consultation and disclosure standards as well as the more general approach to entrepreneurial development).

[134] The Commission was over-stretched and sometimes slow to act. The Council of Ministers tended to add unnecessary levels of complexity to protect national divergence. Further delays arose in the co-decision procedure with the Council and European Parliament. Between May 1999 and Oct 2000, first readings took an average of 8 months, second readings more than 2 years and conciliation an additional 2–3 months. These figures were longer in the financial area. Further delays then arose in national transposition and implementation at the Member State level. 14–15. Separate problems also arose with regard to resources and training especially within the Commission and Parliament. 17–18.

[135] Financial services and securities legislation should be based on eight 'overarching' conceptual principles that should be consistently applied. These consisted of: (a) maintaining confidence in European securities markets; (b) maintaining high levels of prudential supervision; (c) contributing to the efforts of macro and micro prudential supervisors to ensure systemic stability; (d) ensuring appropriate levels of consumer protection proportionate to the different degrees of risk involved; (e) respecting the subsidiarity and proportionality principles set out in the Treaty; (f) promoting competition and ensuring that the Community's competition rules were fully respected; (g) ensuring that regulation is efficient as well as encouraging innovation; and (h) taking into account the wider international dimension of European securities markets.

[136] In giving effect to these 'overarching principles', legislative activity should be restricted to developing more general 'framework principles' in each key area (Level 1). This would, in turn, be based on the establishment of new open, transparent consultation mechanisms that would include strengthening dialogue with market participants and end-users, publication of consultation results, the adoption of staged deadlines and early cooperation with both the European Parliament and national regulators.

The objective would be to produce a series of new legislative measures that would set out the general framework principles to be given effect in each key area. These would be adopted through the existing co-decision procedures although additional efforts would be made to ensure that this was achieved in as quick and flexible a manner as possible. The framework measures would also include a definition of implementing powers to operate at Level 2.

[137] At Level 2, the Commission would consult with the European Securities Committee (ESC) on the adoption of technical implementing measures. Separate advice would be prepared

implementing relevant measures at the national level would be promoted (Level 3).[138] Strengthened enforcement would also be secured through Commission action across Europe (Level 4).[139] The general effect of these recommendations would be to improve both the legislative process at the European level as well as the common content and effective implementation of these measures at the domestic and national levels.[140]

To ensure that these proposals were capable of being given full effect, the Committee separately recommended that clear mandates were established for the two new committees, full transparency was ensured, strong monitoring and reporting maintained, active and well-defined involvement encouraged and national regulatory structures appropriately reformed. A

by the European Securities Regulators Committee (ESRC) in consultation with market participants, end-users and consumers. This would be considered by the Commission and proposals sent to the ESC which would vote on their adoption within a maximum period of 3 months. If approved, the measures would be adopted by the Commission and become binding. If the Commission's proposals were rejected or no opinion was delivered within the three month period, the measures would be submitted to the Council for approval. If rejected by the Council, the Commission would either have to re-submit its draft measures, submit amended proposals or proceed through the traditional legislative procedures involving a directive or regulation. The European Parliament would be kept fully informed of relevant procedures and would be able to adopt a resolution in the event that implementing powers were exceeded. On the revised procedures agreed with the Parliament (n 129).

The ESC would act as a regulatory committee under Art 202 of the Treaty and vote on the Commission's proposals within fixed deadlines of usually three months but also act in an advisory capacity in connection with Level 1 framework principles and Level 2 ESRC mandates. Membership of the ESC would be at Secretary of State level.

The ESRC would act as an advisory committee to the Commission at Level 2 and as an independent coordinator of national action at Level 3. The ESRC would be established as an independent advisory group composed of representatives from national securities regulators. The ESRC would replace the earlier functions of FESCO although on a more formal basis. Voting within the ESRC would be on a qualified majority rather than unanimous basis. This was considered necessary to avoid lowest common denominator agreements and to be consistent with the ESC. On committee establishment (n 143).

[138] National implementation would be improved through strengthening cooperation between national regulators within the ESRC. This would, in particular, involve the production of joint interpretation recommendations, consistent guidelines and common standards especially in areas not covered by relevant European legislation, peer review and comparability of national regulatory practice to ensure consistent adoption and implementation.

[139] Enforcement would be strengthened to ensure full and effective compliance with all measures adopted. This would essentially be carried out by the Commission although the Committee stressed that Member States, national regulators and private sector agencies could assist in this process. The European Parliament was also encouraged to support these efforts. 40.

A separate Monitoring Group would be established to oversee the continuous operation of the four level regulatory process proposed. This monitoring system would operate separately from remedial action. The Monitoring Group would be made up of two external nominees from each of the main institutions concerned. A separate full review of the process was to be undertaken in 2004.

[140] On infringement proceedings generally, I Wouters 'Towards a European Securities Commission? Reflections in an International and Transatlantic Perspective' in M Andenas and Y Avgerinos (eds) 'Financial Market Supervision in Europe: Towards a Single Regulator' (Kluwer Law London 2001).

number of further institutional benefits would then follow including more effective use of scarce resources, faster decision taking and a higher concentration of political and administrative effort and commitment.

It has to be accepted that while the Committee generally referred to its recommendations as being 'regulatory' directed, many of these were essentially legislative or institutional in content and effect. The underlying objective was to ensure that the legislative processes within Europe were made more timeous, flexible and responsive with the existing institutional obstacles identified being removed or, at least, reduced in so far as possible. This would then have consequential regulatory benefits at the national level. The core recommendations are nevertheless still essentially institutional and corrective rather than substantive in content.

Although directed at the securities area, these proposals are also capable of more general application assuming that surrogate banking and insurance committees can carry out the same functions as the ESC and ESRC in their respective sectors. As many of the main recommendations made were not concerned with or directed at securities markets specifically, it is surprising that equivalent institutional arrangements in the banking and insurance area were not considered or, at least, referred to expressly at that time.[141] The Committee presumably felt constrained by its original ECOFIN mandate and subsequent directions. One possible reason for the securities focus may also have been the perceived lack of progress achieved in that area as against the other main financial sectors and consequent potential benefits that may be quickly realized. Even allowing for this, the final financial programme will only be of value if all necessary intra-sector and cross or inter-sector progress is achieved. The Lamfalussy recommendations are accordingly of considerable value although only as part of the larger integration efforts undertaken.

(5) Progress Reports and 2005 White Paper on Financial Services

A number of Progress Reports were subsequently issued by the Commission on the measures proposed to give effect to the Financial Services Action Plan.[142] These considered the legislative progress of each of the measures recommended in the 1999 programme as well as further measures subsequently adopted. Each set of provisions was assessed having regard to the

[141] (n 13) and Ch 1 (nn 25 and 55).

[142] Commission, *First Progress Report* (29 Nov 1999); Commission, *Second Progress Report* (31 May 2000); Commission, *Third Progress Report* (8 Nov 2000); Commission, *Fourth Progress Report* (1 June 2001); Commission, *Fifth Progress Report* (30 Nov 2001); and Commission, *Sixth Progress Report* (3 June 2002); Commission, *Seventh Progress Report* (2 Dec 2002); Commission, *Eighth Progress Report* (3 June 1003); Commission, *Ninth Progress Report* (25 Nov 2003); and Commission, *Tenth Progress Report* (1 June 2004).

revised strategic objectives adopted including wholesale and retail markets, prudential rules and supervision as well as larger single financial market issues. Related market developments and particular difficulties in the adoption of specific measures were also noted.

The reports confirm that substantial progress was possible in each of the main strategic areas identified by the Commission as part of its Action Plan. By the mid-term review in 2002, a substantial number of measures had already been adopted. These included the decisions to establish the ESC and the ECSR[143] and the Electronic Money Directive and Winding-up Directives for insurance undertakings and banks[144] as well as other amendment measures.[145] Despite setbacks in connection with some measures including the Parliament's rejection of the Take-over Directive, legislative progress was possible in connection with a number of other important measures.[146]

[143] Decision of 6 June 2001 setting up the European Securities Committee (C (2001) 1493) and Decision of 6 June 2001 setting up the Committee of European Securities Regulators (C (2001) 1501). (n 137).

[144] Electronic Money Directive 2000/46/EC adopted 18 Sept 2000; Directive on the Reorganization and Winding-up of Insurance Undertakings 2001/17/EC adopted 19 Mar 2001; and Directive on the Winding-up and Liquidation of Banks 2001/24/EC adopted 4 Apr 2001 (n 28).

[145] Directive 2000/64/EC amending the Insurance Directives and Investment Services Directive to permit information exchange with third countries adopted 7 Nov 2000; Directive 2001/97/EC amending the Money Laundering Directive adopted 4 Nov 2001; Directive 2001/65/EC amending the fourth and seventh Company Law Directives to allow fair value accounting adopted 31 May 2001; Directives 2001/107/EC and 2001/108/EC on UCITS adopted 21 Jan 2002; Directives 2002/12/EC and 2002/13/EC amending the solvency margin requirements in the Insurance Directives adopted 5 Mar 2002.

[146] In connection with wholesale markets, the later reports noted the progress achieved on the Prospectuses Directive (COM(2001) 280, 30 May 2001) updating the Regular Reporting Requirements (work continued following first consultation summer 2001 and second consultation April 2002) (n 43). On securities and derivatives markets, the Report referred to the Market Abuse Directive (COM(2001) 281 30 May 2001 with ECOFIN political agreement on 7 May 2002) and revised Investment Services Directive (COM(2000) 729 Final, 15 Nov 2000 with first consultation 2001 and second consultation Apr 2002). On financial statements, Regulation on International Accounting Standards (COM(2001) 80, 13 Feb 2001 with Parliamentary opinion on 12 Mar 2002) and modernization of accounting provisions in 4th and 7th Company Law Directives (to follow Oct 2002). On securities settlement, Financial Collateral Arrangements Directive (COM(2001) 168 Final, 27 Mar 2001, Council common position on 5 Mar 2002 with second Parliament reading early 2002). On cross-border restructuring, Directive on Take-over Bids (new proposal following rejection of compromise text of 6 June 2001 by Parliament on 4 July 2001), Report of the High Level Group of Company Law Experts (new recommendations on take-over bids and examination of conclusions of review on EU corporate governance practices), proposals for 10th Company Law Directive (original proposal 1985 blocked on issue of workers' participation with new proposal to follow September 2002) and proposal for 14th Company Law Directive (new proposal 2003). On investors, Directive on the Prudential Supervision of Supplementary Pension Funds (COM (2000) 507 provisional, 11 Oct 2000, Parliament opinion 4 July 2001).

On open and secure retail markets (strategic objective 2), Directive on the Distance Marketing of Financial Services (COM(1999) 385, 23 July 1999, political agreement 27 Sept 2001, Parliament second reading ongoing), Directive on Insurance Intermediaries (COM

As a result of this, the Barcelona European Council reaffirmed the objectives of the Action Plan in March 2002 with further work to be taken forward by the ECOFIN Ministers at their meeting in Oviedo in April 2002.[147] At the Oviedo meeting, the finance ministers invited the Commission to propose arrangements to facilitate consistent implementation of relevant EU legislation, called for strict use of the competition rules and insisted on the need for increased endeavours on consumer confidence and protection. In connection with the collapse of Enron, the ministers agreed that most of the regulatory issues raised were already being dealt with under the FSAP including in connection with standards and reporting although the further work to be carried out by the Commission was welcomed on auditor independence, auditing strategy priority, financial analysts and credit rating agencies. The High Level Group of Company Law Experts were also invited to recommend best practices in corporate governance and auditing.[148]

The Commission subsequently produced a separate Green Paper on financial services policy in May (2005) and then a follow-up White Paper in December 2005.[149] These attempted to develop ideas for the further integration of EU financial markets with the focus on consolidation and implementation of the existing rules already agreed under the FSAP and on cooperation rather than proposing new laws as such. They also examined means of improving cross-border access to retail financial services and asset management.

(2000) 511 Final, 20 Sept 2000, common position Council 19/3/2002, second reading Parliament 8 Apr 2002), Legal Framework for Payments in the Internal Market (proposal to follow) follow-up to FIN/NET (follow-up on COM/2001/6650 ongoing) and follow-up to Action Plan to prevent fraud and counterfeiting in payment systems (COM(2001) 11, 9 Feb 2001) and Work on Insurance Guarantee Schemes (ongoing since Feb 2002).

On prudential rules and supervision (strategic objective 3), revised capital adequacy directive (proposal 2004 following Basel Committee recommendations), Directive on Financial Conglomerates (COM(2001) 213 Final, 24 Apr 2001, Parliament opinion 14 Mar 2002, ECOFIN political agreement 7 May 2002, Parliament second reading 2002), Reinsurance Supervision (ongoing), Insurance Solvency II (ongoing) and Third Money Laundering Directive.

On wider conditions for optimal single financial market (strategic objective 4), Directive on taxation of savings income on interest payments (new proposal 18 July 2001 with negotiations with third countries continuing), Commission initiative on taxation of cross-border occupational pensions (COM(2001) 214, 19 Apr 2001) and implementation of the Dec 1997 Code of Conduct on business taxation (submitted ECOFIN Nov 1999).

147 The Barcelona priorities included implementing the FSAP by 2005 and by 2003 for securities and risk capital markets. The Council and the Parliament were to have approved the Directives on market abuse, collateral, distance marketing of financial services, insurance undertakings, prospectuses, financial conglomerates and pension funds and the regulation on International Accounting Standards.

148 Sixth Report (n 146) 3.

149 Commission, *Green Paper on Financial Services Policy (2005–2010)* COM(2005) 177; and Commission, *White Paper on Financial Services Policy (2005–2010)* COM(2005). For comment, Internal Market Commissioner Charlie McCreevy commenting on the importance of the Green Paper on 3 May 2005 (IP/ May 527).

The objective of the Green Paper was to set out a series of new ideas for the further integration of European financial markets. The paper was principally concerned with the implementation of all of the existing rules agreed under the FSAP and with improving cooperation between national regulatory authorities. A number of specific recommendations were also made with regard to improving cross-border access to retail financial services and asset management.

Under the Green Paper, the Commission's emphasis would be on consolidating progress towards European financial integration over the next five years although no substantial new legislative programme (an 'FSAP 2') was expected. The Commission considered that one of the most significant achievements made during the previous six years had been the progress secured in creating an integrated, open, competitive and efficient European financial and capital market. Conclusion of the legislative phases of the FSAP had been one of the Commission's top priorities since its launch in 1999. While progress on other parts of the Lisbon agenda had been disappointing, major achievements had been possible in the financial services area. Almost all the main legislative components had been adopted with success likely on the conclusion of the outstanding measures. The Commission would build on this work with the emphasis moving to implementation and enforcement and with possibly some targeted legislative intervention to be considered although only following extended consultation and a full impact assessment.

The December 2005 White Paper attempted to restate a number of key objectives and priorities for financial services policy over the 5 year period between 2005 and 2010. The key idea was referred to as 'dynamic consolidation' based on a new practical, ambitious and reflective approach to financial integration. The Commission accepted that the challenge was now to consolidate progress and work together on applying better regulatory disciplines to create the best financial framework in the world. The new strategy was described was being practical, economics driven and citizen focussed.

The White Paper builds on the May 2005 Green Paper and a July 2005 Exchange of Views. It also reflects the Report by the Financial Services Committee to the EU Finance Ministers on 2 June 2004 on financial integration within Europe, the ECOFIN Council Conclusions of 11 October 2005 and the Report by the Economic and Monetary Affairs Committee of the European Parliament on the current state of integration of EU financial markets.[150] The main priorities were stated to be concerned with dynamic consolidation, removal of barriers, effective implementation and enhanced

[150] http://www.europarl.eu.int/meetdocs/2004–2009/documents/pr/553/553131/55311en.pdf. See also 'Common actions for growth and employment: the Community Lisbon Programme' COM(2005) 330 final, 20 July2005.

supervisory cooperation and convergence. The Commission was also concerned to expand the EU's external influence in global capital markets and to maintain an effective monitoring process with the results being published by the Commission on an annual basis.

The December 2005 White Paper accordingly represented a reformulation or restatement of the Commission's policy in the financial area for 2005–2010. This was essentially based on consolidation, better regulation, supervisory convergence, competition, and global contribution. This then represents an extension but also reassessment and reformulation of the Commission's new policy approach in this area. A number of particularly important elements were added including, in particular, the use of better regulation based on open consultation and impact assessments as well as the adoption of a more risk based and principles driven approach to regulation, regulatory revision and simplification with only minimum legislative intervention. The main policy components within the White Paper represented a new maturity and sophistication in Commission policy. Much of this is now market, cost and effect rather than simple intervention driven. The Commission is no longer trying to introduce common requirements simply to achieve harmonized European rules at all levels and in all areas.

The White Paper also demonstrates a new sense of responsibility and involvement on the part of the Commission. Rather than only act as a simple agent of absolute harmonization, the Commission has assumed a more intermediate role in which it tries to assist relevant stakeholders discuss and agree on areas of necessary intervention and most appropriate solution. The Commission's function has then become more formulative, advisory and participatory. The Commission is concerned to promote discussion and achieve the most appropriate response rather than simply impose a common minimum decision on all parties regardless of its policy objectives or effect.

These are accordingly useful documents although possibly somewhat light in terms of regulatory content and substance at this stage. They nevertheless contain a number of important new control components and represent the beginning of an extended revision and consolidation phase within European financial integration. All of this is to be strongly supported.

E. PROGRAMME COMMENT

A basic system of mutual access has been created across Europe based on the principle of mutual recognition which was developed by the Commission during the 1980s in place of the earlier full harmonization approach.[151] Mutual recognition is supported by the corresponding principles of

[151] Sections A and B and Ch 6, sections C and D.

minimum harmonization and home country control (although some care has to be exercised in the use of these terms).[152]

In the financial area, this new approach has allowed common agreement to be achieved on certain minimum regulatory or control requirements and outline (although essentially) limited operational and supervisory provisions.[153] This has allowed a single market in banking and financial services to be the constructed on the basis of the mutual recognition of national authorization and licensing systems although only the most minimum regulatory and supervisory framework has been created in each financial sector area with considerable differences remaining in terms of substantive regulatory content and operational market supervision. This has partly occurred through inconsistent interpretation and adoption or simple failure to implement at the national level in certain cases.

Of possibly more importance has been the lack of substantive content provided for in many key areas at the European level.[154] The combined

[152] Minimum harmonization can either be used generally to refer to the selection of necessary areas for legislative intervention at the European level or with the imposition of certain fixed minimum levels of protection within particular directives or the other secondary measures adopted. It then has an alternative external (programme structure) and internal (substantive content) usage. Under the original policy programme outlined in the Commission's 1985 White Paper, 'minimum harmonization' was concerned with the essential areas in which some European harmonization was required. This then corresponded with those areas in which national territories may continue to restrict action contrary to the more general Treaty provisions on free movement. Mutual recognition, in contrast, refers to those areas in which no such restrictions may be imposed and host Member States are required to give effect to the relevant provisions imposed under the law of the home territory under the jurisprudence of the European Court of Justice. Minimum harmonization is then (strictly) the obverse rather than complement or supplement to mutual recognition. Commission, White Paper (n 3), paras 64 and 65. (n 19). See also Ch 6, sections C (1) and (2).

While minimum harmonization is substantive in function, home country control is allocatory and corresponds with the division of power or authority between national agencies within a split or mixed (parallel) supervisory system such as that that operates within a regional trading regime. While it could also be argued that minimum harmonization was already implied in *Cassis de Dijon*, this is incorrect to the extent that *Cassis* was only concerned with initial product production and first placement on the market. Home country control had to be included in the financial area due to the need to provide for the continuing supervision of financial institutions after their initial market entry or authorization. Commission, White Paper (n 3), para 103. For further discussion, Ch 6, sections C and D.

[153] Section B.

[154] With regard to regulatory content, significant differences may still arise, for example, with regard to suitability assessment procedures, supporting documentation and practices on authorization. Specific requirements with regard to internal controls, record and decision taking procedures may also differ as well as detailed rules on capital adequacy credit risk (including, for example, country or sovereign risk, industry risk, geographic risk, transfer risk, default risk and event risk), market risk (including basis risk, yield spread risk, transaction risk, translation risk, availability risk, quantity risk, inventory risk, inflation risk, extension risk, performance risk, repayment risk, discontinuity ('jump') risk, timing risk, forced sale risk and underwriting risk), currency (or foreign exchange) risk, settlement and delivery risks, interest rate risk, more complex financial derivatives related risks, commodity risks and operational risk as well as legal risks, business risks and 'environmental' risks and liquidity rules.

effect of minimum harmonization with mutual recognition is that host territories are not permitted to apply any more onerous requirements in pre-harmonized areas to overseas firms even if only the most minimal of direction has been provided under the relevant directive. Considerable discretion and freedom of action is then left in giving effect to the agreed basic standards imposed. With the significant differences that already exist in underlying legal, regulatory and enforcement systems and supporting control and compliance cultures, the result has been that the assumed operational or regulatory equivalence that should have arisen under mutual recognition has simply not emerged in many areas.

Despite the mandatory operation of the market access system created, no corresponding mutual review or agreed market support arrangements have been established. Enforcement is still Commission controlled with non-implementation (and the fragmentation factor) still being too high in a number of areas. There has also been no clear or, at least, publicly expressed agreement on cross-border support operations in the event that an entity from one Member State experiences (or causes) financial difficulties in another territory.[155]

Considerable economic benefits will follow from the creation of a single market in financial services although the larger welfare gains that arise must be protected from possible market and systemic collapse. Whether the balance between immediate economic advantage and longer-term market and economic stability has been properly achieved remains to be seen.

Significant inconsistencies may also arise with regard to local supervisory practice. Only the most minimal of direction is, for example, provided with regard to consolidated supervision the conduct of which may vary considerably in practice (n 49). Some Member States (including the UK) have also since extended this to include 'significant business unit' supervision (in addition only to legal subsidiaries) as well as more complex forms of new 'conglomerate supervision.' (nn 51 and 52). The main European directives also contain no provision with regard to regular prudential reporting, the number, content and filing of returns and the nature and timing of management meetings. Other information collection practices may vary with local inspection and verification rules and procedures. More formal search and seizure practices may also be different while administrative and criminal sanctions and civil recovery regimes will necessarily vary.

The scope of market access more generally in any territory may be effected by differences in the local definitions of key terms with regard to relevant institutions, products and activities. Certain financial products are also not covered by existing directives such as new derivative structures under the 1993 ISD (including commodity derivatives). The main financial directives also only apply to cross-border establishment by branching rather than by subsidiaries as provided under the Treaty which may create further problems in terms of scope of market access and the exercise of rights in a host territory. Section E (1) and (n 156).

155 K Lanoo 'Supervising the European Financial System' (May 2002) Financial Markets Group, Special Paper No 137. See also Commission 'Report on Financial Stability' (May 2000) prepared by ad hoc working group of the Economic and Financial Committee, Economic Papers, No 143; and Commission, 'Report on financial crisis management' (July 2001).

A number of provisional comments can be made with regard to the limitations and gaps that remain within the final programme of secondary measures adopted in the banking and financial area in Europe. These can be considered in terms of the basic access, regulatory and supervisory issues already identified in this text with some further comments being made with regard to more general systems weaknesses and market support as well as programme completion and institutional direction secured.

(1) Market Access

In terms of market access, the financial programme is largely complete except in relation to subsidiaries. Market access in respect of establishment and services has been secured through the concept of mutual recognition which was been developed in association with the connected principle of home country control under the banking and financial directives. This, however, has not been extended to apply to subsidiaries and agencies as provided for in Article 52 of the Treaty. The effect of this is that non-branch establishment remains to be governed by the basic provisions contained in Article 52. As this has been held to have direct effect and is capable of non-discriminatory application, financial institutions are, at least in theory, capable of challenging national authorization requirements in host Member State courts. To the extent that such subsidiaries were not already authorized in their home Member State, however, the host authorities would be able to insist on separate licensing and authorization. An extended Cassis doctrine would not apply insofar as the subsidiary had not already been authorized to conduct financial business in its home territory. The subsidiary would then, by analogy, not have been legitimately put on the market for the first time in the home territory. The subsidiary would be able to challenge any discriminatory provision although not those of a non-discriminatory prudential nature.[156]

Problems in terms of access do nevertheless still arise with regard to the legality of the notification procedures imposed, a possibly too liberal inter-

[156] The separate authorization required in respect of subsidiaries may also be justified on the basis of an extended general good concept insofar as all prudential requirements may be considered necessary to protect the general good. Under the general good criteria, the host authorities could insist on compliance with their licensing and authorization requirements on the basis that the subsidiary has not already complied with equivalent provisions in the home territory. If this was correct, adoption of the general good may no longer be a device for simply determining the allocation of responsibility between the home and host Member States. It would include all general regulatory requirements which can be justified on a systemic or depositor interest basis. Which rules would apply would be determined having regard to whether the home authorities had already applied the relevant provisions. As they would have done so in relation to branches, host rules would be inapplicable. They would, however, be capable of full application in the case of subsidiaries. Ch 3, section B; and Ch 6, section D.

pretation of the scope of the general good by the Court and the legality and effectiveness of the reciprocity rules imposed in practice.

Some gaps have also arisen with regard to the scope of particular directives such as in connection with commodity derivatives and advice under the original ISD although these have been dealt with through the replacement MIFID.[157] Other problems arise in connection with lack of specification of particular definitions.[158]

(2) Market Control

With regard to market control, a substantial set of supervisory and regulatory provisions has been adopted. While the regulatory measures within the control policy adopted operate on a minimum harmonization basis, financial market supervision is generally conducted through home country control.

Separate regulatory provisions are imposed both in respect of initial authorization and on a continuing basis thereafter. These are generally suitability and capital based with a general and indeterminate requirement being imposed in respect of internal systems and controls. The suitability rules are extended to include directors and managers and shareholders with parallel controls being imposed in relation to non-financial holdings by banks and investment firms. While capital regulation was only imposed initially in relation to credit risk, this has subsequently been extended to include market risk, interest rate risk and foreign exchange risk.

An impressive set of core requirements has accordingly been developed in this area although the focus on capital controls as the principal regulatory control requirement is unfortunate. Capital may be of value in encouraging higher internal risk management control and compliance generally as well as in providing some indirect loss cover although it can never be sufficient by itself.[159]

The focus of modern financial regulation must be on proper internal risk management analysis and compliance supported by high levels of disclosure and market discipline. This has been reflected in recent trends at the international level although only marginally within Europe, for example,

[157] (n 39).

[158] Problems may, for example, still arise with regard to the definition of 'credit institution' under the Banking Consolidation Directive. While this defines a credit institution as an undertaking that accepts deposit from the public and grants credits on its own account, inconsistencies may arise where national legislation expands the definition of, for example, 'deposit' or 'banking business' with the supporting statutory exemptions and exclusions. Case C-366/97 *Romanelli* of 11 Feb 1999, Ch 4 (n 117). See, for example, sections 5 and 6 of the Banking Act 1987 in the UK as restated in Schedule 2 to the Financial Services and Markets Act and supporting Regulated Activities Order.

[159] Walker, Capital Postscript (n 25).

through the qualified recognition of internal risk modelling for capital adequacy purposes.[160]

The omission of further direction in this regard is defensible to the extent that the Community only ever intended to establish a minimum framework on top of which national mutual recognition would operate. To that extent, internal control techniques and procedures can be left to Member State judgement. Insofar as this may create divergent standards across Europe, however, this is unfortunate. Proper internal risk management and control should be the focus of financial regulation and supervision. Relying on more traditional static capital requirements only diverts attention from this core activity within financial institutions. Although again defensible in light of the highly distinct of the nature of markets across Europe and levels of sophistication in place, this is still regrettable insofar as it significantly undermines the overall effectiveness of the European control programme adopted.

While core measures have also been adopted in other key areas of market control and, in particular, with regard to deposit protection and relevant insolvency procedures, these should again be reviewed to ensure that they operate in a complete and complementary manner with the other basic provisions adopted. The content of the overall programme should also be subject to a much more fundamental continuing examination and review process to ensure that all residual gaps and areas of inconsistent operation are identified and corrected.[161] Although a nominally solid series of minimum standards has been established, it is clear that on any more detailed examination only the most skeletal framework of relevant provision has been constructed. While this does confirm the operational value and success of the mutual recognition doctrine as an integration device, serious concerns still arise with regard to the overall effectiveness and quality of the financial regulation secured across Europe at the national level.

The capital adequacy rules for banks and securities companies will have to be further revised following the new measures to be adopted by the Basel Committee on Banking Supervision and EU CRD.[162] Related inconsistencies may also arise in connection with the various policies adopted with regard to liquidity requirements at the Member State level. Although market liquidity is generally reserved to the host territory under the key directives, the adequacy of the liquidity requirements imposed may have

[160] This area has attracted more recent attention especially under the new Basel II capital rules and implementing European Capital Requirements Directive (CRD) although it still requires proper dedicated attention at the international, regional and national levels. (n 25).

[161] Fundamental inconsistencies, for example, may still remain with regard to the scope, content, timing and use of prudential returns, the degree and nature of the individual supervision conducted in respect of particular institutions especially in the banking area and with regard to the number, quality and experience of individual personnel within Member States' supervisory agencies. See also (n 154).

[162] Walker 'Capital Postscript' (n 25).

more effect in practice on the stable and continuing operation of financial markets than capital or other prudential controls. This reservation should be reviewed.

(3) Market Supervision

With regard to financial supervision, the adoption of a basic home country control concept has allowed almost full market access to be secured in respect of branches and services. While a home country control rule has then been adopted, substantial reserve powers are conferred on host authorities. The exchange of information and cooperation requirements as well as verification procedures also mean that in practice, much supervision will be conducted on a shared rather than a pure home or host basis.

Despite the more detailed deficiencies that arise, it must be stressed that a substantial and credible programme of market access and control has been established across Europe. It is only regrettable that more attention has not focused on operational aspects of bank and other financial institution supervision as well as on proper market (or lender of last resort (LLR)) support.[163]

Despite the adoption of certain common minimum provisions with regard to such matters as inspections and verifications, it is possibly in the area of operational market supervision that least progress has been achieved in developing common provisions. No requirements are, for example, imposed in connection with the preparation, content and filing of regular returns. The accurate completion, collection and processing of these returns is an essential part of supervisory practice in almost all countries.[164] No common provisions have been agreed in connection with the importance of management contact and management meetings. Basic provisions could have been considered concerning the timing, purpose and attendance of such meetings. Developing effective working relations between supervisors and management within locally incorporated institutions as well as the host operations of foreign institutions is of crucial importance. The inclusion of some minimum directions or requirements in this regard should have been considered. While minimum requirements with regard to the imposition of sanctions in connection with basic regulatory offences are also provided for, no separate direction is given with regard to the mainte-

[163] Section E (5). Ch 6 (n 13).

[164] While it is understood that the issue of prudential returns was considered by the Commission at any early stage, it was decided not to attempt to develop common standards, at least, initially. This was possibly considered necessary having regard to the other more important areas in which common agreement was required such as scope of supervision (definitions), capital and inspections. Difficulties in this area may have obstructed disagreement in connection with other matters. This decision should, however, now be reconsidered.

nance and operation of more complete enforcement policies at the domestic level. This is again a crucial aspect of local supervisory practice.

Separate difficulties arise in connection with the institutional and agency arrangements set up in each country. No common agreement was arrived at the European level in connection with the training and competence of national supervisory personnel. There has been no agreement on resources and agency structure or capacity although some minimum provision has been included with regard to inter-authority exchange of information. More developed standards on contact and cooperation could have been considered, for example, on the model of the Basel Committee on Banking Supervision. To the extent that European authorities intended to rely on such international standards, this could have been expressed to avoid misunderstanding and inconsistent or contrary national practice. This issue has become of more significance in recent years as the statements of best practice agreed by the Basel Committee have become more complex and substantial. Separate comparable provisions have also been agreed in connection with securities and insurance supervision by the International Organization of Securities Commissions (IOSCO) and the International Association of Insurance Supervisors (IAIS). To the extent that these measures are to be understood to be incorporated and applied within Europe either in whole or in part, this should be made clear.

While the Commission's current consolidation work and Financial Services Action Plan framework are important, a further regulatory *Refonte* will be required in early course to correct a number of the more significant technical deficiencies in the programme while the larger systems revision being undertaken is still too superficial and essentially consumer protection rather than market and payments system stability based.

(4) Mutual Review

The more general difficulty that arises at the European level is in monitoring effective operational consistency and sufficiency of regulatory and supervisory practice across the Member States. This is related to but distinct from the adoption and implementation of individual measures. While the Commission is responsible for monitoring implementation practices, it is generally agreed that insufficient resources have been allocated to ensuring that all specific regulatory measures are given full effect at the national level.[165] The need for continuous and proper enforcement of implementation deficiencies was stressed again by the Lamfalussy Committee.[166] While

[165] It is understood that this was, in particular, to be monitored within DG XIV specifically at one stage although this was not continued due to demand on resources. Interview with Senior Commission official.

[166] Section D (4) and (n 138).

the Lamfalussy recommendations in this regard were endorsed by the Council, no specific action has yet been taken in this regard.

The more general and complex issue that then arises is with regard to ensuring that a necessary degree of effective regulation and supervision is secured in each Member State. This is not dependent upon the implementation of specific provisions rather than the overall or total effect of all regulatory and supervisory action adopted. This will be affected by a number of more subtle factors such as training, resources and competence as well as strict transposition. It was originally proposed that some 'mutual review' or 'peer review' mechanism would be set up within Europe.[167] Although appropriate arrangements were agreed at the international level, it was decided not to adopt any equivalent provision within Europe. The operation of the mutual recognition rule is also understood to mean that national authorities cannot deny market access to banks or financial institutions from other Member States where they satisfy the minimum standards imposed under the financial directives. The effect of this is that while particular authorities may have serious concerns with regard to the extent and quality of the supervision conducted in other Member States, this cannot be used as a basis on which to qualify the underlying Treaty rights conferred on financial institutions.

(5) MARKET SUPPORT AND SYSTEMS FAILURE

Some coordination has been agreed in the areas of depositor and investor protection in the banking and securities areas. The objective is to provide minimum levels of compensation in the event that banks or securities firms fail. After early negotiation, it was agreed that this would operate on a partial rather than full cover basis. Individual investors would then be protected up to agreed limits although some incentive to protect their savings and investments would be retained with professional or wholesale investments being excluded. Market discipline would in this way be preserved and the dangers that would otherwise arise with moral hazard avoided.

167 It is understood that this was proposed by the British authorities during the late 1980s. The concern was that inadequate or insufficient overall supervisory practices would not be maintained in each Member State. The discussions that took place were conducted as part of the larger international negotiations within the Basel Committee. The Committee had incorporated mutual review provisions in its 1983 Revised Concordat. The information requirements supporting this review were strengthened in the 1990 Information Supplement while the operation of all of the Committee's supervisory best practices were restated as absolute minimum rules under the 1992 Minimum Standards. These were adopted in response to the closure of BCCI in July 1991. Walker (n 25), Chs 1 and 2. On subsequent EU use of peer review with accession territories (n 117).

Apart from in connection with this partial depositor and investor protection regime, there has been no more general agreement on larger market support including, in particular, cross-Europe lender of last resort (LLR) responsibility. Even with the establishment of the European Central Bank, no formal central support or lender of last resort function has been established.[168] Full market access has been created across Europe although market support is still to be managed and determined at the national level. Considerable difficulties may arise in practice where a crisis begins as a result of the activities of a large bank or banking group in another Member State. Difficulties may then be created both in providing appropriate support within the local territory where the crisis arises and in the market of the parent institution. Significant problems with regard to division or allocation of cost and responsibility may then arise in such cases while local authorities will have had no control over the access provided to the overseas firm or group under the relevant European provisions. In such cases, market access and market support will clearly conflict.[169]

A system of mutual access will accordingly have been created across Europe based on mandatory mutual recognition. This mutual recognition is, in turn, based on agreement on certain minimum regulatory or control requirements with almost no common operational or supervisory provisions having been specified. Despite the mandatory operation of the market access system created, there is also no corresponding mutual review or agreed market support arrangements. In addition to the underlying access and control conflict which necessarily arises in this area, this can now be understood to include separate regulatory and supervisory elements as well as further review and support components.

(6) Programme Completion and Institutional Revision

A significant amount of further work has been undertaken in recent years to attempt to complete the programme of secondary measures agreed in connection with capital and securities markets specifically as well as more general financial services. In addition to the Commission's Financial Services Action Plan and the securities related recommendations in the Lamflaussy Report, the Committee of Wise Men made a number of specific recommendations with regard to European legislative and regulatory reform. These institutional or agency related revisions can be considered with the larger reforms proposed including the possible assumption of

[168] Walker (n 25), Ch 3 and (n 161; and (n 170 below). See also Ch 6 (n 13).

[169] This creates a separate access and support conflict. Ch 1 (n 4) and section B (2).

supervisory responsibility by the ECB or for the establishment of a separate 'European Financial Services Authority'.[170]

The completion work undertaken to date has accordingly been partly substantive and partly institutional. The substantive or regulatory efforts undertaken have focused on filling in the main regulatory gaps such as with regard to take-overs, prospectuses and market abuse. Some further regulatory improvements have been put forward such as in connection with insurance solvency requirements and banking and securities capital adequacy rules. More generally, the Commission has been concerned with filling in selective substantive gaps rather than any more detailed or sophisticated process of substantive regulatory or supervisory revision. Rather than correct any of the omissions identified, these have either been ignored or simply built into the larger financial framework constructed to date.

More substantive institutional revision such as through the assumption of more formal responsibility by a single agency including either the ECB or a new European banking or financial authority may correct some of the more operational difficulties referred to. Most reform proposals, however, must retain existing national regulatory structures on a subsidiarity basis. Any new European framework would then continue to develop policy and more general administrative or operational guidelines at the European level with specific institutional or market functions being discharged at the national or local level. Even with the more radical institutional reforms proposed, ultimate operational regulation and supervision must continue in practice to be conducted at the domestic level.

It would accordingly appear that the recent revision work undertaken both in connection with secondary programme completion and potential institutional revision may be of relatively limited effect. The substantive

170 (n 155). Under the final Maastrict provisions, the European Central Bank was only given a limited supervisory role. ECB Statute, Art 25 and EC Treaty, Art 105. Possible future involvement was provided for under the 'enabling clause' contained in Art 106(6). The Draft Statute of the European System of Central Banks had included prudential supervision as a fifth basic task of the ESCB although this was deleted. See generally European Shadow Financial Regulatory Committee 'EMU, the ECB and financial supervision' (Oct 1998, Statement No 2); K Lanoo 'Financial Supervision in EMU' *Yearbook of International Financial and Economic Law* (Kluwer Law London 1998) 145; C Hadjiemmanuil and M Andenas 'Banking Supervision and European Monetary Union' JIIB (vol 1, no 2) 84; T Padoa-Schioppa 'EMU and Banking Supervision' Lecture to LSE, Financial Markets Group, 24 Feb 1999 (reproduced *International Finance* vol 2, no 2, 295–308); Lanoo 'Does Europe need an SEC?' (1999), European Capital Markets Institute, Occasional Paper No 1; Lanoo,'Challenges to the structure of financial supervision in the EU' (July 2000) CEPS Working Party report; Lanoo,'EU Securities Market Regulation—Adapting to the needs of an integrated capital market' (Mar 2001) CEPS Working Party Report. See also Padoa-Schioppa 'Towards a European Banking Regulatory Framework' Speech at Conference on 'New equilibria between financial intermediaries, savings and firms' organized by Impresa Magazine, Milan, 23 Oct 1987; and Padoa-Schioppa 'Self vs Public Discipline in the Financial Field' (July 2002) Financial Markets Group, Special Paper No 142.

work may correct some residual gaps in the secondary programme in place. The institutional reforms proposed may also improve legislative adoption at the European level and possibly allow some further coordination of activity at the national level. Whether this will be sufficient to correct all of the residual inconsistencies and more detailed regulatory and supervisory gaps and inconsistencies identified is nevertheless unclear.[171] No separate improvements are proposed in connection with the further problems that arise in terms of mutual review and market support at this time.

The most important recommendation made as part of the recent completion work was possibly in connection with the Lamflaussy Level 3 coordination of activity between national authorities. This is expressly, however, restricted to giving effect to the new Level 2 implementing rules (based on the Level 1 framework principles). This was also at least initially, restricted to securities rather than banking and insurance programme related work. It has to be accepted that it is unclear whether attempting to facilitate this limited coordination can of itself correct all of the deficiencies identified in terms of regulatory and supervisory content, mutual review and market support and especially without any specific new agency mandate in this regard. Even then, this will certainly be of only limited effect to the extent that it is restricted to capital market programme work. Rather than correct, this may only confirm existing cross-sector inconsistencies and gaps within Europe. The result may simply strengthen rather than correct the sector disparities that exist.

The separate difficulty that arises with regard to the current completion programme is whether all of the necessary measures can be agreed and adopted within the ambitious timetables set. Creating specific deadlines does assist promote political agreement and consensus. Pressure is placed on national representatives within the Council and Parliament to attempt to arrive at appropriate compromises by the deadlines fixed. This assumes, however, that suitable draft measures are already available for approval. The pressure on limited Commission resources and the ambitious nature of the programme timetables adopted have meant that substantive quality may

[171] Concerns have been expressed with regard to the gap that has arisen between the political commitment for financial reform and the pace of adoption and implementation. It was considered that progress in creating a single financial market will be even more difficult than the single currency. The process has been further complicated by the 'horse trading' among Member States in the European Parliament and the Commission (n 134). For comment, 'A meeting of minds on markets—views are converging on EU financial services', *Financial Times*, 28 Nov 2002 (editorial). See also (nn 86, 115 and 134). A 'growing disenchantment' had apparently arisen among market participants with the Financial Services Action Plan. Two separate papers were also published by the Paris-based Eurofi Association of Financial Services companies and by Sir Nigel Wicks in the UK. Both reports stressed the need to base an open and integrated financial market on market forces and consultation. The Eurofi Report moved from the original single European regulator proposal to a decentralized structure to be set up within 5–10 years after the end-2005 deadline for the FSAP. On committees (n 13).

suffer in many cases. It is essential that each new measure is fully and carefully considered. Political ambition should not be allowed to undermine or lessen supervisory or regulatory quality.[172]

F. PROGRAMME CLOSE—CONTENT, COMPLETION, AND CORRECTION

A considerable amount of work has been undertaken in the banking and financial area. A number of difficult issues have been considered and considerable clarification achieved. A far from complete and coherent programme has, however, been produced to date. Much of this is still selective and partial while some of the further measures to be produced may only reflect inappropriate political and administrative compromises rather than specific regulatory intent and value.

The main challenge that remains is securing proper programme completion (including existing programme revision) and full programme implementation and review. This will involve ensuring that all residual gaps or deficiencies are corrected and that the programme agreed is then applied and operates in an effective and consistent manner within all Member States in practice. A necessary degree of commitment must be made and resources allocated at the European and national levels to ensure that this is achieved. The final objective must be the full and effective implementation of all necessary measures and the construction of an appropriate level of operational comparability, equivalence and consistency in national regulatory and supervisory practice across all territories within the EU.

Even if any new formal institutional structures cannot be agreed or are considered to be unnecessary or inappropriate indefinitely, closer cooperation and coordination of activity at all operational levels must be ensured. To be effective ultimately, the European financial system may have to move from formal (but still only nominal and superficial) mutual recognition to more substantial mutual review and cooperation or coordination of relevant activity in all operational areas. Traditional mutual recognition may then have to be replaced over time by increased mutual assistance and mutual support and reliance as authorities attempt to develop more effective common operational and administrative systems involving closer cooperation and coordination of all relevant activity.

172 (n 134). On policy and programme reform, Chs 6 and 7. For policy and programme review, Ch 8.

PART FIVE

Financial Policy Comment

6

Banking and Financial Policy—Mutual Recognition and Judicial and Programme Contribution

The European Community (and larger European Union)[1] constitute the most substantial and complex system of regional trading and financial integration attempted to date. This has, in particular, included the provision of a full right of market access in all areas of goods and services (as well as establishment, workers and capital). This is, in turn, based on the underlying Treaty entitlements and supporting rights of market entry (or passport) contained in each of the main financial and equivalent goods and services directives. This privileged right of market access is supported by the construction of a parallel supervisory and regulatory control regime (generally) based on the concepts of minimum harmonization and home country control. The Community has in this way attempted to balance the conflicting issues that arise with securing privileged market access at the same time as secure proper market control and stability within any integrated internal market place.

One of the particular difficulties that had to be overcome in the banking and financial area specifically was that a basic vacuum had been left in the Treaty of Rome with regard to the structure and content of the new policy framework to be constructed. Despite the lack of direction and guidance provided and the earlier problems that arose in trying to apply a full harmonization approach in such a complex and politically sensitive area, a significant amount of progress has since been possible in correcting this original Treaty omission. This has partly been achieved through the work of the European Court of Justice in the construction of a new law of free movement within Europe. This was generally carried out through the liberal interpretation of the underlying rights and obligations created under the Treaty of Rome. Through this process of generous or extended judicial examination, the Court has been able to a significant extent, to clarify, if not, create a number of new rights (and obligations) in addition to the core entitlements (and requirements) set out in the original Treaty provisions.

1 On the legal identity of the European Community and European Union, Ch 1 (n 1) and Ch 2, sections F and G.

Although not specifically designed for use in the financial area, this new corpus of judicially developed law is capable of equal application. Some adjustments have nevertheless to be made in using the more general principles that have emerged in the banking and financial area. Unfortunately, financial market specific related decisions have only recently begun to be issued due to the selective and accidental nature of the litigious process although the cases that have arisen have already allowed the Court generally to confirm the application of the same basic principles in this area. Under the more general doctrine of the unity of the European Community and European law, a substantial body of law is beginning to emerge as part of this new *acquis communautaire*.

A significant contribution has also been made by the European Commission (Council and Parliament) through more general policy work and the application of the principles developed by the Court through the secondary programme rules included within the main banking and financial directives. In carrying out its executive and legislative functions, the Commission, in particular, has assisted in the development or, at least, clarification of a number of new strategic or structural rules (design principles) based on the key ideas of mutual recognition, minimum harmonization and home country control. These have since become the core control components or integration devices within this new framework.

Despite the successes achieved to date, a number of difficulties remain in determining the content and operation of the final or, at least, provisional policy and programme adopted in the banking and financial area. Whether the final Treaty, judicial and programme results secured are complete and coherent remains to be confirmed. Further difficulties also arise in securing the effective and consistent implementation (adoption, application and operation) of these measures at the national level. A basic control or oversight gap or omission accordingly also arises in this regard.

The purpose of this Chapter is to attempt to draw some conclusions with regard to the validity and value of the new policy framework constructed to date. The importance of European integration is initially reviewed and the issues that arise from a policy perspective reconsidered. The origin, validity, meaning[2] and function as well as application and operation of mutual recognition is examined in further detail especially in light of the importance of this integration principle within the new control framework erected. This includes the qualified Treaty and judicial basis for mutual recognition and its historical evolution during the 1980s. The related principles of minimum harmonization and home country control are considered and the sub-stages or sub-processes involved within mutual recognition

[2] In clarifying its use and application, at least, five possible meanings can be assigned to mutual recognition. Section D (1).

examined in turn. Some of the residual difficulties that arise within the secondary programme rules adopted are highlighted. More specific comments are also made with regard to the development and content of the more general policy response constructed over time within the Community. Final conclusions are drawn with regard to the clarity, value and effectiveness of the final result achieved.

A. EUROPEAN INTEGRATION

European history has generally been dominated by political tension and conflict. Disputes have most often been resolved through military engagement and territorial consolidation and attachment.[3] This has also included such other fundamentally non-consensual or non-democratic means as political (crown) succession and linkage (essentially inter-marriage) in addition to simple military acquisition and accession. In contrast with these earlier more general (non-accountable) historical processes, the post-War European period has been characterized by the adoption and application of a series of new functionally specific economic and democratic processes. Within the European Community, in particular, the underlying philosophy has been based on functional integration and volunatary economic and political cooperation rather than non-consensual direction or dominance.[4] The essence of the new Europe can then be understood in terms of the establishment of a new (continuous) process of deepening social, economic and financial integration support by a shared institutional structure that is itself in the process of moving towards some form of more complete democratic inclusion and accountability.

The structure and content of this new European integration can be understood in terms of a number of distinct stages of economic and monetary connection or relation. Possible levels of economic integration generally consist of a free trade area, customs union, common market, economic union, monetary union (as well as economic and monetary union) and full political union.[5] The three main components within this are trade integration, monetary (currency) and supporting economic integration and ultimately political integration. The initial objective of establishing the EEC can be understood in terms of the creation of a single trading market based on a customs union and the full free movement of goods and services with certain other supporting economic policies. While this process is still not complete, this was the original and immediate goal of the Treaty of Rome.

[3] Ch 1 Introduction and (n 8); and Ch 2, (nn 4–6) and section A. On the meaning and nature of integration, Ch 1 (n 14) and Ch 2, sections (B), (C) and (D).

[4] Ch 1 Introduction; and Ch 2, section A and (n 7).

[5] Ch 1 (nn 6 and 7); and Ch 2, section B (nn 28–30 and 33–35).

This was clearly reflected in the discussions that supported the negotiation of the original Treaty provisions in 1957 and subsequent adoption of the Single Act in 1986. Since then, economic and monetary union has been taken forward under the Maastricht Treaty. More substantial institutional reform and expansion were also considered under the proposed European Convention arrangements while further political union is still promoted by various interest and lobby groups.[6]

The construction of a single market across Europe can be justified in terms of a number of economic and consequent social advantages.[7] These are principally based on reduced transactions costs and increased growth and competition which produce consequent higher earnings and investment with related social benefits in terms of improved employment levels and standards of living. Care must nevertheless be taken to ensure that these benefits are fairly distributed between participating territories and regions while an unnecessarily obstructive or inconsistent body of regulations and directives are not adopted that could otherwise undermine the attainment of the economic and social advantages otherwise available. One of the particular residual difficulties that arises is avoiding conflicts through the pursuit of an inconsistent or possibly incoherent social market programme as against a more complete open market policy such as that adopted in federal territories and certain other national and regional economies.[8]

Financial integration then represents one aspect of the larger political and economic integration process still under construction within Europe.[9] This relates specifically to the inter-linkage of each of the main financial sectors on a cross-border basis as well as the further approximation or harmonization of supporting monetary and regulatory policies. Whatever level of integration is achieved in the intermediate to longer term, banking and financial markets will act both as important productive sectors within the economy as well as essential support channels for the rest of the new regional market place and national sub-markets involved.

A significant amount of work has been undertaken in the creation of a single market in financial services within Europe although a number of important omissions and difficulties remain both with regard to the structure and content of the programme of secondary measures adopted and its effective adoption and implementation at the national level. The new policy developed is stated to be based on the three core principles or components of mutual recognition, minimum harmonization and home country control. Despite the apparent clarity and validity of these ideas, the underlying legal

[6] Negotiations were held on the 'White Paper' for a New Europe and the European Convention which began in June 2002. Ch 1, section F (2) (nn 91, 92, and 93).

[7] Ch 2, sections B, C and D.

[8] Ch 1, section E (4) and (5) and (nn 75–78).

[9] Ch 2, sections A and B.

base and substantive and operational content of the law in this area is more complex. Banking and financial policy has, in particular, to be understood in terms of both the relevant principles of European law as applied and expanded by the European Court of Justice as well as the key provisions contained within the programme of secondary measures constructed although significant difficulties remain with regard to each. The development, content and value of both of these aspects of the new policy under construction are considered in the following sections.

B. BANKING AND FINANCIAL POLICY

The purpose of this book has been to attempt to consider the nature, content and effectiveness of the underlying policy adopted within Europe in the banking and financial area. The nature and content of the policy referred to itself may, however, have been far from clear. Five separate issues can accordingly be identified in clarifying the basic idea of banking and financial policy and the specific subject matter covered. These relate to the nature (definition and scope) of the policy covered, the particular and more general integration objectives or purposes concerned, the larger design principles adopted and more specific programme rules developed in the financial directives as well as the overall results or effects achieved.

(1) Definition and Scope

The text has been concerned with banking and financial markets and specifically with the supervision and regulation of their structure and operation. For this purpose, supervision has been understood to refer to the more general oversight function conducted by financial authorities and the more specific compliance activities involved in ensuring that financial institutions comply with all relevant regulatory obligations imposed on them under law, secondary legislation or other administrative practice. Regulation refers to the particular obligations imposed that limit or control the activities carried on by financial institutions and the consequent risks and exposures generated.[10]

This supervisory and regulatory policy can be distinguished from the more general financial policy developed within Europe which also includes monetary and economic policy, exchange rate controls and the free movement of capital. Financial supervision and regulation then form a sub-function or sub-functions within financial policy and financial control more generally.[11]

[10] Ch 1 (n 2).

[11] Ch 2 (nn 114 and 168). Reference to banking and financial policy includes supervisory and regulatory policy as well as more general financial policy to the extent relevant.

The core issue that arises within any regional system is one of securing effective market access or entry. To the extent that the essential function of any regional trading system is to facilitate market entry between the participating territories concerned with regard to all aspects of the products or services covered, a number of local restrictions will have to be adjusted to secure this purpose.[12]

The difficulty that arises within any regional trading system is that the parallel objectives of market access and market control will necessarily conflict. To the extent that any restraints or conditions with regard to such matters as quotas, charges or any other similar measures (of equivalent effect) are removed to allow the free passage of all relevant goods and services, this may undermine the effectiveness of the control systems that would otherwise have applied within the local market place. These may include technical requirements with regard, for example, to product composition and marketing or the content and quality or validity of the services provided. Within the financial area, this will, in particular, include the market entry (authorization) or licensing rules designed to protect depositors and investors as well as the stability of the financial system more generally. Privileged or permissive market access will then conflict with market control and stability. Some reconciliation has accordingly to be secured to ensure that the relevant market (and sub-markets) involved continue to operate in a stable and effective manner. The extent to which this is secured within any regional system will necessarily determine its relative success or failure.

The further but related issue that arises with regard to banking and financial markets specifically is that they are inherently unstable and prone to collapse in the absence of supporting control systems or structures. Banks, in particular, are subject to individual failure as a result of the underlying maturity transformation or mismatch involved in holding and managing deposit based assets.[13] The result of any failure to secure proper market

[12] This creates a basic access and control conflict within any regional trading system. Preface and Ch 1 (n 4) and section B (2). On the difference between regional and global systems Ch 1 (n 23) para 2.

[13] The two main difficulties that arise are with regard to the inherent instability of banks specifically and the risk of contagion between banks and the ultimate risk of systems or systemic collapse more generally.

Banks lend medium to long term on the basis of sight or other short-term funding. Banks will generally keep a reserve to cover any ongoing withdrawal demands. This will either be in the form of cash or some other easily realizable asset. Historically, this reserve has generally represented about one third of the total deposit value of the bank. In the event that additional claims are made in excess of this reserve, the bank will either attempt to borrow from other banks or approach the local central bank for emergency funding (under its lender of last resort arrangements). Ch 1 (n 21).

Under traditional lender of last resort theory, the general rule is that funding will be made available provided that the individual bank concerned is only illiquid and not insolvent. Funding should only otherwise be provided where the collapse of the particular bank could create a larger systemic threat to the local banking system. See generally, Henry Thornton *An*

control may then be the collapse of each of the local markets involved as well as the regional market place as a whole.

An appropriate banking and financial policy must accordingly be adopted within any regional trading system to secure proper market access, market efficiency and market stability.

(2) Objective and Purpose

The general objective of any regional trading system is integration. The benefits of this can be understood both in terms of the economic advantages that will arise from immediate increased market penetration as well as the larger political goals secured in the form of closer union.[14]

The economic advantages of free movement of goods and services can be understood in terms of lower costs of production and increased earnings and investment for firms and improved competition, choice and quality or value for money for customers. Free movement of production factors including capital and labour can also improve allocation and create new opportunities for investment and product or service development and innovation.

Enquiry into the Nature and Effects of the Paper Credit System of Great Britain (1802); and Walter Bagehot *Lombard Street* (1873). See also Thomas M Humphrey 'Lender of Last Resort: the Concept in History' 75:2 Fed Res B Richmond Econ Rev 8 (March/April 1989)

In the event that support funding is not available from the central bank, an individual bank may collapse. Once its reserves are exhausted, it will only hold continuing or outstanding loan obligations on its balance sheet which it will generally not be able to call in early (for contractual reasons) nor dispose of by way of sale or transfer (for legal reasons). Loan sales are inherently difficult to effect due to the intangible nature of the claim. These have generally to be assigned with most legal systems imposing a number of restrictions or conditions on the transfer. Legal assignments under English law are governed by the Law of Property Act 1925 which requires, in particular, an unconditional and confirmed obligation, a written legal instrument and notice to the debtor (or debtors). Other partial forms of transfer are possible such as through equitable assignments or such other devices as participation (or sub-participation) and outright novation (replacement) although these are not generally satisfactory from a legal or economic perspective.

The further commercial difficulty that arises is that the acquirer of any outstanding loan obligation will insist on some reduction (or discount) on its balance sheet value as the new creditor will not be able to make the same original credit assessment as the disposing bank. These discounts may be substantial in practice depending upon the apparent quality of the main assets within the loan book. Where the residual value is considered to be particularly limited, the assets may only be disposed by way of a 'firesale' with only a fraction of the original total amount advanced being paid in consideration of the transfer.

In the event that one bank collapses, this may effect the stability of other banks with whom it either has a direct credit relation or possibly indirectly where a bank run arises (with depositors trying to withdraw their funds to prevent perceived imminent loss). If this contagion (domino or knock-on effect) is sufficient, this may lead to a large number of banks being threatened and ultimately the stability of the financial system as whole being undermined. See generally Walker 'Financial Conglomerates—The Next Generation' *The International Lawyer* (vol 30, no 1, Spring 1996), 57–96.

Banks are accordingly inherently unstable in themselves which instability may be transferred more generally through a process of contagion and ultimate systemic collapse. Ch 1 (n 21).

[14] Ch 1 sections A and B (5); and Ch 2, sections B, C, and D.

The basic objective of any regional financial system is to promote market integration with the consequent economic, social and political benefits that this creates. This must, however, be facilitated without undermining the stability of the local and regional markets concerned. It is accordingly necessary to ensure both effective market access within the regional framework as well as proper market control. This market control then includes both market supervision (or oversight) and regulation (or control).

While integration constitutes the main objective of any regional programme, the more specific sub-objectives or sub-purposes will then consist of market access, market regulation and market supervision.

(3) Design Principles

The overall integration strategy and more general principles that direct policy construction and application may be identified separately. This is not necessary where the policy instruments or rules adopted are clear and simple in themselves although this becomes of importance in more complex situations such as with regard to the banking and financial components in any regional system.

Within Europe, the new approach to market integration adopted by the Commission is stated to be based on the core principles of mutual recognition, minimum harmonization and home country control.[15] It must be stressed, however, that these are not Treaty nor case law derived legal principles as such. They do have some Treaty precedence and are implied in certain judicial decisions. They are not, however, separate, autonomous self-validating legal rules or principles as such.[16]

The Commission had originally adopted an integration approach based on full harmonization that involved agreeing detailed measures governing all aspects of product and service production or provision. The difficulties and delays that arose with this during the 1960s and 1970s, however, forced the Commission to attempt to find a new approach by the early 1980s. Since then, the Commission has attempted to construct a new framework to promote European regional integration on the basis of mutual recognition and minimum harmonization (and with home country control in certain cases including, in particular, in the banking and financial area).[17] These then constitute parallel linked provisions that have been used to direct the construction of a new integration framework especially since the Commission's 1985 White Paper.[18]

[15] Ch 5, section A.

[16] Ch 3, sections C and D.

[17] Ch 2, section H; and Ch 5, section A and (n 18).

[18] Commission *Completing the Internal Market—White Paper from the Commission to the European Council* (Milan 18-29 June 1985), COM (85) 310 final (14 June 1985). Section C (2) and (nn 42 and 43).

It is often stated that this new approach is based on these essential principles. This is correct to the extent that they have been used as more general design principles that have determined the structure and content of the overall framework adopted. Aspects of particular principles have also been incorporated within the secondary programme adopted including the main financial directives.[19] Care must nevertheless be exercised in stating that the secondary programme is itself based on these three principles.[20] They only represent more general precepts or doctrines that have been applied in the construction of the new legislative programme adopted.

To this extent, rather than treat them as fixed legal rules, they are best considered as more general strategic, framework or design principles on which the overall integration approach has been constructed.

(4) PROGRAMME RULES

Having identified the scope of relevant policy, objectives and more general governing design principles involved, a programme of specific secondary measures has been constructed to give these effect. The significance of this is that these programme provisions amplify and define the circumstances in which the underlying Treaty rights concerned can be exercised in any particular case.[21]

In the banking and financial area, this means ensuring that the rights of freedom of establishment and the free provision of services on a cross-border basis may be properly exercised in practice. A core right of market access is then provided for under each of the main financial directives (although this is still based on underlying Treaty provision). The directives also ensure a proper degree of market control through the imposition of a number of common provisions with regard, in particular, to the licensing and continuing supervision of relevant institutions. This is necessary to the extent that the maintenance of effective local control systems would otherwise fall within the scope of the general good and justify national (host) intervention. A set of minimally established common provisions has then been provided for to allow the underlying Treaty rights to be exercised effectively in practice.

[19] Ch 5, sections A and B. Ch 6, sections D (1), (2) and (3).

[20] Section C (1). Mutual recognition and minimum harmonization are properly concerned with the distinction (or selection) between essential and non-essential areas of harmonization as determined by relevant judicial principles which are, in turn, determined by the scope of the permitted mandatory requirements as defined by the Court. This then specifies the areas within which further legislative harmonization or approximation of laws is required. Member States are not entitled to enforce local requirements that restrict trade outside these permitted areas of public interest. Ch 3, sections C and D; and Ch 6, section D (4) and (5) further.

[21] On the legal efect of directives Ch 4 (n 94).

The programme rules adopted then provide for mutual recognition and incorporate the principles of minimum harmonization and home country control in the banking and financial area. The directives must, however, also define the scope of the right of mutual recognition conferred in terms of the particular activities and financial firms covered (such as credit institutions, investment firms and insurance undertakings). Qualifications and exceptions are also generally included.[22] Any conditions applicable are clearly specified (including in relation to authorization requirements and continuing capital rules). Other continuing operational conditions (such as with regard to reporting and notification) are set out. These programme rules then establish the minimum requirements to be complied with in practice to benefit from the mutual recognition provided.

The financial directives accordingly include a number of specific separate programme rules that give effect to the more general integration and financial objectives as well as separate design principles identified.[23] These, in turn, give effect to the underlying Treaty rights that constitute the law of free movement within Europe.

(5) Policy Operation and Policy Application and Implementation

The overall resultant policy adopted within Europe is accordingly a complex mix of Treaty rights and underlying judicial principles as well as secondary programme expansion. The essential rights and obligations created are dependent on underlying Treaty provision, the precise scope and meaning of which are determined by Court ruling. Their exercise and function can then be further developed in the secondary programme measures adopted. The core policy under discussion is accordingly dependent on a combination of Treaty based definition, judicial expansion and programme inclusion and application.

The more general design principles on which the secondary programme are based are of value although insufficient in their own terms to explain or define relevant banking and financial policy. European banking and financial law can only be properly understood having regard to more generally applicable Treaty rights and judicial principles as well as the more detailed supporting secondary programme provisions created.

The exercise of these rights can also be dependent on local implementation, in particular, to the extent that the programme is based on directives (rather than regulations or decisions). A significant amount of discretion has been included within the financial secondary programme constructed such as with regard to suitability rules, capital and other financial requirements and the content and filing of financial returns. The result of this is

[22] Ch 5, section B.
[23] Section B (3).

that a far from uniform set of operational provisions may be applied at the national level. Further difficulties may consequently arise as a result of inconsistent implementation or implementation and adoption failures.

Member States are required to report implementation measures to the Commission which exercises a certain monitoring function over national practice. In light of the limited resources available to the Commission, however, it has been impossible in many areas to maintain any substantial or continuing effective role in this regard and only in the most extreme of situations has action been taken until recently.

The final policy position produced will accordingly also be effected by national implementation inconsistency and omission as well as administrative action (or inaction) by the Commission. This is in addition to the underlying Treaty right, judicial interpretation and secondary expansion and application issues referred to. Banking and financial policy may then be effected by up to five separate possible sources or sets of determining factors. Each of these has consequently to be taken into consideration in understanding and assessing relevant policy in any particular situation.

C. MUTUAL RECOGNITION

The essential policy adopted in the banking and financial area can be stated or explained in terms of the *New Approach* set out in the Commission's 1985 White Paper which was described as being based on mutual recognition and minimum harmonization. European integration is sometimes (although less accurately) stated to be based on mutual recognition alone. This is possibly best treated as a summary or short form reference only.[24]

The purpose of this section is to consider in further detail the meaning and nature of mutual recognition. For this purpose, the origin and validity, nature and content, function, relations and operation of mutual recognition may be considered separately.

(1) ORIGIN AND VALIDITY—*CASSIS DE DIJON* (1979)

In light of importance of the concept of mutual recognition within Europe, it is necessary to consider its origin and validity in further detail. The accepted basis is the case law of the European Court. The Court did not,

[24] This created a useful political 'catch phrase' (or 'sound-byte') which allowed the Commission and other EU institutions to promote the adoption and development of this new integration principle during the 1980s and subsequently. It was this apparent simplicity (and apparent or assumed validity) that facilitated the more general adoption of mutual recognition as the dominant integration doctrine within Europe. Ch 5, section A and Ch 6, section C (1) and (2) below. See also Kenneth Armstrong 'Mutual Recognition' in Catherine Bernard and Joanne Scott *The Law of the Single Market—Unpacking the Premises* (Hart Publishing London 2002).

however, refer to mutual recognition as such in the leading case of *Cassis de Dijon* in 1979. The concept was implied in paragraph 14 of the judgement (which referred to the lawful production and first placement of goods on the market) but not developed further.[25] The facts had not raised any question of equivalence as such (as there had been no express comparison of the effectiveness of the German and the French requirements with France having no comparable rules in place). More significantly, the issue of comparability or equivalence was also strictly *obiter* as the Court had already decided the case on the basis of the inadequacy of the German Government's arguments for the maintenance of its product content rule as against the more general principle of free movement.[26]

The Court did not then refer to the principle of mutual recognition expressly in *Cassis*. It did note earlier in the judgement that appropriate information could be provided through labelling (with regard to origin and content)[27] which implied prior home country action (or pre-compliance) although any idea of comparability or equivalence was not considered further until the later (paragraph 14) reference to prior lawful production and first placement. Any obligation on the part of Member State governments to confirm the nature and content of any protection already secured in the country of export (mutual or pre-review) was also not expressly raised by the Court. The paragraph 14 reference was accordingly *obiter* and can therefore only be considered to amount to a sort of anticipatory or preparatory statement that looked to subsequent decisions in which the issues of prior-compliance and pre-review could be developed more clearly.[28]

[25] (n 28 and 32) and Ch 3, section C (3).

[26] The decision in *Cassis* can be considered to be based on the core elements of authority, derogation (mandatory requirements) and assessment. Ch 3 (n 75). The Court initially recognized the authority of the host territory to regulate matters not subject to any prior common provision at the European level (numbered para 8, para 1). The Court accepted that further measures could be retained where they satisfied certain recognized public interests even where these restricted trade (numbered para 8, para 2). The Court then examined the arguments advanced by the German Government in defence of the maintenance of the restrictions in the present case and rejected them principally on the basis of proportionality (paras 9–13). Having conducted this assessment, the Court concluded that the measures were an unlawful restraint on trade (numbered para 14, para 1). The subsequent reference to lawful production and first placement was accordingly unnecessary and strictly *obiter* (numbered para 14, para 2). A slightly different structure of examination would be followed in later decisions which would include the further aspect of equivalence and home country review. These would then generally be based on authority and derogation (together), assessment and pre-compliance or review in which the comparability of the home and host rules would form part of the actual *ratio*. Ch 3 (nn 70 and 72).

[27] *Cassis*, paras 9–13.

[28] The two key issues that arise with *Cassis* and any extended concept of mutual recognition are prior or pre-compliance and mutual or pre-review.

From a judicial perspective, the issue of mutual recognition arises as part of the Court's examination of the sufficiency of the arguments advanced in support of a holding of legitimate or permitted mandatory requirement. The Court will recognize the authority of the host territory to act in the absence of common rules but also the possible maintenance of some restric-

The issue of comparability and equivalence would be raised, in particular, more directly in the facts of such later cases as *Fietje* (which involved a comparison between two sets of national requirements in connection with product labelling).[29] Even then, there would be no more complete judicial development (or reconciliation) of all of the separate issues involved with the concept of mutual recognition as such.[30]

tion where this can be properly justified (n 26). In conducting this examination, the Court will look to the purpose and content of the restriction and determine, in particular, whether it is necessary and proportionate. As part of this exercise, the Court may look to the degree of protection already secured in the country of origin to the extent that this may be of relevance. This was not strictly relevant in *Cassis* as the French Government had imposed no equivalent requirement and the Court decided the case on the basis of its rejection of the separate arguments advanced by the German Government. The German rules were not compared with the French rules (or absence of any rules) as such but assessed in their own terms. No question of comparability accordingly arose.

To the extent relevant, the issue of prior or pre-compliance will accordingly arise as part of the Court's assessment of relevant mandatory requirement. Within this, the Court could have looked to the relevance and validity of the arguments advanced having regard only to local conditions and needs (in the host territory) without reference to the position in any other Member State. This would have involved a sort of unitary or solo local country or host country only assessment. Rather than consider the prevailing conditions in the country of import (the host territory) alone, however, the Court decided that it had to consider any degree of equivalent protection already secured in the country of export (the home country). The assessment of relevant mandatory requirement (already a judicial creation) is then further extended in this way to include an examination of pre-compliance with the home country rules.

The separate issue that arises is one of pre-review and adjustment (which is concerned with whether Member States are subject to an express obligation of prior mutual review and revision). The Court does not expressly state that Member States must examine the systems already in place in all other territories. The Court does, however, include a review of the protections already provided by such systems in its assessment of legitimate mandatory requirement. The Court does not then create or impose any express obligation of pre-review (or mutual review) although this does arise as a necessary consequence of both the Court's assessment of mandatory requirement and inclusion of prior home country compliance within that. For Commission discussion under its 1980 Communication, Ch 3 (n 83)

Two distinct but connected issues accordingly arise in terms of the Court's assessment of the effects of any prior home country compliance (as part of its examination of available mandatory requirements) and whether Member States are under any separate obligation of mutual or pre-review. The need for prior compliance is referred to in *Cassis* (in para 14 and the earlier discussion of labelling) although this is still *obiter*. The issue of pre-review is not referred to directly but is implied in the *obiter* para 14 statement. In neither case, is mutual recognition referred to as such. Mutual recognition would then be subsequently developed by the Commission as an independent principle as part of its new integration strategy. The effect of this would be to convert mutual recognition into a new independent obligation of general application without reference to any underlying particular Treaty provision and its associated definitions and derogations (nn 30 and 32). On US pre-emption (n 57).

[29] Case 27/80 *Fietje* [1980] ECR 3839, [1981] 3 CMLR. Ch 3 (n 72). *Gilli and Andres* and similar cases would follow *Cassis* without any issue of protective comparability. It is only in some of the later cases that any specific issue of comparability between national measures and the prior compliance with home country rules would be expressly considered. For further discussion, Ch 3, section C (3).

[30] The practice of comparing national requirements would be developed further over time by the Court in a number of decisions under Art 28 (ex 30). See, for example, the cases referred to in Ch 3 (nn 73 and 74). Rather than provide any original or separate validation of the prin-

The idea of mutual recognition was subsequently most substantially developed in the Commission's 1985 White Paper.[31] In its earlier 1980 Communication on *Cassis*, the Commission had referred to the Court's paragraph 14 statement with regard to lawful production and first placement and developed this into an independent free standing principle. To the extent that the first separate reference to mutual recognition was in the White Paper, it has to be regarded as only constituting an executive or administrative construct under European law. This would then be given some further judicial support subsequently although the Court would continue only to consider specific Treaty provisions and not attempt to convert this into any more general doctrine. While the supposed juridical base would remain *Cassis*, care has accordingly to be exercised in light of the limitations of the original judgement in these terms.[32]

There is some but only limited Treaty support for this new harmonization principle. Mutual recognition was referred to with regard to diplomas, certificates and formal qualifications (Article 47(ex 57))[33] as well as to companies (Article 293 (ex 220)).[34] In each case, however, the recognition to be secured does not operate through the Treaty directly but assumes some process of prior identification, negotiation and common agreement. There is accordingly indirect Treaty precedent for mutual recognition although this cannot be construed (and is not used) as providing any direct legal basis for the more general use of the principle as an independent integration doctrine or device across Europe.

The adoption of mutual recognition as an integration principle has also been supported by the Council of Ministers in various statements since the

ciple of mutual recognition as such, these decisions continued to apply the basic principles established under *Cassis* (authority, derogation and assessment) to which prior compliance would be added as part of the assessment exercise to the extent necessary (nn 26 and 28). The Court would then appear to have been careful only to consider (interpret and apply) relevant Treaty provisions and not to attempt to develop any more general doctrine of mutual recognition beyond its legal (Treaty) authority to do so. For comment on the US position with regard to federal pre-emption of state law (nn 54 and 57).

[31] (n 18).

[32] *Cassis* should possibly be referred to as the legal origin of the principle. More accurately, it is the origin of the principles of comparability and equivalence that would be developed by the Court in subsequent decisions (nn 26 and 28).

[33] Art 47 (ex 57) provides for the recognition of diplomas, certificates and other evidence of formal qualifications. This was to operate on the basis of Council directives in each of the major areas concerned. Mutual recognition was accordingly provided for although this was to work through secondary measures rather than directly under the Treaty.

[34] Art 293 (ex 220) provided for the mutual recognition of companies and firms. This was even more generally stated with Member States only being required to enter into negotiations with one another. This would only take effect through an intergovernmental mechanism. An initial Convention on the mutual recognition of companies and legal persons was entered into in 1968. For further discussion, Goldman 'The Convention Between Member States of the European Community on the Mutual Recognition of Companies and Legal Persons' [1968/69] 6 CMLR 104.

early 1980s although this communiqué acceptance and application again does not create any separate legal foundation for its subsequent or more general use.[35] The Council did, in particular, endorse the Commission's White Paper programme although this cannot be seen as a legal validation of mutual recognition as a separate enforcement or legislative device as such.

It would then appear that mutual recognition was initially only an executive or administrative policy construct that was loosely based on some more general (anticipatory or preparatory) judicial statement and reference rather than clear legal authority. Mutual recognition has no express Treaty basis and only arose as a sort of necessary implication from the Court's assessment of whether any national measure fell within the scope of its permitted mandatory requirements. Even then, this only becomes relevant once the Court has denied the right of the Member State to ignore the protection already secured within the territory of origin.[36] Rather than expressly endorse the Commission's full policy of mutual recognition as such, the Court would continue to develop its examination and assessment practice separately with comparability being restricted only to form one part of its review of whether national measures should be permitted as necessary and proportionate mandatory requirements in each individual case.

(2) NATURE AND CONTENT—THE 1985 WHITE PAPER AND NEW APPROACH

The Commission had originally followed a full harmonization approach to European integration more generally.[37] This was based on the adoption of a number of secondary measures (regulations or directives) in implementation of the General Programmes for goods and services provided for under the Treaty. The main programmes were adopted in 1961 and 1962. In the 1985 White Paper, the Commission recognized that some progress had been possible on this basis.[38] Difficulties had nevertheless arisen in certain areas while the recessionary pressures of the 1970s had led many Member States to adopt a more protectionist and restrictive policy especially with regard to non-tariff barriers. The associated negotiation process for each separate secondary measure had also become cumbersome and prone to delay especially with the practice of attempting to

[35] European Council Communiqués following Copenhagen Summit (Dec 1982), Fontainebleau (June 1984), Dublin (Dec 1984) and Brussels (Mar 1985). Section C (2).

[36] (n 28).

[37] Ch 5, section A.

[38] The Commission refers to the harmonization approach which had been the basis for Community action during the first 25 years producing unprecedented progress in the creation of common rules on a Community wide basis. White Paper, para 61.

incorporate detailed technical specifications within new directives. This was also, of course, subject to veto due to the unanimity requirement under Article 100 (94) of the Treaty.[39]

The need for more substantial progress was generally accepted by the beginning of the 1980s. The European Council pledged itself to the completion of the Internal Market as a priority in Copenhagen in December 1982. This was restated at Fontainebleau in June 1984, Dublin in December 1984 and Brussels in March 1985. The Commission subsequently produced a Consolidation Programme in June 1984 that identified a number of proposals to be adopted by the Council with a view to completing the single market by 1992. This was taken forward under the 1985 White Paper which attempted to construct a new policy for the removal of all physical, technical and fiscal barriers.[40] The White Paper was implemented through various Treaty amendments under the Single European Act in 1986 which provided, in particular, for the inclusion of a new Article 8a (18) on the Internal Market and for the introduction of qualified majority voting in associated measures.[41]

As part of its new approach, the Commission had decided to focus on mutual recognition and equivalence rather than full harmonization.[42]

[39] Para 48.

[40] (n 18). See also Ch 3 (nn 93–5).

[41] For criticism of the Single Act on the basis that it qualified the scope of the original Treaty provisions by focusing only on the completion of the 'Internal Market', Pescatore 'Some Critical Remarks on the "Single European Act"' 24 CMLR 9 (1987), 11. Pescatore argues that the effect was to substitute the one sided notion of an internal market based on arbitrary selection of Treaty objectives for the well balanced and complex concept of the Common Market. Pescatore also criticized the decision not to give the definition of the Internal Market set out in Art 8a direct effect. The Luxembourg Conference (which negotiated the Single Act) adopted a separate 'Declaration on Art 8a' which confirmed that setting the date of 31 Dec 1992 did not create any automatic legal effect. This was despite the Commission's recommendation that Art 8a should have direct effect. Ehlermann and Glaesner nevertheless claimed that the Internal Market represented a new substantive legal concept and that proceedings may be commenced against the Council under Art 175 if it failed to act. Toth argued that the Declaration was only an interpretative communication with no legal effect. Pescatore, 12. See also, N Forwood and M Clough 'The Single European Act and Free Movement' 11 ELR (1986) 383, 399–404; CD Ehlermann [364–72]; and HJ Glaesner 'The Single European Act: Attempt at an Appraisal' 10 Fordham ILJ (1987), 446. Claus-Dieter Ehlermann was Director General of the Commission Legal Service and Hans-Joachim Glaesner Director General of the Council Legal Service; AG Toth 'The Legal Status of the Declarations Annexed to the Single European Act' 23 CMLR (1986), 803.

[42] The White Paper refers to the Commission moving from the concept of harmonization towards that of mutual recognition and equivalence (para 13). With the acceptance of the essential equivalence of the objectives of national legislation, mutual recognition could be an effective strategy for bringing about a common trading market (para 63). Following the rulings of the Court of Justice, both the European Parliament and the Doodge Committee had stressed the principle that goods lawfully manufactured and marketed in one Member State must be allowed free entry into other Member States (para 77). Immediate and full recognition must be the rule where harmonization of supporting regulations and standards was not considered essential. See also (n 60) and Ch 3 (n 97).

Approximation of laws under Article 100 would still be required although it was proposed that this would be on a majority rather than unanimous basis.[43] The Commission accepted that while pure mutual recognition could remove barriers to trade, it would be inadequate for the purpose of constructing an expanding and competitive European market by itself.[44] The Commission also noted that a harmonization policy on its own would be over-regulatory, take a significant amount of time to implement and be inflexible and constrain innovation.[45] The new approach to be adopted would accordingly proceed on the basis of the mutual recognition of non-essential standards and with legislative harmonization through directives under Article 100 being restricted to core health and safety requirements that would be obligatory in all Member States. The separate 'mutual acceptance' of national standards would be promoted through the agreed notification and standstill procedure set up under Directive 83/189/EEC in connection with non-standardized areas pending further European harmonization.[46]

Article 100 (94) was superseded by Article 100a (95) which was inserted into the Treaty by the Single European Act 1996. Article 100 (95) was not formally repealed although its requirement for unanimity meant that most new measures would be adopted under the qualified majority voting provided for in Article 100a (95).[47] Certain types of measures were

[43] Para 13. Art 100 provides for the approximation of such provisions laid down by law, regulation or administrative action in Member States as directly affect the establishment of the common market. Art 100 (94) then provided the basis for the adoption of harmonization measures in any area relevant to the operation of the Common Market where no other express provision was set out in the Treaty. The scope of the Common Market was defined in Art 3 to include attainment of the four freedoms (goods, persons (workers and establishment), services and capital) as well as the promotion of common policies in agriculture, transport and social services and the protection of competition. Art 235 separately provided for the adoption of measures whenever necessary to achieve a Community objective where no express legislative power was contained in the Treaty.

Following the adoption of the General Programme for the elimination of technical barriers to trade in May 1969, a number of directives were adopted under Art 100 (see OJ Eng Spec Ed 2d Ser 1974, 25). Almost 200 directives had been adopted by the mid-1980s in such areas as motor vehicles (over 60 measures alone), foodstuffs, cosmetics and pharmaceuticals, dangerous products, consumer electrical goods, mechanical products and weighing equipment.

[44] Para 64. Section D (2) and (n 77).

[45] ibid.

[46] Paras 65 and 75. Directive 83/189/EEC on the provision of information on technical standards and regulations (OJ L 109/8 (25 Apr 1983)). This provides for the prior notification to the Commission of any regulations that set a 'technical specification' which includes any requirement as to product quality, performance, safety, testing, packaging or labelling. The Commission would notify all other Member States. The adoption of a new specification could be made subject to a six months delay to consider its effect and the need for possible amendment. The Commission could also demand a delay for up to one year to allow it to propose a harmonization directive. Directive 83/189/EEC was subsequently replaced by Directive 98/34/EC (OJ L 204 (21 July 98), 37)). See also Ch 3 (n 97).

[47] Under Art 100a, the Council is by qualified majority to adopt measures for the approxi-

excluded from the scope of the new harmonization procedure and a further opt-out provision provided for (although this was generally not used in practice).[48] Article 100b (now repealed) also provided for Commission review of any non-harmonized laws after 1993 and an automatic recognition procedure. The review was conducted by the Commission although it was decided that it would be sufficient to proceed through the continued application of the case law of the European Court without the need for any further legislative recognition device.[49] Rather than adopt some form of automatic recognition measure with regard to residual non-harmonized areas, the Commission produced a further notification requirement under Decision 3052/95/EC.[50] This provided for the disclosure of the non-application of mutual recognition. Under the Decision, Member States were to give notice within 45 days where they intended not to apply mutual recognition in any particular area after 1 January 1997.[51]

In connection with the harmonization of technical standards, the Commission had adopted a series of new techniques as part of its larger *New Approach* to the completion of the Internal Market. The difficulty that had arisen was that there was demand for a large number of new consumer and environmental protection measures by the early 1980s especially following the significant technological advances that had taken place. The Commission had tried to deal with this through its traditional full harmo-

mation of the provisions laid down by law, regulation or administrative action in Member States which have as their object the establishment and functioning of the internal market. This was to be on a proposal by the Commission and in cooperation with the European Parliament and after consulting the Economic and Social Committee.

[48] Art 100a could not be used with regard to fiscal provisions, free movement of persons and employed persons (Art 100a(2)). Under Art 100a(4), Member States may decline to adopt all or part of a harmonized measure where this was justified by an Art 36 interest or the need to protect the environment or working environment. This was not used in practice due to the complex trigger and Court review involved. For comment, M Waelbroeck 'The Role of the Court of Justice in the Implementation of the Single European Act' 11 Michigan LJ (1990), 671, 684–8.

[49] Commission Communication 'Management of the Mutual Recognition of National Rules After 1992' COM(93) 669 final.

[50] Decision 3052/95/EC establishing a procedure for the exchange of information on national measures derogating from the principle of the free movement of goods within the Community (OJ L 321 (30 Dec 1995), 1)). The Decision applies to any measure which either imposes a general ban on goods, refuses to allow goods to be placed on the market, requires the modification of the model or type of product concerned or withdraws the product from the market. In the event that notification is given, the Commission may either commence infringement proceedings, attempt to harmonize the measure at the European level or take no action. This will depend upon the nature of the measure (temporary or permanent) and whether substantive differences exist in terms of local practice which cannot be dealt with through mutual recognition. The Commission only received 34 notifications in 1996, 69 in 1998 and 26 in 1999. Commission 'Report on the implementation of Decision 3052/95/EC in 1997 and 1998' COM(2000) 194 final.

[51] This was modelled on the earlier transparency obligation set out in Directive 83/189/EEC (n 46).

nization approach although this would become increasingly inadequate in light of the extent of the changes that had occurred and calls for an increased degree of appropriate protection on the European basis. The new response was partly constructed on the basis of Directive 83/189/EEC which had provided for the notification to the Commission and the other Member States of any new 'technical specifications' which could be made subject to a six month or one year implementation delay.[52]

Having recognized the potential value of mutual recognition, the Commission began to develop a new more substantial approach to technical harmonization.[53] This would be based on selective harmonization in essential areas and the development of appropriate technical standards by relevant standardization bodies. The new technical specifications produced would not be mandatory although the sufficiency of local requirements would have to be recognized (under the principle of mutual recognition) where these conformed to the harmonized standards set.[54] This new approach to technical harmonization was approved by the Council in May 1985.[55] Relevant minimum standards were set out in a number of framework directives in various areas.[56] Where relevant European measures had

[52] (n 46).

[53] See, eg, Commission Communication to the Council and Parliament on a new approach to standardization policy (COM(85) 19). See also Commission, 'Technical Harmonization and Standards: A New Approach' (Bull EC 1-1985).

[54] Member States were required to recognize the sufficiency of other national standards on an interim basis until new 'harmonized' standards could be produced. Once a standard had been approved by the Commission and published in the Official Journal, all Member States had to accept goods that were conform. Where a Member State disputed the conformity of a standard to the safety objective set out in a framework Directive, the Member State had to substantiate the contention. This reversal in the burden of proof effectively bypassed any continuing problems with unanimity. Any existing European standards would have absolute priority. Any others, would be subject to the new Commission acceptance procedure. New standards would be developed by recognized bodies made up of representatives of industry, government, consumer and trade union interests. Relevant bodies included CEN (the European Committee for Standardization) and CENELEC (the European Committee for Electro-technical Standardization) as well as other more specialist agencies such as the ETSI (the European Telecommunications Standards Institute). A number of new agencies have been set up subsequently at the same time as staff and financial resources expanded and decision taking procedures improved. See, eg, Commission, Green Paper on European Standardization (28 Jan 1991). Community systems were also set up for the authorization and certification of laboratories and the establishment of appropriate standards for testing, inspection and certificate issuance. Commission, 'Global Approach to Certification and Testing' and Council Resolution of 12 Dec 1989 (OJ C 10 (16 Jan 1989)). For further discussion especially with regard to the US response to the development of these new standard setting functions within Europe, Bermann, Goebel, Davey and Fox *Cases and Materials on European Law* (West United States 1993) 442–7. For further comment (n 57).

[55] Council Resolution of 7 May 1985 (OJ C 136/1 (4.6.1985)).

[56] See, eg, Directive 88/378?EC of 3 May 1988 on the safety of toys (OJ L 187/1 (16 July 1988)); Directive 89/392/EC of 14 June 1989 on safety of machinery (OJ L 183/9 (29 June 1989)). Appropriately certified products are marked 'CE.' See generally F Burrows *Free Movement in European Law* (Clarendon Press Oxford 1987).

established a new standard, Member States would not be able to impose higher requirements unless this could be justified on public interest grounds.[57]

Mutual recognition would then become a key part of the Commission's integration strategy within Europe during the 1980s. The use of mutual recognition in other areas apart from goods has been monitored by the Commission.[58] The importance of mutual recognition was more recently restated within the most recent proposals for the completion of the Single Market such as in the Commission's *Action Plan for the Single Market*.[59]

The new integration approach to be adopted has accordingly been based on the principle of (legislative) minimum harmonization in essential areas with (judicial) mutual recognition being applied and enforced in connection with all other non-essential aspects of standards application and compliance. A revised or partial mutual recognition principle also operated in the form of mutual acceptance during the transitional period in essential areas. In the White Paper, the Commission appears to have been careful not to state that existing European law was based on the principle of mutual recognition as such.[60] The Commission nevertheless recognized the value of mutual recognition in preventing national authorities from imposing standards in non-essential areas and confirmed the Commission's commitment to reinforce this through the use of its enforcement powers under the Treaty.[61]

The 1985 While Paper was accordingly important in clarifying two core issues with regard to the content and operation of the Commission's new approach. The Commission intended to rely on what it referred to as 'the

[57] See, eg, Case 148/78 *Publico Ministero v Ratti* [1979] ECR 1629 (a 1963 Italian law on dangerous solvents could not be enforced following adoption of the 1973 European Directive). See also Case 88/79 *Public v Grunert* [1980] ECR 1827 (French meat preservatives); Case 282/87 *Buet v Public* [1989] ECR 1235 (French prohibition on home canvassing of book sales); and Case 60/86 *Commission v United Kingdom* [1988] ECR 3921 (dim-dip lighting not included with relevant European directives). For discussion of the issue of pre-emption from a US perspective, Bermann, Goebel, Davey and Fox (n 54) 454–64. The position in the US would appear to be that while the Supreme Court has tried to develop various legal doctrines to justify federal pre-emption, the current view is that federal and state regulation may co-exist and pre-emption will only take place where there is evidence of a congressional intent to that effect.

[58] Commission's first biennial report, 'Application of the Principle of Mutual Recognition in Product and Services Markets' See also Commission Communication, 'Management of the Mutual Recognition National Rules After 1992' COM(93) 669final.

[59] Commission 'Mutual recognition in the context of the follow-up to the Action Plan for the Single Market' (June 1999). See also Commission *Action Plan for the Single Market* SEC (97) 1 final. Ch 5 (n 4) and section D.

[60] See, eg, para 58 where it proposes that the general principle should be approved that a product should be sold freely if it is lawfully manufactured and marketed in one Member State. The European Parliament and the Dooge Committee are, however, referred to as being more mandatory in this matter. See, eg, para 77. (n 42).

[61] Paras 65 and 77.

principle of mutual recognition' to prevent Member States from enforcing national provisions in non-essential areas. This was on the basis that equivalent protection would already have been provided in the country of origin. This was subject to mandatory requirements although these generally correspond with the scope of essential as opposed to non-essential regulations and standards. This accordingly followed the simplified approach to *Cassis* as developed in its 1980 Interpretative Communication and subsequent case law on Article 30 (ex 28).

The second issue highlighted was the new strategy to be adopted with regard to legislative harmonization in essential technical areas. This would focus on key areas of health and safety standards (which corresponded with the scope of permitted mandatory requirements). This legislative harmonization would then proceed on the basis of only confirming certain essential or minimum requirements with technical conformity being determined by external assessment agencies. While the non-legislative (non-essential) aspect of the new strategy was based on the Commission's extended interpretation of *Cassis*, selective and essential (legislative) harmonization would be developed by the Commission separately or, at least, on a parallel basis.

(3) Integration Function

The three components of mutual recognition, minimum harmonization and home country control can also be considered in functional terms. For this purpose, the correspondence between the three key design principles (of mutual recognition minimum harmonization and home country control) and the basic issues or objectives that arise within any regional trading system can be identified. The core functions discharged by each of these integration devices can then be considered at both a simple and a more complete or developed level of examination.

(a) Regional Correspondence

The objective of any regional system is to provide for either full or privileged market access in any particular sector or with regard to any specific range goods or services at the same time as ensure that an appropriate level of market or product control is secured. This corresponds with the basic access and control conflict identified.[62] The two core objectives of any regional system are accordingly access and control. In considering control in connection with financial markets, this also involves both market regulation and market supervision.[63] From this, the three core issues to be dealt

[62] Ch 1 (n 4) and section B (2).
[63] Section B (2). Market regulation refers to the imposition of specific rules or regulations

with within any regional financial arrangement can be considered to consist of market access, market regulation and market supervision.

If the three core policy components of mutual recognition, minimum harmonization and home country control are then re-considered having regard to the underlying objectives identified within any regional trading arrangement (access, regulation and supervision), the three clearly correspond. The general purpose of mutual recognition is to promote market access. Minimum harmonization establishes a basic level of regulatory control. Home country control further provides for the assignment or allocation of supervisory responsibility to the home or parent territory.

While the Court or the Commission may not have specifically intended that this correspondence of objectives and function should arise, this is of value in explaining or, at least, better understanding how the three core policy components fit together within the larger policy framework constructed.

(b) Essential Functions

In terms of more specific function within this correspondence of operations, mutual recognition can be considered to carry out a validation (certification or legitimization) function, minimum harmonization a regulatory (or substantive control) function and home country control an allocation (oversight or compliance) function.

In carrying out its access role in the banking and financial area, mutual recognition operates by validating the effectiveness of the authorization (license) held by the incoming bank or financial firm and supporting supervisory system. Minimum harmonization specifies the areas of activity that are to be subject to prior legislative harmonization or approximation and sets the base level of protection to be provided. It is accordingly concerned with determining the particular body and level of regulatory or control provision to be applied in any sector. Home country control provides for the division of supervisory function between national authorities and is therefore allocatory in function.

This correspondence is supported by the terms of the 1985 White Paper and the preambles to the financial directives although not referred to expressly in these terms.[64]

on financial institutions either through law, secondary enactments or administrative practice. Supervision refers to the corresponding process of oversight or review to ensure compliance with the regulations imposed or more general market stability. Ch 1 (n 2).

[64] Section C (2).

(c) Corrective Relations

While this objectives and functional approach is of assistance in understanding the operation and value of each component, this simple correspondence breaks down on any more detailed examination. While minimum harmonization secures a proper identification of the core elements of any national regulatory system (including initial authorization, continuing financial compliance and corrective action), many (if not most) detailed substantive and operational aspects of the system are omitted in the main financial directives. A series of fundamental regulatory and supervisory gaps or omissions then arise with regard to the level of detailed protection provided or failure to include any specific measure within the European financial programme constructed.

These gaps in terms of full systems rules and compliance and enforcement are dealt with in practice by applying the relevant home country provisions. While a simple concept of home country control based on allocation of supervisory authority can be developed,[65] this has now to be extended to include both regulatory and supervisory omissions within the European financial framework. For these to have effect, the concept of mutual recognition has consequently also to be extended beyond the validation of the areas of minimum harmonization secured to include all other aspects of the financial regulation and supervision conducted within the home or parent territory not dealt with on the EU level.

Under this (further) analysis, home country control becomes a more complete and substitute concept applying to all aspects of national regulatory (detailed and full systems) requirements as well supervisory (oversight and enforcement) practices. Mutual recognition then operates as an essential validation mechanism for all of this rather than simply be restricted to areas of minimum harmonization or the scope of the basic home country licence. Home country control additionally carries out a further corrective regulatory (substantive) and supervisory (oversight and compliance) function. This applies to both the initial authorization and continuing oversight of the activities of a bank or other financial institution. The validation function within mutual recognition is also then extended to apply to all aspects of the home country authority.

The essence of the new approach adopted by the Commission in the financial area is accordingly based on home country control. Although implied in *Cassis*, this only corresponds in the financial area with the idea of first placement in terms of initial authorization. Banks and other financial institutions also require substantial ongoing supervision. It is this continuing element of both regulatory and supervisory compliance that

[65] Section D (3).

distinguishes financial services from other products.[66] Mutual recognition is then applied to validate the effectiveness of both this initial and ongoing regulatory compliance within the host territory. This effectively extends the de facto jurisdiction of the home supervisory and regulatory system into that of the host through local withdrawal or exemption. Minimum harmonization still only relates to the essential standards established in mandatory areas (exempt from the scope of mutual recognition under the jurisprudence of the Court) with all other regulatory requirements being dealt with under a combined process of mutual recognition and home country control.

D. COMPONENT STRUCTURE

Despite the simplicity of the Commission and political references to the three core programme components of mutual recognition, minimum harmonization and home country control, their relationship and operation is still far from clear in practice.

These integration devices or components are possibly best considered as Commission, executive or administrative constructs that are designed to develop or promote the new revised integration policy adopted.[67] Their legal authority does not derive from any express juridical base although, to the extent necessary, they have been validated by subsequent Court, Council and secondary legislative application and acceptance. They nevertheless remain important more general policy or design principles rather than operational rules or principles.

The meaning and relationship between each of the three core policy components is considered in further detail in the following sub-sections.

(1) Mutual Recognition— Meaning

It must be accepted that mutual recognition is a deceptively complex concept. While it appears to have a simple and obvious meaning, the term has not been judicially or otherwise officially defined.[68]

Depending upon how the term is used, mutual recognition may be considered to have a number of separate meanings. In connection with its judicial relevance, mutual recognition is concerned with the assessment of

[66] This is despite the assimilation between financial and other products adopted in the White Paper. White Paper, para 103.

[67] (n 24) and section C (1) and (3).

[68] A more general provisional definition may be constructed on the basis of a statement of official (country) agreement as to the validity and application of a foreign law and financial regulatory system within the local or host jurisdiction. On relevant official European documents, section C (1) and (2).

comparability or equivalence of national protective measures. This will be considered by the Court as part of its examination of mandatory requirements and determination as to whether any identified national interests should take precedence over the fundamental principle of free movement.[69] The Court is, however, careful not to refer to mutual recognition as such and this judicial examination of comparability or equivalence must be understood as only forming one part of the Court's larger assessment exercise under the particular Treaty article.

In its 1980 Communication on the decision in *Cassis de Dijon*, the Commission took this assessment of comparability and equivalence and converted into a free standing and independent legal principle.[70] Although not expressed in these terms in the original judgement, the effect of the paragraph 14 reference could be understood to mean that Member State governments are to be placed under an obligation to review other national provisions and to make any necessary adjustments to their own laws or practices.[71] This was then used with minimum harmonization to construct the new integration approach developed under the 1985 White Paper.

Mutual recognition is also often used to refer to the process of cross-identification and cross-validation of the exercise of national powers within directives and, in particular, the financial directives. This is concerned, for example, with confirming the validity of the extended scope of each of the separate licences (or passports) created under the directives that allow banks and financial firms authorized in one Member State to conduct relevant business in all others. This creates a sort of 'internal' usage as distinct from its more general 'external' application as part of the Commission's new integration strategy.[72]

Mutual recognition can also be used more generally (although less accurately) to refer to the Commission's *New Approach* to European regional integration. This is less precise to the extent that minimum harmonization and home country control (especially in the financial area) are independent and separate operational principles and not sub-functions or sub-operations within mutual recognition.[73]

The term can again be used more generally to refer to any act of mutual or reciprocal comparison and acceptance where ever it arises.

From this, mutual recognition can be used for the purposes of external judicial specification (within a larger dependent act) or as an independent legal principle. It can also be used for more general composite policy purposes or to refer to a particular internal act of mutual acceptance or validation

[69] Ch 3, section (3) (C) and (D)); and Ch 6, section C (1).
[70] Section C (1).
[71] (n 28). See also Ch 3, section C (3) and (n 83).
[72] Section C (3).
[73] Sections C (2) and D (2) and (3).

within a European legislative measure. It can also be used more generically to refer to any act of conditional acceptance or recognition.

Care must accordingly to be exercised in using the term. It is not that any particular usage is wrong, only that the intended meaning should be made clear in each case. Historically, the most correct linguistic usage is (arguably) the Commission's independent obligation of review and adjustment as set out in its 1980 Communication although the legal validity of this is still questionable being dependent on the Court's limited original and subsequent development of the ideas of comparability and equivalence under its case law.[74]

Whatever specific meaning is intended, mutual recognition can be considered to carry out a validation function and correspond with the need for privileged or facilitated market access within a regional system. While originally restricted to being used only with minimum harmonization as set out in the financial directives, this has since had to be extended to include all other more detailed regulatory and operational rules.[75]

In light of the complexity of this validation function, mutual recognition is possibly best considered to constitute a process rather than a single activity. Depending upon how the term is used, mutual recognition can also be considered to involve a number of sub-operations or sub-functions. This is considered in further detail below.[76]

(2) Minimum Harmonization

Similar definitional difficulties arise with regard to minimum harmonization although not to the same extent as with mutual recognition. Minimum harmonization can generally either be used to refer to the selection of core areas for legislative intervention (harmonization or approximation) or the fixed minimum level of protection set under any particular directive adopted. This again creates a sort of parallel external and internal usage.

In the 1985 White Paper, the Commission stressed that an integration strategy based purely on mutual recognition would be inadequate to build an expanding market based on competitiveness in which a 'continental scale' uniform market could be constructed.[77] The new approach would then involve both mutual recognition and minimum legislative harmonization in parallel more generally[78] as well as home country control in the financial area specifically.

[74] Ch 3, section C (3); and Ch 6, section C (1) and (2).
[75] Section D (3).
[76] Section E and Ch 7, section E (5).
[77] White Paper, para 64. Section C (2) and (nn 42 and 44).
[78] A clear distinction was drawn between Internal Market initiatives in areas where it was essential to harmonize and those that may be left to mutual recognition of national regulations

With regard to minimum harmonization, the White Paper refers to legislative harmonization in future being restricted to laying down essential health and safety requirements which were to be obligatory in all Member States. Conformity with this would then entitle a product to free movement (para 65, indent 2). Where barriers to trade were created by justified divergent national regulations concerning health and safety of citizens and consumer and environmental protection, legislative harmonization would be confined to laying down essential (but not strictly minimum) requirements (para 68). Where harmonization of regulations would still be required, enterprises would only have to meet a single set of harmonised rules for their products to enjoy free circulation throughout the Community (para 79).

Minimum harmonization may then be concerned with either the selection of necessary areas for further legislative action through the establishment of common European provisions or with the agreement and imposition of certain fixed minimum levels of protection within the directives adopted in each area.

As noted, this is essentially regulatory or substantive in function to the extent that it provides for the imposition of specific minimum levels of compliance obligation on the firms or individuals covered.[79] In so doing, this corresponds with the need for some regulatory or other substantive control provision to be established within a regional trading system.[80]

(3) Home Country Control

In the banking and financial area, the new element within the Commission's integration strategy was the principle of home country control. Banking and financial services were considered under the White Paper to amount to 'financial products' which were comparable with the treatment of industrial and agricultural products under *Cassis*. Mutual recognition would then be possible on the basis of the minimum coordination of certain core rules in this area.[81] This harmonization was to be 'guided' by the separate principle

and standards. Where national regulations were excessive, they would be treated as unjustified barriers under Arts 30–6 (28–34). Legislative harmonization would be restricted to essential mandatory requirement areas. Even where European standards had not been adopted, this absence would not to be allowed to be used as a barrier to free movement. During the transitional period, while standards were being developed, the mutual acceptance of national standards would be the guiding principle subject to an agreed notification procedure. White Paper, para 65. Section C (1) and (2) and (n 54).

[79] Section C (3)(a).

[80] Section C (3)(b).

[81] Para 102. See generally Eva Lomnicka 'The Home Country Control Principle in the Financial Services Directive and the Case Law' Ch 11 in Mads Andenas and Wulf-Henning Roth *Services and Free Movement in EU Law* (OUP 2002).

of home country control which meant attributing primary authority for the supervision of a financial institution to the competent authorities of the Member State of origin with the territory of destination having a more limited but still complementary role.[82] Home country control was accordingly allocatory in function and corresponded with the division of power or authority within a mixed supervisory system such as that set up within a regional trading block.[83]

While it could be claimed that the new allocation provision separately introduced in the financial area was directly implied in *Cassis*, this is incorrect to the extent that *Cassis* was only concerned with initial production and first placement. Home country control is necessary to provide for the continuing supervision of financial institutions in addition to their initial authorization which is itself a considerably more complex process than setting or imposing minimum product (content) rules. This then constitutes a new supplementary rule developed for use in the financial area.

Although the principle of home country control may also appear to have been ancillary to essential coordination under the White Paper, this would be treated as a separate and independent principle in later Commission statements. The banking and financial programme would then be stated to be based on the three connected principles of mutual recognition, minimum harmonization and home country control. In terms of historical development, while these three principles were only clearly articulated during the latter half of the 1980s, they were anticipated, or, at least, implied in some of the earlier initiatives undertaken. The original draft directive produced by the Committee of Experts in July 1972 was based on the principle of full harmonization. The measure nevertheless only attempted to establish a basic minimum common framework for bank regulation and included the principle of cooperation that would form an important element of subsequent home country control.

[82] Minimum harmonization within the financial area especially with regard to the supervision of ongoing activities was to be guided by the principle of home country control (para 103). This means attributing the primary task of supervising the financial institution to the competent authorities of its Member State of origin to which all necessary supervisory information would have to be communicated. The authorities of the destination Member State would have a complementary although essentially limited role. There would have to be a minimum harmonization of surveillance standards although the need to reach agreement on this was not to be allowed to delay further the necessary and overdue decisions to be taken. The proposal for the First Banking Directive separately refers to the final result as involving the overall supervision of credit institutions operating in several Member States being conducted by the competent authorities of the territory of their head office in consultation, as appropriate, with the authorities of the other countries concerned (preamble 3). Credit institutions would then be exempt from any national authorization requirement when setting up branches in other Member States (preamble 10). For Court comment in Case C-233/94 *Germany v European Parliament and Council*, Ch 4, section D (1) and (n 163). Lomnicka (n 81).

[83] Section C (3) (a) and (b). In connection with home control in the area of deposit guarantee, Ch 4 (n 163).

With the proposal for the First Banking Directive (77/780/EEC) in 1974, almost all of the final policy bases or components were identified.[84] The main policy shift from the original draft 1972 Directive to the proposal for the First Banking Directive in 1974 was to move from a fully comprehensive or consolidated single measure to a framework approach in which the necessary common standards would be constructed through a number of separate functionally specific directives. The 1974 proposal refers to it being necessary to proceed by successive stages rather than within a single Directive.[85] The proposal continues that the result of this process should be to provide for the overall supervision of a credit institution operating in several Member States by the competent authorities in the territory where it has its head office in consultation as appropriate with the authorities of the other State concerned. This clearly anticipates the operation of a full home country control rule although not referred to in these terms at that stage. The proposal did anticipate the adoption of uniform authorization requirements across the Community although at that stage it was only necessary to specify certain minimum requirements.[86] This would appear to have assumed that full harmonization would be possible although through a number of measures rather than with a single Directive. The subsequent adoption of a minimum rather than full harmonization approach may then have been the new element.

The original 1974 proposal also referred to credit institutions having their head office in one Member State being exempt from national authorization in setting up branches in other Member States.[87] This clearly anticipates the single passport created under the Second Banking Directive in 1989[88] which operates on the basis of the mutual recognition of the sufficiency of the authorization and supervision effected by all other Member States. The adoption of only the essential harmonization necessary and sufficient to secure mutual recognition was expressly set out in the Second Banking Directive.[89] The Second Banking Directive also provided for a more sophisticated division of responsibility between the home and host authorities.[90] These provisions have since been restated within the May 2000 Banking Consolidation Directive.

[84] First Council Directive 77/780/EEC on the coordination of laws, regulations and administrative provisions relating to the take up and pursuit of the business of credit institutions of 12 December 1997 (OJ L 322 12.12.1997, 30). Ch 5, sections A and B and (nn 6 and 24).

[85] Preamble 3.

[86] Preamble 8.

[87] Preamble 10. This again implies home country control as under Preamble 3.

[88] Second Council Directive 89/646/EEC on the coordination of laws, regulations and administrative provisions relating to the taking up and pursuit of the business of credit institutions of 15 Dec 1998 (OJ L 386, 30 Dec 89, p 1). Ch 5, section B and (n 22).

[89] Preamble 4.

[90] Preamble 10 and Arts 13 and 14.

The Commission's policy in the banking and financial area accordingly moved from a full harmonization approach (based on a single measure) to one relying on a number of separate functionally specific directives. This original and framework harmonization approach then anticipated authorized institutions being exempt from the equivalent supervisory and regulatory systems applicable in other territories having complied with the provisions of their country of origin. This precurses subsequent mutual recognition and the underlying principle of home country control which was clearly considered necessary from an early stage in the financial area. It is this need for subsequent continuing review and oversight through the supervisory process that principally distinguishes financial services from many other products or activities subject to free movement. Almost all of the final policy components were accordingly anticipated by 1972 except for minimum harmonization which would replace full coordination of all relevant provisions as a form of politically acceptable compromise policy under the 1985 White Paper and 1986 Single Act.

The importance of this policy or regulatory anticipation cannot be underestimated. The original integration mechanism adopted in the goods area in 1979 was *Cassis* free circulation based on initial lawful production and first market placement. The original principles of mutual recognition and the minimum harmonization subsequently developed would then be extended in the financial area to include home country control (which is essentially concerned with the continuing supervision effected by the parent authorities). The inclusion of this new integration component, however, effectively transfers the original market-entry based composition and placement rule into a post-entry continuing compliance condition. Rather than simply add a new compliance element, this changes the nature of the relationship between the firm concerned and the home and host territory and between and the home and host territories themselves. The simple pre-entry product rules (lawful production and placement) are converted into a much more substantial continuing post-entry validation system. Mutual recognition is then almost replaced rather than supplemented by a new doctrine of 'license recognition' (or possibly 'license validation' or 'systems validation').

To the extent that home country control effectively converts mutual recognition into a new doctrine (of license recognition or license or systems validation), it can be considered to be separate and independent. Home country control would then imply both mutual recognition (through the cross-validation of the license or authorization provided within each territory) and minimum harmonization (being the defined basis on which the reciprocal recognition would be provided). Mutual recognition can only suggest rather than fully imply home country control to the extent that its pre-market entry product composition and marketing conditions cannot be naturally extended to include full post-entry supervision and continuing regulation. While compliance with relevant authorization conditions may be considered to parallel initial composition and placement requirements, this would not extend to include subsequent continuing regulatory and supervisory compliance. A full doctrine of home country control would nevertheless still imply underlying mutual recognition.

Whether home country control should continue to be considered as an ancillary and dependent or fully independent doctrine or mechanism remains unclear at the present time.[91] The extent to which home country control may be considered to have assisted in the development or adoption of mutual recognition is also difficult to determine. The use of home country control in the financial area was considered as early as 1974 and 1975. This, in particular, reflected the work of the Basel Committee on Banking Supervision which had been set up in December 1974 to consider the construction of a new framework of measures for the cross-border supervision of the activities of internationally active banks. While the initial principle agreed was one of joint responsibility, the original 1975 First Concordat produced by the Committee provided for the division of primary responsibility between the parent and host authorities in connection with various particular functions including bank solvency and liquidity. This was supplemented by a general cooperation and exchange of information requirement.[92] This would subsequently be extended into an express home country control rule with regard to capital adequacy and consolidated supervision under the 1983 Revised Concordat and later papers.[93]

The difference between the emerging Basel and parallel European requirements was that the European provisions would include a market access right or entitlement in addition to basic allocation of responsibility. The inclusion of an access element was clearly set out in the proposal for the First Banking Directive in 1974[94] although it was also implied in the comprehensive common licensing and supervision system to be set up under the original first directive proposed by the 1972 Committee of Experts.[95] It

[91] The existing writing clearly supports its continued use as an ancillary and consequently dependent mechanism (in addition to mutual recognition and minimum harmonization). The reflects the original Commission position. Whether this should be continued depends upon how each of the separate provisions is defined. Sections C(1), (2) and (3).

[92] Basel Committee, 'Report on the supervision of banks' foreign establishments' (September 1975); Basel Committee, 'Principles for the supervision of banks' foreign establishments' (May 1983); Basel Committee, 'Information flows between banking supervisory authorities' (Apr 1990); Basel Committee, 'Minimum Standards for the supervision of international banking groups and their cross-border establishments' (July 1992); and Basel Committee, 'Core Principles for effective bank supervision' (Apr 1997).

[93] GA Walker *International Banking Regulation—Law, Policy and Practice* (Kluwer London 2000), Ch 2.

[94] (n 84).

[95] Ch 5 (nn 9 and 103) The same policy would also appear to have been anticipated by the earlier Working Group that reported in 1967/68.

was accordingly intended that home country control would form the basis of the emerging banking and financial services programme from an early stage. This precursed the possible use of mutual recognition elsewhere by between 8 and 12 years. It is also clear that while home country control can be considered to imply mutual recognition, the basic and original scope of mutual recognition would not include the post-entry continuing supervision and regulation included within home country control.

(4) General Good

The banking and financial programme is generally described as being based on the three core principles of mutual recognition, minimum harmonization and home control.[96] This must nevertheless also be considered to include the principle of the 'general good'. While the Commission had not intended including any express reference to the general good within the proposal for the Second Banking Directive, this had to be included, in particular, at the insistence of the French and Italian representatives during the working group stages.[97]

The current conditions with regard to the operation of this derogation in the services and establishment area are set out in the Court's dicta in *Gebhard* and *Gouda*.[98] These generally require that a measure is non-discriminatory, non-harmonized, recognized, not duplicatory, necessary and proportionate. These can then be considered to consist of a series of scope and application rules.[99] Despite the apparent rigidity of the derogation

[96] White Paper, paras 103–7.

[97] It was considered that the jurisprudence of the Court already implied such a rule and, in particular, with the public interest requirement set out in the 1986 Co-insurance Cases. See Ch 4, section A (1). Interview with Paolo Clarroti, former Head of the Banking and Financial Division within DG XV.

[98] Ch 3, section D (4).

[99] With regard to scope, the measure must not be pre-harmonized nor already be secured by a parallel country of origin requirement. Pre-harmonization removes the authority of the host state to act. The relevant measures are then governed by the common European standards set. Care must nevertheless be exercised in that the general good will strictly only correspond with non-essential areas left to be governed by the jurisprudence of the Court. Section C (1). Essential areas will be governed by European provision which will generally disapply the general good. This may nevertheless be important in residual non-harmonized essential areas as anticipated by the Court.

The country of origin condition raises the difficult issue of equivalence. If the intended objective has already been secured by a country of origin rule, the need for the host requirement becomes redundant. This assumes the primacy of the home country laws as against the host territory. The effect of this is to create a primacy doctrine where issues of possible justification arise in non-essential areas governed by the general law of free movement. The application rules include necessity and proportionality. These operate as interpretation restrictions to ensure that the derogation is only applied on a strict and narrowly construed basis. Although not substantive in content directly, their application may involve a detailed examination of the content and operation of the underlying free movement restriction involved.

conditions set, difficulties continue to arise with regard to both their content and operation. The supporting analysis and examination of the Court in the financial area have also raised some concerns.[100]

Despite this, the doctrine of the general good remains an essential corrective within the overall integration policy constructed. It is necessary that a parallel derogation is provided for with regard to indistinctly applicable measures that would not otherwise be covered by the strict exceptions provided for under the Treaty. The scope of derogation should also be extended as the breadth of the parallel restriction is reconsidered. The only unfortunate aspect is that this requires European Court of Justice ruling and determination. This then creates consequent difficulties in terms of legal and operational certainty. The cost and delay that litigation involves with this commercial uncertainty can also necessarily further damage market integration.[101]

(5) Host Country Control

As with the general good, host country control is generally not included as one of the core components. This may be explained in terms of the politically and intellectually simpler expression of the new integration strategy being based on the three parallel principles of mutual recognition, minimum harmonization and home country control. The existence of a separate host country control element within the post-1985 framework adopted must nevertheless be recognized although albeit in a limited form.

The Banking Consolidated Directive 2000/12/EC operates by assigning the prudential supervision of credit institutions to the competent authorities of the home Member State although this is stated to be without prejudice to the other provisions of the Directive.[102] The Directive does not provide for a home country control rule as such but extends the scope of home country authority to include prudential supervision. Prudential supervision is unfortunately again not otherwise defined although this is generally understood to relate to financial (capital and liquidity) and the main suitability and systems and control requirements imposed on banks.

The non-discrimination requirement creates a minimum floor test. This is strictly unnecessary as the general good will only be considered in cases where an indistinctly (non-discriminatory) applicable provision is concerned. Where overt discrimination arises, possible derogation will only be available in accordance with the express Treaty exceptions provided.

[100] Ch 4, section A. See also Michel Tison 'Unravelling the General Good Exception: the Case of Financial Services' Ch 12 in Mads Andenas and Wulf-Henning Roth *Services and Free Movement in EU Law* (OUP 2002). See also Siofra O'Leary and Jose M Fernandez-Martin 'Judicially Created Exceptions to the Free Movement of Services' Ch 6 in Andenas and Roth.

[101] Ch 1, section B (4) and (n 46).

[102] Directive 2000/12/EC May 2000 relating to the taking up and pursuit of the business of credit institutions 2000/12/EC, Art 26(1). Ch 5, sections B and C and (nn 29 and 65).

The host authorities are stated to be made expressly responsible for liquidity and other measures relating to monetary policy provided that these do not operate on a discriminatory manner.[103] This has also formerly included market risk in advance of the adoption of the Capital Adequacy Directive. Rather than operate on an express home country control basis, the banking directives are accordingly based on the separate definition of home and host competencies. This is supported by the direction that both sets of authorities are required to cooperate closely in the general supervision of the activities of credit institutions.[104] This is further confirmed by the coordination requirement in connection with verifications either generally or in support of the consolidated supervision of financial groups.[105] The dominant operational principles may accordingly be better described as being a combination of assigned and shared competence rather than simple home country control. In addition to the express powers set out in the financial directives, the scope of host country control will also necessarily include measures covered by the general good.[106]

The difficulties that arise in determining the scope of relevant derogation and consequent integration damage or default created in terms of legal and commercial certainty will then again arise with regard to any emerging doctrine of host country control. Any final resolution or reconciliation of all of the internal difficulties and deficiencies that arise with the European financial programme will accordingly require further clarification of the scope of this important integration component.

E. OPERATION

Mutual recognition is a complex concept and is capable of being used in number of different ways.[107] Its content and operation will clearly vary depending upon the context and meaning intended. In each case, however, mutual recognition can possibly be best treated as a process which involves a number of operations or sub-operations rather than as a single activity. On any more detailed examination, a number of sub-operations or sub-functions may then be identified within the term.

[103] Art 27.
[104] Art 28.
[105] Arts 29 and 56(7). Art 56(7), in particular, extends to credit institutions, financial holding companies, financial institutions, ancillary banking financial services undertakings, mixed-activity holding companies, Art 55 subsidiaries (mixed-activity holding companies) and Art 52(10) subsidiaries (non-consolidated entities).
[106] Section D (4).
[107] Sections C (1) and (3) and D (1).

Two of the most substantial uses of the term arise with regard to the Commission's construction of an (external) independent legal principle from *Cassis* and the (internal) cross-validation of national provisions within a particular directive.[108] In each of these cases, five separate potential sub-operations can be identified in terms of initial issue or regulatory identification (or definition), mutual review (or pre-review), standards measurement (or pre-compliance), regulatory adjustment (or disapplication) and systems review (or validation).

(1) Definition or Identification

The relevant area of law, regulation or administrative practice to be covered must initially be identified. This involves defining the scope of the relevant primary law (including statute or constitutional provision), secondary legislation and administrative principles or practice.

This will vary having regard to the nature of the issue to be dealt with. In European terms, this will depend upon whether the particular area falls within the scope of necessary public interests (reasonable measures or mandatory requirements) as identified by the Court in *Dassonville* and *Cassis*.

To the extent that an essential matter is concerned, the Commission will attempt to produce relevant common requirements at the Community level through legislative action. To the extent that a non-essential area is involved, Member States will be required to look to the protection already provided in the country of origin in applying their own local provisions (pre-review or pre-compliance).[109]

In each case, the proper classification of the specific subject matter will depend upon the Court's still evolving definition of mandatory requirements.[110] In the first case, mutual recognition applies to the internal cross-validation of national provision under the legislative measure adopted and, in the second case, to the disapplication of local requirements in light of the protection already provided in the country of origin.

(2) Mutual Review or Pre-Review

In so far as a non-essential area is involved, under the Court's jurisprudence Member Sates are, in effect, required to examine each other's systems to determine whether a country of origin requirement in any particular case already secures the same objective and provides an equivalent degree of

108 Section D (1).
109 (n 28).
110 Ch 3, sections C and D; and Ch 6, section D (4).

protection as the corresponding measure to be applied in the host state or country of import. This then involves an act of mutual review or pre-review on the part of national governments in advance of any enforcement action.

In cases such as *Cassis* and in similar decisions, the Court does not impose this obligation expressly. There is also no underlying Treaty basis for this. This obligation of mutual or pre-review arises by necessary implication from the direction that a product lawfully produced and first placed on the market on one territory is entitled to full free movement.[111]

No separate obligation of pre-review arises with regard to essential measures as the Commission will generally have already tried to adopt common European standards in these areas through legislative intervention.

(3) Standards Measurement

The quality of the relevant provision in each case must then be measured or assessed. The provision must ensure an adequate or sufficient level of protection having regard to the specific objectives intended. The issue that arises is then one of the level or degree of protection secured.

In connection with non-essential measures, the degree of necessary protection will be determined by the Court or, at least, in accordance with comparable jurisprudence and precedent.

With regard to essential measures, the relevant minimum standard will be set out in the directive concerned. This will ultimately be dependent upon political negotiation and agreement.

(4) Regulatory Adjustment or Disapplication

The specific regulatory obligations to be imposed in any particular case must then be confirmed.

Once common European standards have been established at the European level, Member States must ensure that they secure the relevant degree or level of protection provided for with regard to the application of their provisions to local firms or individuals. This is necessary to the extent that the directive will have been addressed to them and require implementation within the local territory.

In connection with firms or individuals from other Member States, the host territory will be required to disapply its provisions with regard to their activities provided only that they comply with the relevant conditions set out in the directive which (in the financial area) will generally relate to home country authorization and continuing supervision. The adoption of common standards at the European level will then result in regulatory

[111] (n 28).

adjustment or the simple disapplication of equivalent provision in the host country.

The European directive will accordingly provide for both the validation of the home country regulation and (by implication) for the disapplication of the equivalent host provision. To the extent that this is set out in a directive that is directed to Member States rather than a regulation (or other measure with direct effect), this will still be dependent upon local implementation. Both the validation and disapplication will nevertheless be provided for under or, at least, implied in the relevant directive.

With regard to non-essential areas, the effect of regulatory adjustment or disapplication will operate through the nonenforceability of the host provisions under the jurisprudence of the European Court of Justice. There will be no automatic adjustment or disapplication of the local provisions although they will become unenforceable under European law as against in incoming firms unless they can otherwise be justified as permitted necessary public interests (or mandatory requirements).[112]

(5) Systems Review and Validation

The effective operation of these parallel systems of recognition will ultimately be dependent upon continuing oversight by the Commission and the Court to the extent necessary.

The Commission will have to monitor both the proper and consistent implementation of relevant European measures in essential areas by Member States as well as the non-enforcement of equivalent national rules in non-essential areas where the necessary degree of protection has already been provided by the host territory. The Court will have to apply its jurisprudence in a consistent manner where it is asked to rule either on the sufficiency of an implementation measure in an essential area or the enforceability of a host rule in a non-essential area.

The full and complete application of mutual recognition is accordingly necessary in areas of both essential and non-essential interests and the Court and the Commission have important complementary roles to discharge in this regard.

F. POLICY COMMENT—TREATY VACUUM AND JUDICIAL AND PROGRAMME CORRECTION

The system of regulation and supervision of banking and financial services set up within Europe represents the most ambitious and, in many respects,

112 Ch 3, sections C and D; and Ch 6, section D (4).

successful attempt to create an extended and integrated system of balanced regional market access and regulation. Although a number of difficulties remain, the significance and value of this achievement cannot be overestimated.

In considering the relevance and importance of the new regional trading system created, it is important to stress both the positive rights to market access created across Europe as well as the new control regime constructed.

The objectives of the Commission were from the beginning expansionary insofar as it intended to create a common and then internal market in banking and financial services. Having moved from an earlier reductionist policy based on heavy harmonization to a more revisionist and integrationist approach involving mutual recognition and the introduction of basic common standards, the Commission has been able to develop a more unified approach to market integration. This new system of open market access and regulatory equivalence is not, however, based on simple regulatory or legal indulgence or tolerance but on the initial underlying agreement achieved in recognising certain core minimum standards across Europe as well as the sufficiency of the authorization and supervisory procedures available in each Member State.

Banking and financial policy specifically is necessarily based on underlying Treaty provision and supporting judicial principle which are then expanded through the secondary programme rules adopted. The programme rules define, clarify and amplify the manner in which the underlying rights are exercised in practice with the overall objective being to create both effective market access and proper market control.

A number of difficulties nevertheless remain in understanding fully the meaning and operation of the policy and programme solution adopted as well as the origin, validity and function of each of the underlying core mechanisms used. Despite this, mutual recognition specifically remains the dominant device within the European integration process. Improvements can be made with regard to its further clarification, revision and reform although its fundamental role and significance should not be underestimated.

The manner in which existing policy adopted in the banking and financial area can be further improved is considered in the following chapter.

7

Judicial and Programme Reconciliation—Construction of a New Integration Framework

Integration policy within Europe and, in particular, in the banking and financial area remains to be governed by both the adjusted judicial principles developed by the European Court of Justice concerning the application and operation of the underlying Treaty rights of free movement as well as the more specific rights given effect to under the programme rules contained in the secondary measures adopted under the conferral provisions set out in the Treaty. Relevant policy is then both (Treaty) right and programme determined.

To the extent that judicial principles operate by confirming the scope of relevant Treaty prohibition (and supporting derogation), they operate negatively and on a reserve or residual basis. Programme or legislative provisions rather operate positively by conferring on individuals and legal persons specific rights of action rather than inaction (although these are ultimately still Treaty derived).[1]

The distinction between these two sources of immediate entitlement can also be considered in internal and external terms. Programme rights operate on an internal basis to the extent that they are conferred and determined in accordance with the provisions set out in the particular measure. Other (non-programme supported) rights are determined in accordance with the application of more general European law and therefore operate outside (and are external to) the secondary legislative framework constructed. This distinction between internal and external entitlements corresponds with that drawn by the Court and the Commission between essential and non-essential areas of intervention for harmonization purposes. This is relevant in determining the proper scope of coverage and application of relevant law in each case.[2]

[1] On the nature of directives and the relationship between Treaty and programme rules, *French Republic v Commission of the European Communities* [1997] ECR I-1627. Ch 4 (nn 93–4). On the meaning and nature of integration, Ch 1 (n 14) and Ch 2, sections (B), (C) and (D).

[2] Chs 3 and 4; and Ch 6, sections C (1) and (2) and (n 78). See also Ch 5 (n 152).

A substantial legal framework has since been constructed on the basis of both of these sources of right or entitlement although a number of significant difficulties remain in each case as well as in attempting to build the two into a single coherent legal framework. A considerable amount of confusion also continues to arise with regard to the nature, content and operation of the rights in each case and with their underlying legal bases as well as the relationship between them.

It is possible that an effective integration strategy and policy framework can be constructed within Europe on the basis of the main mechanisms developed to date (including the core underlying principles of mutual recognition, minimum harmonization and home country control). For this purpose, however, the proper meaning and function of each and their relationship *inter se* must be clearly understood and a coherent and complete programme of integration rules (and sub-rules) constructed around them.

The purpose of this chapter is to attempt to determine whether any clear link (or reconciliation) is possible between these two separate policy sources and whether any new (or, at least adjusted or revised) integration strategy and framework can be constructed that combines the benefits of the existing approach developed to date at the same time as remove any residual confusion and correct any continuing omissions and deficiencies. The separate contributions of the Court and the Commission are initially reviewed. The relationship between the two policy sources is considered and residual integration difficulties identified. The basis for the construction of a new or, at least, revised policy basis is examined in further detail.

A. JUDICIAL BALANCE

The essential policy contribution of the Court is concerned with the determination of the proper limits of the rights of free movement created under the Treaty. The Court has set these limits by extending the scope of relevant Treaty prohibition against restrictions on free movement to include a range of measures beyond overt discrimination.

It had originally been assumed that the tests (or triggers) to be applied in each area of free movement would generally operate on either an express or implied discrimination basis.[3] The Court has then significantly extended these provisions to include a range of indistinctly applicable measures in various areas. The result of this is that a number of national requirements are still treated as unenforceable even where there is no difference in application in terms of nationality or place of residence. A number of the decisions produced in this area can be understood in terms of indirect

[3] Ch 1, section E (3) and (n 74); and Ch 3, sections C and D and (n 129).

discrimination (such as in *Commission v Greece*[4] and the tax cases)[5] where non-nationals are subject to some additional obligation although the provisions are applied equally. The Court has nevertheless gone beyond this in other cases (such as *Dassonville, Cassis, Gebhard, Säger* and *Kraus*) only to look at the effect of the restriction on cross-border trade.[6] The Court has consequently either adopted a discrimination (direct or indirect) or full effects test with regard to the prohibition of national measures restricting rights of free movement depending upon the particular facts and policy considerations involved.

While certain inconsistencies remain, the Court's jurisprudence can be reconsidered or re-assessed having regard to the basic approach adopted under the original GATT arrangements. This applied a full effects doctrine to restrictions on initial market access (or entry) and then a discrimination based test to subsequent internal regulatory provision (after entry had been secured).[7] Decisions such as *Gebhard* and *Säger* can then be understood in terms of entry restrictions. In these cases, an extended effects based restriction is applied. This would also include *Alpine* and *Schindler* in the financial services area.[8] Other rulings can then be understood in terms of internal regulation to which a discrimination (rather than effects test) would be applied.

Difficulties nevertheless remain in determining the proper limits of the extended restrictions imposed. The Court has attempted to clarify this with regard to goods in *Keck* although a number of separate difficulties arise with the decision and, in particular, with regard to the in law and in fact proviso attached.[9] The Court could also have adopted the same approach in such cases as *Alpine* and *Bosman* with regard to services and workers although it declined to do so. Rather than consider these as being theoretically inconsistent or mutually exclusive, they are best considered as representing different consequences of a parallel or equivalent analysis. The restrictions in these cases can be considered to have affected market access or entry directly with the result that the relevant Treaty prohibition applied.

Residual difficulties also arise with regard to the scope of supporting derogation. Some clarification on the *Dassonville* reasonableness formulation was provided with the list of mandatory requirements set out in *Cassis*. *Commission v Germany* (*Co-insurance*) public interest was then restated as the four *Gebhard* conditions (of non-discrimination, general interest, suitability and necessity).[10] The professional rules justified by the general good

4 Case C-198/89 [1991] ECR I-727. Ch 3 (n 32) and section D (2).

5 Ch 3 (n 159).

6 Ch 3, sections D (2) and (5).

7 Ch 3, section C (1) and (n 46).

8 Ch 4, section A (2) and (3).

9 Ch 3, sections C (4) and (5).

10 Ch 3 (nn 153).

in the area of services in *Van Binsbergen* similarly evolved into overriding reasons relating to the public interest, appropriateness and proportionality in *Gouda*.[11]

The effect of these provisions would appear to be to develop a parallel jurisprudence based on the underlying concepts of public requirement or public interest with regard to possible exemption or derogation. Difficulties nevertheless remain with regard to the proper scope and content of each relevant set of possible derogations. While an objective test is also, for example, generally adopted with regard to appropriateness or proportionality, the Court has on occasion allowed Member States to undertake a more subjective assessment such as in *Schindler*. The ability of the Court to create new bases (such as in *Alpine*) or to assess matters on an essentially uninformed or poorly informed basis (such as in *Parodi*) are also of concern.

The difficulty of attempting to develop a coherent jurisprudence in such complex areas on the basis of selective judicial opportunity must be taken into account. Considerable uncertainties nevertheless remain with regard to the proper scope and content of Treaty prohibition and the supporting rights of national derogation. This creates significant consequent problems in terms of legal certainty and predictability which, in turn, substantially increase cost and delay. This will then act as a significant disincentive for market operators with the overall effect being materially to undermine the underlying integration intent or effect of the European internal market process as a whole.

B. PROGRAMME SUPPORT

A number of difficulties also remain with regard to secondary programme content and operation. These are specifically concerned with the scope of relevant access rights, regulatory content, operational supervision, programme completion and institutional revision as well as systems failure and market support.

Particular difficulties continue to arise with regard to market access. Subsidiaries are excluded from the main financial directives contrary to the terms of the underlying Treaty provisions in the services and establishment area. The scope of residual Treaty (as opposed to programme) rights in this area remains untested.[12] Problems also arise with regard to the definition of the key financial institutions including 'credit institution,' 'investment firm,' 'insurance undertaking' and related or subsidiary definitions as well as in

[11] Ch 3 (nn 179 and 180).

[12] Ch 1, section C (3); and Ch 5, sections B and C and (nn 152 and 154) and section E (1) and (n 156).

the products covered such as commodity derivatives and potentially new electronic finance instruments or arrangements.

The inclusion of only minimum provision in terms of regulatory detail within the directives also creates difficulties in terms of content and substance. Minimum direction or guidance is, for example, provided with regard to suitability, management structures and control systems. Significant disparities also continue to arise in connection with capital adequacy rules either where concessions have been provided or stricter standards have been adopted in harmonized as well as non-harmonized but related areas.[13] Separate inconsistencies arise where particular areas are expressly excluded from the scope of minimum harmonization such as with regard to liquidity.[14]

With regard to continuing supervision, separate issues arise in connection with operational practice, consolidated supervision and enforcement policies. In connection with operational rules and practices, no common provisions exist on such matters as returns (including content and filing), management meetings (purpose, attendance and timing) and intervention powers. The scope, nature and operation of consolidated supervision has only been dealt with at the most minimum level through the Consolidated Supervision Directive and restated (but unamended) Consolidated Banking Directive.[15] No common provisions have been attempted in connection with supporting enforcement policy. Continuing difficulties also remain with regard to inconsistencies in terms of training and competence, resources and agency structure, areas of inter-agency communication and exchange of information as well as operational consistency and sufficiency more generally. The necessary consequence of these disparities is that the scope and content of operational supervision can vary significantly between Member States. The additional or ancillary effect of mutual recognition is then to require mutual acceptance of these differences in connection with harmonized areas while the understanding or assumption is that mutual recognition also precludes any more general mutual review.

Further difficulties arise in connection with the proposed completion programmes adopted in connection with capital markets and financial services more generally. As well as specific concerns with the quality of

[13] See, eg, the additional sections set out in the UK IPRU (BANK) chapter of the FSA's Handbook of Rules and Guidance. This includes chapters BO (proxies for market risk in the banking book), CM (commodities risk), DU (common treatment for counterparty risk), TC (counterparty risk in the trading book), TL (incremental for large exposures), CD (credit derivatives), SE (securitization and asset transfers), LM (mismatch liquidity) and LS (Sterling stock liquidity) as well as VA (valuation), NE (collateral and netting), OS (outsourcing) and PN (provisioning policy statements). The Handbook is available on http://wwwfsa.gov.uk. See Walker 'Banks and Banking' *Financial Services Regulation* (Butterworths, 5 vols Loose Leaf), Division 4. See also Walker 'Banks' in M Blair and Walker (eds) *Financial Services Law* (Oxford University Press Oxford 2006), ch 12.

[14] Contrast FSA chs LM (Mismatching liquidity) and LS (Sterling stock liquidity).

[15] Ch 5, section C (nn 29 and 65). See also Ch 5, section E and (nn 152–154).

particular measures, significant problems may arise as a result of forced political compromises and timing pressures to comply with relevant administrative deadlines. While useful improvements have been recommended in connection with the revision of the supporting institutional structures, at least, in connection with securities markets under the Lamfalussy proposals, parallel progress was not immediately possible in the other main financial sector areas as well as in terms of cross-sector cooperation and coordination of relevant activity more generally.[16]

The related failure to agree any common market support (lender of last resort) mechanism is also a cause of significant concern. While a single European market has been created, no formal or, at least, express or visible attempt has been made to establish any extended financial support system. This had been left to be dealt with at a national discretionary level pre-European Monetary Union (EMU). No further guidance has since been provided in connection with the operation of the European Central Bank in this area post-EMU.[17] The result may be that a local domestic crisis possibly triggered through mandatory mutual recognition may cause regional contagious effects that are not controlled through any coordinated national or central support mechanism. Mutual recognition, of itself, may then act as a cause or, at least, catalyst for both national and regional crisis without any coordinated support facility being in place to deal with the consequences of such an event.

C. POLICY RELATION AND RECONCILIATION

In addition to the separate sets of difficulties that exist within each major policy area, problems arise in understanding the proper relationship or link between them. A substantial body of commentary and comment has emerged in connection with the law governing the free movement of goods as well as establishment, services and workers (and to a much lesser extent capital and payment).[18] While some examination has emerged in the banking and financial area, this has been considerably less extensive. There has also only been limited specific consideration of the relationship between the more general law of free movement and supporting secondary programmes especially in the financial area.

[16] Ch 5, section D (4) and (5). Some success has been possible subsequently through the creation of a new technical committee system post-Lamfalussy. Ch 5, section D (4) (nn 137 and 143). The success or otherwise of this initiative is nevertheless unclear at this time. On the structure and work carried out by these new committees, Ch 1 (nn 25 and 55).

[17] Ch 1, section D (4) and (n 65); and Ch 5, section E (5) and (n 170).

[18] See generally S Weatherill and P Beaumont *EU Law* (3rd edn Penguin London 1999); AM Arnull, AA Dashwood, MG Ross and DA Wyatt *European Union Law* (4rd edn Sweet & Maxwell London 2000); P Craig and G de Búrca *EU Law* (3rd edn OUP Oxford 2002).

The essential link between the two sets of judicial and programme policies in the financial and other areas is the doctrine of mutual recognition. Unfortunately, considerable confusion continues to arise with regard to its meaning, relevance and value and the relationship between mutual recognition and the related mechanisms of minimum harmonization and country control.[19]

With regard to judicial policy construction, mutual recognition is concerned with the legal unenforceability of national requirements that restrict any right of free movement subject to available derogation. Although derived from *Cassis* (or, more accurately, anticipated by *Cassis*), considerable care has to be exercised in this regard. The ideas of equivalence and necessary pre-review and withdrawal of local restriction were not referred to nor implied in *Cassis* directly to the extent that no comparable national measures were involved. The idea of equivalence was only anticipated in the para 14 obiter statement which was then subsequently taken up in *Fiejte* and later decisions.[20]

The Court has also been careful not to refer to mutual recognition as such. This rather represents a Commission or EU institutional creation, construction or extraction that has subsequently been developed into a more general integration approach, policy or philosophy.[21] While this may subsequently have been considered to form a natural part of the more general process of judicial (and executive or legislative) policy construction or evolution within the EU, care must be exercised in understanding the origin and nature of the principle in this case.

Unfortunately, mutual recognition has also over time been assigned a number of separate meanings. It is, in particular, capable of being applied within both judicial and programme policy discussion. In connection with the general law of free movement, mutual recognition refers to the disapplication of local laws that restrict cross-border trade and do not fall within any recognized exemption. Mutual recognition is then used as an external prohibition device (subject to possible derogation). With regard to programme directives or other measures, mutual recognition refers to the cross-identification and cross-validation of national provisions under specific secondary provisions such as the financial directives. Mutual recognition is then used as an internal validation device that requires the disapplication of equivalent requirements in all other Member States.

Mutual recognition can also be used as an independent legal principle or to refer to the Commission's new integration approach as under the 1985

[19] Ch 1 (n 60) and Ch 6, sections C and D.

[20] Ch 3, section C (3) (nn 70 and 72); and Ch 6, section C (1) and (2) and (nn 26, 28 and 32).

[21] Ch 6, section C (2) and (3) and (n 24).

White Paper and more generally to refer to any act of mutual comparison or acceptance.[22] Its specific meaning and relative advantage and disadvantage in each particular case must accordingly be taken into account.

The essential link between the two main integration policy sources is mutual recognition although considerable care has to be exercised in explaining its origin, validity and relevance. The proper nature of the integration process involved in the financial area and more generally can only be understood if any confused meaning or usage is avoided.

D. POLICY DEFECT AND OMMISSION

Before constructing any new integration strategy within Europe, it is necessary to identify any residual process obstacles or difficulties that may arise. These are generally concerned with continuing policy confusion, implementation and effect and monitoring and enforcement limitations and deficiencies

(1) Policy Confusion

The existing gaps and uncertainties in relevant policy must initially be corrected in so far as possible. The original source of all rights and obligations remains the European Treaties and the Court's interpretation and expansion of these provisions. Consideration should then be given to producing a set of more formal and consolidated provisions in each key area such as banking, securities and insurance. These would go further than the existing consolidation given effect to under the SLIM programme[23] to the extent that they would clarify, correct and develop the law in each area building on the underlying Treaty rules, existing legislative provisions, the Court's official interpretation of each of these sets of provision to the extent relevant and any further amendments or corrective measures considered appropriate. These 'restatements' (or *refontes*) could then be validated either through a European Parliament and Council process or delegated simplified special committee procedure.

A similar exercise has already been attempted to some extent through the use of Commission Interpretative Communications in certain areas.[24] These are of considerable value although unauthoritative and non-substantial in themselves. The scope of these measures could then be developed further by building in all of the relevant or particular entitlements and conditions set

[22] Ch 6, section D (1).

[23] Ch 5, section C and (nn 59 and 60).

[24] Commission Interpretative Communication, Freedom to provide services and the interests of the general good in the Second Banking Directive (97/C 219/04). Ch 4 (n 2) and section B.

out in the supporting secondary directives and relevant judicial principles in each area while the measures themselves could be issued in a formal binding format.

An emerging new integration strategy could then be constructed in each key area on the basis of such integrated restatements which would include both underlying Treaty and secondary programme expansions as well as supporting judicial confirmations or conditions. Any continuing gaps or uncertainties could be dealt with through legislative correction. This could either be affected directly by the Parliament and Council or through a special simplified approval process based on the work of a specialist committee such as in the banking, securities or insurance area.

The objective of these restatements would be to produce a complete and coherent body of relevant provision in any particular area. The immediate advantage would be legal certainty and predictability. The consequent practical benefit would be ease of adoption and application by all relevant parties which would, in turn, significantly stimulate and support the integration process in any particular financial, commercial or other sector area.

(2) Implementation Review

Having produced such restatements, the most specific difficulty that arises is securing full implementation and enforcement. In practice, this is initially dependent on national adoption and application although this can be supported both by the application of a consistent enforcement policy by the European Court of Justice as well as a continuing review and disciplinary or sanction regime being given effect to by the Commission.

One of the particular difficulties that has arisen historically has been in connection with the limited resources of the Commission especially in monitoring and taking consequent corrective action in connection with implementation infractions by Member State governments. While Member States are generally required to report implementation action under most directives, the subsequent processing, assessment and review work undertaken by the Commission has varied. It was, for example, originally proposed that a special implementation monitoring unit would operate within each of the financial services areas within DG XV although this was not pursued and resources were reallocated at an early stage.

Continuing implementation review accordingly remains a significant problem. Even where implementation failures have been identified, the capacity and practice of the Commission in pursuing disciplinary actions under the Treaty against Member States has varied considerably. This remains a significant problem that has to be addressed within any new integration framework.

(3) Operational Effectiveness and Equivalence

Apart from in terms of implementation review and sanction, the related issue that arises is with regard to ensuring necessary equivalence of national practice in both harmonized (essential) and other non-harmonized (non-essential) areas. The basic assumption upon which judicial (non-essential) and programme (essential) mutual recognition is based is that a sufficient degree of underlying equivalence already exists between the national measures concerned. Where this equivalence is not already present, it is assumed that the integration policy adopted will result from a natural process of national convergence over time.

In essential areas where directives or other secondary measures are adopted, the basic convergence level is fixed through the establishment of a set of agreed minimally harmonized standards. This means that only an agreed floor or base level of protection is set out in the relevant secondary instrument. This is defined in terms of the common minimum standards agreed. Member States will generally then be given a significant amount of discretion in giving this effect to secure the required level of protection to be achieved.

Once these minimum requirements have been complied with, other Member States will not be able to restrict market entry to relevant products, persons or services. In non-essential areas, national provisions may only be enforced where they satisfy the strict conditions set out by the Court under the relevant free movement case law.

The fundamental omission within the mutual recognition based system adopted within Europe is that no continuing review mechanism or procedure has been set up to ensure that a necessary degree of minimum or sufficiently consistent level of equivalence is secured in each area in practice. Considerable substantive and operational disparities may necessarily arise in giving effect to any programme of secondary measures due to the minimum levels set and the high degree of discretion inherent in the use of directives as a harmonization measure.

The result of this, in practice, will be that considerably distinct levels of market supervision may be effected. In the absence of any central Commission review function, equivalence adjustments can be given effect to through a flexible application of relevant provisions by the Court. This is, however, still dependent on subsequent necessary litigation and consequent judicial reference which is itself prone to additional cost, delay and associated legal uncertainty.

Mutual recognition remains a highly flexible and valuable integration device. It is, however, essentially incomplete to the extent that it is based on an assumption of either pre-existing or necessarily resultant or consequent operational equivalence. Where this does not exist or follow (in both essential and non-essential areas), the effectiveness of the degree of market integration achieved will necessarily be undermined if not wholly destroyed. This will, in particular, mean that the effectiveness of any applicable control system such as in connection with financial market supervision and regulation may be threatened. The consequence may be domestic or host financial closure, contagion and either country or regional systematic crisis and collapse. It is accordingly essential that any continuing system of mutual recognition is subject to proper continuing review to ensure that a necessary degree of equivalence is secured in all cases in practice.

(4) Commission, Committee, and Mutual Review

The operational review referred to may be undertaken by the Commission or some other central agency. Consideration could, for example, be given to establishing one or more review bodies that could be specifically mandated to identify, monitor and assess equivalence results in particular areas or sectors. Alternatively, this could be delegated to particular sector committees such as those set up in the banking and financial area. The authority and obligations of each body or committee would, however, have to be clearly set out in necessary secondary legislation and appropriate accountability and transparency arrangements set up.

Where the Commission continues to lack the necessary resources and the use of some delegated agency or committee systems is considered undesirable or inoperable for any reason, the main, if not only, alternative would be some form of continuing Member State review. Member States could then be permitted (or possibly required) to monitor equivalence in key areas and to report to the Commission or some other appropriate committee or body. In the event that it was agreed that undesirable levels of imbalance (inequivalence) had arisen, appropriate adjustments could be made principally through either EU or local host legislative amendment or revision and clarification through the restatements referred to above.

The general effect of this would be to create a system of 'mutual review' in addition to the underlying system of 'mutual recognition' to operate in essential and non-essential areas across Europe. Whether such mutual review is excluded by mutual recognition is unclear at present although it is arguably not. Mutual recognition only operates where a sufficient degree of minimum cross-compliance or cross-equivalence is available. Mutual review may then be implied in mutual recognition. For political reasons, however, it may have been considered undesirable to adopt an express policy in this regard, at least, during the earlier stages of the integration process. This may nevertheless be re-introduced now to ensure the longer term effective operation of the integration initiative under development across Europe. This would certainly be the case in the absence of any further extended programme of full harmonization, which of itself, may be considered undesirable or, at least, inoperable at this time.

To the extent that mutual recognition is based on assumed levels of underlying equivalence of necessary standards and protection, it is accordingly necessary that some continuing review mechanism is set up to ensure the longer-term effective operation of each of the financial, commercial, industrial or other systems or sectors and sub-systems or sub-sectors involved. Necessary equivalence should not simply be assumed. This must be monitored and appropriate adjustments made as necessary, in particular, through the secondary programme measures in place. The advantages of mutual recognition in terms of simplified legislative programming, automatic and mandatory operation and ease of political acceptance or compromise could be achieved at the same time as necessary levels of equivalence secured in all key financial, commercial, industrial and other areas. In the absence of such a review mechanism, mutual recognition will continue to suffer from the core defects of inconsistent application and uneven equivalence. The overall final result would then be dependent upon operational or political accident rather than managed and controlled intent.

Some from of continuing implementation and equivalence review mechanism should accordingly be considered. In the absence of any Commission or other central function, some form of agreed mutual review between Member States should be discussed as a compliment or supplement rather than substitute to underlying mutual recognition in essential and non-essential policy areas.

(5) Corrective Action

Where this restated system of mutual review reveals continuing difficulties either in terms of implementation gaps and deficiencies or no or substantially ineffective or defective equivalence having been secured, an appropriate corrective action procedure must be available.

Correction would generally operate through policy and programme revision. This would mainly be effected, in practice, by reporting relevant problems to the Commission which would take necessary action either by legislative or possibly administrative amendment or action against Member States for failure to implement. Simplified procedures may also be available through the use of the various sector committees in operation including, for example, the 'Banking Advisory Committee' (and its replacement the European Banking Committee (EBC) and the Committee of European Banking Supervisors (CEBS)), the new European Securities Committee (ESC) and Committee of European Securities Regulators (CESR) or proposed Financial Conglomerates. Appropriate policy revision could then be effected through the appointed advisory committee with any necessary administrative adjustments being given effect to through the relevant regulatory committee.

Where the necessary mandates of the particular committees are not clear or appropriate, they would have to be revised. This would, in particular, include replacing the Banking Advisory Committee with a new EBC and CEBS on the model of the securities equivalents set up under Lamfalussy.[25] The objective of this revision would be to clarify the two main functions concerned of policy examination and revision (on the one part) and the more specific conduct of cross-border supervision and regulation on a coordinated or common basis (on the other).

Where a sufficient response was not possible either through policy or administrative correction (at the Commission or committee level), Member States may have to be given an ultimate right of unilateral corrective action. This would parallel the unilateral rights of action available under the Basel Committee on Banking Supervision papers governing the cross-border supervision of internationally active banks as introduced under the 1983 Revised Concordat and restated in the 1992 Minimum Principles.[26]

Under European law, this would correspond with the scope of the host authorities' right of action as determined under the conditions governing the general good as set out in the jurisprudence of the European Court of Justice. While this generally relates to recognising continuing rights of regulatory intervention on a more general basis, it might be expressly accepted that host authorities have a residual right of unilateral action in circumstances where emergency corrective measures are required. The effect of this would be to clarify both the rights of European intervention as well as bring relevant European provision more into line with best global practice.

Each of these issues of continuing policy confusion, implementation and equivalence review, residual national oversight authority and possible corrective action would have to be considered as part of any new more general integration strategy or framework.

25 Ch 5, section D (4). See also Ch 1 (n 55); and Ch 2 (n 111).

26 A 'dual mechanism' was introduced under the 1983 Revised Concordat. This required that supervisors monitor each others' activity. In the event that the parent or host authorities were not satisfied with the scope or content of the supervision conducted by the other, they either had to extend their supervision accordingly or deny the bank concerned the right to conduct overseas or local activities as appropriate. This dual key mechanism was strengthened through a restated right of host country corrective action under Principle 4 of the 1992 Minimum Standards. This was principally designed to allow such host authorities as the Bank of England (at that time) and the New York Federal Reserve Bank the right to take action against incoming banks where this was considered appropriate. The 1992 Minimum Standards were agreed following the global closure of BCCI in July 1991. Basel Committee 'Principles for the supervision of banks' foreign establishments' (May 1983); and Basel Committee 'Minimum Standards for the supervision of international banking groups and their cross-border establishments' (July 1992). For discussion, GA Walker *International Banking Regulation—Law, Policy and Practice* (Kluwer London 2001), ch 2.

E. NEW INTEGRATION STRATEGY

Having considered the main difficulties that arise in terms of policy content and financial integration, it is possible to begin to construct a new or, at least, revised or adjusted integration strategy and framework. The objective must be to remove any continuing uncertainties and inconsistencies within each of the main judicial and programme policy areas at the same time as attempt to develop a more coherent overall integration framework based on a clearer examination of all relevant sources of right and obligation.

In so doing, it is possible to incorporate all existing laws and principles available under the current mutual recognition based approach as well as build in further additional or corrective elements as necessary.

An appropriate new strategy can then be considered on the basis of regulatory and policy correction, policy restatement, policy and systems review, institutional revision and a revised policy base (including an adjusted or restated core doctrine of mutual or functional convergence or equivalence in addition to the current mutual recognition). Each of these is considered in further detail below.

(1) Policy Review and Revision

The law governing the operation of banking and financial activities within Europe would initially have to be clarified.[27] This would require, in particular, a review of governing Treaty, judicial and programme rights and obligations. Each of the main official body participants involved would have an obligation to cooperate in this regard.

The Court should attempt to clarify its still evolving policy and, to the extent possible, attempt to produce a clearer and more consistent jurisprudence in this area. This would require, in particular, clarification of the principles governing the scope of restriction in each of the major free movement areas (goods, services, establishment, workers and capital) as well as a clearer articulation of the principles determining the scope of possible supporting derogation. The Court has a responsibility to attempt to produce as clear and consistent a body of relevant law as possible.

The Commission is also responsible for the production of a clear and coherent body of draft programme rules in all essential areas where Community measures are required. The Council and European Parliament must then assist in the adoption of a unified body of secondary measures that gives proper service to the each of the relevant sectors and sector objectives concerned. Other legislative or separate political objectives or compro-

[27] Section D (1).

mises should not be allowed to distort the construction of effective sector regimes.[28]

(2) Policy Restatement

Once the main sources of relevant law have been clarified insofar as possible, comprehensive or consolidated 'restatements' should be produced that would go considerably further than the more limited amendments (*refontes*) currently being considered.[29] The model for these would be the Interpretative Communications issued by the Commission in a number of areas although these would be extended to include all relevant Treaty, programme and judicial entitlements.[30] Insofar as possible, these should also be separately validated through Council and Parliamentary approval or, at the minimum, issued as *sui generis* documents.

The objective would be to produce as complete and coherent as possible a restatement of all relevant provisions in each major area. One could be produced, for example, in each of the main financial sectors of banking, securities and insurance as well as possibly cross-sector activities (financial conglomerates) and capital (and payment) policy. These could also build in relevant market practice and agreed best practice to the extent necessary. Any residual uncertainties and gaps would be disclosed through the preparation process. These could then be corrected through necessary legislative intervention either through the issuance of separate amendment provisions (*refontes*) or (preferably) through reissued 'Restatements.'

(3) Implementation Review, Mutual Review, and Corrective Action

An appropriate policy and systems review mechanism must be established to ensure that the restated law operates effectively in practice.[31] This would require a review of both national implementation action of all relevant European obligations as well as an assessment of the operational effectiveness of the supervision and regulation secured. Implementation review could principally be effected through the continued reporting of necessary

28 The inclusion of the Commission, Council and European Parliament in the legislative process is necessary on the basis of proper representation and democratic inclusion and accountability. See generally, Wyatt and Dashwood (n 18) Ch 2; Weatherhill and Beaumont (n 18) Chs 2, 3 and 4; Craig and de Búrca (n 18) Ch 2. The disadvantages of this inclusive process are nevertheless delay, possibly defective drafting (through lack of resources or proper technical or specialist support), policy confusion or ineffective provision through legislative or political compromise or the danger of more general veto or amendment for separate political reasons. On concerns with regard to the current degree of political commitment to the integration process, Ch 5 (n 171). See also Ch 5 (nn 115, 132 and 134).

29 Section D (1). See also Ch 5 (nn 152, 154, 156 and 158).

30 (n 24).

31 Sections D (2).

action taken by Member States to the Commission. The Commission would be responsible for monitoring the necessary work taken. Continuing implementation reports could be produced and published as appropriate.

Of more importance in terms of the operational effectiveness of the systems of sector supervision created would be to ensure that a necessary degree of operational equivalence was secured in practice. The system at present generally operates on the basis of an assumption of consequent equivalence that may or may not exist or apply.[32] Significant differences may continue to arise in terms of the scope, content and quality of the market supervision and regulation effected, in particular, due to the limited nature of the minimum harmonization initially provided for under the relevant directives and the operation of the automatic validation provided for under mutual recognition. Effective market control will only be possible if a necessary degree of equivalence is ensured in practice which must be confirmed rather than simply assumed.[33]

Necessary corrective action must also be available in the event that either implementation is absent or defective or equivalence inadequate or not present at all. Action can either be taken by the Commission directly such as under the infringement proceedings available under the Treaty[34] or through policy or administrative review and revision. The possibility of a unilateral right of action may also be considered.[35]

(4) Policy Support and Institutional Revision

Necessary supporting institutional structures will be required to ensure that the new strategy operates effectively in practice. In the absence of any central Commission function and adequate resources, this should principally be given effect to through a revised committee structure within the European Community. The model for this would principally be the new advisory (policy) and regulatory (operational) committees set up for securities under the Lamfalussy Report. A policy and regulatory committee should be set up in each of the main sector areas (including banking, securities and insurance) with a separate cross-sector (conglomerate) and possibly capital (and payment) committee.[36]

The main objective in terms of policy review would be to monitor and assess the completeness and coherence or otherwise of the programme rules adopted and their relationship with supporting Treaty and judicial principles. The policy committee would be required to review the general content and operation of the law in each area as set out in the sector restatements

[32] Ch 1 (n 60) and Ch 7, section D (3).
[33] Section D (3).
[34] Ch 3, section A and (nn 7–12).
[35] Section D (5).
[36] Ch 3, section D (4). This was achieved in 2003 and 2004. Ch 1 (n 55); and Ch 2 (n 111).

issued. The advisory function involved could then involve policy review, assessment and revision.

The work of the advisory or regulatory committee could also be extended to include implementation and equivalence reviews. This may be considered appropriate having regard to the limited personnel and financial resources of the Commission. Using a specific sector committee would also have the further advantages of being more immediate, informed, arguably more accurate, cost effective (efficient) and effective (due to the additional technical expertise and incentives involved).

The regulatory committee would be responsible for producing draft rules or other measures and for ensuring that the agreed system of cross-border supervision and regulation operated effectively in practice. This would include, in particular, working on a joint basis in connection with the supervision of individual financial institutions or groups. The committee could then be responsible for the application of relevant provisions at the individual firm or group level. Its functions could include information exchange, coordination and agreed corrective action as well as the possible adoption of more substantial operational rules or regulations in connection with specific aspects of supervisory and regulatory action.

Corrective action in any individual case could initially be considered at the regulatory committee level. Only in the absence of agreed joint action may unilateral intervention be required. As noted, any separate policy correction could be dealt with through the policy committee or at the Commission level.

(5) REVISED POLICY BASE—MUTUAL OR FUNCTIONAL EQUIVALENCE AND ADJUSTMENT

One of the major difficulties that has arisen is the confusion that has developed concerning the proper meaning and operation of the main integration principle of mutual recognition and the associated principles of minimum harmonization and home country control. Mutual recognition, in particular, can be used in a number of different ways[37] especially with regard to its external non-enforcement function in connection with non-essential areas and its internal programme function of cross-validation. It must also be accepted that its main uses involve a number of separate operations and sub-operations[38] while its effect is necessary limited or qualified in practice. Separate difficulties arise with regard to the meaning of the related operational principles of minimum harmonization and home country control and the relationship between the three core integration components.[39]

[37] Section C and Ch 6, section D (1).
[38] Ch 6, section (E); and Ch 7, section E (5).
[39] Ch 6, sections D (2), (3) (4) and (5).

In light of the difficulties and uncertainty that have arisen, the construction of any new integration framework would require the development of a restated or clarified core operational doctrine in place of mutual recognition. In developing a new principle or doctrine, it is necessary initially to recognize its separate external (judicial) as well as internal (programme) function. The objective of the new external doctrine would be to allow for the joint or common mandatory non-enforcement of relevant national measures in non-essential areas where this would otherwise constitute a restriction on free trade and not fall within any of the permitted derogations.[40] This corresponds with the original statement of mutual recognition produced by the Commission following the judgment in *Cassis*.[41]

In developing a new integration doctrine, this could be referred to as 'mutual convergence' or 'functional convergence' (or possibly 'regulatory adjustment' or, more generally, 'technical adjustment'). The objective would be to provide for the mandatory cross-recognition and validation of separate national measures and their consequent non-application and enforcement in non-essential areas (or essential areas where no relevant European standards had been developed) as well as in other essential programme areas.

Mutual or functional convergence would, in turn, be based on a new common test or standard of 'functional equivalence' and a continuing operational process of 'functional adjustment.'[42] This adjustment mechanism could then be applied with regard to internal (essential) and external (non-essential) measures. This could again be based on a number of underlying sub-doctrines or sub-processes of pre-identification, pre-review, pre-compliance, disapplication and adjustment.

The corresponding internal doctrine could, for example, be referred to as 'programme adjustment' which would involve the cross-validation of essential areas subject to some level of harmonization under relevant European directives. This would parallel or correspond with the use of mutual recognition as an internal cross-validation mechanism within specific legislative instruments. This would then be based on a mandatory system of common, joint or automatic validation or cross-validation. This would, in turn, be based on the sub-doctrines of regulatory (or mutual)[43] identification, regulatory definition, regulatory validation, regulatory disapplication and regulatory adjustment. The external doctrine could then be referred to as

[40] Ch 3, sections C (1) and (2). See also Ch 1 (n 60).
[41] Ch 3, section C (3) and (n 83). See also Ch 6 (nn 26 and 28).
[42] Section D (3); and Ch 8, sections B, C and D.
[43] It may be appropriate (although not necessary or objectionable) to avoid use of the term 'mutual' as this implies some element of conditional reciprocity or exchange of benefit. This is not relevant where the cross-validation of (essential and non-essential) measures takes place under more general European law or specific directives. The operation of this system is then mandatory and not dependent upon any exchange of rights or entitlements in particular cases.

'regulatory or technical adjustment' and operate on the basis of an equivalent set of sub-doctrines or sub-processes.

The objective of creating this new core operational doctrine or principle (and supporting sub-doctrines or sup-processes) would be to clarify the application and operation of this integration tool in all cases and remove the earlier confusion that arose. This would still have to be subject to separate mutual review both with regard to necessary implementation and to ensure that an appropriate degree of operational equivalence was secured in practice in all cases.[44] This may then include either central, agreed common or unilateral corrective action as appropriate.

This adjustment element of the revised operational doctrine would then be made up of the following separate components depending upon whether it was being used with regard to essential or non-essential (and non-harmonized) areas:

(a) Internal or Secondary Programme Adjustment

Programme adjustment would operate in essential areas. The scope of application of relevant rights and entitlements as well as supporting obligations would be set out in the relevant Community directives or other legislative measures. On compliance with the relevant conditions (internal minimum harmonization), the parties concerned would be able to exercise the relevant rights conferred. This would include the automatic cross-recognition and cross-validation of relevant national provision.

Programme adjustment would operate on the basis of the following sub-doctrines or sub-principles:

(i) Programme (or Mutual) Identification and Definition

It would be necessary initially to identify the relevant commercial, industrial or financial right covered. The specific subject matter would be set out in the relevant directive. This would include a full definition of the relevant right or entitlement and supporting terms, conditions and obligations.

(ii) Programme (or Mutual) Assessment

The relevant standard to be achieved would also be set out in the directive. This would correspond with the earlier more general principle of minimum harmonization. This might be referred to as 'internal minimum harmonization' or 'programme harmonization' to clarify its internal application and operation.

Although only selected minimum levels of protection may have been specified in earlier directives or other measures, the scope and detail of the

[44] Section D (3).

standards set should be extended over time to ensure that a proper level of equivalence is ensured in practice. The main difficulty that can arise with a simple minimum harmonization process is that insufficient scope of coverage or detailed content is provided. It is in these cases that uneven or insufficient levels of operational equivalence may arise in the absence of a separate review or adjustment mechanism. The operation of the minimum standards set and consequent equivalence must accordingly be monitored and adjusted on a continuing basis.[45]

(iii) Programme (or Mutual) Validation

The issuance of directives in particular areas would have the effect of cross-recognising and cross-validating national measures in connection with each right or activity. This automatic cross-validation would only be conditional upon proper implementation and compliance with the relevant directive or other measure at the national level. In the event that this was not effected in any Member State, issues of direct effect and sanction would arise under EU law.

(iv) Programme (or Mutual) Disapplication or Withdrawal

The automatic cross-validation of national requirements would have the necessary effect of disapplying the application and enforcement of the equivalent local (host) requirement. A system of mutual or mandatory disapplication would accordingly apply.

(v) Programme (or Mutual) Adjustment

Any consequent or necessary adjustments would also have to be made within each set of national regulatory or technical requirements in light of the cross-validation of other Member States' provisions and the consequent disapplication or non-enforceability of the local requirement.

The degree of further adjustment required would vary in each case and be dependent, in particular, on the scope of the minimum harmonization already achieved. Adjustment would generally be required where this fell within the scope of the minimum harmonization achieved although difficulties may arise in practice in determining whether specific national requirements fell within a particular area of harmonization or where the matter could be treated as non-harmonized and therefore fall outside the scope of the adjustment process.[46]

[45] Sections D (2) and (4) and E (3) and (4).

[46] This may, for example, occur in connection with the capital requirements. While basic minimum common obligations may have been imposed with regard to the core items of credit risk and market risk, disagreement may arise with regard to ancillary risks (such as commodity or operational risk) as well as more sophisticated aspects of larger risk management processes (such as trading book proxies or provisioning adjustments). Whether the host terri-

(b) Regulatory or Technical Adjustment

In non-essential areas or in essential areas where no common European provisions have been adopted, a more general external adjustment doctrine would apply. This would correspond with the non-enforceability of national measures in accordance with the jurisprudence of the European Court of Justice.

For clarificatory purposes and to distinguish it from internal programme operations, this might be referred to as 'regulatory adjustment' (in connection with financial and similar areas) or more general 'technical adjustment' (in all other standards areas). The objective in this case would be to provide for the non-enforcement of local (host measures) in other cases not covered by relevant Community directives or other measures where these would otherwise be considered contrary to the law of free movement and not fall within the scope of any permitted derogation.[47]

This revised or clarified doctrine of regulatory or technical adjustment would then operate on the basis of the following sub-doctrines or sub-principles:

(i) Pre-identification (or Regulatory Identification) and Definition

A general system of pre-identification would operate whereby all areas involving the application of local (host) territory requirements that may restrict trade, establishment or services would fall within the doctrine of regulatory or technical adjustment where they were not otherwise covered by a relevant Community directive or other measure. This pre-identification would correspond with the scope of any restrictive measure not otherwise permitted under the jurisprudence of the Court. Where the issue was dealt with under a relevant directive or other measure, this would be subject to programme adjustment.[48]

(ii) Pre-review (or Regulatory Review)

It is implied in the doctrine of equivalence suggested (or anticipated) in *Cassis* that Member States would, in practice, be required to confirm whether a particular person or firm had already complied with corresponding

tory will be able to apply its separate provisions in each case would depend upon whether they were considered to fall within or outside the scope of the original minimum harmonization achieved. This may cause considerable difficulties in particular cases in practice. (nn 13 and 14).

More general difficulties may also arise where the implementation achieved in any particular Member State goes beyond the minimum required under the relevant EU rules agreed. In such cases, this will still constitute an EU harmonized area and mutual recognition with therefore apply. The legal effect of this 'super-equivalence' may depend on the relevant measure.

[47] Ch 3, sections C and D.
[48] Section E (5)(a).

requirements in their home territory before any host measures may be enforced.[49] This was not expressed by the Court although this necessarily follows from the operation of the principle of equivalence suggested. Member States are not to be required generally to review the requirements imposed in all other territories although they are required to confirm whether any equivalent measure has been imposed in any particular case in advance of any enforcement action. A more limited doctrine of pre-enforcement or pre-review may then operate.

(iii) Pre-compliance (or Regulatory Compliance)

In the event that a person or firm has already complied with equivalent obligations imposed in the home territory, this pre-compliance would prevent the enforcement of the corresponding local provision. This would correspond with the sub-doctrine of programme (or mutual) validation referred to above in connection with essential activities covered by particular directives or other measures. The effect would be to provide for the automatic and mandatory recognition in the validation of the home requirements in such cases.

(iv) Disapplication (or Regulatory Disapplication) and Withdrawal

The application of the equivalent host measures would then be prevented through a process of mandatory unenforceability or disapplication. This would correspond with the sub-doctrine of programme (or mutual) disapplication referred to above.[50]

(v) Adjustment (or Regulatory Adjustment)

A similar process of necessary and immediate adjustment would also take place again depending upon the scope of the particular measure and the degree of the pre-compliance already secured. The revised core doctrine of regulatory and technical adjustment would then again be supported by appropriate mutual review and corrective action mechanisms.

F. NEW FRAMEWORK COMMENT— EUROPEAN FINANCIAL MARKETS AND FINANCIAL INTEGRATION

The creation of a single financial market place constitutes only one part of the larger integration process or dynamic still under construction within Europe. This nevertheless represents a core commercial sector in its own right while financial markets provide a range of essential support services

[49] Ch 3 (n 75); and Ch 6 (nn 26 and 28).
[50] Section E (5)(a)(iv).

in all other trade and commercial areas. The effective and stable operation of the banking and financial markets accordingly remain core objectives or components of the larger European integration initiative.

A significant amount of progress has been possible in the construction of a new single market place based on both a combination of privileged market access and balanced market control. Market access is defined in terms of the law of European free movement which extends, in particular, to goods, workers, services, establishment and capital. These rights are provided for under the European Community Treaty although expanded in the relevant secondary measures adopted including the main financial directives. Market control is achieved through the common regulatory standards introduced under minimum harmonization within each of the main directives as well as through supporting judicial derogation (under the principle of the public interest or general good). A number of difficulties nevertheless remain in constructing a complete, coherent and consistent body of law in this area. Work must accordingly continue in the clarification of all relevant judicial principles and supporting programme rules.

This revision could, in particular, be conducted through the construction of a new integration strategy that would principally be based on an underlying revision programme, the production of a series of legislative and interpretative restatements, a new review mechanism, adjusted institutional or committee structure and a revised or enhanced doctrine of mutual convergence or functional convergence. All of these recommendations are possibly not strictly necessary for the completion of the financial integration already under construction. They would nevertheless focus necessary effort at the same time as assist with both the initial completion process already under way and the more general achievement of an effective longer term final result.

Whether all of the other commercial, social or political objectives of the European Union are attainable within the short to medium term, the completion of the single market in banking and financial services is still possible. This would both support and stimulate the completion of all of the other separate initiatives concerned as well as the larger integration process as a whole at the same time as create a new regional and global model for cross-border market integration elsewhere based on both open market access and proper market control.

PART SIX

Policy Effect and Revision

8

Policy Postscript—Financial Integration Revision

The purpose of this postscript is to review and restate some of the key ideas developed in this text. A number of complex issues necessarily arise in constructing a single banking and financial market within Europe. Certain key difficulties have to be overcome in creating any form of integrated market place which problems become even more complex in the financial area. Despite the constraints identified, it is possible to construct a new framework based on a revised integration policy and strategy.

A basic market access and control conflict necessarily arises with the construction of any form of regional trading system or arrangement.[1] As existing national levels of market, technical and consumer protection are disapplied to permit market entry to incoming firms, relevant levels of local regulatory control may be significantly reduced or wholly undermined. Consequent market stability (and investor protection) will then be dependent on the extent to which any compensatory common (regional) control arrangements have been established.[2] The privileged rights of market access created under the regional trading system must accordingly be balanced with appropriate new (central) or, at least, revised and coordinated (national) market control systems and structures.

This conflict becomes of particular significance in the banking and financial area due to the importance of the functions that financial institutions carry out within any economy and the inherently unstable nature of the intermediation process (due, in particular, to the underlying maturity transformation or mismatching mechanism involved with banks funding medium to long term borrowings from sight or demand deposits as well as with the volatility of the separate securities based capital markets).[3]

An additional policy vacuum also exists within Europe in this area under the European Community Treaty which is aggravated by the separate control gap that arises with the absence of any central regulatory or supervisory agency or function within the regional trading system created.[4] In

1 Introduction and Ch 1, (n 4) and section B (2).
2 Ch 1, section B (2); Ch 6, sections C, D and E; and Ch 7, sections (D) and (E).
3 Introduction and Ch 1, sections A and B.
4 Introduction and Ch 1, section B (3) and (5).

light principally of the importance and sensitivity but also technical complexity of the financial sector, market regulation also continues to be carried out at the national or host state level, at least, at this stage in the European integration programme.[5]

Each of these core issues must be properly managed in developing any new more complete and coherent integration framework within Europe.

In constructing a new integration strategy in this area, a number of further more specific issues have also to be resolved. These include policy confusion and programme defect, lack of policy and programme transparency, access and coherence as well as the absence of any central or effective cooperative (delegated) institutional structure, proper market support and effective corrective action procedures.

A number of significant inconsistencies continue to undermine the clarity and coherence of many of the basic Treaty and supporting judicial principles that make up the law of free movement within Europe.[6] Particular difficulties arise both in determining the scope of relevant prohibition and possible supporting derogation or exception.[7]

With regard to substantive programme construction, only the most minimal regulatory framework has been created under the current legislative format. The use of minimum harmonization and mandatory mutual recognition have meant that significant gaps have arisen while uneven adoption, interpretation and implementation levels have resulted in significant differences arising across Member States.[8] The assumed operational or regulatory equivalence or convergence that should have arisen under a mutual recognition based integration policy regime has simply not emerged in many areas.[9]

Policy and programme content are also far from transparent which creates significant problems in terms of access and reliance.[10] Inability to exercise relevant rights then damages legal predictability and certainty which necessarily undermines consequent market reliance and integration.[11]

Separate difficulties arise in terms of institutional support.[12] This is relevant both with regard to policy construction and operational cooperation as well as more general legislative adoption and enforcement. Policy

[5] Introduction Ch 1, section B (3) and (5) and Ch 6, section D. On integration, Ch 1 (n 14) and Ch 2, sections (B), (C) and (D).

[6] Ch 1, sections C (2) and E (3) and (n 74); Ch 3 and 4; and Ch 7, section A.

[7] Chs 3 and 4; and Ch 7, sections A and D.

[8] Ch 1, section D; and Ch 7, section B.

[9] Ch 1, section D (4) and (n 60); Ch 6, section C; and Ch 7, section D (3).

[10] Ch 1, section B (4); Ch 5, sections E (1), (2) and (3); Ch 6, section D (2); and Ch 7, section B.

[11] Ch 1, section B (4) and (n 46); and Ch 2, section B; and Ch 7, section D.

[12] Ch 1, sections C (5) and D (5); Ch 5, section E (5); and Ch 7, section E (4). On the ECB, Ch 1 (n 45). On the revised committee structure, Ch 1 (n 55).

remains to be developed at the European level. The existing procedures are, however, slow and inflexible and prone to unnecessary political interference and damage.[13] Although technical advice has generally been taken and market opinion considered during the consultation phases set up, this essential input may then be distorted (or simply ignored) as part of the politically controlled negotiation, decision-taking and adoption procedures that follow. While the degree of relative advantage and disadvantage that this process may produce may be appropriate (or, at least, acceptable) in certain integration fields, this may have serious detrimental consequences in the banking and financial area in particular especially with the inherent dangers of closure, contagion and systemic collapse that already exist. The legislative process in such a sensitive and technical area should accordingly be as quick, flexible and politically neutral as possible.

Significant difficulties also remain in terms of lack of sufficient operational contact and cooperation between national authorities concerning the day-to-day supervision of financial institutions as well as market support.[14] The possible creation of a central agency is still being discussed although this is generally resisted on cost, bureaucracy and subsidiarity grounds. In the absence of any central coordination function, more effective operational relationships have to be established between national competent authorities.

Separate significant difficulties arise with regard to the enforcement resources and record of the Commission against non-compliant and repeatedly recalcitrant Member States.[15]

A. FINANCIAL INTEGRATION

Despite these difficulties, it is possible to begin to construct a new, or, at least, revised or adjusted integration strategy in banking and financial policy and with regard to the law of free movement more generally.

This would, in particular, be based on underlying policy and programme revision, an extended form of consolidated policy restatement, a new or, at least, adjusted institutional structure (including a reformed legislative process and technical committee system) and a series of revised corrective action mechanisms and supporting review or sanction procedures.

13 Ch 1, sections C and D; and Ch 5, section D and (nn 131–4).
14 Ch 5, section E (6); Ch 7, sections D (5) and E (4); and Ch 1, section D (5) and (n 65).
15 Ch 7, section D (5) and E (3).

(1) SUBSTANTIVE POLICY CORRECTION

Any new or adjusted integration framework must initially be based on proper policy review, revision and restatement.[16]

The residual uncertainties and inconsistencies that exist within the law of free movement must be corrected as completely, quickly and as transparently as possible. This could be most easily achieved through the adoption of an adjusted 'free trade' (GATT or GATS based) model that would apply an effects trigger to market entry restrictions and a discrimination test to subsequent internal market regulation.[17] This could then be subject to a 'reclassification' proviso that would allow regulatory measures to be reassessed as entry restrictions in more complex situations. The result is to combine a simple set of basic new 'free movement' rules with the possibility of a more sophisticated (competition law style) market examination and analysis being conducted in more difficult cases where nominally non-discriminatory internal measures still have a restrictive effect on cross-border market entry and consequent free trade.

A simpler set of derogation conditions should also be adopted. The existing non-discrimination and non-harmonization conditions are tautologist to the extent that any discriminatory restriction can only be justified under the terms of the express provisions set out in the Treaty while 'pre-harmonized' areas are already subject to assessment under the terms of the relevant secondary measure concerned. Relevant derogations are generally (but not exclusively) available in non-essential (or, at least, non-harmonized) areas. Necessity and proportionality also only represent particular aspects of the traditional interpretative doctrine of strict construction (*contra proferentem*) that would automatically apply in connection with any statutory or fundamental treaty rights' limitation. Such natural rules of construction have simply been elevated to distinct operational conditions under the present formulations. This can be considered only to cause confusion and imbalance. Any additional requirement that an exemption falls within an existing class of recognized public interest is also both circuitous, unnecessary and simply inaccurate to the extent that the Court has continued to recognize further areas of exemption or exclusion in appropriate cases. The list will accordingly never be closed and will rather be assessed in terms of the core tests that should properly apply in each case. The relevant derogation conditions should be revised and clarified accordingly.

The remaining proper condition (test or doctrine) for possible derogation should be prior (or, at least) parallel home country control and compliance.

[16] Ch 7, sections D (1) and E (1).

[17] Ch 1, section E (3) and (n 74). Ch 3, sections C (2) and (n 46) and C (5) (nn 128 and 129); and Ch 7, section E (5).

This corresponds with the doctrine of 'pre-compliance' implied in *Cassis* or, at least, the Commission's re-statement of the Court's judgement in *Cassis*.[18] This requires that where a sufficient degree of regulatory protection (or functional equivalence) has already been secured under the home rules, the host territory will not be able to 're-apply' its corresponding provisions. The relevant test will then become 'functional equivalence' in terms of which the resultant comparative result or effect of a measure is assessed having regard to the underlying interest (or interests) to be protected and the extent to which this has already been secured through the application of the home requirements. The relevant derogation rules (including the 'general good' in the financial area) should be reconsidered and restated in these terms.

The decision in *Cassis* may also be considered to imply a separate doctrine (or sub-doctrine) of 'pre-review' which is concerned with whether Member States are subject to an implied obligation to assess other countries' requirements.[19] Rather than take the form of a general obligation (rather than right) of 'mutual review,' this can be understood to constitute a more specific pre-condition before individual enforcement action can be taken in any particular case. This would operate as a form of procedural safeguard that would prevent Member States from commencing enforcement actions before they have determined whether an equivalent degree of protection has already been secured through application of the home country rules. Any new free movement derogation doctrine could then be further clarified by including such a pre-review requirement as an additional procedural condition within the revised operational rules to be imposed.[20]

Having developed an adjusted free trade prohibition (subject to reclassification) and supporting new derogation doctrine, every effort should be made to apply these on as consistent a basis as possible across all areas of free movement. A coherent and consistent body of free movement jurisprudence must be constructed as soon as possible.[21] While the application of the same principles in connection with distinct rights and particular circumstances may produce different results, a consistent legal framework can nevertheless be constructed and applied in this way. This will then increase legal predictability and improve legal certainty which will, in turn, facilitate operational access, reliance and adoption and consequent market integration.

[18] Ch 3, section C (3) and (n 70); and Ch 6, section C (1) and (n 28).
[19] Ch 6, section C (1) and (n 28).
[20] Ch 6, section D (4).
[21] Ch 3, section D (5).

(2) PROGRAMME REVISION

The existing body of secondary legislative measures (in essential integration areas) must be reviewed and revised as appropriate. A substantial secondary programme has been adopted although a number of significant gaps and deficiencies remain.[22]

A considerable amount of work has been undertaken in the completion of the European legislative framework (especially as part of the Financial Services Action Plan (FSAP) and post-Lamfalussy reform work).[23] This is not, however, directly concerned with the amendment or correction of individual measures or the operational relationship between each of the existing sets of provisions already in place. Although some more limited amending directives (*refontes*) were being considered by the Commission in advance of the FSAP, this work had to be suspended or postponed. The only major area in which this work was continued was in connection with the revision of the Investment Services Directive and final MIFID (now included as part of the post-Lamfalussy reforms and the larger FSAP).[24]

The Commission has accordingly moved from an earlier policy of programme revision to one of programme completion without correcting any of the significant residual problems that remained within the secondary measures in place. This separate revision work (as opposed to more original legislative function) is essential and should be continued (or recommenced) as soon as possible and to the extent that resources and timing permit.

A number of substantive difficulties accordingly remain in connection with each of the main sets of sector directives including, in particular, the Banking Consolidation Directive and the former Investment Services Directive (as well as the corresponding insurance measures). The deficiencies identified relate to, for example, definitional difficulties, scope of relevant access rights, regulatory content, operational supervision, programme completion and institutional revision as well as adequate protection against systems failure and market support.[25] Each of these should be re-considered both independently (within the scope of operation of the particular measure) and collectively (as part of the larger financial services programme under construction).

The objective must be to produce as complete and coherent a body of secondary programme measures as possible in all essential areas that will

[22] Ch 1, section C (3); Ch 5, sections E and F; and Ch 7, section B.

[23] Ch 5, sections D (1) and (4).

[24] Ch 5, sections B and D (4). The revision of the ISD eventually resulted in the adoption of the Markets in Financial Instruments Directive (MIFID) 2004/39/EC. Ch 5 (n 39).

[25] Ch 5, section E (5).

then be supported by the parallel judicial principles and jurisprudence developed by the Court in corresponding non-essential areas.[26]

(3) SUBSTANTIVE POLICY CORRECTION

Consideration should be given to setting out the new substantive policy framework produced in a series of consolidated 'restatements' that would confirm all of the relevant Treaty, secondary and interpretative provisions that apply in each major area (including banking, securities and insurance as well as possibly conglomerates and capital and payment). A clear and accessible body of relevant provision must be produced, in particular, to promote commercial and legal awareness, access and reliance.[27]

One option would be for such restatements to operate through the creation of a series of new regulatory 'handbooks' or 'rulebooks' within each major financial sector. (These might be referred to as 'regulatory rules' or '*erules*' or '*frules*.') These could take the form of a virtual (hypertext mark-up language (http)) based set of consolidated financial rules that would include all relevant Treaty provisions, sector restatements (*refontes*) and supporting guidance and commentaries (such as interpretations or communications). These could be made available on a central site and extended to include relevant implementation measures within each Member State. These national 'implementation reports' (or modules) could either be incorporated within the commentaries or guidance produced or included as separate sections or attachments. All of this would significantly increase access and transparency and promote implementation and compliance.

Similar sets of 'virtual' provisions are already available, for example, through the UK Financial Services Authority's Handbook of Rules and Guidance[28] and with the Compendium of Standards produced by the Financial Stability Forum at the international level.[29] These virtual formats are of particular value where either a large amount of material (possibly made up of a number of separate sections) is to be produced (or re-produced) or papers from a number of separate sources or other bodies (and jurisdictions) are involved.

The new handbooks or rulebooks could be prepared by the main relevant sector technical committees in the banking, securities, insurance, capital (and payment) and conglomerate areas. These committees would still operate under the general direction and oversight of the Commission although strictly in accordance with the mandates conferred under the

[26] Ch 3, section E; Ch 5, sections E and F; and Ch 7, sections D (1) and E (1), (2) and (5).
[27] Ch 1, section B (4) and (n 46); and Ch 7, sections D (1) and E (1) and (2).
[28] Available http://www.fsa.gov.uk/handbook.
[29] http://www.fsforum/standards.

particular financial (or separate establishment and appointment) directives (which could also then be amended to the extent necessary).[30]

The objective would in each case be to provide a fully consolidated set of relevant rules and regulations applicable in all financial areas. The effect of the construction of such 'virtual' handbooks or rulebooks over time would be to facilitate the adoption of a much more intensive and substantial intra-sector convergence process than is currently possible under existing mutual recognition and minimum harmonization. This process could also be managed directly by the technical bodies concerned (without separate political interference) and operate through the parallel development of a common set of regulations, interpretations and supporting national practices as appropriate.

While the Commission has already moved generally from a full harmonization to a mutual recognition based approach to European integration (with an intermediate 'framework' approach in the financial area), this would now be supplemented by a new more specific sub-policy or doctrine of 'functional convergence,' 'regulatory convergence' or 'committee convergence' (or possibly even 'rules convergence' or 'administrative' or 'regulatory harmonization').[31]

Apart from being technically informed and managed and more cooperative and cost effective, the advantage of such a committee (and rules) based convergence process would be that it would avoid any consequent significant inconsistencies or imbalances arising (due to lack of regulatory or functional equivalence). Interpretative and implementation problems would also be avoided as more consistent and uniform sets of common rules were constructed over time.

Even if a full common rulebook process could not be adopted immediately (for political, cost or resource reasons), the emphasis of any new integration policy must be on more substantial technical and regulatory convergence. While the original 'mutual recognition' approach adopted has been of considerable value in promoting increased market access and penetration in many areas, the continuing market control problems that exist with uneven adoption and implementation levels secured must now be corrected through the use of some form of supplementary or complementary integration device or mechanism. One useful option would be through such a more technical and committee based 'functional convergence' or 'regulatory convergence' process.

[30] On recent institutional reforms within the EU, Ch 1 (n 55) and Ch 2 (n 111).
[31] Ch 1, section D (4) and (n 60). Ch 5, section A and (n 10).

(4) Revised Legislative and Institutional Structure

A revised legislative system should be set up to allow for the adoption of key measures in a faster and more flexible manner.[32] This must be as technically informed (both through the inclusion of appropriate official and market representation) as well as politically neutral as possible (to avoid unnecessary 'non-financial' market-based considerations distorting or damaging the new control systems being created). This would have to operate within the existing procedural and institutional structures already in place although a revised 'technical' (fast track) process should still be introduced. The objective would be to produce general 'structural' or 'framework' measures at the European level that would then be transferred to the relevant sector committees for expansion and restatement.[33]

The absence of any central administrative function and lack of cooperation between national authorities could be dealt with through the revised technical committee structures to be set up. This could be further refined in practice to include the creation of both a policy and a regulatory agency within each committee area. These two functions could be carried out by the same committee although it may be preferable for administrative and membership reasons to assign them to two separate bodies. It may, for example, be considered necessary to separate policy formulation and implementation activities within the new framework.

The policy committee could develop more general laws and regulations to apply in particular areas as well as prepare (or manage the preparation of) the consolidated handbooks referred to. (The handbooks could either be prepared by the policy committee directly or a sub-group within the committee or by separate 'regulatory committee' or 'handbook (or rules) committee'). Even if a full common handbook approach was not to be followed, the policy committee could focus on substantive convergence and the production of more detailed European 'secondary' level measures to be implemented at the national level either directly or indirectly through the separate regulatory committee.

The regulatory committee would support this policy development and could also possibly coordinate the supervision of individual institutions or groups on a cross-border basis. The 'European Securities Regulatory Committee' could, for example, carry out this function in the securities area while the 'Contact Group' would be reconstituted as a regulatory committee in the banking area (with a re-constituted 'Banking Advisory Committee' acting as the policy unit). Separate policy and regulatory committees should then be established in the insurance and conglomerate

[32] Ch 1, section C (4); Ch 5, section D (4) and (n 132); and Ch 7, sections E (4).

[33] Ch 7, sections D (4) and E (4). See also (n 30).

areas as well as possibly in connection with capital and payments (including settlement).

(5) CORRECTIVE ACTION AND ADJUSTMENT

A revised corrective action procedure should be adopted to support these other policy, operational and institutional reforms.[34] While this would still be centrally Commission managed, this could operate at the Member State or firm level with complaints being referred to the Commission (or one of the sector committees) for action. A more effective system of 'mutual review' could then be constructed that would parallel 'mutual recognition' (acceptance or validation) at the Member State level. This would assist correct both for the lack of necessary Commission resources as well as possible problems in terms of political sensitivity in pursing infraction proceedings against recalcitrant Member States.

Under this new oversight regime, national governments and agencies and commercial operators would monitor implementation and convergence. In the event that significant difficulties arose either with regard to implementation or consequent convergence (technical or regulatory equivalence), relevant incidents would be referred to the Commission to be dealt with under the existing infraction procedures set out in the Treaty. (Consideration might also be given to allowing Member States some possible unilateral (solo) right of action in emergency situations although disciplinary and sanction proceedings would generally continue to be determined at the Commission level.)

With the revised committee and oversight structure proposed, there may be no need to consider the issue of necessary consequent equivalence separately. It is essential that some form of continuing 'functional adjustment' is undertaken to ensure that any significant operational inconsistencies do not arise. A necessary degree of operational equivalence could nevertheless be produced under the coordination of common interpretations and supporting guidance of relevant European measures (in both essential and significant non-essential areas) especially if implementation coordination and reporting are also to be included within the restatements referred to.

'Functional convergence' (or 'regulatory convergence' or 'committee convergence') would then supplement mutual recognition as an intermediate but more complete and substantive form of integration mechanism. As the main secondary programmes of measures have already been produced in most essential areas, work in this area would then focus on achieving a more intimate form of functional or regulatory convergence in practice.

[34] Ch 7, sections D (5) and E (3).

While some of these recommendations have already been given effect to under the Lamfalussy Committee proposals and subsequent committee reform work undertaken,[35] the objective of this new strategy more generally would be to construct a revised framework that would operate in a more complete and coherent manner and apply across all financial sectors and activities. It would also allow for the adoption of a consistent and parallel approach in both essential and non-essential areas that would be based on a new common underlying integration policy (defined in terms of 'functional convergence,' 'functional equivalence' and 'functional adjustment').[36] This would more completely and clearly balance the underlying access and control conflict identified.

B. POLICY RECONCILIATION

One of the most significant difficulties that has arisen with the progressive nature of the policy developed within Europe is that a 'dual' or combined approach has effectively been followed (since the mid-1980s) with Commission harmonization work focusing on 'essential' areas with 'non-essential' matters (as well as non-harmonized essential areas) being left to be governed by underlying Treaty provisions and the still evolving jurisprudence of the European Court of Justice.[37]

Two separate sources of policy content and structure then arise with problems of inconsistent substantive content and application being created. While the Commission has attempted to produce directives and other secondary (non-Treaty) measures in a number of key areas and, in so doing, to ensure in so far as possible that these are consistent with relevant judicial decisions, the Court is still restricted by the selective nature of the litigious process and the need to apply the law to the particular facts only. Some more general guidance and direction have been provided in appropriate situations through the inclusion of more general or 'anticipatory' language in individual decisions such as in *Cassis de Dijon* although the value and validity of this must be necessarily limited. To the extent that the authority of the Court is constrained by the terms of the powers conferred under the Treaty (and by the nature of the judicial process itself), it may never be possible to coordinate fully the work of the Court and the Commission directly.[38]

A provisional policy reconciliation may nevertheless be constructed through the use of 'functional equivalence' as a common test or standard in

[35] (n 30) and Ch 5, section D(4).
[36] Ch 1, section D (4); and Ch 8, sections B, C and D.
[37] Ch 6, section C.
[38] Ch 3, Introduction.

both essential and non-essential harmonization areas.[39] This does reflect the general approach (or result) that has been followed in some cases although a clear and consistent policy has still not been adopted in this regard. With the adoption of such a new common single test or condition, a fully integrated 'new policy' or 'new strategy' may be possible in the financial area.

This new governing standard would then operate within a larger integration framework based on functional equivlance or convergence (or possibly 'mutual convergence' or 'technical or regulatory convergence') supported by a continuing process of 'functional adjustment.'

C. POLICY CONFLICT AND RESOLUTION

The basic access (or integration) and control conflict identified within any regional system can initially be resolved through the construction of a revised programme of secondary measures based on combined 'mutual recognition' (with minimum harmonization and home country control) and 'functional' (or regulatory or technical) convergence. While mutual recognition (with minimum harmonization) would establish the basic legislative framework to apply, functional convergence would allow a considerably more substantial substantive operational body of relevant common provisions to be developed in all areas of regulatory control. A parallel structural (framework) and more substantial content (rules) based solution could then be constructed.

This core legislative and regulatory programme (based on mutual recognition and functional convergence) would then be supported by the consistent application of the adjusted free trade prohibition to any other restrictions on market entry with any possible exemptions or permissions being determined in accordance with the revised 'derogation rules' proposed. Within this, the core test would become 'pre-compliance' which would be assessed having regard to the degree of underlying 'functional equivalence' already secured by applying the home country rules.

The final assessment in each case (secondary programme or more general free movement) could then be made in terms of functional equivalence with a common (or, at least, more approximate) result being possible in both essential legislative and non-essential (judicial) areas which would be supported by the consistent application of the parallel principles developed.[40]

[39] Ch 1, section D (4) and (n 60); and Ch 7, sections C and D (3) and E (5).
[40] Ch 7, sections C, D (3) and E (5); and Ch 8, section B.

D. NEW INTEGRATION FRAMEWORK

A revised and strengthened integration strategy and framework can accordingly be constructed using the new doctrine of 'mutual convergence' or 'functional convergence' proposed. The revised system would then be based on three sub-processes or principles of 'functional (or regulatory) convergence,' 'functional equivalence' and 'functional adjustment.'

The purpose or objective of the new initiative would be functional (technical or regulatory) convergence in all core financial, industrial and commercial sectors and other social and political programme related areas. The common test or standard to be applied in both essential and non-essential areas would be 'functional equivalence' with the overall strategy being subject to a continuing process of 'functional adjustment' to ensure that a necessary degree of operational equivalence was achieved at all times in practice.

Policy revision in non-essential areas would be governed by an adjusted 'free trade' prohibition subject to a 'reclassification proviso' (in more complex cases). A revised derogation regime would operate on the basis of the common test of 'functional equivalence' (or possibly 'mutual effect' or 'common benefit or protection'). A more general doctrine of (*Cassis* derived) 'pre-compliance' and a separate procedural 'pre-review' condition would also generally apply.

The underlying secondary measures in place would be subject to 'programme revision' (including revised 'programme access,' 'programme (or regulatory) content' and 'programme operation' (or possibly 'programme supervision or effect')). A separate doctrine of 'programme completion' or revision would continue to apply to ensure that no major (or even minor) gaps or deficiencies arose.

Institutional adjustment would be determined in accordance with a new 'committee review programme,' (which would involve the creation of a specialist policy formulation body in each significant regulatory and technical area), a new 'operational support structure' (based on enhanced financial or technical supervisory cooperation and coordination in practice) and integrated or effective 'market support' (including the provision of regional 'lender of last' resort in the financial area in appropriate cases).

Any revised corrective action programme would continue to be based on 'central oversight' (Commission monitoring) although this would be subject to supplementary 'mutual review' and 'regulatory or (technical) reporting' and possible 'mutual (or unilateral) action' in necessary cases (possibly determined in accordance with the terms of some form of 'solo action' clause to be included in each financial or other technical directive).

It would still be essential to ensure that an appropriate or sufficient degree of 'functional (or operational) equivalence' arises in all cases. While this could be dealt with under some form of separate review process, this may naturally arise with the more complete and substantial nature of the underlying degree of regulatory and technical convergence possible under the new integration regime to be constructed. In the event of further difficulties or delays arising, these could be dealt with through a more general 'policy and programme adjustment process.'

It would accordingly be possible to re-activate and complete the integration process already underway in the financial and other areas within Europe through the adoption and application of a new framework based on these new integration doctrines or devices. The advantage of identifying and defining each separately in this way would be to clarify their availability and operation and with this further re-enforce and strengthen the larger integration process already under construction.

E. CLOSING COMMENT—A NEW BEGINNING

Despite the historical, political and technical difficulties that have arisen in the banking and financial area, it is possible to begin to construct a new integration strategy and framework. This should generally be based on policy and programme revision, consolidated regulatory restatement and the establishment of an adjusted institutional and corrective action structure. Economic and financial integration are necessarily complex and sensitive issues. An effective solution is nevertheless possible that balances enhanced market access with proper market control in this key area of European integration.

In so doing, the underlying objective of the revision programme must be to attempt to advance necessary integration insofar as possible by making full use of the existing principles and practices already in place at the same time as correct any continuing or residual omissions and deficiencies that arise through the adoption and application of a number of new or revised doctrines or processes (and sub-doctrines and sub-processes). This would, in particular, include the creation and use of the new doctrine of mutual or functional convergence (based on underlying functional equivalence and functional adjustment). This would then operate as a necessary complement or supplement to the retention and continued application of the existing dominant doctrine of mutual recognition.

With these revisions and adjustments, it should be possible to begin to construct a new integration strategy and approach based on a more immediate and intimate form of functional convergence and equivalence. This would then operate as an intermediate form of integration between 'full harmonization' and minimum standards based 'mutual recognition'. While mutual recognition would continue as the dominant framework principle, a significantly more substantial and effective degree of underlying regulatory and technical convergence should be possible under the new equivalence driven integration approach and policy proposed.

Bibliography

1. EUROPEAN REGULATIONS, DIRECTIVES AND DECISIONS

Council Directive 68/360 (1968 JO L257/13, 1968 OJ Spec. Ed (II), 485)

Council Directive 73/183/EEC of 28 June 1973 on the abolition of restrictions on freedom of establishment and freedom to provide services in respect of self-employed activities of banks and other financial institutions

Council Directive 73/239/EEC

Council Directive 75/368 of 16 June 1975

Council Directive 83/189/EEC on the provision of information on technical standards and regulations (OJ L 109/8 (25.4.1983))

Council Directive 83/850/EEC of June 13 1983 on the supervision of credit institutions on a consolidated basis

Council Directive 85/577/EEC concerning the protection of consumers in respect of contracts negotiated away from business premises (OJ 1985 L 372, p. 31)

Council Directive 88/378/EEC of 3 May 1988 on the safety of toys (OJ L 187/1 (16.7.1988))

Council Directive 89/299/EEC on the own funds of credit institutions 17 April 1989 (OJ L 124, 5.5.1989, p 16) as amended by Directive 91/633/EEC of 3 December 1991 (OJ L 339 , 11.12.1991, p 33) and Directive 92/16/EEC of 16 March 1992 (OJ L 75, 21.3.1992, p 48)

Council Directive 89/392/EC of 14 June 1989 on safety of machinery (OJ L 183/9 (29.6.1989))

Council Directive 89/647/EEC on a solvency ratio for credit institutions of 18 December 1989 as amended by Directive 91/31/EEC

Council Directive 91/633/EEC of 3 December 1991 as amended by Directive 91/633/EEC of 3 December 1991 and Directive 92/16/EEC of 16 March 1992

Council Directive 92/121/EEC on the monitoring and control of large exposures of credit institutions of 21 December 1992

Council Directive 92/350/EEC on the supervision of credit institutions on a consolidated basis of 6 April 1992

Council Directive 93/6/EEC of 15 March 1993 on the capital adequacy of investment firms and credit institutions

Council Directive 93/22/EEC of 10 May 1993 on investment services in the securities field

Council Directive 95/26/EC of 29 June 1995 amending Directives

77/780/EEC and 89/646/EEC in the field of credit institutions, Directives 73/239/EEC and 92/49/EEC in the field of non-life insurance, Directives 79/267/EEC and 92/96/EEC in the field of life assurance, Directive 93/22/EEC in the field of investment firms and Directive 85/611/EEC in the field of undertakings for collective investment in transferable securities (UCITS) with a view to reinforcing prudential supervision 95/26/EEC

Council Directive 98/34/EC (OJ L 204 (21.7.98), 37))

Council Directive 2000/64/EC amending in the Insurance Directives and Investment Services Directive to permit information exchange with third countries adopted 7 November 2000

Council Directive 2001/65/EC amending the fourth and seventh Company Law Directives to allow fair value accounting adopted 31 May 2001

Council Directive 2001/97/EC amending the Money Laundering Directive adopted 4 November 2001

Council Directives 2001/107/EC and 2001/108/EC on UCITS adopted 21 January 2002

Council Directives 2002/12/EC and 2002/13/EC amending the solvency margin requirements in the Insurance Directives adopted 5 March 2002

Council Resolution of 7 May 1985 (OJ C 136/1 (4.6.1985)).

Council Resolution on new policy priorities regarding the information society, adopted on 8 October 1996

Directive on Financial Conglomerates (COM(2001) 213 Final, 24/4/2001, Parliament opinion 14/3/2002, ECOFIN political agreement 7/5/2002, Parliament second reading 2002), Reinsurance Supervision (ongoing), Insurance Solvency II (ongoing) and Third Money Laundering Directive (report to follow).

Directive on Insurance Intermediaries (COM(2000) 511 Final, 20/9/2000, common position Council 19/3/2002, second reading Parliament 8/4/2002), Legal Framework for Payments in the Internal Market (proposal to follow) follow-up to FIN/NET (follow-up on COM/2001/6650 ongoing) and follow-up to Action Plan to prevent fraud and counterfeiting in payment systems (COM(2001) 11, 9/2/2001) and Work on Insurance Guarantee Schemes (ongoing since February 2002)

Directive on Take-over Bids (new proposal following rejection of compromise text of 6/6/2001 by Parliament on 4/7/2001)

Directive on taxation of savings income on interest payments (new proposal 18/7/2001 with negotiations with third countries continuing), Commission initiative on taxation of cross-border occupational pensions (COM(2001) 214, 19/4/2001 ongoing) and implementation of the December 1997 Code of Conduct on business taxation (submitted ECOFIN November 1999, ongoing).

Directive on the Distance Marketing of Financial Services (COM(1999) 385, 23/7/1999, Political agreement 27/9/2001, Parliament second reading ongoing)

Directive on the Prudential Supervision of Supplementary Pension Funds (COM(2000) 507 provisional, 11/10/2000, Parliament opinion 4/7/2001)

Directive on the Reorganisation and Winding-up of Insurance Undertakings 2001/17/EC adopted 19 March 2001

Directive on the Winding-up and Liquidation of Banks 2001/24/EC adopted 4 April 2001

Draft Directive for the coordination of the legal and administrative provisions for the taking up and exercise of the 'independent operator' activities of credit institutions, July 1972 (XIV/508/72-D, Orig, D)

Electronic Money Directive 2000/46/EC adopted 18 September 2000

Financial Collateral Arrangements Directive (COM(2001) 168 Final, 27/3/2001, Council common position on 5/3/2002 with second Parliament reading early 2002)

First Council Directive 11 May 1960 (OJ, English Special Edition 1959/1962, p. 49)

First Council Directive 77/780/EEC on the coordination of laws, regulations and administrative provisions relating to the taking up and pursuit of the business of credit institutions of 12 December 1977

First Life Directive 79/267/EEC of 5 March 1979 (OJ No L 63, 13.3.1979, p 1)

Investment Services Directive 93/22/EEC (OJ 1993 L 141, p. 27)

Investment Services Directive (COM(2000) 729 Final, 15/11/2000 with first consultation 2001 and second consultation April 2002)

Market Abuse Directive (COM(2001) 281 30/05/2001 with ECOFIN political agreement on 7 May 2002)

Proposal for 14th Company Law Directive (new proposal 2003)

Proposal for a European Parliament and Council Directive amending for the third time Directive 83/189/EEC laying down a procedure for the provision of information in the field of technical standards and regulations (COM(96) 392 final of 30 August 1996; OJ No C307, 15.10.1996, p. 11). Council Directive 78/473/EEC of 30 May 1978 (OJ 1978, L151, p. 25)

Proposals for 10th Company Law Directive (original proposal 1985 blocked on issue of workers' participation with new proposal to follow September 2002)

Prospectuses Directive (COM(2001) 280, 30/05/2001), updating the Regular Reporting Requirements (work continues following first consultation summer 2001 and second consultation April 2002)

Regulation 1612/68 (1968 JO L257/2)

Regulation on International Accounting Standards (COM(2001) 80, 13/2/2001 with Parliamentary opinion on 12/3/2002) and modernisation of accounting provisions in 4th and 7th Company Law directives (to follow October 2002)

Second Council Directive 63/21/EEC of 18 December 1962 (OJ, English Special Edition 1963–4 p. 5)

Second Council Directive 89/646/EEC on the coordination of laws, regulations and administrative provisions relating to the taking up and pursuit of the business of credit institutions of 15 December 1989

Second Life Directive 90/619/EEC of 8 November 1990 (OJ No L 330, 29.11.1990, p 50)

Second Non-Life Directive 88/357/EEC of 22 June 1988 (OJ No L 172, 4.7.1988, p 1)

Third Life Directive 92/96/EEC of 10 November 1992 (OJ No L 360, 9.10.92, p 1

Third Non-Life Directive 92/49/EEC of 18 June 1992 (OJ No L 228, 11.8.1992, p 1)

2. EUROPEAN CASE LAW

Case 52/59 *Procureur du Roi v Debauve* [1980] ECR 833

Case 7/61 *Commission v Italy* [1961] ECR 317, [1962] CMLR 39

Case 26/62 *Van Gend en Loos v Nederlande Administratie der Belastingen* [1963] ECR 1, [1963] CMLR 105

Case 6/64 *Costa (Flaminio) v ENEL* [1964] ECR 585, [1964] CMLR 425

Cases 56 & 58/64 *Consten SARL & Grundig-Verkaufs GmbH v Commission* [1966] ECR 299, [1966] CMLR 418

Case 56/65 *STM/MBU* [1966] ECR 235

Case 7/68 *Commission v Italy* [1968] ECR 423

Case 24/68 *Commission v Italy* [1969], ECR 193, [1971] CMLR 611

Cases 2 and 3/69, *Sociaal Fonds voor de Diamantarbeiders v SA Ch. Brachfeld & Sons* [1969] ECR 211, [1969] CMLR 335

Case 5/69 *Volk v Vervaecke* [1969] ECR 295

Case 11/70, *Internationale Handelsgesellschaft mbH v Einfuhr-und Vorratsstelle für Getreide und Futtermittel* [1970] ECR 1125, [1972] CMLR 255

Case 2/73 *Geddo v Ente Nazionale Risi* [1973] ECR 865, [1974] 1 CMLR 13

Case 34/73 *Variola v Amministrazione delle Finanze* [1973] ECR 981

Case 120/73 *Gebrüder Lorenz GmbH v Federal Republic of Germany et Land de Rhénanie-Palatinat*, [1973] ECR 01471

Case 152/73 Sotgui *v Deutsche Bundespost* [1974] ECR 153

Case 190/73 *Officier van Justitie v J.W.J. van Haaster* [1974] ECR 01123
Case 2/74 *Reyners v Belgium* [1974] ECR 631, [1974] 2 CMLR 305
Case 8/74 *Procureur du Roi v Dassonville* [1974] ECR 837, [1974] 2 CMLR 436
Case 12/74 *Commission v Germany* [1975] ECR 181, [1975] 1 CMLR 340
Case 33/74 *Van Binsbergen v Bestuur van de Bedrijfsvereniging voor de Metaalnijverheid* [1974] ECR 1299, [1975] 1 CMLR 298
Case 39/75 *Coenen v Sociaal Economische Raad* [1975] ECR 1547, [1976] 1 CMLR 30
Case 48/75 *Procureur de Roi v Royer* [1976] ECR 497 [1976] 2 CMLR 619
Case 65/75 *Ricardo Tasca* [1976] ECR 291, [1977] 2 CMLR 183
Case 87/75 *Bresciani v Amministrazione Italiana delle Finanze* [1976] ECR 129, [1976] 2 CMLR 62
Cases 88–90/75 *Societa Sadam* [1976] ECR 323, [1977] 2 CMLR 183
Case 188/75 *Watson & Belmann* [1976] ECR 1185, [1976] 2 CMLR 552
Case 13/76 *Donà v Mantero* [1976] ECR 1333, [1976] 2 CMLR 578
Case 71/76 *Thieffry v Conseil de L'Ordre des Avocats a la Cour de Paris* [1977] ECR 765, [1977] 2 CMLR 373
Case 74/76 *Iannelli & Volpi SpA v Ditta Paolo Meroni* [1977] ECR 557, [1977] 2 CMLR 688
Case 111/76 *Officier van Justitie v Beert van den Hazel* [1977] ECR 00901
Case 11/77 *Patrick v Ministre des Affaires Culturelles* [1977] ECR 1199, [1977] 2 CMLR 523
Case 13/77 *GB–INNO v ATAB* [1977] ECR 2115
Case 82/77 *Openbaar Ministerie v Van Tiggele* [1978] ECR 25, [1978] 2 CMLR 528
Case 106/77 *Amministrazione delle Finanze dello Stato v Simmenthal SpA* [1978] ECR 629, [1978] 3 CMLR 263
Case 148/77 *H. Hansen v Hauptzollamt Flensburg* [1978] ECR 1787 [1979] 1 CMLR 604
Case 15/78 *Société Générale Alsacienne de Banque v Koestler* [1978] ECR 1971
Case 115/78 *Knoors v Secretary of State for Economic Affairs* [1979] ECR 399, [1979] 2 CMLR 357
Case 82/77 *Openbaar Ministerie v Van Tiggele* [1978] ECR 25, [1978] 2 CMLR 528
Cases 110–111/78 *Ministère Public and Chambre Syndicale des Agents Artistiques et Impresarii de Belgique, ASBL v Willy van Wesemael and others* [1979] ECR 35, [1979] 3 CMLR 87
Case 118/78 *C.J. Meijer BV v Department of Trade, Ministry of Agriculture, Fisheries and Food and Commissioners of Customs and Excise* [1979] ECR 1387, [1979] 2 CMLR 398

Case 120/78 *Rewe–Zentrale AG v Bundesmonopolverwaltung für Branntwein (Cassis de Dijon)* [1979] ECR 649 [1979] 3 CMLR 494
Case 136/78 *Ministère Public v Auer* [1979] ECR 437, [1979] 2 CMLR 373
Case 148/78 *Pubblico Ministero v Ratti* [1979] ECR 1629, [1980] 1 CMLR 96
Case 152/78 *Commission v France* [1980] ECR 2299, [1981] 2 CMLR 743
Case 5/79 *Procureur Générale v Hans Buys, Han Pesch and Yves Dullieux and Denkavit France SARL* [1979] ECR 3203, [1980] 2 CMLR 493
Case 15/79 *Groenveld (P.B.) BV v Produktschap voorVee en Vlees* [1979] ECR 3409, [1981] 1 CMLR 207
Cases 16–20/79 *Criminal Proceedings against Joseph Danis and others* [1979] ECR 3327, 3 CMLR 492
Case 21/79 *Commission v Italy* [1980] ECR 1, [1980] 2 CMLR 613
Case 34/79 *R. v Henn and Darby* [1979] ECR 3795, [1980] 1 CMLR 246
Case 62/79 *SA Compagnie Générale pour la diffusion de la Télévision, Coditel, and others v Ciné Vog Films and others* [1980] ECR 881, [1981] 2 CMLR 362
Case 88/79 *Ministère Public v Grunert* [1980] ECR 1827
Case 140/79 *Chemial Farmaceutici v DAF SpA* [1981] ECR 1, [1981] 3 CMLR 350
Case 788/79 *Criminal Proceedings against Herbert Gilli and Paul Andres* [1980] ACR 1071, [1981] 1 CMLR 146.
Case 27/80 *Fietje* [1980] ECR 3839, [1981] 3 CMLR 722
Case 30/80 *Kelderman* [1981] ECR 517
Case 53/80 *Officier van Justitie v Koninklijke Kaasfabriek Eyssen BV* [1981] ECR 409, [1982] 2 CMLR 20
Case 155/80 *Summary Proceedings against Sergius Obel* [1981] ECR 1993, [1983] 1 CMLR 390
Case 193/80 *Commission v Italy* [1981] ECR 3019
Case 203/80 *Casati* [1981] ECR 2595, [1982] 1 CMLR 365
Case 272/80 *Frans-Nederlandse Maatschappij voor Biologische Producten* [1981] ECR 3277, [1982] 2 CMLR 497
Case 279/80 *Criminal Proceedings against Alfred John Webb* [1981] ECR 3305, [1982] 1 CMLR 719
Case 6/81 *Diensten Groep v Beele* [1982] ECR 707
Case 8/81 *Ursula Becker v Finanzamt Münster-Innenstadt* [1982] ECR 00053
Cases 62 and 63/81 *Société anonyme de droit français Seco et Société anonyme de droit français Desquenne & Giral v Etablissement d'assurance contre la vieillesse et l'invalidité* [1982] ECR 223
Case 75/81 *Joseph Henri Thomas Blesgen v Belgian State* [1982] ECR 1211, [1983] 1 CMLR 431
Case 76/81 *SA Transporoute et Travaux v Minister of Public Works* [1982] ECR 417

Case 220/81 *Criminal Proceedings against Timothy Frederick Robertson and others* [1982] ECR 2349, [1983] 1 CMLR 556
Case 261/81 *Walter Rau Lebensmittelwerke v de Smedt Pvba* [1982] ECR 3961, [1983] 2 CMLR 496
Case 286/81 *Oosthoek's Uitgeversmaatschappij BV* [1982] ECR 4575. [1983] 3 CMLR 428
Case 29/82 *F. Van Luipen en Zn BV against a Disciplinary Measure Adopted against it* [1983] ECR 00151
Case 94/82 *Criminal Proceedings against De Kikvorsch Groothandel-Import-Export BV* [1983] ECR 947, [1984] 2 CMLR 323
Case 218/82 *Commission v Council* [1983] ECR 4063
Case 237/82 *Jongeneel Kaas v The State (Netherlands) and Stichting Centraal Organ Zuivelcontrole* [1984] ECR 483, [1985] 2 CMLR 53
Case 271/82 *Ministère Public v Auer* [1983] ECR 2727, [1985] 1 CMLR 123
Case 294/82 *Einberger v Hauptzollamt Freiburg* [1984] ECR 1117
Case 107/83 *Ordre des Avocats du Burreau de Paris v Klopp* [1984] ECR 2971, [1985] 1 CMLR 99
Case 182/83 *Robert Fearon and Co Ltd v The Irish Land Commission* [1984] ECR 3677, [1985] 2 CMLR 228
Case 207/83 *Commission v United Kingdom* [1985] ECR 1201, [1985] 2 CMLR 259
Case 220/83 *Commission v France* [1986] ECR 3663, [1987] 2 CMLR 113
Case 252/83 *Commission v Denmark* [1986] ECR 3713
Case 270/83 *Commission v France* [1986] ECR 273, [1987] 1 CMLR 401
Cases 60 and 61/84 *Cinéthèque SA v Fédération Nationale des Cinémas Français* [1985] ECR 2605
Case 110/84 *Commune de Hillegom v Cornelis Hillenius* [1985] ECR I-03947
Case 112/84, *Humblot v Directeur des Services Fiscaux* [1985] ECR 1367, [1986] 2 CMLR 338
Case 178/84 *Commission v Germany* [1987] ECR 1227, [1988] 1 CMLR 780
Case 197/84 *Steinhauser v City of Biarritz* [1985] ECR 1819, [1986] 1 CMLR 53
Case 205/84 *Commission v Germany* [1986] ECR 3755, [1987] 2 CMLR 69
Case 206/84 *Commission v Ireland* [1986] ECR 3817, [1987] 2 CMLR 150
Case 63/85 *Commission v Italy* (1988) ECR 29, [1989] 2 CMLR 601
Case 148/85 *Direction Générale des Impôts and Procureur de la République v Forest* [1986] ECR 3449, [1988] 2 CMLR 577
Case 205/85 *Commission v Germany* [1988] ECR 3755, [1987] 2 CMLR 69

Case 221/85 *Commission v Belgium* [1987] ECR 719, [1988] 1 CMLR 620
Case 407/85 *Drei Glocken v USL Centro–Sud* [1988] ECR 4233
Case 60/86 *Commission v United Kingdom* [1988] ECR 3921
Case 98/86 *Ministère Public v Mathot* [1987] ECR 809, [1988] 1 CMLR 411
Case 222/86 *UNECTEF v Heylens* [1987] ECR 4097, [1989] 1 CMLR 901
Case 286/86 *Ministère Public v Deserbais* [1988] ECR 4907, [1989] 1 CMLR 516
Case 292/86 *Gullung v Conseil de l'Ordre des Avocats* [1988] ECR 111[1988] 2 CMLR 57
Case 308/86 *Ministère Public v Lambert* [1988] ECR 4369)
Case 18/87 *Commission v Germany* [1988] ECR 5427, [1990] 1 CMLR 561
Case 81/87 *R v HM Treasury and Commissioners of Inland Revenue, ex parte Daily Mail and General Trust plc* [1988] ECR 5483, [1988] 3 CMLR 713
Case 143/87 *Stanton v INASTI* [1988] ECR 3877, [1989] 3 CMLR 761
Case 196/87 *Steymann v. Staatsecretaris van Justitie* [1988] ECR 6159, [1989] 1 CMLR 449
Case 282/87 *Buet v Ministère Public* [1989] ECR 1235
Case 298/87 *Proceedings for Compulsory Reconstruction against Smanor* [1988] ECR 4489
Case C-3/88 *Commission v Italy* [1989] ECR 4035, [1991] 2 CMLR 115
Cases 54 and 91/88 and 14/89 *Criminal Proceedings against Eleonora Nino and others* [1990] ECR 3537, [1992] 1 CMLR 83
Case C-23/89 *Quietlynn and Richards v Southend BC* [1990] ECR I-3059, [1990] 3 CMLR 55
Case C-61/89 *Criminal Proceedings against Marc Gaston Bouchoucha* [1990] ECR I-3551, [1992] 1 CMLR 1033
Case C-113/89 *Rush Portuguesa Lda v Office Natinal d'Immigration* [1990] ECR I-1417, [1991] 2 CMLR 818
Case C-154/89 *Commission v France* [1991] ECR I-659
Case C-180/89 *Commission v Ita*ly [1991] ECR I-709
Case C-198/89 *Commission v Gree*ce [1991] ECR I-727
Case C-213/89 *R v Secretary of State for Transport, ex parte Factortame Ltd and others* [1990] ECR I-2433, [1990] 3 CMLR 1
Case C-246/89 *Commission v United Kingdom* [1991] ECR I-4585, [1991] 3 CMLR
Case C-288/89 *Stichting Collective Antennevoorziening Gouda v Commissariaat voor de media* [1991] ECR I-4007
Case C-312/89 *Union Départment des Syndicats CGT de l'Aisne v SIDEF Conforama* [1991] ECR I-997
Case C-332/89 *Ministère Public v Marchandise* [1991] ECR I-1027

Case C-339/89 *Alsthom Atlantique SA v Sulzer SA* (1991) ECR I-107

Case 340/89 *Vlassopoulou v Ministerium fürJustiz, Bundes-und Europaangelegenheiten Baden-Wurttenberg* [1991] ECR 2357, [1993] 3 CMLR 221

Cases C-6/90 and C-9/90 *Andrea Francovich and Danila Bonifaci and others v Italian Republic* [1991] ECR I-05357

Case C-76/90 *Manfred Säger v Dennemeyer & Co Ltd* [1991] ECR I-4221, [1993] 3 CMLR 639

Case 159/90 *Society for the Protection of the Unborn Child v Grogan* [1991] ECR I-4685

Case C-204/90 *Bachmann v Belgium* [1992] ECR I-249 [1993] 1 CMLR 785

Case C-370/90 *R v Immigration Appeal Tribunal and Surinder Singh, ex parte Secretary of State for the Home Department* [1992] ECR I-4265, [1992] 3 CMLR 358

Case C-106/91 *Ramrath v Ministère de la Justice* [1992] ECR I-3351, [1992] 3 CMLR 173, [1995] 2 CMLR 187

Case C-112/91 *Werner v Finanzamt Aachen-Innenstadt* [1993] ECR I-429

Cases C-306/88, 304/90 and 169/91 *Stoke- on- Trent CC v B&Q plc* [1992] ECR I-6457, [1993] 1 CMLR 426

Cases C-267 and 268/91 *Criminal Proceedings Against Keck and Mithouard* [1993] ECR I-6097 [1995] 1 CMLR 101

Case C-330/91 *R v Inland Revenue Commissioners, ex parte Commerzbank AG* [1993] ECR I-4017, [1993] 3 CMLR 457

Case C-19/92 *Dieter Kraus v Land Baden, Wuerttenberg* [1993] ECR I-1663

Case C-275/92 *Her Majesty's Customs and Excise v Gerhard Schindler & Jörg Schindler* [1994] ECR I-1039

Case C-292/92 *Ruth Hünermund and others v Landesapothekerkammer Baden-Württemberg* [1993] ECR I-6787

Case C-319/92 *Salmone Haim v KVN* [1994] ECR I-425

Case C-334/92 *Teodoro Wagner Miret v Fondo de Garantía Salarial* [1993] ECR I-06911

Case C-379/92 *Matteo Peralta* [1994] ECR I-3453

Case C-391/92 *Commission v Greece* [1995] ECR I-1621, [1996] 1 CMLR 359 and [1995] All ER (EC) 802

Cases C-401 and 402/92 *Criminal Proceedings Against Tankstation't Heukske vof and J. B. E. Boermans* [1994] ECR I-2199, [1995] 3 CMLR 501

Case C-1/93 *Halliburton Services BV v Staatssecretaris van Financiën* [1994] ECR I-1137, [1994] 3 CMRL 377

Case C-17/93 *Openbaar Ministerie v Van der Veldt* [1994] ECR I-3537 [1995] 1 CMLR 621

Case C-18/93 *Corsica Ferries Italia Srl v Corpo dei Piloti del Porto di Genova* [1994] ECR I-1783

Case C-23/93 *TV 10 SA v Commisariaat voor de Media* [1994] ECR I-4795

Case C-41/93 *French Republic v Commission* [1994] ECR I-01829

Cases C-46/93 and C-48/93 *Brasserie du Pêcheur SA v Bundesrepublik Deutschland and The Queen v Secretary of State for Transport, ex parte: Factortame Ltd and others* [1996] ECR I-01029

Cases C-69 and 258/93 *Punto Casa SpA v Sindaco del Commune di Capena* [1994] ECR I-2355

Case C-279/93 *Finanzamt Köln-Altstadt v Roland Schumacker* [1995] ECR I-225, [1996] 2 CMLR 450

Case C-293/93 *Criminal Proceedings against Ludomira Neeltje Barbara Houtwipper* [1994] ECR I-4249

Case C-320/93 *Lucien Ortscheit GmbH v Eurim-Pharm Arzeimittel GmbH* [1994] ECR I-5243, [1995] 2 CMLR 242

Case C-381/93 *Commission v France* [1994] ECR I-5145

Case C-384/93 *Alpine Investments BV v Minister van Financiën* [1995] ECR I-1141, [1995] 2 CMLR 209; [1995] All ER [EC] 543

Case C-387/93 *Giorgio Domingo Banchero* [1995] ECR I-4663 [1996] 1 CMLR 829

Case C-412/93 *Société d'Importation Édouard Leclerc-Siplec v TF1 Publicité SA and M6 Publicité* [1995] ECR I-179, [1995] 3 CMLR 422

Case C-415/93 *Union Royale Belge des Société de Football Association ASBL and Others v Jean-Marc Bosman* [1995] ECR I-4921, [1996] 1 CMLR 645

Case C-418/93 *Semeraro Casa Uno Srl v Sindaco del Commune di Erbusco* [1996] ECR I-2975

Case C-484/93 *Svensson and Gustavsson v Ministre du Logrment et de l'Urbaniseme* [1995] ECR I-3955

Case C-55/94 *Reinhard Gebhard v Consiglio dell 'Ordine degli Avvocati e Procuratori di Milano* [1995] ECR I-4165: [1996] 1 CMLR 603

Case C-80/94 *Wielockx v Inspecteur de Directe Belastingen del Golfo* [1995] ECR I-2493

Case C-84/94 *United Kingdom of Great Britain and Northern Ireland v Council of the European Union* [1996] ECR I-05755

Case C-101/94 *Commission v Italy* [1996] ECR I-2691

Case C-107/94 *P. H. Asscher v Staatssecretaris van Financiën* [1994] ECR I-1137, [1996] 3 CMLR 61

Cases C-140-142/94 *Dip Spa v Commune di Bassano del Grappa* [1995] ECR I-3257, [1996] 4 CMLR 157

Cases C-178/94, C-179/94, C-188/94, C-189/94 and C-190/94 *Erich Dillenkofer, Christian Erdmann, Hans-Jürgen Schulte, Anke Heuer, Werner, Ursula and Trosten Knor v Bundesrepublik Deutschland* [1996] ECR I-04845

Case C-193/94 *Criminal Proceedings against SofiaSkanavi and Konstantin Chryssanthakopoulos* [1996] ECR I-00929
Case C-233/94 *Federal Republic of Germany v European Parliament and Council of the European Union* [1997] ECR I-02405
Case C-268/94 *Portuguese Republic v Council of the European Union* [1996] ECR I-06177
Case C-272/94 *Criminal Proceeding against Michel Guiot & Climatec SA* [1996] ECR I-1905
Cases C-418-421, 460-462 and 464/93, 9-11, 14-15, 23-24 & 332/94 *Semeraro Casa Uno Srl v Sindaco del Commune di Erbusco* [1996] ECR I-2975, [1996] 3 CMLR 648
Case C-3/95 *Reisebüro Broede v Gerd Sandker*[1996] ECR I-6511
Case C-18/95 *F. C. Terhoeve v Inspecteur van de Belastingdienst Particulieren Ondernemingen Buitenland* [1999] ECR I-345
Case C-28/95 *A.Leur-Bloem v Inspecteur der Belastingdienst/ Ondernemingen Amsterdam 2.* [1997] ECR I-04161
Cases C-34-36/95 *Konsumentonbudsmannen (KO) v de Agostini (Svenska) Forleg AB* [1997] ECR I-3843
Case C-53/95 *INASTI v Kemmler* [1996] ECR I-704
Case C-57/95 *France v Commission (Re Pension Funds Communication)* [1997] ECR I-1627, [1997] 2 CMLR 935
Case C-70/95 *Sodemare SA v Regione Lombardia* [1997] ECR I-3395, [1998] 4 CMLR 667
Case C-127/95 *Norbrook Laboratories Ltd v Ministry of Agriculture, Fisheries and Food* [1998] ECR I-01531
Case C-222/95 *Société Immobilière Parodi v Banque H Albert de Bary* [1997] ECRI-3899
Case C-250/95 *Futura Participations SA Singer v Administration des Contributions* [1997] ECR I-2471, [1997] 3 CMLR 483
Case C-316/95 *Generics BV v Smith Kline and French Laboratories Ltd* [1997] ECR I-7231, [1998] 1 CMLR 1
Case C-358/95 *Tommaso Morellato v Unita Sanitairia Locale (USL) No I1 di Prodenone* [1997] ECR 1-1431
Case C-368/95 *Vereinigte Familiapress Zeitungsverlags-und Vertriebs GmbH v Heinrich Bauer Verlag* [1997] 3 CMLR 1329
Case C-398/95 *Syndesmos Ton en Elladi Touristikon Kai Taxidiotikon Grofeion v Ypourgos Ergasias* [1997] ECR I-3091
Cases C-51/96 and C-191/97 *Christelle Deliege v Ligue Francophone de judo et Disciplines Associées ASBL, Union Européenne de judo (C-51/96) and Francois Pacquée (C-191/97)*, [2000] ECR I-02549
Case C-57/96 *H. Meints v Minister Van Landbouw, Natuurbeheer en Visserij* [1997] ECR I-6689, [1998] 1 CMLR 1159
Case C-67/96 *Albany International BV v Stichting Bedrijfspensioenfonds Textielindustrie* [1999] ECR I-05751

Case C-90/96 *David Petrie and Others v Università degli studi di Verona and Camilla Bettoni* [1997] ECR I-06527

Case C-108/96 Criminal Proceedings against Dennis Mac Quen, Derek Pouton, Carla Godts, Youssef Antoun and Grandvision Belgium SA [2001] ECR I-00837

Case C-264/96 *Imperial Chemical Industries plc (ICI) v Kenneth Hall Colmer (Her Majesty's Inspector of Taxes)* [1998] ECR I-4695, [1998] CMLR 293

Case C-288/96 *Federal Republic of Germany v Commission* [2000] ECR I-08237

Case T-90/96 *Automobiles Peugeot SA v Commission* [1997] ECR II-00663

Cases C-115/97 and C-117/97 *Brentjens' Handelsonderneming BV v Stichting Bedrijfspensioenfonds voor de Handel in Bouwmaterialen* [1999] ECR I-06025

Case C-124/97 *Markku Juhani Läärä, Cotswold Microsystems Ltd and Oy Transatlantic Softward Ltd v Kihlakunnansyyttää (Jyväskylä) and Suomen Valtio (Finnish State)* [1999] ECR I-60007

Case C-131/97 *Annalisa Carbonari and Others v Università degli studi di Bologna, Ministero della Sanità, Ministero dell' Università e della Ricerca Scientifica and Ministero del Tesoro* [1999] ECR I-01103

Case C-140/97 *Walter Rechberger, Renate Greindl, Hermann Hofmeister and Others v Republik Österreich* [1999] ECR I-03499

Case C-147/97 and C-148/97 *Deutsche Post AG v Gesellschaft für Zahlungssysteme mbH (GZS) (C-147/97) and Citicorp Kartenservice GmbH (C-148/97)* [2000] ECR I-00825

Case C-162/97 *Criminal Proceedings against Gunnar Nilsson, Per Olov Hagelgren and Solweig Arrborn* [1998] ECR I-7477

Case C-212/97 *Centros Ltd v Erhvervs-og Selskabsstyrelsen* [1999] ECR I-1459, [1992] 2 CMLR 551

Case C-219/97 *Maatschappij Drijvende Bokken BV v Stichting Pensioenfonds voor de Vervoeren Havenbedrijven*, [1999] ECR I-06121

Case C-255/97 *Pfeiffer Großhandel GmbH v Löwa Warenhandel GmbH* [1999] ECR I-2835

Case C-307/97 *Compagnie de Saint-Gobain v Finanzamt Aachen-Innenstadt* [1999] ECR I-6161

Case C-366/97 *Criminal Proceedings against Massimo Romanelli and Paolo Romanelli* [1999] ECR I-00855

Case C-424/97 *Salomone Haim v Kassenzahnärztliche Vereinigung Nordrhein* [2000] ECR I-05123

Cases T-186/97, T-187/97, T-190/97 to T-192/97, T-210/97, T-211/97, T-216/97, T-217/97, T-218/97, T-279/97, T-280/97, T-293/97 and T-147/99 *Kaufring AG and Others v Commission* [2001] ECR II-01337

Cases T-204/97 and T-270/97 *EPAC—Empresa para a Agroalimentaçäo e Cereais, SA v Commission* [2000] ECR I-02267

Case C-67/98 *Questore di Verona v Diego Zenatti* [1999] ECR I-7289.

Case C-379/98 *PreussenElektra AG v Schhleswag AG* [2001] ECR I-02099

Case C-367/98 *Commission v Portuguese Republic* [2002] ECR I-04731

Case C-405/98 *Konsumentombudsmannen (KO) v Gourmet International Products AB (GIP)* [2001] ECR I-01795

Case C-473/98 *Kemikalieinspektionen v Toolex Alpha AB* [2000]

Case C-478/98 *Commission v Kingdom of Belgium* [2000] ECR I-07587

Case C-136/99 *Ministre du Budget and Ministre de L'Economie et des Finances v Société Monte Dei Paschi Di Siena* [2000] ECR I-06109

Case C-167/99 *European Parliament v d'aménagement et d'équipement de la region de Strasbourg and Ville de Strasbourg* [2003] ECR I-03269

Cases C-223/99 and C-260/99 *Agorà Srl and Excelsior Snc di Pedrotti Bruna & C. v Ente Autonomo Fiera Internazionale di Milano and Ciftat Soc. Coop. Alr.* [2001] ERC I-03605

Case C-240/99 *Forsakringsaktiebolaget Skandia* [2001] ECR I-01951

Case C-294/99 *Athinaiki Zythopoiia AE v Elleniko Dimosio* [2001] ECR I-06797

Case C-306/99 *Banque Internationale pour L'Afrique Occidentale SA (BIAO) v Finanzamt für Großunternehmen in Hamburg* [2003] ECR I-00001

Case C-309/99 Wouters [2002] ECR I-01577

Case C-335/99 PCR). *HFB Holding für Fernwarmetechnik Beteiligung Sgesellschaft mbH & Co. KG and Others v. Commission* [1999] ECR I-08705

Case C-340/99 *TNT Traco SpA v Poste Italiane SpA and Others* [2001] ECR I-04109

Case C-390/99 *Canal Satélite Digital SL v Adminstraci?n General del Estado, and Distribuidora de Televisi?n Digital SA (DTS)* [2002] ECR I-00607

Case C-439/99 *Commission v Italian Republic* [2002] ECR I-00305

Case C-482/99 *French Republic v Commission* [2002] ECR I-04397

Case T-228/99 and T-233/99 *Westdeutsche Landesbank Girozentrale and Land Nordrhein-Westfalen v Commission*, [2003] ECR II-00435

Case T-331/99 *Mitsubishi HiTec Paper Bielefeld GmbH v Office for Harmonisation in the Internal Market (Trade Marks and Designs) (OHIM)* [2001] ECR II-00433

Case C-11/00 *Commission v European Central Bank* [2003] ECR I-07147

Case C-15/00 *Commission v European Investment Bank* [2003] ECR I-07281

Case C-153/00 *Criminal Proceedings against Paul der Weduwe* [2002] ECR I-11319

Case C-208/00 *Überseering BV v Nordic Construction Company Baumanagement GmbH* [2002] ECR I-09919
Case C-209/00 *Commission v Federal Republic of Germany* [2002] ECR I-11695
Case C-278/00 *Hellenic Republic v Commission* [2004] ECR I-03997
Case C-324/00 *Lankhorst-Hohorst GmbH v Finanzamt Steinfurt* [2002] ECR I-11779
Case C-339/00 *Ireland v Commission* [2003] ECR I-11757
Case C-457/00 *Kingdom of Belgium v Commission* [2003] ECR I-06931
Case C-463/00 *Commission v Kingdom of Spain* [2003] ECRI-04581
Case C-473/00 *Cofidis SA v Jean-Louis Fredout* [2002] ECR I-10875
Case T-87/00 *Bank für Arbeit und Wirtschaft AG v Office for Harmonisation in the Internal Market (Trade Marks and Designs) (OHIM)* [2001] ECR II-01259
Case T-158/00 *ARD v Commission* [2003] ECR II-03825
Case T-195/00 *Travelex Global and Financial Services Ltd, formerly Thomas Cook Group Ltd and Interpayment Services Ltd v Commission* [2003] ECR II-01677
Case C-8/01 *Assurandør-Societetet et v Skatteministeriet* [2003] ECR I-13711
Case C-63/01 *Samuel Sidney Evans v The Secretary of State for the Environment, Transport and the Regions and The Motor Insurers' Bureau* [2003] ECR I-14447
Case C-79/01 *Payroll Data Services (Italy) Srl, ADP Europe SA and ADP GSI SA* [2002] ECR I-08923
Case C-187/01 and C-7/02 *Gemeente Leusden (C-187/01) and Holin Groep BV Cs (C-7/02) v Staatssecretaris van Financiën* [2004] ECR I-05337
Cases T-195/01 R and T-207/01 R. *Government of Gibraltar v Commission* [2001] ECR II-03915
Case T- 213/01 R. *Osterreichische Postsparkasse AG v Commission* [2001] ECR II-03963
Case T-214/01 R. *Bank für Arbeit und Wirtschaft AG v Commission* [2001] ECR II-03993
Case T-216/01 R. *Reisebank AG v Commission* [2001] ECR II-03481
Case T-219/01,*Commerzbank AG v Commission* [2003] ECR II-02843
Case T-306/01 R. *Abdirisak Aden, Abdulaziz Ali, Ahmed Yusuf and Al Barakaat International Foundation v Council of the European Union and Commission* [2002] ECR II-02387
Case C-222/02 *Peter Paul, Cornelia Sonnen-Lütte and Christel Mörkens v Bundesrepublik Deutschland* [2004] ECR I-09425
Case C-224/02 *Heikki Antero Pusa v Osuuspankkien Keskinäinen Vakuutusyhtiö* [2004] ECR I-05763

Case C-334/02 *Commission v French Republic* [2004] ECR I-02229
Case C-442/02 *CaixaBank France v Ministère de l'Économie, des Finances et de l'Industrie* [2004] ECR I-08961
Case T-56/02 *Bayerische Hypo- und Vereinsbank AG v Commission* [2004] ECR 00000
Case C-8/03 *Banque Bruxelles Lambert SA (BBL) v Belgian State* [2004] ECR I-10157
Case C-445/03 *Commission v Grand Duchy of Luxemburg* [2004] ECR I-10191
American Land Title Assn. v Clarke, 968 F. 2d. 150 (1992)
Ashby v White (1703) 3 LD Raym 320
Atkinson v Newcastle &Gateshead Waterwork Co (1877) to Ex. D. 44.1 (CA).
Bourgoin SA v Ministry of Agriculture, Fisheries and Food [1985] 3 All ER 585, [1986] QB 716
B&Q plc v Shrewsbury BC [1990] 3 CMLR 535
Davis v BromleyCorp [1908] 1 KB 170
Davis v Radcliffe [1990] to All ER 538, [1990] 1 WLR 81
Dunlop v Woollahara Municipal Council [1981] 1 All ER 1202, [1982] AC 158
Generics BV v Smith Kline and French Laboratories Ltd [1997] ECR I-7231, [1998] 1 CMLR 1
Paul v. Virginia, 231 U.S. 495 (1869)
Payless v Peterborough CC [1990] 2 CMLR
Payless DIY v Peterborough CC [1991] 2 CMLR 577
Stoke City Council v B&Q plc [1990] 3 CMLR 31
Three Rivers District Council v. Governor and Company of the Bank of England [1996] 3 All ER 558 and 634), [2000] 2 WLR 15) [2001] UKHL 16, (2000) 2 WLR 1220
Turner v Sterling (1671) to Vent 24, 86 BR 287
Wellingborough BC v Payless [1990] 1 CMLR 773
Yuen Kun-Yeuv AG of Hong Kong [1987] 2 All ER 705, [1988] AC 175

3. INTERNATIONAL COMMITTEE AND INTER-GOVERNMENTAL PAPERS

BIS, *The International Interbank Market: A Descriptive Study* (July 1983)
BIS, *Recent Innovations in International Banking*, (April 1986)
BIS, *Recent Developments in International Interbank Relations* (October 1992)
BIS, *Large Value Funds Transfer Systems in the Group of Ten Countries*, (1992)

BIS, *Delivery versus Payment in Securities Settlement Systems* (1992)

BIS, A *Discussion Paper on Public Disclosure of Market and Credit Risks by Financial Intermediaries* (September 1994)

BIS, *Macro Economic and Monetary Policy Issues Raised by the Growth of Derivatives Markets* (November 1994)

BIS, *Issues of Measurement Related to Market Size and Macro Prudential Risks in Derivatives Markets* (February 1995)

BIS, *International Banking and Financial Market Developments* (November 1994)

BIS, *International Banking and Financial Market Developments* (July 1995)

BIS, *65th Annual report* (12 June 1995)

BIS, *Delivery versus Payment in Securities Settlement Systems* (1992)

BIS, Press Release of 7th April 1997

BIS, *International Banking and Financial Market Developments* (July 1998)

Basel Committee, 'Consolidation of banks' balance sheets: aggregation of risk-bearing assets as a method of supervisory bank solvency' (October 1978)

Basel Committee, 'Consolidated Supervision of Bank's International Activities' (March 1979)

Basel Committee, 'A Framework for Measuring and Managing Liquidity' (1992)

Basel Committee, 'Information flows between supervisory authorities' (April 1990)

Basel Committee, 'Measuring and Controlling Large Credit Exposures' (1991)

Basel Committee, 'The Management of Banks' Off-balance Sheet Exposure: A Supervisory Perspective' (March 1986)

Basel Committee, 'Minimum Standards for the Supervision of International Banking Groups and their cross-border establishments' (Summer 1992)

Basel Committee, *Preliminary Response to the Request of the G7 Heads of Government at the June 1995 Halifax Summit* (September 1995)

Basel Committee, 'Prevention of Criminal Use of the Banking System for the Purpose of Money Laundering' (1988)

Basel Committee, 'Principles for the supervision of banks' foreign establishments' (May 1983)

Basel Committee, 'Principles for the Supervision of Financial Conglomerates' (September 1992)

Basel Committee, 'Prudential Supervision of Banks' Derivatives Activities' (December 1994)

Basel Committee, 'Report on Banking Secrecy and International Cooperation in Banking Supervision 1981' (July 1982)

Basel Committee, 'Report to the Governors on the supervision of banks' foreign establishments' (September 1975)

Basel Committee, 'Report on International Convergence of Capital Measurement and Capital Standards' (July 1988)

Basel Committee, 'Report on International Developments in Banking Supervision 1981' (July 1982)

Basel Committee, 'Report on International Developments in Banking Supervision 1982' (March 1983)

Basel Committee, 'Report on International Developments in Banking Supervision 1984' (April 1985)

Basel Committee, 'Report on International Developments in Banking Supervision,' Report Number 5 (September 1986)

Basel Committee, 'Report on International Developments in Banking Supervision,' Report Number 6 (September 1988)

Basel Committee, 'Report on International Developments in Banking Supervision,' Report No 7 (September 1990)

Basel Committee, 'Report on International Developments in Banking Supervision,' Report No 8 (September 1992)

Basel Committee, 'Report on International Developments in Banking Supervision,' Report No 9 (September 1994)

Basel Committee, 'Report on International Developments in Banking Supervision,' Report No 10 (June 1996)

Basel Committee, 'Report on Third International Banking Supervisory Conference' (September 1984)

Basel Committee, 'Market Risk Amendment' (January 1996)

Basel Committee, 'Overview of the Amendment to the Capital Accord to Incorporate Market Risks' (January 1996)

Basel Committee, 'Supervisory Framework for the Use of 'Backtesting' in Conjunction with the Internal Models Approach to Market Risk Capital Requirements' (January 1996)

Basel Committee, 'Responding to the Challenge—Supervision Global Financial Markets' (April 1996)

Basel Committee, 'Risks in Computer and Telecommunications Systems' (1989)

Basel Committee and IOSCO, 'Framework for Supervisory Information about the Derivative Activities of Banks and Securities Firms' (1995)

Basel Committee and IOSCO, 'Public Disclosure of the Trading and Derivatives Activities of Banks and Securities Firms' (1995)

Basel Committee and the Offshore Supervisors' Group, 'The Implementation of the Concordat—Practical Aspects of Information Flows' (1996)

Tommaso Padoa-Schioppa, Chairman of the Basel Committee on Banking Supervision, and Edward J Waitzer, Chairman of the Technical Committee of IOSCO, letter addressed to Mr Jean Arthuis, Ministre de l'Economique et des Finances (April 16, 1996)

Basel Committee and Offshore Supervisors' Group, 'The Supervision of Cross-Border Banking Committee on Payment Systems, Settlement Risk in Foreign Exchange Transactions' (March 1996)

Basel Committee and IOSCO, *Response of the Basle Committee and of the International Organisation of Securities Commissions to the Request of the G-7 Heads of Government at the Halifax Summit*, (May 1996)

Basel Committee, *Compendium of Documents* (April 1997)

Basel Committee, *Core Principles for Effective Banking Supervision* (September 1997)

Basel Committee, *Promoting Financial Stability—Submission for the G-7 Heads of Government at the 1998 Birmingham Summit* (March 1998)

Basel Committee, 'Banks' Interactions with Highly Leveraged Institutions' (January 1999)

Basel Committee, *Core Principles Methodology* (October 1999).

Committee on Payment Systems, *Settlement Risk in Foreign Exchange Transactions* (March 1996)

European Commission, *Easier Cross-Border Payments: Breaking Down the Barriers*, Working Document, March 1992

Finansinspektionen and the Basel Committee, *New Challenges for Supervision of Cross-Border Banking and Domestic Markets* ICBS, December 1996, Part II 'Improving Supervisory Methods'

Heads of State and Government of the G7 and the President of the European Commission, Halifax, Nova Scotia Summit (June 15–17, 1995), Communiqué

Heads of State and Government of the G7 and the President of the European Commission, Halifax Summit, Background Document 'Review of International Financial Institutions'

Governors of the Central Banks of the G10 Countries, Press Communiqué, 12 February 1995

Finance Ministers, *Final Report to the G-7 Heads of State and Government on Promoting Financial Stability* (June 21, 1997)

G7 Finance Ministers, *Final Report to the G7 Heads of State and Government on Promoting Financial Stability* (June 21, 1997)

G7 Finance Ministers, *Financial Stability—Supervision of Global Financial Institutions* (May 1988)

G7, *Report by Finance Ministers of the G7* (June 1999)

G10, *The Resolution of Sovereign Liquidity Crises* (May 1996)

G10, *Financial Stability in Emerging Market Economies* (April 1997)

G10, *Report on the Implementation of the Concerted Strategy for Strengthening Financial Systems in Emerging Market Countries* (November 1997)

G22, *Summary of Reports on International Financial Architecture* (October 1998)

G22, *Report of the Working Group on Transparency and Accountability* (October 1998)
G22, *Report of the Working Group on Strengthening Financial Systems* (October 1998)
G22, *Report of the Working Group on International Financial Crises* (October 1998)
G22, *Comments on the Reports on the International Financial Architecture* (August 1999)
G30, *Clearance and Settlement Systems in the World's Securities Markets* (March 1989)
G30, *Report on Derivatives* (July 1993)
G30, *Global Institutions, National Supervision and Systemic Risk* (1997)
G30, *The Future of Global Financial Regulation* (1998)
IMF, *International Capital Markets: Developments, Prospects, and Policy Issues* (August 1995)
IMF, *International Capital Markets: Developments, Prospects and Key Policy Issues* (1995)
IMF, *International Capital Markets: Developments, Prospects and Key Policy Issues* (1996)
IMF, *Special Data Dissemination Standards* (March 1996)
IMF, *General Data Dissemination System* (December 1997)
IMF, *International Capital Markets: Developments, Prospects and Key Policy Issues* (1997)
IMF, *International Capital Markets: Developments, Prospects and Key Policy Issues* (1998)
IMF, *Toward a Framework for Financial Stability* (January 1998)
IMF, *International Capital Markets: Developments, Prospects and Key Policy Issues* (1999)
IMF, *World Economic Outlook: Interim Assessment* (December 1997)
IMF, *Code of Good Practices on Fiscal Transparency* (April 1998)
IMF, *Code of Good Practices on Transparency in Monetary and Financial Policies* (July 1999)
IMF, *Annual Report* (1999)
IMF, *World Economic Outlook* (October 1999)
IMF *Orderly and Effective Insolvency Procedures* (1999)
IOSCO, *Capital Standards for Securities Firms* (1989)
IOSCO, *Contract Design of Derivatives Products on Stock Indices and Measures to Minimise Market Disruption* (1992)
IOSCO, *Cooperation between Market Authorities* (March 1996)
IOSCO, *Default Procedures* (March 1996)
IOSCO, *The Implications for Securities Regulators of the Increased Use of Value at Risk Models by Securities Firms* (1995)
IOSCO, *Mechanisms to Enhance Open and Timely Communication*

Between Market Authorities of Related Cash and Derivatives Markets During Periods of Market Disruption (1993)

IOSCO, *Principles for Memoranda of Understanding* (1991)

IOSCO, *Principles for the Supervision of the Financial Conglomerates*, IOSCO Doc 7 (October 1992)

IOSCO, *Recommendation on the Recognition of Bilateral Netting Agreements in the Calculation of Capital Requirements for Securities Firms*, (March 1996)

IOSCO, *Report on Issues Raised for Securities Regulators by Under-Regulated and Uncooperative Jurisdictions* (1994)

IOSCO, *Report on Margin Requirements for Equities and Derivatives Based on Equities* (Summer 1996)

IOSCO, *Report on Money Laundering* (1992)

IOSCO and Basel Committee, *Framework for Supervisory Information about the Derivatives Activities of Banks and Securities Firms* (1995)

IOSCO and Basel Committee, *Public Disclosure of the Trading Activities of Banks and Securities Firms* (1995)

IOSCO, *Response to the Challenge—Supervising Global Financial Markets* (April 1996)

IOSCO, *Developments for Consideration by the G-7 Ministers at the Birmingham Summit* (May 1998)

Letter by Edward J Waitzer, Chairman of the Technical Committee of IOSCO to the Honourable Paul Martin, PC, MP, Ministry of Finance, Ottawa, and Annex (*Background to the G7 Finance Ministers on International Cooperation in the Regulation and Supervision of Financial Institutions and Markets: The Work of the International Organisation of Securities Commissions (IOSCO)*)

IOSCO, *Annual Report for 1997*

IOSCO, *Developments for Consideration by the G-7 Ministers at the Birmingham Summit* (May 1998)

OECD, *The Internationalisation of Banking: The Policy Issues* (1983)

OECD, *Banking and Electronic Fund Transfers* (1983)

OECD, *International Trade in Services: Banking* (1984)

OECD, *Trends in Banking in OECD Countries* (1985)

OECD, *Banking and Monetary Policy* (1985)

OECD, *Competition in Banking* (1989)

OECD, *Systemic Risks in Securities Markets*, (1991)

OECD, *Banks Under Stress* (1992)

OECD, *Transformation of the Banking System: Portfolio Restructuring, Privatisation and the Payment System* (1993)

OECD, *Financial Market Trends* (November 1996)

OECD, *The OECD Report on Regulatory Reform* (1997)

Tripartite Group of Banking, Insurance and Securities Regulators, 'Progress Report on the Supervision of Financial Conglomerates' (April 1994)

Tripartite Group of Banking, Insurance and Securities Regulators, 'Report on the Supervision of Financial Conglomerates' (July 1995)

UNCITRAL, *A Model Law on Cross-border Insolvency* (1997)

UNCTC, *Transnational Banks:Operations, Strategies and their Effects in Developing Countries* (1981)

UNCTC, *Transnational Banks and the International Debt Crisis* (1991)

UNCTC, *Transnational Banks and the External Indebtedness of Developing Countries: Impact of Regulatory Changes* (1992)

Working Group on EC Payment Systems, *Issues of Common Concern to EC Central Banks in the Field of Payment Systems*, European Community, September 1992

Working Group on EC Payment Systems, *Payment Systems in EC Member States*, European Community, September 1992

World Bank, *The East Asian Miracle: Economic Growth and Public Policy* (1993)

World Trade Organisation, *WTO Director-General Hails Financial Services Accord* Press, Release/18, 26 July 1995

4. UNITED KINGDOM GOVERNMENT AND OFFICIAL REPORTS

Seventh Report from the Select Committee on Nationalised Industries, *The Bank of England*, HC [1975–6]

Minutes of Evidence taken before the House of Lords Select Committee on the European Communities (Sub-Committee A) (Wednesday 10 May 1976) (unpublished))

Memorandum submitted by the Bank of England, Minutes of Evidence Taken before the Select Committee on Nationalised Industry (Sub Committee C) (February 1976)

Bank of England, *Supervision of the Markets in Money, Foreign Exchange, Currency Deposits and Gold* (June 1978)

Report to the Committee set up to Consider the System of Banking Supervision, June 1985 (Cmd 9550)

Report into the Supervision of the Bank of Credit ad Commerce International (October 1992)

Treasury and Civil Service Committee, Fourth Report, 'Banking Supervision and BCCI: International and National Regulation' HC (1991–92)

Report of the Inquiry into the Supervision of the Bank of Credit and Commerce International (1992) HC 192

Report into the Supervision of the Bank of Credit and Commerce International (October 1992)

Treasury and Civil Service Committee, First Report, 'The Role of the Bank of England' HCP (1993–94)

Bank of England, *Banks in 1992* (May 1993)
Bank of England, *Derivatives: Report of an Internal Working Group* (April 1993)
Bank of England, 'The Bank's Review of Supervision' (1995)
Bank of England, *Report of the Board of Banking Supervision Inquiry into the Circumstances of the Collapse of Barings* (July 1995)
Bank of England, *Banking Act Report 1995/1996*
Board of Banking Supervision, *Report of the Board of Banking Supervision Inquiry into the Circumstances of the Collapse of Barings*, Bank of England (July 1995)
SIB, *Equity Market Review Report* (21 June 1995)
Futures Industry Association Global Task Force on Financial Integrity, *Financial Integrity Recommendations for Futures and Options Markets and Market Participants* (June 1995)
Bank of England, *Banking Act Report 1996/97*
Bank of England, *The Board of Banking Supervision's Report on Barings: The Post Barings Recommendations—A Report*, Press Notice, Supervision and Surveillance Division (January 1996)
The Treasury Committee, *Barings Bank and International Regulation* HC 65-I Session (1996–1997)
Arthur Andersen, *Findings and Recommendations of the Review of Supervision and* Surveillance (July 1996)
Bank of England, *A Risk Based Approach to Supervision (the RATE framework)* (March 1997), *A Risk Based Approach to the Supervision of Non-EEA Banks (the SCALE framework)* (July 1997) and *A Risk Based Approach to Supervising Foreign Exchange and Other Market Risks* (July 1997)
Sir Andrew Large, Chairman of the SIB, *Report to the Chancellor on the Reform of the Financial Regulatory System* (July 1997)

5. UNITED STATES AND OTHER GOVERNMENTAL REPORTS

Minutes of Board of Governors of Federal Reserve Bank, (1974: 41–2)
Deutsch Bundesbank, *Banking Act of the Federal Republic of Germany* (1991)
Senator John Kerry and Senator Hank Brown, *The BCCI Affair*, Report to the Committee on Foreign Relations, United States Senate, 30 September 1992
Board of Governors of the Federal Reserve System, *The Federal Reserve System—Purposes and Functions*, (1994)
Department of Finance, 'Finance Minister Announces Six Point Canadian Plan to Deal with Global Financial Turmoil', Press Release 98/094 (29 September 1998), Canada

Chang, R and A Velasco, *Financial Crises in Emerging Markets: A Canonical Model*, NBER Working Paper No 6606 (June 1998)

Cole, HL and TJ Kehoe, *A Self-Fulfilling Model of Mexico's 1994–95 Debt Crisis*, Federal Reserve Bank of Minneapolis, Research Report No 210 (April 1996)

Dooley, M, *A Model of Crises in Emerging Markets*, NBER Working Paper No 6300 (December 1997)

Eichengreen, B, *Toward a New International Financial Architecture—A Practical Post-Asia Agenda*, Institute for International Economics (February 1999)

Government of France, *Facing International Instability: Twelve Proposals for European Initiative* (1998)

United States General Accounting Office, *GAO Report—Mexico's Financial Crisis: Origins, Assistance, and Initial Efforts to Recover* (GAO/GGD-959–56, 23 February 1996)

Goldstein, M and P Turner, 'Banking Crises in Emerging Economies: Origins and Policy Options,' *BIS Economic Paper* No 46 (October 1996)

Testimony of R Helfer, Chairman of the FDIC, Before the Committee on Banking and Financial services, US House of Representatives reproduced in 'A Brief History Of Unadopted Regulatory Restructuring Proposals' *Banking Policy Report*, Volume 15, Number 11, p 7

Honohan, P, 'Banking System Failures in Developing and Transition Economies: Diagnosis and Predictions,' *BIS Economic Paper* No 39 (January 1997)

Litan, R et al, 'Statement of the Shadow Financial Regulatory Committee on International Monetary Fund Assistance and International Crises', Shadow Financial Regulatory Committee, Statement No 145 (4 May 1998)

McKinnon, R and H Pill, 'Economic Liberalisations and Overborrowing,' *American Economic Review Papers and Proceedings* [1997] 87: 189–93

Meltzer, A, 'Asian problems and the IMF', Testimony prepared for the Joint Economic Committee, US Congress (24 February 1998)

Singapore Ministry of Finance, *Report on Barings Futures (Singapore) Pte Ltd* (6 September 1995)

Bureau of National Affairs, Inc, *Banking Report*, July 3 1995

Testimony of Chairman Alan Greenspan, Before the Committee on Banking and Financial Services, U.S. House of Representatives, 22 May 1997, p 1

6. UNITED KINGDOM STATUTES IN FORCE

The Banking Act 1979

The Banking Act 1987

Financial Services Act 1986
Financial Services and Markets Act 2000

7. NON-UK STATUTES

McCarrant-Ferguson Act 1945
The Bank Holding Company Act 1956
Federal Reserve Act 1919
Financial Services Competitiveness Act 1995
The Foreign Bank Supervision Enhancement Act 1991
International Banking Act 1978

8. BOOKS

Acres, W Marston, *The Bank of England from Within* (1931)

Ring Adams, J and D Frantz, *A Full Service Bank—How BCCI Stole Billions Around the World* (1992)

Aeckhoute, P, *The European Internal Market and International Trade* (Clarendon Press Oxford 1994)

Affros, RC (ed), *Current Legal Issues Affecting Central Banks* (1992)

Aguirre, E and JJ Norton (eds), *Reform of Latin American Banking Systems* (2000)

Alcock, A, *The Financial Services and Markets Act 2000: A Guide to the New Law* (Jordans Bristol 2000)

Alibber, R, *The Reconstruction of International Monetary Arrangements* (1987)

Altman, EI and AW Sametz (eds), *Financial Crises: Institutions and Markets in a Fragile* Environment (1978)

Andenas, M, L Gormley, C Hadjiemmanuil, and I Harden, *European Economic and Monetary Union: The Institutional Framework* (Kluwer Law International London 1997)

Andenas, M and Y Avgerinos, *Financial Market Supervision in Europe: Towards a Single Regulator?* (Kluwer Law International London 2003)

Andenas, M and F Jacobs, *European Community Law in the English Courts* (Clarendon Press Oxford 1998)

Andenas, M and Roth Wulf-Henning, *Services and Free Movement in EU Law* (OUP Oxford 2002)

Andenas, M and A Türk, *Delegated Legislation and the Role of Committees in the EC* (Kluwer Law International London 2000)

Arner, D and S Gou (eds), *Tawian Financial Reform* (Kluwer Law London 2004)

Andersen, TJ, *Euromarket Instruments: A Guide to the World's Largest Debt Market* (1990)

Argy, V, *The Post War International Money Crisis—An Analysis* (1981)

Bagehot, Walter, *Lombard Street* (1873)

Bakker, Age FP, *The Liberalisation of Capital Movements in Europe—The Monetary Committee and Financial Integration, 1954–1994* (Kluwer Dordrecht and London 1996)

Arnull, A, *The European Union and its Court of Justice* (OUP Oxford 1999)

Balassa, B, *The Theory of Economic Integration* (Allen & Unwin London 1961)

Baylis, John and Steve Smith, *The Globalization of World Politics* (2nd edn Oxford 2001)

Bedts, R, *The New Deal's SEC: The Formative Years* (Columbia University Press New York 1964)

Bell, G, *The Euro-dollar Market and the International Financial System* (1973)

Benink, H, *Financial Integration in Europe* (Kluwer Academic Publishers Dordrecht 1993)

Bermann, George A, Roger J Goebel, William J Davey, and Eleanor M Fox, *European Community Law* (1993)

Bernstein, P, *Capital Ideas* (Free Press New York 1992)

Bhagwati, J, *In Defence of Globalisation* (OUP Oxford 2004)

Bieber, R, R Dehousse, J Pinder, and J Weiler (eds), *1992: One European Market?* (Nomos 1988)

Bingham, Lord Justice, *Inquiry into the Supervision of Bank of Credit and Commerce International* (HMSO London 1992)

Bitner, JW, *Successful Bank Asset/Liability Management* (1990)

Blair, M et al, *Blackstone's guide to the Financial Services & Markets Act 2000* (Blackstone Press London 2001)

Blair, M and GA Walker, *Financial Services Law* (OUP Oxford)

Blair, M and GA Walker, *Financial Markets and Exchanges Law* (OUP Oxford)

Blair, W, A Allison, K Palmer, P Richards-Carpenter, and G Walker, *Banking and Financial Services Regulation* (3rd edn Butterworths 2002 1998)

Boyle, A, *Montagu Norman* (1967)

Bowe, M, *Eurobonds* (1988)

Bratton, W, J McCahery, S Picciotto, and C Scott, *International Regulatory Competition and Coordination* (Clarendon Press Oxford 1996)

Brenton, P and M Vancauteren, *The Extent of Economic Integration in Europe: Border Effects, Technical Barriers to Trade & Home Bias in Consumption* (CEPS WP No 171, August 2001)

Breyer, S, *Regulation and Its Reform* (Harvard University Press Cambridge 1982)

Broadie, A, *The Scottish Enlightenment* (Birlinn Edinburgh 2001)

Brown, LN, *The European Court of Justice* (Sweet & Maxwell London 1983)

Bryant, R, *International Financial Intermediation* (1987)

Buchanan, J, *Liberty, Market and State: Political Economy in the 1980s* (Wheatsheaf Brighton 1986)

Burrows, *Free Movement in European Law* (1987)

Buxbaum, R, G Hertig, A Hirsch,and K Hopt, *European Business Law: Legal and Economic Analysis on Integration and Harmonisation* (Walter de Gruyter Berlin 1991)

Buxbaum, R, G Hertig, A Hirsch, and K Hopt, *European Economic and Business Law: Legal and Economic Analysis on Integration and Harmonisation* (Walter de Gruyter New York 1996)

Campbell, D (ed), *Financial Services in the New Europe* (1992)

Campbell, D (ed), *International Insurance Law and Regulation* (1994)

Cameron Markby Hewitt, *EC Insurance Law* (1991)

Campbell, D, *Financial Services in the New Europe* (Graham & Trotman London 1994)

Caprio, G and D Vittas, *Reforming Financial Systems—Historical Implications for Policy* (1997)

Cavanagh, J, D Wysham, and M Arruda (eds), *Beyond Bretton Woods: Alternatives to the Global Economic Order* (Pluto Press London 1994)

Chalmers, D and E Szyszczak, *European Union Law, Volume II: Towards a European Policy?* (Ashgate Aldershot 1998)

Chalmers, EB, *Readings in the Eurodollar* (1969)

Chorafas, DN, *The Commercial Banking Handbook* (1998)

Chryssochoou, D, *Democracy in the European Union* (Tauris Academic Studies London 1998)

Clapham, J, *The Bank of England: A History* (CUP Cambridge 1970)

Clapham, Sir John, *The Bank of England, 1797–1914* (1944)

Clay, H, *Lord Norman* (1957)

Clendenning, EW, *Eurodollar Market* (1970)

Clifford Chance, *Insurance Regulation in Europe* (1993)

Corrigan, G, *Financial Market Structure: A Longer View* (1987)

Cox, J, R Hillman, and D Langevoort, *Securities Regulation: Cases and Materials* (3rd edn Aspen Law & Business Gaithersburg 2001)

Craig, P and G De Búrca, *EU Law: Texts, Cases and Materials* (OUP Oxford 2nd edn 1998)

Craig, P and G De Búrca, *The Evolution of EU Law* (OUP Oxford 1999)

Craig and Harlow (eds), *Law Making in the European Union* (1998)

Ehle and Meier, *EWG-Warenverkehr* (1971)

Cranston, R, *Principles of Banking Law* (OUP Oxford 1997)
Cranston, R, *The Single Market and the Law of Banking* (Lloyd's of London Press London 1991)
Cranston, R, *The Single Market and the Law of Banking* (2nd edn Lloyd's of London Press London 1995)
Cutler, T, C Halsem, J Williams, and K Williams, '1992—The Struggle for Europe' (Berg Oxford 1989)
Dale, R, *International Banking Deregulation: The Great Banking Experiment* (1992)
Dale, R, *The Regulation of International Banking* (1984)
Dale, R, *International Banking Deregulation: the Great Banking Experiment* (Blackwell Oxford 1992)
Dale, R, *Risk and Regulation in Global Securities Markets* (1996)
Dam, KW, *The Rules of the Game: Reform and Evolution in the International Monetary System* (University of Chicago Press Chicago and London 1982)
Danthine, JP, F Giavazzi, X Vives, and EL von Thadden, *The Future of European Banking* (Centre of Economic Policy Research London 1999)
Dassesse, M, S Isaacs, G and Penn, *EC Banking Law* (2nd edn Lloyd's of London Press London 1994)
Davies, E, J Kay and C Smales, *1992: Myths and Realities* (London Business School London 1989)
Davis, EP, *Debt, Financial Fragility and Systemic Risk* (1992)
Davis, P, *Debt, Financial Fragility and Systemic Risk* (Clarendon Press Oxford 1995)
Dehousse, R, *The European Court of Justice* (Macmillan Basingstoke 1998)
Den Boer, M, A Guggenbühl, and S Vanhoonacker, *Coping with Flexibility and Legitimacy after Amsterdam* (European Institute of Public Administration Maastricht 1998)
Dermine, J (ed), *European Banking in the 1990s* (Blackwell Oxford 1990)
Di Giorgio, G, C Di Noia, and L Piatti, *Financial Market Regulation: The Case of Italy and a Proposal for the Euro Area* (Financial Institutions Center Pennsylvania 2000)
Dobson, W and P Jacquet, *Financial Services Liberalization in the WTO* (Institute for International Economics Washington 1998)
Downes, P and R Vaez-Zadeh (eds), *The Evolving Role Central Banks* (1991)
Duff, A, *Subsidiarity within the European Community* (Federal Trust for Education and Research London 1993)
Dyker, D(ed), *The European Economy* (Longman London 1992)
Dyson, K, *The Politics of the Euro-Zone* (OUP Oxford 2000)
Edwards, F and H Patrick, *Regulating International Financial Markets: Issues and Policies* (Kluwer Academic Publishers Boston 1992)

Edwards, RW, *International Monetary Collaboration* (Transnational Publishers New York 1985)
Edwards, V, *EC Company Law* (Clarendon Press Oxford 1999)
Eichengreen, B, *European Monetary Unification: Theory, Practice and Analysis* (Massachusetts Institute of Technology Press Cambridge 1997)
Eichengreen, B, *Should the Maastricht Treaty be saved?* (Princeton University Princeton 1992)
Emerson, M, M Aujean, M Catinat, P Goybet, and A Jacquemin, *The Economics of 1992* (OUP Oxford 1988)
Emiliou, N and D O'Keeffe, *The European Union and World Trade Law* (John Wiley & Sons USA 1996)
Engler, H and J Essinger, *The Future of Banking* (Pearson Education London 2000)
European Commission, *Economies of Scale: Impact on Competition and Scale Effects* (Kogan Page EarthScan London 1997)
Evans, Graham and Jeffery Newnham, *International Relations* (Penguin, 1998)
Evans, P, D Rieschemeyer, and T Skocpol, *Bringing the State back in* (CUP Cambridge 1985)
Fabozzi, FJ and A Konishi (eds), *The Handbook of Asset/Liability Management* (Irwin Chicago and London 1996)
Fair, D and R Raymond, *Competitiveness of Financial Institutions and Centres in Europe* (Kluwer Law International Dordrecht 1994)
Fay, S, *The Collapse of Barings* (1996)
Feeney, P, *Sterling Commercial Paper: the Banker's Dilemma* (1986)
Ferran, E and C Goodhart, *Regulating Financial Services and Markets in the Twenty First Century* (Hart Publishing Oxford 2001)
Ferrarini, G, *European Securities Markets: The Investment Services Directive and Beyond* (Kluwer Law International London 1998)
Ferrarini, G, *Prudential Regulation of Banks and Securities Firms: European and International Aspects* (Kluwer Law International London 1995)
Financial Times, *Behind Closed Doors: the biggest bank fraud in history (a collection of special feature articles)* (1991)
Fforde, J, *The Bank of England and Public Policy, 1941–1958* (1992)
Finsinger, J and M Pauly, *The Economics of Insurance Regulation: A Cross-National Study* (1986)
Fisher, FF, *International Bonds* (1981)
Franke, HH, *Europäische Währungsunion: Von den Konzeption zur Gestaltung: Beihäfte zu Kredit und Kapital H.14/1998* (Dunker & Humblot Berlin 1998)
Fraser, R and Long, *The World Financial System* (Longman Harlow 1993)
Freedman, M, *Roosevelt and Frankfurter: Their Correspondence 1928–1945* (Little, Brown & Company Boston 1967)

Frieden, J, D Gros, and E Jones, *The New Political Economy of EMU* (Rowman & Littlefield Lanham 1998)
Friedland, J, *The Law and Structure of the International Financial System: Regulation in the US, EEC and Japan* (Quorum Books Westport 1994)
Galbraith, J, *The Great Crash 1929* (Houghton Mifflin Boston 1997)
Gambetta, D, *Trust: Making and Breaking Cooperative Relations* (Blackwell Oxford 1988)
Gapper, J and N Denton, *All that Glitters—The Fall of Barings* (1996)
Gardener, EP, *Theory and Practice in Banking Supervision: Some Reflections* (Institute of European Finance University of North Wales 1986)
Gardener, EP (ed), *UK Banking Supervision and Evolution, Practice and Issues* (Allen & Unwin London 1986)
Gart, A, *Regulation, Deregulation, Reregulation: The Future of the Banking, Insurance and Securities Industries* (John Wiley & Sons New York 1994)
Gart, A, *Regulation, Deregulation and Reregulation—The Future of the Banking, Insurance and Securities Industires* (1994)
Geisst, C, *Exchange Rate Chaos—Twenty-Five Years of Finance and Consumer Democracy* (Routledge London 1995)
Genetay, N and P Molyneux, *Bancassurance* (1999)
Giavazzi, F, S Micossi, and M Miller (eds), *The European Monetary System* (CUP Cambridge 1988)
Gilbody, J, *The UK Monetary and Financial System* (Routledge London 1991)
Gilligan, G, *Regulating the Financial Services Sector* (Kluwer Law International London 1999)
Giovanoli, M, *International Monetary Law* (OUP Oxford 2000)
Giovanoli, M and G Heinrich, *International Bank Insolvencies: A Central Bank Perspective* (Kluwer Law International London 1999)
Giuseppi, J, *The Bank of England: A History from its Foundation in 1694* (Evans Bros London 1966)
Goacher, D, *The Monetary and Financial System* (Bankers' Books London 1990)
Goldstein, M, *The Asian Financial Crisis: Causes, Cures, and Systemic Implications* (Institute for International Economics Washington 1998)
Goodhart, C, *Money, Information and Uncertainty* (Macmillan London 1989)
Goodhart, C et al, *Financial Regulation: Why, How and Where Now?* (Routledge London 1998)
Goris, P, *The Legal Aspect of Swaps—An Analysis Based on Economic Substance* (Graham & Trotman London 1994)
Gormley, L, *Prohibiting Restrictions on Trade within the EC* (1985)

Gould, J, *Legal and Institutional Aspects of the International Monetary System: Selected Essays* (1984)

Gowland, A, *The Regulation of Financial Markets in the 1990s* (Elgar Aldershot 1990)

Graaf, F, *Euromarket Finance: Issues of Euromarket Securities and Syndicated Eurocurrency Loans* (1992)

Grahl J and P Teague, *1992: The Big Market* (Lawrence & Wishart London 1992)

Gros, D, *EMU and Capital Markets: The Institutional Framework* (Institut für Kapitalmarktforschung Frankfurt April 1998)

Gros, D and N Thygesen, *European Monetary Integration* (2nd edn Longman Harlow 1998)

Grubel, H, *World Monetary Reform—Plans and Issues* (1964)

Gruson, M and R Reisner (eds), *Regulation of Foreign Banks: United States and International* (2nd edn)

Hadjiemmanuil, C, *The European Central Bank and Banking Supervision* (Centre for Commercial Law Studies London 1996)

Haas, E, *The Uniting of Europe: Political, Social and Economic Forces, 1950–57* (Stanford University Press 1958)

Haas, EB, *Beyond the Nation State* (Stanford University Press 1964)

Hall, MJB, *Financial Deregulation: A Comparative Study of Australia and the United Kingdom* (1987)

Hall, MJB, *Banking Regulation and Supervision: A Comparative Study of the UK, USA and Japan* (1993)

Hayek, FA, *New Studies in Philosophy, Politics, Economics and the History of Ideas* (University of Chicago Press Chicago 1978)

Hazen, T, *The Law of Securities Regulation* (West Publications St Paul 1996)

Held, D, McGrew, D Goldbatt, and J Perraton, *Global Transformations: Politics, Economics and Culture* (Polity 2001)

Herman, A, *The Scottish Enlightenment* (Fourth Estate London 2001)

Herring, RJ and RE Litan, *Financial Regulation in the Global Economy* (1995)

Hirst, P and G Thompson, *Globalization in Question: The International Economy and the Possibilities of Governance* (Polity Press Cambridge 1996)

Hodges, M, J Kirton, and J Daniels, *The G8's Role in the New Millennium* (Ashgate Aldershot 1999)

Hogan, WP and IF Pearce, *The Incredible Eurodollar* (1982)

Hooke, AW, *The International Monetary Fund—Its Evolution, Organisation and Activities* (IMF Pamphlet Series No 37 1982)

Hoschka, T, *Cross-Border Entry in European Retail Financial Services: Determinants, Regulation and the Impact on Competition* (St Martin's Press New York 1993)

Howells, P and K Bain, *Financial Markets and Institutions* (Longman London 1990)

Jansen, M, *History of European Integration, 1945–1975* (University of Amsterdam Amsterdam 1975)

Jeunemaitre, A, *Financial Markets Regulation: A Practitioner's Perspective* (Macmillan Press Basingstoke 1997)

Joerges, C, *The Market Without the State?—States Without a Market?: Two Essays on the Law of the European Economy* (EUI Florence 1996)

Johnston, RB, *The Economics of the Euro-Market* (1983)

Kane, DR, *The Eurodollar Market and the Years of Crisis* (1983)

Kane, E, *The Gathering Crisis in Federal Deposit Insurance* (1985)

Kapstein, EB, *Governing the Global Economy—International Finance and the State* (1994)

Kapteyn, P and P Verloren Van Themaat, *Introduction to the Law of the European Communities* (2nd edn Kluwer Law International Deventer 1989)

Kole, Karen V and Anthony D'Amato, *European Union Law Anthology* (1998)

Kenen, P, *Economic and Monetary Union in Europe: Moving beyond Maastricht* (CUP Cambridge 1995)

Keohane, R and S Hoffman, *The New European Community—Decision-making and Institutional Change* (Westview Press Boulder 1991)

Keohane, R, *Neo-Realism and Its Critics* (Columbia University Press 1986)

Kerr, IM, *A History of the Eurobond Market: the First 21 Years* (1984)

Keynes, JM, *The General Theory of Employment, Interest and Money* (Harcourt, Brace & World New York 1936)

Kindleberger, C, *Manias, Panics and Crashes: A History of Financial Crises* (1989)

Kingdon, J, *Agendas, Alternatives and Public Policies* (Little, Brown & Company Boston 1984)

Kirsch, CE, *The Financial Services Revolution—Understanding the Chaning Role of Banks, Mutual Funds and Insurance Companies* (1998)

Lannoo, K, *Does Europe need an SEC?* (European Capital Markets Institute Madrid November 1999)

Lannoo, K, *Challenges to the Structure of Financial Supervision in the EU* (Centre of European Policy Studies Brussels 1999)

Lannoo, K, *Challenges to the Structure of Financial Supervision in the EU* (Centre of European Policy Studies Brussels July 2000)

Lannoo, K, *Financial Supervision in EMU* (Centre of European Policy Studies Brussels 1999)

Lasok, D, *The Trade and Customs Law of the European Union* (Kluwer Law London 1998)

Lasok, KPE, *The European Court of Justice: Practice and Procedure* (Butterworths London 1984)

Lastra, R, *Central Banking and Banking Regulation* (Financial Markets Group London School of Economics London 1996)

Lastra, R, *The Reform of the International Financial Architecture* (Kluwer Law International London 2000)

Lee, R, *What is an Exchange? The Automation, Management and Regulation of Financial Markets* (OUP Oxford 1998)

Lewis and Davis, *Domestic and International Banking* (Philip Allan Deddington 1987)

Lindberg, L, *The Political Dynamics of European Economic Integration* (Stanford University Press 1963)

Lindberg L and S Scheingold, *Europe's Would-be Polity: Patterns of Change in the European Community* (Prentice-Hall 1970)

Lindberg L and S Scheingold, *Regional Integration* (Harvard University Press 1970)

Lipgens, W, W Loth, and A Milward, *A History of European Integration, vol. 1, 1945–1947, The Formation of the European Unity Movement* (Clarendon Press London 1982)

Lipgens, W, *Documents on the History of the European Integration,* Volumes 1–3 (De Gruyter Berlin 1986)

Lipgens, W and W Lath, *Documents on the History of European Integration,* Volume 4 (De Gruyter Berlin 1991)

Llewellyn, D, *The Regulation and Supervision of Financial Institutions* (Institute of Bankers Gilbart Lectures on Banking London 1986)

Lo, AW, *The Industrial Organization and Regulation of the Securities Industry* (University of Chicago Press Chicago 1996)

Loss L and J Seligman, *Fundamentals of Securities Regulation* (4th edn Aspen Law & Business Gaitherburg 2001)

Louis, JV, *The Euro in the National Context* (British Institute of International & Comparative Law London 2002)

Louis, JV et al, *Banking Supervision in the European Community* (University of Brussels Brussels 1995)

McCormick, M, *Origins of the European Economy* (CUP Cambridge 2001)

McCraw, T, *Prophets of Regulation* (Harvard University Press Cambridge 1984)

McCrudden, C, *Regulation and Deregulation: Policy and Practice in the Utilities and Financial Services* (Clarendon Press Oxford 1999)

McDonald, RP, *International Syndicated Loans* (1982)

McDonald F and S Dearden, *European Economic Integration* (3rd edn Longman New York 1999)

MacDonald, R, *Consolidated Supervision of Banks* (Bank of England London 1998)

Macdougal, D, *The World Dollar Problem—A Study in International Economics* (1957)
McVea, H, *Financial Conglomerates and the Chinese Wall* (1993)
Machlup, F, *A History of Thought on Economic Integration* (Macmillan London 1977)
Madden, JT and M Nadler, *The International Money Markets* (1968)
Maduro, MP, *We the Court* (Hart Publishing Oxford 1998)
Majone, G, *Regulating Europe* (Routledge London 1996)
Moloney, N, *EC Securities Regulation* (OUP Oxford 2002)
Mansfield, R et al (eds), *Banking Law Guide* (Butterworths London 2006)
March, J and J Olsen, *Rediscovering Institutions* (Free Press New York 1989)
Marks, G, F Nielsen, L Ray, and J Salk, *Governance in the European Union* (Sage London 1996)
Marsh, D and G Stoker, *Theory and Methods in Political Science* (Palgrave Basingstoke 1995)
Martenson, GC, *The Eurodollar Market* (1964)
Maycock, J, *Financial Conglomerates: The New Phenomenon* (1986)
Mayes, D, L Halme, and A Liuksila, *Improving Banking Supervision* (Palgrave Basingstoke 2001)
A Mayss and A Reed, *European Business Litigation* (Ashgate Dartmouth 1998)
Micklitz, H and S Weatherill, *European Economic Law* (Ashgate Aldershot 1997)
Minsky, HP, 'A Theory of Systemic Fragility' in EI Altman and AW Sametz (eds), *Financial Crises: Institutions and Markets in a Fragile Environment* (1978)
Mitchell, C, *The Sterling Commercial Paper Market* (1988)
Moffit, M, *The World's Money: International Banking from Bretton Woods to the Brink of Insolvency* (1984)
Mohammed, S, *European Community Law on the Free Movement of Capital and the EMU* (Kluwer USA and Canada 1999)
Moley, R, *The First New Deal* (Harcourt New York 1966)
Molle, W, *The Economics of European Integration* (4th edn Ashgate Aldershot 2001)
Moloney, N, *EC Securities Regulation* (OUP Oxford 2002)
Morgan, G and D Knights, *Regulation and Deregulation in European Financial Services* (Macmillan Press Basingstoke 1997)
Morgan Guaranty Trust Company, *World Financial Markets* (March 1978 p 6 and September 1978)
Molyneaux Philip and Nidal Shamroukh, *Financial Innovation* (1999)
Murray-Jones A and A Gamble, *Managing Capital Adequacy: A Handbook of International Regulations* (1991)

Newman, P, *The New Palgrave Dictionary of Economics and the Law* (Macmillan Reference London 1998)

Nielsen, P, *Services and Establishment in European Community Banking Law* (DJOF Publishing Copenhagen 1994)

Norton, JJ *International Bank Supervisory Standards: the Case of the Basle Committee and Capital Adequacy Standards* (1994)

Norton, JJ *Devising International Bank Supervisory Standards* (1995)

Norton, JJ *Banking Law Manual* (1995)

Norton, JJ, M Andenas, and M Footer (eds), *The Changing Nature of International Law in the Twenty-First Century* (1998)

Norton, JJ (ed), *Yearbook of International Financial and Economic Law 1998* (Kluwer Law International London 1999)

Norton, JJ and M Andenas, *Emerging Financial Markets and the Role of International Financial Organizations* (Kluwer Law International London 1996)

Oatley, T, *Monetary Politics: Exchange Rate Cooperation in the European Union* (University of Michigan Press Ann Arbor 1997)

Oditah, F, *The Future for the Global Securities Markets—Legal and Regulatory Aspects* (Clarendon Press Oxford 1996)

Ogus, A, *Regulation—Legal Form and Economic Theory* (Clarendon Press Oxford 1994)

O'Keeffe, D and P Twomey, *Legal Issues of the Maastricht Treaty* (Chancery Law Publishing Bath 1994)

Oliver, Peter, *Free Movement of Goods in the EEC* (1998)

Page A and R Ferguson, *Investor Protection* (Weidenfeld & Nicolson London 1992)

Paraskevopoulos, C, *European Union at the Crossroads* (Edward Elgar Cheltenham 1998)

Parrish, M, *Securities Regulation and the New Deal* (Yale University Press New Haven 1970)

Paul N and R Croly, *EC Insurance Law* (Cameron Markby Hewitt 1991)

Peacock, A, *The Regulation Game* (Basil Blackwell Oxford 1984)

Peterson, J and M Shackleton, *The Institutions of the European Union* (Oxford University Press Oxford 2002)

Pollock, G, *Euronotes and Euro-Commercial Paper* (1987)

Porter, ME, *The Competitive Advantage of Nations* (Free Press New York 1990)

Prechal, S, *Directives in European Community Law* (Clarendon Press Oxford 1995)

Prochnow, HEV (ed), *The Eurodollar* (1970)

Quinn, BS, *The New Euromarkets* (1975)

Rawnsley, J, *Going for Broke—Nick Lesson and the Collapse of Barings Bank* (1995)

Ray, C, *Slater Walker—An Investigation of a Financial Phenonomon* (1977)

Revell, J, *The British Financial System* (Macmillan London and Basingstoke 1973)

Revell, J, *Solvency and Regulation of Banks: Theoretical and Practical Implications* (1975)

Richards, JH, *International Economic Institutions* (1970)

Rider, B and M Andenas, *Developments in European Community Law* Vol 1/1996 (Kluwer Law International London 1997)

Ritchie, A, *James M. Landis: Dean of the Regulators* (Harvard University Press Cambridge 1980)

Rosamond, B, *Theories of European Integration* (Palgrave Basingstoke 2000)

Rose-Ackerman, S, *Rethinking the Progressive Agenda: The Reform of the American Regulatory State* (Free Press New York 1993)

Salmon, T and Sir Nicholl William, *Building European Union—A Documentary History and Analysis* (Manchester University Press Manchester 1997)

Sarwal, AK, *KPMG International Handbook of Financial Instruments and Transactions* (1989)

Saunders A and I Walter, *Universal Banking—Financial System Design Reconsidered* (1997)

Savage, Katherine, *The History of the Common Market* (Longman & Harlow 1969)

Sayers, RS, *The Bank of England, 1891–1944* (1976)

Scott, HS and PA Wellons, *International Finance—Transactions, Policy and Regulation* (1998)

Smidt, Rene, *European Central Bank* (Kluwer Law 1998)

Schmidtchen, D and R Cooter, *Constitutional Law and Economics of the European Union* (Edward Elgar Cheltenham 1997)

Scott, H and P Wellons, *International Finance: Transactions, Policy and Regulation* (8th edn Foundation Press New York 2001)

Securities Association, *Investment Services Directive: A Commentary and Analysis* (Whitefriars Press London March 1989)

Seligman, J, *The SEC and the Future of Finance* (Praeger New York 1985)

Seligman, J, *The Transformation of Wall Street: a history of the Securities and Exchange Commission and modern corporate finance* (Houghton Mifflin Boston 1982)

Servais, D, *The Single Financial Market* (European Commission Luxembourg 2nd edn 1991)

Singer, P, *One World: The Ethics of Globalisation* (2nd edn Nota Bene Yale 2004)

Smits, R, *The European Central Bank: Institutional Aspects* (Kluwer Law International The Hague 1997)

Snowden, PN, *Emerging Risk in International Banking* (1985)
Snyder, F, *International Trade and Customs Law of the European Union* (Butterworths London 1998)
Spulber, D, *Regulation and Markets* (Massachusetts Institute of Technology Press Cambridge 1989)
Solomon, S, *The Confidence Game: How Unelected Central Bankers are Governing the Changed World Economy* (1995)
Soros, G, *The Crisis of Global Capitalism* (1998)
Spero, J, *The Failure of Franklin National Bank* (Columbia University Press New York 1980)
Spierenburg, D and R Poidevin, *The History of the High Authority of the European Coal and Steel Community: Supra nationality in Operation* (Weidenfeld & Nicolson London 1994)
Spruill, C, *Conglomerates and the Evolution of Capitalism* (1983)
Steil, B, *The European Equity Markets: The State of the Union and an Agenda for the Millennium* (Royal Institute of International Affaires London 1996)
Stigum, M, *Money Market* (1983)
Stuyck, J, *Financial and Monetary Integration in the European Economic Community: Legal, Institutional and Economic Aspects* (Kluwer Law Deventer 1993)
Sundararajan, V and TJT Balino (eds), *Banking Crises: Cases and Issues* (1991)
Swann, EJ (ed), *The Development of the Law of Financial Services* (1993)
Taylor, M, *Peak Practice: How to Reform the UK's Regulatory System: Implementing 'Twin Peaks'* (Centre for the Study of Financial Innovation London October 1996)
Taylor, M, *Twin Peaks: A Regulatory Structure for the New Century* (Centre for the Study of Financial Innovation London December 1995)
Taylor, P, *International Organization in the Modern World—The Regional and the Global Process* (Pinter New York 1993)
Tennekoon, R, *The Law & Regulation on International Finance* (1991)
Thornton, Henry, *An Enquiry into the Nature and Effects of the Paper Credit System of Great Britain* (1802)
Tinbergen, J, *International Economic Integration* (Elsevier London 1954)
Toth, AG, *Oxford Encyclopedia of European Community Law*: Vol I (OUP Oxford 1990)
Tridimas, T, *The General Principles of EC Law* (OUP Oxford 1999)
Triffin, R, *The World Money Maze—National Currencies in International Payments* (1966)
Truell, P and L Gurwin, *BCCI—The Inside Story of the World's Most Corrupt Financial Empire* (1992)
Tygier, C, *Basic Handbook of Foreign Exchange* (Euromoney London 1983)

Usher, J, *The Law of Money and Financial Services in the European Community* (Clarendon Press Oxford 1994)

Valdez, S, *An Introduction to Western Financial Markets* (Macmillan Business Basingstoke 1993)

Van Houtte, H, *The Law of Cross-Border Securities Transactions* (Sweet & Maxwell London 1999)

Vaughan, EJ and CM Elliott, *Fundamentals of Risk and Insurance* (1989)

Vickers, J and G Yarrow, *Privatization: An Economic Analysis* (Massachusetts Institute of Technology Press Cambridge 1988)

Viner, J, *The Customs Union Issue* (Carnegie Endowment for International Peace New York 1950)

Vittas, D, *Financial Regulation: Changing the Rules of the Game* (World Bank Washington 1992)

Waelbroeck, *Les reglementations nationals de prix et le droit communautaire* (1975), p 23

Walker, GA, *International Banking Regulation: Law, Policy and Practice* (Kluwer Law International London 2001)

Wallace, H and W Wallace, *Policy-Making in the European Union* (OUP Oxford 4th edn 2000)

Walsh, T, *The Customs Code of the European Union* (Butterworths London 1997)

Weatherill and Beaumont, *EC Law* (2nd edn 1995, 532–5; and 3rd edn 1999)

Weiler, J, *The Constitution of Europe: 'Do the New Clothes has an Emperor?' and other Essays on European Integration* (CUP Cambridge 1999)

Wendell, F, *Issues Related to the Regulation of Broker–Dealers under the Investment Advisers Act and the Status of Investment Advisers under the Securities Exchange Act* (The American Law Institute Washington 1997)

Williamson, J, *The Failure of World Monetary Reform, 1971–74* (Nelson Sunbury-on-Thames 1977)

Wilson, K, *The History of the Idea of Europe* (Routledge London 1995)

Woolf, M, *Why Globalisation Works: the Case for the Global Market Economy* (Yale University Press 2004)

Wymeersch, E, *Further Perspectives in Financial Integration in Europe* (Walter de Gruyter Berlin 1994)

Zhang, PG, *Barings Bankruptcy and Financial Derivatives* (1995)

Ziegler, P, *The Sixth Great Power: Barings, 1762–1929* (1988)

Zilioli, C and M Selmayr, *The Law of the European Central Bank* (Hart Publishing Oxford 2001)

9. JOURNAL AND NEWSPAPER ARTICLES AND CHAPTER CONTRIBUTIONS

Agence Europe, 18.7.80, p 11

'European law problem for the Bank of England,' *The Times* (8.1.1972), p 24, col D

'EEC wants rules on banking harmonised,' *The Times* (16.1.1974), p 16, col 3

'Banking harmonisation,' *The Times* (30.6.1973), p 19, col 6

Abrahamson J and J Sivono, 'A Tale of Two Shutdowns' 10 *BJIBFL* (1995), 560

Abrams, C, 'The Investment Services Directive—who should be the principal regulator of cross-border services?' (1995) 11 European Financial Services Law 317

Abrams, C, 'The Second Banking Directive and the Investment Services Directive: when and how can the single European passport be used for cross-border services?' (1997) 10 European Financial Services Law 248

Ackerman, F, D Mounts, and D Thomas, 'Automated compliance systems' (1999) 1 Journal of Financial Regulation and Compliance 48

Adams, G, 'The single market in financial services—an Orwellian approach' (1996) 3 European Financial Services Law 149

Alexander, K, 'The International Supervisory Framework for Financial Services: An Emerging Regime for Transnational Supervision' (2000) 1 Journal of International Banking Regulation 33

Alibar, RZ, *International Banking: Growth and Regulation' Colombia Journal of World Business* (Winter 1975), 10 (4): 9–15

Alter and Meunier-Aitsahalia, 'Judicial Politics in the European Communion—European Integration and the Path breaking *Cassis de Dijon* Decision', *Comparative Political Studies* (January 1994), vol 26, no 4, 535 at footnote 1

Anason, D, 'Financial Council's Power, Scope, Makeup Criticised' *American Banker* June 27, 1997, p 3

Andenas, M, 'Current Developments' (1994) 43 *ICLQ* 731; and (1996) 45 *ICLQ* 230 at 234–5

Andenas, M, 'Rules of Conduct under the Principle of Subsidiarity' (1994) 14 *Co Law* 61

Andenas, M, 'Rules of conduct and the principle of subsidiarity' (1994) 14 Company Lawyer 61

Andenas, M, 'Cross border cold-calling and the right to provide services' (1995) 8 Company Lawyer 249

Andenas, M, 'Italian Nationality Requirement and Community Law' (1996) 17 Company Lawyer 219

Andenas, M, 'Directive on deposit guarantee schemes challenged' (1995) 1 Company Lawyer 18

Andenas, M, 'Current Developments: EC Law, IV. Insurance and Banking' (1996) 45 International & Comparative Law Quarterly 230

Andenas, M, 'Financial Market Regulation and the Case Law' (1998) European Business Law Review 203

Andenas, M, 'The Financial Market and the Commission as legislator' (1998) Company Lawyer 98

Andenas, M, 'The Financial Market and Commission as Legilsatory' (1999) 19 *CoLaw* 98.

Andenas, M, 'Liability for Supervisors and Depositors' Rights – the BCCI and the Bank of England in the House of Lords' (2001) 3 Euredia 388

Andenas, Mads and Jukka Snell, 'Keck and Free Movement of Services' *ABLR* (1998)

D'Arista, J, 'U.S. Banks Abroad,' *FINE: Financial Institutions and the National Economy*, Compendium of papers prepared for the FINE study, Book II, p. 812

Arlman, P, 'European Equity Markets after the Euro: Competition and Cooperation across new Frontiers' (1999) 2 International Finance 139

Armstrong, K, 'Integrating Law: An Introduction' (1998) 2 Journal of Common Market Studies 147

Arnull, A, 'Does the Court of Justice have inherent jurisdiction?' (1990) 27 Common Market Law Review 683

Arnull, A, 'What Shall We Do On Sunday?' (1991) 16 EL Rev 112 [ ]

Arner, D, 'The Mexican Peso Crisis: Implications for the Regulation of Financial Markets,' *Studies in International Financial and Economic Law* (1996)

Arner, D, 'The Mexican Peso Crisis of 1994–95: Implications for the Regulation of Financial Markets' 2 NAFTA Rev., 28 (1996)

Avgerinos, Y., 'Essential and non-Essential Measures: Delegation of Powers in EU Securities Regulation' (2002) European Law Journal 269

Avgerinos, Y, 'European System of Central Banks: Monetary Policy, Independence, Banking Supervision and Future Perspectives' (1999) 4 Journal of International Banking and Financial Law 144

Avgouleas, E, 'The Harmonisation of Rules of Conduct in EU Financial Markets: Economic Analysis, Subsidiarity and Investor Protection' (2000) 1 European Law Journal 72

Avgouleas, E, 'The Implementation of the Insider Dealing Directive in Greece' (1997) 4 European Financial Services Law 131

Bank of England, 'International Conference of Banking Supervisors' (1979) BEQB

Bank of England, 'Developments in co-operation among banking supervisory authorities' (1981) BEQB

Bank of England, 'International Conference of Banking Supervisors' (1975 BEQB 298

Bank of England, 'Offshore Financial Centres' (1982) BEQB

Bank of England, 'Regulation in the City and the Bank of England's Role' (1978) BEQB

Bank of England, 'Developments in Wholesale Payment Systems' (1992) BEQB 449

Bank of England, 'The Development of a real-time gross settlement system' (1994) BEQB 34

Barber, T and Simonian, H, 'Germany's financial vision' (12 February 2001) Financial Times 20

Barents, R, 'The Internal Market Unlimited: Some Observations on the Legal Basis of Community Legislation' (1993) 30 Common Market Law Review 85

Barents, Rene, 'New Developments in Measures Having Equivalent Effect', p. 271 at 272

Barnard, J, 'The Securities Law Enforcement Remedies Act of 1989: Disenfranchising shareholders in order to protect them' (1989) 65 Notre Dame Law Review 32

Beckers, S, L Rijckmans, Y Stam, and S Storm,'Euronext: a Dutch Perspective' (2001) 7 Journal of International Banking & Financial Law 323

Bell, Geoffrey 'How will the City fare in Europe?', *The Times* (25.10.1972), p 25, col D

Benston, G, 'Consumer Protection as Justification for Regulating Financial Services Firms and Products' (2000) 3 Journal of Financial Services Research 277

Beraud, 'Les measures d'effet equivalent au sens des articles 30 et suivants du Traite be Rome' [1968] RTDE 265

Bermann, Goebel, Davey and Fox, op cit, n, 442–7

Bevan, T, 'Banking Conglomerates: Revolution or Evolution?' (1985) Aug. Barclays Bank Review 56

Bjorklend, Mattias, 'The Scope of the General Good Notion in the Second EC Banking Directive According to Recent Case Law' European Business Law Review (July/August) 1998, p. 227 at p235

Bjorkland, Matias, 'The Scope of the General Good Notion of the Second EC Banking Directive According to Recent Case Law' EBLR (July/August 1999) 227 at 236

Blair, W and GA Walker, 'Negotiable Instruments,' in P Cresswell et al (eds), *The Encyclopaedia of Banking Law* (December 1997), Div F

Blair, W, A Allen, K Plamer, P Richards-Carpenter and G Walker, *Banking and Financial Services Regulation* (1998)

Blake, David, 'Government to bring in new code for control of banking,' *The Times* (30.10.1975), p 19, col A

Blake, David, 'Supervisory role vital, Bank Governor says,' *The Times* (29.11.1975), p 19, col D

Blanden, Michael, ' "Last chance" to alter EEC banking rules' *Financial Times* (21.11.1973)

Bloch, E, 'Eurodollars: An Emerging International Money Market' *Bulletin No 39*, Institute of Finance, NYU Graduate School of Business (April 1966)

Blunden, G, 'The supervision of the UK banking system' (1975) BEQB, No 2, 190

Blunden, G, 'The Supervision of the UK Banking System' *Journal of the Institute of Bankers* [Vol. 96, Part 4], August 1975, p. 213

Blunden, G, 'Control and Supervision of the Foreign Operations of Banks' in JE Wadsworth, JSG Wilson, and H Fournier (eds), *The Development of Financial Institutions in Europe, 1956–1976* (1976), Ch XIII

BNA 'Daiwa Bank to Pay $340 Million in Plea Bargain Over Coverup Charges' 66 *Banking Rep.* 367 (March 4, 1996)

BNA 'Financial Modernization—Senate Faces Increasing Pressure to Consider Banking Reform Bill,' Banking Law Report (Vol. 17, No 11, p 4)

BNA Op-Sub Debate Heats Up As Regulators Consider Merits of H.R.10' Banking Policy Law Report (Vol. 17, No 12, p 5)

BNA 'Financial Modernization—Senate Enters Financial Services Reform Debate by Holding Hearings,' Banking Law Report (Vol. 17, No 14, p 5)

Boland, V and F Guerrera, 'FSA staff brand iX plan a 'nightmare" (8 September 2000) Financial Times 1

Bradley, C, 'Competitive Deregulation of Financial Services Activity in Europe after 1992' (1991) 11 Oxford Journal of Legal Studies 545

Brentford, P, 'Constitutional Aspects of the Independence of the European Central Bank' (1998) 1 International & Comparative Law Quarterly 75

Buiter, W, 'Alice in Euroland' (1999) 2 Journal of Common Market Studies 181

Bureau of National Affairs, Inc., *Banking Report*, July 3 1995

Burns, AS, 'Reflections on an Economic Policy Maker' American Enterprise Institute, Washington, DC (1978)

Calvo, GA and E Mendoza, 'Reflections on Mexico's Balance of Payments Crisis: A Chronicle of Death Foretold', Journal of International Economics [1996] 41: 235–64

Capelli, F, 'Les Nalentendus Provoques Par L'arret sur le Cassis de Dijon', Revue du Marche Commun (1981), 421–435

Carli, 'Eurodollars: A Paper Pyramid' Quarterly Review, Banco Nazionale de Lavoro, 95–109 (1971)

Centeno, M and A Mello, 'How Integrated are the Money Market and the Bank Loans Market within the European Union?' (1999) 18 Journal of International Money & Finance 75

Chalmers, D, 'Free Movement of Goods within the European Community: an Unhealthy Addiction to Scotch Whisky?' (1993) 42 ICLQ 26
Chalmers, D, 'Repackaging the Internal Market—The Ramifications of the *Keck* Judgment' (1994) 19 ELRev 385
Clifford Chance, 'Challenging times for exchanges' (1999) 10 Journal of International Banking & Financial Law 413
Clifford Chance, 'Commission Forms Forum Groups to Develop Action Plan' (1999) 11 Journal of International Banking & Financial Law 452
Clifford Chance, 'FSA Proposals for new Customer Classification Regime' (2000) 3 Journal of International Banking & Financial Law 103
Coase, RH, 'The problem of Social Cost' (1960) 3 The Journal of Law and Economics 1
Coates K, and C Ffinch, 'A single passport for insurers—where next?', EFSL, June 1994
Conti, C, 'The Impact of new technologies on the financial services industry' (1997) 11 European Financial Services Law 284
Cooke, P, 'The role of the banking supervisor' (1982) BEQB 547
Cooke, P, 'The international banking scene: a supervisory perspective' (1983) BEQB
Cooke, P, 'Some current concerns of a banking supervisor' (1985) BEQB
Cremona, M, 'A European Passport for investment services' (1994) Journal of Business Law 195
Crockett, A, 'Market discipline and financial stability' (2001) 10 Financial Stability Review 166
Crosby, S, 'The Single Market and the Rule of Law' (1991) 16 European Law Review 451
Dach, 'Legal Nature of the Euro-Dollar System' AJCL 13 (1964)
Dale, R, 'Japan's 'Glass-Steagall' Act' [1987] JIBL,
Dale, R, 'Regulating Bank's Securities Activities: A Global Assessment' (1991) *JISM*
Dale, R, 'Reflections on the BCCI Affair: A United Kingdom Perspective' (1992) 26 International Law 949
Dale, R, 'Bank Regulation after BCCI' [1993] 1 JIBL
Dale, R, 'Regulating investment business in the Single Market' (November 1994) 4 Bank of England Quarterly Bulletin 333
Dale, R, 'The Regulation of Investment Firms in the European Union (Parts 1–2)' (1994) 10–11 Journal of International Banking Law 394
Dale, R and S Wolf, 'The Structure of Financial Regulation' (1998) 4 Journal of Financial Regulation and Compliance 326
Dalhuisen, JH, 'Liberalisation and Re-Regulation of Cross-Border Financial Services: Part I' (1999) 5–6 European Business Law Review 158
Dalhuisen, JH, 'Liberalisation and Re-Regulation of Cross-Border Financial Services: Part II' (1999) 7–8 European Business Law Review 284

Dalhuisen, JH, 'Liberalisation and Re-Regulation of Cross-Border Financial Services: Part III' (1999) 9–10 European Business Law Review 354

Darling, A, Labour's Spokesman on the City in 'Through the Looking Glass' *Euromoney*, March 1996, No 323, pp 63–65

Dashwood, A., 'The Principle of Direct Effect in European Community Law' (1978) 16 Journal of Common Market Studies 229

Dashwood, A, 'The Cassis de Dijon line of authority' in *In Memoriam J.D.B. Mitchell* (1983), 145 at 152

Dassesse, M, 'The Regulatory Implications of the Location of Financial Services under EU Law' (2001) 10 Journal of International Banking & Financial Law 473

Davies, H, 'Law and Financial Regulation' (1993) 4–5 Journal of International Financial Markets 193

de Witte, Bruno, 'Direct Effect, Supremacy and the Nature of the Legal Order' in Paul Craig and Grainne de Búrca, *The Evolution of EU Law* (1999), ch 5, pp. 178–80.

Deakin, S and G Slinger, 'Hostile Takeovers, Corporate Law and the Theory of the Firm' (1997) 24 Journal of Law and Society 124

Deane-Johns, S, 'Recent Developments in the UK and European E-Securities Framework' (1999) 2 Business Law Review 29

De Grauwe, P, 'Monetary Policies in the Presence of Asymmetries' (2000) 4 Journal of Common Market Studies 593

Dehousse, '1992 and Beyond: The Institutional Dimension of the Internal Market Programme' [1989/1] *LIEI* 109

Demarigny, F, 'Disentangling the Single Market' (2000) 4 The Financial Regulator 32

Deutsche Bank Research, 'Regulation and banking supervision: Caught between the nation state and global financial markets' (29 June 2000) 86 EMU Watch 1

Dimson, E and P Marsh, 'Calculating the Cost of Capital' (1982) 2 Long Range Planning 112

Dona, 'Les measures d-effet equivalent a des restrictions quantitatives' [1973] RMC 224

Dufey, G and T Chung, 'International Financial Markets: A Survey' in RT Kuhn (ed), *International Finance and Investing* (1990), ch 3

Eackhout, P, 'Recent Case-law on Free Movement of Goods: Refining Keck and Mithouard' (1998) 2 European Business Law Review 267

Editorial Comments, 'Executive Agencies within the EU: The European Central Bank—a model?' (1996) 33 Common Market Law Review 623

Edward, D, 'Establishment and Services: An Analysis of the Insurance Cases' (1987) ELRev 231

Ehlermann, CD, 'The European Community, its law and lawyers' (1992) 29 Common Market Law Review 213

Ehlermann, CD, 'The Internal Market following the Single European Act' (1987) 24 Common Market Law Review 361

Ehlermann, CD in Groeben, Boeckh and Thiesing, *Kommentar zum EWG-Vertrag* (1974), Vol 1, 263

Ehlermann, CD 'Das Verbot der MaSnahmen gleicher Wirkung in der Rechtsprechung des Gerichtshofes' in *Feschrift für Ipsen* (1977), 579

Ehlermann, CD [364–372]

Eichengreen, B, 'European Monetary Unification' (1993) 1 Journal of Economic Literature 31

Einzig, P, 'Dollar Deposits in London' *The Banker* (1960) 110

Emiliou, N, 'Opening Pandora's Box: the Legal Basis of Community Measures before the Court of Justice' (1994) 5 European Law Review 488

Endo, K, 'The Principle of Subsidiarity: from Johannes Althusius to Jacques Delors' (1994) 6 Hokkaido Law Review 553

Engler, H, 'Global Markets Prompts Need for Closer Co-operation' *Reuters Financial Service*, July 3, 1996

Estrella, A, 'A Prolegomenon to future Capital Requirements' (1995) 2 Federal Reserve Bank of New York Economic Policy Review 1

European Shadow Financial Regulatory Committee, 'The European Shadow Financial Regulatory Committee: a new initiative' (1999) 2 Journal of International Banking Regulation 137

Evanoff, D, 'Preferred Source of Market Discipline' (1993) 10 Yale Journal on Regulation 347

Falkner, R, 'Insurance' in D. Campbell (ed), *Financial Services in the New Europe* (1992)

Fell, P, 'The Single Passport—an Overview' (1994) 11 European Financial Services Law 176

Ferrarini, G, 'The European Regulation of Stock Exchanges: New Perspectives' (1999) 3 Common Market Law Review 569

Ferrarini, G, 'Towards a European Law of Investment Services and Institutions' (1994) 6 Common Market Law Review 1283

'Supervision of financial markets' *Financial Regulation Report* (August 1996)

The Financial Times, 'New central bank group to 'police' Euro markets' 13 February 1975, p. 26e

The Financial Times, 'The Ten choose Blunden', Men and Matters, 13 February 1975

Fisher, R, 'Banking Reform and Regulatory Relief' Annual Review of Banking Law (1998), Vol. 17, pp 2–8

Foot, M, 'Michael Foot—executive director, Bank of England' Global Compliance Monitor (September 13, 1996), Vol. 1, No 4, p. 11

Forwood, N and M Clough, 'The Single European Act and Free Movement' 11 ELR (1986) 383, 399–404

Fox, J, 'Lead Regulator Plan Seen as Way to Avert Barings-Style Debacle' The American Banker, March 11, 1996, p 2

Freidbacher, 'Motive Unmasked: The European Court of Justice, The Free Movement of Goods and the Search for Legitimacy' (1996) 2 ELJ 226

Friedman, M, 'The Euro-Dollar Market: Some First Principles' *The Morgan Guaranty Survey* (October 1969), pp 4–14

Frydl, 'The Debate over Regulating the Eurocurrency Markets', Federal Reserve Bank of New York Quarterly Review, Volume 4, No 4, Winter 1979–80

Frydl, 'The Eurodollar Conundrum', Federal Reserve Bank of New York Quarterly Review, Volume 7, No 1, Spring 1982

Galanopoulou, V., 'Recent Developments in Financial Services Regulation: A Good Example for the European Regulators?' (1999) European Business Law Review 408

Garten, HA, 'Universal Banking and Financial Stability' 19 Brook J Int'l L., 159

Garzaniti, L, 'Single Market-Making: EC Regulation on Securities Markets' (1993) 3 Company Lawyer 43

Gerven, 'The Recent Case Law of the Court of Justice concerning Articles 30 and 36 of the EEC Treaty' [1977] CMLR 5

Giddy, IH, 'Measuring the World Foreign Exchange Market' Colombia Journal of World Business (Fall 1979), 14 (3)

Glaesner, HJ, 'The Single European Act: Attempt at an Appraisal' 10 Fordham ILJ (1987), 446

Linda Goldberg, 'Predicting Exchange Rate Crises: Mexico Revisited' *Journal of International Economics* [1993] 36:413–30

Goldman, B, 'The Convention Between Member States of the European Community on the Mutual Recognition of Companies and Legal Persons' [1968/69] 6 CMLR 104

Goodhart, C and D Schoenmaker, 'Should the Functions of Monetary Policy and Banking Supervision be separated?' (1995) 4 Oxford Economic Papers 539

Gormley, '*Cassis de Dijon* and the Communication from the Commission', *European Law Review* (1981), 6, 454

Gormley, LW, 'Actually or potentially, directly or indirectly? Obstacles to the free movement of goods', Yearbook of European Law (1989), 9, 197–208

Gormley, L, 'Reasoning Renounced? The Remarkable Judgement in *Keck & Mitouard*' (1994) EBLRev 63

Gormley, L, 'Assent and respect for judgements: *Uncommunautaire* reasoning in the European Court of Justice' in Cramer, Micklitz, and Tonner (eds), *Law and Diffuse Interests in the European Legal Order*

Graham, G, 'Banking regulator highlights failings' *The Financial Times*, 8 March 1996

Graham, G, 'Bank urges regulation changes' *Financial Times*, 22 February 1997

Grauwe, P de, 'The Development of the Eurocurrency Market' 12 Finance and Development, 14 (September 1975)

Green, D, 'Enhanced Co-operation among Regulators and the Role of National Regulators in a Global Market' (2000) 2 Journal of International Financial Markets 7

Griffin, P, 'The Delaware Effect: Keeping the Tiger in its Cage: The Experience of Mutual Recognition in Financial Services' (2001) 3 Columbia Journal of European Law 337

Grubel, 'A Proposal for the Establishment of an International Deposit Insurance Corporation', *Princeton Studies in International Finance*, No 133, July 1979

Guericke, A, 'Deposit Guarantee and Investor Compensation Directives' (2000) 1 Journal of International Banking Regulation 61

'Guth Underlines Micro Economic Risks for Private Banks in Recycling Funds', *International Herald Tribune,* 16 June 1980

Hadjiemmanuil, C and M Andenas, 'Banking Supervision and European Monetary Union' (1999) 2 Journal of International Banking Regulation 84

Haines, P, 'The Investment Services Directive—Progress to Date' (1995) 2 European Financial Services Law 30

Hall, MJB, 'BCCI: The Lessons for the Bank Supervisors' [1992] 1 JRPL

Hall, MJB, 'A Review of the Board of Banking Supervisors' Inquiry into the Collapse of Barings' BJIBFL, October 1995

Hall, MJB, 'A Review of the Board of Banking Supervision's Inquiry into the Collapse of Barings' *Loughborough University Banking Centre Research Paper* (September 1995)

Hall, MJB, 'A Review of the Board of Banking Supervision's Inquiry into the Collapse of Barings—Part II' BJIBL, November 1995

Harding, C, 'Member State Enforcement of European Community Measures: The Chimera of 'Effective' Enforcement' (1997) 4 Maastricht Journal of European and Comparative Law 5

Hatzopoulos, Vassilis, 'Case C-384/93 *Alpine Investments BV v Minister van Financien*, Judgment of 10 May 1999, NYR, (1995)' 32 CMLR 1427

Hawkesby, C, 'The Institutional Structure of Financial Supervision: A Cost-Benefit Approach' (2000) 3 Journal of International Banking Regulation 36

Hayward, P, *Prospects for International Cooperation by Bank Supervisors (With Background Note on the Basle Committee on Banking Supervision)* in J.J. Norton, *International Bank Supervisory Standards: the Case of the Basle Committee and Capital Adequacy Standards* (1994)

Heigel, C, 'Case Comment: Independent Insurance Agents of America, Inc.

v. Ludwig and Variable Annuity Life Insurance Co v Clarke: The Banking-Insurance War in Search of a Judicial Truce' 55 Ohio St. L.J.

Herranz, IR, 'Distance Marketing of Consumer Financial Services' (2001) 16 Banking & Finance Law Review 303

Hertig, G, 'Imperfect Mutual Recognition for EC Financial Services' (1994) 14 International Review of Law and Economics 177

Hertig, G, 'Regulatory Competition for EU Financial Services' (2000) 2 Journal of International Economic Law 349

Hill, A, 'Greed and fear return' (8 June 2002) Financial Times 12

Hopt, K, 'Special Issue on the Economic Law of the Member States in an Economic and Monetary Union: Report' (1976) 13 Common Market Law Review 147

Hoskins, M, 'EEC Banking Law: Plugging the Gaps' (1992) 1 Journal of International Banking Law 56

Hudson, A, 'The European Netting Directive' (1996) 11 European Financial Services Law 309

Hugon, 'Why the Eurodollar?' *Bankers' Magazine* (1978) 222

Humphrey, Thomas M, 'Lender of Last Resort: the Concept in History' 75:2 *Fed.Res.B. Richmond Econ.Rev.* 8 (March/April 1989)

Hunnings, N, 'Amending the EC Treaty: the Commission proposals-II' (2000) 6 Perspectives on European Business Law 10

Hutton, R, 'The Regulation of Foreign Banks—A European Viewpoint', *Columbia Journal of World Business*, Winter 1975

Issac, WM, 'Greenspan Hasn't Made Good Case for Bank Regulation Czar' *American Banker*, April 10, 1997, p 9

Jachtenfuchs, M, 'The Governance Approach to European Integration' (2001) 2 Journal of Common Market Studies 245

Jackson, H and E Pan, 'Regulatory Competition in International Securities Markets: Evidence from Europe in 1999—Part I' (2001) 2 Business Lawyer 653

Jackson, P, 'Unified Supervision: the UK Experience' (2000) 3 The Financial Regulator 50

Jarvis, K, 'Does the fiduciary bell toll?' (1996) 2 Company Lawyer 51

Joris, JL, 'Will the European Company work?' (2002) 2 International Financial Law Review 19

Kapstein, EB, 'Supervising International Banks: Origins and Implications of the Basle Accord' Essays in Int'l. Fin, N. 185, Princeton University (December 1991)

Karmel, R, 'Glass-Steagall: Some Critical Reflections' (1980) Banking Law Journal 97

King, D, 'Judicial Expansion of National Banks' Insurance Powers: The Resurrection and Statutory Interpretation of Section 92 of the National Bank Act' 19 Iowa J Corp L

Kirchgässner, G, 'Constitutional Economics and its Relevance for the Evolution of Rules' (1994) 47 Kyklos 321

Kirchhof, P, 'The Balance of Powers between the National and European Institutions' (1999) 3 European Law Journal 225

Kirsch, CE, *The Financial Services Revolution—Understanding the Chaning Role of Banks, Mutual Funds and Insurance Companies* (1998)

Klopstock, FH, 'The International Money Market: Structure, Scope and Instruments' 20 *Journal. of Finance* (1965)

Klopstock, FH, 'The Wiring of the Eurodollar Market' Euromoney, August 1970

Klopstock, FHG, 'Outlook for the Euromarket' International Currency Review, March/April 1973

Krause, H, 'Germany wins Compromise on EU Takeover Rules' (2001) 7 International Financial Law Review 18

Krugman, P, 'A Model of Balance-of-payments crises', Journal of Money, Credit and Banking [1979] 11: 311–25

Laffont, J and J Tirole, 'The politics of government decision-making: A theory of regulatory capture' (1991) 4 Quarterly Journal of Economics 1089

Lambert, R and A Simon,'An Ideal Regulatory Model for dealing with Retail Financial Institution Runs and Failures' (2000) 4 Journal of Financial Regulation and Compliance 309

Landis, J, 'The Legislative History of the Securities Act of 1933' (1959) 28 George Washington Law Review 29

Landsmeer, A and M Van Empel, 'The Directive on deposit-guarantee schemes and the Directive on investor compensation schemes in view of Case C-233/94' (1998) European Financial Services Law 143

Lang, J, 'European Community Constitutional Law: The division of powers between the Community and the Member States' (1988) Northern Ireland Legal Quarterly 209

Langton, J, '$6 trillion market with a crucial capital role' *Sunday Observer*, 14 July 1991

Lannoo, K, 'A European Perspective on Corporate Governance' (1999) 2 Journal of Common Market Studies 269

Larosière, J and D Lebègue, 'Bringing harmony to Europe's markets: Euro-zone states should hasten the integration of their financial systems' (14 September 2000) Financial Times 17

Lasok, KP, 'Freedom to Provide Insurance Services in the Light of the Co-insurance Cases' (1988) Modern Law Review 706

Lastra, R, 'Lender of Last Resort' (1999) 2 ICLQ 340

Lee, BE, 'The Eurodollar Market Revisited' 156 The Bankers' Magazine, 64 (Autumn 1973)

Leleux, P, 'Corporation Law in the US and in the EEC' (1967–8) 5 Common Market Law Review 133

Lenaerts, K, 'Regulating the regulatory process: 'delegation of powers' in the European Community' (1993) 18 European Law Review 23

Lenaerts, K and A Verhoeven, 'Towards a Legal Framework for executive rule-making in the EU? The Contribution of the new Comitology Decision' (2000) 3 Common Market Law Review 645

Levitt, M, 'Does Europe want a single market?' (2001) 4 The Financial Regulator 20

L'Heveder, C, 'The Investment Services Directive and its implications for participants in Europe's financial markets' (1996) 1 Journal of International Banking & Financial Law 5

Licht, A, 'Regulatory Arbitrage for Real: International Securities Regulation in a World of Interacting Securities Markets' (1998) 38 Virginia Journal of International Law 563

Lichtenstein, C, 'International Standards for Consolidated Supervision of Financial Conglomerates: Controlling Systemic Risk', Brooklyn J Int' L, [Vol. XIX: 1 1993]

Little, 'The Eurodollar Market: Its Nature and Impact' *Federal Reserve Bank of Boston*, New England Economic Review, May/June 1960

Llewellyn, D, 'Re-engineering the Regulator' (1996) 3 The Financial Regulator 21

Lomax, R, 'Supervision in the Single Market' (1993) 3 Central Banking 36

Lomnicka, E, 'EC Harmonisation of Investor Compensation Schemes' (1994) 1 European Financial Services Law 17

Lomnicka, E, 'The Home Country Control Principle in the Financial Services Directives and the Case Law' (2000) 11 European Business Law Review 324

Long, W, 'European Initiatives for On-Line Financial Services: Part 1' (1999) 8 Journal of International Banking & Financial Law 324

Long, W, 'European Initiatives for On-Line Financial Services: Part 2' (1999) 9 Journal of International Banking & Financial Law 373

Long, W, 'European Initiatives for On-Line Financial Services: Part 4' (2000) 3 Journal of International Banking & Financial Law 84

Longstreth, B, 'Averting a Chain Reaction Disaster in the Money World' Bus. & Soc'y Rev., Summer 1983

Louis, JV, 'A Monetary Union for Tomorrow?' (1989) 2 Common Market Law Review 301

Lovett, WA, 'Lessons from the Recent Peso Crisis in Mexico' (1996) 4 Tul.J.Int'l & Comp L. 143

Lutz, 'The Eurocurrency System' Quarterly Review, Banco Nazionale de Lavoro, Vol. 27, No 110, 183–200 (1974)

McConnell, B, 'Treasury Expected to Back Referee Among Regulators' The American Banker (April 25, 1997), p 3

MacDougall, M, 'Daiwa: A Message for Foreign Banks in the United States' 11 BJIBFL (1990), 51

McGee and Weatherill, 'The Evolution of the Single Market—Harmonisation or Liberalisation?' (1990) 53 MLR 578

MacNeil, I, 'The Future for Financial Regulation: the Financial Services and Markets Bill' (1999) 62 Modern Law Review 725

McVea, H, 'Financial Conglomerates and Conflicts of Interest: Resolving the Regulatory Dilemma' (1996) 47 Northern Ireland Law Quarterly 239

Macey, JR, 'The Inevitability of Universal Banking' 19 Brook.J.Int'l L., p 203

Machlup, 'Five Errors about Eurodollars' Euromoney, July 1972

Maduro, P, '*Keck*: The end? The beginning of the end? or just the end of the beginning?' (1994) 1 Irish Journal of Eur Law 33

Magnette, P, 'Towards 'Accountable Independence'? Parliamentary Controls of the European Central Bank and the Rise of a New Democratic Model' (2000) 4 European Law Journal 326

Mahmood, S, 'Chinese Walls—An Evolutionary Process' (1999) European Financial Services Law 67

Majone, G, 'The Rise of the Regulatory State in Europe' (1994) 3 West European Politics 77

Majone, G, 'Regulating Europe: Problems and Perspectives' (1989) 3 Jarhbuch zur Staats- und Verwaltungswissenschaft

Malloy, M, 'Banking in the Twenty-First Century' (2000) 25 The Journal of Corporation Law 789

Mann, M, 'The SEC's International Enforcement Program and Bilateral and Multilateral Initiatives', 961 P.L.I. Corp 7, 24 (1996)

Marks, G and L Hooghe, 'Optimality and Authority: A Critique of Neoclassical Theory' (2000) 5 Journal of Common Market Studies 795

Masclet, J-C, 'Les articles 30, 36 et 100 du traite Cee a la lumiere de l'arret *Cassis de Dijon*', Revue de Droit Europeen (1980), 611–34.

Mattera, 'Libre circulation des marchanises et articles 30 a 36 du Traite CEE' [1976] RMC 500

Mattera, A, '"*Cassis de Dijon*": Une nouvelle approche pour la realisation et le bon fonctionnenent du marche interieur', Revue du Marcat Commun (1980), 505–513

Mayer, HW, 'The BIS Concept of the Eurocurrency Market' Euromoney, May 1976, 60–6

Meiji and Winter, 'Measures having an equivalent effect to quantitative restrictions' [1976] CMLR 79

Metcalpe, L, 'Reforming the Commission: Will Organizational Efficiency Produce Effective Governance?' (2000) 5 Journal of Common Market Studies 817

Mikesell, RF, 'The Eurodollar Market and the Foreign Demand for Liquid Dollar Assets' 4 Journal of Money, Credit and Banking, 643 (August 1972)

Minsky, HP, 'A Theory of Systemic Fragility' in EI Altman and AW Sametz (eds), *Financial Crises: Institutions and Markets in a Fragile Environment* (1978)

Mitchell, GW, 'How the Fed Sees Multinational Bank Regulation,' The Banker (July 1974), 124(581): 757–60 at 759

Mohamed, S, 'A Critical Assessment of the ECJ Judgment in Trummer and Mayer' (1999) 9 Journal of International Banking & Financial Law 396

Mohamed, S, 'A Single Regulator for the E.C. Financial Market' (2001) 8–9 Journal of International Banking Law 203

Monney, P, 'Governing Globalised Businesses: Achieving New Business Models' (1999) 9 International Business Lawyer 366

Moravcsik, A 'Preferences and Power in the European Community: A Liberal Intergovernmentalist Approach' (1993) 4 Journal of Common Market Studies 473

Moravcsik, A and K Nicolaidis, 'Explaining the Treaty of Amsterdam: Interests, Influence, Institutions' (1999) 1 Journal of Common Market Studies 59

Morison, Ian, 'The City may have to swallow its pride,' The Times (10.5.1972), p 25, col A

Morison, Ian, 'Regulating banking—The wink and a nod may not be enough,' The Times (4.10.1972), p 19, col A

Morison, Ian, 'EEC entry 'may pose a threat to City banking'', The Times (25.10.1972), 23, col H

Mortelmans, K, 'Article 30 of the EEC Treaty and Legislation Relating to Market Circumstances: Time to Consider a New Definition' (1991) 28 CNLRev 115

Mwenda, K and A Fleming, 'International Developments in the Organisational Structure of Financial Services Supervision: Part II' (2002) 1 Journal of International Banking Law 7

New York Times, 3 September 1974

Norton, J and C Olive, 'Globalization of Financial Risks and International Supervision of Banks and Securities Firms: Lessons from the Barings Debacle' (1996) 2 International Lawyer 301

Norton, JJ, 'Capital Adequacy Standards: A Legitimate Regulatory Concern for Prudential Supervision of Banking Activities?' in (1989) Ohio St LJ 1299

Norton, JJ, 'Up against 'the Wall'—Glass–Steagall and the Dilemma of a Deregulated 'Regulated' Banking Environment' (1987) 42 *Business Lawyer*

O'Leary, Siofra, 'The Free Movement of Persons and Services' in Craig and de Burca, op cit, n 18, Ch 11.

O'Niell, N, 'Supervision of Financial Conglomerates' [1994] Journal of International Business Law

Obstfeld, Maurice, 'Destabilising Effects of Exchange Rate Escape Clauses', Journal of International Economics [1997] 43: 61–77

Ogus, A, 'Competition between National Legal Systems: a Contribution of Economic Analysis to Comparative Law' (1999) 48 ICLQ 405

Julcin Ozkan, S and Alan Sutherland, ' A Currency Crisis Model with an Optimising Policymaker', Journal of International Economics [1998] 44: 339–64

Padoa-Schioppa, T, 'EMU and Banking Supervision (1999) 2 International Finance 295

Pelkmans, 'The New Approach to Technical Harmonisation and Standardisation' (1986–87) 25 JCMS 249

Perkinns, 'The Divorce of Commercial and Investment Banking: A History' (1971) 88 Banking LJ

Perry, D, 'Insurance Regulation: past, present and future' in EJ Swann (ed), *The Development of the Law of Financial Services* (1993)

Pescatore, 'Some Critical Remarks on the 'Single European Act'' 24 CMLR 9 (1987), 11

Philipe, H, 'Towards a Unified European Securities Market' (1997) 4 The Financial Regulator 11

Philippart, R and G Edwards, 'The Provisions on Closer Co-operation in the Treaty of Amsterdam: The Politics of Flexibility in the European Union' (1999) 1 Journal of Common Market Studies 87

Pollack, M 'Delegation, Agency and Agenda Setting in the European Community' (1997) 1 International Organization 99

Pollack, M, 'International Relations Theory and European Integration' (2001) 2 Journal of Common Market Studies 221

Quinn, B, 'The UK approach to controlling risk in large-value payment systems' (1993) 33 BEQB

Raffer, K, 'Applying Chapter 9 Insolvency to International Debts: An Economically Efficient Solution with a Human Face', World Development [1990] 18: 301–11

Reich, N, 'Protection of Diffuse Interests in the EEC and the Perspective of Progressively Establishing an Internal Market' (1988) 11 JCP 395

Reich, N, 'Binnenmarkt als Rechsbegriff' (1991) Europäisches Zeitscrift für Wirtschaftsrecht 203

Reich, N, 'Competition Between Legal Orders: A New Paradigm for EU Law?' (1992) 5 Common Market Law Review 861

Reich, N, 'The 'November Revolution' of the European Court of Justice: *Keck*, *Meng* and *Audi* Revisited' (1994) 31 CMLRev 459

Reynolds, 'KM, House Panel Wraps Hearings on Financial Modernisation Bill' The Bond Buyer, 31 July 1997, p 5

Richardson, G, 'International banking in turbulent times: some lessons from recent experience' BEQB March 1983

Romano, R, 'Empowering Investors: A Market Approach to Securities Regulation' (1998) 107 Yale Law Journal 2359

Roth, WH, 'Case C-79/90 Manfred Säger v Dennemeyer & Co. Ltd.' (1993) 1 Common Market Law Review 145

Roth, WH, 'Case C-233/94, Federal Republic of Germany v. European Parliament and Council of the European Union' (1998) 4 Common Market Law Review 459

Roth, WH, 'EEC Treaty Article Fifty-Nine and its Implications for Conflicts Law in the Field of Insurance Contracts' (1992) 2 Duke Journal of Comparative and International Law 131

Rowley, Anthony, 'EEC's laws seen as danger to City banks,' The Times (6.6.1973), 24, col E

Sachs, J, A Tornell and A Velasco, 'Financial Crisis in Emerging Markets: The Lessons from 1995', Brookings Papers on Economic Activity [1996] 1:147–215

Sakaibara, 'The Euro-currency Market in Perspective' 12 Finance and Development, 11 (September 1975)

Sargent, JA, 'Pressure Group Development in the EC: The Role of the British Bankers Association' 20 JCMS (1982), 269

Saunders, A and I Walter, *Universal Banking—Financial System Design Reconsidered* (1997)

Scharph, F, 'The Joint Decision Trap: Lessons from German Federalism and European Integration' (1988) 66 Public Administration 239

Schooner, H and M Taylor, 'Convergence and Competition: The Case of Bank Regulation in Britain and the United States' (1999) 20 Michigan Journal of International Law 595

Seidel, 'Der EWG-rechtliche Bergriff der 'MaSnahmen gleicher Wirkung wie eine mengenmassige Beschrankung' [1976] NJW 2081

Shah, AK, 'International Bank Regulation: Objectives and Outcomes—An Interview with Peter Cooke, former Chairman of the BASLE Committee, 1977–1988' BJIBFL June 1996

Sherwood, A, 'The impact of electronic trading on regulatory surveillance' (1997) 4 Journal of Financial Regulation & Compliance 299

Siebert, H and M Koop, 'Institutional Competition versus Centralisation: Quo Vadis Europe?' (1993) Oxford Review of Economic Policy 15

Slover, T, 'Tequila Sunrise: Mexico Emerges from the Darkness of Financial Crisis' *Studies in International Financial and Economic Law* No 15 (1998)

Smedresman, PS and AF Lowenfeld, 'Eurodollars, Multinational Banks, and National Laws' 64 NY UL Rev 733 (1989)

Smith, *Glass–Steagall Act, A History of Its Legislative Origins and Regulatory Construction* (1975) 92 Banking LJ

Smits, R, 'Banking Supervision in the Monetary Union' (1999) 2 Journal of International Banking Regulation 122

Smout, C and J Barrass, 'International Regulatory Cooperation', *Financial Stability Review*, Autumn 1992

Smout, C and Barrass, J, 'International regulatory co-operation' (1996) 1 Financial Stability Review 44

Snell, J and Andenas, M, 'Exploring the Outer Limits-Restrictions on the Free Movement of Goods and Services' (1999) 7–8 European Business Law Review 252

Stanley, P (1996) 33 CMLRev 713, 719–21

Steiner, J, 'Direct Applicability in EEC Law—A Chameleon Concept' (1982) 98 Law Quarterly Review 229

Stengel, A, 'Is Regulation Effective Enough to Combat Fraud?' (1998) 8 Journal of International Banking Law 276

Stigler, G, 'The Theory of Economic Regulation' (1971) 2 Bell Journal of Economics 3

Stiner, J, 'Drawing the Line: Uses and Abuses of Art 30 EEC' (1992) 29 CNLRev 749

Sun, JM and J Pelkmans, 'Regulatory Competition in the Single Market' (1995) 1 Journal of Common Market Studies 67

Sykes, A, 'Regulatory Competition or Regulatory Harmonisation: a Silly Question?' (2000) 2 Journal of International Economic Law 257

Tanzer, G, 'Developing Uniform Standards to Allow a Global Passport for Mutual Funds—IOSCO's Role' (2000) 5 International Business Lawyer 229

Taylor, M, 'Hedgefund Regulation' [May 1999], BJIBSL, pp 183–187

Theil, R, 'The EC Investment Services Directive: A critical time for investments firms' (1994) 2 Journal of International Banking & Financial Law 61

Thieffry, G, 'The State of European Securities Regulation' (2001) 5 International Financial Law Review 15

Thieffry, G, 'Towards a European Securities Commission' (1999) 10 International Financial Law Review 14

Thieffry, G and J Walsh, 'Securitisation: The New Opportunities Offered by Economic and Monetary Union' (1997) 12 Journal of International Banking Law 463

Thomson, CJ, 'The Basle Concordat: International Collaboration in Banking Supervision'

'Conglomerates Challenge Regulators' *Thompson's International Banking Regulator* (5 May 1997), Vol. 10, No 18, p 1

Thorkildsen, T, 'Power to draw up Conduct of Business Rules after the ISD' (1995) 15 Company Lawyer 102

The Times, 'Bonn sets pace for central banks in task for stemming liquidity failures' 10 September 1974 p 17

The Times, 'New City committees set up by the Bank' June 1974

The Times, 'Experts work on early warning system to avoid bank collapses' 13 February 1975, p 17

Timmermans, C, 'How can one improve the quality of Community legislation?' (1997) 34 Common Market Law Review 1229

Tison, M, 'What is 'General Good' in EU Financial Services Law?' (1997) 2 Legal Issues of European Integration 1

Toth, AG, 'The Legal Status of the Declarations Annexed to the Single European Act' 23 CMLR (1986), 803

Truman, EM, 'The Mexican Peso Crisis: Implications for International Finance' 82 Fed.Res.Bull. 199 (March 1996)

Tsebelis, G and G Garrett, 'The Institutional Foundations of Intergovernmentalism and Supranationalism in the European Union' (2001) 2 International Organization 357

Turing, D, 'General Principles of Risk Control' (2000) 2 Journal of International Banking & Financial Law 38

Usher, J, 'Financial Services in EEC Law' (1988) 1 ICLQ 144

Van den Bergh, R, 'The Subsidiarity Principle in European Community Law: Some Insights from Law and Economics' (1994) 1 Maastricht Journal of European & Comparative Law 337

van Themaat, 'De artikelen 30–36 van het EEC-Verdrag' R.M. Themis 4/5, 378

Vives, X, 'Restructuring Financial Regulation in the European Monetary Union' (2001) 1 Journal of Financial Services Research 57

Frank Vogl, 'German sees City as hub of EEC banking,' The Times (5.5.1972), p 1, col H

Von Rosen, R, 'Clearing up Europe's Exchanges' (9 February 2001) Financial Times 19

Vos, E, 'Reforming the European Commission: What Role to play for EU Agencies?' (2000) 5 Common Market Law Review 1113

Waelbroeck, M, 'The Role of the Court of Justice in the Implementation of the Single European Act' 11 Michigan LJ (1990), 671, 684–88.

Waitzer, E, 'Supervision of financial markets' *Financial Regulation Report* (August 1996)

Wallich, HC, *Federal Reserve Bulletin* (November 1974), 60 (11):760 cited in Spero, op cit, n. 19, pp 155–6

Walker, GA, 'Consolidated Supervision' BJIBFL [1996] 74–83 and 131–139

Walker, GA, 'Financial Conglomerates—The Next Generation' The International Lawyer Vol. 30, No 1 (January 1996), p 45

Walker, GA, 'Financial Derivatives: Global Regulatory Developments' [1996] JBL January, p 66

Walker, GA, 'The Joint Forum doesn't add up' The Financial Regulator Vol. 3, No 2 (Sept 1988), p 45.

Walker, GA, 'Conglomerate Law and International Financial Market

Supervision' Boston University Annual Review of Banking Law [Vol. 17: xxx, 1998], p 287
Walker, GA, 'So Close But So Far' FT-FRR (May 1999), p 1
Walker, GA, 'Accord at Last', FT-FRR (June 1999), p 1
Walker, GA, 'A New Beginning,' FT FRR (June 1999), p 1
Walker, GA, 'A New Capital Adequacy Framework' FT-FRR (August/September 1999), pp 3
Walker, GA, 'Working Groups and Global Standards' FRR (October 1999), p 1
Walker, GA, 'The New Global Rule Book' FRR (November 1999), p 1
Walker, GA, 'Financial Stability Standards' FRR (November 1999), p 3
Walker, GA, 'New Dawn (New Risk),' FRR (January 2000), p 1
Walker, GA, 'Not Another Country Club,' FRR (April 2000), p 1
Walker, GA, 'Hedge Fund Control' FRR, May 1999, p 1
Warren, MG III, 'The Common Market Prospectus' (1989) 4 Common Market Law Review 687
Watson, J, 'International Co-operation in the field of Financial Regulatory Enforcement: Part 1, The UK Approach' (1999) 11 Journal of International Banking & Financial Law 467
Watson, J, 'International Co-operation in the field of Financial Regulatory Enforcement: Part 2, The EU Approach' (2000) 1 Journal of International Banking & Financial Law 13
Watson, J, 'International Co-operation in the field of Financial Regulatory Enforcement: Part 3, IOSCO and Transnational Regulatory Cooperation' (2000) 5 Journal of International Banking & Financial Law 157
Watson, J, 'International Co-operation in the field of Financial Regulatory Enforcement: Part 4, The current State of Play and the Future' (2000) 6 Journal of International Banking & Financial Law 187
Weiler, J, 'The Community System: The Dual Character of Supranationalism' (1981) 1 YBEL 267
Weatherill, S, 'After Keck: Some Thoughts on how to Clarify the Clarification' (1996) 33 Common Market Law Review 885
Weiler, J, 'The Transformation of Europe' (1991) 8 Yale Law Journal 2403
Welby, J, 'Do Business Ethics Matter' (1992) 3 International Company and Commercial Law Review 46
White, 'In Search of the Limits of Article 30 of the EEC Treaty' (1989) 26 *CNLRev* 235, 246–7
Willis, 'The Banking Act of 1933 in Operation' (1935) 35 Colum L Rev
Willman, Arpo, 'The Collapse of the Fixed Exchange Rate Regime with Sticky Wages and Imperfect Substitutability Between Domestic and Foreign Bonds', European Economic Review [1988] 32: 1817–38
Wils, 'The Search for the Rule in Article 30 EEC: much ado about nothing?' (1993) 18 ELRev 475

Woodworth, GW, 'Understanding the Eurodollar Market' 154 Bankers' Magazine, 32 (August 1971)

Woolfson, P, "Bancassurance' and Community Law: Current Status and Expected Developments' [1994] 12 Journal of International Business Law

Woolfson, P, 'Electronic commerce and the Single Market in financial services in Europe: What changes for success?' (1997) 4 Journal of Financial Regulation and Compliance 306

Wouters, J, 'Conflict of Laws and the Single Market for Financial Services (Part I)' (1997) 2 Maastricht Journal of European and Comparative Law 161

Wouters, J, 'Conflict of Laws and the Single Market for Financial Services (Part II)' (1997) 3 Maastricht Journal of European and Comparative Law 284

Wouters, J, 'Rules of conduct, foreign investment firms and the ECJ's case law on services' (1993) 13 Company Lawyer 194

Wymeersch, E, 'The EU Directives on Financial Disclosure' (1996) 2 European Financial Services Law 34

Zaring, D, 'International Law by other means: The Twilight Existence of International Financial Regulatory Organizations' (1998) Texas International Law Journal 282

Zavvos, G, 'Regulation of the European Securities Markets: The Challenges in the post-Barcelona Era' (2002) 30 Kangaroo Group Newsletter

10. SPEECHES, CONFERENCES, PRESS RELEASES AND SPECIAL PAPERS

Bandilla, R, Legal Consequences of the Single Currency (Contribution to the FIDE Congress, Helsinki, 1–3 June 2000)

Becht, M, European Disclosure for the Next Millennium (Paper for CEPS Task Force, 7 December 1999)

Bergsten, F and R Henning, *Global Economic Leadership and the Group of Seven* (1996) Institute for International Economics

Bergsten, F, 'How to Target Exchange Rates', *Financial Times* (20 November 1998)

Bergsten, 'Missed Opportunity', *The International Economy* [1998, 12] No 6 (November 1998) pp. 26–27

Bolkestein, F, The EU's Economic Test: Meeting the Challenges of the Lisbon Strategy (Speech delivered at the 17th Annual State of the International Economy Conference, London, 19 November 2001)

Breuer, R, Convergence of supervisory practices—a banker's view (Paper presented at the conference of European Banking Supervisors, Copenhagen, 20 November 2000)

Brimmer, AF, 'International Finance and Management of Bank Failure: Herstatt vs Franklin National,' American Economic Association and the American Finance Association, September 16, 1976

Brown, G, 'Impose New Codes of Conduct', *Wall Street Journal* (6 October 1998), a22

Brown, M and E Gardener, *Bancassurance and European Banking Strategies: An Exploratory Analysis using DEA of the Concept and Treatment of 'Relative Efficiency',* Paper presented to the Annual Conference of the European Association of University Teachers in Banking and Finance, University of Modena, Italy, September 1994

Camdessus, M (former IMF Managing Director), 'From the Asian Crisis Toward a New Global Architecture,' Address to the Parliamentary Assembly of the Council of Europe, Strasbourg (23 June 1998)

Camdessus, M, Stable and Efficient Systems for the 21st Century: A Quest for Transparency and Standards (Paper presented at the 24th IOSCO Annual Conference, Lisbon, 25 May 1999)

Camdessus, M, 'Global Financial Reform: The Evolving Agenda,' Council of Foreign Relations, New York (June 4, 1999)

Camdessus, M, 'The IMF We Need,' Georgetown (2 February 2000)

President WJ Clinton, 'Speech on the Global Finance Crisis,' Council of Foreign Relations (14 September 1998)

President WJ Clinton, 'Remarks to World Economic Forum,' Davos, Switzerland (January 29, 2000)

Corsetti, G, P Presenti, and N Roubini, 'What caused the Asian currency and financial crisis?' (March 1998)

Crocket, A, Banking Supervision and Financial Stability (The William Taylor Memorial Lectures No 4, 1998)

Dale, R, *Deposit Insurance: Policy Clash over EC and US Reforms*, London School of Economics Financial Markets Group, Special Paper Number 53 (1993)

Davies, H, Building the Financial Services Authority; What's New? (Travers Lecture, London Guildhall University Business School, 11 March 1999)

Davies, H, Convergence of Supervisory Practices (Paper presented at the Conference of European Banking Supervisors, Copenhagen, 20 November 2000)

Davies, H, EMU and Financial Markets: Winners, Losers and Regulators (Paper presented at the Financial Times EMU Conference, London, 21 November 1997)

Davies, H, Introductory remarks (Paper presented at the Eurofi Conference, Paris, 15 September 2000)

Davies, H, Why regulate? (Henry Thornton Lecture, City University, 4 November 1998)

Davies, H, Euro-Regulation (European Financial Forum Lecture, Brussels, 8 April 1999)

Davies, H, Global Markets, Global Regulation (Paper presented at the 25th IOSCO Annual Conference, Sydney, 17 May 2000)

Duisenberg, W, Financing in the European Capital Markets (Speech delivered at the Waarborgfonds Sociale Woningbouw, Utrecht, 14 June 1999)

Duisenberg, W, The ECB and the accession process (Speech delivered at the Frankfurt European Banking Congress, 23 November 2001)

Duisenberg, W, The euro as a catalyst for legal convergence in Europe (Speech on the occasion of the Annual Conference of the International Bar Association, Amsterdam, 17 September 2000)

Duisenberg, W, The future of banking supervision and the integration of financial markets (Speech delivered at the conference 'Improving integration of financial markets in Europe', Turin, 22 May 2000)

Dunnett, R, The transition to Stage Three: Impact on the Financial Markets (Lecture given at the Workshop on Institutional Aspects of the EMU at King's College London, 26–27 January 1996)

Edwards, S, 'Abolish the IMF', *Financial Times* (13 November 1998), a1

Edwards, S, 'Capital Controls Are Not the Reason for Chile's Success', *Wall Street Journal* (3 April 1998), a19

Farrant, R, 'The Lead Regulator Model and Group Supervision' *Financial Regulation into the Next Decade—Minimising Systemic Risk*, One Day Conference, 7 November 1996

Fischer, S, The Asian Crisis: A View from the IMF (Paper presented at the Midwinter Conference of the Bankers' Association for Foreign Trade, Washington, 22 January 1998)

Foot, M, 'International Regulatory Cooperation Post-Barings', Speech, 7 March 1996

FSF, 'First Meeting of the Financial Stability Forum,' Press Release (6 April 1999)

FSF, 'Second Meeting of the FSF,' Press Release (15 September 1999)

FSF, 'Broadening Representation in the Financial Stability Forum' Press Release (21 June 1999)

FSF, 'Terms of Reference: FSF Study Group on Deposit Insurance' Press Release (19 November 1999)

'G Force' *FT* (13 September)

'G7 prepares to give birth to its GX baby' *FT* (20 September 1999),

Gardener, EP, *Theory and Practice in Banking Supervision: Some Reflections*, IES Institute of European Finance, RP 86/2

Garten, J, 'In This Economic Chaos, a Global Bank Can Help', *International Herald Tribune* (28 September 1998), p 8

Gemnill, G, The Danger of Markets Collapsing (Speech submitted at the conference 'The Role of Regulation in Global Financial Markets', City University Business School, London 13–14 July 2000)

Goodhart, CHA, P Hartmann, DT Llewellyn, L Rojas-Suarez, and SR Weisbrod, *Financial Regulation: Why, How and Where Now?*, Monograph for the Central Bank Governors Meeting at the Bank of England, 6 June 1997

Goodhart, C, The Organisational Structure of Banking Supervision (Financial Market Group Seminar, LSE, 30 October 2000)

Gretschmann, K, The Subsidiarity Principle: Who is to do what in an Integrated Europe? (Paper submitted to the Jacques Delors Colloquium, Subsidiarity: The Challenge of Change, Maastricht, March 1991)

Grundman, S and W Kerber, Information Intermediaries and Extending the Area of Informed Party Autonomy—Securities and Insurance Markets (Paper presented at the Conference 'Party Autonomy for the Internal Market', King's College, 11–13 May 2000

Guth, 'Trends in International Banking', Speech, 34th International Banking Summer School, Timmendorfer Strand, 31 August 1981

IMF, Interim Committee, *Communiqué* (4 October 1998)

IMF, Executive Board, 'Work Programme on Strengthening the Architecture of the International Monetary System' (30 October, 1998)

IMF, 'Progress Report—Developing International Standards' (March 1999)

IMF, 'International Standards and Fund Surveillance—Progress and Issues' (16 August 1999)

IMF Executive Board, 'International Standards and Fund Surveillance—Progress and Issues' and IMF, 'A Guide to Progress in Strengthening the Architecture of the International Financial System' (22 December 1999)

Ingves, S, Assessing Financial Sector Soundness: the Role of the IMF (Paper presented at the Conference of European Banking Supervisors, Copenhagen, 20 November 2000)

Issing, O, The Euro—Four Weeks After the Start (Speech delivered at the European-Atlantic Group, House of Commons, London, 28 January 1999)

Kalomiris, C, *Blueprints for a New Global Financial Architecture* (1998)

Kaufman, H, 'Preventing the Next Global Financial Crisis', *Washington Post* (28 January 1998), a17

Kaufman, 'Proposals for Improving the Structure of Financial Supervision and Regulation. Outline of remarks before the Brookings Institution Symposium on Limiting Model Hazard in Financial Rescues', Washington (4 June 1998)

Krantz, T, The danger of Price Fragmentation (Speech delivered at the conference '24-Hour Securities Trading and the growth of ECNs', London 9–10 November 1999)

Krugman, P, 'What Happened in Asia' (1998)

Lamfalussy, A, Presentation on the Special Roundtable on the findings of the Committee of Wise Men on the Regulation of European Securities Markets (Centre of European Policy Studies, 29 November 2000)

Large, A, *Systemic Risk and the Securities Regulator*, SIB Press Release 012/96, 27 March 1996

Llewellyn, D, *The Regulation and Supervision of Financial Institutions*, The Gilbart Lectures on Banking (1986)

Louis, JV, The EMU, and after? (Paper delivered at the Federal Trust Conference 'Consolidating EMU', London, 9 June 2000)

McMahon, K, Mansion House London 26 May 1982

Maughan, D, 'Global Capital Markets and the Implications for Financial Institutions' Presentation at Harvard Law School (September 1993)

Meister, E, How should regulatory and supervisory responsibilities be shared among the national functional regulators? (Lecture held at the Multinational Banking Seminar, New York, 9 June 2001)

Michau, J, Workshop No 4, *Information Sharing Between Securities Regulators (Market Surveillance and Insider Trading)*, XV th Annual Conference, November 1990

Muckenfuss, C, *Handling Distressed Banks in the United States*, paper presented to the International Conference of Banking Supervisors, Washington DC, 24–25 September 1981

Muller, HJ, 'The Concordat: A Model for International Cooperation' International Conference of Banking Supervisors (London 5–6 July 1979), p 65

Norgen, C, Securities Markets in the Information Age (Address at the 26th Annual IOSCO Conference, Stockholm, 23–29 June 2001)

Padoa-Schioppa, T, EMU and Banking Supervision (Lecture at the London School of Economics, Financial Markets Group, 24 February 1999)

Padoa-Schioppa, T, Reflections on recent financial incidents (Speech at the Third Joint Central Bank Research Conference on Risk Measurement and Systemic Risk, Basel, 8 March 2002)

Padoa-Schioppa, T, Remarks at the roundtable: Mid-term review of progress towards European financial integration (Brussels, 22 February 2002)

Padoa-Schioppa, T, Securities and banking: bridges and walls (Lecture at the London School of Economics, 21 January 2002)

Phillips, Susan, member of the Board of Governors of the Federal Reserve System, at the Exchequer Club in Washington on 18 June 1997

Radelet, S and J Sachs, 'The Onset of the East Asian Financial Crisis' (1998)

Rubin, R, 'The Asian Financial Situation,' Georgetown University (21 January 1998)

Rubin, R, 'Strengthening the Global Financial System,' Brookings Institute (14 April 1998)

Sainz de Vicuña, A., Legal Consequences of the Single Currency (General Report at the FIDE Congress, Helsinki, 1–3 June 2000)

Schoenmaker, D, *Home Country Deposit Insurance*, London School of Economics Financial Markets Group, Special Paper Number 43 (1992)

Schoenmaker, D, *Externalities in Payment Systems: Issues for Europe*, London School of Economics Financial Markets Group, Special Paper, September 1993

Shepard-Walwyn, T, 'The Future of Financial Services Regulation, Some Reflections from the Inside', Paper to the LSE Financial Markets Group, 11 November 1996

Solans, E, Financial Markets in the European Monetary Union (Speech delivered at the 28th Annual Financial Markets Seminar, Valencia, 8 June 2001)

Soros, G, 'Avoiding a Breakdown: Asia's Crisis Demands a Rethink of International Regulation', *Financial Times* (31 December 1997), p 12

Spaventa, L, Regulation for financial markets (Speech delivered at the FESE European Financial Markets Convention, June 2000)

Stark, J, The ECB and other European Institutions and the Future of the Euro (Address at the 3rd Euro Capital Markets Forum, Amsterdam, 2 April 2001)

Summers, L, Rising to the Challenge of Global Economic Integration (Remarks to the School of Advanced International Studies, Washington DC, 20 September 2000)

Teietmeyer, H, *International Co-operation and Co-ordination in the Area of Financial Market Supervision and Surveillance* (11 February 1999)

Van Miert, K, EU Competition Policy in the Banking Sector (Speech delivered to the foreign bankers in the Belgian Bankers' Association, Brussels, 22 September 1998)

Vargas, F, The Convergence of Banking Supervisory Practices (Paper given at the conference of European Banking Supervisors, Copenhagen, 20 November 2000)

Wallich, HC, 'Institutional Cooperation in the World Economy', Chicago, 5 May 1983, issued as Press Release by Federal Reserve Board Washington, DC

Wallich, Henry C, 'Central Banks as Regulators and Lenders of Last Resort in an International Context: A View from the United States', *Key Issues in International Banking Series*, No 18 (Federal Reserve Bank of Boston, October 1977)

Welteke, E, Regulating European Financial Markets (Speech delivered at the European Banking Conference, Frankfurt, 17 November 2000)

Wisbey, G, The Challenge of Technology—Regulation of Electronic Financial Markets (Speech delivered at the conference 'The Challenges facing Financial Regulation', Cambridge, 6–7 July 2000)

Wyplosz, C, 'Globalised Financial Markets and Financial Crises,' Conference paper, 'Coping with Financial Crises in Developing and Transition Countries: Regulatory and Supervisory Challenges in a New Era of Global Finance' Amsterdam, (March 1997)

Wyplosz, C, Economic policy Coordination in EMU: Strategies and Institutions (Paper presented at the Deutsch-Franzosisches Wirtschaftspolitisches Forum, Bonn, 11–12 January 1999)

Zuberbühler, D, The Financial Industry in the 21st Century (Speech delivered at the Jubilee International Conference of Banking Supervisors, Basle, 21 September 2000)

11. ACADEMIC PAPERS AND ELECTRONIC DOCUMENTS

Adonis, A and S Jones, Subsidiarity and the Union's Constitutional Future (Centre for European Studies Discussion Paper No 2, Nuffield College, 1991)

Alexander, K, The Role of the Basle Standards in International Banking Supervision (ESRC Centre for Business Research Working Paper No 153, Cambridge, March 2000)

Alfon, I and P Andrews, Cost–Benefit Analysis in Financial Regulation (FSA Occasional Paper Series No 3, September 1999)

Benink, H, The Future of Banking Regulation in Developed Countries: Lessons from and for Europe (mimeo, 2000)

Briault, C, The Rationale for a Single National Financial Services Regulator (FSA Occasional Paper Series No 2, May 1999)

Briault, C, Revisiting the Rationale for a single National Financial Services Regulator (FSA Occasional Paper Series No 16, February 2002)

Caprio, G, Bank Regulation: The Case of the Missing Model (World Bank Policy Research Working Paper No 1574, January 1996)

Crooke, A, 'Securities Markets attack EU Prospectus Reforms' (http://www.legalmediagroup.com, 9 September 2001)

Cukierman, A, Accountability, Credibility, Transparency and Stabilization Policy in the Eurosystem (mimeo, January 2000)

De Sousa, P, Independent and Accountable Central Banks and the European Central Bank (European Integration Online Papers No 9, http://eiop.or.at/eiop/texte/2001-009a.htm, 2001)

Di Giorgio, G and C Di Noia, Designing Institutions for Financial Stability: Regulation and Supervision by Objective for the Euro Area (mimeo, November 2000)

Dutzler, B, OLAF or the Question of Applicability of Secondary Community Law to the ECB (European Integration online Papers No 1, http://eiop.or.at/eiop/texte/2001-001a.htm, 2001)

Eatwell, J and L Taylor,International Markets and the Future of Economic Policy (Centre for Economic Policy Analysis Working Paper No 9, August 1998)

Endo, K, Subsidiarity and its Enemies: To what Extent is Sovereignty contested in the mixed Commonwealth of Europe? (European University Institute Working Paper No 2001/24, 2001)

European Shadow Financial Regulatory Committee, The Regulation of European Securities Markets: The Lamfalussy Report (Statement No 10, Madrid, 26 March 2001)

Evans, H, Plumbers and Architects: A Supervisory perspective on international financial architecture (FSA Occasional Paper Series No 4, January 2000)

Fender, I and J Von Hagen, Central Bank Policy in a more perfect Financial System (Zentrum für Europäische Integrationsforschung Policy Paper B03, 1998)

Gardener, EP, Theory and Practice in Banking Supervision: Some Reflections (IES Institute of European Finance, Research Paper 86/2, 1986)

Goodhart, C, An incentive Structure for Financial Regulation (LSE, Financial Market Group Special Paper No 88, July 1996)

Goodhart, C, Myths about the Lender of Last Resort (mimeo)

Gruson, M, Convergence of Bank Prudential Supervision Standards and Practices within the European Union (Centre for Commercial Law Studies, Studies in International Financial & Economic Law No 23, 1999)

Hall, B, European governance and the future of the Commission (Centre for European Reform Working Paper No 5, May 2000)

Hardouvelis, G, D Malliaropoulos, and R Priestley, EMU and European Stock Market Integration (Centre of Economic Policy Research Discussion Paper No 2124, April 1999)

Joerges, C, The Market without the State? The 'Economic Constitution' of the European Community and the Rebirth of Regulatory Politics (European Integration online Papers No 19, http://eiop.or.at/eiop/texte/1997-01920htm, November 1997)

Karmel, R, The Case for a European Securities Commission (mimeo, 1999)

Kumar, A, The Regulation of Non-Bank Financial Institutions (World Bank Discussion Paper No 362, 1997)

Latter, T, Causes and Management of Banking Crises (Bank of England, Centre for Central Banking Studies Handbook No 12, 1997)

Leino, P, The European Central Bank and Legitimacy: Is the ECB a Modification of or an Exception to the Principle of Democracy? (Harvard Jean Monnet Working Paper No 1/01, 2001)

Llewellyn, D, The Economic Rationale for Financial Regulation (FSA Occasional Paper No 1, April 1999)

Mayes, D and J Vesala, On the Problems of Home Country Control (Bank of Finland Discussion Paper No 20/98, 1998))

Niemeyer, J, An Economic Analysis of Securities Market Regulation and Supervision: Where to Go after the Lamfalussy Report? (Stockholm

School of Economics Working Paper Series in Economics and Finance No 482, December 2001)

Panourgias, L and M Andenas, Euro, EMU and the UK Law (Report submitted for the Euro-Spectator Project, April 2001)

Parti, A and G Schinasi, European Monetary Union and International Capital Markets: Structural Implications and Risks (International Monetary Fund Working Paper No 97/62, May 1997)

Simpson, D, G Meeks, P Klumpes, and P Andrews, Some cost–benefit issues in financial regulation (FSA Occasional Paper Series No 12, October 2000)

Steil, B, Regional Financial Market Integration: Learning from the European Experience (Royal Institute of International Affaires London 1998)

Stephan, P, Regulatory Cooperation and Competition: The Search for Virtue (University of Virginia School of Law, Legal Studies Working Paper No 99; 12, June 1999)

Shepheard-Walwyn, T, The future of financial services regulation: some reflections from the inside (LSE, Financial Markets Group Special Paper No 94, 1997)

Tison, M, Conduct of Business Rules and their Implementation in the EU Member States (Gent University, Financial Law Institute Working Paper 2000-14, 2000)

Tison, M, The Investment Services Directive and its Implementation in the EU Member States (Gent University, Financial Law Institute Working Paper 1999-17, 1999)

Tison, M, Unravelling the General Good Exception: The Case of Financial Services (Gent University, Financial Law Institute Working Paper 2000–3, 2000)

White, W, What have we learned from recent Financial Crises and Policy Responses? (Bank of International Settlements Working Paper No 84, January 2000)

Wymeersch, E, The Harmonisation of Securities Regulation in Europe in the New Trading Environment (Gent University, Financial Law Institute Working Paper 2000-16, July 2000)

Yataganas, X, Delegation of Regulatory Authority in the European Union: The relevance of the American model of independent agencies (Harvard Jean Monnet Working Paper No 3/01, 2001